Radical Economics

General Editor: SAM AARONOVITCH

Debates between economists are not just technical arguments amongst practitioners but often reflect philosophical and ideological positions which are not always made explicit.

Discontent grew with the prevailing economic orthodoxy as the long period of economic expansion in the advanced capitalist economies came to an end in the 1970s; disenchantment was expressed in open discussion about the 'crisis' in economics and in the rise of various kinds of radical economic theory, often using the general title of 'political economy'.

Many economists have looked for a more fruitful point of departure in the ideas of Marx and the classical economists and also in such contemporary economists as Kalecki and Sraffa. Although it is possible to identify a broad radical stream, it does not mean that there are no significant controversies within this radical approach and, indeed, it would be unhealthy if this were not the case.

Can radical economic theory interpret the world better than the current orthodoxy which it challenges? And can it show also how to change it? This is a challenge which this series proposes to take up, adding to work already being done.

Each book will be a useful contribution to its particular field and should become a text around which the study of economics takes place.

Radical Economics

Published

Michael Bleaney, *The Rise and Fall of Keynesian Economics*
Keith Cowling, *Monopoly Capitalism*
Michael Howard, *Profits in Economic Theory*
Antal Mátyás, *History of Modern Non-Marxian Economics*

Forthcoming

Amit Bhaduri, *Macroeconomics*
Krishna Bharadwaj, *Classical Theories of Value and Distribution*
Terry Byres, *The Political Economy of Poor Nations*
Matthew Edel, *Urban Economics*
Paul Hare, *Planning the British Economy*
Michael Howard and John King, *A History of Marxian Economics, Volumes I and II*
David Purdy, *The Theory of Wages*
Malcolm Sawyer, *The Economics of Michal Kalecki*

HISTORY OF MODERN NON-MARXIAN ECONOMICS

From Marginalist Revolution through the
Keynesian Revolution to Contemporary Monetarist
Counter-revolution

Second edition

ANTAL MÁTYÁS D. Sc. (Econ.)

Head of Department of the History of Economic Thought,
Karl Marx University of Economics, Budapest

MACMILLAN

Originally published in Hungarian as
A MODERN POLGÁRI KÖZGAZDASÁGTAN TÖRTÉNETE,

Közgazdasági és Jogi Könyvkiadó, Budapest

Translated by István Véges

Translation revised by Hugo Radice (Parts 1–9) and Peter Tamási (Part 10)

First hardback English Language edition published by
Akadémiai Kiadó, Budapest 1980

Second, revised and enlarged English Language edition published 1985 by
Macmillan Education Ltd as a co-edition with Akadémiai Kiadó
Budapest

Published by
MACMILLAN EDUCATION LTD
Houndmills, Basingstoke, Hampshire RG21 2XS
and London
Companies and representatives
throughout the world

Printed in Hungary

British Library Cataloguing in Publication Data
Mátyás, Antal
History of modern non-Marxian economics :
from marginalist revolution through the
Keynesian revolution to contemporary
monetarist counter-revolution.
1. Economics
I. Title   II. A modern polgári
közgazdaságtan története. English
330   HB171

ISBN 0–333–38957–3
ISBN 0–333–36608–5 Pbk

CONTENTS

5

Part Two

Further development of the equilibrium theory of price formation

8

10

PREFACE

This work is the revised English version of a textbook used at the University of Economics, Budapest. Hence, its original aim was to contribute to the training of Marxist economists who should be well-versed not only in the political economy of Marxism, but also in non-Marxian economic literature. This is an indispensable requirement to be met by the economists of socialist countries, especially in our days when economic, scientific, cultural and political co-operation among countries with different social systems is expanding, and Marxist economists have steadily increasing opportunities to come into contact with their non-Marxist colleagues. Besides, their research work also makes it necessary for them to study non-Marxian literature.

As the book explains the principal concepts of non-Marxian economics to economists with training in Marxist theory, the exposition of the individual theories necessarily differs from the approach applied by professors of economics in non-socialist countries.

The author presents the economic theories in terms of their historical development. It is for this reason that he briefly outlines how, as early as the 70s of the past century, Menger, Jevons and Walras laid the foundations of the price and income distribution theories, which are still prevailing in today's non-Marxian economics. He singles out from the teachings of earlier authors only those elements which are also present in a modern form in non-Marxian literature. He is convinced that this historical approach to the individual theories facilitates their better understanding. His work, however, differs from the corresponding textbooks used at the universities of non-socialist countries in that the author not only points out the main turning-points in the history of the development of economic theories, but also discusses them in more detail than the authors of the above-mentioned textbooks. This is because the author cannot possibly assume that his students have already become acquainted with these theories in other economics courses, and thus their exposition has to be included in his lectures on the history of economic thought.

What does this work offer the non-Marxist reader? First, a detailed, exact and objective treatment and a systematic arrangement of the theories discussed with reference to the role they play in the history of economic thought, and, second, a comparative analysis of non-Marxian and Marxian economics. It evaluates, on the basis of Marxism, the theories discussed, reveals their interrelationships, points out the main stages of their development and shows to what extent they reflect the reality of capitalist economy, and it analyses their real elements and problems, and offers some possible solutions to them from a Marxist point of view.

The book cannot, of course, undertake to cover all fields of modern non-Marxian economics. Though it has attempted to include a rather wide range of them, these fields have become far too ramified to make it possible for any author to summarize all of their aspects in a single book. Publishing here the results of about two decades of research, the author has singled out from the complexity of non-Marxian ideas primarily those basic economic concepts which have come to occupy a prominent place in economic textbooks and theoretical reviews in non-socialist countries. It is, by the way, worth noting that the few books written in the past one or two decades by Marxist and non-Marxist authors on the history of modern non-Marxian economics are also far from providing a comprehensive picture of all the fields and problems of this discipline.

The author wishes to express his gratitude to Mr. István Véges for his conscientious work in rendering the author's ideas into English as faithfully as possible. He would also like to acknowledge his debt to Mr. Hugo Radice, lecturer at Sterling University, for the meticulous revision of the translation and for his other valuable assistance.

Budapest, November 1984

Professor Antal Mátyás

Head of Department of the
History of Economic Thought,
Karl Marx University of
Economics, Budapest

Part One

THE FOUNDATIONS OF MODERN NON-MARXIAN ECONOMICS

Chapter 1

A GENERAL SURVEY OF SUBJECTIVE ECONOMICS IN THE 1870s

The foundations of modern non-Marxian economics were laid independently and almost simultaneously in the 1870s by three economists, the Austrian Menger, the Swiss–French Walras and the English Jevons. Their views were diametrically opposed to those of the classical school of economic thought.

Let us examine and compare the most important characteristics of the theories of, on the one hand, the early classical economists, among them primarily the English classical economists representing the most developed ideas, and on the other hand, the founders of modern non-Marxian economics.

The starting-point for the investigations of the representatives of classical economics was *production*. This was due to the following historical circumstances:

1. They were economists of the progressive bourgeoisie still closely connected with production.

2. They fought against obsolete production relations impeding the development of the productive forces, and against the practices of landlords which hindered progress.

3. They were engaged in an ideological struggle against an idle class which, owing to the emergence of a capitalistic *rentier* system, did not take part in the production process. Thus, they were able to make use of the findings of their investigations setting out from production in the struggle they fought against landlords and in the critique they levelled against obsolete production relations impeding development.

As a result of their starting from production, the outstanding representatives of the English classical economic school arrived at the *labour theory of value*. It was on this theory that they based their ideas. The most consistent representative of this school was Ricardo. He directed his attacks from the basis of the labour theory of value against the landlord class and their practices which put a brake on capitalist accumulation.

The economists of the classical school tried to remove the obstacles in the way of the development of the forces of production. This was the reason why they laid special emphasis in their theoretical investigations on problems relating to *economic development*. One of the first representatives of modern non-Marxian growth theory, the English economist Harrod, writes: "... the old classical economics contains in roughly equal proportions what I define as static and dynamic elements."[1] Adam Smith held the view that the wealth of nations, the amount of

---

[1] R. Harrod: *Towards a Dynamic Economics*, New York, 1966, p. 15.

products needed to satisfy the demands of social consumption, increases as a result of the growth in the number of population and in the productivity of labour. Ricardo, however, made a central question of his investigations the way in which the incomes of individual classes develop in the course of capital accumulation, and whether this process promotes or hinders capital accumulation as the basis for any economic development.

The struggle for social progress, for the consolidation of the capitalist economic system and for removing the obstacles in the way of capitalist development turned the attention of the economists of the classical school to the analysis *of the long-term phenomena and processes of the economy,* in the investigation of which he assigned a great role to the labour theory of value.

What were, by contrast the characteristics of the new theory of non-Marxian economics as evolved in the 1870s? Though the views of the three founders of this school differed in many respects, nevertheless they held one thing in common, namely, that in the explanation of economic phenomena they broke away from production as a starting-point and started instead from the side of *consumption* and *wants*. "The starting-point of all investigations of economic theory"—Menger begins his basic work—"is human nature suffering from wants. Without wants there would be no economic activities, no social economy and no science underlying it. The study of wants (their recognition and understanding) is crucial to economics."[2] Setting out from wants, they searched for laws governing the satisfaction of the wants of *individual consumers,* and tried to reduce the objective economic processes ultimately to a subjective factor, that is, to the sensation of satisfaction that the consumers derive from fulfilling their wants.

Unlike the economists of the classical school, each of the three founders of the new economics was concerned with the investigation of short-term phenomena, but none of them examined the problems of growth. They took the level of technical knowledge and the quantity of the available resources as given, and expected that a rise in social welfare would result not from the free unfolding of the factors of growth, but from the optimal allocation of the available resources. They wished to find, by means of marginal analysis, an answer to the question of how the consumer employs, with the given pattern of his wants, the resources available to him so as to optimize their satisfaction. They sought the conditions for maximizing the satisfaction of wants in the fields of households, exchange and production. Although the entrepreneur's endeavour to maximize his profit also appears in Walras, this entrepreneur, responding to the signals of the market, fulfils eventually the desires of the consumer who is maximizing his own position. That is, the representatives of the marginalist revolution also created their value theory which would be suitable to solve that task.

In reforming the concept of value, they left production out of account and wished to find an answer to the question of how the consumer assessed, from the point of view of the satisfaction of needs, each unit of a given quantity of goods. They were of the opinion that by this interpretation of value they could account for the price the buyer was willing to pay for a given quantity of goods placed on the market, that is, for the formation of prices during the market period, so called by Marshall. They included production only as the next step in their investiga-

[2] C. Menger: *Grundsätze der Volkswirtschaftslehre,* 4th ed., Wien–Leipzig, 1923, p. 1.

16

tions. They assumed that the available factors of production could be used for the production of various kinds of products alternatively. And by means of the value theory, they also wished to explain how the functioning of the law of value allocated the given resources among the production of the different kinds of goods so as to ensure the maximum satisfaction of needs. This would ensue if the subjectively interpreted value and the production costs coincide in all fields of the utilization possibilities. Thus the new value theory explains both the magnitude of the price in a given market situation and the centre of price fluctuations.

Our criticism in this respect is not directed against the practice that these economists investigated the short-term phenomena of capitalism and thus analysed also price formation in the short run. The examination of the short-term phenomena of capitalist economy is a task that Marxian political economy still has to solve. What we maintain, however, is that it is impossible to investigate short-term phenomena, for example, concrete price phenomena, merely from the angle of the consumers' subjective motives. Individual price phenomena have to be interpreted as instances of a price movement governed by the law of the labour theory of value, that is, as forms of manifestation of a deeper interrelationship, while also taking into account that their size is influenced by several factors other than the law of value. Marx writes on this: "The exchange, or sale, of commodities at their value is the rational state of affairs, i.e. the natural law of their equilibrium. It is this law that explains the deviations, and not vice versa, the deviations that explain the law."[3]

In elaborating the principles of using available resources to ensure the maximum satisfaction of wants, the founders of subjective economics brought about, in essence, *the arche-type of the theory of the optimal allocation of resources*. They formulated certain rules of rational economic action which go far beyond the scope of the satisfaction of wants, and contain elements which also crop up in modern programming methods. It was with these achievements that Menger, Jevons and Walras laid the foundations of modern non-Marxian economics.

Let us try to set out the social background to these new developments in modern non-Marxian economics.

As soon as the bourgeoisie had gained their final victory over the landlords, the struggle of the working classes against the capitalist class took on "practically as well as theoretically, more and more outspoken and threatening forms."[4] Already during the lifetime of Ricardo the early English socialists began to use the ideological weapon for fighting against landlords, i.e. the labour theory of value, as a tool of the critique of the capitalist system. After Ricardo's death, with the sharpening of the class struggle, the bourgeoisie increasingly vulgarized the labour theory of value. In his statement on Mill's value concept, which was aimed at further developing Ricardo's value theory, the Hungarian economist Farkas Heller says: "... Mill himself was unaware of how far he moved away from Ricardo in explaining the costs of production."[5] In the decades following

[3] K. Marx: *Capital*, Vol. III, Moscow, 1962, p. 184.
[4] K. Marx: *Capital*, Vol. I, Moscow, 1954, p. 15.
[5] F. Heller: *A közgazdasági elméletek története* (The history of economic theories), Budapest, 1943, pp. 71–72.

Ricardo's death, the labour theory of value fell to pieces in non-Marxian economics. The theoretical system had to be established on another basis, different from the labour theory of value which was getting more and more dangerous to the bourgeoisie. The emergence of subjective economics was the logical consequence of the development of a trend of ideas reflecting the sharpening of class struggle. Its stages were marked by the activities of such well-known thinkers as Bentham, Say, Senior, Bastiat. Jevons refers, among others, to Bentham, to his utility mechanism, his attempt to evaluate pleasure and pain, and to Bastiat who held that the ultimate subject of economics was human desires, and desires, efforts and satisfaction constituted the circle within which political economy had to move. He also referred to Senior, who represented wealth as the totality of scarce goods which directly or indirectly give pleasure, or remove pain. Walras attributes the principles of his theory to his father, August Walras, and regards Cournot as his master in applying the tools of mathematics to economic analysis.

Then, around the middle of the last century, several studies were published which paved the way for a radical change in value theory. Thus, among others, A.J.E.J. Dupuit, a French civil engineer, the chief supervisor of the roads and bridges in Paris, tried to point out—primarily in connection with the pricing policy for public services—that should a public institution increase the supply of its services, it must diminish their prices. R. Jennings, with the law of the variation of sensations, had already stated that the consumer does not derive the same satisfaction from each unit of a stock of goods. And we could go on enumerating the forerunners of the new value concept. The subjective interpretation of value appears in an already elaborated form in Gossen's book published in 1854, in which he formulates exactly the laws of his doctrine. Gossen's views were completely ignored in his lifetime. It was only later, after his death, that Jevons became aware of the significance of Gossen's theory through a work of the Hungarian economist Gyula Kautz[6]: he then admitted the similarity between Gossen's views and his own.

Thus the way had already been paved for Menger, Jevons and Walras.

Despite the approximate coincidence in time, it is not likely that the emergence of the subjective economic tendencies in the 1870s was a direct reaction to the appearance of Marx's *Capital*. Jevons had already worked out his theory by 1962, and none of the founders of the subjective school was concerned with Marx's teachings. It was only their followers who took up the fight against them.

The change that took place in the theoretical system of non-Marxian economics undoubtedly reflects the changes in the structure and institutions of the capitalist economy. It would be historically unjustified to link the emergence of subjective economics to the rise of monopoly capitalism. Lenin characterizes the 1870s and 1880s as the climax of the development of free competition, a period when monopolies existed only in their embryonic state.[7] It can, however, be related to the spread of corporate forms of undertaking, primarily the joint-stock companies. This is how Marx sees the structural transformation of the capitalist economy: "the abolition of capitalist private industry on the basis of the capitalist

---

[6] J. Kautz: *Theorie und Geschichte der Nationalökonomik*, Wien, 1858, Propyläen, Vol. I, p. 9.
[7] V. I. Lenin: *Imperialism, the Highest Stage of Capitalism*, Moscow, 1970, p. 22.

system itself..."[8] "... [the joint-stock companies] represent a mere phase of transition to a new form of production."[9] The joint-stock company form "... reproduces a new financial aristocracy, a new variety of parasites..."[10] It is, then, the spread of this corporate form that finds expression in the subjective economics of the 1870s. This manifests itself, among other things, in the fact that its representatives divorce capital ownership from the function of capital, on the one hand, and capitalist entrepreneur from passive capital owner, on the other, and further that by ignoring the cost side they determine the value of the means of production, i.e. capital goods, like stock prices, as capitalized return. This analogy is also emphasized by Wieser, another prominent representative of the Austrian School besides Menger, its founder: "The greater the dividend expected from a stock, the higher will be the value put upon the stock. This illustration of stocks and dividends is, on the whole, the best that could be given to explain productive value."[11] Starting from consumption rather than production also shows that, with the spread of the corporate form, "... the capitalist disappears as superfluous from the production process."[12]

Changes in the endeavours of the bourgeoisie also explain the emergence of the tendencies of subjective economics. The task is no longer to fight against obsolete social relations, but how to behave in the most rational way under the new capitalist relations. It needs therefore theories which provide guidance how to make optimum use of resources, how to produce more goods with less cost, and how to gain thereby the largest possible profit.

[8] K. Marx: op. cit., Vol. III, p. 429.
[9] Ibid.
[10] Ibid.
[11] F. Wieser: Natural Value, New York, 1930 (reprint of the 1893 edition), p. 71.
[12] K. Marx: op. cit., Vol. III, p. 380.

Chapter 2

THE SUBJECTIVE INTERPRETATION OF VALUE

The three founders of modern non-Marxian economics sought the conditions for maximizing the satisfaction of wants in the fields of households, exchange and production. It was also in accordance with this aim that they formulated their value theory as a category of optimization. Therefore it seems expedient also to approach the theories of value, price and income distribution as evolved in the 1870s from the angle of the optimum allocation of resources.

The principle of the optimum allocation of resources is, according to Kenneth Boulding, a prominent American representative of today's non-Marxian economics, the *principle of equal advantage:* "The market economy is governed by a principle which we may call the principle of equal advantage."[13]

The development of modern non-Marxian value, price and income distribution theories compared to the subjective theories of the 1870s, is virtually nothing else but a more elaborate formulation of this principle.

In Boulding's opinion, the principle of equal advantage presupposes that in the continuous utilization of some means or resources in a given field of human activity, the allocative efficiency of these means or resources is diminishing. Now, if the economic subject finds that with some of his means or resources suitable for an alternative use he can achieve better results in another field than where he is employing them, then this means that he has gone too far in their present use. Since he aims at achieving optimum results, he will find it worth transferring part of his means and resources from a less to a more advantageous use. In this way, he will gain more advantage than he has sacrificed. But as a result of continuous re-allocation, the efficiency of the use of his means and resources will rise from where he has withdrawn them owing to a decrease in their quantity used, while where he now employs them, their efficiency will fall as a result of the increase in their quantity. He will finally reach a point at which the advantage gained will just equal the advantage sacrificed. It is by this allocation of his means and resources that our economic subject has achieved the optimum result, a situation in which the last unit of the means and resources used in any field ensures him the same advantage.

The principle of equal advantage emerges in modern non-Marxian economic theory whenever the economic subjects wish to attain a certain objective by the optimum allocation of those means and resources suitable for being used in an alternative way.

[13] K. Boulding: *Economic Analysis,* New York, London–Tokyo, 1966, p. 87.

In the subjective economic theories of the 1870s, the individual consumer is faced with the aim: the maximum satisfaction of his wants. And the principle of diminishing efficiency appears in the form of the principle of *diminishing pleasure*[14]; or, in the Marshallian formulation: the law of satiable wants. Marshall says: "There is an endless variety of wants, but there is a limit to each separate want."[15] This means that in the course of their successive satisfaction, the individual wants will sooner or later reach the point of satiety. And since the satisfaction of his wants gives pleasure to the consumer, the intensity of pleasure will diminish in the course of their continuous satisfaction. Drinking the second glass of water does not give the same pleasure as the first one.

To illustrate the principle in question by an example in figures: if drinking the first glass of water gives our individual, say, 10 units of pleasure, the second will be the source of only 8, the third of 6, the fourth of 4, the fifth of 1 unit of pleasure. The principle of diminishing pleasure was formulated by the German Gossen as early as 1854. It was in his honour that Wieser, and after him non-Marxian economics called it *Gossen's first law*. The similarity between the principle of diminishing pleasure and the Weber–Fechner Law well known in psycho-physiology is conspicuous. According to this law, the greater the intensity of an initial stimulus, the more it must grow to cause an appreciable difference in the response to it. If, however, the stimulus is repeated within a definite period of time at constant intensity, the intensity of the subsequent response will diminish. In the doctrine of diminishing pleasure the stimulus is the increase in the stock of goods, and the response is the pleasure obtained from the satisfaction of wants.

It is on the principle of diminishing pleasure that Menger's, Jevons's and Walras's value theories are based. According to their theories, a consumer evaluates any unit of a given stock of commodity in terms of the pleasure its consumption gives him. In other words, it is the degree of accomplishing the aim that gives value to the means, the unit of the commodity. Though from the point of view of the satisfaction of wants each unit of a given commodity has a different value according to whether it is consumed earlier or later, the assumption being that each unit of the given stock is homogeneous and thus perfectly substitutable, the consumer will not attach, in a subjective way, different values to each unit. He will evaluate them all alike, attributing to each of them the same significance as to the last unit of the given stock of the commodity. Each unit will count, from the point of view of achieving his aim, the satisfaction of his want as if it were the last one. Should any unit of a given stock of a commodity, say, 5 glasses of water, get lost, it is always the want of the last unit, the fifth glass of water, that remains unsatisfied. The consumer can replace the previous units, if they are lost, by the last one. The subjective significance for the consumer of the last unit available to him is *marginal utility*, and thus, in the subjective valuation of the consumer, any unit of the stock is measured in terms of marginal utility. The name marginal utility comes from Wieser, an economist of the Austrian School following in the footsteps of Menger. He writes: "In the following I shall call the utility of goods

[14] In Jevons's formulation: "Increase of the same kind of consumption yields pleasure continuously diminishing up to the point of satiety." W. S. Jevons: *Theory of Political Economy*, 3rd ed., London, 1888, Preface, p. xxxii.

[15] A. Marshall: *Principles of Economics*, 8th ed., London, 1930, p. 93.

crucial to the value of the unit of goods, since it is just at the margin of economically possible use, economic marginal utility, or in brief, marginal utility."[16] It is this term coined by Wieser to denote value interpreted as a subjective judgement of the consumer that has come to be established in non-Marxian economics.

The greater the stock of a given commodity available to a consumer, the farther he can go in satisfying his want of that commodity, and the smaller will be the marginal utility of that commodity; but marginal utility will become higher if the size of his stock of that commodity is smaller. It is the so-called utility function which expresses the way in which the subjective significance of each unit of a given stock of a commodity depends on the size of that stock.

For marginal utility to assume a positive magnitude, it is necessary that the commodity should be available to the consumer in a limited quantity, that is, to use a term of non-Marxian economics, the good should be scarce. "... for a commodity to have value it is necessary that the danger should really exist that some of our wants may be left unsatisfied if part of that stock of commodity is lost, and the greater the danger of some of our wants remaining unsatisfied, the greater must be its value."[17] It is in this sense that Wieser writes: "Value means that pleasure is associated with anxiety..."[18]

The scarcity of goods expressed in marginal utility is the theoretical basis on which the theories of Menger, Jevons and Walras are constructed.

The concept of marginal utility expressing the scarcity of goods is in practice a first derivative, and Jevons already defines it as such. If u is the total utility of quantity x of a commodity, then marginal utility (Jevons calls it the final degree of utility) is the increment of total utility $\dfrac{du}{dx}$ which is obtained if quantity x is changed by an infinitely small unit, dx. As such it expresses the movement of total utility as a function of the size of a stock of a commodity. Now the principle of diminishing pleasure in Jevons's formulation is this: with the quantity of a stock of a commodity increasing, its total utility will also increase, but at a diminishing rate.

[16] F. Wieser: *Über den Ursprung und die Hauptgesetze des wirtschaftlichen Werthes*. Wien, 1884, p. 128.

[17] F. Heller: *A határhaszon* (Marginal utility), Budapest, 1904, p. 4.

[18] F. Wieser: *op. cit.*, p. 87.

Chapter 3

JEVONS'S ATTEMPT TO DETERMINE THE EQUILIBRIUM EXCHANGE RATIO BY MEANS OF MARGINAL UTILITY

Menger's, Jevons's and Walras's exchange value, i.e. price theories are built upon the marginal utility concept. We shall provide the explanation of price formation, i.e. of the evolution of equilibrium exchange value based on marginal utility, by presenting Jevons's theory, since his (and Walras's) theory is more advanced than that of Menger and of the Austrian School in general. With Walras's theoretical system we shall deal in Chapter 8, Part One. Relying on the principle of equal advantage, Jevons, like Walras, tries to determine the equilibrium exhange ratio (equation of exchange) by means of the theory of marginal utility.

Let A and B, says Jevons, represent two trading bodies engaged in exchange. A has wheat, B has beef. A has in his possession quantity a of wheat, and B quantity b of beef. Thus, taking the stock of commodities of the two parties as given, he entirely disregards production, and wishes to determine the equation of exchange of the two commodities without taking into account the costs of production. Also known in Jevons's model, are the utility functions of wheat and beef both for A and B. Now, given these data, Jevons says, the exchange equilibrium can be determined.

He tries to determine the margin of exchange for both parties to the exchange by means of marginal analysis, and then breaks down the process of exchange into subsequent acts of exchange: they procure the quantities needed not at the same time, but subsequently, in small quantities. The exchange takes place at as yet unknown but constant exchange ratios.

In each exchange act A gives up quantity dx of his stock of wheat in exchange for quantity dy of beef obtained from B. A is willing to continue the exchange as long as it can improve his position, that is, as long as he can get more utility by means of dy received than he has to sacrifice by giving up dx. But in the course of continuous exchange his stock of wheat will diminish, and consequently the marginal utility of wheat will increase, while, with his stock of beef increasing, the marginal utility of beef will fall. The utility received will steadily decrease, and the utility given up will rise, i.e. the two utilities will come closer to each other. The margin of exchange is marked by the point where the utilities of the last dy received and the last dx given up are equal. In a similar way, says Jevons, we can determine the margin of exchange for B at the exchange ratio of $\dfrac{dx}{dy}$

The two parties will continue the exchange until they have derived all benefit that the exchange can offer them. "This point of equilibrium will be known by the

23

criterion that an infinitely small amount of commodity exchanged in addition, at the same rate, will bring neither gain nor loss of utility."[19]

According to Jevons's theory, every seller also has an "own demand" for his product, since he does not sell his whole stock of commodities but retains part of it for his own consumption, depending on the size of the exchange ratio. This is conceivable of course in the case of simple exchange. But own consumption is of no importance to a capitalist. It would be absurd to assume that a capitalist evaluates the commodity offered for sale subjectively.

Jevons also tries to demonstrate the determination of the exchange margins for both parties in a diagrammatic form. Graphical representation is rendered difficult by the fact that finite magnitudes have to be substituted for infinitely small ones.

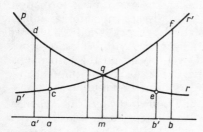

Source: W. S. Jevons: *The Theory of Political Economy,* London, 1888, p. 97.

Figure 1

Curve *pqr* (See Fig. 1) represents the formation of the marginal utility of the commodity to be bought, and curve *p'qr'* that of the own commodity, as a function of the increase in their quantity for *A*. While the curve represents the increase in the quantity of the commodity to be bought moving from point *a* towards point *b*, it shows the quantity of the own commodity moving in the opposite direction, from *b* towards *a*.

For the sake of simplicity, let the exchange ratio be 1:1. In this case, the quantities of the commodity received and given up are demonstrated by the same distance. By giving up quantity *a'a* of his own product and getting quantity *a'a* of the other party's commodity, exchange party *A* obtains utility *ad* in exchange for utility *a'c*. The utility gained is greater than the utility sacrificed. Proceeding along the line towards point *q*, they converge. Beyond point *q* the utility gained is less than the utility sacrificed. Thus, at point *q*, Jevons obtained *A*'s demand and supply at the exchange ratio of 1:1.

He determines *B*'s demand and supply in a similar way at the ratio of 1:1, by means of the utility function of the two commodities. If at the exchange ratio of 1:1 *A*'s demand equals *B*'s supply, and *B*'s demand equals *A*'s supply, then the exchange ratio of 1:1 was an equilibrium exchange ratio.

Let us express in the form of an equation that at the margin of exchange the utilities gained and sacrificed become equal for both parties, assuming that for this, *A* had to give up quantity *x* of his own product and to receive quantity

[19] W. S. Jevons: *op. cit.,* p. 96.

24

y of B's product, while in B's case, conversely, he had to give up quantity y of his own product and receive quantity x of A's product.

$$\varphi_1(a-x)\,dx = \psi_1 y\,dy, \text{ whence } \frac{\varphi_1(a-x)}{\psi_1 y} = \frac{dy}{dx},$$

where $\varphi_1(a-x)$ is the marginal utility of the stock of wheat left over after the exchange for A, and $\psi_1 y$ is the marginal utility of the stock of beef bought for A. Conversely, $\psi_2(b-y)\,dy = \varphi_2 x\,dx$, whence

$$\frac{\varphi_2 x}{\psi_2(b-y)} = \frac{dy}{dx},$$

where $\psi_2(b-y)$ is the marginal utility of the stock of beef left over after the exchange for B, and $\varphi_2 x$ is the marginal utility of the stock of wheat bought for B.

We seek therefore an exchange ratio of $\dfrac{dy}{dx}$ at which, with the advantages equalizing for both parties, A demands just the same quantity of B's product as B offers for sale, and B demands just the same quantity of A's commodity as A offers for sale. We have two equations and four unknowns, dy, dx, x and y. Since the exchange ratio was constant throughout, $\dfrac{dy}{dx}$ can be substituted for $\dfrac{y}{x}$, and thus we obtain $\dfrac{\varphi_1(a-x)}{\psi_1 y} = \dfrac{y}{x} = \dfrac{\varphi_2 x}{\psi_2(b-y)}.$ And Jevons comes to the conclusion: "The two equations are sufficient to determine the results of exchange; for there are only two unknown quantities concerned, namely x and y, the quantities given and received."[20]

But Jevons's equations do not provide a definite solution from the point of view of the marginal utility theory. The equilibrium exchange ratio is undetermined. The task would be to determine an exchange ratio at which both parties have found maximum total utility, when the ratio of marginal utilities equals the exchange ratio for both parties. If, however, the $\dfrac{dy}{dx}$ assumed at the start was not the equilibrium exchange ratio, quantity dx of wheat and quantity dy of beef exchanged can already lead to equilibrium for one party, but not yet for the other. But the latter can always offer his partner some exchange ratio at which they can continue the exchange with advantage to both of them. They then change the exchange ratio until finally the ratios of the marginal utilities are equal for both, and neither is interested in continuing the exchange. Thus an equilibrium position is eventually brought about. In this case, however, $\dfrac{dy}{dx}$ will not equal $\dfrac{y}{x}$, and thus cannot be substituted for in the equation. It is absolutely not necessary—writes Wicksell—that "the relation between the marginal utility of the two commodities (which, in equilibrium, should be the same on each side) will be also the same as the proportion in which the *whole* quantities exchanged stand to each other... this

[20] W. S. Jevons: *op. cit.*, p. 100.

ratio can, within certain limits, very indefinitely, and in each particular case the relation between the marginal utilities of the goods at the margin of exchange will be different, though always the same on both sides for the persons exchanging."[21] The size of the equilibrium exchange ratio depends on the exchange ratio assumed to exist at the beginning of the exchange process. Obviously, the equation ratio will be different at the end of the exchange if at the beginning the exchange ratio was favourable for *A*, who obtained more beef for giving up little wheat, and different again if at the beginning the exchange ratio was more favourable for *B*, and thus his stock of wheat increased for giving up little beef. If at the beginning of the exchange the assumed ratio was not an equilibrium ratio, an alteration in the exchange ratio may modify the distribution of goods between the two trading parties in the course of the exchange, and thus its effect will be the same as if they had begun the exchange with different stocks. The problem was first analysed by Edgeworth. Detailed discussion of it can also be found in Marshall and Wicksell.

Marshall stresses that "the uncertainty of the ultimate position of equilibrium does not depend on the fact that one commodity is being bartered for another instead of being sold for money. It results from our being obliged to regard the marginal utilities of all commodities as varying."[22]

[21] K. Wicksell: *Vorlesungen über Nationalökonomie*, Jena, 1913, p. 101. Also published in English: *Lectures on Political Economy*, London, 1951, Vol. I.,
[22] A. Marshall: *op. cit.*, London, 1930, p. 793.

Chapter 4

MARSHALL'S ATTEMPT TO BUILD THE DEMAND FUNCTION ON THE PRINCIPLE OF DIMINISHING UTILITY

According to Marshall, whether a commodity is bartered for another, or is sold in exchange for money, we can obtain a definite solution independent of the initial exchange ratio only if we take the marginal utility of one good to be constant: in the case of a market economy, money.

Let us examine more closely what the assumption of the constancy of the marginal utility of money implies.

Take the demand equation $D_x = f(p_x, y)$, where D_x is the demand for commodity x, p_x is the price of x, and y is the income of the consumer. The constancy of the marginal utility of money means, in Marshall's view, that the amount of money spent on buying a commodity will affect the income of the consumer to a negligible extent, and so will, at least within a certain range, a change in the price of the commodity too. As a consequence, the supply of a certain quantity of goods placed on the market will be brought into equilibrium with demand by the same price, irrespective of whether the exchange was begun at an equilibrium price or not.

Let us illustrate what we have stated by a simple arbitrary example. Let us assume that the utility function of the commodity x is known:

The utility of the 1st unit is 20,
the utility of the 2nd unit is 18,
the utility of the 3rd unit is 16,
the utility of the 4th unit is 14,
the utility of the 5th unit is 12.

Marshall also holds the view that at the margin of purchase the utility sacrificed and gained must be equalized. Thus, the marginal utility of the commodity brought must be equal to the marginal utility of the money paid, which is simply the price multiplied by the marginal utility of money.

But what exactly is the marginal utility of money? If we consider money only in its function as a medium of circulation, the marginal utility of money is understood by the advocates of the theory to be the utility of goods that can be bought for the last unit of money income. Thus, when purchasing goods, the consumer compares the marginal utility of the commodity to be bought with the utility of alternative commodities which he could buy for the same amount of money, and weighs up the utility gained in relation to the utility sacrificed.

Denoting the marginal utility of commodity x by MU_x, and the marginal utility of money by MU_M, then at the margin of purchase the following equation must obtain:

$$MU_x = p_x MU_M$$

According to Marshall, MU_M can be taken to be constant in the exchange if the consumer spends only a fraction of his income on buying the commodity in question.

Let us suppose that of commodity x three units are brought on to the market, our consumer is the only buyer, and he does not take advantage of his monopoly position, but behaves as if undisturbed competition were prevailing on the demand side. Let the marginal utility of money be constant, say, 2. In this case the price at which the consumer is willing to buy the three units of the product, or to use Marshall's expression, the demand price of the three units is given by:

$$p_x = \frac{MU_x}{MU_M} = \frac{16}{2} = 8 \text{ shillings.}$$

In case the three units are supplied, the equilibrium price is 8 shillings.

Let us assume that neither party knows the equilibrium price of the three units of product x. Our consumer begins to make his purchases not at the equilibrium price, but at a price of 9 shillings, and is willing to buy 2 units of commodity x at a price of 9 shillings, because the marginal utility of the two units of commodity x, 18, divided by the marginal utility of money, 2, equals exactly the price of 9 shillings. He pays, then, 18 shillings for the two units. However, at a price of 9 shillings supply exceeds demand. Consequently, the price must fall. At a price of 8 shillings, our consumer will buy the third unit of the commodity, too and the equilibrium between demand and supply will thus be established. Since we have taken the marginal utility of money to be constant, the fact that the initial price was not an equilibrium price and thus our consumer paid 26 shillings instead of 24 for the three units of commodity x, did not affect the magnitude of the equilibrium price, and so it has remained invariably 8 shillings, independently of the initial price. The demand function has not changed either. Our consumer is willing to buy three units of commodity x at a price of 8 shillings.

Let us assume now that the marginal utility of money alters in the exchange, since the earlier purchases at a non-equilibrium price appreciably influenced the size of the consumer's money income. In our demand function the magnitude of y changes, and the demand function shifts with each change in y. Suppose now that the expenditure of 18 shillings at a price of 9 shillings has increased the marginal utility of money from 2 to 2.5. Therefore, the consumer is willing to pay for the third unit of the commodity not 8, but $\frac{16}{2.5} = 6.4$ shillings. The formula $p_x = \frac{MU_x}{MU_M}$ makes it obvious that at a marginal utility of 16 of the third unit of product the demand price of the three units of product will change depending on the change in MU_M, that is, on the price our consumer has paid for the previous units, on the sum he has spent on purchasing them.

In his work published in 1880, it is only the demand function that Marshall

28

wishes to explain by the principle of diminishing utility, i.e. the theory of diminishing marginal utility.

On the basis of the principle of diminishing utility he wants to answer the question why the demand curve is negatively sloped. The demand function as interpreted by Marshall is just one variant of it; the other is attributed to Walras.

In his demand function Marshall takes quantity to be the independent variable, and the so-called demand price to be the dependent variable. According to Marshall, the *demand price* of a given quantity of a commodity is the price at which the market is just willing to take up the quantity in question. With the increase in the quantity of the commodity placed on the market, the demand price will decline to express, as it were, the diminishing of marginal utility to the individual consumers. If we knew the utility function of commodity x, then the quotient of the marginal utility of x and of the marginal utility of money assumed to be constant would express how the demand price of commodity x declined as its quantity increased. Or, conversely, if we know, says Marshall, in what quantity and at what price the consumer is willing to make his purchase, that is, if we know his individual demand function, then, given the constancy of the marginal utility of money, the change in the demand price will express, with the quantity being changed, the change in the marginal utility of the commodity in question, i.e. the "law" of diminishing utility in the case of the individual concerned. "... let us translate this law of diminishing utility into terms of price", says Marshall.[23] Marginal utility expressed in terms of price can now be defined as the maximum amount of money that the consumer is willing to pay for the additional unit of the commodity in question.

It is diminishing utility, writes Marshall, that explains why the demand price declines as the quantity of the commodity rises, why the demand curve slopes negatively. At the same time, the principle of diminishing utility ensures that at a given price only one single equilibrium point exists and that it is stable, and all consumers tend to advance towards that point. In other words, it ensures the secondary condition of maximizing total utility.

If it were really possible to draw up each consumer's demand function in respect of individual commodities, and thereby to construct the marginal utility function, then the so-called *consumer's surplus* could also be found. This concept created by Marshall is essentially the expression of the fact that the utility gained exceeds the utility sacrificed. In Marshall's words: "... the satisfaction which he [i.e. the consumer—A. M.] gets from its purchase generally exceeds that which he gives up in paying away its price; and he thus derives from the purchase a surplus of satisfaction. The excess of the price which he would be willing to pay rather than go without the thing, over that which he actually does pay, is the economic measure of this surplus satisfaction. It may be called *consumer's surplus*."[24]

Let us take an example. The purchaser is willing to buy just one pound of tea at a price of 10 shillings a pound, and an additional pound only when its price drops to 9 shillings a pound. At 9 shillings a pound our individual can buy 2 pounds of tea for 18 shillings, which is $10+9 = 19$ shillings' worth to him. In this way, he can achieve 1 shilling of consumer's surplus. Consumer's surplus expresses

---

[23] A. Marshall: *op. cit.*, p. 94.
[24] A. Marshall: *op. cit.*, p. 124.

that in the exchange each party gains, gives up something that has less utility to him in exchange for something having more utility to him.

If it were really possible to measure consumer's surplus, then the difference in its size in the case of individuals belonging to different social classes would reflect the difference between their social positions. Assume that a poor and a rich man equally like tea. But the rich man buys it at the same price as the poor one, though the marginal utility of money to him is smaller. Thus he gives up less utility than the poor man to derive the same satisfaction from it.

Marshall is credited with the first formulation of the price elasticity of demand. Like every elasticity, the price elasticity of demand is also a relationship between percentage changes, the ratio of the percentage change in price to that in the quantity demanded: $\dfrac{dQ}{Q} : \dfrac{dp}{p}$. Marshall points out that the elasticity of demand is affected, among other things, by the individual's social position. For a given price, the demand elasticity of the same commodity will be different for the various consumer strata, according to their wealth position, size of incomes, etc. If, e.g., the price of meat, milk, tobacco, wool, etc. declines, the demand for them will considerably rise among the low-income consumers, and thus their demand for these goods is elastic within a certain price range. Within the same range of prices, however, the demand for these goods will not grow as a result of lower prices among the well-to-do social strata, who are in a position to satisfy their wants of the goods even if their prices are higher. Therefore, their demand for the goods in question is inelastic at such prices. The situation is just the reverse in the case of luxury goods. It is only the richest that can afford to buy them at a high price. At a lower price the demand for them will be elastic among those having medium income or property, but will be inelastic with the wealthiest stratum. The latter will be able to buy them even at higher prices. And the demand will also be inelastic with the poor, who are not able to buy these goods even at lower prices.

Marshall also pointed out that the statement that the elasticity of demand changes as a function of the price level is equally valid for any commodity and any purchaser, independently of their social position. "The elasticity of demand is great for high prices, and great, or at least considerable, for medium prices, but it declines as the price falls, and gradually fades away if the fall goes so far that satiety level is reached."[25] However, even in the case of the same product different prices will be regarded as high or low, according to different social classes.

Marshall represents the elasticity of demand by means of co-ordinate geometry in the following way (Fig. 2):

Let us reduce the price MP by PR, and the demand will rise from $0M$ to $0M'$, that is, by RP'. Now the elasticity of demand can be expressed as follows:

$$\frac{P'R}{0M} : \frac{PR}{PM}$$

Written in a product form:

$\dfrac{P'R}{PR} \cdot \dfrac{PM}{0M}$. Since $\dfrac{P'R}{PR} = \dfrac{TM}{PM}$, we can substitute the latter: $\dfrac{TM}{PM} \cdot \dfrac{PM}{0M} = \dfrac{TM}{0M}$.

---

[25] A. Marshall: *op. cit.*, p. 103.

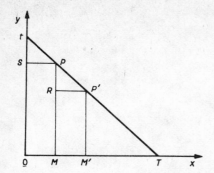

Figure 2

But $\dfrac{TM}{0M} = \dfrac{TP}{tP} = \dfrac{0S}{St}$, where $0S$ is the price and St the distance between the point of intersection of the demand curve with the price axis and price. The value of the fraction $\dfrac{0S}{St}$ shows that the elasticity of demand will rise as the price increases.

Chapter 5

GOSSEN'S SECOND LAW

In determining the demand price of tea, Marshall tried, on the basis of the principle of diminishing marginal utility, to find an answer to the question what price our consumer is willing to pay for the quantity of tea offered for sale. But in basing the general theory of demand on the principle of diminishing marginal utility, a difficulty arises as soon as it is assumed that the consumer has a demand for several goods to be satisfied from his given income.

Our consumer wants to buy commodities x, y, ... z, and in such proportions and quantities that the total utility $U = U_x(q)_x + U_y(q)_y + ... + U_z(q)_z$ should be at a maximum. If he could obtain the goods free of charge, he would get as much of each commodity as would make its marginal utility zero. But our consumer buys from his money income y at the given prices of p_x, p_y ... p_z.

The limiting condition is: $y = p_x q_x + p_y q_y + ... + p_z q_z$.

The task is to determine how our consumer should spend his income, with the prices given, in an optimum way; how much he should buy of each of the commodities so that his total utility be at a maximum within those limits. The relevant problem can be solved mathematically by introducing the so-called Lagrange multiplier. But a solution without applying mathematics is also possible. Our consumer will continue to buy, on the basis of equal advantage, each of the commodities at the prevailing prices until the following equation is satisfied:

$$p_x MU_M = MU_x, \quad p_y MU_M = MU_y ....p_z MU_M = MU_z.$$

But the marginal utility of money must be the same in each of its uses, or else our consumer is in a position to improve his situation by withdrawing money from the purchase of such goods where the marginal utility of money is smaller, and employs the money so withdrawn in buying goods where its marginal utility is greater. He attains the maximum satisfaction of his wants by buying goods in a proportion in which, at established prices, the unit of money last spent on buying any commodity will give him the same increment in utility, that is, a proportion at which the marginal utility of money will be the same whatever use it is put to.

Expressed in a formula: $\dfrac{MU_x}{p_x} = \dfrac{MU_y}{p_y} = ... = \dfrac{MU_x}{p_z} = MU_M.$

In mathematical terms, the marginal utility of money will appear as the Lagrange multiplier.

This principle of the equalization of the marginal utility of money is called by non-Marxian economics, following Lexis, Gossen's second law.

In deriving Gossen's second law, we assumed the measurability of marginal utility by its own subjective units. This concept of utility is called the *cardinal* interpretation of utility.

One variant of the cardinal interpretation of utility represents the utilities of certain goods as independent of the utilities of other goods, and regards the marginal utility of a commodity as the function of its own quantity.

The proportionality of prices and marginal utilities expressed in Gossen's second law, assuming the independent utilities of individual goods, offered besides Marshall's experiment discussed above, a further possibility for the followers of the marginal utility theory to draw up a marginal utility function. If a series of situations can be found in which the prices of two goods, x and y, are different, and different quantities of x are consumed but always the same quantity of y, then in the equation

$$\frac{p_x}{p_y} = \frac{MU_x}{MU_y}$$

MU_y is constant, and thus the movement of MU_x is expressed by $\frac{p_x}{p_y} \cdot MU_y$, that is, by the change in relative prices. Though the magnitude of the marginal utility is indefinite, it would still be possible to determine the form of the marginal utility function. It was under such considerations that Ragnar Frisch tried to demonstrate the change in the marginal utility of money as a function of the change in money income. (For more details see Part Five, Chapter 2.)

Let us assume that p_x diminishes and the marginal utility of money is constant, i.e. that a fall in p_x does not affect the consumer's real income. In this case MU_x also has to decline. But MU_x will fall if our consumer, given his scale of wants, buys more of commodity x. We obtain the same result even if a fall in p_x does affect the consumer's real income, diminishing thereby the marginal utility of money, but the prices of other goods are raised accordingly to ensure that the consumer's real income remain at an unchanged level. Consequently, if the price of a good decreases, the individual's demand, with his real income remaining unchanged, must rise. This effect is called in economic literature, in honour of the Russian economist Slutsky, the *Slutsky, or substitution, effect*.

But what will happen if a fall in p_x also changes the individual's real income and the economist takes into account the relationship of use-values. Assume, for example, that the price of margarine falls. Thus, with margarine becoming cheaper, it ought to oust its substitutes. But, as a result of the price fall, the consumer's real income will rise. Given a higher real income, the demand for certain commodities will rise, for others it will fall. Thus the consumer will buy a better quality substitute, for example, butter instead of margarine. On the other hand, the increasing quantity of butter will diminish the marginal utility of those commodities for which butter is a substitute. This will diminish the marginal utility of margarine and increase the marginal utility of those which are complementary to butter. Owing to the fall in the price of margarine, the consumer will re-arrange his expenditures in order to restore the equilibrium matching the new situation —this is expressed in Gossen's law. In the new equilibrium situation he may buy less margarine and more butter. In this case, the rise in real income resulting from the fall in the price of margarine diminishes the demand for it. Marshall recognized that there were goods the demand for which, with their prices being changed, was uncertain, owing to the effect of these changes on the consumer's real income. In this connection he writes: "Sir R. Giffen has pointed out, a rise in the price of bread makes so large a drain on the resources of the poor labouring families and raises so much the marginal utility of money to them, that they are forced to curtail their consumption of meat and the more expensive farinaceous foods: and, bread being still the cheapest food which they can get and will take, they consume more, and not less of it."[26] In this case, the demand curve for bread will not be negatively sloped and cannot be derived from the principle of diminishing utility. Though emphasizing that such cases are rather rare, Marshall insists on the necessity of assuming the marginal utility of money as given, in order to eliminate the effect of the change in the marginal utility of money on the demand for a commodity, as a result of a change in the price of that commodity. That is, "he neglected the effect on demand of the changes in real income which result from changes in price."[27] Assuming the constancy of the marginal utility of money, if the price of a commodity declines, the demand for it must rise to satisfy the equation $MU_x = p_x MU_M$. The uncertainty of the effect of a change in price, through the changes in real income, on the demand for a given commodity is a further reason why Marshall assumed in his demand theory the marginal utility of money to be constant.

[26] A. Marshall: *op. cit.,* ρ. 132.
[27] J. R. Hicks: *Value and Capital,* Oxford, 1965, 2nd ed. reprinted, p. 32.

Chapter 6

THE LAW OF COSTS ACCORDING TO THE FOLLOWERS OF THE MARGINAL UTILITY THEORY

The representatives of the marginal utility theory initially raised the problem of value as separated from production. Similarly, they abstracted from production when they made the attempt to provide an explanation, based on value theory, of the problem of price formation. But a full exposition of value and price theory makes it also necessary to include reproduction, even in a theoretical system starting from the consumption side. In doing so, the adherents of the marginal utility theory had to provide a subjective interpretation of production costs. "For the costs of production are nothing in the world but the total of the production goods which had to be used up in order to produce a good, they are the capital goods, labor, etc., that have been consumed in that process."[28] But have the factors of production any value from the point of view of the marginal utility theory, since they cannot be consumed directly? Yes, they have, as they do contribute to the consumer's attaining his aim, to the satisfaction of his wants, by taking a direct or indirect part in producing consumer goods. Thus their value derives from the significance the consumers attach to the consumer goods produced with the contribution of the factors of production, or in other words, it depends on the extent to which a consumption good produced with their participation contributes to the satisfaction of the consumer's wants. According to the marginal utility theory, the value of the factors of production is determined by the subjective value of the consumption good in whose production they participate. Böhm–Bawerk writes: "In the light of our understanding of the value of goods it is self-evident that a production good, like any other good, can acquire value for us only when we recognize that the gaining or losing of some utility, of some satisfaction of want, depends on our possessing or not possessing that good."[29] Wieser writes similarly: "The value of production goods is determined by the value of their products or by the value of the return."[30] The derivation of the value of production factors from the value of product is called *economic imputation* in non-Marxian economics after Wieser. The greater the quantities of the factors of production available to society, the greater the quantities of consumer goods which can be manufactured by making use of them, and, consequently, the further the consumers can go in satisfying their wants, the smaller will be the subjective value of a consumption good and thus the value of factor services and the magni-

---

[28] E. Böhm-Bawerk: *Capital and Interest*, Vol. II, South Holland, Ill., 1959, p. 168.
[29] E. Böhm-Bawerk: *op. cit.*, p. 169.
[30] F. Wieser: *Natural Value*, New York, 1930, p. 70.

tude of production costs, too. In this way, production costs are completely separated from production and are resolved into the intensity of satisfaction. Some economists go to the length of seeing in this interpretation of production costs a Copernican change in economics. Böhm–Bawerk writes of the proposition that value is determined by the costs of production: "Its authority remained almost unquestioned, right down to the present day."[31] It was, in his view, only recently that people realized that the relationship was just the reverse: it is on the value of the product that the cost of production depends.

The value of factor services is the entrepreneur's production cost, on the one hand, and the income of the factors of production, on the other. Thus the representatives of the marginal utility theory also base the interpretation of the process of income distribution on the subjective explanation of value as a uniform theoretical basis of value theory.

Deducing production costs from the value of the product can also be encountered in modern programming methods: the accounting price attributed to certain resources, the so-called shadow price, expresses to what extent these resources have contributed to achieving the aim. In the following, we shall subject to criticism this interpretation of production costs, as indeed it was criticized by one of the most prominent English economists of the turn of the century, Alfred Marshall. We must note, however, that the recognition of the significance of the production factors from the point view of attaining a certain aim constitutes an essential element of the modern theory of the optimum allocation of resources, an indispensable element of programming methods. It expresses whether the factors of production capable of alternative uses have been allocated in an optimum way among various possible uses, whether or not too many have been used in one case and too few in another. Already Wieser wanted to apply the principle of economic imputation in the determination of this problem. "No part of a stock of resources should be used in one productive branch to produce a less important product while the same resources can also be used in another branch to turn out a more important product"[32]—he writes in expounding the significance of economic imputation. Such a valuation, however, means the measurement of the significance of resources from the point of view of attaining the aim, on the basis of the role that they play in the production of commodities, and not the determination of the actual value of the resources themselves.

The derivation of production costs from the value of products provides the basis for an interpretation, not uncommon even today, of the costs of products turned out by means of production factors suitable for a variety of alternative uses. This cost concept was developed by Wieser. "People have a limited stock of all production goods compared to their actual wants. If they use up some circulating capital, or labour, in a certain productive branch, they divert them from alternative uses; fixed capital itself and indestructible land, too, are lastingly tied up in the branch of production concerned."[33] "To say that any kind of production involves cost, simply implies that the economic means of production, which could doubtless

[31] E. Böhm-Bawerk: *op. cit.*, p. 168.
[32] F. Wieser: *Über den Ursprung und die Hauptgesetze des wirtschaftlichen Werthes*, Wien, 1884, pp. 148–149.
[33] F. Wieser: *op. cit.*, p. 100.

have been usefully employed in other directions, are either used up in it, or are suspended during it."[34] Or, in other words, if, by means of scarce factors capable of alternative uses, we increase the output of a product by one unit, we must go without producing a certain quantity of another product. Thus the production cost of an additional unit of product is the subjective value of the quantity of other goods forgone, i.e. a utility sacrifice. Wieser's cost theory was later adopted and further developed by Green and Davenport in the United States. According to Green,[35] the costs of production are made up of the costs of alternative opportunities forgone. If we engage the resources available to us in attaining a certain aim, we must give up devoting our factors to achieving other objectives. Thus the essence of production costs is nothing else but the sacrifice of alternative uses. This interpretation of costs has become known in Anglo-American economic literature, after Green and Davenport, by the term *opportunity cost*.

This cost concept, separated from and going beyond production has, in asserting the principle of equal advantage, an important role to play in the modern theory of the optimum allocation of resources. This concept performs a significant function in the original theory, created within the marginal utility theory already in the second half of the last century, of optimizing the use of means and resources.

The application of this concept may be demonstrated by an example faithfully reflecting the ideas of the Austrian School. Let us start from the economy of Robinson Crusoe, who tries to satisfy his wants by his own production. Let production be represented by hunting, in the course of which he uses one factor, his own labour. This has alternative uses: he may hunt either beaver or deer. Assume that Robinson Crusoe equally takes one hour to kill either one beaver or one deer, and devotes 10 hours a day to hunting. Let him first devote all these 10 hours to hunting beaver only, and nothing to hunting deer. In 10 hours a day he is able to kill 10 beavers. The marginal utility of beaver is small. If he diverted one hour from hunting beaver and used it for hunting deer, he would gain a great amount of utility by giving up a small amount. The opportunity cost of the first deer killed is much smaller than its subjective value. Or conversely, the value of the beaver last killed is much smaller than its opportunity cost, the value of the deer thus forgone. "If the value of products ... is less than that of the costs, too much has been produced; ... Where the value of the product exceeds that of the costs, too little has been produced."[36] In hunting deer, one hour of labour has much more subjective significance than in hunting beaver. It is worthwhile for him to reallocate his labour time. As the number of hours of labour spent on deer hunting increases, and that spent on beaver hunting decreases, the value thus obtained will decline, and the value sacrificed, i.e. the size of opportunity cost, will rise. An optimum allocation of time between beaver and deer hunting is reached when the utilities gained and lost are in equilibrium. Value and subjectively interpreted cost are equal in both uses: the value of the deer equals its opportunity cost, i.e. the value of the beaver forgone, and the value of the beaver equals its opportunity cost, i.e. the value of the deer forgone. The hour of labour last used results in this

[34] F. Wieser: *Natural Value*, New York, 1930, p. 175.
[35] D. I. Green: Pain Cost and Opportunity Cost, *The Quarterly Journal of Economics*, 1894, Vol. VIII.
[36] F. Wieser: *op. cit.*, p. 176.

case in the same increment of satisfaction in both of its uses. "Products ... must be produced exactly at cost value, if they are to find the most economically advantageous distribution of production."[37] Wieser's investigations of the optimum allocation of factors capable of alternative uses and available in given quantities lay the foundation for formulating the function of production possibilities, the so-called transformation function.

The derivation of production costs from the value of output, and its interpretation as utility given up, completely resolves the costs of production into intensities of satisfaction. This interpretation of costs was not uniformly accepted by each of the earlier representatives of the subjective value theory. We must appeal in the first place to Marshall, who vigorously opposed the resolution of production costs into the sensations of satisfaction and the one-sided emphasis on wants as the starting-point of economic investigations. His arguments are based on the idea that it is human activities that give rise to new wants. And, in his view, man is led by the endeavour, which can be found in all social classes, to achieve something excellent for its own sake. "Although it is man's wants in the earliest stages of his development that give rise to his activities, yet afterwards each new step upwards is to be regarded as the development of new activities giving rise to new wants, rather than of new wants giving rise to new activities."[38] What "... may claim to be the interpreter of the history of man, whether on the economic side or any other, ... is the science of activities and not that of wants".[39]

Marshall wants to reduce the money costs of production to human activities, but he wishes to approach human activities from their subjective aspect. This leads us to another interpretation of costs in subjective economics, the so-called *real cost theory*.

Real costs are the supply prices of individual production factors, that is, prices needed to ensure a certain size of supply of the individual factors. Wages are, according to Marshall, the supply price of labour. They are paid in order to induce the worker to perform labour, to undertake the disutility accompanying it, to compensate him for the fact that even if he finds pleasure in work, he will, sooner or later, get physically and mentally tired of the continuous working process, that he works under unhealthy conditions, with disagreeable fellow workers instead of devoting his time to amusement and rest. However, such an interpretation of the supply of labour can at best express that the worker, while undertaking a job, weighs up all advantages and disadvantages of that job, and is willing to take up work even for lower wages where the advantages that cannot be expressed in money terms offset the higher wages paid in other workplaces. This circumstance at most diverts the size of wages from the value of labour power; but the subjective interpretation of the supply price of labour divorces wages from the reproduction costs of labour power. Anyway, what is determinant behind the worker's intensity of sacrifice is his social position. The fact that the worker's intensity of sacrifice is a function of his social position and not the other way round, also finds expression in Marshall's interpretation when he writes: "When a workman is in fear of hunger, his need of money (its marginal utility to him)

37 F. Wieser: *op. cit.,* p. 177.
38 A. Marshall: *op. cit.,* p. 89.
39 A. Marshall: *op. cit.,* pp. 89–90.

38

is very great; and, if at starting, he gets the worst of the bargaining, and is employed at low wages, it remains great, and he may go on selling his labour at a low rate."[40]

But it is to Marshall's credit that in the interpretation of the long-term supply price of labour he already goes beyond the subjective approach and connects it with the reproduction costs of labour power. In the long run, "... wages tend to retain a close though indirect and intricate relation with the cost of rearing, training and sustaining the energy of efficient labour."[41] Wages so interpreted by him also have a role to play in the increase in the size of the labour force. "The total numbers of the people change under the action of many causes. Of these causes only some are economic; but among them the average earnings of labour take a prominent place; though their influence on the growth of numbers is fitful and irregular."[42]

Another element of the real cost in Marshall's interpretation is the effort related to saving, the supply price of "waiting". The man who diverts part of his income from personal consumption is, to use Marshall's term, waiting. Waiting is the source of capital accumulation and interest is the incentive for deferring consumption. "Everyone is aware that the accumulation of wealth is held in check, and the rate of interest so far sustained, by the preference which humanity have for present over deferred gratifications, or, in other words, by their unwillingness to 'wait'."[43]

According to Marshall, saving is made virtually by the whole of society. In his opinion, in the England of his time, a significant part of savings was made by rentiers, professional men and hired workers. He also blames English classical economists for regarding savings "... as made almost exclusively from the profits of capital."[44] Though he admits that there are people who save for the sake of increasing their wealth, he nevertheless holds the view that most people divert part of their incomes from present consumption to ensure that their families will be better off in the future than they were before. Thus he tries to reduce the significance of business saving, saving made for profit considerations, and sees the primary motive for saving in the consumer's endeavour to improve his future position. That is why he links the desire to save to the size of the rate of interest. He maintains that there are individuals who endeavour to accumulate capital in order to provide a certain income. They save less if the rate of interest rises (the Sargant effect). But it is "a nearly universal rule that a rise in the rate of interest increases the desire to save."[45]

In actual fact, however, the bulk of saving is made not for consumption but for business considerations, i.e. in order to increase capital providing surplus value. Such saving is not regulated by changes in the rate of interest.

Again, it is Keynes who later points to the fact that the magnitude of saving depends primarily on the magnitude of real income, and thus the undertaking of a "sacrifice" relating to saving presupposes a definite class position, namely, that the individual gets an income which enables him not only to consume but

---

40 A. Marshall: *op. cit.*, p. 335.
41 A. Marshall: *op. cit.*, p. 532.
42 A. Marshall: *op. cit.*, p. 143.
43 A. Marshall: *op. cit.*, p. 581.
44 A. Marshall: *op. cit.*, p. 229.
45 A. Marshall: *op. cit.*, p. 236.

also to save. The alleged sacrifice which saving implies cannot justify the existence of a return on capital. And anyway, what sacrifice does saving mean to the capitalist class when it does not prevent them from living in the greatest possible wealth, and when a luxurious way of life is increasingly becoming a requirement of their business activities.

The arguments put forward by certain economists on how to promote capital formation reveal in fact that it is the working classes who make the sacrifice of saving. As Keynes points out, one of the main arguments of neo-classical economists—given the great disparities in wealth—was that "the increase in wealth... depends on the abstinence of the rich."[46] Thus capital accumulation presupposes the low income, the low living standards of the working masses to enable the capitalists to make greater profits, from which to make their investments. Under such circumstances it is not the capitalists but the working classes that make sacrifices in relation to saving and investment.

It is the worker's efforts and waiting that jointly constitute, according to Marshall, the real cost of a good. "... the efforts and sacrifices which are the real cost of production of a thing, underlie the expenses which are money cost."[47] Thus, according to Marshall, it is on costs interpreted subjectively that the supply price of a given quantity of goods depends, that is, the price at which the producers are willing to sell just the adequate quantity of the goods concerned.

Land has, according to Marshall, no supply price. The supply of land does not mean any sacrifice to the landlord. Marshall does not regard ground rent as a real cost; it does not take part, in his view, in determining price. On the contrary, it is the excess of price over real costs as such that is a function of price formation. Marshall makes no attempt to provide a moral justification of the ground rent.

However vulgar Marshall's explanation of the production cost is—since, like the cost interpretation of the marginal utility theory, it deprives the cost of production of its social content and represents as cost what in real fact is surplus value—, the fact that it did not resolve cost into intensities of pleasure made it possible for him to criticize the economic analysis which one-sidedly starts out from marginal utility. He quotes Jevons according to whom the "cost of production determines supply. Supply determines final degree of utility. Final degree of utility determines value."[48] If, however, the costs of production are not the intensity of pleasure and are not determined by marginal utility, then, Marshall draws from Jevons's argument the conclusion that value is determined by production cost. He writes: "Now if this series of causations really existed, there could be no great harm in omitting the intermediate stages and saying that cost of production determines value."[49]

Marshall does not really accept this causal sequence. Though he does not resolve costs and thus the supply side into sensations of pleasure and indeed makes marginal utility dependent on the magnitude of costs, their magnitude is still determin-

[46] J. M. Keynes: *The General Theory of Employment, Interest and Money*, London, 1936, p. 373.
[47] A. Marshall: *op. cit.*, p. 352.
[48] A. Marshall: *op. cit.*, p. 817.
[49] A. Marshall: *op. cit.*, p. 818.

ed in his theory by the size of demand. His value theory rests on a dual basis; value is jointly determined by marginal utility and subjectively interpreted cost. "We might as reasonably dispute whether it is the upper or the lower blade of a pair of scissors that cuts a piece of paper, as whether value is governed by utility or cost of production."[50] In his view, marginal utility only determines value in the case of the elimination of production, that is, of a given size of supply and of perishable goods. The cost of production, however, would be the only determinant of value if the size of costs did not depend on the volume of output and through it the size of demand, that is, if entrepreneurs produced at constant returns.

[50] A. Marshall: *op. cit.*, p. 348.

Chapter 7

A CRITIQUE OF THE MARGINAL UTILITY THEORY

1. Does the marginal utility theory contain any rational element? Leaving aside for the time being the concept of utility, and approaching the theoretical system based on it merely from a methodological point of view, we must acknowledge as a rational element the attempt of the representatives of the theory to use marginal, differential analysis in their economic investigations. In this respect we can find in it certain elements of the modern theory of the optimum allocation of resources: the principle of equal advantage resting on the comparison of advantages gained and sacrificed, and the valuation of resources based on economic imputation, on the degree of attaining the objectives set, i.e. the principle of determining the accounting price or shadow price of factors. Though the shadow price of factors does not express the value of capital goods, or the value of labour power, it does indicate their significance for the realization of the objective at the margin of their use on the basis of the role they have played in the production of use-values.

But the three founders of subjective economics regarded the consumer's endeavours to maximize the satisfaction of their wants as the final cause of economic phenomena, and thought that the disclosure of the individual's relationship to things was the key to understanding all socio-economic phenomena. Thus their starting point was the individual with his scale of needs.

In approaching economic phenomena from the satisfaction of wants, the subjective sensations of needs are factors working only from the demand side.

No doubt, these wants can be mitigated and their intensity decreased if the quantity of the good in question increases. Also, the consumer is able to distinguish between degrees of intensity in satisfying his vital wants. Within the limits of his income, he is willing to pay a higher price for goods needed for the satisfaction of his wants of greater intensity. Writing about Gossen's first law, Péter Erdős attempts to strip it of the subjective element and unravel its inherent rational core: "... the utility of a good depending on its quantity, ... more exactly, the diminishing trend of the intensity of need and of utility ... is a fundamental truth because, among other things, as opposed to the uncertainty of individual cases, on a social scale, as a statistical rule, in the phenomena of elasticity of demand with respect to price and income, it appears with a high degree of regularity and consistency."[51] It is also true that the consumer, though his various wants are owing to their

[51] P. Erdős: *Wages, Profit, Taxation. Studies on Controversial Issues of the Political Economy of Capitalism,* Akadémiai Kiadó, Budapest, 1982, Chapter II.

quantitative differences incommensurable, endeavours to achieve a certain proportionality in their satisfaction. And this is the rational core of Gossen's second law. However, the consumers' wants exert an influence on price formation only if these wants turn into effective demand.

It is a realistic element in the false trading problem recognized by Marshall that demand for a given good changes differently if only one element of the demand function, viz. price, alters at an unchanged real income, and thus the consumer moves along an unchanged demand function, and again differently if both elements of that function, i.e price and real income, change, and thus the demand function is also shifted. Accordingly, the price at which the market will absorb a given quantity of products will be different in the two cases. The analysis carried out by Marshall, was, however, a partial one. He investigated the market only for one particular good and regarded the market for all the other goods, with a *ceteris paribus* assumption, as unchanged, whereas exchange takes place in all markets at non-equilibrium prices, that is, in one market below, in another above the equilibrium price, and thus their impact on the consumers' real income is unpredictable. It is also possible that the effects acting on real income equalize one another. In any case, it is the effects upon the demand side that is in question here, and they concern the centre of price fluctuations and the social value only in so far as the average of individual values changes through the adjustment of the output of individual goods to the demand for them.

But any analysis based on the individual consumer's intensity of wants disregards the fact that man has always performed his activities within a definite social framework. It is on the character of this social framework and the position he assumes within it that his relationship to things depends, and his social position also determines the scale of his wants.

Starting out from the intensity of wants of individual consumers cannot provide an explanation for the socially determined nature of needs. We cannot by this means answer the question why there are similarities in the structure of wants of individuals belonging to a given social group, and why we find a certain degree of equality in the demand structure of individuals belonging to the same social stratum. Even if the demand structure of the individual reflects the scale of his needs, the latter is obviously not the final cause of a given demand structure. Behind it we cannot fail to notice as a determining element laws governing the wants of the social stratum of which the individual is a member. It is exactly these laws that scientific analysis must explore. Gossen's second law cannot provide any information about the laws determining the demand structure for the very reason that it is built on a general principle entirely independent of social position. Some of the followers of non-Marxian economics also acknowledge the socially determined nature of wants. The Veblen effect expresses the fact that the individual's scale of needs, the structure of his demands are substantially modified by social influences. In his consumption habits, the individual tends to imitate the members of the social group to which he belongs. Even if such statements do not reach as far as the class roots inherent in the laws governing the demand structure, they call attention at least to the necessity of not choosing the isolated individual as a starting-point for economic investigations.

The theory which regards wants as final causes does not provide an answer to the question of what makes new wants come about. Marx reveals a mutual relationship between production and consumption. He points out that production does not exist without consumption, or else production would have no sense. A product can become a genuine product in consumption only, and consumption, by reproducing wants, stimulates production. The founders of subjective economics laid one-sided emphasis on this component of the relationship only. They disregarded the other component of the interdependence, namely, that it is production that provides the objects of consumption, it is production that determines the way people consume and brings about new needs. "The need felt for the object is induced by the perception of the object. Production accordingly produces not only an object for the subject, but also a subject for the object."[52] Marx emphasizes that it is production that plays a determinant role in the relationship of the two: "consumption is thus a phase of production."[53]

2. In the theoretical system based on the satisfaction of wants of individual consumers, social relations of production expressed in economic categories are lost. The followers of the Austrian School, or Walras himself, are even reluctant to see in the price phenomenon a sort of social utility judgement, an average of individual estimates. They see prices as the manifestation of individual utility judgements. The Austrian Böhm–Bawerk sees in them the utility judgement of the marginal consumer, and Walras that of all individual consumers. Of the three founders it is Jevons who speaks of a kind of averaging of marginal utilities. Walras and his followers severely critized Jevons, because "... he left the basis of realities—says Walras—and placed his argument on the basis of fictitious averages."[54]

But from the fact that the ultimate aim of production is the satisfaction of wants in any social system, we are not to draw the conclusion that economic analysis should start from wants. Its task is to reveal the social form of the interrelationship of production and wants typical of the economic system under consideration, to find out the economic mechanism through which these wants exert an influence on production under that economic system. Since the social form of the interrelationship of production and wants, the economic mechanism transmitting the impact of wants, varies according to the economic system, it cannot be deduced from the relationship of the consumer to scarce goods independently of the social system he lives in.

The marginal utility theory aims to explain the interconnections of capitalist economy, the capitalist form of relationship between production and consumption, or, in the explicit formulation of the Austrian School, the law of cost, by means of consumer psychology. But in this interpretation the cost doctrine appears to be a "law" devoid of all social content, independent of any economic systems, including even the one governing Robinson Crusoe's economy. Robinson, like a capitalist entrepreneur, compares the relative shares of value that can be imputed to the contribution of capital, labour and land in their various uses, and, as a result of these considerations, decides on the optimum allocation of the factors available

[52] K. Marx: Introduction: Production, Consumption, Distribution, Exchange (Circulation). In: *A Contribution to the Critique of Political Economy*, London, Lawrence and Wishart, 1971, p. 197.
[53] K. Marx: *op. cit.*, p. 199.
[54] L. Walras: *Éléments d'économie politique pure*, Lausanne–Paris, 1900, p. 171.

to him, on what products and how much of each product he will produce. The difference appears at most in the fact that in a capitalist economy the law of opportunity cost asserts itself through the price mechanism determined by marginal utility, while in Robinson Crusoe's economy with the elimination of the price mechanism, it operates directly by a valuation based on marginal utilities.

It must also be noted, by the way, that the consumer's relation to scarce goods as represented in the marginal utility theory is really not independent of history. This consumer endeavours consciously to make an optimum use of his resources in consumption, exchange and production. The advocates of that theory attribute the behaviour of a capitalist entrepreneur to the consumer in circumstances in which capitalist relations do not prevail, or indeed, no production relations exist at all, as for example in Robinson Crusoe's economy.

In a capitalist economy the basis of the relationship of production to consumption is the profit motive. The capitalist will obtain his profit by adjusting his production process to existing demand. But the profit motive cannot be deduced from some abstract psychological consumer attitude; it is the product of the structure of capitalist society. The capitalist wants more and more profit not because he wants to consume more; he is stimulated only by the increase in abstract wealth. He intends to use the surplus value already realized to secure more surplus value. Production for production's sake, so characteristic of a capitalist economy, does not originate from the psychological attitude of the consumer.

The representatives of the marginal utility theory see the basic form of human relationships in exchange relations. Smith and Ricardo tried to reveal the laws governing exchange from the social division of labour; marginal utility theory, instead of starting out from the social division of labour, only stresses with respect to exchange that the individual engages in exchange to improve his position as a consumer. Thus it resolves class relations into exchange relations. In Böhm-Bawerk's representation, even the worker makes his choice among the possibilities offered to him and decides on the most favourable one before selling his labour power, that is, before becoming a worker. "Conditions in our modern economy are such that the workers almost never possess sufficient means to exploit their own labour themselves in a production process occupying years. They are thus faced by the alternatives of selling their labour and of exploiting it on their own account in production processes that are limited to such brevity and inefficiency as their scanty supply of available means dictates. Naturally they will make whichever choice is more favourable."[55] The capitalist will sell that stock of commodities "that he does not use for the satisfaction of his momentary personal needs."[56] And the subjective value of the stock of goods produced will be shared by each class to the extent to which the production factors owned by it have contributed to the output of these goods.

Thus, if we approach class relations from the aspect of the satisfaction of wants, of the production of goods to meet those wants, then the essential difference between classes, i.e. exploitation, will disappear. For goods to be produced, labour, capital and land are equally needed. "Here 'capital' is a factor like all

55 E. Böhm-Bawerk: *op. cit.*, Vol. II, pp. 308–309.
56 E. Böhm-Bawerk: *op. cit.*, Vol. II, p. 359.

the rest, and the distribution between work and property has disappeared from view."[57] But the specific historically determined character of individual incomes linked to definite production relations will also disappear. The subjective value of the goods produced in Robinson Crusoe's economy is divided into parts of income attributable to labour and capital goods just as is the subjective value of goods produced in a capitalist economy. In Böhm–Bawerk's view, capitalist production begins from the time when Robinson Crusoe started using means of production instead of producing goods with his bare hands and the forces of nature.

What further problems arise in the marginal utility theory?

3. Let us begin with the doctrine of diminishing marginal utility. Like the law of diminishing returns it is a static principle. Diminishing returns disregard the development of technology, and diminishing marginal utility leaves out of account changes in the wants and tastes of consumers. Let us give up taking the scale of wants as given, and we shall see that with the tastes of consumers changing, the marginal utility of a good may increase with the increase in quantity or decrease with the decrease in quantity. If our consumer takes a fancy to a commodity, the marginal utility curve of that commodity will shift upwards. Then its quantity may rise from Q to Q_1 (Fig. 3), and marginal utility will rise simultaneously. The case is just the opposite if the marginal utility curve of the commodity shifts downwards, indicating that the consumer's liking of that good diminishes. In this case marginal utility may decrease even with the quantity falling.

4. As regards the shape of the demand curve, the Marxist Robert Hoch holds the view that it depends, especially in the case of more or less independent goods, or groups of goods, basically on two factors: (a) how demand develops in such income categories in which those belonging to them were buyers before, and will continue to be buyers after the price change; (b) what new strata will be included and excluded by the price change.[58] The negatively sloped shape of the demand curve is explained partly by the dependence of utility on quantity, as pointed out by Péter Erdős, and partly by the fact that, with a fall in price, even such strata will have access to the consumption of a particular commodity which would not have been able to buy it at a higher price. The lower the price, the broader masses of people will be able to buy the commodity in question.

5. The greatly limited applicability of the traditional demand curve used in theoretical models, and the difficulties of the traditional interpretation of demand elasticity, were pointed out by Morgenstern, among others. In his opinion, "the points on the individual demand curve are a set of simultaneous alternative maximum offers for those quantities that are linked to the individual prices."[59] This means that each point in the same and the immediately subsequent period is valid only with the elimination of the other points. The individual expresses his readiness to buy one or the other quantity at appropriate prices at a given point of time. "Therefore, whatever the form of a one-variable demand curve, ... it is

[57] J. Robinson: *Economic Philosophy*, London, 1962, p. 55.

[58] See R. Hoch: *Consumption and Price, with Special Regard to the Theories and Practice in the Socialist Countries*, Budapest, 1979, p. 138.

[59] O. Morgenstern: *Spieltheorie und Wirtschaftswissenschaft*, Wien–München, 1963, pp. 133–134.

valid only for one single transaction,"[60] and the original demand function can no longer be used for the following transaction. If, for example, the individual has bought quantity q_i at a price of p_i, and the price increases to p_{i-1}, he will

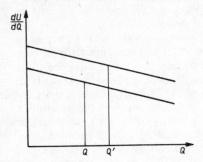

Figure 3

not buy anything though, according to his original demand curve, he ought to buy quantity q_{i-1} when $q_i > q_{i-1}$. If, however, the price decreases from p_i to p_{i+1}, then at this price the individual will not buy quantity q_{i+1}, which is larger than q_i as shown by the original demand curve, but quantity $q_{i+1} \cdot p_{i+1} - p_i q_i$.

It is on this basis that Morgenstern attacks the interpretation found in the economic literature on the elasticity of demand. "While the concept of elasticity" —he writes—"is of course fully suitable to describe the slope of a given demand curve, it is unsuitable for the purpose it was destined to perform, namely, to describe the reaction of demand to short-run price changes."[61] It would be possible to move along a given demand curve only if the same demand curve were restored as a result of the individual getting new income, or if his wants were reproduced. "The concept of restoring the curve is, however, not part of the usual demand theory."[62]

As far as aggregate demand is concerned, Morgenstern comes to similar conclusions. Analysing one of the simplest cases, he assumes that the market is a closed one, and each buyer purchases just one unit of a given commodity, and the maximum sum of money they are ready to pay for it differs from buyer to buyer. Given price p_i, each buyer who is willing to pay a price of p_i or more, will create demand for it. The magnitude of demand is q_i at a price of p_i. All those who have made their purchases at a price of p_i, will withdraw for some time from the market until their demand curve is restored. Thus, in the short run, only one part of the original demand curve is valid, namely the part which contains the maximum offer of those who are ready to buy only at a price lower than p_i. Thus the quantities along the original curve must be decreased by the quantity that has already been bought at the price of p_i, since at any possible lower price along the original demand curve every buyer will appear again in the market with

60 O. Morgenstern: *op. cit.*, p. 138.
61 O. Morgenstern: *op. cit.*, p. 153.
62 O. Morgenstern: *op. cit.*, p. 164.

47

his demand, even those who have already bought at a higher price. Thus, at a price of p_{i+1}, which is lower than p_i, the actual size of demand will be not q_{i+1}, but only $q_{i+1}-q_i$. In this way, however, instead of the original demand curve we shall get another, strongly reduced curve, the elasticity of which differs from the elasticity of the original curve. The subsequent response of demand to a decrease in price cannot be read off the original demand curve.

According to Morgenstern, it is only in wide, open markets, where frequently changing masses of people make their purchases and the prices are formed continuously, that the traditional concept of the elasticity of demand can be used, since in such markets it is likely "that the demand curve, at least as regards its slope and position, can always be restored by itself."[63] In such a case, it does not create any problem to specify the period to which the demand curve applies.

6. A serious difficulty that marginal utility theory has to face is the determination of the total utility of a stock of a commodity. In relation to this problem, two conflicting views exist within the Austrian School, those of Böhm–Bawerk and Wieser. According to Böhm–Bawerk, the total utility of a stock of goods is the total of the subjective significances of its individual units. This conception contradicts the principle of marginal utility, which says that each unit of a stock of a commodity counts as if it were the last unit. It is in this sense that Wieser interprets the total utility of a stock of a commodity, that is, the stock multiplied by its marginal utility. As Leo Illy points out, it is essentially Wieser's conception that is behind the statements of the later followers of the marginal utility theory.[64] Wieser's definition, however, contradicts reality. It implies that a stock of a commodity with a marginal utility of 0 will also have a total utility of 0.

7. According to the representatives of an earlier version of the marginal utility theory, the total utility of a stock of different commodities is the sum total of the partial utilities of the quantities of individual commodities. This statement was criticized by the followers of a later, revised version of the marginal utility theory because it supposed that the utility functions of the individual goods were independent of one another, and could therefore be added up. The utility function of this interpretation is called the *additive utility function*. The economists who further developed marginal utility theory were to point out, as we shall see, that the utility functions of different goods are closely interrelated and cannot be added up.

The additive treatment of utility functions further presupposes that the needs for different commodities have a common measure which enables them to be added up. Gossen's second law is also based on the assumption that the utility increments per unit of money last spent on buying different goods can be compared in an exact way by means of some sort of common measure. This idea formed the basis for Jevons's exchange-value theory, the law of cost discussed above, and as we shall see for Walras's general equilibrium theory, too. In actual fact, there is no common measure for the utilities derived from the satisfaction of the various wants. It is simply inconceivable to reduce to a common denominator the utilities derived from the consumption of bread, meat, wine, etc., to get hold of them merely quantitatively by some abstract intensity of satisfaction, in isolation from

[63] O. Morgenstern: *op. cit.*, p. 173.
[64] L. Illy: *Das Gesetz des Grenznutzens*, Wien, 1948, p. 41.

48

their qualitative differences. Though the individual does compare his various wants, he can only do so with more or less uncertainty, since there is no common yardstick to measure them. It is impossible to weigh up exactly by marginal analysis the infinitely small utility increments. And yet, marginal utility theory carries out operations with these utility intensities, adds them up and multiplies them. Not only is the consumer unable to compare exactly the utility intensities of the various goods, but he cannot even be supposed, as Marshall expects of the individual buying tea, to give an exact answer to the question of how much he is willing to buy at a given price. Since utility judgements cannot be measured, we cannot expect the consumer of a given commodity to tell us exactly to what extent the marginal utility to him of that good will fall with an increase in its quantity.

8. According to the representatives of the marginal utility theory, and of its founders (it is primarily Walras of whom this statement is characteristic), if every consumer distributes his income with the greatest possible rationality among the various goods he buys, that is, if he realizes in his own household the maximum satisfaction of his needs, then this ensures that maximum welfare will also be realized on a social level.

This statement was criticized by some non-Marxian economists who pointed out that it had validity only within the limits of the existing distribution of income. But when applied to class relationships, marginal utility theory, the principle of equal advantage, can be used as a critique of capitalist income distribution. Marginal utility theory reflects the inequalities of capitalist distribution relations in such a way that, as a result of their lower money incomes, the marginal utility of money is much greater to working-class people than to the capitalist class. By re-distributing incomes in favour of the working class, social welfare can be increased. Pigou also draws this conclusion from marginal utility theory: "... suppose that there is one rich man and ten poor ones. A pound is taken from the rich man and given to the first poor one. Aggregate satisfaction is increased. But the rich man is still richer than the second poor man. So the transfer of a pound to him again increases aggregate satisfaction. And so on, until the originally rich man is no richer than anybody else."[65]

Wieser also questions whether the maximum of social welfare could be reached under capitalist conditions. In his view, the existing order of the distribution of wealth prevents the prices of goods from really expressing their social utilities. Since in the market it is not want but effective demand that counts, production is aimed in the first place at satisfying the desires of wealthy consumers, and such goods will primarily be produced which are better paid for, and not such as are better needed by society.

9. According to the marginal utility theory, consumer behaviour is motivated by the pleasure the consumer derives from the satisfaction of his wants, and, in order to achieve maximum satisfaction, our consumer must behave in a definite way. His behaviour is described as determinate behaviour. It is by means of such determinate actions that the theory tries to explain market relations, the formation of prices. But such an explanation presupposes that consumer behaviour is not

[65] A. Pigou: Some Aspects of Welfare Economics, *The American Economic Review*, June 1951, pp. 299–300.

influenced by the phenomena to be explained. The satisfaction gained from the consumption of goods is independent of market relations, of price relations. But subsequent surveys have provided evidence that the individual does not have a perfect knowledge of commodities, and is unable to assess correctly the satisfaction he can derive from the consumption of a given commodity. In appraising the useful qualities of a good he has to rely on external circumstances, publicity, advertisements, sales talks, and even on the level of prices. But these factors may mislead him in correctly assessing the subjective significance of goods to him, and make him desire products that do not give him the satisfaction expected. Desire and satisfaction may deviate, but consumer behaviour in the market is directed by his desires which, no longer closely related to the satisfaction wished for, can be manipulated by these external circumstances (advertisements, level of prices, etc.). The idea of consumer's sovereignty collapses. It turns out that the consumers' purchases are directed by the sellers. But if the desires of the consumers can be manipulated to such an extent, how can a theoretical system be built on consumer behaviour as a solid basis?

10. Let us now examine the problem of economic imputation. Böhm–Bawerk rejects the value- or price-determining function of the cost of production by saying that it is movement in a vicious circle, since production cost also has its own cost of production. This objection to the determination of value by production cost is fully justified. Marxian political economy reduces the cost of production to labour. Subjective economics, however, resolves it into a sensation of satisfaction. Böhm–Bawerk wishes to justify the derivation of factor value from the value of output by tracing goods back to primary factors for which the law of cost has no validity. He mentions two such primary factors: the natural productive forces of land and labour. He does not classify capital goods among primary factors because they can be reproduced by labour and the use of land, and are thus subjected to the law of cost. But the value of primary factors that are not subjected to that law, can, it appears, only be interpreted by means of economic imputation.

Even Marxian political economy does not associate the formation of the price of virgin land with production inputs. In virgin land there is no labour embodied, and consequently it cannot have value. Nor can the problem be explained by the theory of economic computation either. According to Marxian political economy, the price of land is capitalized land rent, and land rent is a form of manifestation of surplus value. The other primary factor, labour, has no value in Marxian political economy either. Labour is the source of value, but has no value in itself. The representatives of the marginal utility theory, however, regard as wages that part of value which can be imputed to labour, and consider the latter, as a final cost element, also to be independent of the law of cost. However, wages are not the value of labour, but of labour power, and labour power is already subject to the law of cost, or more exactly to the law of value. But if this were admitted, there would be a contradiction in the theory of economic imputation. What, then, determines the value of labour power? The value of consumer goods necessary to reproduce it. The value of consumer goods that can be imputed to the worker's labour is in no relationship whatsoever with the value of consumer goods needed to reproduce his labour power. Hence, if we treat wages as the value of labour power, then we have already exempted one of the two primary factors from the competence of economic imputation. Consequently, the representatives of the

50

marginal utility theory had to deny, in the interest of economic imputation, that wages expressed the reproduction cost of labour power. "Through a very strange error in judgment," writes Wieser, "the classical school of political economy has put forward the proposition that the exchange value of human labour also is determined by costs of production. The costs of production of human labour would be the costs of producing the labourer. What a monstrous idea! Can it be that there is a 'production' of labourers in the same sense as there is a production of material things?"[66]

Marx had already defended the English classical economists earlier against similar attacks, and his words also refer to Wieser's indignant outcry: "Doubtless, Ricardo's language is as cynical as can be... To put the cost of manufacture of hats and the cost of maintenance of men on the same plane is to turn men into hats. But do not make an outcry at the cynicism of it. The cynicism is in the facts and not in the words which express the facts ... if they reproach Ricardo and his school for their cynical language, it is because it annoys them to see economic relations exposed in all their crudelity, to see the mysteries of the bourgeoisie unmasked."[67] Or elsewhere: "It is not a base action when Ricardo puts the proletariat on the same level as machinery or beasts of burden or commodities, because (from his point of view) their being purely machinery or beasts of burden is conductive to 'production' or because they really are mere commodities in bourgeois production."[68]

The interpretation of production cost as opportunity cost is closely connected with the theory of economic imputation, the derivation of the value of production factors from the value of physical product. If we examine the significance of certain factors for attaining an objective, it is important to consider to what extent other ends must be forgone in order to achieve to a certain degree the realization of that objective. This concept has its significance from the point of view of programming. It is used, among other things, in foreign trade too—the pioneer of this application was Haberler—to determine what goods are worthwhile to trade abroad. But the concept of opportunity cost exceeds the scope of production, can be construed wherever resources capable of alternative uses have to be allocated among different ends. In the Jevonsian exchange act the goods received were the opportunity cost of the goods given up. The concept of opportunity cost also emerges in the cash-balance theory, according to which the individual decides how much of his money he will use to buy commodities and how much to form reserves. We also come across opportunity cost in Keynes when the individual weighs up how much of his savings he will use for buying bonds, and how much for preserving his wealth in money. In so far as opportunity cost is used in connection with production, its magnitude depends on the production cost, but is not directly a production category. Costs from the point of view of production cannot be classified by means of the opportunity cost concept.

66 F. Wieser: op. cit., p. 186.
67 K. Marx: The Poverty of Philosophy, Moscow, [no date], p. 48.
68 K. Marx: Theories of Surplus-Value, Part II, Progress Publishers, Moscow, 1968, p. 119.

Chapter 8

WALRAS'S AND CASSEL'S GENERAL EQUILIBRIUM THEORY

THE WALRASIAN CONCEPT

In his price theory Marshall provided only a partial analysis, examining price formation in the market of one commodity, and disregarding, by making *ceteris paribus* assumptions, the fact that the processes taking place in the market of one commodity also affect the markets of other commodities, and the processes taking place in those markets will influence the market of the commodity under consideration. Walras, on the other hand, attempts to grasp exactly the general relationship prevailing in the market. He constructed a general equilibrium theory in which everything is connected with everything else. Thus, among other things, a change in the price of a given consumption good affects the demand for other goods; the demand for a given commodity is a function of its own price, but also of the prices of all other consumer goods, and depends in addition on the magnitude of incomes which are, according to him, the prices of productive services. The prices of productive services are in turn affected by the demand for consumer goods, in the production of which they participate, since the demand for productive services is derived from the demand for products. This is called *derived demand*.

In the Walrasian model, capital function is completely divorced from capital ownership, the capitalist entrepreneur from the owner of capital. The central figure of the model is the capitalist entrepreneur who does not possess capital goods; he can only produce if he buys in their markets the services of the factors of production—of labour, capital and land. (Factors *n* in the model mean varieties of the three factors of production.) Their price is the income of the factor owners and the production cost of the entrepreneurs. By means of the factor services the entrepreneurs proceed to manufacture consumer goods. It is only later that Walras includes the production of the means of production and takes into account depreciation, too. The consumer goods produced are sold by the entrepreneurs on the consumer goods market to the owners of the factors of production, who buy them with the income received for their services. Reproduction in the model to be presented is simple, incomes being entirely spent on buying consumer goods. In this way, the total revenue of the owners of productive services is the total amount of the prices of consumer goods, that is, total price sum of consumer goods = total production cost. In a general equilibrium situation the price of every consumer good must be equal to the cost of its production. In the Walrasian model the most important link in the general interrelationship is this: owing to their close interdependence, the two markets mutually act on each other.

In constructing his general equilibrium theory, Walras takes certain elements of the system as given, such as the utility functions of the consumers with respect to the commodities demanded, or the productive services offered by them. In the latter case he presupposes that the productive services of the factors have direct utilities to their owners, that is, they offer something that they themselves could use as consumers. Also taken as given in the model are the quantities of the available factors of production, and, further, the technical coefficients which in the first two editions of his basic work Walras assumes to be fixed. In his presentation, the rows are as follows:

$$a_t, \ a_p, \ a_k \ \ldots$$
$$b_t, \ b_p, \ b_k \ \ldots$$
$$c_t, \ c_p, \ c_k \ \ldots$$

These technical coefficients express the quantities of factors t, p, k used up in producing one unit of the consumer goods a, b, and c. With these things taken as given, Walras deduces from the defined behaviour of consumers and entrepreneurs the magnitude of the unknowns, the prices of the consumer goods m, the prices of the productive services n, the demand for the consumer goods m, and the supply of the productive services n, in the state of general equilibrium. Consumer behaviour is characterized by the consumers' endeavour to maximize the satisfaction of their wants, and entrepreneurial behaviour by the entrepreneurs' "endeavour *to avoid* losses and secure profits..."[69]

In analysing the Walrasian model, mention must also be made of the fact that Walras left out of account, or possibly did not even recognize, the relationship between the utility functions of particular goods. He disregards the uncertain effect of a change in price on demand through a change in real income. Nor does he take into account the social effects bearing upon the individual utility functions, in the course of which the purchases of an individual are also affected by the purchases of other individuals. Thus in his system the individual demand curves can be added up. He assumes that the cost functions of all firms in a given industry are identical, that is, he disregards competition within an industry. Owing to the assumption of fixed technical coefficients, he does not reckon with the advantages of large-scale production, nor with the external effects of other firms or industries influencing the output of the firm in question. He also leaves out of account production relations between commodities, i.e. joint supply, when two or more products can only be produced simultaneously. Abstraction from all these circumstances is the precondition for an unambiguous solution. The Walrasian model supposes an undisturbed competition, free of all monopolistic elements, in which prices are given for the individuals operating on the market.

Walras sets up as many equations as the number of unknowns. His equations are partly behaviour equations, which express the reaction of the economic subjects to price changes (demand–supply equations), partly equations expressing the conditions of equilibrium (demand = supply, price = cost). When later he assumes the technical coefficients to be variable, technical equations are also added to these types of equation.

69 L. Walras: *op. cit.*, p. 194.

The first set of equations represents the demand equations for m consumer goods. It expresses how much of these consumer goods the individual consumers, aiming to maximize the satisfaction of their wants, buy at different incomes and at different prices. The Walrasian demand equations reckon with the fact that the demand for a particular consumer good is a function not only of its own price, but also of the prices of all other consumer goods, as the source of the demand for each of them is consumer income. In this way, there is a close relationship not only between the markets for consumer goods and for productive services, but also between the markets for the individual consumer goods.

$$D_a = f_a(p_a, p_b, p_c \ldots; p_t, p_p, p_k \ldots)$$
$$D_b = f_b(p_a, p_b, p_c \ldots; p_t, p_p, p_k \ldots)$$
$$D_c = f_c(p_a, p_b, p_c \ldots; p_t, p_p, p_k \ldots)$$

The next set of behaviour equations represents the market supply equations for productive services. They show what quantities of productive services are supplied by factor owners trying to achieve maximum satisfacton of their wants at different prices of consumer goods and productive services.

$$O_t = f_t(p_a, p_b, p_c \ldots; p_t, p_p, p_k \ldots)$$
$$O_p = f_p(p_a, p_b, p_c \ldots; p_t, p_p, p_k \ldots)$$
$$O_k = f_k(p_a, p_b, p_c \ldots; p_t, p_p, p_k \ldots)$$

where D_a, D_b, D_c stand for the demand for consumer goods. O_t, O_p, O_k for the supply of productive services, p_a, p_b, p_c for the prices of consumer goods and p_t p_p, p_k for the prices of productive services.

The third set of equations expresses that in equilibrium the price of a consumer good equals its cost of production:

$$p_a = a_t \cdot p_t + a_p \cdot p_p + a_k \cdot p_k \ldots$$
$$p_b = b_t \cdot p_t + p_b \cdot p_p + b_k \cdot p_k \ldots$$
$$p_c = c_t \cdot p_t + c_p \cdot p_p + c_k \cdot p_k \ldots$$

Walras arbitrarily assumes p_a to be unity, and regards it as the measure of prices, a *numéraire*. He gives the prices of other commodities in terms of that *numéraire*.

The last set of equations contains the requirement that the demand for productive services should equal the already derived supply of productive services.

Walras deduces the demand for productive services from the demand for consumer goods by means of the given technical coefficients.

$$
\begin{aligned}
D_t &= a_t \cdot D_a + b_t \cdot D_b + c_t \cdot D_c + \ldots = O_t \\
D_p &= a_p \cdot D_a + b_p \cdot D_b + c_p \cdot D_c + \ldots = O_p \\
D_k &= a_k \cdot D_a + b_k \cdot D_b + c_k \cdot D_c + \ldots = O_k
\end{aligned}
$$

.
.
.

We have altogether $2m + 2n$ equations and $2m + 2n - 1$ unknowns. Since Walras took the price of one consumer good to be 1, he only has to determine the price of $m-1$ consumer goods. It turns out, however, that not all of the $2m + 2n$ equations are independent of one another. One of the equations depends on the others. Let us multiply each of the equations of the last set by p_t, p_p and p_k, and each of the equations of the third set by D_a, D_b and D_c. The left sides of the equations are equal, consequently their right sides must also be equal:

$$
\begin{aligned}
O_t \cdot p_t + O_p \cdot p_p + O_k \cdot p_k \ldots &= D_a + D_b \cdot p_b + D_c \cdot p_c \ldots, \text{ whence} \\
D_a &= O_t \cdot p_t + O_p \cdot p_p + O_k \cdot p_k \ldots - (D_b \cdot p_b + D_c \cdot p_c \ldots)
\end{aligned}
$$

Thus, D_a can be deduced from the rest of the equations, and so there will remain $2m + 2n - 1$ unknowns. Note that on the basis of the equality of aggregate demand for consumer goods and total income we could have omitted any other equation.

It is a characteristic requirement of Walras's general equilibrium that if we take the prices formed for consumer goods and productive services, then the demand for consumer goods is such that the demand for productive forces deduced from it is exactly equal to the supply of productive services offered at identical prices. At the same time, with these prices of consumer goods and productive services the prices of consumer goods must equal the costs of their production. In equilibrium the available factors of production are used optimally: the total utility of the quantity of consumer goods produced and productive services retained is at a maximum for the persons acting in the market.

The above price model is designed to determine the ratio of prices by the ratio of marginal utilities. But what does the price level depend on? Walras, as we have seen, singles out an arbitrary commodity which plays in his system the role of the measure of prices and denotes its price with an arbitrarily chosen cardinal number. It is in relation to that number that he expresses the prices of other commodities by means of the price ratio. The commodity playing the role of the measure of prices is not demanded as such. The person who sells a commodity in order to possess an article acting as a *numéraire* does so either because he wants to consume that article directly, or because he wants to spend it on buying other goods. According to this so-called Walras's law, whether the economy is in equilibrium or not, the price sums of the commodities demanded and supplied are always equal irrespective of the price level. In this presentation the demand for and the supply of commodities are independent of the price level. If we double, treble, etc. all prices, those of both consumer goods and productive services, we always obtain, according to the Walrasian model, the same relationships. The so-called *homogeneity postulate* expresses that the demand for goods and the supply of productive services are, for Walras, only a function of the price ratios and not of the price level. The demand and supply functions are zero-degree homogeneous functions of the price level. And if we find, on the basis of the equality of the price sums of the commodities demanded and supplied, those price proportions at which the demand and supply are in equilibrium in the market for all but one commodity, then at the same price proportions the equilibrium between demand and supply will also be established in the market for the commodity not considered. If the commodity not considered is a good performing the role of the measure of prices, then the price ratios which create equilibrium in the market of other commodities will also bring about equilibrium in the market of money-commodity. But according to the homogeneity postulate, the price ratios required by the equilibrium situation may develop at any price level. Thus the price level in the price model discussed is completely indeterminate.

An approach of non-Marxian economics made the attempt, as we shall see later, to determine the price level by assuming that money is demanded because people want to form cash reserves. The desire to hold cash is aimed at creating a money reserve with definite purchasing power which represents a certain proportion of national income. In this case, with a given quantity of money, the price level is, according to the theory, not arbitrary, as it has a definite equilibrium level. At a price level lower than that, the given quantity of money represents too high purchasing power. People do not wish, as a rule, to hold such high cash reserves, they rather spend their surplus money, so the demand for goods, and the supply of money increase. At a price level higher than the equilibrium level, the purchasing power represented by the given quantity of money is too low. People wish to fill up their money reserves and thereby increase the supply of goods and the demand for money.

For Marx professing the labour theory of value and assuming metal-money circulation, the determination of the price level did not raise the problem that crops up in the Walrasian model. The absolute level of the price of a given commodity is determined, as a rule, by the quantity of the precious metal which contains the same amount of labour as the commodity in question.

How can this intricate system of simultaneous equations be solved?, asks Walras. In his view, the market continuously produces the solution. By the method of *tâtonnement* ("groping") he tries to show how his system of simultaneous equations would be solved theoretically. In his theory, the auctioneer puts up a certain arbitrary set of prices for both consumer goods and productive services.

Those taking part in the market process let the auctioneer know what quantity of consumer goods or productive services they are willing, given the put-up prices, to offer for sale or to buy in order to optimize their positions. If these prices prove to be non-equilibrium prices, the auctioneer will put up a new series of prices, now corrected in a definite direction. And finally he will hit upon the equilibrium prices. "What must then, be proved," he asks, "in order to find out if the theoretical solution and the solution provided by the market are identical?"[70] And he answers, that what must be proved is "merely that the rise and fall [i.e. the rise and

[70] L. Walras: *op. cit.*, p. 130.

fall of prices—A.M.] provide the method by which to solve the system of simultaneous equations of the equilibrium of demand and supply, that is, the method of *tâtonnement*."[71] Following Walras, Oscar Lange tries to show in a study written in the 1930s how the market mechanism provides the solution to the simultaneous equations. In a study of his written later he remarks, in connection with Walras, that the task had become much easier by his time. The electronic computer can simulate the iterative process which is inherent in the "groping" of the market mechanism and eliminates the deviation from equilibrium.[72]

But the Walrasian *tâtonnement* raises a serious problem from the point of view of the marginal utility theory. In Walras's model marginal utilities always vary in the course of continuous exchange. In this case, however, according to the logic of the marginal utility theory, it is the sales and purchases transacted at initial, not equilibrium prices, that influence the final result. Walras's solution to this problem differs from that given by Marshall. In Walras's model the buyers and sellers stipulate between them that in case prices turn out not to be equilibrium prices, no transactions are effected. The persons engaged in the market modify their contracts. They become binding, and purchases and sales are transacted only when an equilibrium is established. Since under these circumstances only one transaction is concluded, the question whether the demand curves are restored in their original form in the course of successive transactions cannot be raised at all. Morgenstern notes that such a theoretical experiment is very interesting, but "does not fit any known market, or if such a market does exist, it is sure to be insignificant."[73]

Walras's achievement is highly appreciated by non-Marxian economists. They call him the Laplace of economics. The idea itself of the mutual independence and interaction of the markets of products and productive services, that is, how the demand for products affects the demand for factor services with given or changing technical coefficients, how the factor income influences the demand for consumer goods, how the demand for a consumer good depends, in addition to the size of its own price, on the formation of the prices of other consumer goods, is all very interesting. All price models which wish to answer the question as to how the optimum allocation of available resources must be effected with given demand functions and what prices will develop with the given size and optimum use of these resources, regard the Walrasian model as their starting-point.

Such models, however, in spite of the rational elements they contain, reveal the class relations of capitalist society in a distorted way, because they approach relationships only from the side of utilities.

In the Walrasian model, there is no relationship whatsoever between the working and capitalist classes. The capitalist is a passive participant of the production process who, like the worker, offers the service of a scarce production factor, capital, to the entrepreneur. Thus worker and capitalist are in a relationship with the entrepreneur only, and the character of their relationship is completely identical: they offer the entrepreneur the services of the factors of labour and capital

[71] L. Walras: *op. cit.*, p. 130.
[72] O. Lange: The Computer and the Market. In: *Socialism, Capitalism and Economic Growth.* Essays presented to Maurice Dobb, Cambridge, 1967.
[73] O. Morgenstern: *op. cit.*, p. 160.

indispensable in the production of commodities. Class relations are replaced by the relations of consumers and entrepreneurs. It is in their capacity as consumers that workers and capitalists offer their productive services of which the entrepreneurs make use in producing commodities. The worker receives as a reward for his work a part of the net product, and the capitalist gets as his income another part of the net product. The capitalist class is entitled to its income, to a share of the new value, because capital is needed to produce commodities; there is a demand for capital, a demand which in turn forms prices for the services of scarce capital. In the third edition of his work Walras explicitly reduces the income of the capitalist class to the use of capital in the production process of commodities, to the marginal productivity of capital.

Even if we accept the fiction of the entrepreneur owning no capital and taking up loans in kind by renting machinery and equipment from the capitalist, he will in fact pay interest on these loans from the surplus value and not from the contribution of capital to producing commodities. In this case, however, the worker is in a relationship not only with the entrepreneur but also with the capitalist. And the position of the worker and the capitalist cannot be characterized merely as a consumer position. The capitalist is in a capitalist partnership relation with the entrepreneur, sharing the surplus value, both of them confronting the worker, as exploiters the exploited.

The fact that they share the surplus value completely disappears from the Walrasian model. Competition ensures that the whole net output is distributed as interest and wages among the factors taking part in production, and thus price is equal to the costs of production. In Walras, there is no profit left for the entrepreneur in equilibrium; "...in an equilibrium state of production the entrepreneurs neither gain profits nor sustain losses."[74]

In the Walrasian model we only have to do with individuals: in the demand functions for consumers it is their individual utility functions that find expression, and likewise in the supply functions of factors. But the individual demand functions and the underlying individual utility functions differ not primarily owing to differences in their individual tastes, but because of the social class position of the individual. The worker's relation to his work, the subjective valuation of leisure on which the supply function of his labour depends, are all functions of established class relations, of the workers' class position. Even the proportion of people who offer their labour, and the proportion of those who offer their services of capital and land, reflect the ownership distribution of the means of production in the Walrasian model. In the Walrasian model the functions expressing the reactions of individuals are the final data of the model. These functions have nothing to do with existing production and ownership relations, they are entirely of an individual character. The interaction of individual reactions is missing, and so is any representation of how the demand and supply functions of individuals act upon each other. In this case, however, they cannot be added up. Walras also fails to demonstrate how the individual sellers compete for the acknowledgement of the social character of their production, and how a uniform price comes to be established as a result of their competitive struggle. The latter problem is left out of account from the very outset, as Walras assumes that all

[74] L. Walras: *op. cit.*, p. 195.

producers in a given industry turn out their products under the same technical conditions.

In Walras's general equilibrium theory, the quantity of the factors of production is taken as given, but the supply of their services changes as a result of the operation of the price mechanism, and this causes their supply to come into equilibrium with their demand. This is a requirement of the general equilibrium theory. But Walras builds the supply functions of the productive services on the marginal utility concept and is therefore compelled to assume that "...the services themselves represent direct utilities to each individual."[75] Consequently, if real income falls, the owners of the factors of production retain part of their services for their own use. Authors commenting on Walras manage somehow to explain the direct utility of productive services in the case of the worker: he could make use of the time he spends on working for the capitalist as leisure too. In practice, however, he cannot do so, because he must use it for the reproduction of his labour powers. This makes it unacceptable to build the supply function of labour on the worker's utility function with respect to the 24 hours of the day. Anyway, the valuation he puts on his leisure is a function of his class position and not of his individual taste. It is conceivable *in abstracto* that the worker should spend his time not on work but on leisure. But the assumption regarding the direct utility of productive services becomes completely absurd as far as the service of capital (or the service of land) is concerned. "...an essential feature of the Walrasian schema is that all of them [the productive services—A.M.] are capable of being consumed by their owners directly", writes Schumpeter critically, who otherwise appreciates him very much. "This creates difficulties that are particularly obvious in the case of specific instruments of production, such as machines. To assume that, potentially at least, a machine can, at the will of its owner, be instantaneously turned into an easy chair is indeed heroic theorizing with a vengeance."[76]

In Marx, market equilibrium reflects the equilibrium of reproduction. Therefore, the demand for and the supply of consumer goods are in equilibrium if the production of the means of production and of consumer goods are in equilibrium. In Walras's model, assuming simple reproduction, the production of the means of production is missing. "Walras for the most part finesses the problem of intermediate goods and operates as if production transformed ultimate resources directly into final commodities."[77] In his model, the decisive criterion of equilibrium is that, given the structure of consumer demand, ensuring maximum total utility, the demand for and the supply of productive services should be in equilibrium, and the price of consumer goods should cover the costs of production. It is only in the market of particular consumer goods that in his model a discrepancy between demand and supply, between price and cost of production is permissible. The aggregate demand for consumer goods always equals aggregate supply, and their total prices equal their total costs even if the economy is not in a state of equilibrium. In fact, if we consider the equilibrium of the production of consumer goods and of the means of production to be the basis of market

75 L. Walras: *op. cit.*, p. 195.

76 J. Schumpeter: *History of Economic Analysis*, London, 1955, p. 1010.

77 R. Dorfman, R. Solow and P. A. Samuelson: *Linear Programming and Economic Analysis*, New-York–Toronto–London, 1958, p. 348.

equilibrium, the aggregate demand for and supply of consumer goods need not equal one another even under simple reproduction. If there is no equilibrium between the outputs of the two sectors (departments), the demand for consumer goods will deviate from their supply, and prices from their values, or the prices of production.

Walras regards equilibrium as an ideal state which never materializes in real life with the exactness of theory, "but is normal in the sense that under free competition things tend towards it both in production and exchange."[78]

More recently, mainly under Keynes's influence, attempts have been made in modern non-Marxian economics to reform the price system based on microeconomics. These attempts have been aimed at showing that in disequilibrium even the free operation of the price mechanism is unable to restore equilibrium immediately, and a cumulative process towards disequilibrium will evolve. Thus, the fiction of the auctioneer is left out of the model, and the assumption that the operators of the market are perfectly informed about the market situation is abandoned. Exchange can thus take place even at non-equilibrium prices and, as a result, a cumulative process sets in, namely, the gap between demand and supply widens and unemployment increases. The reform of price theory taking place in our days will be dealt with in detail in Part Ten, Chapter 6.

A lasting disruption of general market equilibrium reflects, however, a lasting disequilibrium of reproduction, and the processes of a lasting boom or slump reflect a lasting disturbance of proportionality between the two departments, the production of capital goods and consumption goods. The price mechanism is unable to prevent this process. In Walras's basic work the decisive circumstance gets lost, namely, that the solution of his equations by the market mechanism is realized only through a general crisis of overproduction, unemployment, capital surplus, a waste of commodities and resources.

THE CASSELIAN CONCEPT

The Walrasian system of simultaneous equations was further developed by the Swedish economist Gustav Cassel. He simplified the Walrasian model and separated it from the marginal utility concept. He thus gave up the theory of value even in its subjective form. He thought that without the marginal utility theory, merely on the basis of the principle of *scarcity,* it was possible to show that if a large quantity, in relation to effective wants, of a particular commodity is placed on the market, the price will fall, and conversely, if a small quantity is marketed, the price will rise. "Values are then replaced by prices, valuation by pricing, and we have a theory of prices instead of a theory of value."[79] It is prices that keep the satisfaction of wants within the limits of the available stock of goods, and thus it is in them that the scarcity of goods finds expression. "This restriction of the demands of consumers... is the object of pricing."[80] "The restriction of consumption must be all the more vigorous, the greater the scarcity of goods in relation to the de-

[78] L. Walras: *op. cit.,* p. 194.
[79] G. Cassel: *The Theory of Social Economy,* London, 1932, p. 49.
[80] G. Cassel: *op. cit.,* p. 74.

mands of consumers ... therefore, prices are largely determined by this scarcity..."[81] Cassel holds that the amount of money that buyers offer for a commodity is the expression of the intensity of their wants. "The exchange economy thus measures the importance of the various wants by the sums of money which are offered for satisfying them."[82] And he maintains that it is possible to establish an actual functional relationship in the demand function by statistical observation. By this he completely deprives price theory of its foundation in value theory.

By rejecting marginal utility theory, Cassel also rejects the Walrasian supply function with respect to factor services, as in his system the available quantities of the production factors are fully employed. He retains, however, the rigid technical coefficients of the Walrasian model. It was the inclusion of fixed technical coefficients in his model that made Walras assume, in order to prove the realization of full employment, that factor services can directly be consumed. Without this assumption, a factor not having the necessary complements would be underemployed.

Criticizing Cassel's model, Neisser and Stackerberg pointed out as far back as the early 1930s that the identity of the number of independent equations and of the number of unknowns did not necessarily present an economically meaningful solution, as it was possible that a mathematical solution to the price model existed only at negative prices or negative quantities.

Dorfman, Solow and Samuelson[83] called attention to the problems relating to the solution of Cassel's model, namely, that the factors of production taken as given were not available to society in adequate proportions. Assuming only two industries in his model, if the ratio of the available capital stock to the labour force is above the capital-labour ratio in the given industry operating with a larger capital stock per head, or if it is below the capital-labour ratio in the industry operating with a smaller stock of capital per head, then we get a negative value for the quantity of the product which makes a more intensive use of the factor that causes the bottleneck.

The solution thus obtained is economically not meaningful. Why do we get a negative value for the quantity of a product? Because in the given case the mathematical solution yields such a large quantity for the other product that, with the available capital and labour, is impossible to produce, and the capital and labour showed to be lacking by the mathematical solution can only be obtained if a negative quantity is produced of the product in question.

Dorfman, Solow and Samuelson also point out that under unemployment a fall in wages need not necessarily lead to full employment. Cassel holds that in the case of unemployment declining wages will bring about a relative fall in the price of the product manufactured by a more labour-intensive production technique. The demand for that product will increase, its output expand and full employment be realized. Dorfman, Solow and Samuelson point out that under full employment two products may be offered for sale in Cassel's model in such a proportion that demand absorbs them at a price covering the production costs only at a negative value of wages. A negative value of wages expresses, given the existing demand

[81] G. Cassel: *op. cit.*, p. 74.
[82] G. Cassel: *op. cit.*, p. 85.
[83] R. Dorfman, R. Solow and P. A. Samuelson: *op. cit.*, pp. 366–375.

structure, that there is a surplus supply of labour relative to available capital. With full utilization of the production factors, with given technical coefficients, a disproportionately large quantity is produced of the labour-intensive product and a disproportionately small quantity of the capital-intensive one. The price of the more labour-intensive product will fall, that of the more capital-intensive one will rise. And since in determining wages it is the relatively reduced price of the more labour-intensive product that is decisively taken into account, and in

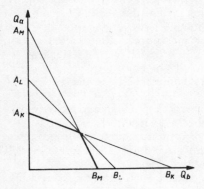

Figure 4

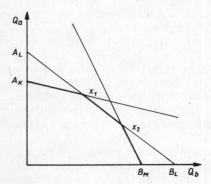

Figure 5

computing the rate of interest it is the relatively higher price of the more capital-intensive product that is considered, the interest rate will rise, and wages may have to fall below zero for the lower price of the more labour-intensive product to cover increased capital costs. It may happen that wages fall so far below zero that the negative element in the cost of the products making too intensive use of labour will exceed the cost of the factor used as a positive cost element. In this case, the price of the product in question will be negative.

If the price model assumes that the two products are manufactured by means of three production factors and, in addition to labour and capital, land together with its own rigid technical coefficients is also included in the model, then a further complication will arise in Cassel's simultaneous equations. Now there are three equations showing that the demand for all the three factors equals the available quantities of factors, but there are only two unknowns in the three equations, the quantities of the two products. Solution is only possible in quite special cases when the three straight lines representing the limiting conditions intersect in one point. Otherwise at any apex of the broken line which limits the production possibilities, only two factors can be used fully, and part of the available quantity of the third factor remains unused (see Figs. 4 and 5).

Dorfman, Solow and Samuelson emphasize that in order to obtain a meaningful solution to the Casselian model it must be stipulated that the values of the variables, the quantities of products and the prices of productive services cannot be negative. In this case, however, apart from the above-mentioned special case, part of the available quantities of the factors of production will remain unused, the price will not cover their production costs. Thus the relationships between the demand for and the supply of the factors of production as well as between prices and production costs cannot be represented in the form of equations, only in the form of inequalities, more precisely, only by using the signs "is greater or equal to" or "is less than or equal to".

Chapter 9

MARGINAL PRODUCTIVITY THEORY

GENERAL CHARACTERISTICS. APPROACHING THE PROBLEM FROM THE VIEWPOINT OF THE HISTORY OF SCIENCE

According to the marginal utility theory, the value of the services of the factors of production in their totality is a function of the degree to which the goods produced with their participation contribute to the fulfilment of the consumer's objective, the best possible satisfaction of his wants. This is shown by the marginal utility of the product which is expressed, according to subjective economics, by the price of the product. Thus, in proportion to the degree of achieving that end, the production factors may also have value. The larger the quantities of them that are available, the larger quantities of goods can be produced; hence the further the consumer can go in achieving his aim, the less will be the marginal utility of the product and through it the value attributable to the contribution of the different factors. And within that, the value of the services of a unit of various factors is determined by the role they play in producing a given good, by the volume of the product depending on their availability, that is, by the subjective value of the quantity of the product imputable to their employment.

Equilibrium theory tries to determine the equilibrium price of factor services by means of demand and supply curves. This theory makes joint factor demand dependent on product demand, and the demand for individual factors on their degree of contribution to production.

The valuation of the services of factors capable of alternative uses according to the significance of the consumers' objectives and the extent to which a factor unit contributes to the fulfilment of these objectives in the various uses, i.e., the role the individual factors play in producing the different goods needed to achieve these aims, is of basic importance in the theory of the optimum allocation of resources. According to this theory, an optimum allocation of the available resources among the various uses occurs if they are employed everywhere up to the limit which ensures identical significance for identical factors everywhere. In other words, the quantity of the commodity imputable to the employment of a given factor unit multiplied by the marginal utility expressing the degree of achieving the aim, i.e. the product price, should be equal in all its uses.

But the product thus obtained is the result of the joint employment of the factors of production. In order to determine the subjective significance of the services of the various factors, it is necessary to find out their separate proportional contributions. The result of the long development of attempts to solve this problem was the production function, which expresses the dependence of a given quantity of product on the factors engaged in its production, $Q = f(K,L)$.

The Austrian School first attempted, on the basis of subjective value theory, to determine the quantity of a commodity imputable to the employment of each of the production factors. Menger finds that the quantities of a commodity that can be "imputed" to the individual factors cannot be determined by completely removing the factor in question from the production process. But it is possible, he thinks, to decrease the quantity of a given factor by a small unit, with the other factors taken to be constant, and to impute the resultant decline in output to the removal of the unit of the given factor.[84] The method suggested by Menger constitutes an attempt to extend the application of marginal analysis from the process of the satisfaction of wants to the process of production. In this attempt Menger supposes that the proportions between the factors of production can be changed. Later non-Marxian economists, in further developing the theory of production, examine how the productivity of factors changes if the quantity of a factor is continuously altered relative to the quantity of the other factors. According to Menger, the significance for the satisfaction of wants of a unilateral change in the quantity of one factor will only be a function of the change in its marginal utility and not in its productivity, too.

Wieser, another outstanding representative of the Austrian School, though recognizing the possibility of varying proportions between factors, attempts to determine the price of factor services by assuming fixed factor proportions. He supposes that the factors are used in different productive branches in different proportions. The relationship expressed in the production function as to how output changes as a result of changing factor proportions, is now applied to productive branches. Wieser assumes that the factors are optimally allocated among the different industries, and thus the marginal significance of each factor for the satisfaction of wants, i.e. its contribution to output multiplied by its marginal utility or price, is identical in all productive branches. He also takes as given the quantities of factors employed in the various productive branches, the volume of products turned out through them and their values or prices. On such assumptions, according to Wieser, the subjective significance of factor services, expressed in his system by their price, could be determined by means of a system of simultaneous equations.[85]

Later, under similar conditions, Cobb, Douglas, and Bronfenbrenner attempted to approach the contribution of the factors of production to the production of commodities on a social scale.

At the turn of the century the most debated question of the theory of production in non-Marxian economics was whether the proportions among factors could be changed: whether it was possible to increase one factor unilaterally, keeping the quantities of the other factors constant, or whether factor proportions should be regarded as fixed. It was Pareto who most vehemently attacked the assumption that the factors were substitutable. Wicksteed, Marshall, Wicksell and, in the third edition of his work, Walras, too, stood for varying proportions.

Then, arising from the varying proportions, a peculiar law of return began to take shape in their works. Wicksteed pointed out that, owing to varying pro-

[84] C. Menger: *Grundgesetze der Volkswirtschaftslehre*, Vienna, 1923, pp. 155–157.
[85] F. Wieser: *Natural Value*, New York, 1930, (reprint of the 1893 edition), p. 88.

portions, the assertion of diminishing returns, can be found in all domains of production. His argumentation is valid in the case of a first-degree homogeneous, i.e. a homogeneous and linear production function. A production function is homogeneous of degree r when, multiplying each of the independent variables by λ the dependent variable increases by λ^r; $f(\lambda K, \lambda L) = \lambda^r f(K, L)$. (It must be noted that if the production function is homogeneous of degree r, the marginal productivities of the factors are homogeneous of degree $(r-1)$, that is, if all factors are multiplied by λ, marginal productivity must increase by the factor λ^{r-1} for output to increase by the factor λ^r.) In the case of a first-degree homogeneous production function, if the independent variables are multiplied by λ, the dependent variable will also increase λ-fold, that is, output will rise in the same proportion in which the dependent variables are increased, $f(\lambda K, \lambda L) = \lambda f(K, L)$. Wicksteed holds the view that, if one factor is unilaterally increased, for example twofold, then obviously output cannot increase twofold, but only to a lesser degree. J. B. Clark writes similarly that "... the diminishing productivity of labour, when used with a fixed amount of capital, is a general phenomenon."[86] Similarly general is the diminishing productivity of capital if its quantity is increased with a given labour force.

Thus, as the factor proportion change, the factor whose quantity is increased becomes a less and less effective substitute for the factor whose quantity remains constant.

Edgeworth pointed out that by changing factor proportions, increasing returns can also occur up to a certain limit. This is the case if a factor is *indivisible*.[87] Such an indivisible factor may be e.g. some equipment which is constructed for a certain quantity of output. Its physical dimensions given, it is physically indivisible. If a smaller than optimum quantity of output is intended, the given equipment may ·not be replaced in the short run by another variety constructed for the production of a smaller quantity of output. Owing to its indivisibility, even if a smaller quantity of output is to be produced, the whole equipment has to be operated, with no part of it left unused. "We cannot install half a blast furnace or half a locomotive (a small locomotive is not the same as a fraction of a large locomotive)."[88]

If this indivisible factor is taken to be constant and output is first increased by employing more of the other factors, then, at the beginning, the indivisible factor will increasingly be brought into use, and the increment in output will grow. If later the variable factors are increased beyond their right proportion to the indivisible factors, it is only then that output will rise at a diminishing rate.

Given a larger volume of output, specialized factors will be applied for this particular volume. If the indivisible factor destined for the larger output volume is fixed, and at the same time the quantities of the other factors are increased, output will rise to a higher level, again first at an increasing and later at a diminishing rate.

[86] J. B. Clark: *The Distribution of Wealth*, New York, 1902, p. 49.
[87] F. Y. Edgeworth: *Collected Papers I*, London, 1925, p. 63.
[88] W. J. Baumol: *Economic Theory and Operations Analysis*, New York, 1961, p. 181.

According to Carver, by changing the factor proportions, an increasing and later a decreasing sphere of returns can be experienced in all fields of production, and also a constant sphere of returns at the border of the two. He speaks of the general law of productivity, of the *law of variable proportions,* which comprises all the three spheres. Ragnar Frisch refers to the above-mentioned development of the spheres of returns as a fact of experience: "The empirical study of a set of production processes shows that production, when one factor is changed with all the others left unchanged, will as a general rule first go through a phase of increasing, and then one of diminishing returns."[89]

In his study written in 1939, Stigler characterizes the case when, as a result of changing factor proportions, only diminishing returns prevail, as "the case of divisible plant that is completely adaptable to changing amounts of the variable productive services... For in this case the conventional law of diminishing returns is almost fully applicable..."[90] He illustrates the divisibility of capital equipment of a given size by the following example: "When the ditch-digging crew is increased from ten to eleven, the ten previous shovels must be metamorphosed into eleven smaller or less durable shovels equal in value to the former ten..."[91]

By synthesizing the elements previously elaborated, modern non-Marxian production theory was created primarily by Ragnar Frisch, Erich Schneider, Suno Carlson and H. Stackelberg in the 1930s. It is mainly on their findings that we shall rely in our subsequent discussions.

Assuming two factors, capital and labour, let us gradually increase one quantity at the given level of technological knowledge, while leaving the quantity of the other unchanged. It is by numerical examples constructed on such an assumption that the representatives of marginal productivity theory endeavoured in the 1930s to illustrate their theory, to demonstrate how total output, the marginal and the average productivity of a factor change if a factor is increased unilaterally.

But a unilateral increase or decrease in a factor presupposes the possibility of varying the proportions between factors.

J.B. Clark mentions that even within a given technological process it is possible to carry out a certain change in proportions: "Though a hundred men can sail a steamship, a hundred and five may sail it better."[92] "In mills, mines, shops, furnaces, etc., there is in this way often a chance to vary, within narrow limits, the number of men who are employed...[93]" "Yet in commerce there is often an appreciable elasticity in the amount of labor that can be employed in connection with a stock of saleable merchandise. In manufacturing and in transporting, too, the working force may often be varied perceptibly, with no change in the amount or in the character of the capital goods that are used in connection with it."[94] He remarks, however, that "such changes must, of course, be kept within compara-

[89] R. Frisch: *Lois techniques et économiques de la production,* Paris, 1963, p. 87. A revised version of the Norwegian edition: "Tekniske og økonomiske produktivitetslover." Mimeographed lectures, University of Oslo.

[90] G. Stigler: Production and Distribution in the Short Run, *The Journal of Political Economy,* Vol. 47, No. 3, June 1939, p. 309.

[91] G. Stigler: *op. cit.,* p. 307.

[92] J. B. Clark: *The Distribution of Wealth,* London, 1902, p. 100.

[93] J. B. Clark: *op. cit.,* p. 101.

[94] *Ibid.*

tively narrow limits."[95] "...but there is no such limit to the number who can work with a fixed amount of capital *if the forms of it can be varied to suit the number of men.*"[96] (Stiegler's example quoted before provides a clear illustration of changes in the form of capital of a given size.) Quoting again Clark, "...the labor changes its forms in the same way."[97] In this view, a change in proportions means a switch-over from one production process to another.

Though Hicks also admits that even within a given technological process it is possible to change factor proportions, yet, in expounding marginal productivity theory, he opts for factor substitution primarily by way of changing the character of the technological process. In his book on wages published in 1932, he writes that "...the whole conception of marginal productivity depends upon the variability of industrial methods..."[98]

The view which holds that factor substitutability takes place by means of a switch-over from one production technique to another, assumes, in the interest of the continuity of substitution, that "there exist a very high number of techniques..."[99] It further supposes that capital goods are malleable; "...at any moment of time, all existing capital goods could be costlessly and timelessly taken to pieces and, using the latest booklet of instructions as our guide, changed into the latest cost-minimizing form..."[100]

Thus, the representatives of the marginal productivity theory describe the capital factor as a homogeneous good independent of its actual form, capable of employing any size of labour force in any production process. Yet, this good, because it is used in producing commodities, is concrete, and thus, as Mrs Robinson remarks ironically, the assumption "that a quantity of 'capital' remains the same when it changes its form is a mystery that has never been explained to this day."[101]

In discussing the two sorts of substitution, Hicks, J. Robinson and others distinguish between short- and long-term marginal products. "Marginal productivity in the short period, when the other factors are fixed not only in amount but in form, will be very different from marginal productivity in the long period."[102]

In connection with the malleability of capital it must be noted that Hicks was one of those who first pointed to the fact that "one of the co-operating factors —capital—is, at any particular moment, largely incorporated in goods of a certain degree of durability. It may have become more advantageous to use other methods, or to invest capital in other directions, than those which are currently practised; but if the capital is at present invested in durable goods, the change in relative profitability cannot immediately be realised. At the moment, only a small portion of the total supply of capital is 'free'—available for investment in new forms...

[95] *Ibid.*
[96] J. B. Clark: *op. cit.*, p. 114.
[97] J. B. Clark: *op. cit.*, p. 159.
[98] J. R. Hicks: *The Theory of Wages*, London, 1932, p. 20.
[99] L. Pasinetti: Switches of Technique and the "Rate of Return", *The Economic Journal,* Sept. 1969, p. 510.
[100] G. C. Harcourt: Some Cambridge Controversies in the Theory of Capital. *The Journal of Economic Literature,* June 1969, p. 374.
[101] J. Robinson: *Economic Philosophy,* London, 1962, p. 60.
[102] J. Robinson: *The Economics of Imperfect Competition,* London, 1954, (reprint of the 1933 edition), p. 236.

But as time goes on, ...larger and larger will therefore become the possibilities of adjustment."[103]

These misgivings of Hicks concerning the malleability of capital and thereby the possibility of varying proportions among the factors of production crop up with greater emphasis in economic literature when attempts are made to use production functions in practice, too, or when, in the course of the development of growth theories, a significant part of technical progress is interpreted as embodied technical progress. (We shall discuss this question in more detail in connection with growth theories.) "The notion of embodied technical progress represents one departure from the assumption of complete homogeneity (malleability) of the capital stock."[104] Embodied technical progress must be incorporated in new capital goods. It is always the latest generations of machinery that are the carriers of technical progress. Once the entrepreneur has decided which of the techniques representing the latest level of technical progress to choose, his capital has assumed a definite, concrete form, and this form cannot be changed overnight. In fact, however, there might be cases when, within a given technique, a certain change in proportions is possible, but, as J.B. Clark, Hicks and others have already pointed out, this possibility is much narrower than when the entrepreneur has not yet been faced with the decision as to which of the available techniques to choose. In the case of an established plant it is possible to change the forms of capital goods only if new investments are made or used-up capital goods are replaced. However, substitution made possible by such steps only affects an insignificant part of the capital stock.

In connection with giving up the notion of the malleability of capital, the Norwegian economist Leif Johansen[105] makes a distinction between *ex-ante* and *ex-post* substitutability. *Ex-ante* substituability is substitution between techniques when the form of capital goods changes. In the case of *ex-ante* substitutability it is assumed that at the given level of technical knowledge the entrepreneurs have a blueprint for any technique suited for any capital–labour ratio. And it is possible for a desired production technique to be introduced only, as already mentioned, in the case of new investments and of the replacement of old capital goods. It is impossible, therefore, to change the form of all tied-up capital goods overnight. Much slighter, even negligible according to the latest opinion, is the possibility of applying *ex-post* substitutability within a given production technique. Phelps[106] tries to make clear the difference between *ex-ante* and *ex-post* substitutability. by his "putty–clay" simile. *Ex-ante* substitutability is putty: the capital good is malleable in the production technique chosen. *Ex-post* substitutability is clay: by choosing the production technique, the formerly putty-like, malleable capital good becomes like clay, can no longer be changed.

As we shall see later, the assumption of the malleability of capital still survives.

103 J. R. Hicks: *The Theory of Wages,* London, 1932, pp. 19–20.

104 J. H. Hahn and R. C. O. Matthews: The Theory of Economic Growth: A Survey, *The Economic Journal,* December 1964, p. 838.

105 L. Johansen: Substitution versus Fixed Production Coefficients in the Theory of Economic Growth: A Synthesis, *Econometrica,* Vol. 27, April 1959.

106 E. S. Phelps: Substitution, Fixed Proportions, Growth Distribution, *The International Economic Review,* Vol. 4, Sept. 1963.

"The assumption of *ex-ante* substitutability but *ex-post* fixed coefficients (putty–clay) is probably the more realistic, but the alternative assumption of malleable capital is analytically far simpler."[107]

Hicks also points to a further possibility of substitution.[108] A change in the relative prices of the factors of production may bring about a shift from the production of goods needing the factor whose price is increasing to a greater extent towards the production of goods needing it to a lesser extent. If the stock of capital increases, those goods whose production needs capital above the average, become relatively cheaper and consequently, their output will be stepped up.

THE LAW OF RETURNS WITH PARTIAL FACTOR CHANGE, OR RETURNS TO PROPORTION

The following table represents a specific type of production function assuming continuous substitution, i. e. the law of returns with partial factor change. It shows how output depends, with a given stock of capital, on the continuous increase in the labour force, how the unilateral increase in the labour force influences the efficiency of production.

The example supposes the existence of all the three spheres of return, that is, the spheres of increasing, constant or decreasing return can equally be found, if the labour force is raised unilaterally.

We have taken the numerical pattern from the work of a present-day author. The formation of total output, marginal and average productivity as a function of the continuous increase in the labour force employed on a given area of land was already illustrated with a numerical pattern by Edgeworth in his study published in 1911.[109]

The relationship shown in the above table can also be represented by a graph:

Labour force	Total output	Marginal productivity	Average productivity of labour
1	10	10	10
2	26	16	13
3	57	31	19
4	92	35	23
5	125	33	25
6	150	25	25
7	168	18	24
8	176	8	22
9	176	0	19
10	170	—6	17

Source: D. Hamberg: *Principles of a Growing Economy*, New York, 1961, p. 500.

[107] G. A. Akerlof and J. E. Stiglitz: Wages and Structural Unemployment, *The Economic Journal*, June 1969, p. 270.

[108] J. R. Hicks: *op. cit.*, p. 23.

[109] F. Y. Edgeworth: *op. cit.*, Vol. I, p. 68.

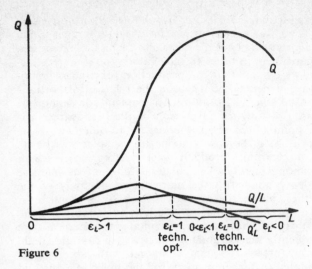

Figure 6

Changes in the marginal productivity of labour indicate the tendency of the formation of total output as the labour force changes continuously. Like all marginal concepts, this too is a differential quotient, the partial derivative of the production function with respect to a variable factor, in our example to labour: $\frac{\partial Q}{\partial L}$. And the marginal products of a factor, according to Carlson's definition, is the increment of the variable factor multiplied by its marginal productivity. In so far as we take the increment of the variable factor to be unity, marginal product will equal marginal productivity.[110]

The marginal productivity of a certain quantity of the variable factor is the slope of the tangent drawn to the total product curve at a point corresponding to the amount of the variable factor. Average product with the same amount of the variable factor, is expressed by the slope of a ray drawn from the origin to the appropriate point on the total-product curve.

Changes in marginal productivity show that with a unilateral increase in the labour force output rises first at an increasing, and then at a decreasing rate. The rise at an increasing rate will change into a rise of decreasing rate, that is, the production function will have its point of inflexion where the marginal-productivity curve reaches its maximum. The second derivative of the production function relative to the variable factor, in our example labour, $\frac{\partial^2 Q}{\partial L^2}$, is the acceleration of output. At the point of inflexion it reverses its sign and, with a further increase in output, will change from positive into negative.[111]

[110] S. Carlson: *A Study on the Pure Theory of Production*, Oxford, 1956, p. 16.
[111] Oscar Lange remarks that the representatives of the neo-classical school assume that the existence of the maximum of the production function $Q = f(K,L)$ follows from the nature of the problem itself, and it is superfluous to examine the conditions of the existence of the maximum of the two-variable function $Q = f(K,L)$. See O. Lange: *Optimal Decisions*, Warsaw, 1971, p. 62.

What does the marginal productivity of a factor depend on? If we disregard technical progress and the improvement of organizational techniques (and, while interpreting the marginal productivity of the particular factors, the representatives of the theory do disregard them in order to move along the same production function), and if, further, we assume that the production function is homogeneous of the first degree, then it depends only upon the relative proportions among factors. "...any marginal productivity is an intensive magnitude dependent only upon relative proportions..."[112]—writes Samuelson of the first-degree production function. Beyond the point of inflexion, the larger the quantity of the variable factor available in relation to the constant one, the smaller will be its marginal productivity. But if the marginal productivity of factors changes with shift in relative proportions among factors, the unilateral, continuous increase in the labour force will not leave unaffected the marginal productivity of the constant factor of capital, either. When the quantity of labour is plentiful in relation to capital stock, and thus the marginal productivity of labour is small, then, looked at from the side of capital, the quantity of capital is too small relative to the labour force, and consequently the marginal productivity of capital is high. The case is reversed if the labour force is too small compared with capital stock. Already Wicksteed had formulated a further property of the homogeneous and linear production function: by changing the relative proportions of factors, the marginal productivity of the variable and constant factors will change in the opposite direction. "...the marginal significance of the increasing factor falls and that of the diminishing factor rises..."[113]

Ragnar Frisch demonstrates, by means of the so-called cross acceleration, i.e. the cross second-order partial derivatives, how the increase in the quantity of the variable factor increases the marginal productivity of the constant factor. "Cross acceleration shows," he writes, "how the marginal productivity of one factor changes when the quantity of the other starts altering."[114] It is also through cross acceleration that he determines the relationship among factors. Two factors are complementary, that is, they presuppose each other, if their cross acceleration is greater than 0, $\dfrac{\partial^2 Q}{\partial L \partial K} > 0$, i.e. the increase in the quantity of one factor increases the marginal productivity of the other. In the case of substitutable factors, cross acceleration is less than 0, $\dfrac{\partial^2 Q}{\partial L \partial K} < 0$, i.e. the increase in the quantity of one factor diminishes the marginal productivity of the other.

Figure 6 also shows that the average-product curve reaches its maximum where it intersects the marginal-product curve. In general, the average value of a given $f(x)$ function, $\dfrac{f(x)}{x}$, is at a maximum or minimum where this value equals the marginal value of the function.

[112] P. A. Samuelson: Prices of Factors and Goods in General Equilibrium, *The Review of Economic Studies*, October 1953, No. 54, p. 3.
[113] Ph. H. Wicksteed: *Commonsense of Political Economy*, London, 1949, p. 862.
[114] R. Frisch: *op. cit.*, p. 59.

$$\frac{d}{dx} \cdot \frac{f(x)}{x} = \frac{xf'(x) - f(x)}{x^2} = 0;$$

$$\frac{xf'(x)}{x^2} = \frac{f(x)}{x^2},$$

$$xf'(x) = f(x), \text{ whence } \frac{f(x)}{x} = f'(x).$$

If the second derivative $f''(x)$ is negative, the value of $\frac{f(x)}{x}$ is at a maximum, and if $f''(x)$ is positive, it is at a minimum.

Now, in the sense of the logic of the marginal productivity theory, we can already answer the question what quantity of product depends on the labour of one worker if, with a given capital stock, a certain size of labour force, say 7 workers, are employed. In other words, what the significance of one worker's labour is in the production of commodities assuming that the labour power of all workers is entirely identical. This is not expressed by average productivity. The magnitude of per capita output is 24 if 7 workers are employed, but the number of the labour force multiplied by the units of average product exhausts the total amount of output, and if the marginal productivity of capital is positive, then nothing is left for the contribution of capital.

The dependence of total output upon one worker's labour input is shown by the fall in output which ensues when we decrease the number of workers employed by one. In this case, total output will drop from 168 to 150, meaning a fall of 18, which is just equal to the marginal productivity of labour in the case of 7 workers being employed. The marginal productivity of labour shows the change in output as a result of changing labour input by one unit, or the significance of one worker in producing commodities. This significance is the greater, the smaller the number of the labour force in relation to capital; and the smaller, the greater the relative size of the labour force. We have arrived at a similar relationship in the case of the utility function. Assuming a given scale of wants, the significance for the satisfaction of wants of one unit of a stock of a commodity is the smaller, the greater that stock; and the greater, the smaller the stock. In this way the followers of that theory also subordinate the significance of factors to the principle of scarcity, that is, along with the theory of consumer behaviour, production theory is also based on the scarcity of goods. "The marginal product of the factors of production is subordinated to the principle of scarcity, i.e. relatively the less quantity of a factor is available, the greater its marginal productivity will be, and vice versa."[115] "In marginal product just as in price... it is the degree of scarcity of production factor A relative to production factor B that is reflected."[116]

[115] A. Fortstmann: *Neue Wirtschaftslehre*, Berlin, 1954, p. 90.
[116] E. Preiser: Erkenntniswert und Grenzen der Grenzproduktivitätstheorie. In: *Bildung und Verteilung des Volkseinkommens*, Göttingen, 1957, p. 195.

When changing the proportions among factors the question arises: where does the sphere of increasing returns end, and where does that of diminishing returns begin? At a point where average productivity or marginal productivity starts decreasing, or else another criterion must be found for this demarcation.

Edgeworth suggests two definitions. "The definition based on marginal production is here distinguished as *primary,* preferred as more directly related to the theory of *maxima.*"[117] According to another definition: "The law of increasing return acts when the *average* product per unit of productive power applied increases, with the increase of productive power ... and the law of diminishing return, in the converse case."[118]

For Frisch, Schneider and Carlson, the criterion of demarcation is whether total output increases by a larger or smaller proportion compared to the percentage increase in the variable factor. Frisch writes that while "marginal productivity raises the question of the unit of measure", the relationship between the percentage changes in particular factors and output is *"independent of all units of measure,* being expressed in the notion of relative growth."[119] The relationship of percentage changes was already mentioned by Johnson in his article published in 1913,[120] in which he called it the *elasticity of production.* The same designation was also used later by Douglas in his work *The Theory of Wages.* Frisch, Schneider and Carlson use different names for it. R. Frisch calls it marginal elasticity and defines it "as the partial elasticity of the production function with respect to the quantity of the factor considered."[121] In Carlson's work the relationship of percentage changes goes by the name "function coefficient". Schneider calls the ratio of the proportional change in product to the proportional change in the variable factor complexes *Ergiebigkeitsgrad,* that is, "degree of productivity".[122] It is also under this name that he discusses elasticity of scale in his work published in 1934.

Let us call the ratio $\dfrac{dQ}{Q} : \dfrac{dL}{L}$ the elasticity of production with respect to labour, or in the following briefly, the production elasticity of labour, and denote it by ε_L. After transformation we obtain: $\varepsilon_L = \dfrac{dQ}{dL} : \dfrac{Q}{L}$, that is, the quotient of marginal and average productivity. The production elasticity of factors is not the same as their marginal productivity. The former, as we have seen, expresses the elasticity of the function of total product with respect to particular factors, that is, by what per cent the dependent variable changes with the percentage

[117] F. Y. Edgeworth: *op. cit.,* p. 61.

[118] F. Y. Edgeworth: *op. cit.,* p. 67.

[119] R. Frisch: *op. cit.,* p. 92.

[120] W. E. Johnson: The Pure Theory of Utility Curves, *The Economic Journal,* December 1913, pp. 483–513.

[121] R. Frisch: *op. cit.,* p. 62.

[122] E. Schneider: *Theorie der Produktion,* Vienna, 1934, p. 10.

change in one independent variable. And the latter expresses the partial derivative of the function of total product with respect to particular factors, the increment of total product, which we obtain by increasing one factor only by an infinitely small unit.

Now, in the view of the above-mentioned authors, we can speak of increasing return if, with a given percentage change in one variable factor, output increases by a greater percentage, in which case the marginal productivity of the variable factor is greater than its average productivity, and therefore its production elasticity is greater than unity. Within this sphere marginal productivity first rises, and then falls, but output will increase throughout by a greater percentage than the variable factor. Of production elasticity we can also say that it first grows in the sphere of increasing return and then decreases, and thus the elasticity of elasticity first assumes a positive value, then 0, and finally a negative value. At the boundary of increasing return the quantities of output and the variable factor increase in the same proportion, the magnitudes of marginal and average productivity are equal. the production elasticity of labour equals 1, average output has reached its maximum (see Fig. 6). To use Frisch's and Schneider's term, we have arrived at the *technical optimum*. The equality of the marginal and average productivity of the variable factor is a characteristic of the sphere of constant return. In the sphere of diminishing return output rises in a smaller proportion than the variable factor, marginal productivity is smaller than average productivity, and the production elasticity of the variable factor is smaller than 1. It is in this sphere that output reaches its maximum, more exactly at a point where the marginal productivity of the variable factor is 0, and thus its production elasticity is also 0. This point is called the *technical maximum*. Beyond technical maximum, the marginal productivity and production elasticity of the variable factor are equally negative, and total output decreases as the variable factor increases.

Since the change in output resulting from the increase in the variable factor also affects the marginal and average productivity of the constant factor and thus its production elasticity, too, it is also possible to determine the spheres of return of the constant factor. For this Frisch assumes that the production function is homogeneous of the first order. In that case the sum of the production elasticities of the constant and variable production factors is 1. If we increase them by 1 per cent each, output will rise by 1 per cent.

Let us now increase the quantity of one factor continuously, assuming a homogeneous and linear production function, while the quantity of the other factor remains unchanged. We shall obtain the same spheres of return for the constant factor as we obtained for the variable factor, only in the opposite direction. When the production elasticity of the variable factor, labour, is $\varepsilon_L > 1$, when labour is too small in relation to the constant factor, then the production elasticity of the constant factor, capital is, $\varepsilon_K = <0$, the marginal productivity of capital is negative, and too much equipment is available in relation to labour. If, leaving the labour force unchanged, we increased the equipment by 1 per cent, output would decrease in absolute terms. The case would be reversed if $\varepsilon_L < 0$; then $\varepsilon_K > 1$. In this case the labour force is too large compared with capital, and, by increasing the labour force only by 1 per cent, output would fall in absolute terms, i.e., the marginal productivity of labour would be negative, whereas with a 1 per cent increase in capital stock, output would increase by more than 1 per cent. At the technical optimum, when $\varepsilon_L = 1$, $\varepsilon_K = 0$, that is, the constant factor is at its technical maximum. When $\varepsilon_L = 0$, that is the variable factor is at its technical maximum, $\varepsilon_K = 1$, the constant factor is at its technical optimum. Between technical optimum and technical maximum the production elasticity of both production factors is less than 1, but greater than 0, and the marginal productivity of both is positive; but it is only within these two limits—at the one limit the variable factor is at its technical optimum and the constant factor at its technical maximum, at the other limit the variable factor is at its technical maximum and the constant factor is at its technical optimum—that the two factors are substitutes for one another in the sense that if the quantity of the one is continuously decreased, the quantity of the other can always be raised by the amount that is needed to keep total output unchanged.

Already at the turn of the century several economists, among them Wicksteed Flux, Walras, Wicksell and Johnson, demonstrated that if the production function is homogeneous of the first order, the sum of the products of the marginal productivity and the quantity of each factor is equal to the magnitude of total production. This relationship has come to be known in non-Marxian economics as Euler's theorem, so named in honour of the great Swiss mathematician. Our relationship based on the homogeneous and linear function, $\varepsilon_L + \varepsilon_K = 1$, already implicitly contains Euler's theorem. Substituting for ε_L and ε_K the quotients of marginal and average productivities, or expressing these quotients in terms of products, we obtain:

$$\frac{\partial Q}{\partial L} \cdot \frac{L}{Q} + \frac{\partial Q}{\partial K} \cdot \frac{K}{Q} = 1;$$

multiplying throughout by Q, we obtain Euler's theorem:

$$\frac{\partial Q}{\partial L} \cdot L + \frac{\partial Q}{\partial K} \cdot K = Q.$$

Let us choose from among the derivations of the above authors that of Walras. He sets out from the assumption that in the case of long-term equilibrium price revenue in all productive branches equals total cost: $Qp = Kp_K + Lp_L$.

In the short run, the possible profit as the difference between the amount of price and production costs, is $Qp - (Kp_K + Lp_L) = \pi$, where π is the amount of profit.

Let us maximize the amount of profit by unilaterally increasing either labour or capital. Total profit will be at a maximum when marginal profit, the partial derivative of profit with respect to both capital and labour, becomes 0.

$$\frac{\partial \pi}{\partial K} = \frac{\partial Q}{\partial K} \cdot p - p_K = 0, \text{ whence } \frac{\partial Q}{\partial K} \cdot p = p_K$$

$$\frac{\partial \pi}{\partial L} = \frac{\partial Q}{\partial L} \cdot p - p_L = 0, \text{ whence } \frac{\partial Q}{\partial L} \cdot p = p_L.$$

Substituting p_K and p_L into the equation expressing the equality of price revenue and total cost in long-term equilibrium:

$$Qp = K \frac{\partial Q}{\partial K} \cdot p + L \frac{\partial Q}{\partial L} \cdot p,$$

simplifying by p, we obtain Euler's theorem:[123]

$$Q = \frac{\partial Q}{\partial K} \cdot K + \frac{\partial Q}{\partial L} \cdot L.$$

Wicksell takes the general integral of Euler's theorem as a partial differential equation, $P = af \frac{a}{b}$, where $f(\ )$ represents any functional form, that is, where P must be a linear homogeneous function of a, the number of the labour force, and of b, the area of land. Out of the infinite number of functions, where this is the case, he chooses one form, $P = a^{\alpha} \cdot b^{\beta}$, where the exponents α and β are two constant fractions whose sum is 1. Thus, in his book published in 1913, Wicksell had already arrived, starting out from Euler's theorem, at the relationship between output and factor quantities set up later by Cobb and Douglas.

The demonstration of Euler's theorem reveals another characteristic of the homogeneous and linear production function, which now we are in a position to summarize, following R. Frisch and others: in the case of a homogeneous and linear production function, the marginal productivity of the factors of production is dependent only upon the ratio between the amounts of the factors employed, but not on their quantities. If the factors are all increased by the same percentage, their marginal productivity does not change, nor does their average productivity and thus their production elasticity, either.

If the quantity of only one factor is increased, its marginal productivity will decrease, but that of the constant factor will increase. When the variable factor is at its technical optimum, the constant factor is at its technical maximum, and vice versa. This relationship we can also obtain by Euler's theorem. Let the marginal productivity of one factor be equal to 0: then the marginal productivity of the other factor will equal its average productivity. Finally, the validity of Euler's theorem will obtain.

These characteristics of the homogeneous and linear production function were essentially formulated already by Wicksteed at the beginning of the century.

The representatives of the marginal productivity theory gladly assume the homogeneous and linear nature of the production function not only because they need it to explain the relations of income distribution but also for its favourable properties, since, with such a production function, it is enough to compute the elasticity of one factor, and this will automatically yield the elasticity of the other factor. Further, the elasticity of substitution, which will be discussed later, is determinate only in the case of the homogeneous and linear production function.

[123] See K. Wicksell: *Lectures on Political Economy*, Vol. I, London, 1934, pp. 127–128.

So far, we have investigated, by means of the production function, how a unilateral change in one factor influences the efficiency of output. With respect to output, a distinction was made between the spheres of increasing, constant and diminishing returns. Different from the law of return based on partial factor change is the return to scale, which expresses how the efficiency of production changes when all factors are changed simultaneously, that is, how output is influenced by changes in the scale or volume of production.

When we start to increase the production factors simultaneously, "at first one may think that constant proportional return should be prevalent in all productions, since it seems rather natural that the output should be doubled, trebled, and so on when the input of all the services is increased twice, three times, etc."[124]

Initially, with increasing output, the advantages of mass production can really be felt, viz., production becomes more and more efficient. Among the factors promoting increasing returns, economic literature refers to indivisibility in the first place. "The existence of indivisibilities upsets the applicability of the principle of constant returns to scale," writes Lerner.[125] In the short run, with given equipment, indivisibility yields increasing returns, because with stepping up the volume of production the equipment constructed for a certain quantity of output can be used more effectively. In the long run, when the equipment itself changes in the process of increasing production, indivisibility makes itself felt in the fact that the larger the scale of output, the more effective production methods can be introduced with ever more specialized equipment, whose application is not profitable for a small scale of output. This is how Mrs. Robinson writes on the subject: "For any kind of production there will be a hierarchy of possible technical methods, each using more highly specialized units of the factors than the last, and production is carried out most efficiently when each separate action in the production process is performed by a unit of a factor of production specially adapted to that particular task. But since the units of the factors are indivisible, the most specialised method of production will involve the largest outlay, and it is not profitable to make use of the full equipment of the highly specialised factors for a very small output. As output increases, a method higher in the hierarchy of specialisation can be adopted, and for this reason cost falls as the output of a commodity increases."[126]

While expanding the input of productive services, returns are also increased due to the fact that "an increased input of the productive services commonly permits a more efficient organisation, at least on the purely technical side of production; a more extensive division and specialization of labour, for instance, may be possible."[127] These factors working in the direction towards increasing returns in the process of expanding the volume of production were first analysed in detail by A. Marshall, who called them summarily *internal economies*.

E.A.G. Robinson points out that with the increase in the scale of productive

[124] S. Carlson: *op. cit.*, p. 21.
[125] A. P. Lerner: *The Economics of Control*, New York, 1947, p. 175.
[126] J. Robinson: *The Economics of Imperfect Competition*, London, 1954, pp. 335–336.
[127] S. Carlson: *op. cit.*, p. 21.

services, the economies of increased dimensions, or as Kaldor calls them in one of his recent studies, the 'space principle', comes into prominence.

Costs do not always grow with scale, and thus "in many cases, the large mechanical unit is both more efficient in operation and cheaper to construct than the smaller."[128] For example "if you take an ordinary container, such as a water tank, and double every dimension, so that it is twice as high, twice as long and twice as broad as it was before the amount of water which the tank will hold has increased with the cube of the dimension; that is, in this case it has increased eight times. But the area of the walls of the tank will only have increased as the square of the dimension. In this case it will have increased four times."[129] Or "where the object has to be moved against the resistance of water or air, as in the case of a ship or of an airship, similar gains are to be found, for while the capacity of a ship increases with the cube of its dimensions, the resistance increases in proportion to the wetted area, which increases as the square of the dimensions. The large ship will, therefore, require less horse-power per ton to move it at a given speed, or with the same horsepower per ton will travel faster than a smaller ship."[130]

In expanding the volume of production by increasing all factors, decreasing returns to scale will begin to assert themselves at a certain scale of inputs. This is an indication that a bottleneck has developed in one of the production factors. "The leadership and control of the business firm and its commercial relations frequently become increasingly difficult when, the size of the firm has passed a certain limit."[131]

But the factors working in the direction of increasing or diminishing returns to scale often change the proportions between the production factors, as we have already seen. The factors cannot be increased simultaneously, and cannot be changed proportionately. Returns deriving from changes in the scale of production and in factor proportions intermingle with one another. Returns increase or diminish, because the scale of output changes and because factor proportions also change. It is to this problem that Boulding calls attention: "Frequently... what appears to be variable return to scale turns out to be nothing but a subtle example of variable marginal physical productivity."[132]

Though the existence of a genuine variability of returns to scale is difficult to prove, nevertheless there is no doubt about it that the efficiency of a larger plant is greater than that of a smaller one, and an excessive increase in the size of a plant, at the existing level of technical knowledge, decreases its efficiency.

According to traditional classification, elasticity of scale, or *Niveauelastizität* in Schneider's, and "conversion coefficient" in Ragnar Frisch's terminology, is the relationship between the percentage increase in output and the percentage increase in all factors "when the quantity of all factors is increased in the same proportion by an infinitely small increment."[133] If its magnitude, $\varepsilon > 1$, then output rises in a larger proportion than the quantity of factors, returns to scale

128 E. A. G. Robinson: *The Structure of Competitive Industry*, London, 1931, p. 32.
129 E. A. G. Robinson: *op. cit.*, p. 29.
130 E. A. G. Robinson: *op. cit.*, p. 30.
131 S. Carlson: *op. cit.*, p. 21.
132 K. E. Boulding: *Economic Analysis*, Vol. I, New York–London–Tokyo, 1966, p. 549.
133 R. Frisch: *op. cit.*, p. 65.

are increasing. Increasing returns to scale obtain until the optimum size of firm is reached. At the optimum size of firm returns to scale are constant, output and factors grow in the same proportion, elasticity of scale equals 1. Now first-degree homogeneous production functions are also characterized by constant returns to scale and an elasticity of scale equal to 1. Further increasing factor inputs, the percentage rise in output will be smaller than that in factors, returns to scale will be diminishing and the elasticity of scale $\varepsilon < 1$.

Schneider also introduces, along with the concept of level elasticity or elasticity of scale, the notion of marginal return to scale, by which he understands such an infinitely small increment of output as is obtained by increasing all factors by an infinitely small unit, leaving their quantitative proportions unchanged.

Instead of returns to scale, Stonier and Hague recommend the term "returns to outlay" in case factor proportions change with the change in the volume of production. The notion "returns to outlay" expresses to what extent production increases with increasing factor outlay.

"Now it is quite possible that although returns to outlay are constant along any scale line, the *proportions* between the factors along that same scale line may alter."[134]

If the production function is not first-degree homogeneous, then, if factor proportions are changed, the marginal productivity of factors need not move in opposite directions.

With increasing or decreasing returns to scale, the marginal productivity of factors is dependent not only upon their relative proportions, but also upon their *absolute size*. Increasing the factors by the same percentage, their marginal productivity will rise with increasing returns to scale, and with decreasing returns to scale, their marginal productivity will decrease.

With non-constant returns to scale, the technical optimum of one factor does not correspond to the technical maximum of the other.

The amount obtained by factor inputs multiplied by the marginal productivity of factors will yield, with diminishing returns to scale less, and with increasing returns to scale more, than the volume of output produced.

It was Wicksell who first pointed out that since in the case of a production function, if all factors are simultaneously increased, there is always a sphere of constant return between the spheres of increasing and decreasing returns, the production function, even if not first-degree homogeneous, may also have a range where its curve closely approaches a straight line: the sum of the products of the marginal productivities of factors multiplied by factor inputs exhausts total output, and thus the production function becomes linear. We shall see from what follows that, according to the theory, competition free of monopolistic elements causes the entrepreneurs to operate in the sphere of constant returns to scale.

[134] A. W. Stonier and D. C. Hague: *A Textbook of Economic Theory*, London, 1965, p. 220.

THE LAW OF RETURNS WITH PARTIAL FACTOR CHANGE IN THE CASE OF A FINITE NUMBER OF PRODUCTION TECHNIQUES WITH A FIXED CAPITAL–LABOUR RATIO FOR EACH TECHNIQUE

The law of returns with partial factor change discussed so far is based on the assumption that *continuous* substitution is possible between factors of production, which presupposes that factor proportions within the production process can be continuously altered, or that an infinite number of production processes, with a capital–labour ratio different in each of them, are available to the entrepreneur, and it is easy for him to switch over from one technique to another. But as soon as the attempt was made to apply marginal analysis to practice, it turned out that it suits modern industrial production better to assume that the entrepreneur can only choose from among a finite number of production techniques, and the factors within each must be used in a technologically determined proportion, and thus it is not possible to apply ex-post substitutability. A new method reflecting these properties came into being to formulate an optimum production programme, the so-called linear *activity analysis,* which is nothing other than the application of linear programming to production. This method was first worked out by Koopmans in his study published in 1951. "In our static model an activity consists of the combination of certain qualitatively defined commodities in fixed quantitative ratios as 'inputs' to produce as 'outputs' certain other commodities in fixed quantitative ratios to the inputs."[135] Activity analysis characterizes all production methods by technical coefficients corresponding to them.

Allen and others pointed out that activity analysis is "to supplement rather than to replace the marginal approach..."[136] "Marginal analysis may be perfectly appropriate", writes Allen at an other place of his work quoted, "as a matter of exposition; it may certainly lead to a statement of the main results in the most illuminating form."[137] Apart from this, the assumption of continuous substitutability in the long run, for a wider range of the economy and, accordingly, the application of marginal analysis with a continuous production function seems to be appropriate. As we shall see below the production function for US industry constructed on the basis of the date of twenty-four years also supposes continuous substitution between the factors of production.

References to the common features of the two methods of analysis can often be found in non-Marxian economics. "...it will turn out that the two types of approach [to the problem of production—A.M.] are really not so different after all and that the analyst whose training is primarily in standard economic theory will find in the programming model a great deal that is familiar to him."[138]

Substitution between production factors in activity analysis takes place in switching over from one production technique to another, or in the combination of different techniques.

[135] T. C. Koopmans: Analysis of Production as an Efficient Combination of Activities. In: *Activity Analysis, Production and Allocation,* New York–London, 1951, pp. 35–36.

[136] R. G. D. Allen: *Mathematical Economics,* London, 1965, p. 619.

[137] R. G. D. Allen: *op. cit.,* p. 341.

[138] W. J. Baumol: *Economic Theory and Operations Analysis,* 2nd. edition, Englewood Cliffs, N. T., 1965, p. 271.

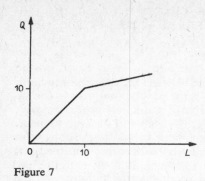

Figure 7

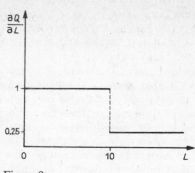

Figure 8

For simplicity's sake let only two production techniques with a rigid capital–labour coefficient for each be available to the entrepreneur:

$$a_{1K} = 10 \qquad a_{1L} = 1$$
$$a_{2K} = 8 \qquad a_{2L} = 1.6$$

Let 100 units of capital be the capital stock at the entrepreneur's disposal. Our entrepreneur wishes to expand his output by increasing labour input by one unit each at his given capital stock. We assume the labour force to be available in any quantity. Let our entrepreneur first adopt the technique in which the labour coefficient is smaller, and the productivity of labour accordingly greater, that is, the first production technique. In this technique 10 units of capital will combine with one unit of labour. As he increases the quantity of labour input by one unit, he mobilizes an increasing share of his capital stock, and output will always increase by one unit. Thus the marginal productivity of labour is 1. Our entrepreneur can fully make use of his 100 units of capital if he employs 10 units of labour. Then the total volume of output will be 10 units. By further increasing labour input at a given capital stock, any additional increase in the volume of output can only materialize if he combines the first technique with the second. He withdraws 10 units of capital from the first production technique, that is, he produces, applying the first technique, 9 units of output by employing 90 units of capital and 9 units of labour. He employs the 10 units of capital withdrawn from the first in the second production technique. Adopting the second technique, he will need 2 units of labour to mobilize 10 units of capital, and then the volume of output will be 1.25 units. At a given capital stock, our entrepreneur employs now 11 units of labour to produce a total volume of 10.25 units of output. The marginal productivity of labour is 0.25, and employment and production, under the continuous withdrawal of capital from the first production technique and employment in the second technique, can be increased up to 20 units of labour and 12.5 units of output, respectively. The marginal productivity of labour, by increasing labour input from 10 units to 20 units, is 0.25 throughout.

Let us now represent graphically the changes in the total product and the marginal productivity of labour as labour input is increased at a capital stock of 100 units.

82

The principle of diminishing returns will assert itself here, too, just as in any model based on marginal analysis, since we have switched over from a production technique ensuring higher labour productivity to a technique ensuring lower productivity. With rigid technical coefficients, however, returns to scale can only be constant.

Dorfman, Samuelson and Solow have demonstrated[139] that Euler's theorem also applies to activity analysis. The amount of commodities attributable to resources available in given quantities will yield according to activity analysis also the sum total of net output.

THE MARGINAL PRODUCTIVITY APPROACH AS A THEORY OF INCOME DISTRIBUTION

According to marginal productivity theory as a theory of income distribution, competition, if free of monopolistic elements, ensures that the marginal product is paid as real income to every factor of production, or, in other words, factor money payment equals marginal product multiplied by product price.

The operation of this mechanism will be illustrated by the example of wages.

When undisturbed competition prevails, the entrepreneur is faced with a given product price and a given level of wages. If he continuously increases labour by one unit, with his capital stock left unchanged, and deducts from the increment of output the share attributable to other factors growing with increased labour force (this residual imputable to labour is called by Marshall the *net marginal product of labour*), his total money revenue will rise by the marginal product of labour multiplied by product price, while his total cost less "incidental expenses" (using Machlup's term) will only increase by the wage of one additional worker. If this latter is more than the increment of his money revenue, the employment of one additional worker would cause a loss to the entrepreneur, and therefore he would not employ him. However, as long as by employing one more unit of labour the increment of his money revenue is greater than the increment of his cost, he will gain by increasing his labour force employed. Assuming that the entrepreneur wishes to maximize the amount of his profit, he may go on employing additional labour up to the limit where the increment of profit becomes zero, that is, the increment of his money revenue, i.e. the marginal productivity of labour multiplied by the product price, is equal to the level of money wages. Then, in the case of a competition free of monopolistic elements, the real wage will equal the marginal productivity of labour.

Let us represent graphically the curve of the marginal value product of labour, showing marginal product multiplied by price figuring as a datum under competition free of monopolistic elements (see Fig. 9).

The area thus obtained under the curve shows the amount of the entrepreneur's total money revenue at a certain employment level after the payment of the cost of the constant factor. Taken the amount of wages to be given, the surplus of the

---

[139] R. Dorfman, R. Solow and P. A. Samuelson: *Linear Programming and Economic Analysis*, New York–Toronto–London, 1958, pp. 166–169.

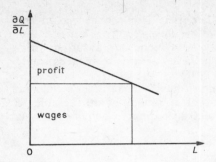

Figure 9

price sum of output over and above total wages paid to the workers employed will be the entrepreneur's profit. Clearly, this will be greatest at a level of employment where the marginal product of labour multiplied by the product price, the so-called marginal value product, drops to the level of money wages.

It is similarly demonstrated for capital, too, that its revenue, interest, equals the marginal product of capital multiplied by the price of the product. "The power of capital to create the product is, then, the basis of interest."[140]

The followers of marginal productivity theory try to trace back total output entirely to the participation of the various factors. This is clearly conceivable only in the case of first-degree, homogeneous production functions. And, as far as income distribution is concerned, they wish to demonstrate that, under the undisturbed assertion of competition, the value of total net product is paid out as wages, interest and land rent to the factor owners, that is, total wages, total interest and total land rent exhaust total net product. In the value of the quantity of output produced there is no room for unearned revenue: undisturbed competition does not permit unearned income.

According to Samuelson[141], the so-called exhaustion theory is not necessarily linked to the first-degree homogeneous nature of the production function. It is much more dependent on the form of the market. As Wicksell already emphasized, if competition is free of monopolistic elements, the total revenue of factors can exhaust net total product even in the case of functions which are not first-degree homogeneous, as competition stimulates the entrepreneurs to operate at the optimum size of the firm. But the existence of monopolistic elements makes it impossible, according to marginal productivity theory, for the factors to be rewarded according to their marginal product multiplied by the price of the product: thus, in the case of first-degree homogeneous production functions, the total revenue of factors does not exhaust total output; but if total net product is paid out as a reward to the factors, the production function cannot be homogeneous and linear.

However, Samuelson's reasoning only expresses that the explanation of the pro-

140 J. B. Clark: *op. cit.*, p. 135.
141 P. A. Şamuelson: *Foundations of Economic Analysis*, Cambridge, 1948, p. 83.

84

cess of income distribution according to the principle of marginal productivity assumes competition to be free of monopolistic elements. In the case of undisturbed competition, however, the demonstration of income distribution on the basis of marginal productivity theory presupposes that the production function is first-degree homogeneous. This is also emphasized by Hicks: "In the days of marginal productivity we needed a constant returns to scale assumption in order to make it possible for the factors to get their marginal products..."[142] This is why Wicksell and Samuelson had to make efforts to prove that the undisturbed character of competition compels the entrepreneurs to operate in the long run at the optimum size of the firm.

With this we have stumbled upon one of the technical snags of marginal productivity theory as a theory of income distribution: "If one assumes a production function with increasing returns to scale, the marginal-productivity theory of distribution goes by the board; for the total of returns to all factors, if they were all paid according to their marginal products, would exceed the total that there was to distribute. It is impossible that every factor should receive its marginal product; some, at least, must get less."[143] But capital accumulation is characteristic of a developed economy, and it goes together with increasing returns: "For my own part I find it hard to believe that increasing returns and growth by capital accumulation are not tied very closely together."[144] These lines shattering marginal productivity theory as a theory of distribution were written by Hicks who significantly contributed, among others by his work published in 1932, to the further development of the theory of income distribution based on marginal productivity theory. Kaldor also writes that "... on an empirical level, nobody doubts that ... in industry—increasing returns dominate the picture..."[143] Once increasing returns have asserted themselves, writes Kaldor quoting Young, "change becomes progressive and propagates itself in a cumulative way."[146] Speaking of factors giving rise to increasing returns, he calls attention to the "dynamic economies of scale", or, using Arrow's phrase, to "learning by doing". He points out that in the ceaseless, repetitive process of productive work new inventions continue to improve, and several new ideas are born.

Neo-classical economics made use of the marginal productivity theory to demonstrate that no unemployment can exist if competition freely asserts itself. Though the pressure of the unemployed diminishes money wages, real wages, they say, will also decline given the price of the product, and consequently the entrepreneur may increase his profit by expanding employment. And money wages, and through them real wages, too, will allegedly decrease until full employment is realized. According to the logic of the theory, unemployment is caused by the behaviour of the workers who, by means of their organizations, keep wages at an artificially high level, preventing them from falling freely.

[142] J. R. Hicks: Thoughts on the Theory of Capital: the Corfu Conference, *Oxford Economic Papers*, June 1960, No. 2, p. 128.
[143] J. R. Hicks: *op. cit.*, p. 129.
[144] J. R. Hicks: *op. cit.*, p. 128.
[145] N. Kaldor: The Irrelevance of Equilibrium Economics, *The Economic Journal*, December 1972, p. 1242.
[146] N. Kaldor: *op. cit.*, p. 1244.

The mechanism depicted also realizes the full employment of the available capital stock under free competition through the movement of the rate of interest. Thus, the free assertion of the mechanisms of capitalist economy ensures the full employment of the factors of production. The economists who believed in the beneficial effect of the automatisms of capitalist economy were given the attribute *neo-classical*, because the economists of the rising bourgeoisie, the early classical economists—of course under completely different historical circumstances—considered full employment as the normal state of capitalist economy. But modern non-Marxian value theory which came into being as the counterpart of early classical economics, and the theoretical system based on it, are so remote from the classical tenets that Schumpeter himself stresses that "there is no more sense in calling the Jevons–Menger–Walras theory neo-classic than there should be in calling the Einstein theory neo-Newtonian."[147]

A CRITIQUE OF THE MARGINAL PRODUCTIVITY THEORY

1. Marginal productivity theory plays an important part in the theory of the optimum allocation of resources, or in the programming method related to it. With its help the representatives of the theory try to answer the question of how to combine the available production factors in an optimal way, how to allocate them optimally among their alternative uses. The concept of marginal productivity is used not only by marginal analysis but also by linear programming. "... if we want to determine the optimal magnitudes of our outputs and the optimal allocation of our bottleneck inputs, we should value the inputs in terms of their marginal (profit) yields..."[148]—writes Baumol in expounding linear programming. If, for example, the primal task of linear programming is to determine which of the products that can be produced with the available factors should be turned out and in what combination and quantity, for the price revenue to be at its maximum, the dual task is the determination of how to produce this quantity of output with minimum expenses. In doing so, the price sum of the output produced is imputed to the scarce resources, and a price of account, a shadow price is calculated for them which expresses the value of the marginal product of the resources concerned.

The optimal allocation of resources is a relationship existing with respect to use-value. Provided the marginal productivity of factors could be ascertained, the theory of marginal productivity might play a crucial role in optimal resource allocation.

It must be noted, however, that marginal product, too, has been produced by the totality of factors. At best we can say that the emergence of marginal product is a function of the availability of the last unit of a production factor or a group of factors. This is how modern non-Marxian economics interprets the marginal productivity of factors: "A causal relationship, in the sense of real effect, cannot be revealed by exploring the determination of marginal product. But it is possible

---

[147] J. Schumpeter: *History of Economic Analysis*, New York, 1955, p. 919.
[148] W. J. Baumol: *op. cit.*, p. 114.

to construe dependence ... marginal productivity theory sets, therefore, dependence against causal relationships."[149]

The theory of optimal allocation of resources, however, in so far as it remains at the enterprise level in trying to specify the marginal productivity of the factors of production, ignores the impact of society on the productivity of individual factors, i.e. the marginal social productivity of factors; this arises from the fact that, owing to the social interrelationships of firms and industries, the productivity or efficiency of production factors may increase in terms of their benefit to society, or that the operation of a factor beneficial to the firm may do harm to society.

By way of introduction to a critique of the theory of marginal productivity as a distribution theory we only want to note that since the marginal productivity of factors is based, according to the theory, on their relative scarcity, the question is bound to arise as to what are the determinants underlying it. Economists specifically concerned with the problem have pointed out that the relative scarcity of factors is not independent of the distribution relations to be explained. Marshall, for example, accepts the statement of the theory of marginal productivity that there is a tendency for the income and marginal productivity of factors to become equal in equilibrium, but denies that marginal productivity theory may serve in itself as a theory of income distribution. In his view, the marginal productivity of any factor of production depends on the conditions under which the factor in question operates. But these conditions themselves depend on several other circumstances. The net marginal productivity of a shepherd is dependent, among other things, upon the area that is available for the purpose of sheep-farming. This in turn is influenced by the demand for land for the purpose of timber production, rye growing or hunting, etc. The net marginal productivity of a shepherd also depends on how many shepherds were employed before him in the given area of land by sheep-farmers. And this in turn is affected by the proportion of the population who have chosen to be shepherds. This again is dependent upon the formation of incomes, which is exactly what marginal productivity theory wants to explain. And these conditions, which, according to Marshall, influence the net marginal product of a shepherd's labour, could be extended still further. Thus he does not accept marginal productivity theory as an independent income distribution theory, since the net marginal product itself of the factors of production has to be traced back to several circumstances, among them to the distribution relations that should be explained.[150]

A similar criticism of marginal productivity theory can be found in Kaldor: "Unless we assume that the 'fixed factors' are fixed by Nature and not as a result of a previous act of choice ... we must again enquire why the fixed factors came to be of such magnitude as they actually are."[151] And the obvious answer is that present factor proportions, which determine the magnitude of their marginal productivities and through them the income of their services, depend on the past prices of factor services. Later, when discussing the problem of measuring capital

[149] H. Runge: *Die Lehre der Grenzproduktivität,* Berlin, 1963, p. 55.
[150] A. Marshall: *Principles of Economics,* London, 1930, pp. 517–518.
[151] N. Kaldor: The Equilibrium of Firm. In: *Essays on Value and Distribution,* London, 1960, p. 39.

goods, we shall come up against the dependence of marginal productivity on distribution relations.

In the passage quoted, Marshall speaks of *net marginal product* wishing to express by this that it is impossible to increase a single factor one-sidedly "without considerable extra outlays in other directions, as for land, buildings, implements, labour of management, etc."[152] especially not within a given production technique. In order to determine the net marginal product of labour, "... we have to take for granted all the expenses of production of the commodity on which he works, other than his own wages."[153]

Mrs. Robinson writes similarly: "... when the number of men employed is increased, other factors will in most cases also be increased."[154] And she also defines net marginal productivity as "the marginal gross productivity caused by employing an additional man with the appropriate addition to other factors, less the addition to the cost of other factors."[155]

A prominent German management economist, Erich Gutenberg, also doubts that output could be expanded by a one-sided increase in one single factor alone. He holds that the intended increase in one factor will make it necessary also to increase a number of complementary factors such as energy, lubricants, fuels, etc. But their change is technologically uniquely determined. From this he comes to the conclusion that "... surplus return in the course of changing the quantities of factors employed can only be ascribed to the totality of these additional factor quantities used. Since these quantities cannot be freely changed, it is impossible to determine ... partial marginal productivity for particular factors."[156] Obviously, if there is no possibility of changing the proportions between certain factors, then their marginal productivities have no sense at all. In this case, even the concept of net marginal productivity introduced by Marshall is of no avail. It is impossible to deduce the marginal productivity of the other factors from their common return, in order to obtain the net marginal productivity of a given factor, if the marginal productivity of the rest of the factors cannot be determined either.

2. But let us assume that the marginal productivity of factors can be determined, and criticize from this aspect the conclusions that can be drawn from the principle of marginal productivity.

To begin with, it seems necessary to clarify that tracing back the price sum of the use-values produced to the participation of a factor of production is a different process from distributing the new value produced among the various classes of society. Even if capital goods do contribute to producing use-values, they by no means participate in creating values. The distribution of the new value produced among social classes is determined not by participation in producing use-values but by the ownership relations of the means of production. In a capitalist economy, for example, as a result of the fact that the worker is deprived of the means of

---

[152] A. Marshall: *op. cit.*, p. 517.
[153] A. Marshall: *op. cit.*, p. 518.
[154] J. Robinson: *The Economics of Imperfect Competition*, London, 1954, p. 238.
[155] J. Robinson: *op. cit.*, p. 239.
[156] E. Gutenberg: *Grundlagen der Betriebswirtschaftslehre*, Berlin–Heidelberg–New York, 1966, Vol. I, p. 313.

production, he gets as his share of the new value produced by him only the value of his labour power, while the capitalist (or landowner) class as the owner of the means of production receives the surplus value which was created by the worker's surplus labour. Even if every capitalist entrepreneur organized production by programming and computed the shadow prices of the factors of production, and combined or allocated the production factors accordingly, this would not change the capitalist character of distribution relations; it would at best result in lenghtening the worker's surplus labour and increasing the amount of surplus value. The explanation of distribution relations based on participation in producing use-values divorces the system of distribution from the existing social order, and deprives incomes of their specific historical and social nature.

The dependence of the process of income distribution on social relations manifests itself in marginal productivity analysis in so far as market forms other than perfect competition prevent the factors of production from getting a money reward corresponding to the marginal productivity of the production factors multiplied by the product price. The market forms other than undisturbed competition explain, in this view, only the deviation from the standard distribution, i.e. the principle of marginal productivity, while non-Marxian economics is unable to detect behind the changes in market forms the historical-economic development giving rise to them.

But the determining role of ownership relations in the process of income distribution also becomes apparent in this representation. According to this theory, the marginal productivity of labour is accorded as wages to the workers taking part in the production process, and the marginal productivity of capital and land will fall to the share of capitalists and landowners as interest and rent respectively, though it was only their capital and land and not they themselves personally that participated in the production process. "The productivity of capital is ... not the productivity of the capitalist," writes Bronfenbrenner.[157] How is it that the marginal productivity of capital and land falls to the share of the capitalist and the landowner, and not of the worker operating the means of production? Obviously, on the basis of the ownership relations of the means of production. But by admitting this, marginal productivity theory swerves from its starting point, distribution according to participation in producing commodities, into a quite different direction, in which it depends already on the ownership relations which class will get the products as income imputed to particular factors.

Basing the distribution relations on participation in producing use-values, has raised serious problems in marginal productivity theory.

As far as the products imputed to labour are concerned, it is not clear whether or not they cover the costs of the reproduction of labour. The principle of marginal productivity cannot relate wages to the reproduction costs of labour power because it would compel the theory to give up economic imputation, the assumption that the value of factors or of their services, the rewards to them, depends on the value of the commodities produced with their participation. In so far as we make the magnitude of wages dependent on the costs of reproduction, we determine them

[157] Quoted by W. Hoffmann: *Einkommenstheorie vom Merkantilismus bis zur Gegenwart* Berlin 1965, p. 237.

independently of the principle of marginal productivity, and hence its magnitude is an external datum from the point of view of marginal productivity theory.

If we interpret wages figuring as a form of manifestation of the value of labour power, and use marginal analysis to determine the conditions for attaining maximum profits, we shall arrive at a causal relationship diametrically opposed to the statement of marginal productivity theory: it is not the marginal productivity of labour that determines the size of wages; rather it depends on the value of labour power what volume of employment, given a certain capital stock, ensures maximum profit for the entrepreneur, that is, the magnitude of the marginal productivity of labour is determined by the value of labour power.

This also shows that we can acknowledge the significance of marginal analysis for the optimum use of factors without accepting marginal productivity theory as a theory of distributing incomes. The advocates of marginal productivity theory, in response to the Marxist objection that in determining wages they leave out of account the reproduction costs of labour power, may, and do in fact, refer to it that equilibrium theory, as it can be seen in the third edition of Walras's principal work or in Marshall, builds only the demand function with respect to productive services upon the marginal productivity principle. In addition, this theory also includes the supply function with respect to productive services in the price model. In accordance with the two varieties of subjective value theory, the supply function of labour appears in two forms. For Walras and the American representatives of subjective value theory, the owner of the production factor, including the worker, is free to choose between two alternatives: the realization of one possibility requires the sacrifice of the other. The worker, for example, makes use of the day's 24 hours available to him in an optimum way, namely he allocates them, at the various levels of his real wages, between work and leisure so that the total utility of consumption goods he can buy for his wages and of the remaining leisure should be at a maximum. Contrary to the so-called opportunity cost approach, wage in the Cambridge variety of the subjective value theory is—as we have seen—a sort of compensation for the effort made in connection with production, and represents a payment for the marginal sacrifice of employment.

But such a supply function of labour is in a sharp contradiction with capitalist reality. Non-Marxian criticism also points out that the length of the worktime is fixed in capitalist enterprises, the worker may not leave his work when he feels that the utility of the goods available to him for his wages and the utility of the leisure sacrificed, or his sensation of sacrificing the last working hour, are just in equilibrium. Moreover, the worker is never free to choose whether to work, and acquire thereby the pleasure of wage goods or to enjoy leisure. He must work to get the value of his labour power. But both varieties of the supply function of labour divorce wages from the reproduction costs of labour power.

The explanation of the process of income distribution on the basis of marginal productivity theory raises a serious problem in connection with the reward to capital. From the viewpoint of subjective value theory Böhm-Bawerk points out that the contribution of capital to producing use-values does not prove in itself that surplus value has also been created because the quantity of the commodities produced and the magnitude of value do not always move parallel with one another. In other words, a unit of product in physico-technical terms and a unit in terms of value are different. According to Runge, "the extreme case may occur

90

in which, owing to increased productivity, the price sum of a larger stock of goods is less than that of a smaller stock of goods offered before the rise in productivity."[158] Böhm-Bawerk raises the question whether the value of a quantity of goods imputable to the contribution of one unit of capital goods is sufficient only to replace the capital used up. It appeared necessary for subjective value theory to prove that the value of this stock of products also contains a surplus over and above the cost of replacement, "why a larger stock and better quality of goods is more valuable than the capital used up in its production."[159]

The source of the problem lies in the fact that by endeavouring to reveal the role of factors in producing commodities, marginal productivity theory is trying to determine the marginal productivity of factors by assuming their quantities as data, and cannot therefore provide an explanation of the forces determining factor supply. In order to demonstrate, on the basis of subjective value theory, that the share attributable to capital also contains a surplus in excess of replacement, they tried to establish what factors keep the supply of capital so scarce compared to the demand for it that, as a result, capital can make a claim to be rewarded. Thus Marshall writes that we must understand the causes "which have kept the supply of accumulated wealth so small relatively to the demand for its use, that that use is on the balance a source of gain, and can therefore require a payment when loaned."[160]

According to the two varieties of subjective value theory, there also exist two approaches to the supply function of capital.

One of them is associated with Marshall. In his view, as we have already mentioned, the source of capital is saving, sacrifice on the part of the consumer; and interest, as one of the real costs of production, is the supply price of this saving as sacrifice. According to him, it is the sacrifice character of saving that restricts capital accumulation to such an extent that the value of a stock of products imputable to its participation ensures interest for the saver in excess of replacement. In this sense, interest is an incentive to accumulation. We have already criticized Marshall's theory of interest. The basic deficiency of his interest concept is that it represents the business savings of capitalists as consumer savings which mean sacrifice to the capitalists as consumers, entitling them to interest as a reward for their sacrifice entailing saving.

Böhm-Bawerk tries to prove from another viewpoint that in economic imputation, in addition to the value necessary to replace it, capital also earns interest.

In his view, it is due to the nature of the consumer, that he discounts future goods against present goods. He puts less emphasis on an intensity of pleasure caused by a stock of commodities available in the future than on the intensity caused by a stock of goods of the same quantity available at present; he attributes less marginal utility to future goods than to present goods. As in business life, where future claims are taken account of at their discounted present value, Böhm-Bawerk's consumer discounts future pleasures at their present value to him. This consumer value judgement is known in English economic literature as *time preference*. Pigou, the late professor of Cambridge University, speaks of the con-

[158] H. Runge: *op. cit.*, p. 32.
[159] E. Böhm-Bawerk: *Capital und Capitalzins,* Vol. II, Innsbruck, 1902, p. 135.
[160] A. Marshall: *op. cit.*, p. 581.

sumers' lack of telescopic faculty: "... everybody prefers present pleasures or satisfaction to future pleasures or satisfactions of equal magnitude even when the latter are perfectly certain to occur. But this preference for present pleasures does not—the idea is self-contradictory—imply that a present pleasure of given magnitude is any greater than a future pleasure of the same magnitude. It implies only that our telescopic faculty is defective, and that we, therefore, see future pleasures, as it were, on a diminished scale."[161]

The intention is obvious: to demonstrate on the basis of consumer value judgement, how interest comes into being as surplus value. Who saves, says Böhm-Bawerk, renounces the pleasure of present goods. For lending present goods, he justly demands more future goods in exchange, that is, a premium, interest. "This agio [i.e. premium—A.M.] is the organically inevitable consequence of a two-fold factor which at all times exerts its influence on the market situation ... first, the superior utility and desirability of present goods as compared with future goods, and second, the fact that present goods are never ... offered in unlimited quantities."[162] If they were not to receive interest, consumers would never save.

Present goods supplied as savings are borrowed by the entrepreneurs, who use them to produce capital goods. It is by their use that production becomes more effective, says Böhm-Bawerk. Thus the producers get more consumer goods than they would if they had carried out production without capital goods, or, in other words, with the aid of the available capital goods they get more consumer goods if, instead of using them directly for producing consumer goods, they first use them to produce more sophisticated capital goods. But capital goods are future goods in Böhm-Bawerk's view; they will become consumer goods only in the future, in the course of the production process, and therefore their value is less compared with present goods. "... the entrepreneur buys the future goods called means of production for fewer units of present goods than the units of future output those means will produce."[163] But capital goods as future goods become, through their use in the production process, present goods, articles of consumption, whereby their value increases. "For his [i.e. the entrepreneur's—A.M.] future good gradually ripens into a present good during the course of the production process, and thus grows into possession of the full value of a present good."[164] "It is quite literally a surplus arising from the potentiality for increment in value which resides in those future goods which are transformed under the hand of the entrepreneur into present consumable goods."[165]

Thus interest, in Böhm-Bawerk's view, in contrast to that of Marshall, is not real cost, not the supply price of saving as sacrifice, since saving itself is not a real sacrifice, but simply a regulator of choice between alternatives, the choice between present and future consumption. Interest is the increase in value of advanced capital goods, surplus value interpreted in a subjective way. It is by distinguishing between present and future goods, by interpreting capital goods as future goods that Böhm-Bawerk tries to explain why the value of products imputable to the

161 A. C. Pigou: *The Economics of Welfare*, London, 1960, 4th ed., pp. 24–25.
162 E. Böhm-Bawerk: *op. cit.*, p. 357.
163 E. Böhm-Bawerk: *op. cit.*, p. 317.
164 E. Böhm-Bawerk: *op. cit.*, p. 318.
165 E. Böhm-Bawerk: *op. cit.*, p. 319.

participation of capital contains surplus value in excess of the value needed to replace capital. Capital is scarce in relation to the demand for it because of the underestimation of future goods, resulting from the nature of consumers. Now the fact that interest is to be paid on savings constitutes a restriction for the entrepreneurs, who can expand production only up to a limit. They can expand it as long as they are able to pay the premium, interest. To use the expression of a modern version of marginal productivity theory, a given stock of capital could be increased up to the technical maximum only if there were no difference in value between present and future goods. At the technical maximum the marginal productivity of capital is 0, and the capitalist would not be able to pay interest on borrowed savings.

Does an underestimation of the future really characterize consumer psychology?

Let us look at the arguments advanced by Böhm-Bawerk. Today the individual lives in difficult conditions, but expects his income to rise in the future. He feels strongly the pressure of his present wants, but he is less anxious about the satisfaction of his future wants. Such consumer behaviour is conceivable but not general, and especially not typical of the well-to-do capitalist class. It is largely a function of social position. A man living in poverty will not save however high a rate of interest is promised to him, simply because he cannot. Prudence depends not on the rate of interest but on income relations.

Owing to a deficiency of willpower and lack of imagination, the individual cannot resist the temptations of the present, says Böhm-Bawerk enumerating his further arguments. It is an irresponsible, careless, irrational consumer behaviour differing from the rational consumer calculation assumed by the theory of the optimum allocation of resources. Such a consumer psychology, as far as its validity for value theory is concerned, is not well-founded from the point of view of marginal utility theory which regards value as a sensation of satisfaction. Discounting the future for the above considerations does not mean at all that a given good gives less pleasure in the future than in the present. It is only the consumer who thinks it does. This is a very shaky foundation for an explanation of the emergence of surplus value.

As a last motive derived from consumer psychology for discounting the future, Böhm-Bawerk mentions the shortness and uncertainty of human life. We can never be sure that what we save today we can consume tomorrow. This consumer motivation cannot be accepted as general either, as it is exactly the shortness and uncertainty of life which induce some people to save, to provide for their families.

Böhm-Bawerk's ideas of consumer psychology concerning the under-estimation of the future gave rise to heated debates in non-Marxian literature, too. Cassel remarks that "naturally these grounds for the under-estimation of future needs are strongest among those classes who are able to provide only very scantily even for the present... But in the higher classes of wage earners more importance is attached to future needs. And in the middle and upper classes there is evidently a strong tendency to put future needs on the same level as present ones."[166]

The basic deficiency of this concept is that the business savings of the capitalist

[166] G. Cassel: *The Nature and Necessity of Interest,* New York, 1957, (reprint of the 1903 edition), p. 141.

cannot be deduced from consumer psychology. In his saving for business purposes, the capitalist does not compare the satisfactions derived from present and future goods, and it is not on the basis of this comparison that he makes his decisions on the magnitude of his savings. Böhm-Bawerk's explanation is the logical consequence of the origin of his investigation being consumer behaviour: if the value of the consumer good produced returns the capital used up in its production with a value added, then the reason for this may be that the consumer prefers consumer goods to capital goods.

The capitalist in fact saves part of his income in order to get more profit by using it for exploitation. "... the appropriation of ever more and more wealth in the abstract becomes the sole motive of his [i.e. the capitalist's—A.M.] operations... *Use values* must therefore never be looked upon as the real aim of the capitalist... The restless, never-ending process of profit-making alone is what he aims at."[167]

Now this passionate chase after abstract wealth, which is the characteristic feature of capitalist production, cannot be deduced from consumer behaviour. Money in the sense of subjective value theory can constitute the object of independent effort, in so far as some people engage in selling in order to hold money to bridge the period between the time they may need to buy goods and the time these goods are produced (see Chapter 3, Part Seven on the cash balance theory), by this an independent marginal utility accrues to money. In this presentation it is clearly not the desire to get rich in absolute terms that stimulates the economic subject to accumulate. Or, according to Keynes, money has a marginal utility of its own in that it is the most secure form holding one's wealth. Keynes tries to find an explanation of the desire of capitalists to get rich in consumer psychology. In his view, given a certain size of income the desire to accumulate wealth comes into prominence due to consumer psychology. The consumer in his turn insists on holding part of his wealth saved in money form since wealth so held is less exposed to losing its value than wealth held in bonds. With Keynes's reasoning, starting from the consumer, we can at best get as far as characterizing the miser, but we cannot explain the aim of capitalist production, the never-ending process of appropriating abstract wealth.

In both explanations, Marshall's and Böhm-Bawerk's, the rate of interest stimulates saving. But how can the existence of interest be explained in a stationary economy where there is no saving and no investment, and only existing capital is replaced? The question was raised in connection with the Marshallian interpretation of real cost: why does the owner of capital get his regular interest on the capital created by a single act of sacrifice? Or, as Mrs. Robinson remarks: "... what Marshall needs is the ratio of profit appropriate to a stock of capital, not to a rate of accumulation."[168] In fact, however, he only explains the latter. In Marshall we cannot find a clear answer to this problem. But the question may also arise in connection with Böhm-Bawerk's theory of interest. If a positive rate of interest stimulates saving, which then becomes investment, we can no longer speak of a stationary economy. Schumpeter holds that in a stationary economy the share

[167] K. Marx: *Capital*, Vol. I, Moscow, 1954, pp. 152–153.
[168] J. Robinson: *Economic Philosophy*, London, 1962, p. 61.

of value imputable to the participation of capital is just enough to replace capital and does not contain interest.[169]

Cassel, however, tries to prove the necessity of interest. References to his idea can also be found in modern economic literature. Saving as the postponement of present consumption is 'waiting' for Cassel, a separate force of production. It makes it possible to devote factors of production, which otherwise would be used to produce consumer goods, to producing capital goods. Thus Cassel also emphasizes that views of capital, that it is the result of deferred consumption. But according to his theory, those who perform saving, receive interest not as a reward for the sacrifice made for saving, not as a premium on present goods as opposed to future goods, but simply because waiting is scarce. And if the rate of interest is too low, people will give up saving. "But a very low rate of interest," Cassel writes, "would have another and an additional effect, namely, that small capitalists would begin, very generally, to consume their capital."[170] In other words, since production takes place in time, the owner of capital has to wait even in the case of simple reproduction until the product is available. If he did not get interest, or the rate were too low, he would not use his capital, as soon as it was available to him again in money form, to replace the means of production used up. Existing capital is kept at a scarcity level in relation to demand by the fact that the capitalists may consume part of their capital if they consider its yield to be very low. Thus, even the maintenance of simple reproduction presuppose the existence of a certain positive rate of interest.

A positive rate of interest is thus not incompatible with the existence of a stationary economy. At a certain low rate of interest there will always be people, according to Cassel who save part of their incomes, while others may consume their capital, and positive and negative saving may equalize in such a way that at a certain positive rate of interest society does not save anything.

Cassel is fully aware of the fact that the consumption of existing capital is possible only for individual capitalists but not for the capitalist class as a whole.

However, this foundation of the existence of a positive rate of interest in a stationary economy, whether it is used in Marshall's or Böhm-Bawerk's theory of interest, assumes that the savers, who for the most part are members of the capitalist classes, compare the rate of interest with deferred consumption, that is, they decide as consumers whether to keep their production at an unchanged level or to cut it. The only realistic element in Cassel's statement on the capitalist's alleged consumer behaviour is that it is impossible even in a stationary economy to carry on production in a capitalist way if there is no surplus value.

In Marxian surplus value theory the question whether a return on capital exists in a stationary economy cannot arise at all. Yet Marx, in the third volume of his *Capital* refers to the case of absolute overproduction of capital when capital stock $C + \Delta C$ produces the same or less profit than capital stock C. But equilibrium does not come about in such an idyllic way by the capitalist using part of the surplus capital for personal consumption, since Marx himself, in connection with capital, does not emphasize the role of waiting, but rather considers it as self-realizing value, and the capitalist as its personification. According to this view, equilibrium

---

[169] J. Schumpeter: *Theorie der wirtschaftlichen Entwicklung*, Leipzig, 1911, p. 326.

is created in a cut-throat struggle for profit, in which some capital would lie idle and indeed would, to a greater or lesser extent, be destroyed. It would be destroyed in its material form, but the greatest, the gravest damage would be done to capital value. The price of commodities on the market would suffer an unheard-of slump, the process of reproduction would discontinue, and disruption would arise. Some of the capitalists would not even be able to realize the costs of production, which would, for that very reason, make the utilization of capital for the purposes of personal consumption impossible for them.

As far as such a justification in the Marshallian model of interest on existing capital is concerned, we must agree with Mrs. Robinson when she writes that "yet to treat owning a stock of capital already in being as a 'sacrifice', to be added to the 'efforts' of the workers is not really very telling."[171] The question concerned is as "hazy ... as has been ever since."[172]

Lerner attempted to find a solution to the other aspect of the problem, namely, that a positive rate of interest induces investment in a stationary economy, and therefore with a positive rate of interest no stationary equilibrium is possible. He made a distinction between the marginal productivity of capital and the marginal efficiency of investment. "If the marginal productivity of capital equals the rate of interest, net investment will be zero..."[173] Investment is stimulated if the rate of interest is smaller than the marginal productivity of capital. "Only in a stationary society does this difference disappear..."[174] In a stationary state "the marginal productivity of capital is therefore measured by, and can be defined as, the *marginal efficiency of investment when the rate of net investment is zero*."[175]

3. In determining the return to capital by means of economic imputation, the question of the measurement of capital has been a serious problem up to this day. Unlike labour and land, the various concrete capital goods have no common natural unit of measure. But the theory of the optimum allocation of resources requires a common yardstick for them, as the available capital goods are optimally allocated between their various uses if so much of each is applied that the significance of the last unit is identical in all uses.

They can be reduced to a common denominator by means of price. But this again will give rise to serious difficulties. The logic of marginal productivity theory requires that, in explaining distribution relations, capital as a factor of production should be represented as a magnitude independent of distribution relations. "And once this valuation problem is faced, the foundations of the neo-classical parable in which the magnitude of 'capital' as a 'factor of production' is independent of the distributions of income become logically insecure."[176] "... it is impossible to conceive of a quantity of capital in general, the value of which is independent of the rates of interest ... and wages."[177] Bhaduri stresses

---

170 G. Cassel: *op. cit.*, p. 148.
171 J. Robinson: *op. cit.*, p. 61.
172 *Ibid.*
173 A. P. Lerner: *op. cit.*, p. 335.
174 *Ibid.*
175 *Ibid.*
176 A. Bhaduri: On the Significance of Recent Controversies on Capital Theory: a Marxian View, *The Economic Journal*, September 1969, p. 532.
177 G. C. Harcourt: Some Cambridge Controversies in the Theory of Capital, *Journal of Economic Literature*, June 1969, p. 371.

that what is involved here is not simply an index problem relating to measurement: "... under the obvious surface of an index-number problem deeper issues lie in connection with the valuation of 'capital'."[178] Using Marxian terminology, the capitalist, while making his business calculations, operates with capital goods valued at their current price. Their market price fluctuates around their price of production, which in turn is influenced by changes in incomes. In determining return to capital, marginal productivity theory is compelled to work with capital values, whose size is affected by income changes and thus by changes in the return to capital, too. This question will be dealt with in detail in a separate chapter.

4. A further problem is the determination of the existence of profit in marginal productivity theory. This is due to the fact that a large number of non-Marxian economists since Say have not been able to get rid of the illusion that interest and entrepreneurial gain—the latter is called profit in non-Marxian economics—derive from different sources. Even the authors of a well-known English textbook reproach the early classical economists because "they did not distinguish profits from interest."[179]

The representatives of marginal productivity theory usually trace back the result of the contribution of capital to interest only. And profit would mean to them entrepreneurial gain in a Marxian sense. In the case of a competition free of monopolistic elements, if the production function is first-degree homogeneous, marginal productivity theory attributes the full value of the net product to the contribution of the factors of production.

Competition does not permit any income without compensation. But what service is rendered by the entrepreneur, and in return for what service does he get his profit?

In order to obtain surplus value, the capitalist entrepreneur manages, organizes production and contributes thereby to the production of goods. But most followers of marginal productivity theory do not regard the function of direction and organization, that is, managerial activity, as a real entrepreneurial function. The entrepreneur can delegate the task of management and organization to salaried employees and thus "...the return to management as such is generally regarded as essentially a wage ... rather than an element in profits..."[180]

It poses a problem for modern non-Marxian economics to specify who performs the entrepreneurial function in the joint-stock company of the 20th century, and what activity can still be regarded as a function of the entrepreneur that cannot be delegated.

On the profit issue there is still great confusion in modern non-Marxian economics even today. Those economists who accept marginal productivity theory as an income-distribution theory do not take a uniform position on the question of profit. In his *Economics* Samuelson mentions that a student of his counted up 14 different profit theories.[181] It is the scientific basis of value theory that is needed in order to fit profit as unearned income into price theory as an organic part.

178 A. Bhaduri: *op. cit.*, p. 533.
179 A. W. Stonier and O. C. Hague: *A Textbook of Economic Theory*, London, 1965, p. 318.
180 B. F. Haley: Value and Distribution. In: *A Survey of Contemporary Economics*, Philadelphia–Toronto, 1949, p. 46.
181 P. A. Samuelson: *Economics*, New York–London, 1955, p. 583.

But the existence of profit is a fact that must be explained. It is obvious, writes Samuelson, that "...in the real world net revenue is not zero for all firms, nor is it tending towards zero. This is true under pure competition as well as impure competition."[182]

J.B. Clark, one of the first representatives of marginal productivity theory, tries to explain the origin of profit as distinct from interest on the basis of marginal productivity theory. He points out that it is only under static conditions that no profit accrues to the entrepreneur. As if he were a forerunner of Schumpeter, Clark emphasizes that the emergence of profit can well be explained in a dynamic economy. A new invention will increase the marginal productivity of factors. And factor income should also increase. But the rise in wages will "...always remain by a certain interval"[183] behind the increase in the marginal productivity of labour, and thus a dynamic process will give a temporary rise in profit. This shows that profit may appear to be the unearned product of labour even if looked upon from the angle of marginal productivity theory. But in this representation profit is only a temporary phenomenon. If the operation of competition were undisturbed, no profit could arise even in a dynamic economy.

An explanation of the origin of profit, having wide currency in today's non-Marxian economics, was provided by Knight's profit theory. In his view, profit would disappear from price only if the entrepreneurs could foresee the future and could thus predict at what price they can realize their products at the time they are put on to the market. "...under such conditions," he writes, "distribution or the imputation of product values to production services will always be perfect and exhaustive and profit absent."[184] In a real economy, however, there is no such thing as perfect foresight. Knight distinguishes risk from uncertainty. In the case of risk we have certain quantitative information about the probability of the outcome of an enterprise, and risks can be covered by insurance. But future uncertainties cannot be predicted. No seller can know in advance how much of a given product his rivals will offer for sale, nor can he be sure of the desires and incomes of his prospective buyers.

The condition for the emergence of profit is, according to Knight, the uncertainty of the future. Production is based on expectations regarding unpredictable future demand. It is on this basis that the entrepreneurs create demand in the present for factor services, and the remuneration of factors as stipulated in the contracts concluded with them does not take place according to their marginal products valued at current prices but according to expected prices depending on uncertain future demand. If the entrepreneurs get higher than expected receipts, it will exceed their costs and they realize a profit; if lower, they will sustain a loss. Profit comes about, therefore, because of erroneous calculations owing to the uncertainty of the future, as a residual above the cost of production, a difference between *ex-ante* or *ex-post,* that is, expected and realized receipts, which entrepreneurs' competition, owing to the uncertainty of the future, cannot eliminate. According to Knight, the size of profit is in an inverse proportion to the optimistic and pessimistic nature of expectations. He holds that the uncertainty of the future

[182] P. A. Samuelson: *Foundations of Economic Analysis,* Cambridge, 1948, p. 87.
[183] J. B. Clark: *op. cit.,* p. 406.
[184] F. H. Knight: *Risk, Uncertainty and Profit,* New York, 1964, p. 198.

would yield a positive profit for all capitalist entrepreneurs if their expectations turned out to be generally pessimistic. In this case, they would expect lower revenue, and thus they would establish factor payments lower than the realized value of their marginal product. In the case of a general optimism, however, profit may become negative, that is, the entrepreneurs may sustain losses.

According to a widespread view in non-Marxian economics, *normal profit* is the supply price of entrepreneurship, that is, the price that is needed to induce people to undertake the uncertainty inherent in any enterprise. The realization of normal profit is rendered possible by the fact that there are few who are ready to bear this uncertainty.

The uncertainty mentioned by Knight is largely connected with the anarchy stemming from production for profit. Knight, however, reverses the causal succession and wishes to explain the existence of profit from uncertainty derived from anarchy. Reality, however, contradicts this view. At a time of crisis, when their profit is extremely low, and some of them even sustain losses, capitalist entrepreneurs are usually pessimistic. At a time of prosperity, however, when profits are high, the entrepreneurs are optimistic.

In contrast to Knight, Samuelson emphasizes that profit in his interpretation cannot be a separate revenue since, owing to the uncertainty of the future, not only the entrepreneurs but the factor owners themselves get unexpected revenue or suffer losses. A worker, for example, who has the bad luck to learn a trade which, owing to technical development, becomes obsolete, will sustain a loss. In the contrary case, however, he will enjoy unexpected revenue.[185]

If we reduce profit to unpredictable uncertainty, then its magnitude cannot be determined either. But this renders any analysis completely unstable. As far as future is concerned, any reasonable assumption can be made, or, as Mrs. Robinson says, it "...enables economists to prove whatever they please."[186]

Those models which do not take uncertainty into account, usually identify profit with the marginal productivity of capital. This position is also adopted by Samuelson. If there is no uncertainty, the interest rate per annum and the percentage rate of profit are "the same thing", he writes in one of his studies.[187] But this means a return to the process criticized by non-Marxian economics, namely, that interest and profit stem from the same source.

5. Let us have a critical look at the statement of marginal productivity theory which maintains that the cause of unemployment is high real wages, and a fall in real wages ensures full employment.

According to the representatives of the theory, a fall in real wages is attained through a fall in money wages.

But lower money wages cause a fall in real wages only on the micro-level.

In general equilibrium theory, the function of marginal productivity is the demand function in respect of factors. And this in turn is derived from the demand function for consumer goods that can be produced by the factors in question. The demand function for consumer goods expresses, assuming a given money

[185] P. A. Samuelson: *Economics,* New York–London, 1955, pp. 586–587.

[186] J. Robinson: *An Essay on Marxian Economics,* 2nd. edition, London, 1966, p. 60.

[187] P. A. Samuelson: Parable and Realism in Capital Theory: the Surrogate Production Function, *The Review of Economic Studies,* June 1962, p. 195.

income of consumers, that the demand for a product changes as the price of that product changes. Now, according to the assumption of the theory, if wages fall, the production costs of consumer goods will also fall, and the supply function shifts downwards and intersects the demand curve at a point of higher output and lower price. In other words, entrepreneurs expand production and employ more workers. A rise in employment reflects, according to the logic of the theory, that real wages have decreased because, under the pressure of the unemployed, the fall in money wages was greater than the fall in the price of the product.

But this reasoning is valid only for the micro-level, i.e. it expresses a relationship that exists only on the firm or industry level. Only if the money wages of the workers of a firm or an industry diminish, can we assume that it has a negligible effect on the consumers' income level included in the demand function, with respect to the products of the firm or industry concerned. But it is completely inadmissible to regard consumer incomes representing data on the micro-level also as data on the macro-level. When there is general unemployment, the general fall in money wages in the demand function with respect to consumer goods cannot leave consumer money incomes unchanged. Their level is bound to decline. But this will cause the demand function to shift downwards, too. With different product prices the demand will be less than before. And the shifted demand and supply curves may intersect at the original scale of output, when neither the level of employment nor the level of real wages changed. But now the price level has fallen. A fall in nominal wages is not a suitable means to cause real wages to be cut as it affects the demand for consumer goods and through it their price level.

Let us assume that real wages will really decrease; does it stimulate employment and improve the surplus-creating possibilities of capital?

Assume that the upswing has come to an end, the new investments have reached maturity and the capacities of consumer goods production have grown. Their full utilization deteriorates the surplus-creating possibilities of capital. But they are also deteriorated if entrepreneurs, in order to maintain the profit margin added to costs, leave a significant part of the expanding capacities unused.

Since in the stage of reproduction under consideration new investments have contracted and the supply of consumer goods has grown, the national income produced will be embodied primarily in such products which are less suitable on a social plane for incorporating surplus value. With declining real wages, a considerable part of the consumer goods produced becomes unsaleable. Though the greater part of the new value remains with the capitalist class, it cannot realize most of it. If, however, the price level is free to fall and thus real wages rise, the capitalists can get rid of their surplus inventories and, as a result, the volume of the surplus value held by them will also diminish.

The realized volume of surplus value would increase only if the capitalist class raised its spendings, primarily its investment outlays. Absolutely false is the view of the representatives of marginal productivity theory, widely held even in our days, that unemployment is caused by a rise in real wages. In fact, the case is not that employment has decreased because real wages have increased but that the real wages of those workers who were lucky enough not to lose their jobs have increased because the weight of department I in total social output has decreased relative to that of department II, and therefore the workers of department II have had to share the supply of consumer goods with fewer department I workers.

And all that has ensued because the surplus-creating possibilities of capital have deteriorated, new investment and employment have fallen, reproduction has contracted because a general crisis of overproduction has set in.

In the case of an upswing, the situation is just the reverse: the output of department I forges ahead relative to that of department II, profit prospects improve, employment and the volume of output increase and, owing to the increased consumer demand of the workers of department I, too many have a claim on the products of department II. If we disregard technical progress, the real wages of the workers employed will decrease. It is not a fall in real wages that has given rise to increased employment, but it is a shift in proportion between the two departments in favour of department I that has induced a decline in real wages.

6. It was from the side of the law of returns that Neisser criticized in 1932 the assumption of marginal productivity theory that wage cuts put an end to unemployment. "The question is still open", he writes, "to what extent this inclusion of the labour force can take place at a given stock of capital... this question depends in the first place on the non-economic, primarily technically determined form of the return function, which at any moment can only be ascertained empirically; consequently, it must be regarded as basically accidental that by such an absorption of the labour force existing unemployment can fully be eliminated."[188] Neisser emphasizes that with the increase of employment and at a given stock of capital, the fall of the marginal productivity of labour to zero already at a time before full employment is realized, "...belongs to the sphere of possibilities, in which case the employment of labour would be impossible at the existing level of productive equipment."[189]

7. As a further criticism of marginal productivity theory as income-distribution theory, we must discuss a difficulty arising from technical progress and affecting the determination of the relative shares of classes in national income. The representatives of marginal productivity theory ignored for a long time the fact of technical progress. It was Hicks[190], who first attempted, in 1932, to provide an explanation within the framework of marginal productivity theory as to how technical progress influences the relative shares of classes in national income. From the point of view of income distribution it would be important to size up the effect of technical progress, since what is characteristic of capitalist economy is not stagnation at a given level of technical knowledge but rather further development in the field of technology. Marx also emphasizes that "The intermediate pauses are shortened in which accumulation works as simple extension of production, on a given technical basis."[191] "Similarly, Kaldor also writes that accumulation does not take the form of 'deepening' the structure of capital (at a given state of knowledge), but rather in keeping pace with technical progress..." We shall discuss Hicks's classification of technical[192] progress in connection with neoclassical growth theories. If technical progress, assuming a given capital–labour

[188] H. Neisser: Lohnhöhe und Beschäftigunsgrad im Marktgleichgewicht, *Weltwirtschaftliches Archiv*, 1932, Vol. 36, p. 441.
[189] H. Neisser: *op. cit.*, p. 442.
[190] J. R. Hicks: *The Theory of Wages*, London, 1932.
[191] K. Marx: *Capital*, Vol. I, Moscow, 1954, p. 629.
[192] N. Kaldor: *Essays on Value and Distribution*, London, 1960, p. 223.

ratio, increase the marginal productivity of capital more than that of labour, then this fact will induce the adoption of more capital-using production techniques at established factor prices. The share of the capitalist class in national income will increase. But owing to the introduction of capital-using, that is, labour-saving production techniques, wages will fall, which in turn will induce the substitution of labour for capital. Hicks points out that if the labour force employed increases in a higher proportion relative to capital than the proportion in which wages have declined relative to interest, the share of the working class in national income will rise, but if the ratio of these two percentage changes, which Hicks calls the *elasiticity of substitution*, is less than 1, the share of the working class, owing to declining wages, will decrease. Substitution effect and the effect of technical progress on the relative shares of classes may offset one another, or one may spoil the effect of the other. The separation of the two effects comes up, as we shall see, against serious difficulties. However, owing to their close interrelationship, the actual development of distribution relations can be explained in a variety of ways on the basis of marginal productivity theory, that is, the theory may size up the expected effect of technical change on the relative shares of social classes differently. Marginal productivity theory is only able to enumerate the possibilities without being capable of scientific foresight.

Hicks further points out that by changing the relative prices of factor services, technical progress diminishes the production cost of those commodities which make a greater use of the relatively cheapening productive services. If the demand for them is more elastic than the demand for products making a more intensive use of the productive services with relatively increasing prices, then this fact will raise the share of the former factor in national income. Owing to the uncertain magnitude of the elasticity of demand, marginal productivity theory is again unable to give a definite answer to the question of how the relative shares of classes will develop in the course of technical progress. We shall more thoroughly discuss this question, including technical progress, within the context of neo-classical growth theories.

It was the indeterminacy of the relative shares of social classes within marginal productivity theory, as a result partly of the micro-economic approach, partly of the inclusion of the effect of technical progress, that, among other things, induced Kaldor to provide an explanation entirely different from marginal productivity theory, for the relative shares of social classes in national income.

Chapter 10

BÖHM-BAWERK'S AND SAMUELSON'S ATTEMPTS TO FIND A MEASURE OF THE VOLUME OF CAPITAL GOODS

BÖHM-BAWERK'S AVERAGE PRODUCTION PERIOD

Böhm-Bawerk's capital theory must be mentioned as a lasting achievement of the Austrian School still gaining wide acceptance in modern non-Marxian economics. It was adopted, among others, by the founder of the Stockholm School, the eminent Swedish economist, Knut Wicksell. Non-Marxian economics simply refers to it as the *Austrian capital theory*. According to Wicksell, it was the problems relating to the measurability of capital that induced Böhm-Bawerk to create his capital theory. Capital goods, unlike labour and land, have no common natural unit of measure. "If capital were also to be measured in technical units... productive capital would have to be distributed into as many categories as there are kinds of tools, machinery and materials, etc., and a unified treatment of the role of capital in production would be impossible..."[193] It would be impossible to "calculate the rate of interest, which in equilibrium is the same on all capital."[194] But instrumental in the creation of Böhm-Bawerk's capital theory might also have been the fact that its author, as has already been mentioned, tried, in the interest of economic imputation, i.e. the derivation of the value of the factors of production and production cost from the value of products, to trace back the production of commodities to the contribution of such factors as he supposed not to be subject to the assertion of the law of cost.

Böhm-Bawerk denied that capital was an independent factor of production. In his view there are only two original factors of production, labour and land. "... land use and labour are the elemental economic forces of production."[195] All other products, capital goods or consumption goods, are themselves products of these two factors.

According to his theory, the original factors are used either directly for the production of consumption goods in so far as they are produced directly, without capital goods, merely by means of labour or the forces of nature, or they are first used for the production of so-called intermediate goods, that is, capital goods. Thus it is only in a roundabout way, through the production of intermediate goods, means of production, that we can get consumption goods, but this is the more efficient way of producing them. "By using the original factors... in a wisely chosen roundabout way, more and better products can be turned out than

---

[193] K. Wicksell: *Lectures on Political Economy*, Vol. I, 1934, pp. 149.
[194] *Ibid.*
[195] E. Böhm-Bawerk: *op. cit.*, p. 83.

if we used them directly, by production without capital."[196] It is this roundabout way of producing consumer goods, the so-called *roundabout method of production,* that gives, according to Böhm-Bawerk, a capitalistic character to production. Capitalist production exists since man began to use capital goods for production.

The more time is devoted to making capital goods prior to producing consumer goods, the more the production of consumer goods is preceded by intervals in which intermediate goods, capital goods, raw materials, machines are produced; that is, the more roundabout, the more efficient is production.

By the roundabout method of production Böhm-Bawerk touches upon a feature of technical progress: the development of the forces of production goes hand in hand with the development of the social division of labour. In the production process a product goes through several stages before it is completed, and for its production the co-operation of more and more productive branches or specialized plants is needed. Through a succession of vertical stages of production, the final product of one production stage will become constant capital in the subsequent stage, and thus, proceeding from stage to stage, one more layer of labour is imposed upon the product of the previous stage, and the larger the number of the successive production stages, the larger becomes the amount of embodied labour. Or, in Böhm-Bawerk's words: "The maturation of intermediate goods to consumer goods requires the continuous addition of the current forces of production. In each stage of the production process new labour is added to the intermediate product taken over from the previous stage to pass it on in a more advanced state to the subsequent stage... It is a natural consequence of this process that the amount of capital invested in any productive branch will grow with the progress of the production stages, or, in other words, with approaching to a stage nearer to maturation."[197]

According to Böhm-Bawerk, a production process is the more capital-intensive, the more roundabout it is; or, if the number of production stages and the amount of the original factors used up in two production methods are the same, then the more capital-intensive of the two methods is the one which uses up the greater part of the original factors in the initial stages.

Böhm-Bawerk tries to ascertain the capital intensity of the production methods available for the production of a good by avoiding the measurement of capital, using the so-called *average production period.* "That production method is the more capital-intensive which makes the utilization of the original factors of production yield fruit at a later time on the average."[198]

Böhm-Bawerk's average production period as exemplified by him can be shown as follows:

Suppose that the production of a consumer good requires 100 labour-days from the earliest production period farthest from maturation until the time the product is completed. (For simplicity's sake, Böhm-Bawerk leaves the other original factor, land, out of account.) Out of the 100 labour-days 10 labour-days are used as so-called "forward" labour (*Vorarbeit*) for the production of intermediate, i.e. capital goods, 10 years before starting the process of producing

[196] E. Böhm-Bawerk: *op. cit.,* p. 86.
[197] E. Böhm-Bawerk: *op. cit.,* p. 117.
[198] E. Böhm-Bawerk: *op. cit.,* p. 94.

consumer goods, at the rate of one labour-day per year. Thus, the means of production brought about by the input of "forward" labour applied in 10 production periods will be directly transformed into the consumer good by the input of 90 labour-days. The input of one labour-day applied in the earliest period produces, without using any means of production, the capital good which as an intermediate good will be further processed in the subsequent period by the input of one labour-day. The amount of labour applied in the earliest period is tied up for 10 periods, and it appears in the product of all subsequent periods until the means of production are completed, to be used directly for the production of the consumer good. In the following period the duration of tying up one labour-day is 9 periods, and so on.

Böhm-Bawerk weights the inputs of labour-days per year according to how far away their use is from the manufacture of the final product. He does not consider the period in which the final product is completed. Then, the sum of the inputs of labour-days multiplied by the number of years for which they were invested, divided by the number of all labour-days used, will yield the average production period. In our example it is $\dfrac{10+9+8+7+6+5+4+3+2+1}{100} = 0.55$, that is, the input of one labour-day is tied up on the average for about half a year.

The length of the average production period is the measure of the capital intensity of the production process. The magnitude of this average period will increase if a significant part of the 100 labour-days is devoted to "forward" labour, that is, to the production of intermediate goods. Let us change the application of the 100 labour-days, following Böhm Bawerk's example, in such a way that in order to arrive at the end product 20 days were applied in the 10th and 9th year each to producing capital goods, then 5 days per year were used in the remaining 8 years, and the direct production of the consumer good required 20 labour-days.

Now the average production period will be:

$$\frac{10\cdot20+9\cdot20+8\cdot5+7\cdot5+6\cdot5+5\cdot5+4\cdot5+3\cdot5+2\cdot5+5}{100} = 5.6,\text{ that is, more than}$$

5 and a half periods, which means that one labour-day is tied up on the average for more than five and a half years.

Let us now translate into the language of Marxian political economy what Böhm-Bawerk says to see whether it contains rational elements. The translation is made easier by the fact that Böhm-Bawerk assumed only one original factor, labour, and thus traced back capital goods and consumer articles as use-values to labour only. In this way, the amount of labour applied to the production of capital goods and consumption articles also expresses, in a Marxian sense, the value of products.

Setting out from the second example, the value of the product of the earliest, or, according to Böhm-Bawerk's numbering, the tenth period, is $v+s = 20$ labour-days. In the following period, this product value appears as a c element, and the 20 days' labour, with 20 labour-days' worth of constant capital, produces 40 labour-days' worth of product. In the 8th period, 40 labour-days' worth of constant capital is used for labour now reduced to 5 days, and 45 labour-days' worth of product is made which appears as constant capital in the 7th period, and so on. Until the production of the consumer good begins, the total value of the means of production finished in the course of "forward" labour is $20+40+45+50+55+60+65+70+75+80 = 560$ labour-days, that is, necessarily the same amount as Böhm-Bawerk's total of labour-days weighted according to the number of periods. Its ratio to the 100 labour-days used expresses the cumulative amount of "forward" labour applied for one labour-day, that is, the quantity of constant capital spent on the average of one day's labour, or transferred to the value of the product made by it. This is the same as the capital value per man if we employed a labour force of 100 men instead of 100 labour-days.

According to the two-sector (department) model expressing Marxian simple reproduction, we can represent Böhm-Bawerk's relationships in the following way. As "forward" labour, that is, labour used in the first sector, 80 days' labour input was applied, and 20 days' labour was used up in the second sector. The production of department I is the value of 560 labour-days, and the production in department II represents total new value, that is, 100 labour-days. Department II uses as means of production the means produced by the 5 labour-days last applied to making the means of production, whose total value is 80 labour-days. Thus:

$$\text{department I} \quad 480c+80(v+s) = 560$$
$$\text{department II} \quad 80c+20(v+s) = 100.$$

The greater the weight of department I in relation to department II, the more roundabout is production, the more capital is required to produce consumer goods. This is, translated into the language of Marxian political economy, the gist of Böhm-Bawerk's theory, the rational core of his capital theory.

Let us examine what Böhm-Bawerk's average production period expresses. It does express the average quantity of constant capital per unit of labour used up, it does not express the total amount of capital tied up per man, because fixed capital passes only part of its value on to the new product. And if the lengthening of the roundabout method of production does not result in an increase in the total amount of fixed capital, there will still be a rise in that amount of value which fixed capital passes onto the product only little by little, without the total quantity of capital being changed. It is no accident that Böhm-Bawerk, in the example illustrating his capital theory and designed to compute the average production period, takes capital into account only as circulating capital. Translating Böhm-Bawerk's model into the Marxian two-sector model presupposes at the outset that fixed capital is fully used up in producing the final product. And this Böhm-Bawerk really presupposes.

In one of his latest studies Hicks mentions that some capital theories, among them Clark's and Walras's, handle capital as fixed capital. Such an interpretation of capital becomes, in his view, useless as soon as they apply it to circulating capital. But Böhm-Bawerk's capital theory, claiming to solve the problem of measuring capital by means of the average production period, is in fact a theory of circulating capital, which simply intends to reduce fixed capital to circulating capital. In Böhm-Bawerk it is first without any means of production that capital goods are produced, goods which go through the production cycle from period to period with new labour being imposed on them in each period until the final

106

product, the consumer good, is completed. In Ragnar Frisch's terminology, this is the *flow input – point output* case. Output is the result of a series of inputs. If we assume that in the production process fixed capital is also produced, which is fully used up in the process of completing the final product, we are still dealing with the flow input — point output case. It is only by such rigid, limiting assumption that Böhm-Bawerk can reduce final product to the stream of inputs used to compute the average period of production. As Hicks also emphasizes it, "Fixed capital, however, is the source of a whole stream of outputs — outputs at different points of time."[199] Applying Ragnar Frisch's terminology, this is the point of flow input – flow output case. Then, however, it is extremely problematic to reduce a given unit of the final product to a factor embodied in fixed capital, and to compute the average period of production, as already pointed out by J. B. Clark and Knight.

In his example Böhm-Bawerk wants to determine the amount of capital by the amount of labour applied in production, taking into account the number of production periods that the product of labour inputs as an intermediate product applied in the different production periods has gone through. But he makes no attempt to approach the labour theory of value, to determine capital value through the amount of labour. He only wishes to reduce capital as a stock of use-values to labour, and in fact regards labour and nature together as the source of capital goods. Since he cannot find a common measure for labour and the force of nature, he simply ignores the force of nature in computing the average period of production, and represents capital goods taken as use-values merely as the product of labour, instead of determining the value of capital goods by means of labour. This derivation stems from the negation of capital as an independent factor of production. The replacement of fixed capital used up also takes place in Böhm-Bawerk in such a way that the process of production of fixed capital through a succession of vertically superimposed periods is first started by labour alone. In real fact, however, as Stigler remarks "... we know of no society, however primitive, which does not possess capital goods."[200] Schneider is right in saying that Böhm-Bawerk sought an answer to the question of how the production process "functions *today* when it is fully developed... This question cannot be settled by means of a historico-genetical explanation, only by a thorough analysis of the role played by durable means of production in an advanced production technique. Such an investigation, however, leads to the basic fact that durable capital goods take part not only in the manufacture of consumer goods, but also in making means of production, and become, in this sense, independent factors of production."[201]

Even if the value of capital is completely the product of labour, capital goods as use-values cannot exclusively be reduced to labour. Even in the production period which was farthest from the production of consumer goods, it was not with bare hands that man proceeded to production. In this case, however, the question of the valuation of capital goods emerges already in the initial stage of

[199] J. R. Hicks: Die Österreichische Kapitaltheorie und ihre Wiedergeburt in der modernen Wirtschaftswissenschaft, *Zeitschrift für Nationalökonomie,* 1972, Vol. 32, Fasç. I, p. 93.
[200] G. Stigler: *Production and Distribution Theories,* New York, 1946, p. 198.
[201] E. Schneider: *Einführung in die Wirtschaftstheorie,* Part IV, Vol. I, Tübingen, 1970, p. 61.

production. Thus this problem cannot be evaded simply by referring to the average period of production.

Wicksell, who otherwise adopts Böhm-Bawerk's capital theory, brings up another problem against Böhm–Bawerk's interpretation of capital. To understand Wicksell's objection, let us start from Böhm-Bawerk's first example. The amount of labour applied in each period of the production of capital goods is 1 labour-day. Let us assume, using Marxian terminology, that the degree of exploitation is 100 per cent, that is, the necessary labour time and surplus labour time are equally half a day in each period. Thus the amount of surplus value is identical in each period, but the value of capital goods rises from period to period. Thus the rate of profit varies between periods. But the capitalist must get the average profit on his capital in each period. Hence, the part products of the various periods must be taken account of at prices of production, and the average period of production must be computed on the basis of the part products so valued. As a recent development of non-Marxian economics, the economists of the Cambridge School pointed out that, owing to the changes in the average rate of profit or interest, those components from which the average period of production is computed have to be weighted differently. As a result, the length of the average period of production will change without the physical amount of capital goods used up in making the final product being changed. The problems relating to this question will be dealt with in detail in the next section. Böhm-Bawerk's capital theory takes only the quantity of capital used up into consideration, and cannot therefore provide a basis for the computation of the average rate of profit, since it is calculated on the basis of total capital stock tied up.

More recently, perhaps because of the problems connected with the re-switching of technique to be discussed in the following section, or owing to the construction of vintage models in growth theory, Böhm-Bawerk's capital theory has come again into prominence. Attention has shifted, as Hicks [202] or Weizsäcker[203] pointed out, from the horizontal structure of capital and production to time, that is, to the vertical structure of capital and production. And the merit of Böhm-Bawerk's capital theory is found to lie in the fact that it reveals the relationships in which production processes are vertically linked with one another.

SAMUELSON'S FACTOR-PRICE FRONTIER

Let us now look at an attempt[204] undertaken in modern non-Marxian economics by Samuelson to come to grips with the determination of the volume of capital.

As we know, the marginal productivity of capital expresses the relation between an infinitely small increment of a physical capital good and the increment of output arising from its employment. This relationship between capital and product determines, according to marginal productivity theory, the size of the market rate

[202] J. R. Hicks: A Neo-Austrian Growth Theory, *The Economic Journal,* June 1970.

[203] C. Ch. Weizsäcker: Die zeitliche Struktur des Produktionsprozesses und das Problem der Einkommensverteilung zwischen Kapital und Arbeit, *Weltwirtschaftliches Archiv,* 1971, Fasc. I.

[204] P. A. Samuelson: Parable and Realism in Capital Theory: the Surrogate Production Function, *The Review of Economic Studies,* June 1962.

of interest, or, in the view of those who identify the two, also of the rate of profit. But the form of capital varies with different production methods. The different capital goods as use-values have no natural measure. The marginal productivities of capital under the application of different production techniques can be compared in natural terms at best in the imaginary world of a *one-commodity economy,* where capital good and product are identical use-values. (For example, when by means of grain, as the only capital good, grain is produced by an infinite number of production methods.) To illustrate their ideas, some representatives of marginal productivity theory actually make use of the fiction of a one-commodity economy. They assume that in such an economy, with the physical capital stock per man rising at the given level of technical knowledge, the marginal productivity of capital expressed in natural terms will steadily decrease, and so will the equilibrium level of the market rate of interest, or of profit, too. Consequently, physical capital stock per man can be arranged according to the size of the rate of interest, or the rate of profit.

Passing over now from a fictitious one-commodity economy to the analysis of real economy, the question arises whether the different capital goods can be represented as abstracted from their actual forms, as some kind of homogeneous good playing the same role as capital goods in a one-commodity economy. If, for example, the different capital goods are reduced in price to a common denominator, will capital per head also increase in terms of price with the decrease of the rate of interest or the rate of profit? By constructing the concept of *surrogate capital,* Samuelson intends to demonstrate exactly this: he wants to replace heterogeneous capital goods by a homogeneous good of the same nature, wishing to prove that capital in the real world of economy, though assuming diverse physical forms, functions in the same way as the homogeneous good of a one-commodity economy: "... the Surrogate (Homogeneous) Capital ... gives the same result as does the shifting collection of diverse, physical capital goods in our more realistic model...[205]

In constructing the concept of surrogate capital he assumes that to produce a given amount and combination of consumer goods there are a number of production techniques available to society. Each technique uses a different capital good and requires a different capital–labour ratio. But for each technique of production the capital–labour ratio is rigid. And the various capital goods not only produce consumer goods but, under the same rigid technical conditions as in the case of producing consumer goods, are also able to reproduce themselves. The output quantities produced by the various techniques are shared by capital and labour. The particular share of each of the two factors can grow, at the given level of technical knowledge, only at the expense of the other. Samuelson constructs for each production technique a so-called *factor-price frontier,* which shows the rate of profit at different rates of wages. He assumes that the profit is fully accumulated, and thus determines the rate of profit for each production technique as a ratio of the net capital good produced to the capital stock consisting of the same capital goods and expresses it, by avoiding the value category, in terms of the same product as in a one-commodity economy. The worker, however, spends all his wages on buying consumer goods. Thus the ratio of new

[205] P. A. Samuelson: *op. cit.,* p. 201.

capital goods, produced and used for accumulation, to consumer goods will vary with changes in the relative shares of social classes. The technical coefficients being known, the factor-price frontier is expressed in Figure 10 by the line $N_\alpha M_\alpha$ for the production technique α. $0N_\alpha$ is the maximum wage which we obtain if the profit rate is 0, that is, if the worker gets the whole net output. Thus the distance $0N_\alpha$ shows the average productivity of labour, the ratio of net output to labour input. The distance $0M_\alpha$, however, represents the highest profit rate which would arise at a wage rate of 0, that is, if the whole net output produced accrued to capital as a revenue. Thus the average efficiency of capital is what we obtain if we divide net output by capital input.

Let the labour coefficient be 2 and the capital coefficient 4 for the production method α, so that the technical ratio between capital and labour is 2. Let the average life-time of capital be 10 years, and thus, by employing 4 units of capital, 40 per cent of the quantity of product will serve for replacement and be embodied in capital goods. If the whole amount of the net output, 60 per cent of the total output is fully paid out as wages, when it is embodied exclusively in consumer goods, then the wage per one unit of labour is half the net output, that is, 30 per cent of the total output. If, however, the total net output accrues as profit or interest to capital, when it is fully embodied in capital goods, the rate of profit is 60 per cent of the total output divided by 4 units of capital, that is, 15 per cent.

Now the corresponding values of the factor-price frontier for the production technique α are easy to compute.

Wages per one unit of labour as the percentage of total output	0	5	10	15	20	25	30
Rate of profit (%)	15	12.5	10.0	7.5	5.0	2.5	0
Total profits as % of total output	60	50	40	30	20	10	0

Let us now choose a production technique β in which the capital coefficient is 5, the labour coefficient 1, and thus the technical ratio between capital and labour is 5. Let the life-time of capital remain 10 years, and thus the net output is 50 per cent of the total output. In this case, we obtain the following corresponding value for the rates of wages and profit, and the amount of profit:

Wages per unit of labour as the percentage of total output	0	5	10	15	20	25	30	35	40	45	50
Rate of profit (%)	10	9	8	7	6	5	4	3	2	1	0
Total profits as % of total output	50	45	40	35	30	25	20	15	10	5	0

The income of the working class will rise, at increasing wages, by the same quantity as the income of the capitalist will decrease. Therefore:

$$Ldw = Kdr, \text{ and thus } \frac{dw}{dr} = \frac{K}{L},$$

where w is the wage rate, r the rate of profit, L the number of the labour force and K the stock of capital.

In this way, Samuelson determines capital per man for a given production technique as the quotient of dw and dr. In our example

for production technique α: $\dfrac{K}{L} = \dfrac{dw}{dr} = \dfrac{0.05}{0.025} = 2,$

for production technique β: $\dfrac{K}{L} = \dfrac{dw}{dr} = \dfrac{0.05}{0.01} = 5.$

Let us draw the graph of the joint factor-price frontier of the production techniques α and β:

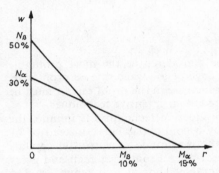

Figure 10

The above tables and the graph reveal that the capital-intensive production technique can only be applied in the case of a high wage rate and a low profit rate. At a wage rate higher than 10 per cent of total output, the production tehnique β is the more economical as it yields a larger amount of profit than technique α. At a wage rate lower than 10 per cent, however, the technique α is the more economical, yielding a larger amount of profit than β. At a wage rate of 10 per cent, both techniques are equally economical, the amount of profit being 40 per cent of the total output in either case.

Constructing the factor-price frontiers also for the production techniques γ, δ, etc., it will be clear that the point of intersection with the wage-rate axis will be found to lie further from the origin, the smaller the labour coefficient, and with the profit-rate axis, the further from the origin, the smaller the capital coefficient. As we can see from Figure 11, α is the most labour-intensive production method, and δ the most capital-intensive one.

Comparing now the factor-price frontiers corresponding to the four production techniques with the continuous decrease in wages, or with the continuous increase in the profit rate, we can see that equilibrium is possible only at the outermost sections, drawn with heavy lines in the graph, of the various factor-price frontiers.

The totality of these sections expresses the optimum factor-price frontiers.

111

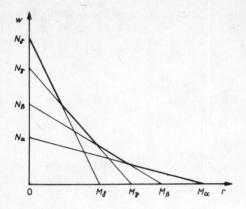

Figure 11

As the graph reveals, any method can be considered as the most profitable production technique only within a certain range of the wage rate or profit rate, and owing to the decrease in the wage rate or increase in the profit rate, it must be replaced, at a certain level, by more and more labour-intensive techniques.

Assuming that the number of available production techniques is infinite, the optimum factor-price frontier is expressed by a continuous curve instead of by sections of a line. How can we now find the magnitude of surrogate capital? "Merely by calculating the slope of the Factor-price Frontier at each and every point and multiplying it by the easily measurable labor at that point."[206] The different physical capital goods belonging to the various production techniques are thus taken account of by Samuelson through the slope of the curve expressing the optimum factor-price frontier, through $\frac{dw}{dr}$, as a homogeneous capital good, which is supposed to have the same properties as the capital good of a one-commodity economy: with diminishing profit rate and increasing wage rate, capital stock per man will increase.

Has Samuelson really succeeded in determining, by means of the quotient $\frac{dw}{dr}$, the movement of physical capital stock per man? Using Marxian terminology, the $\frac{dw}{dr}$ ratio for a given production technique would only express the quantity of capital per man if, on the one hand, the organic composition of capital were the same in the production of both consumer and capital goods, and thus value did not need to be transformed into the price of production. Samuelson assumes this to be the case by stipulating that both consumer goods and capital goods are produced with the same technical coefficients for each production technique.

[206] *Ibid.*

112

On the other hand, for the $\dfrac{dw}{dr}$ ratio to yield the amount of capital per man, the rate of profit must be computed, according to the logic of marginal productivity theory, only on the basis of constant capital advanced.

If, however, the organic composition of capital varies in producing consumer goods and capital goods with different production techniques, the profit rates must be integrated into an average profit rate, when it is no longer possible to ignore the value category, and capital per man must be taken into account at prices of production. Changing the wage rate continuously will, owing to the resulting change in the average profit rate, also change the production price of both consumer and capital goods, and to a different extent. Thus the physical stock of capital valued at production prices will yield different magnitudes.

Consequently, it is impossible to determine the magnitude of the physical stock of capital even within the same production technique arrived at by means of the $\dfrac{dw}{dr}$ ratio.

According to Samuelson, each production technique counts as a separate economic system, and if the organic composition of capital is different for each production technique in producing consumer and capital goods, an average profit rate will develop for each production technique and thus the latter will have its own separate price system.

Now let us include the different production techniques adopted to manufacturing the same product within an economic system. Let us assume that the capitals employed in the individual production techniques contribute to the formation of the average profit rate only to a negligible extent, and thus its magnitude may be regarded as an external datum for the various techniques.

If two techniques are thus compared with one another, we may ask whether, even with the inclusion of the price system, the basic assumption of marginal productivity theory, which Samuelson tries to verify by avoiding the price system, finds its justification or not. According to this assumption, at a low rate of profit or of interest only the more capital-intensive technique, and at a higher profit rate or interest rate only the more labour-intensive technique, will be taken into account, and thus the rate of profit or rate of interest expresses the physical marginal productivity of capital.

It was exactly the dependence of the price of production on changes in distribution relations that Sraffa made use of in criticizing marginal productivity theory.[207] For this reason, he revived Böhm-Bawerk's capital theory, according to which the product, whether a consumer good or a means of production, goes through several superimposed stages of production before it is finished. The production methods necessary to produce a given product vary according to the number of these stages, or to the distribution of labour inputs among the various production stages. From this it follows that the technical composition of capital in terms of value, that is, the organic composition of capital, will vary in the successive production stages, according to the production technique. In each stage of production, the product is sold to the subsequent stage for further processing at a price compris-

207 P. Sraffa: *Production of Commodities by Means of Commodities*, Cambridge, 1960.

ing cost plus average profit, and thus the amount of profit, moving from one stage on to the other, will increase on the analogy of compound interest.

Let us now change the level of the average profit rate as an external datum continuously for both production methods available to turn out the same product. At the individual stages of the vertical structure this will change the production prices of intermediate products differently. And the production price of the final product will be the resultant of these prices. Comparing the two techniques of production while changing the average profit rate, we shall find the product cheaper now in the first, and now in the second production technique. Indeed, at a given level of the profit or interest rate, both techniques may be equally cheap even though in terms of the value of their capital-labour ratio they differ. Sraffa calls the values of the rate of profit at which the products of both techniques are equally economical, *switch points*.

Similarly, by continuously changing the profit or interest rate, first the one, then again the other technique becomes more 'capital-intensive', or the amount of capital per man will come to be the same in terms of prices of production for both techniques without the amount of physical capital goods per man employed by them being changed.

Under given distribution relations, the production techniques may be arranged according to the order of magnitude in terms of prices of production of the capital per man employed by them. But this arrangement absolutely need not correspond uniquely to the order in which the production techniques, with changes in the profit or interest rate, will be optimal. At a certain profit or interest rate a production technique employing a smaller amount of capital per man in terms of price of production and one employing a larger capital per man in terms of price of production may be equally optimal. And, by changing the profit rate, we may again and again rearrange the production techniques according to the amount of capital per man valued at price of production. It is possible that with a fall in the profit rate not the capital-intensive but, in contrast to the logic of the marginal productivity theory, the less capital-intensive production technique becomes more profitable.

Sraffa used, by the way, the effect of distribution relations on the price of production, to which he may have been alerted by the controversy between Ricardo and Malthus, not only for criticizing marginal productivity theory, but also for criticizing Böhm-Bawerk's average production period concept, emphasizing that the length of the latter is also influenced by changes in distribution relations.

It was in 1966 that in the *Quarterly Journal of Economics* the controversy between the followers of marginal productivity theory and its critics, primarily the Cambridge economists, flared up. In the debate even such an eminent representative of marginal productivity theory as Samuelson was compelled to accept the arguments of the opposing party. Moreover, it was Samuelson himself who illustrated by an example the effect of changes in the profit rate on the price of production of the final product, and revealed thereby the above-mentioned problems of marginal productivity theory.

114

In this example[208] Samuelson assumes that champagne is produced by two different production techniques. In the first period of both techniques of production work is begun without any capital goods, merely by using labour. In the first period of technique I two workers prepare grape juice which, in the second period, in the process of fermentation, becomes wine without any labour input. Wine in the third period is transformed into champagne by 6 workers. Using technique II, in the first period of production seven workers are employed, who prepare one unit of brandy. In the following period brandy ferments to be champagne by itself, without any labour input.

Samuelson takes the wage rate, independently of changes in the profit rate, to be a constant, unity. Then he begins to increase the profit rate and examines how the product price develops depending on the production techniques used. At less than 50 per cent rate of profit technique II is more economical than I. If the profit rate is 50 per cent, both techniques are equally economical, the 50 per cent rate of profit being the switch point. Adopting technique I, 2 units of wages $+1$ unit of profit equal 3 units' worth of grape juice. On fermentation, the 3 units' worth of grape juice plus profit will yield $3+1.5 = 4.5$ units' worth of wine. The 4.5 units' worth of wine as circulating capital will be processed by 6 workers, and thus the value of champagne will be 4.5 units of circulating capital $+6$ units of wages $+5.25$ units of profit $= 15.75$ units of price. Using technique II, the value of brandy is 7 units of wages $+3.5$ units of profit $= 10.5$ units of price, and on fermentation, the value of the champagne is 10.5 units' worth of brandy as circulating capital $+5.25$ units of profit $= 15.75$ units of price. Technique II is more capital-intensive than technique I. At a profit rate lower than 50 per cent, technique II is cheaper and more capital-intensive than technique I. Between 50 and 100 per cent, technique I will be cheaper and, at the same time, less capital-intensive. At 100 per cent profit rate both techniques are again equally economical, but technique II is more capital-intensive than technique I. At 150 per cent profit rate, technique II is again more economical and more capital-intensive. At 200 per cent profit rate, capital per man is equal for both techniques, and II is the more economical. At a profit rate higher than 200 per cent, technique I is the more capital-intensive and II is the more economical.

Has Sraffa anything to say for Marxian political economy? Yes, he has. If we express the organic composition of capital not in terms of value, but in terms of price of production, then it changes together with distribution. With changing distribution relations the different industries will always develop a different ranking of compositions. An industry which under a certain structure of distribution had a composition below the average in terms of price of production, may—given a different structure of distribution—have a higher than average composition. Taking into account the vertical structure of capital, the effect of a change in distribution relations will make itself felt in a more cumulative way, the nearer we are to the stage of production of the final product. It will thus turn out that a change in distribution relations would leave the price of production of a commodity produced in an industry with average organic composition unchanged only if all elements of the capital employed in it were also produced in industries with an average organic composition. In the contrary case, with a change in distribution, there will be a change in the price of production of capital goods used in the industry with a hitherto average organic composition in terms of prices of production, and therefore in the price of production of the product, too. Moreover, the industry concerned, as has already been mentioned, may even cease to be of an average organic composition in terms of price of production.

[208] P. A. Samuelson: A Summing up, *The Quarterly Journal of Economics*, November 1966, p. 579.

Part Two

FURTHER DEVELOPMENT OF THE EQUILIBRIUM THEORY OF PRICE FORMATION

Chapter 1

THE TRANSFORMATION OF SUBJECTIVE VALUE THEORY INTO THE LOGIC OF RATIONAL CHOICE

The subjective economic tendencies evolved in the 1870s tried to explain economic interrelationships by setting out from consumer behaviour, represented as a function of the process of satisfying wants. Some representatives of the Austrian School, making more extensive use of the psychological method, believed that their basic propositions could be established in an empirical way from consumer self-interest, confirmed by subjective experience. The principal idea of their theoretical system was the assumption that wants exceed the available means, which necessitates an economic use of them. They must be used in such a way that, allowing for diminishing marginal utility as a given want is increasingly met, the individual may derive maximum satisfaction from them.

The aims of the economic subjects, however, are obviously not independent of production relations, and do not stem merely from the psychic characteristics of the consumer. The drive for profit cannot be derived from consumer behaviour. The capitalist does not strive to attain the greatest possible profit because he wants to maximize his consumption.

The extension of marginal analysis from the domain of satisfying needs to the sphere of production has made it clear, however, that investigations into the optimal utilization of the scarce factors of production have led to similar relationships in production as did research into the conditions of the optimal satisfaction of needs. Thus, for example, the principle of equal advantage at the margin of exchange also applies to production. This similarity is expressed by Phelps Brown when he writes: "... the outlay of the entrepreneur can be submitted to a rule exactly symmetrical with that which governs the outlay of consumers..."[1]

The realization slowly begins to gain ground that the relationships revealed by marginal analysis based on the optimizing behaviour of consumers or entrepreneurs are not specific relationships of the satisfaction of wants or of production, but the general rules of a rational use of scarce resources. Compared with the methods applied by the representatives of early subjective economics, the behaviour of the economic subject is now being examined on a broader basis. Goods are no longer regarded as scarce merely from the point of view of the satisfaction of needs. The economic subject has specific objectives of his own. His aim may be the maximum satisfaction of needs, the maximization of his profit or anything else. But to achieve his aims he has resources at his disposal to a limited extent only, but with alternative uses at the same time. The consumer can spend his scarce income on

---

[1] E. H. Phelps Brown: *The Framework of the Pricing System*, Oxford, 1936, p. 116.

buying various combinations of commodities, the entrepreneur can produce a given quantity of products by different combinations of capital and labour and also various product combinations by the quantity of capital and labour available to him. Now economics is found to have its principal task in revealing how rationally acting individuals should allocate their scarce resources among alternative uses so as to achieve their objective to the maximum extent, or to ensure the attainment of this objective at the minimum cost inputs. It is in this sense that in his famous methodological book Professor Robbins formulates the subject-matter of economics: "Economics is the science which studies human behaviour as a relationship between ends and scarce means which have alternative uses."[2]

Thus, any economic action is a choice between alternatives, different combinations of goods and factors. Or, in Robbins's words: "... when time and the means for achieving ends are limited *and* capable of alternative application, *and* the ends are capable of being distinguished in order of importance, then behaviour necessarily assumes the form of choice."[3] Accordingly, any valuation is a comparison of alternative possibilities with respect to the realization of aims.

Robbins, Mises and others emphasize that the rules of rational action thus revealed apply not only to the economy, but to any field of human activity where it is necessary to use scarce resources optimally in order to achieve a definite objective. "The conception we have adopted," writes Robbins, "may be described as *analytical*. It does not attempt to pick out certain *kinds* of behaviour, but focuses attention on a particular *aspect* of behaviour, the form imposed by the influence of scarcity."[4] And then he continues: "We do not say that the production of potatoes is economic activity and the production of philosophy is not. We say rather that, in so far as either kind of activity involves the relinquishment of other desired alternatives, it has its economic aspect."[5] Therefore, they wish to extend economics to the general discipline of human activity. "... it is from political economy that the general science of human activity, praxeology is born."[6] Such endeavours point to the direction of a complete formalization of political economy. The social content becomes lost to an even greater extent than in the economic theory based on consumer behaviour.

Following the merging of subjective value theory into the logic of rational choice, a change has also taken place in the attitude of some economists towards economic laws. In the relationships revealed by the ends–means approach, they become aware of the general rules of rational economic action, and some tend to perceive only logical necessities in the conclusions arrived at from the premises set up by them. These logical necessities, according to the extreme view of certain economists, do not even need to be verified by confrontation with reality. Pantaleoni insists that "theory need not conform to reality, provided it is logical."[7] According

[2] L. Robbins: *An Essay on the Nature and Significance of Economic Science*, London, 1935, (2nd edition), p. 16.

[3] L. Robbins: *op. cit.*, p. 14.

[4] *Ibid.*

[5] L. Robbins: *op. cit.*, p. 17.

[6] L. von Mises: *Nationalökonomie, Theorie des Handels und Wirtschaftens*, Genf, 1940, p. 3.

[7] Quoted by E. James: *Histoire de la pensée économique en `X^e` siècle*, Paris, 1955, Vol. II, p. 363.

to J. Marchal, the science of rational economic action consists in "setting up a theory which has only logical sources."[8] Mises writes in a similar fashion: "The general science of human activity ... is a-priori knowledge and not an empirical science."[9]

Kaldor, on the other hand, criticizes these premises and emphasizes that in scientific theory "the basic assumptions are chosen on the basis of direct observation of the phenomena the behaviour of which forms the subject-matter of the theory..."[10] In his view, the basic assumptions of modern, non-Marxian economics, however, are either of a kind that are unverifiable, such as when the producers strive to maximize their profits and the consumers their utility, or of a kind which are directly contradicted by observation, for example, linear-homogeneous and continuously differentiable production functions, perfect divisibility, etc.

Let us add to Kaldor's propositions that even if the premises of the theoretical system resting on the ends–means relationship were verifiable, their basic deficiency remains, namely, that it is man's relation to things that are manifest in them, and thus the scope of the conclusions drawn from them is limited, referring at best to the field of private economy, and within it primarily to the behaviour of the entrepreneur. It provides the answer in the first place to the question only of the conditions for the entrepreneur to achieve maximum profit with minimum cost within his own economy. But they tend to extend the relationships revealed in examining the behaviour of the individual even to the social plane. They imagine that if every individual acts rationally in his own economy, then, assuming undisturbed competition, the optimum utilization of the available scarce resources will also materialize on a social level. Thus, the organization realized within the capitalist firm is extended to the capitalist economy as a whole, that is, the same takes place on the social plane as in the individual's economy. On such assumptions, they think, it is possible to discover the laws of capitalist economy by exploring the rational behaviour of the economic units, households and firms. This micro-approach in price theory reflects the narrow view of modern non-Marxian economics in not going beyond the surface, the sphere of the market: they only see the competition of individuals where social laws of price formation, demand and supply assert themselves through competition.

The ends–means approach is subject to the same deficiency as the method applied by the earlier representatives of subjective tendencies in economics to reveal economic interrelationships. It is impossible to derive the laws of capitalist production relations from conclusions drawn from premises expressing man's relation to things. The nature of the social and the production relations of the individual striving to achieve optimum results is also lost in the ends–means approach. By representing labour, more exactly labour power, merely as a scarce good, in much the same way as capital goods—on the grounds that the owners of both of them equally aim at achieving optimum results—,the adherents of that theory conceal the economic subject's actual class position which, serving as a framework for his behaviour, also determines it. They see in the individual's social relations

8 J. Marchal: *Cours d'économie politique*, Paris, 1949, p. 223.

9 L. von Mises: *op. cit.*, p. 39.

10 N. Kaldor: The Irrelevance of Equilibrium Economics, *The Economic Journal*, December 1972, p. 1238.

only market relations such as exist between sellers and buyers. Further, this approach conceals the fact that the scope and manner of the rational use of scarce resources are determined by the existing production relations, that the optimum use of scarce resources on a social scale cannot really take place unless the means of production are in social ownership, since capitalist private property and the irreconcilable conflicts between the working and capitalist classes counteract this process. It further disguises what Marx brilliantly demonstrated in the third volume of *Capital,* that the principles of a rational economy are distorted in the practice of the capitalist firm. The identification of individual and social rationality, the explanation of socio-economic relationships by the behaviour of the rational economic subject, was to be severely criticized by Keynes under the impact of the great economic crisis, at a time when even non-Marxian economists lost their confidence in the efficiency of the mechanisms of capitalist economy.

Non-Marxian value and price theory can account for the effects of social relations on the rational use of scarce resources in production and consumption only super-ficially, identifying them with the effect of market forms, in just the same way as it represents the interrelationships of economic subjects merely as exchange relations. It takes into consideration the social conditions of individual action at best as various market forms, without going beyond the limitations of a narrow micro-economic view.

Marxian political economy does not underestimate the science of rational action, *praxeology*. The various programming methods can be applied success-fully even under the conditions of socialism, and indeed, it is primarily under socialism that they can be adopted on a social level. But it does not identify political economy with praxeology. It assigns to praxeology an appropriate place in eco-nomics, regarding it as an auxiliary discipline of political economy. It may have an important role to play as a deductive method of exploring an economy in which actions are really rational. But in drawing conclusions in a deductive way, it is only the accepted and established rules of rational action that should be applied, also taking into account the scope within which the conclusions derived from the prem-ises have validity. If the research covers capitalist economy, then the premises must reflect the features characteristic of capitalist production relations. And by confronting these conclusions with reality, the validity of the premises should also be verified.

Theoretical conclusions, however, can never fully conform to reality as they are merely its abstract reflections expressing only its essential features, while actual economic processes also contain a large number of accidental elements. From this, however, it would be inappropriate to conclude that the statements of a theory do not require the test of practical applicability, that the only precondition of their validity is their logical structure. It is possible to draw logical conclusions from false premises, to build up a system whose elements logically fit together, which however does not reflect reality, or if it does, reflects it only superficially

Chapter 2

ATTEMPTS AT CONSTRUCTING THE DEMAND CURVE BY THE INDIFFERENCE-CURVE APPROACH

THE CONTRIBUTIONS OF EDGEWORTH, FISHER AND PARETO

One of the sets of technical tools used in revealing the rules of rational action, first applied to the exploration of consumer behaviour, is indifference-curve analysis. It evolved in the wake of the critique of marginal utility theory and of the endeavours to eliminate its deficiencies. Its foundations were laid by Edgeworth and later by Pareto and Irving Fisher. Utility is immeasurable, said the critics of that theory, and so consequently is the consumer's objective, too. And it was this objective, the conditions of the maximum satisfaction of which the adherents of marginal utility theory set out to determine.

The criticism further pointed out that marginal utility theory represented the utility of one unit of a given commodity as a function of its own quantity, thus building the demand function on the principle of diminishing utility. According to this theory, the utility functions of the various goods can be aggregated; the total utility of the stock of goods consisting of different commodities is merely the sum of the partial utilities of stocks of individual commodities. Edgeworth, Pareto and Fisher called attention to the fact that individual goods are closely interrelated with regard to the satisfaction of wants, and thus "the utility of one commodity is a function of the quantities of all commodities,"[11] and these goods either strengthen or weaken each other's effect. In the case of complementary goods, such as tea and milk, bread and butter, meat and potatoes, etc., the utility of one unit of such a commodity may increase without a decrease in the quantity of that commodity if we also buy a complementary commodity. Bread yields greater satisfaction when consumed with butter or marmalade than without them. The case is reversed with substitutes. The utility to the consumer of one unit of his stock of beef may decrease even without an increase in this stock if, for example, he also buys some pork, etc. Or, as Fisher writes: "If the quantity of bread is increased, the ordinate (marginal) utility for the *same quantity* of biscuit decreases, and of butter increases."[12] The critique of marginal utility theory emphasizes that a *generalized utility function* is needed which deals with the above relationships.

The technical apparatus for exploring consumer behaviour taking account of the relationships between commodities was invented by Edgeworth. He examined the direct exchange of two commodities between two individuals on the assumption that marginal utility is measurable. The solution found by Edgeworth was to be

---

[11] I. Fisher: *Mathematical Investigations in the Theory of Value and Prices*, New Haven, 1925, (reprint of the 1892 edition), p. 64.
[12] I. Fisher: *op. cit.*, p. 65.

123

used extensively by the modern theory of market forms for the explanation of price formation in the case of bilateral monopoly.

Edgeworth's problem was the following: two individuals, A and B, are engaged in continuously exchanging two commodities, x and y. In doing so, the quantity of the good given up will steadily decrease, while the quantity of the good received will steadily increase. Consequently, the marginal utility of their own good will continuously increase while that of the good received will continuously decrease, and thus the exchange ratio will be different after each act of exchange. Can we determine at what exchange ratio equilibrium will come about in direct exchange? The problem is the same as that already raised by Jevons. But Edgeworth's answer differs from Jevons's although he determines the margin of exchange in a similar way as Jevons: both will continue to exchange as long as the combined utility of the stocks of goods left and received increases for both of them, that is, as long as the utility of dx given up in the successive exchanges is smaller to A than the utility of dy received, or

$$\frac{\partial U}{\partial x} \cdot dx < \frac{\partial U}{\partial y} \cdot dy.$$

To B, however, the utility of dy given up is smaller than the utility of dx received, that is,

$$\frac{\partial V}{\partial x} \cdot dx > \frac{\partial V}{\partial y} \cdot dy, \text{ where } \frac{\partial U}{\partial y} \text{ and } \frac{\partial U}{\partial x}$$

are the marginal utilities of y and x to A, and $\dfrac{\partial V}{\partial x}$ and $\dfrac{\partial V}{\partial y}$ are the marginal utilities of x and y to B.

At the margin of exchange the utilities of the commodities given up and received will be the same to both individuals, and thus neither can improve his welfare by the last act, total utility being unchanged to both parties.

$$\frac{\partial U}{\partial x} \cdot dx = \frac{\partial U}{\partial y} \cdot dy, \text{ and } \frac{\partial V}{\partial x} \cdot dx = \frac{\partial V}{\partial y} \cdot dy.$$

If we plot the quantity of one commodity on one axis and that of the other on the other axis of a graph, and the total utilities to A and B of the different commodity combinations on a third axis, then x and y may have several sets of combinations whose total utility to A or B is the same. Now if we connect these commodity combinations with curves on a two-axis graph, we get curves for both A and B, to use Edgeworth's term, curves of constant satisfaction, or, in other words, *indifference curves* for both individuals. Moving along an indifference curve, A or B will choose different sets of combinations, in which the decline in total utility, as a result of the decrease in the quantity of one commodity, is always counterbalanced by a rise in total utility owing to the increase in the quantity of the other commodity. Thus, in the exchange the equilibrium equation is in fact the equation of the indifference curves for both parties.

There are an infinite number of indifference curves for both exchanging parties. Let us now combine the indifference maps representing the sum of the two individuals' indifference curves, following the procedure widely used in non-Marxian economics for representing Edgeworth's idea, in Pareto's *box diagram*. We assume that the total quantity of each of the two commodities is constant and it is "only their distribution between individuals that changes."[13] Let us now, following Pareto, reverse the indifference map of one individual and connect the axes. Thus the origin of the graph is the lower left-hand corner of the box diagram for one individual, and the upper right-hand corner of the box diagram for the other. In this representation the equilibrium point in the exchange of the two individuals can only be the tangent point of two indifference curves, where the ratio of the marginal utilities of the two commodities is equal for both parties. It is at this ratio of exchange expressing the identity of the marginal utility ratio for both parties that an equilibrium position can come about. But there are several such tangent points, and thus an equilibrium exchange ratio can come about at any point of the so-called *contract curve* connecting the different tangent points (see Figure 12). According to Edgeworth, the equilibrium exchange ratio, at which the marginal utility ratios for both parties are equal, is indeterminate in the case of a direct exchange between two parties, for it depends on their bargaining positions, on how they started, depending on their individual cleverness, the exchange, or on the way the exchange ratios changed in the course of the successive exchange acts. But the final exchange ratio is obviously also influenced by the original quantity of the two parties' own products. All that can be said about the equilibrium point is that it lies somewhere along the contract curve. Edgeworth defined the contract curve as "the locus of bargains which it is not the interest of both parties to disturb...",[14] as the marginal utility ratio of the two commodities is the same for both parties all along the contract curve.

Edgeworth already deals with the relationships of utility functions, and provides a general utility function: $U = f(x, y \ldots z)$, which expresses how total utility depends on the quantity of the various goods available to the individual. Thus, marginal utility is already the partial derivative of the utility function, and the value of the second cross derivative, for example $\dfrac{\partial^2 f}{\partial x \partial z}$, shows the relationship of commodities: if it is larger than 0, the two commodities complement one another; if it is less than 0, they compete with one another.

Let us see how Fisher determines consumer's equilibrium.

For the consumer it is his income and the product price that constitute constraints for his choice. This Fisher represents by the so-called income line. Given a \$ 25 consumer income per annum, "any point on the straight line AB will represent a consumption combination of A and B purchasable for \$ 25. AB may be called a partial income line."[15] The consumer "will select his combination in such a manner as to obtain the maximum utility, which is evidently at the point... *where*

[13] V. Pareto: *Manuel d'économie politique*, 2nd ed., Paris, 1927, p. 190.
[14] F. Y. Edgeworth: *Collected Papers Relating to Political Economy*, London, 1925, Vol. II, p. 306.
[15] I. Fisher: *op. cit.*, p. 72.

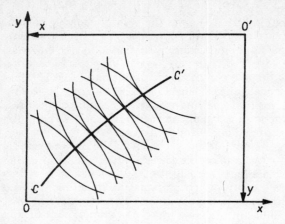

Figure 12

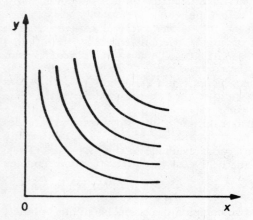

Figure 13

AB is tangent to the indifference curve. At this point he gets the most for his money."[16]

This analysis will be developed further below, and is illustrated in Figure 13.

In drawing the indifference curves, Edgeworth and Fisher assumed that utility was measurable and tried to deduce the indifference curves from the utility surface on the assumption of its measurability. Pareto, however, took over from Edgeworth the indifference-curve approach not only to deal with the relationship

[16] *Ibid.*

126

between utility functions, but already with a view to eliminating the measurability of utility. "Edgeworth ... assumed the existence of utility *(ophélimité)*,[17] and derived the indifference curves from it, while I, just on the contrary, take the indifference curves as given, and derive from them all that I need for the equilibrium theory."[18]

Pareto recognized that the indifference-curve approach makes it possible for him not to assume the measurability of utility in describing consumer behaviour. It is sufficient if we suppose the consumer to be able to rank the different combinations of commodities according to their total utilities. He replaced the utility function based on the measurability of utility by the so-called *index function,* which is not aimed to express by how much a given combination of commodities has more utility than another, but only assigns a utility index to the different sets of combinations corresponding to their position in the consumer's ranking. "Let us give each of these combinations", he writes, "an index number which has to satisfy the following two conditions, but is otherwise arbitrary: 1. two combinations between which the choice is indifferent should have the same index number. 2. Of two combinations the one which is preferred to the other should have a higher index number."[19] Thus, the cardinal interpretation of utility supposing the intensity of utility to be measurable, is replaced by the *ordinal* interpretation of utility.

Thus, Pareto does not derive the indifference curves from utility surfaces taken to be measurable, but connects with curves the combinations having the same utility index number. He assumes that the combinations of goods in an indifference map can be continuously changed, so that every indifference curve is continuous, and it is also possible to change over continuously to a higher indifference curve.

But Pareto is still haunted by the marginal utility concept. He still wants, in Edgeworth's fashion, to express the relationship of utility functions by the aid of marginal utility. The modern version of the indifference-curve approach was elaborated primarily by Hicks and Allen in the 1930s.[20] They tried to eliminate Pareto's inconsistencies and completely to divorce the indifference-curve approach from the marginal utility concept and to change it into the logic of rational choice, to develop it as a technical device which can also be applied to other fields of activity. We shall demonstrate the modern version of the indifference-curve approach through Hicks's works.

[17] Instead of utility Pareto uses the term *ophélimité*. He points out that economics began to use utility in a sense different from its everyday meaning. "Morphine is not a utility in the ordinary sense since it is harmful to the morphine addict; at the same time it is a utility to him economically since it satisfies one of his wants even if it is harmful to him." W. Pareto: *op. cit.,* p. 157. In order to avoid confusion between its economic and everyday usage, he suggests that "economic utility should be denoted by the word *ophélimité*."(*Ibid.*)

[18] V. Pareto: *op. cit.,* p. 169.

[19] *Ibid.*

[20] See: R. G. D. Allen and J. R. Hicks: A Reconsideration of the Theory of Value, *Economica,* February and May 1934.

HICKS'S CONTRIBUTION TO THE FURTHER DEVELOPMENT OF THE THEORY

The main characteristics of the indifference-curve approach

In exploring consumer behaviour Hicks, like Pareto, supposed the consumer to be able only to decide which combinations he prefers in relation to a point on the plane representing various combinations of two commodities, which other combinations he considers as inferior, and which he holds to be equal to it.

The ranking of combinations supposes a consistent behaviour on the part of the consumer and requires that his choices should be transitive. If he prefers combination A to combination B, and combination B to combination C, then he also has to prefer combination A to combination C.

Hicks also holds that the area surrounded by the two axes on the graph can be filled in by indifference curves. The indifference map thus obtained shows the individual's scale of preferences which Hicks tries to explain without assuming the measurability of utility intensities, merely by ranking (ordering) the different combinations of commodities. Thus he describes consumer behaviour by means of the consumer's choice among them.

With the aid of indifference-curve analysis he only wishes to state that total utility is the same all along the indifference curve, and the farther a given curve is from the origin, the greater the total utility it represents. Since total utility cannot be measured, the distance between the curves does not express the magnitude of difference between the total utilities of different combinations.

An indifference curve expresses that the constant total utility of two goods depends on their different combinations, i.e.

$$U = f(x, y) \text{ is constant.}$$

If moving along an indifference curve we increase the quantity of commodity x by dx, then the quantity of commodity y must be decreased by a quantity of dy, if total utility is not to change, such that

$$\frac{\partial U}{\partial x} \cdot dx + \frac{\partial U}{\partial y} \cdot dy = 0.$$

The tangent gradient drawn to the curve is, using Hicks's term, the *marginal rate of substitution* between the two goods. "We may define the marginal rate of substitution of x for y as the quantity of y which would just compensate the consumer for the loss of a marginal unit of x."[21] Other authors, for example Schneider, Baumol, etc., take, in defining the marginal rate of substitution, the quantity of the substitute to be the unit. "We shall call that quantity of No. 2 commodity", writes Schneider, "whose loss is just compensated for, in the judgement of the household, by the increase by one unit of No. 1 commodity, the marginal rate of substitution of No. 2 commodity in relation to No. 1 commodity."[22]

---

[21] J. R. Hicks: *Value and Capital,* Oxford, 1965, p. 20.
[22] E. Schneider: *Einführung in die Wirtschaftstheorie,* Tübingen, 1969, Vol. II, p. 16.

128

The marginal rate of substitution between two products depends on the ratio of their marginal utilities, that is,

$$\frac{\partial U}{\partial x} \cdot dx = -\frac{\partial U}{\partial y} \cdot dy,$$

from which the marginal rate of substitution of y for x:

$$\frac{dy}{dx} = -\frac{\dfrac{\partial U}{\partial x}}{\dfrac{\partial U}{\partial y}}.$$

The followers of the theory maintain that even if marginal utility is immeasurable, the marginal utility quotients can be determined by the marginal ratio of substitution between two products, that is, through a relation between things. Thus the indifference-curve analysis tries to represent the significance of a commodity at the margin for the satisfaction of wants not in terms of the intensity of satisfaction, but through its substitutability for another commodity. The concept of the marginal rate of substitution is, according to Stackelberg, "no longer a fictitious but an empirical magnitude..."[23]

If we continuously substitute one unit of x for y, the quantity of y will decrease and that of x will increase, the significance of x will steadily decrease relative to y, and one unit of x will substitute for less and less y. We have arrived at a relationship similar to the one expressed by the production function; the relative significance for the satisfaction of wants of one unit of a given commodity depends on its relative scarcity. In changing the proportions, the principle of diminishing utility is replaced by *the principle of the diminishing marginal rate of substitution*.

Stackelberg emphasizes that despite all similarity the principle of diminishing marginal utility is not identical with the concept of the diminishing marginal rate of substitution. "... the diminishing marginal rate of substitution is compatible with increasing marginal utilities...,"[24] since the marginal rate of substitution allows for the interrelationships of utilities. In the case of complementary commodities, if they are at the same time also in a mutual substitution relationship, the marginal rate of substitution can decrease even if the marginal utility of both goods increases, provided the utility of the good to be substituted for shows a higher rise than that of the substitute.

Now we are in a position to summarize the main characteristics of the indifference-curve approach as outlined by Hicks.

Two indifference curves cannot intersect, nor can they be tangent to one another, because if they have one common point, all the other points will be common, too.

Every indifference curve is negatively sloped. For if we assume that the marginal utilities of both products are positive, then the increase in the quantity of one commodity will require that the quantity of the other should be decreased for total utility to remain unchanged. A positively sloped indifference curve would imply that the quantities of both commodities should be increased for the consumer to be

[23] H. Stackelberg: *Grundlagen der theoretischen Volkswirtschaftslehre*, Bern, 1948, p. 116.
[24] H. Stackelberg: *op. cit.*, p. 117.

left on the same curve. This case can only emerge if the marginal utility of one commodity is negative, because it is a harmful good, a dis-commodity. If its quantity is increased, total utility will decrease. For total utility to be left unchanged, the other good, the one with positive marginal utility, must also be increased.

Finally, the indifference curve is convex to the origin. It is the diminishing marginal rate of substitution that finds expression in its convexity.

How do we find the optimum combination of commodities for the consumer?

In exploring consumer behaviour in the system of indifference curves, the maximization of the degree of attaining the consumer's aim no longer involves the assumption of the measurability of utility. It only supposes that the consumer is able to rank the different commodity combinations with respect to the degree of realizing his aim.

In order to determine the optimum commodity combination for the consumer, the limiting factors must also be known. Pareto discusses under the heading "obstacles" the limitations which prevent the consumer from maximizing his total utility without any restraint. The theory, assuming the free assertion of competition, distinguishes two limiting factors on the part of the consumer: his income and the prices of products. These "obstacles" to attaining maximum total utility are expressed in the form of the so-called *budget equation*:

$$y = p_x q_x + p_y q_y,$$

where y is the consumer's income, p_x and p_y the prices of commodities x and y and q_x and q_y the quantities of x and y that can be bought.

Representing the budget equation in a two-dimensional graph form (see Figure 14), we obtain the *budget line* (called *price line* by Hicks). It expresses what quantities of x and y the consumer can buy at given prices, supposing that he spends his entire income. In other words, the budget line is the locus of points representing those combinations of x and y whose price sum is of the same magnitude.

If the consumer bought only commodity y, he could get quantity $\dfrac{y}{p_y}$ for his income; if he bought only commodity x, he could get quantity $\dfrac{y}{p_x}$. The straight line connecting the two points is the budget line. Its slope, $\dfrac{y}{p_y} : \dfrac{y}{p_x}$, is the ratio of prices.

Let us draw the budget line within the system of indifference curves (see Figure 15). Now our consumer can spend his entire income on purchasing all those combinations which are at the points of intersection of the budget line and the indifference curves. Striving to maximize his welfare position, he moves towards higher and higher indifference curves. The budget line just touches the highest achievable indifference curve. The combination at the point of tangency means for the consumer the greatest possible total utility that can be attained under the limiting conditions.

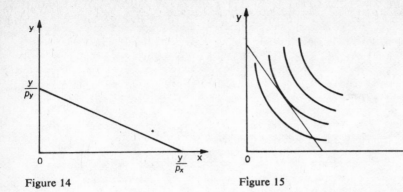

Figure 14

Figure 15

The slope of the budget line as a tangent expresses at the point of tangency the marginal rate of substitution between the two goods. Thus, in an optimum case for the consumer, the marginal rate of substitution will equal the price ratio of the consumer goods in question. Characterizing the consumer's rational choice, we may say that he will be able to increase utility by changing the combinations of goods that are accessible to him at his given income and at the established prices of consumer goods as long as the decrease in the quantity of x can be offset, from the point of view of the satisfaction of his wants, by an increase in the consumption of y by a smaller quantity than can be bought for the money released as a result of his decreasing the consumption of x. Total utility attainable with a given income will be maximized at a combination of consumer goods in which they are, in respect of satisfying wants, substitutes for one another at the margin, in proportion to their price ratios. In other words, the substitution ratio relating to satisfactions must be equal to the substitution ratio relating to the market (exchange). Here again we come across the principle of equal advantage at the margin, but this time in the context of a general utility function and without assuming the measurability of utility.

The assumption of convexity in connection with indifference curves implies that any point on the curve may be a stable equilibrium point. This will be clear if we realize that a budget line can be drawn as a tangent to any point of the curve, that is, any combination can be optimal in a certain price–income situation. The convexity of the curve also means that the consumer will buy a given commodity combination only in a certain price–income situation. A given budget line can touch only one indifference curve, and only at one single point at that.

The income–consumption curve

Hicks examines what will happen if, with the prices of two products being unchanged, the consumer's money income changes, say, increases. Then the budget line will shift parallel to itself, touching higher and higher indifference curves. Hicks calls the curve connecting the points of tangency the *income–consumption*

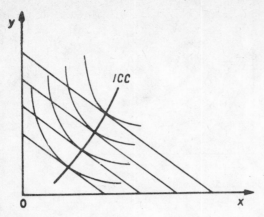

Figure 16

curve. This curve "shows the way in which consumption varies when income increases and prices remain unchanged"[25] (see Figure 16).

If the income elasticity of demand is constant, the income–consumption curve is a straight line. Otherwise, depending on the income elasticity of demand it will slope downwards or upwards. By summing the individual income–consumption curves, Hicks seeks to construct the social income–consumption curve.

As a result of an increase in income, and assuming unchanged prices, the demand for certain goods will rise, for others will decline. This effect was already formulated by the Russian economist Eugen Slutsky as early as 1915: "It is ... necessary to proceed to a classification of goods: those whose quantity increases with the increase of income can be said to be *relatively indispensable*, those whose quantity diminishes with the increase of income, *relatively dispensable*. For example, ... a poor family in consequence of a slight increase of income consumes more meat, more sugar, more tea, and less bread and potatoes."[26]

Hicks calls the former goods *superior,* and the latter *inferior goods*. With the increase of his income, a consumer can achieve more satisfaction if instead of cheaper, lower-quality goods he buys more expensive, higher-quality goods. (Butter instead of margarine, more meat and less potatoes, etc.) If, on the other hand, his income declines, his demand for inferior goods will rise and for superior goods will drop. Owing to the decrease in his income the consumer will be compelled to buy cheaper, lower-quality goods instead of more expensive, higher-quality goods. Thus the demand for inferior goods changes in a direction opposed to changes in income, while the demand for superior goods changes in the same direction as income. Hicks calls this effect of the increase and decrease of income the *income effect*.

In graphical representation, if a commodity is of the inferior type, the income–

[25] J. R. Hicks: *op. cit.,* p. 9.
[26] E. E. Slutsky: On the Theory of the Budget of the Consumer. In: *Readings in Price Theory,* Chicago, 1952, p. 38. (Translation of the original study published in Italian.)

132

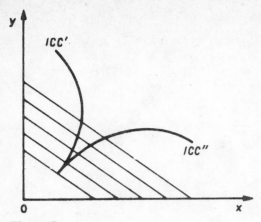

Figure 17

consumption curve bends backwards, expressing that with the increase in income the demand for the commodity concerned will decline at a certain level of income (Figure 17).

Curve ICC'' shows that commodity y is an inferior good while curve ICC' indicates that commodity y is a superior good.

The price–consumption curve. An attempt to derive the demand curve by means of indifference-curve analysis

If, at a given money income, the price of a good, say x, is changed, then the budget line will cut the axis of commodity x at a point which is the farther from the origin, the lower the price of x. The curve, using Hicks's term the *price–consumption curve,* connecting the points of tangency of the so obtained budget lines and indifference curves "shows the way in which consumption varies when the price of x varies and other things [i.e. money income and the price of the other commodity—*A. M.*] remain equal."[27] (See Figure 18.)

Hicks tries to derive the *individual demand curve* of individual goods from the price–consumption curve. In his view, we only have to read off the graph where the budget line, deviating as a result of, say, a change in the price of x, touches the various indifference curves, and what amounts of demand for x are attached to the different points of tangency. This would make it possible, in Hicks's view, to construct the individual's demand curve for various goods. And the summation of individual demand curves would add up to the market demand curve of the good in question.

[27] J. R. Hicks: *op. cit.*, p. 30.

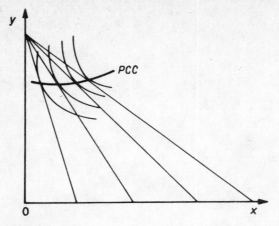

Figure 18

The two effects of a price change. Their separation represented graphically

Hicks writes of "the really important thing which Slutsky discovered in 1915, and which Allen and I rediscovered in the nineteen-thirties, that content can be put into the distinction by tying it up with actual variations in income..."[28] First they examine how the demand for commodity x would change, for example owing to a decrease in its price, at a constant marginal utility of money, that is, at unchanged real income. Marshall considered the marginal utility of money to be constant on the assumption that the consumer spends only a fraction of his income on buying commodity x. Slutsky, Allen and Hicks, however, want to counterbalance the effect of a change of price on the marginal utility of money by changing money income. Slutsky writes that the price increase of a commodity must be accompanied by "an increment of income equal to the apparent loss"[29] if real income is not to change. "... if after an increase of the price of bread wages increase only by the amount of apparent loss, the demand for bread on the part of the wage-earners will not be maintained at the original level, on the contrary, it will fall."[30] At the same time, the demand for other goods, which are substitutes for the good increasing in price, should rise as they have become cheaper compared to it, and therefore more attractive. And conversely, the demand for a commodity will rise with a decrease in its price, assuming unchanged marginal utility of money, i.e. real income, while the demand for other commodities, in relation to which the commodity with a decreasing price has become relatively cheaper and thus relatively more attractive, must fall. This is the *substitution effect*. Non-Marxian literature calls the Slutsky theorem the statement that the demand for a commodity

[28] J. R. Hicks: *A Revision of Demand Theory*, Oxford, 1956, p. 14.
[29] E. E. Slutsky: *op. cit.*, p. 42.
[30] *Ibid.*

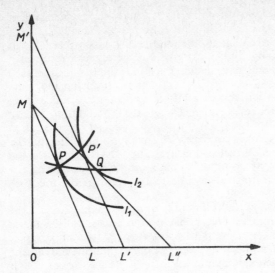

Figure 19

will move contrary to changes in its price if we disregard the effect which a price change exerts on the consumer's real income. These authors then examine how the demand for commodity x would change, merely as a result of the change in the marginal utility of money, that is, at unchanged price proportions and at a corresponding rise in real income. The latter is the so-called *income effect*.

Taking into account the combined substitution and income effects of a price change, Slutsky comes to the conclusion that "the demand for a relatively indispensable good ... is necessarily always normal, that is, it diminishes if its price increases, and increases if its price decreases... The demand for a relatively dispensable good ... can be abnormal in certain cases, that is, it can increase with the increase of price and diminish with the decrease of price."[31]

Hicks attempts to separate the substitution effect and income effect of price changes by applying indifference-curve analysis. The original price–income situation is expressed in his diagram by the budget line $L\,M$ (Figure 19). The budget line touches the highest indifference curve at point P. Now let the price of x fall, and the new budget line $L'\,'M$ will touch a higher indifference curve at point Q. At Q the demand for x is higher compared with that at point P, and this increase in demand is due, according to Hicks, partly to the *income*, partly the *substitution effect*. The income effect expresses that "a fall in the price of a commodity... makes the consumer better off, it raises his 'real income', and its effect along this channel is similar to that of an increase in income."[32] Hicks separates this from the substitution effect by drawing the tangent $L'M'$, parallel to the old budget line,

[31] E. E. Slutsky: *op. cit.,* p. 41.
[32] J. R. Hicks: *Value and Capital,* Oxford, 1965, p. 31.

to the new indifference curve, touching it at point P'. As the slope of the tangent drawn to point P' is the same as that of the old budget line, the tangency point P' expresses the income effect of the price change, the amount by which the demand for x would have increased at unchanged price proportions merely as a result of a change in real income, that is, owing to a change-over to a higher indifference curve. Hicks interprets real income in a subjective way: every point on the same indifference curve means identical real income as it yields identical total utility; a change-over to a higher indifference curve means greater total utility, hence higher real income.

Point P' lies on the income–consumption curve PP', while point Q lies on the price-consumption curve PQ. Since the price–consumption curve comprises the total effect of a price change, "... as we go up on to higher indifference curves, the price–consumption curve through P must always lie to the right of the income–consumption curve through P."[33]

As a result of a fall in the price of x, the full change in the demand for x, that is, the movement from P to Q along the price–consumption curve, will be made up of the following partial effects: the movement from P to P' which expresses the income effect, the change-over to a higher indifference curve, and the movement from P' to Q, that is, the movement along the same indifference curve, which shows the substitution effect, the rise in the demand for x with the given income as a consequence of the fall in its price. At a given real income, that is, moving along the same indifference curve, with the demand for x rising, the demand for y must fall. Hence the name, substitution effect. By separating the two effects in a two-dimensional diagram, Hicks demonstrates that, if the income effect is filtered out from the effect of a price change on the demand for a commodity, the demand curve of that commodity, owing to the substitution effect, is always negatively sloped.

"... the substitution effect is absolutely certain—it must always work in favour of an increase in the demand for a commodity when the price of that commodity falls. But the income effect is not so reliable."[34] In the case of inferior goods it works in a direction opposed to the substitution effect.

Hicks's demand curve contains both effects of a price change. Does false trading not cause therefore a problem for Hicks? In his view, "... if there is a change in price in the midst of trading, the situation appears to elude the ordinary apparatus of demand-and-supply analysis."[35] But Hicks ascribes only a secondary significance to the problem of false trading. A price reduction increases the demand for superior goods through the income effect. But a price change has its double effect, according to Hicks, also on the seller's part. The seller has a given stock of a commodity, part of which he wants to retain for his own consumption. If the price of his commodity falls, he retains, in compliance with the substitution effect, more of his stock for own consumption and decreases its supply. But, owing to the price fall, his position deteriorates, and therefore he decreases his demand for superior goods, and if his commodity was such a superior good, he will retain less of it for own consumption and will increase the supply of his own product. The income

[33] J. R. Hicks: *op. cit.*, p. 33.
[34] J. R. Hicks: *op. cit.*, p. 32.
[35] J. R. Hicks: *op. cit.*, p. 128.

136

effect of the price reduction, which gives rise in price theory to the problem already discussed, increases, according to Hicks, not only the demand for superior goods, but also increases their supply, and the two effects may counterbalance each other, in which case only the substitution effect ensuring a stable equilibrium will remain.

The demand curve of Giffen goods

Giffen goods[36] are those inferior goods in whose case the income effect counteracts the substitution effect. Therefore, if their prices fall, the demand for them will decrease, and if their prices rise, the demand for them will also rise. But Hicks points out that the demand for Giffen goods may also be normal both at high and

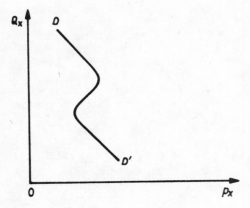

Figure 20

low prices, because the consumer spends, whether the prices are high or low, only a fraction of his income on purchasing inferior goods, and thus the substitution effect may offset the income effect. The backward-sloping part of the curve indicates that range of prices within which the negative income effect asserts itself (Figure 20).

Hicks also emphasizes that on a social scale the summation of the individual demand curves of Giffen goods may become normal. The backward-sloping part of the individual demand curve falls, with different strata, into different intervals, and thus in their social summation normal reactions may outweigh abnormal reactions.

[36] Robert Giffen, an English statistician, observed that in low-income households the demand for bread increased with a rise in its price. In Germany, in the 1920s, a similar observation was made in the case of potatoes.

137

A CRITIQUE OF THE INDIFFERENCE-CURVE ANALYSIS

1. The indifference-curve approach is undoubtedly an ingenious attempt to analyse the behaviour of the consumer wishing to optimize his welfare position, and to derive, in investigating consumer behaviour, the individual, or in the case of summation, the social demand curve. However, in criticizing that theory[37] we must emphasize that the construction of the demand curve on the basis of the ordinal interpretation of utility promotes the theory of demand no better than its derivation by means of the cardinal interpretation of utility. Common to both approaches is the individual starting-point which Hicks justifies by saying that "market demand has almost exactly the same properties as individual demand."[38] The *individual's given* scale of wants independent of any social influences, and yet represented by marginal utility theory as the *final* cause of demand is replaced by the *individual's* equally *given* scale of preferences also not liable to any change as a result of external influences, a scale the factors responsible for whose formation are also unknown. Moreover, the unchangeability of the scale of preferences is one of the basic conditions of indifference-curve analysis. If we admit the changeability of the scale of preferences, the individual's choices will no longer be consistent, his scale of preferences cannot be determined, and his satisfaction cannot be maximized. Common to both approaches is the method of introspection, too. The only difference that can be found between them is that the introspective cardinalism of marginal utility theory is replaced by the introspective ordinalism of the indifference-curve analysis.

If the analysis does not go beyond the individual's scale of preferences, it is impossible to reveal the socially determined laws governing changes that occur in the structure of demand. As regards the effect of a change of income on the structure of demand, indifference-curve analysis can only point to a few general relationships independent of the consumer's social position, for example, that with the increase of real income the individual steps up his demand for superior goods and decreases it for inferior goods, and *vice versa*.

Anyway, the individual demand curves that the theory wishes to derive from the scale of preferences could only be summed to yield a social demand curve if they were *independent* of each other. But the individual demand curves are *closely interconnected,* they influence each other. Certain individuals' demand for certain products may rise even without their incomes and the prices being changed, simply because other individuals have made purchases of these products. Owing to the interdependence between individual demands, the social demand function cannot be constructed merely by means of their summation. "... in most of the empirical cases, it seems, what is typical is that they are not of an additive nature."[39]

2. While the representatives of the indifference-curve approach pretend to discard the cardinal interpretation of utility, they in fact steal it back into the theory. They think that the marginal utility quotients can be determined through indifferent

---

[37] A penetrating critique in Marxist literature of the indifference-curve approach can be found in Robert Hoch: *Consumption and Price, with Special Regard to the Theories and Practice of the Socialist Countries,* Budapest, 1979, Chapter 7.

[38] J. R. Hicks: *op. cit.,* p. 34.

[39] O. Morgenstern: *Spieltheorie und Wirtschaftswissenschaft,* Wien–München, 1963, p. 146.

combinations, i.e. through the relationships of commodities. In reality, the case is just the opposite. In forming the indifferent combinations, the consumer must be familiar with the increments in total utility as he must be able to determine whether with the increase in the quantity of commodity y and decrease in the quantity of commodity x the positive and negative increments of total utility will offset one another or not. But the positive or negative increment of total utility is marginal utility. Therefore, the consumer must precisely be aware of the magnitudes of the marginal utilities of x and y. Thus the theory is compelled to assume, writes Carell, that "... the household takes an exact account of utility and knows about any commodity combination, how many times greater in it is the marginal utility of one commodity relative to the marginal utility of other commodities."[40]

3. On the analogy of the behaviour of the entrepreneur seeking maximum profit, indifference-curve analysis also represents the household as striving to maximize a uniform aim. Such representation of the behaviour of the household raises two problems. First, can a conscious optimization endeavour be found in the consumer's purchases in choosing his commodity combinations to satisfy his wants?

No doubt, the consumer wants to improve his welfare position within the limits of his possibilities. At the same time, there are a lot of routine elements, insistence on his established consumption habits, in his behaviour. It would be hard to decide which element is predominant. If we think how difficult it is for the consumer to change his habits, to switch over from buying familiar products to buying new ones even with better properties, it appears that the latter element is more prevalent.

Another, equally difficult problem is this: if the consumer were really intended to achieve an optimum position when combining different consumer goods, *what does he want to maximize?* In order to represent the relationship between utilities, the indifference-curve approach assumes that the consumer compares the total utilities of different commodity combinations. Consequently, he endeavours to maximize a uniform objective. But does such a uniform objective really exist in the household? The indifference-curve approach rejects the measurability of utilities, but by representing the maximization of total utility as the consumer's objective, it assumes that the concrete utilities of the different goods somehow add up to a sort of abstract total utility, which is tantamount to tacitly accepting that the different concrete utilities have some sort of common measure.

What we can say with some certainty is that in combining the different commodities available to him at his income, the consumer really exhibits some endeavour to satisfy his wants in order of urgency, not to meet his less intensive needs before his more urgent ones are satisfied. But all this does not mean that the significance of satisfying the various needs could be estimated according to a common measure, and the different commodity combinations ranked exactly according to their total utility. Since there is no common measure, the comparison of wants according to their urgency is rather uncertain, and so is the ranking by consumers. It is rather because of uncertain ordering than conscious estimation that several commodity combinations may appear to be indifferent to the consumer. And we

[40] E. Carell: Der Ordinalismus in der Nutzentheorie, *Zeitschrift für die gesamte Staatswissenschaft*, 1955, p. 44.

cannot claim to be sure that the consumer is able to tell which combination accesible to him with his income will yield him the greatest utility.

4. In order to choose the combination yielding the assumed maximum total utility, the theory of indifference curves makes use of marginal analysis. To avoid the measurability of marginal utility, it tries to grasp the marginal utility of goods as a relationship of commodities, as a marginal utility ratio. This made it necessary to construct indifference curves, which resolve the relations between utilities entirely into substitutability. It also represents complementarity within the framework of substitutability: the complementarity of two goods through their substitutability for a third good. The resolution of relationships into substitutability is entirely in harmony with the concept of abstract total utility. To satisfy abstract total utility any good can be used, thus they are substitutes for one another. As Hans Mayer writes: "the more generally the total objective is formulated, the less it is determined in qualitative differentiation or composition, and the more it is given only in quantitative terms, ... the more commodity combinations can be related as means of realization to the total objective. If we set out from a non-differentiated total need or total satisfaction, we can relate to it any possible goods, substituting one for an other."[41]

But the consumer is stimulated in his activities not by an abstract total want but a variety of qualitatively different needs for the satisfaction of which he needs goods of different kind and quality. Even if commodity combinations that are indifferent to the consumer should be conceivable, they are by no means indifferent in the sense that the continuous abstention from the satisfaction of one want could be offset by the greater satisfaction of another want. It may occur that somebody restricts his expenditure on food in favour of better clothing. But by having a new, fashionable suit available, his sensation of hunger will not diminish. Only goods that can equally be used to satisfy the same want are in a substitution relationship with one another so that with a continuous decrease in the quantity of the good that is substituted for, the want satisfied by it will not remain unsatisfied as a result of the increase in the quantity of the other good.

5. By the way, a consumer who regularly buys his necessities on the market with his income at given prices can hardly be supposed to make himself independent of income and price relations, and to rank commodity combinations exclusively on the basis of their significance for the satisfaction of his wants, while he must pass judgement on a multitude of combinations never experienced before. He is also unlikely to choose the optimum commodity combination suiting his income and corresponding to the prevailing prices only after he has constructed his scale of preferences solely with a view to satisfying his wants. In reality, a housewife, in making her household budget, takes into account only the combinations attainable by her within the limitations of her income and the established prices, and does not strive to rank combinations that are either inaccessible or too low to her.

The problems discussed above arise when the indifference-curve approach is applied to the investigation of consumer behaviour. But the attempts made to

---

[41] H. Mayer: Der Erkenntniswert der funktionellen Preistheorie, *Die Wirtschaftstheorie der Gegenwart,* Vol. II, Wien, 1932, pp. 214–215.

apply indifference curves go far beyond consumer behaviour. Owing to its praxeological character, this approach is widely used by non-Marxian economics in the field of production to represent, among other things, bargaining between bilateral monopolies. The difficulties arising from its use appear differently, depending on the fields of application.

REVEALED PREFERENCE

The indifference-curve approach tried to construct the individual's scale of preferences by means of introspection. Revealed-preference theory rejects the assumption of the indifference-curve analysis also criticized by us that "the consumer is able without knowing anything about the processes taking place on the market and about the exchange value of goods to decide which of two given baskets of goods is preferable, or whether both of them are indifferent to him."[42] Samuelson[43] was the first to work out a procedure with the aid of which, merely by observing the market behaviour of the consumer, the indifference curve could allegedly be constructed. Now the consumer's scale of preferences manifests itself through his market behaviour, and thus we are faced with a new interpretation of utility, the *revealed-preference* approach or, to use Blaug's terminology behaviourist ordinalism.

Its theoretical assumptions are as follows:

I. The consumer always prefers a larger commodity stock to a smaller one. Of two stocks consisting of identical goods the larger is, as also stated by Pareto, the one which contains more of at least one commodity, but not less of the other commodities.

II. The consumer's choices are transitive.

III. In a given price–income situation the consumer chooses one commodity combination. This combination, as opposed to other combinations available to him with his income and at given prices, is in the situation of revealed preference. The price–income situation is expressed by the budget line.

IV. By changing price–income relations, the consumer may be led to choose any combination.

It follows from assumption III that, taking two goods, x and y, any combination chosen can only be associated with one price ratio $\frac{p_x}{p_y} = f(x, y)$. This, by the way, also follows from the consumer's equilibrium determined by the indifference-curve approach: in seeking an optimum welfare position, the consumer chooses the combination which lies at the point of tangency of the budget line and the indifference curve. But to a certain point of the given indifference curve only one budget line can be drawn as a tangent.

Observing at what relative prices the consumer buys the different combinations

[42] P. Schönfeld: Grundzüge der Theorie der faktischen Preferenz, *Zeitschrift für Nationalökonomie*, Wien, 1962, Vol. XXII, Fasc. 3, p. 299.

[43] P. A. Samuelson: Consumption Theory in Terms of Revealed Preference, *Economica*, November 1943.

of x and y, we can see that these price proportions express, according to Samuelson, the marginal rate of substitution, that is, the slope of the indifference curve passing through the individual combinations at the combination concerned. Putting the marginal rate of substitution for the price proportions, we obtain

$$\frac{dy}{dx} = f(x, y).$$

The revealed-preference approach wishes now to construct the indifference curve through the various marginal rates of substitution thus given.

According to Samuelson, the case is a simple one if the elasticity of the indifference curve is 1. In this case the indifference curve is a rectangular hyperbola, and the product of the co-ordinates of any of its points, $x \cdot y$, yields a constant amount. Then $\frac{dy}{dx}$ will change proportionately with the ratio $\frac{x}{y}$, because, if elasticity as the quotient of marginal and average magnitude is 1, then marginal magnitude will equal average magnitude.

$$\text{Thus } \frac{dx}{dy} = \frac{x}{y}, \text{ or } \frac{p_x}{p_y} = \frac{y}{x}.$$

If now the values of x and y are known at a given point A, then the combinations indifferent to the combination at A can be constructed. Samuelson uses the Cauchy–Lipschitz method by which the authors wished to prove that there exists a solution to a differential equation.

But the elasticity of indifference curves is usually not unity, and thus, according to Samuelson, the marginal rate of substitution must be determined by observation for every point, and it is by observation that the indifference curve must be constructed.

Suppose that the consumer buys commodity combination A with his income at the price ratio of $\frac{p_x}{p_y}$. How can the combinations which are in an indifference relationship with combination A be grasped?

By mere observation an answer can only be given to the question what combinations our individual considers to be inferior or superior to A, but not what combinations he regards as equal to A. It cannot be the criterion of indifference between A and B, says Little, if our consumer, according to the evidence of observation, has preferred A to B as may times as he has preferred B to A. In this case it would be impossible to distinguish indifference from inconsistency.[44] Samuelson sees a way out in separating the combinations that are better or worse than A, and it is at the margin of the two that the combinations indifferent in relation to A are found to lie.

[44] I. M. D. Little: *A Critique of Welfare Economics*, 2nd ed., Oxford, 1965, p. 23.

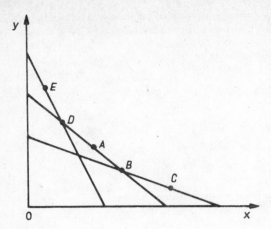

Figure 21

If in a given price–income situation the consumer chooses combination A, he may do so partly because he finds A cheaper than the other combinations, and partly because he values A more than any other combinations. If he were in a position to buy other combinations with his income and at given prices, and he still buys A, then A is clearly more valuable to him than any other attainable combinations. A is, compared to them, in the situation of revealed preference. If we draw the budget line expressing the price ratio and the consumer's income, combination A will obviously lie on it. Our consumer sets less value on the other combinations lying on and below the budget line than he sets on A, because he could have bought them with his income and yet he chose A.

Further expanding the sphere of combinations less favourable than A, we must wait for a price–income situation in which the consumer chooses combination B lying on the original budget line. (Figure 21). Let us now draw the budget line corresponding to the new price–income situation, the line which will cut the old one clearly at point B. In the new situation, our consumer cannot afford A and chooses B instead. On the other hand, he considers B to be more favourable to him than all the other combinations which lie on or inside the new budget line. But then he will underestimate these combinations in relation to A, too, provided his behaviour is transitive, as he underestimated B in relation to A. In the original situation he could have bought either A or B, and yet he decided on A. The sphere of combinations less favourable than A can further be extended by choosing out of the observed price–income situations those in which our consumer will choose a combination C on the new budget line which is now even more unfavourable than B. We can observe our consumer either in such a price–income situation in which he chooses combination D lying left of A on the original budget line which he, in the initial conditions, valued less than A, then, with further changing the price and income relations he chooses combination E on the budget line passing through D. But he values E less than D and, consequently, less than A,

143

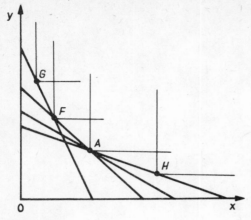

Figure 22

too. With the change in the price–income situation the possibility to compare the combinations successively chosen is ensured by the fact that the preferred new combination is always at the point of intersection of the old and new budget line.

The margin of combinations chosen as less favourable than A is thus represented by non-continuous line-sections convex to the origin. Then, by increasing the number of observations, we obtain a continuous curve convex to the origin.

Let us now draw the margin of combinations that are more favourable than A. It will be clear right in the original situation that any combination which contains more of one commodity, but not less of any other, than A is more favourable than A. These combinations lie 'north-east' of A. Now, from the shape of the area left for the indifference curve to be constructed, we can infer that the curve is negatively sloped and convex to the origin.

If the budget line is in a position as represented in Figure 22, also passing through the original point A, and our consumer chooses combination F, he clearly prefers this to A, as he could also afford A in the new situation. But the combinations 'north-east' of F are more valuable than F, and thus more valuable than A, too. If then, in a further new price–income situation our consumer chooses point G on the budget line passing through F, then he prefers combination G and all combinations 'north-east' of it to F, and this to A, too, provided his behaviour is transitive. Our consumer may also choose combination H lying left of A on the new budget line passing through A if point H lies on the section of the new budget line which is above the old one. Then he will also prefer the combinations 'north-east' of point H to A. The comparability of successively chosen combinations is now ensured by the fact that the new budget line cuts the old one at the previously chosen combination.

The margin of combinations better than A is represented again by non-continuous line sections convex to the origin. With the increase in the number of observations this also assumes the form of a continuous curve convex to the

144

origin. Little pointed out that the curves embracing combinations that are less or more favourable than A converge to one another and constitute the indifference curve of combination A.

A few comments on the revealed-preference approach

1. Putting the approach in question into practice comes up against serious difficulties. On the one hand, the investigations must cover a rather long period of observations, since our individual cannot afford often to buy durable consumer goods making up part of the commodity combinations attainable by him. In the long run, however, the consumer's scale of preferences will also change. It will change as a result of the appearance of new products, of changes in his social position, age, family circumstances, etc. On the other hand, the consumer's choices can significantly be influenced even in the short run by advertising, packing, seller's persuasion, etc. Inconsistency is unavoidable also in the short run if only because people like variety, and our consumer will not buy the same commodity combination even at given prices and unchanged income week by week. All this counteracts the consistency of his choices and the possibility of determining his scale of preferences. It is a condition of consistent choice, writes Little, that "the consumer provided his income and prices remain unchanged, must always buy exactly the same combination of goods."[45]

And in observing the consumer's behaviour in various periods, asks Mrs. Robinson, "how can we tell what part of the difference in his purchases is due to the difference in prices and what part to the change in his preference that has taken place meanwhile?"[46], that is, how far his choices are consistent over time and how far they contradict each other.

2. We must, by the way, emphasize that the revealed-preference approach only describes the consumer's behaviour; it does not reveal the motive behind the individual's choice. Marginal utility theory wanted to grasp the essence behind economic phenomena, but erroneously regarded the consumer's satisfactions to be the real essence. By confining itself merely to the observation of consumer behaviour and showing no interest in the motive governing it, the revealed-preference approach abandons the investigation of the essence even in its subjective form.

[45] I. M. D. Little: *op. cit.*, pp. 283–284.
[46] J. Robinson: *Economic Philosophy*, London, 1962, p. 50.

Chapter 3

AN ATTEMPT TO DERIVE THE SUPPLY CURVE FROM THE BEHAVIOUR OF THE PROFIT-MAXIMIZING ENTREPRENEUR

INTRODUCTORY REMARKS

By means of the indifference-curve approach non-Marxian economics, as we have seen, wants to find an answer to the question of how the consumer must allocate his available income, at given prices, in purchasing different commodities so that they yield maximum total utility to him. By observing the behaviour of optimizing consumers, the followers of that theory try to derive the individual and, by summation, the social demand function from the indifference curves.

At the same time, they want to construct the supply function by setting out from the behaviour of the entrepreneurs wishing to attain maximum profit. In this context, equilibrium theory tries to find solutions to two problems:

1. Assuming that a given commodity can be produced by different combinations of factors of production, what factor combination, taking factor prices to be given, must be used in producing a particular quantity of output with minimum cost to the entrepreneur? The theory claims to have found an answer to this question in the use of so-called *isoquants*.

2. After we have found out the minimum cost of producing different outputs, we must discover how production cost depends on the volume of production. The theory tries to solve this problem by the *cost function*.

Let us begin by analysing the first problem.

THE SYSTEM OF ISOQUANTS

The indifference-curve approach expresses the consumer's choice among different commodity combinations.

The theory supposes that, moving along the same indifference curve, the decrease in total utility as a result of the decrease by dx in the quantity of, say, commodity x, equals its increment as a result of the increase by dy in quantity y.

Already Wicksteed pointed out that, owing to the mutual substitutability between factors, "the same material product may result from different combinations of productive agents ... a marginal subtraction of one may be compensated by a due marginal addition of another ..."[47] It was on the analogy of indifference curves of consumption that Johnson constructed, in 1913, indifference curves of production.[48]

---

[47] P. H. Wicksteed: *Commonsense of Political Economy*, London, 1949, p. 358.
[48] W. E. Johnson: The Pure Theory of Utility Curves, *The Economic Journal*, 1913, p. 508.

The indifference-curve theory of production evolved in its present-day form in the 1930s as a result of the research done primarily by R. Frisch, E. Schneider, S. Carlson, J. R. Hicks. The indifference curves of production have come to be usually referred to in modern economics as *isoquants,* a name given by R. Frisch.

"... an isoquant is a curve drawn in a factor diagram [representing different combinations of factors—*A.M.*], along which curve the quantity of the product is the same."[49] Assuming two factors, capital and labour, any point of an isoquant represents different combinations of capital and labour, but by any combination the same quantity of product can be produced: $Q = f(K, L)$ is constant.

Carlson distinguishes three types of isoquants depending on the relationship they express between factors:

1. The factors are continuous but limited substitutes for one another;
2. The factors can be combined only in a technically determined proportion, and there is no substitution relation between them within a given production method; it is only between production methods, or their combinations, that they are substitutable. This substitution, however, is not continuous.
3. The factors are perfectly substitutable one for the other.

Let us examine the different types of isoquants separately.

The system of isoquants in the case of factors with continuous but limited substitutability

The main characteristics of the system of isoquants

If, moving along the same curve, we continuously decrease the quantity of one factor, then we can, according to our assumption, increase the quantity of the other without changing the magnitude of total output. Along the curve, the following relationship asserts itself:

$$dL \frac{\partial Q}{\partial L} + dK \frac{\partial Q}{\partial K} = 0.$$

Its construction, which is identical with that of the indifference curve, clearly reflects the praxeological character of the procedure expressed in it: both express, in the interest of attaining the given aim, a choice between means applicable in different proportions in the various fields of activity.

The basic characteristics of isoquants are identical with those of indifference curves.

Let us summarize these characteristics following the authors first using the system of isoquants:

1. "... no isoquants can intersect one another."[50] We can add that they cannot even touch one another, because if they have one common point, all the other points must also be common.

---

[49] R. Frisch: *Lois techniques et économiques de la production,* Paris, 1963, p. 50.
[50] S. Carlson: *A Study on the Pure Theory of Production,* Oxford, 1956, p. 19.

2. "Given two factors, the isoquants will decrease in substitution,"[51] which means that the slope of the curve is negative. If the quantity of one factor is increased, that of the other must be decreased for total output to remain unchanged.

3. The isoquant, too, "will be shaped like an indifference curve, being convex downwards."[52] This characteristic stems from the diminishing marginal rate of substitution for both the indifference curve and the isoquant. Just as the gradient of the tangent drawn to the indifference curve expresses the substitutability between two consumer goods at the margin, the gradient of the tangent to the isoquant shows the marginal rate of substitution between factors. "... the quantity of the first factor whose decrease is just offset by an increase by one unit of the other factor, that is, leaves total output unchanged, is called the marginal rate of substitution of the first factor for the other."[53]

In the system of indifference curves the marginal rate of substitution expressed the quotient of marginal utilities, while in the system of isoquants it expresses the quotient of marginal productivities. It follows from the relationship $dL\dfrac{\partial Q}{\partial L} +$

$+ dK\dfrac{\partial Q}{\partial K} = 0$ that the marginal rate of substitution of capital for labour is:

$$\frac{dL}{dK} = -\frac{\dfrac{\partial Q}{\partial K}}{\dfrac{\partial Q}{\partial L}}$$

Let us now, following Schneider, continuously substitute capital for labour. The quantity of labour will decrease relative to capital, the marginal productivity of labour will increase, the quantity of capital will increase relative to labour, and the marginal productivity of capital will decrease. Thus the numerator of the quotient of marginal productivities determining the magnitude of $\dfrac{dL}{dK}$ decreases, and its denominator increases. Therefore, in the case of continuous substitution, the marginal rate of substitution will decrease. As the principle of diminishing utilities was replaced by that of the diminishing rate of substitution in the system of indifference curves, in just the same way, the principle of diminishing return is replaced by that of the diminishing marginal rate of substitution in the system of isoquants.

Yet there are certain differences between the two systems.

First, if we represent the total utility of the individual combinations on a third axis in the system of indifference curves, we can only find out that the utility surface will be higher as we change to a higher indifference curve, while the height of the utility surface is indeterminate. In the system of isoquants, however, the

[51] R. Frisch: *op. cit.*, p. 78.
[52] J. R. Hicks: *Value and Capital*, Oxford, 1965, p. 91.
[53] E. Schneider: *Einführung in die Wirtschaftstheorie*, Tübingen, 1969, Vol. II, p. 177.

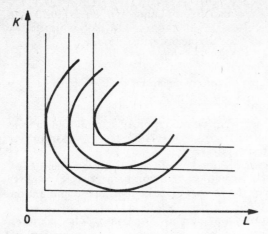

K

0   L

Figure 23

height of the output surfaces will be determinate if we express on the third axis
the volume of output resulting from the different combinations of factor inputs.

Secondly, in the system of indifference curves we suppose that the marginal
utility of products will be positive throughout if their quantities are increased.
Thus, the curve approaches the axis asymptotically. But in the system of isoquants,
as both Frisch and Schneider point out, as a result of a change in proportions
between factors, the marginal productivity of the factor whose quantity is excessively increased relative to that of the other will become negative. This is
reflected by the backward-bending part of the isoquant (see Figure 23): in this
range of the curve, for total output to be left unchanged, if the quantity of the
factor with a negative marginal productivity is increased, the quantity of the other
factor with a positive marginal productivity must also be increased. Thus, in the
positively sloped part of the curve there is no substitutability between factors in
the sense that a decrease in the quantity of one factor could be offset by an increase
in the quantity of the other. The factors can be substitutes in this sense only in
that part of the curve where the marginal productivities of both of them are
positive. As we have already seen, one margin of substitution is the technical
optimum of the variable factor, and the technical maximum of the constant
factor, where therefore the marginal productivity of the constant factor is 0, and
the other margin of substitution is the technical maximum of the variable factor
and the technical optimum of the constant factor, and thus the marginal productivity of the variable factor is 0. At the two margins of substitution, therefore, the
marginal rate of substitution of capital for labour, or labour for capital is 0.
"Thus the economically relevant scope of substitution only consists of one part
of the isoquant, a part which is bounded by two points at which the tangents
drawn to the isoquant become parallel with the axes v_1 and v_2 respectively."[54]
(Schneider represents the two production factors by v_1 and v_2.) The second and

[54] E. Schneider: *Theorie der Produktion*, Vienna, 1934, p. 26.

third characteristics of the isoquants are also clearly valid only within these two points. The points of tangency, therefore, of all tangents to isoquants drawn parallel to the axes mark the margins of the surface of substitution.

The determination of the cost-minimizing factor combination for producing a given output

We can now raise the question proper: what combination of capital and labour must be chosen to produce a given output, in other words, up to what margin is it worthwhile to substitute one factor for the other?

It is worthwhile to change the factor proportions, to substitute one factor for the other, as long as the cost of the given output quantity decreases thereby. To produce a given quantity of output, the factors must be used in a combination which ensures minimum cost.

Assuming an entrepreneur divorced from capital ownership, who acquires capital only by a loan transaction or by hiring capital goods, the cost to him of acquiring capital is interest. We further assume that competition is undisturbed and thus the rewards to factors, that is the costs of capital and labour, are given for him. If we set out, following Schneider, from one margin of the substitution possibilities where, for example, the marginal productivity of capital is 0, we shall find that near this margin at a very low positive marginal productivity of capital, one unit of labour can substitute for very much capital, since the marginal productivity of labour is very high. Clearly, the decrease in total cost, as a result of decreasing the volume of capital in the course of substitution, is much greater than the increase in total cost, as a result of increasing labour by one unit: $dLp_L < dKp_K$, where p_L and p_K represent wage and interest rates. By continuously substituting labour for capital, the marginal productivity of labour will decrease and that of capital will increase, one unit of additional labour input will substitute for ever less capital, and the magnitudes of dLp_L and dKp_K will move nearer to one another. But as long as $dLp_L < dKp_K$, it is worthwhile to substitute labour for capital, as this will cause total cost to decrease. And in the process of substituting labour for capital, total cost will be minimum when the decrease and increase in total cost are equal:

$$dLp_L = dKp_K, \text{ whence } \frac{dK}{dL} = \frac{p_L}{p_K}.$$

From this follows that the cost of producing a given output will be at a minimum in the case of a factor combination in which, to quote Hicks, "the price ratio between any two factors must equal their marginal rate of substitution."[55] Owing to its similar construction, we obtain the same result in analysing consumer behaviour, too: maximum total utility is yielded to the consumer by a combination of goods in which the marginal rate of substitution equals the price ratio of consumption goods.

[55] J. R. Hicks: *op. cit.*, p. 86.

Writing in our formula expressing the condition for minimizing total cost the ratio of marginal productivities in place of the marginal rate of substitution, we obtain

$$\frac{p_L}{p_K} = \frac{\dfrac{\partial Q}{\partial L}}{\dfrac{\partial Q}{\partial K}},$$

which shows that if minimum cost is to be achieved, "the ratio of marginal productivities must equal the price ratio of factors."[56]

By further transforming the above formula, we can also characterize the cost minimum by two more forms. One is

$$\frac{\dfrac{\partial Q}{\partial L}}{p_L} = \frac{\dfrac{\partial Q}{\partial K}}{p_K};$$

cost is minimized when the same output increment arises from each unit of payment for the hire of labour and capital, i.e., whether we hire capital or labour, the unit of money last spent will yield in both cases the same increment of output. In Stackelberg's words: "the marginal productivity of money is the same irrespective of using labour or capital."[57] We have arrived in the field of production also at a relationship similar to Gossen's second law derived in the household, suggesting at the same time that Gossen's second law does not reflect a specific feature of consumer behaviour. We can find a similar relationship in production in Walras, for example, when he derives Euler's theorem. The point in question is the general principle of the rational utilization of scarce means, the principle of the equalization of advantage.

Finally, we obtain, as the reciprocal of the above-discussed formula, the fourth determination of minimum cost based on the principle of equalization of advantage:

$$\frac{p_L}{\dfrac{\partial Q}{\partial L}} = \frac{p_K}{\dfrac{\partial Q}{\partial K}}.$$

Thus, whether labour or capital is unilaterally increased, the increment of total cost (the so-called marginal cost), is equal in both cases as a result of producing the last unit of output at the point of minimum cost.[58]

In constructing the supply curve, we defined the problem to be solved by the system of isoquant curves as an aspect of a programming task: what factor combination will yield a given output with minimum cost? Expressed in the lan-

[56] R. Frisch: *op. cit.*, p. 144.
[57] H. Stackelberg: *Grundlagen der theoretischen Volkswirtschaftslehre*, Bern, 1948, p. 47.
[58] S. Carlson: *op. cit.*, p. 33.

guage of programming, we minimized factor inputs at a given value of the objective function.

$$Kp_K + Lp_L \text{ minimum}$$
$$Q = f(K, L) \text{ constant}$$
$$K \geqq 0, \ L \geqq 0.$$

The dual problem of programming can also be represented in the system of isoquants: what factor combination will ensure maximum output at given cost:

$$Q = f(K, L) \text{ maximum}$$
$$Kp_K + Lp_L \text{ constant}$$
$$K \geqq 0, \quad L \geqq 0.$$

The solution is similar to the first variant: by changing the labour–capital combination that he can afford with his given money capital, for example by decreasing the labour force and increasing the capital stock, the entrepreneur is able to step up his total output so long as a unit decrease in labour can be offset by increasing capital by a lesser quantity than he can hire at the existing levels of wages and interest with the savings resulting from the wages of dismissed labour, that is, until the marginal rate of substitution between factors equals their price ratio.

Let us now represent both programming problems graphically (Figures 24 and 25).

The limiting condition, i.e. that the entrepreneur can hire labour and capital at given factor prices only to the extent of the capital available to him in money form, is expressed, to use Ragnar Frisch's term, by the so-called *iso-cost line*. Its equation is: $Kp_K + Lp_L = c,$ where c is the amount of money capital available to the entrepreneur. The iso-cost line is the locus of those labour and capital combinations which can be bought for a constant total expenditure.[59] The iso-cost line corresponds in the system of isoquants to the budget line in the system of indifference curves. They are constructed in a similar way. The points of intersection of the iso-cost line on both axes signify that quantity of labour or capital that could be bought with the given money capital if the entrepreneur spent it on buying either labour or capital only. The slope of the iso-cost line expresses the given factor–price ratio.[60]

If the cost of a given quantity of output is to be minimized, the isoquant of that quantity is constructed, and then, with the slopes corresponding to the ratio of factor prices, the iso-cost lines are drawn, each expressing a definite level of total cost. Where the isoquant touches the lowest iso-cost line, the factor combination at the point of tangency will ensure the minimum cost of producing the output in question. If, however, with the available amount of money maximum output is to be achieved, the iso-cost line representing the amount of money in question is drawn in the system of isoquants, and the factor combination at the point of tangency of the iso-cost line and the highest isoquant will make it possible to produce maximum output at a given total cost.

[59] *Ibid.*
[60] S. Carlson: *op. cit.*, p. 35.

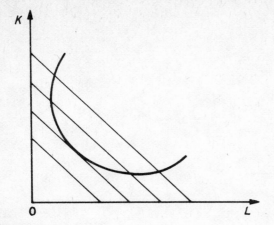

Figure 24

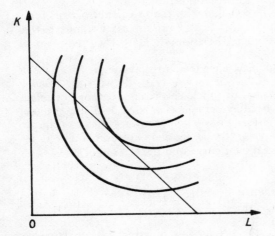

Figure 25

If we connect the factor combinations representing the minimum cost of producing, at established factor prices, different outputs as expressed in the isoquants, i.e., if we connect the points of tangency of the individual isoquants and iso-cost lines, we shall get, using Ragnar Frisch's terminology, the so-called *expansion curve or,* as it is now more commonly called, the *least-outlay curve* (Figure 26). It is this curve which expresses what factor combinations will produce given quantities of output at minimum cost.[61] The least-outlay curve corresponds to the income–consumption curve in the system of indifference curves.

[61] R. Frisch: *op. cit.*, pp. 149–150.

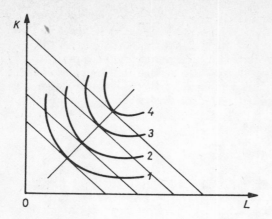

Figure 26

At given factor prices, the points of tangency of the different isoquants and iso-cost lines express an identical ratio of marginal productivities. Thus, at given factor prices, the least-outlay curve will coincide with the so-called *isocline curve*. The designation "isocline" curve stems from Ragnar Frisch, and it connects the points of the same slope of the isoquants, those points at which "the ratio of marginal productivities is constant."[62]

If competition is free from monopolistic elements, so that factor prices mean data for the entrepreneur, the least-outlay curve will coincide with the *isocline* curve. And if at the same time a change in the scale of output does not affect optimal capital–output ratio, the least-outlay curve is expressed by a straight line. In reality, "even with constant factor prices, optimal input proportions can change with the scale of output..."[63] In this case, the locus of factor combinations representing minimum outlay is expressed by a curve and not a straight line.

A few remarks on the isoquant system based on continuous substitution

1. In the simplified form used by us, the production function tries to reveal a functional relationship between the quantity of output Q and the factors K and L. Even at the given level of technical knowledge different relationships may exist between the given quantity of factors and output depending on the way the factors are organized. However, in the production function, at the existing state of technical knowledge, only one single quantity of output can be assigned to the given quantities of factors K and L, the output that can be produced if K and L are used in an optimal way. Such a function tacitly assumes that a certain *purely technical optimization* has already been carried out. This is also realized by Carlson

[62] R. Frisch: *op. cit.*, p. 78.
[63] R. I. Eckhaus: Notes on Invention and Innovation in the Less Developed Countries, *The American Economic Review*, May 1966, p. 99.

when he writes that "the output of an automobile factory, for instance, may vary for different organizations of the same workers and tools at the assembly line. If we want the production function to give only one value for the output from a given service combination, the function must be so defined that it expresses the maximum product obtainable from the combination at the existing stage of technical knowledge. Therefore, the purely technical maximization problem may be said to be solved by the very definition of our production function."[64]

Likewise, a previous technical optimization is also presupposed in that, from the factor combinations constituting our isoquant $Q = f(K, L)$ constant, the technically non-efficient methods have already been eliminated, those which can produce a given output either by using up a larger quantity of both factors, or more of one factor but not less of the other factor, than the efficient combinations lying along our isoquant. The thus eliminated, non-efficient factor combinations cannot be taken into account at any factor price. Thus, the traditional production function assumes that the greater part of the technical optimization problem has already been performed before the analysis begins. In reality, "... the choice of an optimal combination of production processes ... is no trivial task. It is, however, one which can be handled by the methods of mathematical programming", writes Baumol.[65]

2. A continuous isoquant presupposes that an infinite number of techniques are available to the entrepreneur, and if factor prices change, the technique used hitherto can easily be substituted, together with its capital stock, for another production technique with different capital goods attached to it. Both assumptions are far from being realistic. We have already criticized the assumption of the easy malleability of capital and have pointed out that activity analysis rejects the assumption that at the given state of technical knowledge entrepreneurs are free to choose among an infinite number of production methods.

3. The different capital goods attached to the various production techniques can be reduced to a common denominator in the system of isoquants only in price. In this case, however, the problem of "reswitching" will crop up: with the change in factor prices the price of capital goods will also change. But then the statement is no longer valid that at a given interest and wage rate only one single technique can be optimal, or that any capital–labour ratio can be the most economical only at one single combination of the interrelated interest and wage rate. It turns out that at certain factor prices not only one single production technique ensures minimum cost, but different, not equally economical production methods may involve the same amount of capital per man in terms of price of production and that with a change in distribution relations, the same production technique may become alternatively either profitable or unprofitable. Moreover, the construction of the isoquant itself also poses a further problem. The prices of capital goods (prices of production) required by the different production techniques depend on the magnitude of the incomes chosen. Determining the prices of capital goods at different incomes, we obtain different magnitudes for

[64] S. Carlson: *op. cit.*, pp. 14–15.
[65] W. J. Baumol: *Economic Theory and Operations Analysis*, Englewood Cliffs, N. J., 1965, p. 271.

the capital engaged in different production techniques. Thus the same technique will lie at different points of the plane. And with the change in capital-goods prices the marginal productivity of capital will vary even within the same production technique. Consequently, the ratio of marginal productivities and thus the slope of the isoquant will also change. This is what Harcourt also refers to when he writes: "... the value of the same physical capital and the slope of the iso-product curve vary with the rates [i.e. income rates—A.M.] ..."[66] Any change in the ratio of wages and interest will change the slope of the isoquant. We can now see that, contrary to the teaching of marginal productivity theory, it is the change in distribution relations that causes the ratio of marginal productivities to change, not the change in the ratio of marginal productivities that gives rise to a change in distribution relation. "The derivation of factor prices", writes Riese, "presupposes the determination of capital; but any determination of capital is possible only when factor prices have already been determined..."[67] On the other hand, the question arises how the isoquant system can be used for optimization when the procedure is based exactly on changing the ratio of factor prices in order to find that point of the given isoquant at which the slope of the curve just equals the ratio of factor prices.

It appears that the isoquant system can be applied for this purpose only in the existing pattern of distribution, and can provide an answer to the question which technique is optimal at prevailing factor prices provided the existing distribution relations do not involve any switch points.

4. As has already been mentioned, marginal productivity theory holds that the employment of any factor must be expanded up to the margin at which marginal profit equals zero, when capital and labour meet the following conditions:

$$MP_K \cdot p = p_K$$
$$MP_L \cdot p = p_L.$$

This requirement assumes that the necessary quantities of capital and labour are available. If, however—and such a situation may develop particularly in the short run—,the quantity of any of the available factors is limited, production must be stopped before the profit rate reaches zero. In this case the traditional means of marginal analysis can no longer be applied. Under such circumstances a new tool of analysis, activity analysis, is needed for the solution of the optimization problem. Economists using marginal analysis regarded the existence of limiting factors as irrelevant from the point of view of the problem to be solved. Though in his work *Theory of Production* published in 1934, Schneider makes mention of the existence of limiting factors, he still sees the economic problems as being soluble through combining continuously substitutable factors. Activity analysis, however, directs attention exactly to the limiting factors available in given quantities, as it is they that determine what the entrepreneur can and cannot do.

5. Kaldor calls attention to the fact that in the case of the scale effect the optimal capital–labour ratio can change with the scale of output independently of changes

[66] G. C. Harcourt: Some Cambridge Controversies in the Theory of Capital, *The Journal of Economic Literature*, June 1969, p. 371.

[67] H. Riese: Das Ende einer Wachstumstheorie, *Kyklos*, 1970, Fasc. 4, p. 765.

in factor price proportions. "... the choice among activities becomes primarily a matter not of price but of the scale of production,"[68] says Kaldor, regarding production with increasing return as typical in modern industry.

The elasticity of substitution and the capital-intensity function

The slope of the isoquant expresses the marginal rate of substitution. With a change in the isoquant slope, i.e. the marginal rate of substitution, factor proportions will also change. The relationship between the change of the marginal rate of substitution and the concomitant change of factor proportions is expressed *by the elasticity of substitution*. It shows by what percentage factor proportions will change as a result of the percentage change in the ratio of marginal productivities, that is in the marginal rate of substitution. The elasticity of substitution was first defined by Hicks in his work *The Theory of Wages,* emphasizing that "the elasticity of substitution is a measure of the ease with which the varying factor can be substituted for others."[69] The elasticity of substitution, as Mrs. Robinson points out, is determined by the technical conditions of production, and it is, in her view, the assertion of the principle of diminishing returns which indicates that there is a limit to the extent to which one factor can be substituted for the other.[70]

A. P. Lerner sought[71] to define the elasticity of substitution graphically in the

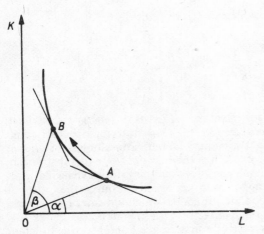

Figure 27

[68] N. Kaldor: The Irrelevance of Equilibrium Economics, *The Economic Journal*, December 1972, p. 1255.
[69] J. R. Hicks: *The Theory of Wages,* New York, 1948, p. 117.
[70] J. Robinson: *The Theory of Imperfect Competition,* London, 1956, p. 330.
[71] A. P. Lerner: Notes on Elasticity and Substitution, II, *The Review of Economic Studies I,* 1933, pp. 68–71.

following way: since capital–labour ratio at a point A on the isoquant curve is indicated by the slope of the line connecting that point with the origin, the elasticity of substitution is the ratio of the relative change of this slope to the relative change of the slope of the tangent drawn to the isoquant at the point in question as we move along the curve setting out from point A (Figure 27).

The inverse of the elasticity of substitution is the elasticity of marginal productivity which expresses by what percentage the ratio of their marginal productivities will change with the percentage change in the proportion between factors.

The elasticity of substitution is:

$$\sigma = \frac{d\left(\dfrac{K}{L}\right)}{\dfrac{K}{L}} : \frac{d\left(\dfrac{dK}{dL}\right)}{\dfrac{dK}{dL}}.$$

In the place of the marginal rate of substitution we can also write the ratio of marginal productivities, or the ratio of factor prices. Then we obtain:

$$\sigma = \frac{d\left(\dfrac{K}{L}\right)}{\dfrac{K}{L}} : \frac{d\left(\dfrac{p_L}{p_K}\right)}{\dfrac{p_L}{p_K}}.$$

Or representing the relationship in question logarithmically:

$$\sigma = \frac{d\left(\log \dfrac{K}{L}\right)}{d\left(\log \dfrac{dK}{dL}\right)} = \frac{d\left(\log \dfrac{K}{L}\right)}{d\left(\log \dfrac{p_L}{p_K}\right)}.$$

It is from the isoquant that the so-called *capital-intensity function* is derived. The assumption is that competition ensures that the rewards to factors correspond to their marginal productivities. Since the capital–labour ratio along the isoquant changes according to the slope of the curve, i.e. the marginal rate of substitution, and the marginal rate of substitution is determined by the ratio of marginal productivities, which, according to non-Marxian economics, equals the ratio of factor prices, they derive from the isoquant a function which indicates how capital per man changes with the change in relative factor prices (Figure 28).

The elasticity of substitution in the case of a first-degree homogeneous function varies only with a change in the ratio between factors. In this case, however, though the elasticity of substitution refers to the given isoquant, if we change from a point on one isoquant representing a certain capital–labour ratio to a point on another isoquant representing another capital–labour ratio, the elasticity of substitution will change in the same way as if we had moved along the original isoquant to the point representing the second capital–labour ratio. In other words, in moving from point A to point D in Figure 29, we find that the elasticity of substitution develops in the same way as if we had moved from point A to point

158

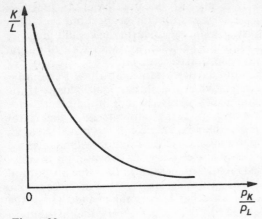

Figure 28

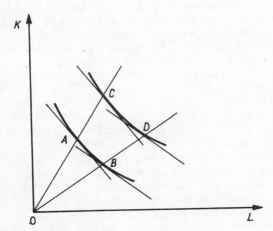

Figure 29

B: the tangents at B and D are parallel. Therefore, the capital-intensity function derived from the isoquant representative of the first-degree homogeneous production function is independent of the scale of output. It shows, independently of the scale of output, how the ratio of factors changes with the change of relative factor prices.

In the case of the scale effect, however, capital-labour ratio may change even at given factor prices with a change in the scale of output. In this case the effect of the change in relative factor prices on the ratio between factors cannot be derived

159

independently of the scale of output by means of the capital-intensity function. With a change in the scale of output the change in factor proportions will differ from that prescribed by the change in relative factor prices in the capital-intensity function set up for the earlier scale of output. Therefore, for every scale of output a different capital-intensity function must be constructed.

By the concept of elasticity of substitution Hicks wanted to show how an increase in the supply of a factor affects relative shares in national income. If the supply of a factor increases, its price diminishes relative to that of the other factor (or factors). If the elasticity of substitution is > 1, the employment of this factor increases relative to the others by more than its relative price has decreased. Therefore, its share in national income will increase. The situation will be reversed when the elasticity of substitution is < 1. If the elasticity of substitution is unity, the relative employment of the expanded factor will increase in the same proportion as its relative price diminishes, or in Hicks's formulation: "... the increase in one factor will raise the marginal product of all other factors taken together in the same proportion as the total product is raised."[72] In other words, the distribution relations will not change.

In moving along the isoquant, the elasticity of substitution will assume different values. The isoquant has a point at which $\sigma = 1$. In general, the less the tangency gradient of the isoquant, that is, the flatter the curve, the smaller the marginal rate of substitution for the isoquant, and the greater the elasticity of substitution.

The elasticity of substitution, assuming the production function to be first-degree homogeneous, is symmetrical for both (all) factors independently of the scale of output. The elasticity of substitution of capital for labour is the same as the elasticity of substitution of labour for capital. Allen also demonstrates this mathematically.[73] The symmetrical character of the elasticity of substitution was already emphasized by Hicks.[74]

This symmetry, however, does not exist if the scale effect changes optimal capital–labour ratio. In this case, the elasticity of substitution also contains the effect of the increase in the scale of output. And since the scale effect may change the optimal factor combination, the elasticity of substitution may be different depending on whether the capital stock or the labour force is increased.

Non-Marxian economics makes not only changes in income distribution but also in production elasticities dependent on the values of the elasticity of substitution. Assuming an increasing capital–labour ratio at σ being greater than unity, the production elasticity of capital will increase and that of labour will decrease. The situation is just the reverse if σ is less than unity. If $\sigma = 1$, production elasticities will not change as capital–labour ratio changes.

1. In appraising the concept of substitution elasticity, we must point out that it expresses merely a technical relationship showing how factor proportions change with the proportions of wage and the rate of interest. Theoretically, it could be used in any theory of income distribution, hence it does not explain in itself the development of distribution relations.

[72] J. R. Hicks: *op. cit.*, p. 117.
[73] R. G. D. Allen: *Mathematical Analysis for Economists*, London, 1966, p. 342.
[74] J. R. Hicks: *op. cit.*, p. 119.

2. In non-Marxian economics it was Keynes who called attention to the fact that on the macro-level the substitution effect of a relative change in money wages is highly uncertain. Hence, the value of σ could explain at best, on the micro-level in what proportion factors are combined by the entrepreneurs as factor prices change. To be more exact, it would not provide any explanation even on the micro-level if optimal factor combination is a function not primarily of relative factor prices but of the scale of output.

3. The derivation of the elasticity of substitution from isoquants is made questionable by the "reswitching" effect, the already mentioned circumstance that with a change in relative factor prices the slope of the isoquant also changes. Valuation of capital per man in terms of price of production makes it absolutely necessary that, with a continuous percentage increase in the interest rate relative to wages, capital per man should continously decrease. As we have seen, in the case of "switch points" at given relative factor prices, any production technique using greater or lesser capital equipment per man valued at production prices may be equally economical.

Leontief's production function

The isoquant curve so far discussed was based on continuous substitution between factors. Let us now examine the shape of the isoquant when the proportion between factors within a given production technique is rigid. This type of production function is called a Leontief production function because in his input–output tables Leontief also assumed such rigid technical coefficients. As we have seen, Walras also worked with rigid technical coefficients in the first version of his general equilibrium theory, and so did Cassel in his revised version of the Walrasian model. Activity analysis as elaborated by Koopmans also regards the assumption of rigid factor proportions within a given production technique as a method which better approaches the production conditions of modern industry. Allen also mentions that "... a construction designed to be used with statistical data, in aiding firms to reach their decisions in full knowledge of the position, would clearly be based appropriately on the alternative analysis in terms of a technology matrix."[75]

While the isoquant curve based on continuous substitution assumes that an infinite number of production techniques are available to the entrepreneur, according to activity analysis he is free to choose only among a finite number of production techniques.

Let us assume that to produce a given product the entrepreneur has four production techniques at his disposal, each of which uses capital and labour in different proportions. Signifying the number of production technique with the first, and the factor with the second index, we can write the technical coefficients of the four production techniques as follows:

$$a_{1K} \quad a_{2K} \quad a_{3K} \quad a_{4K}$$
$$a_{1L} \quad a_{2L} \quad a_{3L} \quad a_{4L}.$$

[75] R. G. D. Allen: *Mathematical Economics*, London, 1965, p. 341.

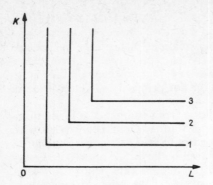

Figure 30

Now we can characterize each production technique by means of a rigid capital and labour coefficient. If the entrepreneur wishes to produce quantity Q of a given product, then, assuming constant returns to scale, the production function can be written as follows:

$$K_1 = Qa_{1K}; \quad K_2 = Qa_{2K}; \quad K_3 = Qa_{3K}; \quad K_4 = Qa_{4K},$$
$$L_1 = Qa_{1L}; \quad L_2 = Qa_{2L}; \quad L_3 = Qa_{3L}; \quad L_4 = Qa_{4L},$$

where K_1, K_2, etc., or L_1, L_2, etc. represent the quantities of capital and labour used up for producing quantity Q of the product in the different production techniques.

Let us first look at one technique.

Solow gave for this case the following formula of the production function:[76]

$$Q = \min\left(\frac{K}{a_{1K}}, \frac{L}{a_{1L}}\right),$$

where a_{1K} and a_{1L} are the capital and labour coefficients respectively, and the designation "minimum" means that with a rigid capital–labour ratio it is always the so-called *limiting factor* constituting the bottleneck that determines the volume of possible output. If, for example, $a_{1K} = 10$ and $a_{1L} = 2$, then the capital–labour ratio is 5:1. In this case, if 200 workers and 800 units of capital are available to the entrepreneur, it is capital that is the limiting factor, and the output that can be produced is 80 units, whereas the available labour force appropriately equipped with capital would make it possible to produce 100 units of output.

Let us represent graphically the isoquant system assuming a rigid capital–labour ratio (Figure 30).

The pairs of lines drawn at right angles to one another express that, irrespective of the increase in the number of workers at a given capital stock, or in capital stock at a given number of workers, output will not change. The apexes signify those combinations of capital and labour at which the available factors are entirely used up.

[76] R. M. Solow: A Contribution to the Theory of Economic Growth, *The Quarterly Journal of Economics,* February 1956, p. 73.

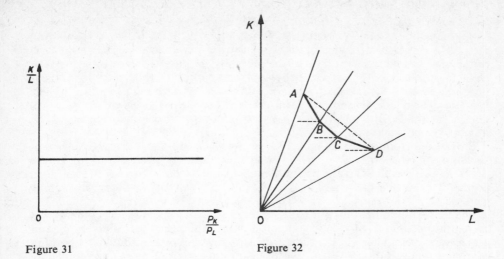

Figure 31   Figure 32

The marginal productivities of both factors at the apex are 0. If, however, there is an excess supply of one factor, then it is the factor representing the bottleneck that has a positive marginal productivity. If its quantity is increased, total output can also be increased.

With Leontief's production function the elasticity of substitution is 0, and the form of the capital intensity function is the following (Figure 31):

Taking now into consideration all the four production methods, we can represent them graphically by four rays from the origin, the slope of each of them expressing the ratio of technical coefficients. Is there any possibility of substitution between factors if several production methods are available to the entrepreneur? Yes, there is, and in such a way that he either changes over from one method to the other, or combines the two. Connecting with a line the neighbouring techniques from among the factor combinations available to produce the same output, we obtain, instead of a continuous curve, an isoquant convex to the origin which comprises four points joined by straight lines (Figure 32).

As shown by Figure 32, any output can be produced by an infinite number of combinations of the production methods. Technically, however, it is only neighbouring production methods that are worth combining. This analysis no longer presupposes that the technically non-efficient methods have already been eliminated before the economist begins to deal with the production function. It is the economist himself who leaves out of his calculations the technically non-efficient methods. Non-Marxian economics tries to determine these methods on the basis of the so-called *Pareto-optimum criterion*. Those methods are non-efficient which, for the production of a given output, use up either larger quantities of both factors than an efficient method, or more of one, and no less of the other factor (or factors). These non-efficient methods lie on the lines connecting any two non-neighbouring methods. With the removal of the non-efficient methods the efficient ones will lie along the non-continuous line-sections convex to the origin.

As has already been mentioned, substitution between factors is also possible in the case of Leontief's production function. In combining two neighbouring methods to produce a certain output, we can always continuously decrease the level of the one, and increase the level of the other, by an appropriate quantity without changing the volume of output. If by applying the first method the entrepreneur produces at level λ_1, he must produce by the second method at level λ_2, where $\lambda_1 + \lambda_2 = Q$. Substitution in this case means changing the levels of the two production methods. But substitution between factors is not continuous everywhere, it is broken at the apexes.

Proceeding from one method to another, we shall find that the marginal rate of substitution between factors again shows a diminishing tendency owing to the isoquant being convex to the origin. And, as we have already seen, the marginal productivity of that factor will also decrease whose quantity has been unilaterally increased.

The factor combination representing minimum cost, or the factor combination making it possible to produce maximum output at a given cost, is determined in graphical representation in the same way as in the case of the isoquant supposing continuous substitution. Also to the isoquant consisting of non-continuous line-sections, an iso-cost line must be drawn as a tangent.

If, however, only one tangent can be drawn to one point on the isoquant, then any change in factor prices will change the optimal combination of factors. But to one apex of such an isoquant an infinite number of tangents can be drawn, so that the factor combinations represented at the apexes may be equally optimal at different factor price ratios. Thus, the optimal factor combination is not sensitive to factor-price changes within a certain limit determined by the angle of two neighbouring segments. If, however, the iso-cost line coincides with a whole segment of the isoquant, several methods may equally be optimal at established factor prices.

In non-Marxian economics it is a generally accepted view that both the production function supposing continuous substitution and Leontief's production function are equally extremes, though Leontief's production function better approaches reality. As a matter of fact, a production function with a certain substitution between factors, even within a given production method, is closest to reality.

The "reswitching" problem also arises with the isoquant consisting of non-continuous line-sections. We have pointed out that at certain factor prices the iso-cost line touches an isoquant at the apex, and it is only the factor ratio corresponding to the point of tangency that ensures minimum cost. But, with the inclusion of the "reswitching" problem it is possible even in that case that at an unchanged factor-price ratio a different capital–labour combination is equally economical; or conversely, the point of tangency expresses unequally economical production methods which, however, use the same amount of capital per man in terms of price of production. The "reswitching" problem also makes it questionable to construct the isoquant consisting of non-continuous line-sections, because a change in factor prices alters the price of capital goods, i.e., the slope of the isoquant changes.

The isoquant in the case of perfect substitution between factors

In this case, the isoquant assumes the following form (Figure 33):

The marginal rate of substitution is constant: whatever the capital–labour ratio, one unit of capital is always substituted for by the same amount of labour, and *vice versa*.

In this case, the elasticity of substitution is infinite, and the capital-intensity function assumes the form represented in Figure 34.

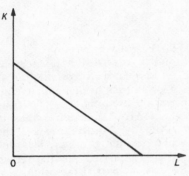

Figure 33

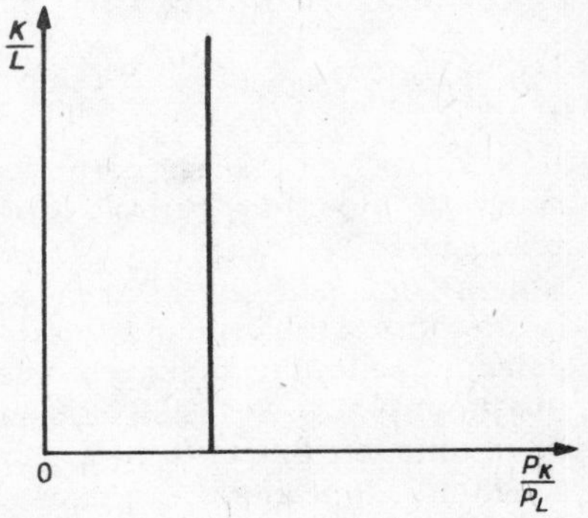

Figure 34

THE COST FUNCTION

General characteristics

Through the isoquant the non-Marxian economics wishes to answer the question of how to combine factors at their given prices for the cost of production to be minimal. If the production function is homogeneous and linear, then the minimum-cost factor combination thus determined is independent of the scale of output. In so far as the production function is not first-degree homogeneous, it only applies to a definite output level.

In constructing the supply curve, non-Marxian economics further tries to reveal the relationship between production and costs, the way costs depend on the scale of output. "After this discussion of minimum cost combinations," writes Carlson, "we may proceed to an examination of the relationship between costs and outputs."[77] And if the system of isoquant curves can be constructed, then the cost function, too, can be derived from it.

The construction of the cost function is due to several authors, but the summary of the results attained and their fitting into the theory of production were primarily the achievements of Frisch, Schneider and Carlson in the 1930s.

[77] S. Carlson: *op. cit.*, p. 41.

Different types of cost functions can be distinguished, depending on the types of production functions they are based on. In the 1930s, these authors regarded the production function resting on continuous but limited substitution as typical in the construction of the cost function.

Following Marshall, economists make a distinction between *short- and long-run cost functions*.

Let us first examine the characteristics of the short-run cost function.

Short-run cost function in the case of continuous substitution

Introductory remarks

In constructing the short-run cost function, Marshall regarded appliances as *constant*. "For short periods people take the stock of appliances for production as practically fixed; and they are governed by their expectations of demand in considering how actively they shall set themselves to work those appliances."[78] Time is too short to make changes in their quantity. Production tries to match increasing demand with the already available equipment. Already Marshall raised the question of how costs change under the conditions of expanding output. The type of production function by which the problem was first analysed was the return function, supposing continuous substitution in the case of partial factor change.

Following Marshall, non-Marxian economics distinguishes two basic types of costs: fixed (constant) and variable costs (Marshall called them "overhead" and "prime costs".) This distinction should not be confused with the Marxian division of capital into constant and variable capital. In non-Marxian economics constant costs include those types of costs which are, in the period under consideration, independent of the volume of output. Variable costs, however, change with the volume of output. Stackelberg emphasizes that time is of crucial importance in distinguishing the two types of costs. "... the longer the period we choose as a basis for our investigation, the smaller the part of total expenditure which should be regarded as constant cost."[79] And conversely, the shorter the period covered by our investigation, the larger the part of total costs which should be considered as fixed. The wages of a worker entitled to two weeks' notice count as fixed costs for a period shorter than two weeks, because even if he is dismissed, his wages must be paid for the two weeks.

This distinction between costs has long been used by business management. Then, with the construction of the supply curve, it has since been applied by non-Marxian economics, too. By making this distinction, non-Marxian economics raises interesting problems. In his famous work *The Economics of Overhead Costs* J. M. Clark points out that the great weight of "overhead" costs prevents the law of value from asserting itself, making it difficult for the economy to recover from a crisis. This is because, owing to the decline in demand, entrepreneurs ought to diminish their outputs in compliance with the law of value. But this would result

[78] A. Marshall: *Principles of Economics*, London, 1930, p. 374.
[79] H. Stackelberg: *Grundlagen einer reinen Kostentheorie*, Vienna, 1932, p. 35.

166

in an increase in fixed costs per unit of output, the growth of cost per unit of product, at a time when entrepreneurs are faced with serious marketing difficulties. Thus, they are likely not to reduce their outputs, but rather to produce for warehousing, being confident that the depression will sooner or later come to an end. But by behaving like that, they will call forth just the opposite effect, because escaping from a crisis presupposes the absorption of surplus inventories. But the law of value will clearly assert itself in spite of the behaviour of entrepreneurs not wishing to contract their production. Some of them will go bankrupt, and output will adapt itself to the contracted demand.

Let us isolate one more of the problems related to the division of costs into fixed and variable costs: how it promotes price discrimination and thereby causes competition to sharpen.

If an entrepreneur, when charging costs plus profit, can fully cover his fixed costs by producing and realizing a quantity Q of output, then, if he further increases his output by quantity ΔQ, he only has to make efforts to realize the variable costs and the corresponding profit. Thus, he can offer for sale the quantity ΔQ at a price excluding fixed costs. And he will make use of this possibility to penetrate the markets of his domestic or foreign competitors, and conquer these markets for his own products.

In the system of cost functions, non-Marxian economics demonstrates the dependence of costs on the volume of output by types of costs. It then illustrates these functions by means of cost curves.

The dependence of average fixed cost per unit of product on the volume of output

As regards the change in fixed costs per unit of output, $Qc_f = C_f$ constant, where c_f is fixed cost per unit of output and C_f the given total fixed cost.

It is obvious that the fixed cost per unit of output will diminish in the course of expanding production by the same percentage as the volume of output increases.[80] The elasticity of the function expressing its change is unity, and is graphically illustrated by a rectangular hyperbola. It was Schneider who, in his work *The Theory of Production*, first called the relationship between the different cost types and the percentage change in production *cost elasticity*.

The dependence of total variable cost on the volume of output

The function expressing the dependence of total variable cost on the volume of output, as pointed out by Schneider, is the inverse of the total-output function constructed under conditions of partial factor change. As total output, owing to the unilateral increase in the individual factor input, rises at a growing rate up to the point of inflexion, then at a constant and finally at a diminishing rate, in the same

---

[80] For an early exposition see J. Viner: Cost Curves, (*Zeitschrift für Nationalökonomie*, 1931, Vol. III). Reprinted in *Readings in Price Theory*, Chicago, 1952, p. 203.

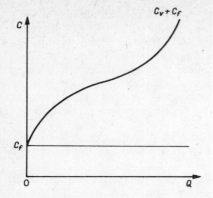

Figure 35

way, the total cost of variable factors rises at a diminishing rate up to the point of inflexion, then at a constant and finally at a growing rate (see Figure 35).

Schneider defines the elasticity of total variable cost in the following way[81]

$$\check{C}_v = \frac{dC_v}{C_v} : \frac{dQ}{Q},$$

where C_v is the total cost of the variable factors. If we regard labour as the only variable factor, C_v will equal total wage cost, Lp_L. In this case, $\check{C}_v$ is clearly the reciprocal of the production elasticity of labour, $\frac{1}{\varepsilon_L}$.

Expressed as the quotient of the marginal and average magnitudes:

$$\check{C}_v = \frac{dC_v}{dQ} : \frac{C_v}{Q},$$

that is, marginal cost divided by average variable cost. Hence average variable cost

$$\frac{C_v}{Q} = \varepsilon_L \cdot \frac{dC_v}{dQ}.$$

Marginal cost;

$$\frac{dC_v}{dQ} = \frac{C_v}{Q} / \varepsilon_L,$$

and total variable cost $= Q \cdot \varepsilon_L \cdot \dfrac{dC_v}{dQ}$.

[81] For more detail see E. Schneider: *Theorie der Produktion,* Vienna, 1934, p. 39.

168

We can now show, following Schneider[82] and Carlson[83] respectively, changes in the elasticity of total variable cost in respect to production, and the interrelationship between marginal and average productivity or between marginal and average variable cost, by stages:

when $\varepsilon_L > 1$, $\dfrac{1}{\varepsilon_L} < 1$, marginal product > average product, marginal cost < average variable cost;

when $\varepsilon_L = 1$, $\dfrac{1}{\varepsilon_L} = 1$, marginal product = average product, marginal cost = average variable cost;

when $\varepsilon_L < 1$, $\dfrac{1}{\varepsilon_L} > 1$, marginal product < average product, marginal cost > average variable cost.

The dependence of average variable cost on the volume of output[84]

The elasticity of average variable cost expresses the relationship between the percentage change in average variable cost and the percentage change in output:

$$\frac{dc_v}{c_v} : \frac{dQ}{Q},$$

where c_v is the average variable cost: $\dfrac{C_v}{Q}$.

The elasticity of the average variable cost

$$EL \cdot \frac{C_v}{Q} = EL \cdot C_v - EL \cdot Q = \frac{1}{\varepsilon_i} - 1,$$

where ε_i is the production elasticity of the group of variable factors if, in addition to labour, other variable factors are also included.

Representing the change in the elasticity of average variable cost by stages

when $\varepsilon_i > 1$, $\dfrac{1}{\varepsilon_i} - 1 < 0$, that is, average variable cost decreases as output increases,

when $\varepsilon_i = 1$, $\dfrac{1}{\varepsilon_i} - 1 = 0$, that is, at the technical optimum, average variable cost is not affected by a change in output,

when $\varepsilon_i < 1$, $\dfrac{1}{\varepsilon_i} - 1 > 0$, that is, average variable cost rises as output increases.

It will reach its minimum clearly at the technical optimum, where it equals marginal cost.

[82] E. Schneider: *op. cit.*, pp. 44–45.
[83] S. Carlson: *op. cit.*, p. 47.
[84] Cf. E. Schneider: *op. cit.*, p. 46; and S. Carlson: *op. cit.*, p. 47.

The elasticity of marginal cost expresses the relationship between the percentage change in marginal cost and the percentage change in the volume of output

$$MC = \frac{c_v}{\varepsilon_i}, \ M\check{C} = EL \cdot \frac{c_v}{\varepsilon_i} = EL \cdot c_v - EL \cdot \varepsilon_i = \frac{1}{\varepsilon_i} - 1 - \check{\varepsilon}_i,$$

where ε_i is the elasticity according to Q of the elasticity of production.

As output increases, marginal cost will decrease as long as total variable cost rises at a diminishing rate. Then its elasticity is negative. This presupposes that ε_i is larger than $\frac{1}{\varepsilon_i} - 1$. As long as $\check{\varepsilon}_i$ is a positive magnitude, marginal cost will decline at a greater rate than average variable cost, because $\check{\varepsilon}_i$ has still to be deducted from $\frac{1}{\varepsilon_i} - 1$, and thus we obtain a greater elasticity in absolute terms than the elasticity of average variable cost. Marginal cost will also decrease as output increases even if $\check{\varepsilon}_i$ is already a negative magnitude, but it is of a greater number and thus is smaller in absolute terms than the equally negative $\frac{1}{\varepsilon_i} - 1$. In this case, however, the elasticity of marginal cost is smaller in absolute terms than the elasticity of average variable cost, $\frac{1}{\varepsilon_i} - 1$ is larger in absolute terms than

$$\frac{1}{\varepsilon_i} - 1 - [-\check{\varepsilon}_i] = \frac{1}{\varepsilon_i} - 1 + \check{\varepsilon}_i.$$

Marginal cost reaches its minimum at the point of inflexion. Here its elasticity is 0, and thus $\check{\varepsilon}_i = \frac{1}{\varepsilon_i} - 1$. Beyond the point of inflexion marginal cost will already rise, the value of ε_i is negative and exceeds $\frac{1}{\varepsilon_i} - 1$ in absolute terms, and thus $\frac{1}{\varepsilon_i} - 1 - [-\check{\varepsilon}_i] = \frac{1}{\varepsilon_i} - 1 + \check{\varepsilon}_i$ already yields a positive value, though average variable cost still decreases up to the technical optimum, i.e. $\frac{1}{\varepsilon_i} - 1$ is still of a negative value.[86]

The dependence of average total cost on the volume of output

Let us examine the dependence of total average cost on the volume of output. Total average cost is composed of two elements: average variable cost and average

---

[85] Cf. S. Carlson: *op. cit.*, p. 46.
[86] S. Carlson: *op. cit.*, p. 47.

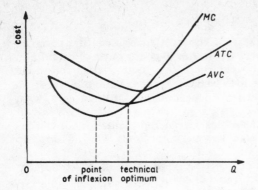

Figure 36

fixed cost. As output increases, average variable cost first decreases, then increases, and average fixed cost decreases throughout. Accordingly, as output increases, average total cost also first decreases, then increases, but it reaches its minimum later than average variable cost: average variable cost already rises while average total cost still falls. The effect of the rise in average variable cost on average total cost is still exceeded for a while by the effect of the fall in average fixed cost, but soon the effect of average variable cost prevails, and average total cost will also rise. It reaches its minimum when the curve representing it cuts the marginal cost curve.

Let us represent graphically the average variable, marginal and average total cost curves (Figure 36).

The question arises: do the three short-run cost functions mentioned above really assume a U-shaped form?

As the question is closely related to the practice of business management, let us turn for an answer to Gutenberg, the well-known German expert in business administration. In some of the cases analysed by him the cost function really proved to be U-shaped. Thus, for example, in the case of internal combustion engines fuel consumption rises first at a diminishing, then at a rising rate, as the revolutions per minute increase. A similar relationship can be found, according to Gutenberg, between the horse-power performance and electric power consumption of electrical engines. In blast furnaces, coke consumption per one ton of crude iron decreases for some time as the output of pig iron increases but, after reaching an optimum point, it begins to rise. In other cases, however, the cost function did not prove to be U-shaped. Relying on the findings of a committee headed by Mason, Gutenberg comes to the conclusion that the thesis "which interprets diminishing costs as a consequence of the improvement in the ratio between factors, and increasing marginal costs as a consequence of the deterioration in the ratio between factors, cannot necessarily be regarded as typical or representative of industrial production."[87]

[87] E. Gutenberg: *Grundlagen der Betriebswirtschaftslehre*, Vol. I, Berlin–Heidelberg–New-York, 1966, p. 381.

Long-run cost function

The production function underlying the long-run cost function is the so-called return to scale. Since all factors are variable in the long run, average total and average variable costs coincide. As output increases, total average cost will decrease up to the optimum size of the firm where it reaches its minimum. If, in increasing output, the size of firm is expanded beyond the optimum size, total average cost will rise (see Figure 37).

Many non-Marxian textbooks of economics give a representation of the relationship between long- and short-run total average cost curves. This relationship is based on the following:

Equipment changes in the long run. If we take various levels of equipment and construct a short-run average total cost curve for each, then the long-run average total cost curve will touch the short-term average total cost curves at

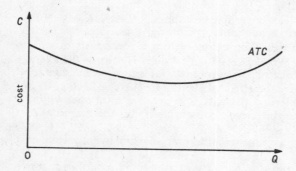

Figure 37

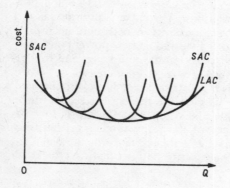

Figure 38

172

certain points, as if giving them a sort of envelope (see Figure 38). Hence the name: *envelope curve*. The long-run average total cost curve touches the short-run average total cost curves up to its minimum point, i.e., up to the optimum size of firm, along their downward sloping parts, while, beyond that optimum size,

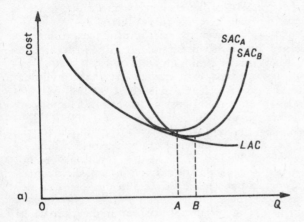

Figure 39 a

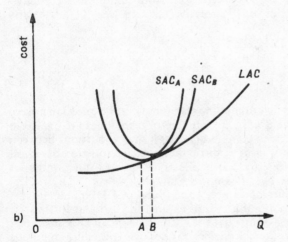

Figure 39 b

the points of tangency will lie along their upward sloping parts. It is only at optimum plant size that the point of tangency on both the short- and long-run average total cost curves represents the point of minimum cost.

This leads to the following conclusions for the behaviour of the firm. Suppose

173

that a given output, A, is to be produced, which is less than the long-run optimum level of output, as in Figure 39a. Then average total cost will not be minimized by operating with equipment of capacity A at the minimum point of its short-run average total cost curve SAC_A, but by expanding all factors, and thus the size of the firm, and operating at less than full capacity, above the minimum point of the new short-run average total cost curve SAC_B. The reason is clear: with *all* factors being expanded, average total cost declines faster as output increases.

Beyond the optimum size of the firm, however, in order to produce a given output, B (see Figure 39b), the average total cost will be smaller if the firm operates equipment of optimum capacity A beyond the minimum point of its short-run average total cost curve SAC_A, than if it operated with capacity B at the minimum point of its short-run average total cost curve SAC_B. Clearly, once the optimum size of the firm has been exceeded, average total cost increases if all factors are expanded to less advantageous levels.

In connection with the long-run cost function we only wish to point out for the time being that it is designed to reveal the dependence of costs on the volume of output at a given level of technical knowledge. Thus the cost function does not take into account that the cost structure depends not only on present-day technology and factor prices; capital stock assumed to be variable in the long run also contains a whole range of plants of various vintages, each vintage reflecting the level of technological development and factor prices existing at the time of its birth. "This brings out the general irrelevance of the traditional long-run average cost curve for a whole industry. Such a curve shows what costs would be at various alternative levels of output if the industry were built from scratch using to-day's technology and minimizing costs at today's relative factor prices. This is clearly irrelevant in most cases."[88]

Cost function based on
Leontief's production function

In the attempts at the practical application of the cost function, the question arises: What will the cost function be like if a limited number of techniques are available to the entrepreneur to produce a given commodity, and if the proportions between factors are rigid. This assumption is more realistic than the cost function based on continuous substitution between factors. Let us illustrate the cost function based on Leontief's production function by a numerical example.

Let an entrepreneur have 110 units of capital and 40 units of labour available, with 5 dollars as a reward for the use of a unit of capital and 1 dollar for the use of a unit of labour. Let us further assume that the entrepreneur can choose among four production methods. The technical coefficients for the individual methods will be the following:

[88] R. Turvey: Marginal Cost, *The Economic Journal,* June 1969, pp. 285–286.

Production methods	a_L	a_K	Cost per unit of output by production methods
I	1	10	51 dollars
II	2	9	47 dollars
III	4	8	44 dollars
IV	8	7	43 dollars

The entrepreneur begins to produce by applying the cheapest process, method IV. In this method, labour is the limiting factor. Only 5 units of output can be produced. Average total cost is 43, and so is the increment in cost, marginal cost, if output is increased by 1 unit. For producing 5 units of output the entrepreneur applying method IV will engage 40 units of labour and 35 units of capital. 75 units of his capital stock will remain unutilized. The entrepreneur would like further to expand his output. This is possible if he combines the cheapest production method, method IV, with method III. In method III, too, labour is the limiting factor, and only 10 units of output can be turned out by using this method. The entrepreneur will further raise his production from 5 units by decreasing by one unit the output produced by method IV, and releases thereby 8 units of labour and 7 units of capital. With the labour thus released as a limiting factor, 2 units of output can be produced by method III. Total cost will increase by 88 units, but will also decrease at the same time by 43 units, and thus with producing the 6th unit, the increment in total cost will be 45. If he wishes still further to expand his output, the entrepreneur will decrease by 1 more unit the output produced by method IV. Applying method III, he can increase production up to 10 units, the marginal cost of producing each unit being 45. Output can further be expanded upwards of 10 units if the entrepreneur combines method III with method II. In the case of method II it is now capital that is the limiting factor, with $12\frac{2}{9}$ units constituting the maximum of output. Let us diminish by 1 unit the output that can be produced by method III. Thus, 8 units of capital and 4 units of labour will be released. By using method II, 2 more units of output can be produced by the factors thus released and those still available. As a result of producing two additional units of output, total cost increases by 94, but decreases at the same time by 44, as the output produced by method III is decreased by 1 unit. Thus the incremental cost of producing the 11th unit is $94 - 44 = 50$. By further decreasing the output produced by method III, he will produce only 8 units by it, while by engaging the factors thus released 4 units will be turned out by method II. The amount of capital employed is $64 + 36 = 100$, and the amount of labour used is $32 + 8 = 40$. There are still 10 units of capital not engaged. By further decreasing by one unit the output produced by method III, two additional units can be produced by method II. Total output is 13 units, 7 produced by applying method III, and 6 units produced by using method II. Thus, by combining the two methods, a larger output can be produced using the same factors than could have been produced by applying methods III or II separately. By combining two methods with different limiting factors in each of them, output can be increased.

Our example reveals that even if we apply the cost function based on Leontief's production function, marginal cost will grow as the volume of output increases.

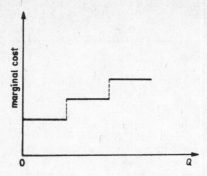

Figure 40

The increase is due to the fact that if the proportion between the available capital stock and the labour force does not correspond to the capital–labour ratio in the cheapest production method, then the fullest possible utilization of the available factors and through it the expansion of output also requires the adoption of more expensive techniques, which, in the course of increasing production, will lead to a rise in marginal cost. Therefore, marginal cost, just as in the case of the cost function based on continuous substitution, will increase. But this increase is not continuous. With a given method, marginal cost is constant, but if the entrepreneur transfers to another, more expensive method, it will rise abruptly, staying unchanged, however, until output increases as a result of adopting a new method.

In graphical representation, the shape of the marginal cost function can be seen in Figure 40.

The discontinuous cost function based on Leontief's production function better expresses the actual change in costs than the cost function assuming continuous substitution. Already in the 1930s, Ivor Jantzen pointed out that the cost curve cannot be continuous if production is carried on in several stages, and the capacity of the equipment varies with the different stages. This is because the full utilization of machinery and equipment with the greatest capacity presupposes that additional equipment should be installed in the stages with smaller capacities as a result of which the cost curve abruptly rises as output increases. Relying on Jantzen, Brehms also concerned himself with this problem in the early 1950s.[89]

The curve of production possibilities—the transformation curve

It is in the context of the cost function that the problem of joint production must be dealt with, when, at the given level of technical knowledge, the entrepreneur turns out different products with the available quantities of factors. By one single machine different products can be produced, and on a given piece of land different plants can be grown, etc. Together with factor quantities, total cost is also given,

[89] H. Brehms: A Discontinuous Cost Function, *The American Economic Review*, Vol. 42, 1952.

and thus the question arises: in what combinations should a firm manufacture, under such circumstances, the different goods at given product prices in order to attain optimum results?

A detailed discussion of the problem of joint production, also considering different market forms, can be found in Stackelberg's work published in 1932.[90]

The solution elaborated on the basis of marginal analysis assumes that the proportions of the products manufactured by the available factors can be changed *continuously*.

For the sake of graphical representation let us assume that the entrepreneur produces only two different products. If he wishes to produce a given quantity of one of them, *x*, he will use the rest of his available factors to obtain the largest quantity of the other product, *y*, consistent with the given output of *x*. The more of *x* he produces, the less of *y* he can turn out, and thus q_y is a unique, continuous, monotonically diminishing function of q_x. The case is just the opposite if the entrepreneur wishes to increase the quantity of *y*. Thus, the two functions will obtain: $q_y = f_1(q_x)$ and $q_x = f_2(q_y)$. The two functions are inverses one of the other, two aspects of the unique relationship between the quantities that can be produced of *x* and *y* with the available resources. The transformation function can be expressed mathematically in this form: $f(q_x, q_y) = 0$, that is, there exists an interrelationship between q_x and q_y. "We define the marginal cost function of the first and the second good respectively as the partial derivatives of the total cost function in respect of x_1 and x_2 respectively [by which Stackelberg understands the quantities of the two products—*A. M.*]. ... Both marginal cost functions are dependent on x_1 and x_2 alike."[91]

Textbooks applying marginal analysis generally regard such cases as normal, in which "the law of diminishing marginal return asserts itself in producing each product"[92], so that the production of the good increasing in quantity rises at a diminishing rate, hence its marginal cost increases, or the production of the good decreasing in quantity diminishes at a rising rate and thus its marginal cost falls. Thus "... it can be taken in the normal case that the production of *y* decreases at an increasing rate as the production of *x* is increased, and conversely."[93] This means that in order to produce an additional unit of a product already increased in its quantity, it would be necessary to renounce an increasingly larger quantity of another product.

Representing graphically the combination of the quantities of two products that can be turned out with the optimum use of the available factors, we obtain a curve concave to the origin, the curve of *production possibilities,* or, to use another term, the *transformation* curve (see Figure 41). The latter designation stems from Hayek, who first used it in an article published in 1936.[94]

90 H. Stackelberg: *Grundlagen einer reinen Kostentheorie,* Vienna, 1932, pp. 53–74.

91 H. Stackelberg: *op. cit.,* p. 66.

92 E. Carell: Die Interdependenz der ökonomischen Grössen und die Bestimmtheit der relativen Preise und ihrer Änderungen bei vollkommener Konkurrenz im nichtstatitonären Zustand, *Schweizerische Zeitschrift für Volkswirtschaft und Statistik,* March 1952, p. 24.

93 R. G. D. Allen: *Mathematical Analysis for Economists,* London, 1966, p. 123.

94 F. A. Hayek: Utility Analysis and Interest, *The Economic Journal,* March 1936, Vol. XLVI, pp. 44–60.

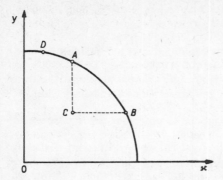

Figure 41

The transformation curve is the locus of *efficient points,* by moving between which we can expand the output of one product only at the expense of the other. Non-efficient points are those lying within the boundary drawn by the transformation curve. This is because if we move 'north-east' of them, the output of one product may grow, while that of the other will not change, or the output of both may rise. In our figure the points lying on the arc of the curve between *A* and *B* are efficient in relation to *C,* while *C* and *D* are not comparable as *D* lies 'north-west' of *C,* and contains more of the one, and less of the other product.

The slope of the curve expresses the marginal rate of substitution between the two products, that is, the quantity of one product which must be given up to increase that of the other by one unit. In Stackelberg's words: "... by the marginal rate of substitution of product *y* for product *x,* we understand the quantity of *x* by which the output of *x* must be decreased if the output of *y* is to be increased by one marginal unit, while ... total cost shall remain unchanged."[95]

What does the marginal rate of substitution or of transformation between two products express from the point of view of production? It expresses *the proportion between the marginal costs* of the two products. And, with the change in proportion between the outputs of the two products, owing to the assumed change in their marginal costs, this marginal rate of transformation will rise as the output of one product continuously increases, and the output of the other accordingly decreases.

It is the interpretation of costs first advanced in the Austrian School and discussed later in English economic literature under the name of opportunity cost that emerges here in a modern form. The marginal cost of the increased output of a product is expressed by the quantity of the other product given up in the interest of the increase by one unit of the first product.

The problem to be solved first, then, is in what proportion the entrepreneur should produce the two products with his available factors so that his total money revenue should be at a maximum at the established prices.

95 H. Stackelberg: *op. cit.,* p. 119.

Here, too, just as in the case of the indifference curves, budget lines must be constructed. The equation of the budget line is $p_x q_x + p_y q_y = R$, that is, it expresses those combinations of products x and y, which, at given product prices, yield a definite amount of money revenue to the entrepreneur. Here, too, the slope of the budget line is the ratio of product prices. And the entrepreneur will attain *maximum money revenue* at a product combination expressed by a point of the transformation curve at which the transformation curve touches the highest budget line. The point of tangency also means the *maximum amount of profit,* for the total cost of all commodity combinations that can be produced by the given factor quantities is identical. At identical total cost, however, the amount of profit will be at its maximum at a commodity combination yielding maximum total money revenue.

After we have maximized money revenue in solving the primal problem, we shall now try to determine, in solving the dual problem, at what combination of two different products a given money revenue can be realized at the least cost. The product combination in question will lie at the point of tangency of the budget line representing the given money revenue and the lowest transformation curve.

In both cases the slopes of the transformation curve and the budget line will coincide at the point of tangency, and therefore the *marginal rate of substitution, i.e. the ratio of marginal costs, will equal the price ratio of the two commodities.*

Let us now eliminate the possibility of a free change in the ratio between the two commodities and suppose that they can be produced within a given production method only by rigid technical coefficients. For the sake of graphical representation assume that only one single factor is needed to produce both commodities, or, what is a more realistic assumption, that there is one common factor used in the production of both commodities. By using the same quantity of the factor concerned in a given production method, the quantities of the two commodities to be produced in a rigid proportion are expressed by a line starting out from the origin. Suppose that four production methods are available. By means of the common factor the products of both commodities can be produced in a rigid proportion which, however, may vary with the methods used. The production possibilities are now represented by concave non-continuous line-sections (see Figure 42). Lange tries to demonstrate the concavity to the origin of the transformation function by assuming that the technically non-efficient methods have already been eliminated. These are the methods by which, with the help of the available factors, either less can be produced of one commodity than by a technically efficient method and the same of the other, or less of both commodities.

We can also change the proportion between the two commodities to be produced by the common factor along the broken-line transformation function either by transferring from one production method to another, or by combining two neighbouring methods. In the latter case, we can change the proportion between the two commodities to be produced at will. In continuous transformation the marginal rate of transformation will also be increasing. But this marginal rate cannot be interpreted at the apexes. The differences already mentioned with the non-continuous isoquants will emerge here, too. If the budget line touches the non-continuous transformation curve at an apex, then the commodity combination at the apex will yield maximum total money revenue at an infinite number of price proportions of the two products. If, however, the budget line coincides with any of the straight sections of the non-continuous transformation curve, then, at a given

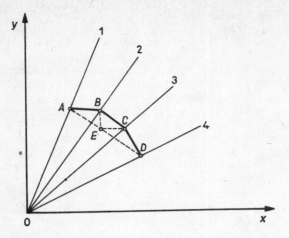

Figure 42

product price proportion, an infinite number of commodity combinations will yield the maximum result.

The transformation curve can be constructed by programming, as shown by Dorfman, Samuelson and Solow.[96] Every efficient point, that is, any point of the transformation function is a maximum solution for each budget line. It is the price amount of $p_x q_x + p_y q_y$ that has to be maximized at different prices. The limiting factors are the quantities of the available factors and the technical coefficients. Solving the programming task for the different prices, we obtain those quantities of the two commodities which yield, at different prices, maximum total money revenue, that is, we get the various efficient points, the points of the function of production possibilities.

The transformation function is based on a cost interpretation called opportunity cost. In connection with the transformation function the conflict of the two cost interpretations of non-Marxian economics comes clearly into prominence, as has already been pointed out by non-Marxian critics themselves. Let us accept for the time being the interpretation of costs as real costs and suppose, following the train of thought of the representatives of that theory, that the disutility of labour is greater in producing commodity x than y, because the production of x involves more inconvenience and trouble than that of commodity y. This fact increases the real cost of x, and the worker producing it has to be rewarded with a higher wage rate than the worker producing y. Consequently, commodity combinations of identical total cost, depending on the proportion in which they contain x and y, cannot use, in contrast to the assumption of the transformation function, the same capital and labour inputs or, to put it in other words, the total cost of commodity combinations produced by a given amount of capital and labour, owing to their

[96] R. Dorfman, R. Solow and P. A. Samuelson: *Linear Programming and Economic Analysis*, New York–Toronto–London, 1958. Chapter 14.

distribution between x and y, cannot be identical. In this case, the transformation function, though resting on the quantity of the available factors and the given state of technical knowledge, cannot be regarded as uniquely determined.[97]

THE EQUILIBRIUM CONDITION ON THE SUPPLY SIDE IN THE CASE OF PURE COMPETITION AT THE FIRM LEVEL

After having analysed the cost function, we are now in a position to provide the answer of non-Marxian economics to the problem raised in price theory, namely, at what level entrepreneurs have to set their outputs, with their given cost functions, to ensure maximum profit.

For a long time, non-Marxian economics regarded pure or perfect competition as the critical market form. Pure competition is a concept created by Chamberlin[98], a pioneer of non-Marxian theory of market forms. By it he wants to express that competition is unalloyed with monopolistic elements. The concept of perfect competition, points out Chamberlin, includes further additional assumptions, the one, for example, that the agents of the market are fully informed about the market situation, there is no uncertainty, the production factors adjust to the changing conditions with ideal fluidity and mobility. According to him,[99] pure competition is characterized by two basic conditions: (1) there are a large number of sellers and buyers with roughly similar economic power on the market; (2) both the goods traded and the sellers themselves are perfectly homogeneous to the buyers. Therefore, it is completely indifferent to them which seller's product they buy.

Owing to these two conditions, price constitutes a *datum* for the individual persons acting on the market. No individual seller or buyer is able to change the market price. If a seller tried, for example, to raise the price of his product, he would lose all his customers. And if he decided to lower its price, all buyers would be eager to buy his product, and since he would be unable to meet the increased demand, the buyers would bid up the price to its general level. Hence, competition develops a uniform price for a given product at a given time and on a given market. And the market absorbs any quantity offered by the individual seller at this uniform price. Whatever quantity of his product the individual seller puts on the market, to whatever extent he increases its supply, it will remain just an insignificant fraction of total supply, and can therefore exercise no appreciable influence on the price. Thus, it is not worthwhile for any seller to decrease the price of his product, to charge a price lower than his competitors, because he can sell any quantity even at the going price. Chamberlin expresses the given character of price for the individual participants of the market by saying that the demand for the products of *individual* sellers is infinitely elastic.

The graphical illustration of a demand function of infinite elasticity can be seen in Figure 43.

[97] M. Blaug: *Economic Theory in Retrospect*, London, 1968, p. 494.
[98] E. Chamberlin: *The Theory of Monopolistic Competition*, Cambridge, Massachusetts, 1947, 5th edition, pp. 7–8.
[99] E. Chamberlin: *op. cit.*, p. 6.

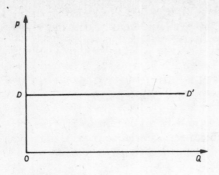

Figure 43   Figure 44

In the short run, with his given machinery and equipment, the entrepreneur increases his output by expanding the quantity of variable factors. He will attain maximum profit, as we know, if he extends the employment of the variable factor up to the point at which its marginal productivity multiplied by the product price falls, owing to the decrease in marginal productivity, to the level of the price of the variable factor, that is

$$\frac{\partial Q}{\partial i} \cdot p = p_i,$$

where i stands for the variable factor, or a group of variable factors.

From this

$$p = \frac{p_i}{\frac{\partial Q}{\partial i}},$$

that is, in the case of maximum profit, product price equals the increment in total costs due to the manufacture of the last unit of product. In other words, as long as owing to the increase in output by one unit the increment in money revenue, which in pure competition is identical with the established price, is larger than the increment in total costs, i.e. *marginal cost,* the entrepreneur can increase the amount of his profit by expanding output. His profit will attain its maximum, his marginal profit will become 0, at that volume of output where marginal cost rises to reach the level of price. The statement that in pure competition "the price of each product will be equal to its marginal cost can also be expressed by saying that each factor of production will be paid a reward equal to the value of its marginal product"[100] (see Figure 44).

For the individual entrepreneur, in pure competition, "his short-run *MC* [marginal cost—A. M.] curve will also be his rational short-run supply curve."[101] This curve shows the limit to which the entrepreneur goes in increasing his output

[100] J. E. Meade: *An Introduction to Economic Analysis and Policy,* Oxford, 1936, p. 106.
[101] J. Viner: Cost Curves and Supply Curves, *Zeitschrift für Nationalökonomie,* 1931, Vol. III, p. 204.

to attain maximum profit at the different levels of price. The equilibrium point can always develop only on the upward sloping part of the marginal cost curve. The point of intersection of the price and the downward sloping part of the marginal cost curve cannot yield an equilibrium point, because, at diminishing marginal costs and given price, the entrepreneur is interested in further expanding his output. Non-Marxian economics then constructs the short-run supply curve of the industry by the horizontal summation of the supply curves of individual firms.

Assuming that the entrepreneur expands his output by increasing two variable factors, i and j, the statement of marginal-productivity value being equal to factor price must be valid for both factors:

$$\frac{\partial Q}{\partial i} \cdot p = p_i, \text{ whence } \frac{\frac{\partial Q}{\partial i}}{p_i} = \frac{1}{p}$$

$$\frac{\partial Q}{\partial j} \cdot p = p_j, \text{ whence } \frac{\frac{\partial Q}{\partial j}}{p_j} = \frac{1}{p}.$$

Consequently,
$$\frac{\frac{\partial Q}{\partial i}}{p_i} = \frac{\frac{\partial Q}{\partial j}}{p_j},$$

that is, even if the equipment cannot be changed in the short run, the use of the variable factors will still continue to take place to satisfy the principle of using the factor combination representing minimum cost. Thus, the formula price = marginal cost already supposes the minimum cost combination of variable factors.

As in consumers' economy, in producers' economy, too, Samuelson distinguishes on the basis of the equality of marginal cost and price the dual effect of price changes, in this case the effect of a change in the price of a factor.[102] If the price of a factor increases, it will cause the marginal cost to increase, too; the upward-shifted marginal cost curve will reach the level of price at a smaller volume of output, therefore output will decrease, and consequently demand will decrease not only for factors with increased prices, but also for those with unchanged prices. This is the so-called *output effect*. The entrepreneur, however, tries to substitute the factors with unchanged prices for higher-priced factors. This is the *substitution effect*. The substitution effect will further decrease the demand for the factor with increased price, and increase the demand for the substitute factors. Hence the demand for the more expensive factor will fall as a result of both effects. The demand for the substitute factor, however, depends upon which of the two effects proves to be stronger. If the output effect exceeds the substitution effect, the demand for factors with unchanged prices will also decline. If, however, the substitution effect is stronger, the demand for the substitute factors will rise despite decreased output.

[102] P. A. Samuelson: *Economics*, New York–London, 1955, pp. 482–483.

Some critical comments on the determination of the equilibrium condition of the firm

In non-Marxian economics the equality of price and marginal cost is the condition for the equilibrium of the firm only. For an industry to reach equilibrium, a further condition must be fulfilled. Before starting to discuss the condition for an equilibrium of the industry, we wish to make some critical statements on the conditions

The price and marginal cost formula expresses only the margin of expanding output, that it is worth increasing output as long as price still covers marginal cost. But it does not express whether the price being equal to marginal cost ensures the firm's conditions for reproduction, whether it covers its costs of production and realizes profit for the entrepreneur. It is possible that the rising marginal cost curve cuts the price axis below the level of the average total cost curve, so that the entrepreneur will not be able to realize even his average total costs and will sustain losses. Since fixed costs have to be borne anyway in the short run, entrepreneurs, according to Stackelberg,[103] will strive, in a time of depression, to cover at least their variable costs, and maintain production until the price drops below the minimum level of average variable costs.

Incidentally, the valuation of a firm's total costs by marginal costs coincides with the actual costs of production only at a volume of output lying at the point of intersection of the marginal and average total cost curves. The points lying to the left of this point of intersection represent less, those lying to the right of it represent more costs.

Therefore, Leo Rogin[104] was wrong in characterizing the achievement of Marshall the economist who was among the first to formulate the short-run equality of marginal cost and price, as a solution to the problem of the classical economists who were unable to reconcile price with cost in the short run, that is, price with the assertion of the law of value. It will be clear from what has already been said that the short-run equality of price and marginal cost does not express the validity of the law of value. Marshall himself notices, by the way, that the short-run equality of price and marginal cost is just one incident of the process in which long-run equilibrium price asserts itself. Though marginal cost includes only variable costs, if price does not cover fixed costs in the long run, too, in addition to variable costs, then the entrepreneurs will slowly discontinue production.[105]

Moreover, the supply curves of individual firms cannot be constructed in isolation, by analysing the firm's activity in itself, if the so-called *external economies* are also taken into account. In this case it ts impossible even to derive the supply curve of the industry from the supply curves of individual firms merely by horizontal summation. The concept of external economies was created by Marshall. It is by means of this concept that in the price theory based on micro-economics it is demonstrated that social production is more than just the mechanical total of the outputs of firms divorced from their social context. As the firm's output constitutes an organic part of total social production and of the division of labour of society, the output of other firms or industries, owing to inter-firm or inter-

103 H. Stackelberg: *op. cit.*, p. 55.
104 L. Rogin: *The Meaning and Validity of Economic Theory*, New York, 1956, p. 558.
105 A. Marshall: *Principles of Economics*, London, 1930 ,p. 376.

industry relations, influences, improves or deteriorates, the production conditions of the given firm. Thus, the production functions of the individual firms, owing to their social interrelations, contain an *invisible input* expressing the services of other firms or industries which they cannot expropriate for themselves. Textbooks, following Marshall, often refer to examples in which the growth in the output of a given industry exerts an effect on the production conditions of the individual firms of that industry. An industry will increase its demand for the necessary means of production if its output increases. Where the effect of this demand makes itself felt, output will also be expanded, which makes it possible for the benefits of large-scale production and the increasing returns to scale to assert themselves: the means of production can be produced more cheaply, the expanding industry will be able to get them at a lower price and thereby to decrease its cost of production. Or the expansion of an industry will give rise to a number of subsidiary industries, which in turn decrease the costs of the basic industry. With the increase in the output of an industry, vocational training will rise to a higher level, it will be possible, e.g., to publish a technical periodical of that industry, etc. All this increases the efficiency of all firms of the industry concerned.

Owing to external economies, the supply functions of the individual firms are closely interrelated, all being dependent on the output of that industry. If, for example, all firms increase their outputs so that their marginal costs reach the level of price, the production of the whole industry will increase, which in turn, owing to the external economies, will cause the cost functions of the individual firms to shift downwards, and they will have to adapt their outputs to the established prices on the basis of their changed cost functions entailing that, as a result of their adaptation, the output of the industry will further increase, further changing thereby each other's cost functions. It is exactly owing to the interrelationship between the output of the industry and the cost functions of individual firms that the supply function of the industry cannot be constructed by a mere horizontal summation of the supply functions of the individual firms, because the firms' supply curves will shift in the course of summation. Nevertheless, the supply of the industry is the total of the supplies of the individual firms.

Can an equilibrium position develop in a firm, and can the supply functions of the firms be summed to form a supply function of the industry in the case of external economies? Neo-classical economics resting on a micro-economic basis has little concerned itself with this question.

One possible answer is that there is a solution if a level of price has developed at which the individual firms jointly put as much of their outputs on the market as the output of the industry constituting the basis of their individual cost curves.

For the sake of graphic illustration suppose that there are n firms operating with identical cost functions in the industry concerned. Each of them produces one n-th of total supply. By means of this *symmetry assumption,* as it is called technically, the problems emerging in analysing the activity of the firm can also be examined at the level of industry. The positively sloping lines, lying one below the other, express the marginal supply curves of the firm under consideration if the output of the industry is Q_1, Q_2, Q_3, etc.

Figure 45 reveals that the increase in the output of the industry from Q_1 to Q_2, Q_3, Q_4, etc. shifts the marginal cost curve of each firm in a downward direction. As the output of the industry increases, equilibrium in the individual firms comes about at those prices at whose intersection with the marginal cost curve each firm, assumed to be identical, puts the quantities $\frac{Q_1}{n}$, $\frac{Q_2}{n}$, $\frac{Q_3}{n}$, etc., on the market, that is, the n firms offer for sale altogether quantities Q_1, Q_2, Q_3, etc., constituting the basis of their cost functions.

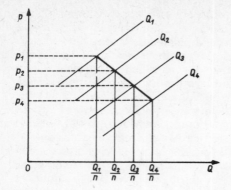

Figure 45

Though the marginal cost curve of individual firms at the given output level of the industry is upward sloping, as can be seen from Figure 45, yet, connecting the point of intersection of the marginal cost curve sloping downwards as the output of the industry increases with the diminishing price, we obtain a negatively, i.e. downward sloping supply curve. It is not a real supply curve though, because it does not indicate how the firm changes its output as prices change, but rather expresses at what prices the individual firms are willing to produce so much of their products that their total output does not change the firms' supply curves, for it contains the effect of external economies called forth by that very output of the industry.[106]

THE EQUILIBRIUM CONDITION ON THE SUPPLY SIDE IN A PURELY COMPETITIVE INDUSTRY

After discussing the equilibrium condition of the firm, let us now examine the condition of equilibrium of the industry under pure competition as set forth in non-Marxian price theory.

This condition is formally similar to the condition formulated by Marxist political economy: an industry comes into a state of equilibrium if new firms do not want to enter that industry, and existing ones do not wish to leave it. According to Marx, adhering to the labour theory of value, this situation arises when all industries realize only average profit. Neo-classical economics, however, which rejects the labour theory of value sees production costs, looked at from the side of demand for the factors of production, as compensation for factor services, determined by the marginal productivity of factors. Marginal productivity theory tries to trace back the quantity of the product, in which value created by labour is embodied, entirely to the services of those factors which go into producing that product.

Thus, it wishes to resolve the new value wholly into production costs. This is, by the way, also required by the theory of optimal resource allocation. In the optimum programme, the magnitude of the maximum value óf output produced, is equal

[106] See R. W. Adams and J. T. Wheeler: External Economics and the Supply Curve; *The Review of Economic Studies*, Oct. 1952, No. 51, pp. 24–39.

to the minimum of the costs of production. "Zero gain", writes Baumol, "is an accounting requirement."[107] If, for example, 1 hour's labour input produces 4 units of net output by using 10 units of capital, then 1 hour's new value is embodied in 4 units of use-value. The capitalit pays to the worker only part of the value created by him in one hour's work, and expropriates the rest without any compensation. Suppose a worker is given the value of 2 units of the product as wages, while the capitalist's surplus value is embodied in the other 2 units. However, interpreting the cost of production as compensation for factor services on the assumption that the marginal productivity of labour is 2 units and that of capital is 0.2 unit, involves that the reward for the service of one hour's work is 2 units of output multiplied by price, and the reward for the service of 10 units of capital is also 2 units of output multiplied by price. According to this view, the new value produced is fully resolved in costs, in the costs of the factors participating in the production of the output embodying the new value. Approaching it from this aspect, equilibrium theory sees the condition of equilibrium of an industry as the requirement that price should cover only the cost per unit of output in all branches of production. Of course, cost per unit of output interpreted as compensation for factor participation is not the true cost in the Marxist sense. Over and above wages, it also contains interest on capital and rent for the land leased, which is in fact surplus value. It is at most from the point of view of the individual capitalist that it can be called cost.

In the equilibrium of an industry price equals average cost, but the condition still prevails that price equals marginal cost, and consequently, marginal cost equals average cost. Thus, in the equilibrium position of an industry, competition compels the entrepreneurs to produce at *optimum firm size*.

At optimum firm size, as we have seen, the minima of both the short- and long-term unit cost curves coincide, and thus the short- and long-term marginal cost curves intersect the short- and long-term unit cost curves at the same point. The two marginal costs are of the same size at the point of intersection and are equal to price in case the industry concerned is in equilibrium. However, the long-term marginal cost curves of the industry cannot add up to a long-term supply curve of the industry because in the long run account must already be taken of the equilibrium of the industry, namely of the fact that price can only cover the unit cost. Assuming that the minimum unit costs of firms are of the same level, the long-term supply curve of the industry can only be a straight line, expressing the fact that the supply price remains unchanged at all possible output volumes.

If in a given industry, price also contained gains over and above the cost per unit of output, then entrepreneurs would leave other industries and rush to establish new enterprises in that industry. Price over and above average cost would mean that in the industry under consideration existing firms would be able to satisfy increased demand only if they expanded their output beyond the optimum size of the firm, producing at decreasing returns to scale, marginal cost higher than unit cost, and the rewards paid to factors, their marginal productivity multiplied by the product price, lower in total than revenue. With the establishment of new firms the supply of the product increases, and its price decreases; the entry of new firms into

---

[107] W. J. Baumol: *Economic Theory and Operations Analysis*, Prentice Hall, 1965, p. 107.

the industry will continue until price falls to the level of average cost at which the entrepreneurs already produce at optimum firm size and at constant returns to scale.

Now, if the firms of an industry produce under different technical conditions, with resources of unequal efficiency and with entrepreneurs at different skill levels, and thus also different costs of production, then, in industry equilibrium, which firm's unit costs should be equal to price? Obviously, those of the marginal firm; "we must study *cost at the margin* in order to discover both the supply price of the commodity and the amount of rent in the industry."[108]

Let us examine this question in somewhat more detail. For simplicity's sake, let us disregard the alternative uses of factors, and assume that the real costs of each unit of the particular factors are identical. Under such circumstances, the firm operating under better conditions will earn surplus income, a rent over and above the cost per unit of output, while a marginal firm will earn only its unit cost. If the price of the product in question falls slightly, then the marginal firm will not earn even its unit cost and will go bankrupt, while intra-marginal firms will continue to produce as price reduction in their case affects only surplus above costs. The cost of the marginal firm is "the cost of the margin of the industry,"[109] and this constitutes the supply price of the product in question.

Intra-marginal firms operating with more efficient factors realize marginal cost over and above their cost per unit of output. In this case, the amount of their unit cost does not express the cost at the margin of the industry. Mrs. Robinson calls their marginal cost *intensive* marginal cost. Thus only firms at the margin operate at optimum firm size. "All intra-marginal firms ... are of more than optimum size"[110] and thus produce at diminishing returns to scale, which, however, since it is the consequence of a better utilization of the more efficient factors, "is obviously in no sense undesirable."[111]

In the neo-classical price model, however, provided the operation of the mechanisms of competition is undisturbed, the cost per unit of output of the intra-marginal firm applying more efficient factors cannot be lower in the long run than that of the marginal firm. According to the assumption of static equilibrium theory, production factors are available to society in a given quantity and quality. This must be assumed if their marginal productivities are to be determined. Under such conditions, the competition of entrepreneurs to catch up with leading firms takes place in such a way that entrepreneurs, in order to obtain better factors, will bid over each other until eventually "all cost savings will tend to be paid out to the more efficient inputs [including the more efficient manager, too—*A. M.*] that make them possible. Hence, since we must include these bonus payments, the costs of the more efficient firms will tend to be driven toward equality with those of the less efficient."[112] Viner wrote about the same problem a few decades earlier as

[108] J. Robinson: *The Economics of Imperfect Competition*, London, 1954, p. 121.
[109] *Ib:d.*
[110] J. Robinson: *op. cit.*, p. 124.
[111] J. Robinson: *op. cit.*, p. 125.
[112] W. J. Baumol: *op. cit.*, p. 210.

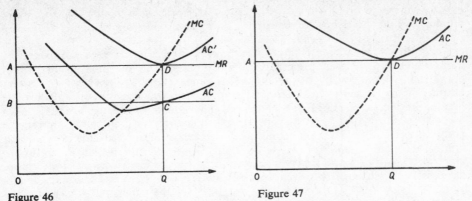

Figure 46   Figure 47

Source: J. Robinson: *The Economics of Imperfect Competition,* London, 1954, p. 125.

follows: "... under long-run static competitive equilibrium, marginal costs and average costs must be uniform for all producers."[113]

In this representation, the intra-marginal units of factors will earn rents as a difference between their revenues and real costs, which economics regards as cost incurred by the entrepreneur. But the regulating role of the firm at the margin will remain because, if the price of the product decreases, it is only the marginal firm that drops out. The rest may decrease the price of their factors, which will cause only their rent above real cost to fall, and thus the factors will not leave the industry.

Competition will now ensure that every firm operates at optimum size. "The average cost of every firm, including rent, will then be at a minimum in equilibrium, and every firm, in this sense, will be of optimum size."[114]

Let us now represent graphically, after Mrs. Robinson, what we have outlined above. Figure 46 represents the intra-marginal firms and Figure 47 the marginal ones.

In both cases, *AC* is the firm's average output cost containing no rent,, *MC* is its marginal cost, *DQ* is the price of the commodity, and *AC'* is the entrepreneur's average cost also including rent. Since the inclusion of rent in total cost increases total cost by a sum independent of the firm's output, the marginal-cost curve will intersect curve *AC'* of the intramarginal firm and curve *AC* of the marginal firm at the minimum point.

"But the most efficient scale of production is not necessarily uniform for everyone. The minimum point of the curve (average total cost curve), although at the same distance from the *x* axis for each producer, may be variously distant from the *y* axis. Qualitative differences in the factors employed will account for this."[115]

The statement, however, that the costs of firms operating under different con-

[113] J. Viner: Cost Curves and Supply Curves. Reprinted in *Readings in Price Theory,* Chicago, 1952, p. 222.
[114] J. Robinson: *op. cit.,* p. 125.
[115] E. H. Chamberlin: *The Theory of Monopolistic Competition,* Cambridge, 1947, p. 22.

ditions will be equal in a long-run equilibrium, contradicts reality. Viner himself emphasizes that statistical observation shows that average cost varies within an industry from firm to firm.[116]

According to Marx, the difference in the conditions and costs of production of industrial firms is based primarily on the difference in the amount of capital employed by them and in their technical equipment. One firm operates with more, another with less developed technical equipment. And it is on capital that the greater productive power of labour depends. The tendency towards the equalization of costs per unit of output as represented in neo-classical price theory reflects reality according to Marxian economics in so far as it suggests that competition tends to eliminate super-profit. It does this, however, not by letting the more efficient factors earn the super-profit produced by the firm working under more favourable conditions. By the real cost of capital goods Marxian economics understands the quantity of labour socially necessary for their reproduction, and if the demand for them raises their price above their value and ensures thereby, to use the term of neo-classical economics, rent for them, then as a result of the assertion of the law of value, the entrepreneurs will expand their outputs until their prices drop to the level of their social value. As capital goods can be reproduced, the competition of firms operating under less favourable conditions to catch up with the technically better equipped firms does not make itself felt in their endeavour to allure the production factors of the more efficient firms by promising them higher rewards for their services, thereby increasing the costs of these firms, but rather in their striving to improve technical equipment, to buy more efficient means of production and to reduce their costs in this way to the level of the more efficient firms. All this is, of course, only a tendency, since the production costs of the firms of an industry never equalize as in the static equilibrium position described by modern non-Marxian economics, because in the meantime technology develops and this keeps up the differences in the production conditions among the individual firms. There are always better firms operating at lower costs, and less efficient firms operating at higher costs, in any industry.

Further analysing neo-classical price theory, let us now, following its representatives, also take into account that the factors of production may be used in alternative ways: they adjust their supply in the various fields of employment not only to real costs, but also to their possible earnings in alternative uses. It is their opportunity cost that is called transfer price or transfer earnings by eonomic literature. The formation of the supply price of a given commodity, the conditions of the emergence of rent in the case of alternative uses of factors was first analysed by Mrs. Robinson in a more detailed way. In this respect, various assumptions may be made. One such assumption is, for example, that each unit of any factor is equally efficient in all but one of its uses. In that particular field of production, the individual units of the factors in question are differently efficient, that is, are specific. In this case, the transfer price of each unit is identical in the given industry, but their prices formed according to their marginal productivity are different. The unit whose earnings are higher than its transfer price obtains rent. And with the industry expanding, such units of the factor concerned must be

[116] J. Viner: *op. cit.*, p. 223.

withdrawn from some other employment which, from the point of view of the new field of utilization, is becoming increasingly unsuitable. The withdrawal of the factor units takes place up to the point at which the reward to the last factor equals its transfer price. In this case, too, what is decisive for the supply price is the costs of that firm, or, in other words, that firm is at the margin of the industry "which employs only marginal units of the factors, that is, units which would cease to be employed in the industry if their earnings were slightly reduced ... In the costs of such a firm there will be no element of rent..."[117]

More complicated is the situation if in the case of a factor "there is a difference between the relative efficiencies of natural units in the industry and their relative efficiences in the industries from which they are drawn."[118] In this case we may assume, for example, that the less efficient units are involved, the less is the difference between their relative efficiencies in the various fields of use. Here again, the least efficient unit will be at the margin. It is this unit whose earnings and transfer price will coincide. But we may also assume the opposite case, in which the difference between their relative efficiencies in the various fields of employment will decrease the more, the more efficient is the unit involved. Then, however, the most efficient unit will be at the margin, the one whose earnings do not contain rent, but only equals the unit's transfer price. Depending, then, on what our assumption is concerning the relative efficiencies of the individual units of factors, the marginal unit will always be different.

Neo-classical price theory includes rent as earnings above the transfer price in the cost per unit of output, too, and thus the unit prices of firms employing factors of different efficiency will tend to be formed at the same level.

Since the costs of all firms of the industry are equal, and in the case of equilibrium in the industry price equals cost per unit of output, the question of the existence of profit justifiably arises.

Under conditions of static equilibrium, the process of realizing surplus value, which is the essence of capitalism, disappears from the theoretical picture. In this model, the passive capitalist, who earns interest, behaves exactly as a consumer; he is not motivated in his actions by the desire to increase abstract wealth. The entrepreneur, however, who performs the function of capital, does not make profit in equilibrium, as we have seen.

This serious contradiction is the consequence of the rejection of the labour theory of value. The operation of the neo-classical price model is based, on the supply side, on the entrepreneurs' endeavour to earn maximum profit. It turns out, however, that in static equilibrium, in the case of pure competition, no profit accrues to the entrepreneurs.

Some economists try to include a certain amount of profit, so-called *normal profit*, in price in such a way that they regard it as part of the cost per unit of output."... it will be useful to include 'normal' profits in average costs,"[119] as we can read in an English economics textbook. They interpret normal profit

[117] J. Robinson: *op. cit.*, p. 121.
[118] J. Robinson: *op. cit.*, p. 113.
[119] A. W. Stonier and D. C. Hague: *A Textbook of Economic Theory*, London, 1965, p. 128.

as the minimum amount of profit which is necessary for the entrepreneur to remain in the industry, and which is, therefore, as they think, a cost of production. Normal profit, according to the above-mentioned textbook, is no average profit, because it does not relate it to the capital advanced. It is independent of average profit as it constitutes the gain of the entrepreneur having no capital, and expresses a sum of money of a given magnitude.[120]

Profit is a necessary condition of capitalist production. But from this it does not follow at all that it should be regarded as production cost, too. Already Marx criticized Adam Smith for holding a similar view: "when saying that profit is no longer explained here by the nature of surplus value, but by the 'interest' of the capitalist. Which is just silly."[121]

Even Knight emphasizes that "... costs are ... other than profit ..."[122] But it is in vain that certain economists interpret profit as cost. Profit is an alien item among costs. They determine the magnitude of the other cost elements by means of marginal productivity theory, while the magnitude of normal profit interpreted as part of the cost per unit of output remains undetermined. The most they can say of it is that as a transfer earning it must reach a magnitude which the entrepreneur would get elsewhere if he left the industry concerned.

But if the capabilities of the entrepreneurs, and thus the magnitude of the profit realized by them, are different, which entrepreneur's profit counts as normal profit in the particular industry? As we have seen, if the entrepreneurs are not equally talented in each industry, owing to the difference between their relative efficiencies in the various industries, then it is equally possible that the actual profit of the worst or the best entrepreneur coincides with his transfer earnings and is therefore regarded as normal profit.

And what determines the amount of the entrepreneurs' profit in general? According to the view widely accepted in non-Marxian economics, if there is no uncertainty in the economy, the entrepreneur might only earn wages of management and interest on their money invested in their firms. In a world of uncertainty, we can speak of profit, but its magnitude, as a result of the interpretation of profit as the psychological cost of bearing immeasurable uncertainty, becomes entirely indeterminate. If we accept the source of profit to lie in immeasurable uncertainty, then such a profit cannot be fitted into a static equilibrium model which presupposes perfect predictability. "The real trouble with Prof. Knight's otherwise excellent book is that it assumes 'perfect competition'. His entrepreneurs bear their uncertainty in a perfectly competitive world ..."[123] Thus, the explanation that normal profit has to be at a level which the entrepreneur would get in another industry, besides not providing an unambiguous answer to the question which entrepreneur's profit should be regarded as normal, cannot say anything definite about its magnitude; thus to settle the issue of normal profit simply by saying that it is formed at the level of transfer earnings is nothing else but dodging the question.

---

[120] A. W. Stonier and D. C. Hague: *op. cit.*, pp. 128–129.
[121] K. Marx: *The Theories of Surplus Value* (selections), New York, 1952, pp. 131–132.
[122] F. H. Knight: *Risk, Uncertainty and Profit*, New York, 1964, pp. 18–19.
[123] P. J. D. Wiles: *Price, Cost and Output*, Oxford, 1956, p. 200.

Equilibrium theory seeks to explain the existence of profit in an economy in which there is no uncertainty and no economic development, simply by giving up the assumption of pure competition: "For profit to arise", writes Jean Marchal, "there must be obstacles to the free play of competition. This shows that there is a profound affinity between profit and monopoly: the pursuit of profit leads to monopoly and only monopoly garnering a regular and lasting profit."[124] It is exactly on the magnitude of profit that non-Marxian economics measures, among other things, the degree of monopoly, i.e. the strength of monopolies. By assuming obstacles to competition to explain the existence of profit, modern non-Marxian economics proves unable to substitute for the labour theory of value any value theory by means of which profit as distinct from interest could appear as an organic part of value, or equilibrium price, in static equilibrium under pure competition.

[124] J. Marchal. The Construction of a New Theory of Profit, *The American Economic Review*, September 1951, p. 552.

Chapter 4

THE OUTLINES AND CRITIQUE OF A MODERN VARIANT OF GENERAL EQUILIBRIUM THEORY

1. The data of the price model discussed coincide in respect of content with those of the Walrasian model. These are: the quantity of the available factors of production; the system of indifference curves expressing the tastes of consumers, including the indifference curves relating to present and future goods, wage goods and leisure; the system of isoquants expressing the technical conditions of production, and, finally, the social structure. The utility functions as data in the Walrasian model are superseded by the system of indifference curves, the rigid Walrasian technical coefficients are replaced by variable technical coefficients as manifested in the continuous isoquant curves.

It is the Walrasian groping method that provides the solution also to the modern variant of the general equilibrium model. The theoretical economist can arrive at a solution by means of the iteration method. He examines what will be the supply of the production factors given a certain series of prices of consumer goods and production factors. It is in this way that he obtains in the price model the expected factor incomes at the prevailing prices. From the factor incomes and the prices of consumer goods he deduces the magnitude of the demand for the latter. Then, by means of the isoquants he constructs the supply function, at the existing factor prices, of the individual consumer goods, and determines at what supply, given the existing prices of consumer goods, the volume of profit will be at a maximum. In this way, he obtains the quantity of consumer goods supplied at the prevailing prices. And, finally, he determines by the isoquants the quantity of labour and capital, i.e., the demand for them, needed to produce the quantity demanded of consumer goods at minimal costs. He wishes to determine the aggregate demand and supply curves for the various consumer goods and production factors by a summation of the individual demand and supply curves. The condition for a general equilibrium to be established is now that such prices of consumer goods and production factors should be formed at which demand and supply are in equilibrium in respect of all consumer goods and production factors, and that the prices thus formed should just equal the cost per unit in the market for all products. These equilibrium prices satisfy a number of marginal conditions, indicating that the resources available to society have been used in an optimal way.

The equilibrium conditions in the modern variant of general equilibrium theory are similar to the conditions formulated by Walras with the difference that they are more sophisticated. In the modern variant, too, the criterion of equilibrium is the formation of a set of prices which satisfies a number of marginal conditions indicating that the consumers and entrepreneurs have optimally used the consumer goods and factors of production available to them. Thus, the theory characterizes the equilibrium position as a state in which each individual in the market has achieved optimum results. It is intended to prove that with such data for the model there can only exist one single such optimal state, and this state is stable in that the economy, when moved away from equilibrium, will always be restored to the same position, provided the data remain unchanged.

Non-Marxian criticism emphasizes that the representatives of equilibrium theory choose the assumptions of the model with a view to deriving from them these characteristics of the equilibrium position.

For an equilibrium position to be established it is necessary, among other things, that no increasing returns to scale should exist, for in that case, in increasing their output at the existing price, the producers could not arrive at an equilibrium position.

The model presupposes a definite form of the functions. The functions, however, say these critics, do not express empirically deduced interrelationships. They are assumed as such by the followers of the theory so that they should permit a stable equilibrium position to be established. Thus, for example, the indifference curves and isoquants convex to the origin, and the transformation curves concave from below, yield, at given relative prices, a stable equilibrium point. The critics are right in saying that such functions arrived at in a deductive way are devoid of any content. Such for example, is, the function which, ignoring the technological peculiarities of the individual sectors of production, wishes to describe in general terms how costs depend on the scale of output. "It is difficult to imagine an analysis which, for example, contains all the complications relevant both to the electricity supply system and to the manufacture of chocolate. Thus, what is needed for decision-making in any particular industry is a cost model specific to that industry, and an understanding of that industry's technology is obviously required for this purpose."[125]

The equilibrium solution supposes that there is no strong income effect to outdo the substitution effect. This, however, is also impossible to reveal merely by logical considerations, without any empirical observations. Owing to the sterile nature of the assumption concerning the reaction of the individuals in the market, derived in a deductive way, behaviourist research is strengthening in non-Marxian economic literature which "proposes to observe and to study the real processes..."[126]

2. The critique also points out that, owing to its static nature, the equilibrium theory of price formation does not take account of the fact that economic processes, including production, take place over time, and the production process begun today will yield its results only in the future; thus the behaviour of entrepreneurs is influenced not only by current changes in prices but also by the expected development of economic processes in the future, by the price of the product at the time when it is ready for sale. And depending on how they evaluate the future in the present, entrepreneurs may react differently to changes in present prices, may divert the economy, depending on their anticipations, far from its

[125] R. Turvey: Marginal Cost, *The Economic Journal,* June 1969, p. 287.
[126] F. Machlup: Theories of the Firm: Marginalist, Behavioral, Managerial, *The American Review,* March 1967, p. 4.

equilibrium position. Already Marshall pointed out that so-called "false trading" begun at a non-equilibrium price, in so far as it influences distribution relations, also influences the formation of the final equilibrium position. Though Hicks attributes, as we have seen, only secondary importance to "false trading", yet more recently the problem has come again into prominence for those who wish to reform neo-classical price theory, to make it capable of explaining why the free working of the price mechanism cannot ensure full employment. According to Don Patinkin, Clower and Leijonhufvud, transactions begun at non-equilibrium prices give rise to a cumulative process, in the course of which aggregate income and aggregate demand decrease, and the equilibrium-restoring effect of the price mechanism becomes weaker. Leijonhufvud, for example, finds the cause of this, as we shall see later, in the imperfect information of the market agents. The representatives of the Walrasian-type general equilibrium model, however, assume that the agents of the market are informed fully and free of charge about the prevailing market situation and, in the knowledge of the current data, they are able, as Keynes writes, to predict the future with a fair degree of certainty[127] and thus the actions of the economic subjects can unambiguously be anticipated from present data. In this model "there is no changing future to influence the present..."[128] Therefore, the role of uncertainty of anticipations, that is, the anarchic nature of capitalist economy is missing.[129]

3. Marxian economics criticizes neo-classical price theory primarily because what matters in it is the individual's relationship to things, and because the fact that this expresses definite production relations is overlooked, production relations as the basis of the price phenomena under consideration are either neglected or distorted. Looked at from this angle, the debate on whether it is correct or not to assume the convexity of the indifference curves or isoquants has relevance only to the surface appearance of production relations.

Based on the fiction of the individual seeking to optimize the realization of his ends by scarce means, the price–income distribution theories make class relations disappear. In much the same way as in Walras, we only deal with consumers and entrepreneurs. The worker and the capitalist offer as consumers the services of certain production factors to the entrepreneur and buy from him the consumer goods produced by means of factor services. Both get their incomes equally as rewards for their own services. By offering the services of scarce factors, they have contributed to the satisfaction of solvent needs. Wage and interest interpreted as cost of production express partly the significance of factor services in satisfying the demand for consumer goods, and partly the direct significance of the worker's leisure, or of the goods withdrawn from personal consumption for the purposes of accumulation, from the point of view of workers or capitalists as consumers.

[127] See J. M. Keynes: The General Theory. Published in the collection of essays *The New Economics*, London, 1963.

[128] J. M. Keynes: *The General Theory of Employment, Interest and Money*, New York, 1936, p. 145.

[129] By creating the concept of pure competition, Chamberlin wishes to express, among other things, that he holds complete prediction to be an assumption contradicting reality, and he therefore leaves perfect competition out of account as it implies complete prediction.

4. And is it really true that a characteristic feature of equilibrium is that both consumers and entrepreneurs have optimized their positions in it? The bulk of consumers are made up of members of the working class. The interests of the working class, however, are opposed to those of the entrepreneurs. While members of the working class wish to maximize their welfare as consumers, and the entrepreneurs their profits, their interests will invariably clash. An increase in the welfare of the working class presupposes an increase in its real wages, and not simply the spending of its wages in an optimum way. However, an increase in real wages at the given level of technological knowledge assumed in the model would decrease the magnitude of profit. If we reject the explanation of distribution relations provided by the theory of marginal productivity, and regard the entrepreneurs' profit as surplus value, no equilibrium position is conceivable in which the classes with conflicting interests have, as a result of competition, optimized their positions.

5. The micro-economic approach in price theory is unacceptable also in respect of the estimation of the significance of the factors in the production of use-values. As we have seen, the efficiency of the utilization of labour or the means of production is increased by the interaction of firms and industries. At the same time, the operation of certain factors may be harmful to society while yielding profit to certain firms. It follows that the social significance of the individual production factors cannot be assessed solely from the point of view of the firms, but only in their social context. The representatives of welfare economics also refer to the favourable or unfavourable effects on the individual's consumption of other members of society. Owing to the social factors affecting the firm's output and the individual's consumption, the individual supply and demand curves cannot be summed (under the above circumstances only a few attempts have been made for the summation of supply curves). Hence, equilibrium theory requires the further assumption that neither production nor consumption should be exposed to external social effects.

6. The irrealistic assumptions of static equilibrium theory cast doubt only on the establishment of the equilibrium position as imagined in it, and not on the existence of equilibrium tendencies in general. In Marxist price theory, it is exactly through tendencies working in the direction of equilibrium that the law of value asserts itself, and the category of value can be analysed in its purity under conditions of equilibrium. Mrs. Robinson also stresses the importance of the equilibrium concept for analysis while criticizing its interpretation by the neo-classical school. "The concept of equilibrium is an indispensable tool of analysis ... its place is strictly in the preliminary stages of analytical argument, not in the framing of hypotheses to be tested against the facts ..."[130]

7. The Marxist determination of the price centre is not based on the behaviour of the individual seeking to attain optimum results with his scarce resources. Under the private ownership of the means of production, a rational economy can only be realized within individual enterprises, but not for society as a whole. Marx examines what price level actually develops in equilibrium between demand

[130] J. Robinson: *Economic Philosophy*, London, 1962, p. 81.

and supply as a result of individual producers performing their activities on a mass scale. It is not individual marginal costs, marginal rates of substitution, but social magnitudes, social value, social production cost, and through them definite production relations, relations between classes with conflicting interests, that find expression in prices formed in equilibrium between demand and supply. Since the equilibrium price as interpreted by Marx reflects a social magnitude, its theory takes account, of course, of the social interaction of individual activities, of the fact that the social efficiency of the activities of individual producers is enhanced by their being performed within the framework of a social division of labour.

And since the laws of capitalist economy assert themselves only through their being violated, an equilibrium position is established, according to Marx, only as an average of past movements. He writes on the operation of the law of value thàt though "supply and demand never equal one another in any given case, their differences follow one another in such a way ... that supply and demand are always equated when the whole is viewed over a certain period, but only as an average of past movements, and only as the continuous movement of their contradiction."[131]

8. Modern non-Marxian price and income distribution theories seek the conditions of an optimal allocation of means, of resources. In constructing the demand and supply curves of products or factor services they want to find the margin up to which, assuming the price of the product or productive service to be given, it is worthwhile for the consumer or the entrepreneur to go in the demand for the product or the productive service, to increase the supply of the productive service or of the product in order to optimize their positions. The behaviour equations of the model express the endeavours of the economic subject to utilize, with ideal rationality, his means and resources at different prices. In this sense, the price phenomenon is an *optimization category,* in which, in the case of equilibrium, such marginal magnitudes are expressed which indicate whether the consumer has spent his income optimally in satisfying his needs and whether the available factors have been used optimally in the production of commodities, as Mrs. Robinson puts it, at both the extensive and intensive margin of production.

This is an important requirement of the optimal allocation of resources, given the assumptions of the general equilibrium model. According to the principle of marginal productivity, the efficiency of the particular factors can only be assessed at the margin of production. It is there that it becomes known whether the same factors have been employed with the same efficiency in all their uses.

In the case of a marginal firm, equilibrium price expresses that unit cost is equal to marginal cost, and in the case of a firm more efficient than the marginal one it expresses (unless its rent-like incomes are included in the production costs) that marginal cost is higher than unit cost.

According to this theory, price must be formed in the long run in each industry in such a way that the *marginal* firm can realize its costs per unit of output. In Marx, however, if the economy is non-monopolistic, price formation takes place in such a way that it realizes cost and average profit in a firm operating under *average* conditions.

[131] K. Marx: *Capital,* Vol. III, Moscow, 1962, p. 186.

Let us now examine the difference between the two views somewhat more thoroughly.

From the supply side, the general equilibrium theory of price formation wishes to reveal the conditions of optimal resource allocation between alternative uses. To solve the problem, it assumes that "there are given productive resources fully specified in physical, engineering terms, a given body of technical knowledge, and a specific list of commodities to be produced."[132] It fixes the circumstance that at a given point of time society has capital goods of different efficiency available together with workers operating with different productivity. Now the question is this: what will be, under such conditions, the magnitude of the supply of an industry at different prices. If society needs a larger quantity of a given commodity, its rising price makes it possible even for firms employing inferior means of production to continue their operation, or stimulates the more efficient firms to extend the margin of their output and thus to produce under less favourable conditions. In this representation, society's demand for the commodity in question influences, by changing prices, the extensive and intensive margins of production, and stimulates to expand or contract production by the necessary quantity. Thus it is the conditions of maintaining production at the margin that find expression in price.

Marx approaches the process of price formation from an entirely different point of view. Since for Marx the greater productivity of labour in industry depends on capital, on the extent to which capital is employed, or independently of the extent of its employment, on the means of production in which it is embodied, on the production process it makes possible to adopt, there is no difficulty in increasing labour productivity by certain capital inputs. Though he does not fail to stress that each firm of an industry operates under different conditions of production, yet he places emphasis rather on the inferior firms catching up with the superior ones. "... as a matter of fact, there is no particular reason why all capital in the same production sphere should not be invested in the same manner. On the contrary, the competition between capitals tends to cancel these differences more and more. The determination of value by the socially necessary labour-time asserts itself through the cheapening of commodities and the compulsion to produce commodities under the same favourable conditions."[133]

This equalization of production conditions, as has already been mentioned, never takes place, because technology develops in the meantime and keeps up the differences among the firms' technical levels. However, it steadily maintains thereby the catching-up process, in the course of which the value of the product turned out by the firms of individual industries is taken into account as social value and, provided that the economic unit is non-monopolistic, as average value, while the individual firms of the industry are considered as average firms, their capitals as social average capital, reflecting, as it were, that the outputs of individual firms constitute an organic part of social production. And since Marx, owing to the labour theory of value, can fit profit into price, competition among industries does not make profit disappear, it only equates the profit rates of the

132 J. Robinson: The Relevance of Economic Theory, *Monthly Review,* January 1971, p. 30.
133 K. Marx: *Capital,* Vol. III, Moscow, 1962, p. 629.

particular industries to form average profit. The centre of price reflects the production conditions of the average firm of the given industry, that is, the social conditions of its production. The profit rate realized under these conditions is the basis for the flow of capitals among individual industries, and the marginal firm can still realize surplus value, because the average firm realizes average profit. As the production conditions of the output of the industry change, so do the production conditions of the average firm, with the price centre changing with them.

It is by no means a characteristic of a steady catching-up process that the particular firms should reach optimum results. On the contrary, by improving their production conditions, they strive to increase their profit. If the less efficient firms drop out in this competition, their missing output will be replaced by the more ambitious firms. The Marxian labour theory of value is not an optimization category. Equilibrium as represented by Marx cannot be characterized by the entrepreneurs' satisfaction.

The static equilibrium theory of price formation fails to capture the competitive struggle of firms to catch up with the leading ones. Or, if this representation does occur, it appears, owing to the fixation of the differences in the efficiency of capital goods and in the labour productivity of the workers employed, in the awkward form that the firms operating with less efficient factors try to entice for themselves the more efficient factors of other firms by promising them higher rewards.

In this representation, having fixed the quantities of, and differences between, factors, a similar situation will arise in all sectors of production as in agriculture owing to the monopoly character of land as a factor of production. It appears, therefore, as if the costs of marginal firms rather than the average of individual values regulate social value.

9. This real competitive struggle between firms is represented, even if in a perverse form, in a passage of Marshall's basic work, [134] where he comes to realize that it is the production costs of the firm operating under average production conditions that are to regulate the market price.

He attempts to find an answer to the question whether industry equilibrium is possible at all in pure competition when the costs of the individual firms, owing to the advantages of large-scale production, or, as he calls them, *internal economies*, are decreasing. Unlike his fellow economists, he answers this question in the affirmative. Yet in a debatable way he assumes that firms like living organisms have their biological life cycles. Having gone through stages of childhood and adulthood, they begin to decline in their old age. Young firms, operating with increasing returns and decreasing costs, expand their outputs. Aged firms, however, operating with decreasing returns and increasing costs, contract their outputs and drop out of the competitive struggle. Equilibrium in an industry, in Marshall's view, can be established in the decreasing-costs case typical of young firms even in pure competition if the price is regulated by the costs of the *representative* firm of an average age. In this case, rising young firms operating with decreasing costs expand their outputs by exactly the same quantity as the fall in industry output as a result of the decline caused by the relatively high production costs of the aged firms. Thus, the output of the industry does not change, it is in equilibrium

---

[134] A. Marshall: *Principles of Economics*, London, 1930.

in just the same way as the output of the representative firm. In Marshall's view, the equilibrium of an industry does not presuppose, in the case outlined above, an equilibrium position of the output of the other firms.

Of the followers of subjective value theory, Marshall was one of the few who represented pure theory intermingled with reality. By introducing the concept of the representative firm he did not wish to answer the question of how to use available resources optimally, but to represent the reality of capitalism, its dynamics, the competitive struggle of capitalists, the process of their differentiation, even if he did it with reference to the alleged biological life cycle of the firms. In the theoretical system based on the logic of rational choice, the realistic concept of the representative firm has not gained general acceptance. Only few economists refer to and make use of it in their investigations.

10. The determination of the price centre by the amount of labour performed under average production conditions does not prevent us from attaching importance to an analysis designed to assess the efficiency of particular factors of production with respect to the production of use-values at the margin of production at established prices. Although what is characteristic of the long-run process is not the persistence of given production conditions, but rather the process of catching up with the better ones, it is important to state at each stage of technical development which of the available production techniques is chosen by the individual firms, how they combine the variable factors in order to minimize their costs, and to what extent they expand their outputs at the established price to maximize their profits. And in such a system, which is capable of running a rational economy with the factors of production even on a social scale,—and this in its entirety is possible only if the means of production are in public ownership—it is highly important to show how to allocate the available resources optimally at each level of technical development among the firms of a particular industry or among the different industries. For this, the marginal productivity of factors, if it can be specified, may provide valuable information. By the rational allocation of the factors of production among the firms of a particular industry, by directing the less efficiently employed factors of certain firms towards firms where they can be used with greater efficiency, the quantity of output that can be produced by the amount of labour at the given level of the forces of production can be increased to a maximum. By the optimal allocation of the production factors between individual industries, channelling the factors less efficiently used in a particular industry into industries which use them more efficiently, the comparison of two industries will reveal, according to the evidence of non-Marxian economics, that, given the same factor employment, a larger quantity can be produced of the product of one industry, and not less of the product of the other. Thus, by the optimal allocation of resources, the labour socially necessary to produce a unit of product can be reduced, and the calculation of factor shadow prices through governing optimal resource allocation, reacts on the social value of products, in fact decreases it.

At the same time, though the quantity of labour used up at the intensive or extensive margin of production also contributes to the emergence of social value, it depends on the size of social value and the price determined by it where the intensive or extensive margin of production will lie, how far the individual firms can go in the use of the production factors, and which firms will just be able to maintain their production at the margin. In general, the deduction of factor shadow prices presupposes the existence of product prices regulated by social value.

Marx, arguing with Ricardo in a chapter of the second volume of his *Theories of Surplus Value,* seeks the margin for profitable capital investment in agriculture. He says that it pays the tenant to increase his additional capital inputs up to the margin where he can still realize a profit rate around the rate of interest in excess of the constant and variable capital advanced. He emphasizes, however, that at the margin of additional capital inputs a profit rate of only around the interest rate is realized, because additional capital inputs can serve the supply of their products only at current market value, that is, at a price which is determined independently of this new production.[135]

11. In Marx, the laws of demand and supply express superficial, market relationships. It is the labour theory of value which asserts itself through them. Neither demand, nor supply can be revealed in its depth without the labour theory of value. The social structure of demand rests basically not on the principle of diminishing utility, but on the relationship of the various classes to one another: primarily on the division of the national income into wages and surplus value, and secondly on the distribution of surplus value. With a change in distribution relations the demand function for the various goods will change, i.e. the quantity of goods which society is willing to buy at a certain price. The explanation of this income-distribution process, however, is built in Marx upon the labour theory of value.

The law of supply expresses, on the other hand, how production adapts itself to demand in such a way that the buyers obtain the product in the long run at social value, that is, at social production price. What is characteristic of the producers' adaptation, as has already been mentioned, is their catching up with the more efficient producers, and thus it is the firm operating under average industry conditions which has to realize average profit through consumer demand. "... absolutely nothing can be explained by the relation of supply to demand before ascertaining the basis on which this relation rests."[136]

Seeking to determine equilibrium price on the basis of market relationships, the followers of the theory represent demand and supply as equivalent factors affecting price. In real fact, however, the motive force of the capitalist economy is the hunt for profit. The regulating role of the law of value asserts itself through the deviation of profit from average profit. The supply side is the active side. And in the long run only those buyers can make purchases who are willing to pay the average profit over and above cost. No credit can be given to the view which attaches the same importance to both the demand and the supply side in explaining the price centre. The representatives of neo-classical price theory, while trying to refute the labour theory of value by referring to cost as a function of the scale of output and demand, characterize long-run equilibrium as a state which emerges in pure or perfect competition at constant returns to scale, that is, under conditions when costs are independent of the scale of output and hence of demand, too. This assumption, as we have already pointed out when quoting Hicks, is also required by the maintenance of the theory of marginal productivity.

[135] K. Marx: *Theorien über den Mehrwert,* 2 Teil, Dietz Verlag, Berlin, 1959, p. 326.
[136] K. Marx: *Capital,* Vol. III, Moscow, 1962, p. 178.

12. As has been shown, the modern variant of general equilibrium theory, too, confines the analysis of economic relationships to the market. But it examines the relations of the product market only *horizontally:* under what sort of distribution of purchasing power the market for final products comes into equilibrium. This approach omits the vertical relationships of the markets of products, and hence their production too.

After the exchange between the two departments, the new value produced—assuming simple reproduction—is incorporated in consumer goods. In general equilibrium theory, the available factors of production or their services are demanded, in the case of simple reproduction, in order to turn out consumer goods. But the demand for productive services to replace the capital goods used up is missing from the picture. In reality, the new value could be incorporated in consumer goods only because the articles of consumption embodying c_2 have been exchanged for means of production incorporating the new value produced in department I, that is, $v_1 + s_1$. These means of production are designed to replace c_2 used up. But from the fact that the incomes produced in department I are spent, in the case of simple reproduction, on purchasing consumer goods embodying c_2, it does not follow at all, as Forstmann writes of the "reproduction of real capital", that "the reward to the factors employed here can be regarded as if they involved the production of consumer goods."[137] The reproduction of the means of production used up in department II is carried out not in the process of producing consumer goods, but means of production. If we analyse the conditions of equilibrium by eliminating multiple counting and by representing the incomes produced as if they were embodied, in the case of their simple reproduction, in consumer goods, so that production is vertically integrated in all directions, it is impossible to reveal the proportionality conditions of reproduction which are the basis of market equilibrium, to disclose under what conditions the two departments can create markets for one another. Yet the creation of equilibrium between the two departments is the condition for establishing general equilibrium in the market of consumer goods in their totality. The fact that market equilibrium is determined by the equilibrium of social reproduction reveals at the same time the inacceptability of a method which claims to characterize general market equilibrium on a micro-economic basis, by the satisfaction of optimizing consumers and entrepreneurs.

[137] A. Forstmann: *Volkswirtschaftliche Theorie des Geldes*, Berlin, 1955, p. 464.

Chapter 5

THE WELFARE EFFECTS OF PURE COMPETITION

According to neo-classical economics, undisturbed competition will direct the economy towards equilibrium, in which the optimal allocation of resources is attained in both consumption and production. Within the framework of the model, maximum welfare is ensured for all members of society. At the beginning, attempts were made to prove this proposition by marginal utility theory, which assumes the interpersonal comparability of utilities, and then, after this assumption was abandoned, the Paretian criterion was adopted to prove the beneficial effect of pure or perfect competition: competition directs the economy towards a state in which the welfare of one individual cannot be increased without harming other people's welfare. It is the characteristics of this optimum state which neo-classical economics tries to formulate without including price relations, merely on the basis of marginal conditions for the optimal use of resources.

According to the *first* efficiency criterion, as a result of the undisturbed assertion of competition, *the consumer goods produced are distributed among the members of society in compliance with the Paretian optimum.*

By means of a graph, the optimum distribution of two consumer goods between two individuals can be shown, given the possibility of extending the analysis to m goods and n individuals. For this purpose, the Paretian box diagram and Edgeworthian contract curve are used. In Figure 48, $0A$ of good x and $0B$ of good y are available to the two consumers. The indifference curves of individual B are drawn contrary to those of individual A: the origin $0'$ of the graph representing B's indifference curves is in the upper right corner.

If they wish to improve their positions, individual A strives to proceed in a 'north-easterly' direction and individual B in a 'south-westerly' direction. Each point of the plane expresses some particular distribution of the two goods between the two individuals. From each point at which the slopes of the two individuals' indifference curves are not identical, it is possible to change to a point at which the two goods are distributed between the two individuals in such a proportion that the slopes of their indifference curves coincide. The marginal rate of substitution between the two goods is now identical for the two individuals; neither can change his position by further adjusting the distribution of the two goods without impairing the other's position. The locus of such points, however, at which the marginal rate of substitution is the same for the two individuals, is the contract curve. Setting out from any point not on the contract curve, a point can always be found on the contract curve at which one individual is better off without making the other worse off than before, or at which both parties are better off. Thus each point on

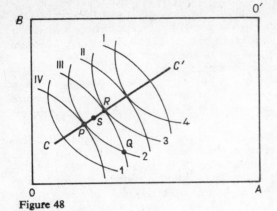

Figure 48

the contract curve represents a Paretian optimum in relation to the points outside the contract curve.

Proceeding on the graph from point Q towards point P, individual A's position does not change, since it remains on indifference curve 2. B's position, however, improves, changing from indifference curve III to indifference curve IV. The situation is just the opposite if our two individuals proceed from point Q towards point R. In this case it is A who changes from indifference curve 2 to 3, while B stays on the indifference curve III. If, however, they change from point Q to point S, that is, to a point of the area bounded by the indifference curves cutting each other, then A's position will improve, because he has reached an indifference curve higher than curve 2, and B's position also improves, because he can rise to an indifference curve higher than curve III.

What ensures, according to neo-classical theory, that the two parties will really remain on the contract curve? The undisturbed state of competition. Under pure or perfect competition, price is given for both. And since in striving to optimize their positions both consumers distribute their incomes among different goods in such a way that the marginal rate of substitution coincides with relative prices, the marginal rate of substitution will be the same for both parties at the same price of the two goods.

A further efficiency criterion under pure competition is, according to the economists of the neo-classical school, that it *ensures the optimum allocation of the factors of production among their alternative uses.* This occurs, in their view, when the marginal rate of substitution between two factors is identical in all their uses. As long as this does not occur, the quantity of output of one product that can be produced may be increased by regrouping the factors among their uses in such a way that the output of the other product does not change, or also increases. Representing now the isoquants of two products in the Paretian box diagram, we shall find that the marginal rate of substitution of the two factors is equal along the so-called production contract curve connecting the points of tangency of the isoquants of the two products. The followers of the theory also sow that proceeding from a point outside the curve connecting the points of tangency towards a nearby point of tangency, the output of one product can be increased without the other decreasing, or the outputs of both firms can be increased.

Let us illustrate the above by Meade's example.[138]

Let the marginal productivity of capital in bread-making be 4 pounds of bread per day, and that of labour also 4 pounds of bread per day. In the manufacture of tea, however, let the marginal productivity of capital be 3 pounds of tea, and that of labour 1 pound of tea.

The marginal rate of substitution between capital and labour is not identical in the two industries, so that total production can be increased by re-allocating the factors. By transferring one unit of labour from the tea industry, where the substitution relation of labour to capital is less favourable, into bread-making, where this relation is relatively favourable, the output of bread-making will increase by 4 pounds, and that of the tea industry will fall by 1 pound. One unit of capital, however, is transferred from bread-making, where the substitution relation of capital to labour is relatively unfavourable, into the tea industry, where this relation is relatively favourable: the output of tea will rise by 3 pounds, while that of bread will drop by 4 pounds. The final result is, therefore, that the same quantity of bread, but 2 pounds more tea will be produced after the re-organization than before.

In the course of regrouping, the marginal productivity of capital rises and that of labour falls in bread-making, while in manufacturing tea the marginal productivity of labour rises and that of capital falls.

Thus, the marginal productivity of the two factors after re-organization are as follows:

In bread-making: 5 pounds of bread per day for capital, and 3 pounds of bread per day for labour.

In the manufacture: 2.5 pounds of tea for capital and 1.5 pounds of tea for labour.

The proportion of the marginal productivities of the two factors are identical in both industries; by further regrouping them the output of neither product can be increased without reducing the output of the other.

What ensures the optimum allocation of the given factors among the various fields of their employment? On the one hand, the entrepreneurs' endeavour to minimize costs: they adjust the marginal rate of substitution to the given factor prices. On the other hand, the flow of factors, which lasts until a given factor obtains the same money income in all fields of its employment.

Another criterion of the efficiency of pure competition is *ideal product combination* in relation to those firms which can produce a variety of products with the factors available to them. Assuming two firms and two products, their output will be distributed optimally between the two firms if they produce the two products in such a proportion that by further changing it, taking their output together, *the output of one product cannot be increased without decreasing the output of the other*.

Let firms A and B produce goods x and y, respectively. The two goods are produced in an optimal proportion if the marginal rate of their transformation is

---

[138] J. E. Meade: *An Introduction to Economic Analysis and Policy*, Oxford, 1936, p. 115.

identical for either firm. In this case, the opportunity cost of x expressed in terms of y, or the opportunity cost of y in terms of x, is identical for both firms. Thus, suppose the opportunity cost of x is higher in firm A than in firm B, for example $3y$ in firm A and $\frac{1}{2} y$ in firm B or, what is the same thing, the opportunity cost of y is less in firm A than in firm B, $\frac{1}{3} x$ in A and $2x$ in B. Then it would be worthwhile for A to contract the output of x and expand the output of y with the factors thus released, since a decrease in the production of x by 1 unit enables it to produce $3y$, while firm B decreases the output of y and increases the output of x, because by decreasing the output of y by 1 unit it will obtain with the factors thus released two additional units of x. In the case of diverging marginal rates of transformation, the two firms may jointly expand the output of both goods until the opportunity cost of these goods is the same for both firms.

Competition also ensures an optimum distribution of the output of the two products between the two firms. Each firm, striving to attain maximum profit, turns out the two products in a proportion in which the marginal rate of transformation equals the relative prices of the products. Under pure competition, however, the prices of the two products are given and identical for the two entrepreneurs; consequently, if relative prices equal the marginal rate of transformation for each firm, then the latter is also the same for both of them.

By connecting the first and third efficiency criterion, we get the combined characteristic of the efficiency of pure competition. Competition ensures that the *marginal rate of transformation of the two* products, that is the marginal rate of their substitution from the point of view of production, *coincides with the marginal rate of their substitution* for each consumer, or in other words, "every competitive equilibrium involves tangency between the transformation locus and some sort of consumers' community indifference curve (an indifference curve which, in some sense, represents the tastes of all consumers taken together)..."[139] Until the two rates are equal, welfare in the Paretian sense can be raised by the modification of the structure of production. Suppose, for example, that a decrease in the output of product x by one unit makes it possible to produce 3 extra units of y, while in consumption one unit of x is replaced by 2 units of y. 3 more units of y are obtained if one unit less of x is produced. The consumer who foregoes one unit of x may be compensated with 2 of the extra units of y, and with the third unit the position of another person can be improved.

Let us now examine these efficiency criteria somewhat more thoroughly.

1. According to neo-classical theory discussed above, if each individual acts rationally in his own household, under the circumstances of undisturbed competition, the optimum use of resources, i.e. the welfare maximum, is also achieved on a social scale.

In our analysis, we have been concerned so far only with individuals and, in the case of particular consumers, only with their individual preference scales. And as we have already mentioned, the basic fact has been ignored that individuals belong to classes with conflicting interests and, while they are striving to optimize their positions, these class interests invariably come into conflict with one another.

In the first criterion, our diagram (Figure 48) interpreted the transition from the points outside the contract curve to those on the contract curve as an improvement

139 W. J. Baumol: *op. cit.*, p. 325.

of welfare. But the Paretian optimum criterion has nothing to say of the welfare effects of the movement along the contract curve when one individual's welfare improves at the expense of the other's. But let us consider social classes instead of individuals. The working class is getting better off at the expense of the capitalist class. Has this caused social welfare to improve? Neo-classical economists applying the Paretian optimum criterion fail to answer this question. Kaldor was the first to attempt, by means of the so-called *compensation principle,* to weigh the effect of changes of economic policy as a result of which some individuals' welfare increases and others' decreases. In doing so, he made use not of the interpersonal comparability of utilities but of the Paretian optimum criterion.[140]

Suppose the economy was in equilibrium, the resources were employed in an optimal way, and the Paretian optimum criterion was realized under the existing distribution relations. Then let a certain economic policy measure, say, the repeal of the Corn Laws, change the distribution relations in favour of the bourgeoisie and to the detriment of the landlords. With a change in distribution relations the structure of demand will also change. The structure of production will adjust itself accordingly: the production of goods demanded primarily by the bourgeoisie will expand in relation to those primarily demanded by the landowning class. The criteria of the optimal distribution of resources will now assert themselves under changed conditions, with the economy having reached another equilibrium position. Is social welfare in the new situation higher than in the old one, or is it not?

According to Kaldor's compensation principle, if the bourgeoisie can compensate the landlords for their losses from the repeal of the Corn Laws, that is, if they can keep the landlords on their original indifference curves while they themselves get better off, even after paying compensation, than they were before the change, then the change increases social welfare.

By the compensation principle Kaldor virtually fixes the original distribution relations and examines whether the change in the economy has really increased social welfare. "... it is always possible for the government to ensure that the previous income distribution should be maintained intact."[141] "A situation," writes Little, "in which some people are only a little better off and some no worse off than in another situation can quite reasonably be said to have the same distribution of real income as that other situation."[142]

The contradictory nature of Kaldor's compensation principle is criticized by Scitovsky.[143] Kaldor emphasizes that the compensation need not in fact be paid. "Whether the landlords, in the free-trade case, should in fact be given compensation or not, is a political question..."[144] To assess an increase in social welfare it is enough if the bourgeoisie is able to pay compensation. Scitovsky stresses that, if those who lose on the change are not paid compensation, they may bribe the winners to abstain from that change. They ensure them the welfare which they

[140] N. Kaldor: Welfare Propositions in Economics. In: *Essays on Value and Distribution,* London, 1960, p. 145.
[141] N. Kaldor: *op. cit.,* p. 144.
[142] I. M. D. Little: *A Critique of Welfare Economics,* Oxford, 1965, p. 100.
[143] T. Scitovsky: A Note on Welfare Propositions in Economics, *The Review of Economic Studies,* 1941, Vol. 9. pp. 77–88.
[144] N. Kaldor: *A Critique of Welfare Economics,* Oxford, 1965, p. 145.

would enjoy after the change, that is, the same indifference curve as they would reach after the change. And if, after paying the bribe, the landlords are still better off than they would have been after the repeal of the Corn Laws, then the situation prior to the change will ensure, on the basis of the Paretian optimum criterion, greater welfare than that after the change.

Scitovsky examines, taking into consideration the post-change distribution relations, the welfare implications of the change taking place in the economy as a result of economic policy and raises the question whether the realization of the post-change distribution relations in the pre-change situation ensures a higher level of welfare than that after the change.

Scitovsky's paradox is that it may be possible for the bourgeoisie to pay compensation to the landlords, and at the same time for the landlords to bribe the bourgeoisie, in other words, that social welfare is increased both by the repeal of the Corn Laws and the transition to free trade and by the abandonment of free trade and the introduction of the Corn Laws.

What underlies the paradox is that the bourgeoisie, even if they should pay compensation, can spend the rest of their incomes on a production structure developing more favourably to them after the change, when they can buy a combination of goods which they could not have afforded out of the incomes accruing to them in the situation prior to the repeal of the Corn Laws. The landlords, however, even if they should pay the sum of money needed to bribe the bourgeoisie, can also spend the rest of their incomes on a production structure developing more favourably to them prior to the repeal of the Corn Laws, and can buy a combination of goods which they could not have afforded out of the incomes accruing to them after the repeal.

Samuelson represented Scitovsky's paradox graphically in his *utility possibility* curves.

Let us suppose that society produces with the production factors available to it two sorts of product, a and b. The landlord class prefers to consume product a, while the bourgeoisie prefers product b. Before the repeal of the Corn Laws, distribution relations favoured the landlords, so that in the optimum structure of production the output of product a had a higher share than that of product b. Let us call this product structure combination I. In the optimum production structure following the repeal of the Corn Laws, however, it is product b which has a greater share, since the distribution relations now favour the bourgeoisie: this product structure will be called combination II.

The welfare of the landlord class in either product combination is at a maximum, in the extreme case, when it obtains the entire volume of production. But this maximum welfare is greater under combination I, containing a greater share of product a, than under combination II with its greater share of product b. Figure 49 represents the welfare of the landlord class along axis y, and of the bourgeoisie along axis x. The two welfare maxima for the landlord class lie on axis y, and clearly the maximum under combination I lies further from the origin.

Let us now re-allocate real income for both combinations from the landlords to the bourgeoisie, decreasing the welfare of the former and increasing that of the latter. In the extreme case, the welfare of the bourgeoisie is maximized when it obtains the entire volume of production, but welfare will be greater under combination II, containing the larger share of product b preferred by the bourgeoisie.

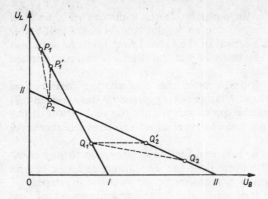

Figure 49

Thus the welfare maxima for the bourgeoisie lie on axis x, with that under combination II further from the origin.

If we now connect for each combination the landlords' maximum welfare point on axis y with the bourgeoisie's maximum welfare point on axis x, we obtain the utility possibility curves. Such a curve is the locus of combinations of the welfare of the two classes which can be achieved by the re-distribution of a particular group of products, in our case a particular combination of products a and b, between the two classes. "No significance attaches to the shape of the curves (this is because the utility scales are arbitrary), except that they must slope down from left to right if they are used to analyse problems in which it is impossible to make one man better off without making another worse off."[145]

If we re-distribute income under both product combinations from one class to the other, we reach a particular distribution in which the welfare of the landlord class is the same at both product combinations, and so is the welfare of the bourgeoisie. This is the point of intersection of the utility possibility curves I and II in Figure 49. With such an income distribution, both parties are indifferent to the changes resulting from the repeal of the Corn Laws.

Now let us suppose that combination I prevails—the Corn Laws are in force— and income distribution is such that the welfare of the two classes is given by Q_1, to the right of the intersection. If the Corn Laws are repealed, and combination II is established with a new distribution of income given by Q_2 then it is possible for the bourgeoisie to compensate the landlords, re-distributing income to Q_2', and still be better off themselves. If however the initial distribution of income is given by P_1 to the left of the intersection, then it would be impossible for the bourgeoisie to compensate the landlords and still be better off themselves, since no point on curve II lies to the 'north-east' of P_1. However, if the repeal of the Corn Laws would establish distribution P_2 under combination II, then it is possible for the landlords to retain the Corn Laws by bribing the bourgeoisie and re-distributing

[145] I. M. D. Little: *op. cit.*, p. 103.

income to P_1': then the bourgeoisie are just as well off as after repeal, and the landlords remain better off.

Thus, under income distributions to the right of the intersection of the two utility possibility curves, the Corn Laws should be repealed, since the bourgeoisie could then compensate the landlords for their loss of welfare. Under income distributions to the left of the intersection, the Corn Laws should be retained, since the landlords can bribe the bourgeoisie with the welfare increase forgone.

Recognizing the contradictory nature of the bribery and compensation criteria, Scitovsky makes the welfare-increasing effect of a change subject to two criteria: 1. the winners should be able to compensate the losers; 2. the losers should not be able to bribe the winners. In other words, under *any* conditions of income distribution prevailing both before and after the change, social welfare should increase as a result of the change.

Such a situation arises when more is produced of both products and thus the two utility possibility curves cannot intersect.

Does social welfare really increase if Scitovsky's double criterion is fulfilled? Instead of the capitalist-landowner relationship let us now take the capitalist-worker relationship. On the basis of Scitovsky's double criterion, social welfare will increase if, as a result of the change, the welfare of the capitalist class increases, and that of the working class decreases, but the capitalist class can potentially compensate the working class, while the working class is unable to bribe the capitalist class. But the validity of the double criterion merely expresses that the output of all products has increased, or only that of certain products without a decrease in others. In this case, *potential* welfare increases, according to Samuelson, at any income distribution. But how social welfare *actually* changes with increased production, depends in fact on how the increased output is distributed among the social classes. Any change in production is generally accompanied by a change in income distribution relations, and vice versa. Owing to the close interrelationship of the two, a given income distribution is matched with a corresponding production structure, and a given production structure has its corresponding income distribution. It is for this reason that Little[146] asserts that the appraisal of changes in production from a welfare point of view is inseparable from the appraisal of the related income distribution relations and he adds a further criterion to Scitovsky's double criterion: income distribution cannot be worse in the new situation than it was before. He leaves, however, the question open on the basis of what theoretical criterion it should be decided which income distribution is to be regarded the more favourable one from the welfare point of view.

When writing that "if corn could by importation be procured cheaper, the loss in consequence of not importing it is far greater on one side that the gain is on the other,"[147] Ricardo expected from the repeal of the Corn Laws, from a change in income distribution relations in favour of the bourgeoisie, the acceleration of capital accumulation. And the development of production and the change in distribution relations in favour of the bourgeoisie wishing to promote the development of the productive forces at the cost of the landowners impeding the develop-

[146] I. M. D. Little: *op. cit.*, p. 101.
[147] D. Ricardo: The Principle of Political Economy and Taxation. In: *The Works of David Ricardo*, London, 1888, p. 203.

14*

211

ment of the productive forces by keeping in force the Corn Laws, were synonymous to him with the growth of social welfare.

2. Further examining the first efficiency criterion, we must state that the identity of the marginal rates of substitution for all consumers is an entirely formal criterion of welfare. This identity exists at any point of the contract curve. It does not give any information on where on the contract curve the two consumers come to an agreement. Clearly, it depends on the incomes of the two individuals compared, on the existing distribution relations, how much of the given quantity of the two products is carved out to the one and how much to the other. Suppose that one of the two persons compared is a worker and the other a capitalist; it is obviously the relatively low indifference curve of the worker and the relatively high one of the capitalist which are tangential to one another. According to the first efficiency criterion, however, all that is needed for maximum welfare to materialize is the optimum use of their incomes by all members of society, however slight these incomes may be. This maximum is merely the maximum attained within the existing order of distribution, and a given welfare maximum is attached to any order of distribution.

Does the transition from a point outside the contract curve really mean the improvement of welfare? Those who maintain that it does regard the consumer preference scale as invariable, and leave out of account the shaping forces of society, the effect which non-Marxian economics calls the externalities affecting consumption. If some people's welfare increases, it does not leave unchanged the welfare of those whose real income has not changed. Already Marx was aware of this effect in his work *Wage Labour and Capital:* "A house may be large or small; as long as the surrounding houses are equally small, it satisfies all social demands for a dwelling. But let a palace arise beside the little house, and it shrinks from a little house to a hut ... the occupant of the relatively small house will feel more and more uncomfortable, dissatisfied and cramped within its four walls."[148] Comparing the relationship between the capitalist and working classes, Marx considers the increase in the welfare of the capitalist class, with the position of the working class left unchanged, not as an increase in social welfare, but as the relative impoverishment of the working class.

3. The criteria listed above show the efficiency of pure competition as divorced from social production relations also in respect of production. We are only concerned with individual, isolated firms, and the fact is completely overlooked that the efficiency of the firm is influenced by the circumstance that it is operating as a member of a social productive organization, by the place it assumes in the interrelationship of the social division of labour. It is forgotten that the productive activity of isolated firms, constituting an organic part of social total production, also may come into conflict with that very social production.

Certain social implications of the activity of isolated capitalist firms, some manifestations of the conflict between private and social interests, were already recognized by some neo-classical economists who, however, did not give up their micro-economic approach to economic relationships. Recognizing these phenomena, they wished to supplement the working of the economic mechanism under conditions of pure competition by certain economic policy measures of the state.

[148] K. Marx: *Wage Labour and Capital,* Moscow, 1954, p. 51.

212

The Marshallian external economies are already indicative of the positive effects of the producers' social relations on the output of the individual firms. In further developing Marshall's idea, Pigou makes a distinction between marginal private and social productivity of particular factors, or between marginal private and social costs of individual firms. If the marginal social productivity of factors exceeds marginal private productivity, this expresses that by employing the factors of production, the firm brings in a benefit to society which the firm cannot appropriate to itself. The reverse case occurs when marginal private productivity of the factors of production surpasses marginal social productivity, or, in other words, when the marginal private cost of a product is less than its marginal social cost. The development of technology has since produced much more convincing examples than those mentioned by Pigou. It will suffice to refer to the increasing pollution of rivers, lakes, seas and the air caused by the activity of certain firms, the resulting damage of which, without being included in the costs of individual firms, is inflicted on society as a whole.

Pigou emphasizes that the divergence of marginal private from social product counteracts optimal resource allocation even under conditions of pure competition. It counteracts it, because "... self-interest will tend to bring about equality in the values of the marginal private net products of resources invested in different ways. But it will not tend to bring about equality in the values of the marginal social net products..."[149] That is, in pure competition, private and social interests clash, since the firms, in carrying on their activities, keep in mind only their private interests and set production at the level where their marginal private cost equals the price level, even if social interest would demand that their outputs be further expanded when the marginal social productivity of factors exceeds their marginal private productivity, or lowered in the opposite case. Thus the pursuit of private interests through the activity of firms striving to maximize their profit does not ensure the maximum of social welfare even under conditions of pure competition.

4. In consumption, as we have seen, different points of the contract curve may be the optimum point depending on the change in income distribution relations. The question is whether the efficiency criteria of production determine the production techniques or the production structure satisfying the Paretian optimum criteria independently of distribution relations.

As far as the coincidence of the marginal rates of substitution between two factors in all their uses is concerned, it appears that the production techniques chosen in compliance with this condition are not dependent on changes in the distribution relations. A certain dependence, however, can be found if the production techniques chosen are not independent of the scale of output, that is, if a change in the scale of output changes relative marginal productivities, the marginal rates of substitution, and thus the production contract curve is not a straight line. In this case, even at an identical level of the marginal rates of substitution, different production techniques will be the optimal ones, depending on the distribution relations and through them on the structure of demand as well as the scale of output of the particular industries. According to the theory, increasing returns to scale are irreconcilable of course with the existence of com-

---

[149] A. C. Pigou: *The Economics of Welfare*, London, 1960, p. 172.

petitive equilibrium. But the marginal rates of substitution between factors can also be changed by diminishing returns to scale.

The fourth, joint efficiency criterion characterizes as welfare maximum the situation in which the marginal rates of substitution between different goods are the same as regards both consumption and production, in which case the social indifference curve touches the social transformation curve. Social welfare is identical at all points along the social indifference curve, the marginal rates of substitution between any two products are the same for all consumers. The social indifference curve is constructed, after Scitovsky, by a specific summation of any two tangent individual indifference curves of a box diagram. In the course of the summation, the two selected indifference curves touch each other at different points and, as a result, the position of the upper right-hand origin of the box diagram will change, too. The changing positions of the origins will describe the social indifference curve. Depending on which two tangent individual indifference curves are combined, the resulting social indifference curve will express different income distribution relations and thus, depending on the distribution relations, the social transformation curve will be tangential to different social indifference curves at different points. As a result of the change in distribution relations, any point of the social transformation function may be optimal. The optimal allocation of resources is optimal always only from the point of view of the prevailing distribution relations. As the system of income distribution changes, always different allocations will become optimal.

So we have arrived at the general conclusion that the efficiency criteria of pure competition as formulated by the representatives of the neo-classical school are merely formal statements. They are formal, because the marginal conditions set up for the individual consumers' or producers' economies are, as we have seen, too general even for the particular economies, lacking any empirical content. They are formal, further, because their realization under *any* system of distribution means the optimum of social welfare in its Paretian sense, and reveals nothing of the welfare effects of a change in the distribution relations.

Otherwise, as has already been shown, the improvement in the situation of individual households and firms does not necessarily mean an increase in social welfare, too, as the two things can conflict even according to the teachings of certain followers of the neo-classical theory.

5. Rejecting the measurability of utilities and thereby their interpersonal comparability, the new variant of equilibrium theory characterizes the equilibrium position as a state in which maximum social welfare is realized in its Paretian sense, Marshall, however, by assuming the interpersonal comparability of utilities, called attention to the fact that, owing to unequal distribution relations, the equilibrium position does not mean the realization of the maximum of social welfare in the strictest sense of the word. On the contrary, social welfare may be increased exactly by a level of supply or demand exceeding the equilibrium level. This is the case, according to Marshall, when the sellers' and buyers' economic positions are not equal. If the buyers are much worse off than the sellers, social welfare can be increased, in Marshall's model, by expanding output beyond its equilibrium size and by selling the products at a loss. Then the resources have not been used optimally in relation to effective demand, but have been used favourably regarding the needs of the mass of people. And social welfare is equally increased

by keeping supply below its equilibrium level when the sellers are worse off than the buyers.

Social welfare, in Marshall's interpretation, demands not only that everybody should use his resources rationally. This welfare can also be increased if the consumers spend their incomes in such a way that they step up demand for the service of the poor, increasing thereby the incomes of the poor, because the same sum of money is of much greater significance for the welfare of the poor than for that of the rich.

In Marshall's view, social welfare may also be increased by state intervention, through upsetting the equilibrium, in the case when in a society there are industries producing at a diminishing, and others producing at increasing returns. In this case, Marshall points out, the productive sector producing at diminishing return should be taxed, and the tax revenue should be used to subsidize the productive sector operating at increasing return.

In the productive sector operating at diminishing return, the tax burden shifts the supply curve of the product upwards, which diminishes the output of the product concerned at a given demand function. As a result of decreasing output, the marginal cost of the product will fall, and thus the supply price not containing tax will also decrease, while the supply price also containing tax will increase to a lesser degree than the tax burden. Therefore, consumers' rent, which, according to Marshall, can also be expressed in terms of money, may decrease less than the tax revenue has increased. This depends on the steepness of the supply curve.

If the government now uses this tax revenue to subsidize the output of products turned out at increasing return, then the productive sector concerned will expand its output, and can offer the increased volume of products at a price lower than their original marginal cost. With the expansion of output, however, the marginal costs and, in conjunction with them, the supply price is bound to decline, and thus the supply price established as a result of state subsidization will decrease by more than the amount of the state subsidy. Therefore, the increase in consumers' rent may exceed the degree of state subsidy. By taxing the productive sector operating at diminishing return and supporting the productive sector operating at increasing return, that is, by diverting price from actual marginal costs and thus by moving the economy away from the equilibrium position, consumers' welfare can be increased.

Thus Marshall[150] acknowledges that the undisturbed assertion of competition does not always ensure maximum social welfare. In this case, government measures are needed to increase it. Marshall's arguments paved the way for the emergence of welfare economics; they show that while the assumption of the interpersonal comparability of utilities does provide some possibility of disclosing the problems stemming from the enormous discrepancies of social distribution relations in a capitalist economy, by the rejection of the interpersonal comparability of utilities even this slight possiblity is lost and social content is increasingly ignored.

[150] See A. Marshall: *Principles of Economics,* London, 1930, Book V, Chapter XIII, pp. 462–476.

Part Three

THE EMERGENCE AND DEVELOPMENT OF THE MODERN NON-MARXIAN THEORY OF MARKET FORMS

Chapter 1

INTRODUCTION

Modern non-Marxian price theory began to concern itself with the emergence of monopoly capitalism after a rather long delay. Until the 1930s, "both the theory of economics as well as the popular conceptions are based essentially upon the English classical theory of competition, of which monopoly forms an exception."[1] Schumpeter also writes that for a long time competition was regarded the normal case, in the sense that it covered the major part of the practice of business life; that deviation from the competition pattern was only fortuitous; and that competition must be the normal case, and appropriate economic policy measures should be applied to ensure that even if the elements of the actual system were not competitive, the whole should operate as a competitive system.[2]

The explanation of the phenomena of capitalist economy on the basis of the theory of pure competition, the insistence on the efficiency of the capitalist economic mechanism under the assumption of pure competition, came more and more into conflict with the reality of capitalism. It was primarily during the great economic crisis that attempts were made in non-Marxian economics to adjust the price and income-distribution theories to the relations of monopoly capitalism.

Pioneers in that field were, in the first place, the American E. Chamberlin and the British J, Robinson. Besides them, the Norwegian economist R. Frisch, the Danish F. Zeuthen, the British R. Harrod and A. L. Bowley as well as the American H. Hotelling and the German H. Stackelberg made, among others, significant contributions to changing non-Marxian price theory in the 1930s.

Piero Sraffa was the first to call attention in his 1926 article, written in a sharp, critical tone, to the deficiencies of the price theory based on pure competition. Robinson and presumably Chamberlin, too, took over some elements from Sraffa.

It was primarily on the aspect of the law of returns that Sraffa began to criticize the theory of pure competition. He pointed out that, as shown by everyday experience, a large number of firms operate under conditions of increasing returns. The large-scale production of modern firms and the resulting advantages in production and marketing are the facts underlying Sraffa's problem of increasing returns. Under these conditions, the greater the scale of output of a firm, the less the cost of production per unit of output. Thus, according to the theory, with

---

[1] F. Zeuthen: *Problems of Monopoly and Economic Warfare,* London, 1930, p. 2.
[2] J. Schumpeter: *The History of Economic Analysis,* New York, 1955, p. 972.

price taken as given, the entrepreneurs should expand their outputs to infinity. But if a firm expands its size to infinity and absorbs the whole market, what remains then of pure competition?

Under conditions of increasing returns, the formula of the equality of price and marginal cost cannot express, in Sraffa's view, the conditions of the firm's equilibrium, because with decreasing cost per unit of output the marginal cost curve will lie below the average cost curve. Therefore, if marginal cost and price were equal, cost per unit of output would be higher than price, and the entrepreneurs would sustain losses.

Practical businessmen, continues Sraffa in his attack against the theory of pure competition, "... would consider absurd the assertion that the limit to their production is to be found in the internal conditions of production of their firm, which do not permit of the production of a greater quantity without an increase in cost."[3] He sees the main impediment to expanding output not in rising costs, but rather in the fact that larger quantities are difficult to sell without a reduction of price, or without an increase in selling costs. By this Sraffa assumes that the particular sellers are able to alter price, and consequently the established market situation is not pure or perfect competition. In his opinion, every seller strives to differentiate his product from those of other firms, to build up in the buyers a preference for his own product, that is, to eliminate the buyers' indifference to the products of particular sellers, which, as is commonly known, is a condition for pure competition. The source of preference for a seller's product may, according to Sraffa, vary greatly, ranging from the buyer's insistence on the product he is used to, to trade marks, trust in the quality of certain products, the firm's reputation or nearness to the market, the buyer's personal relationships, etc. As a result of preferences derived from these factors, buyers are willing to pay more for a commodity just to get it from a particular seller, even though they could get it cheaper from another. In this case, however, the general market for a given commodity is divided into a series of markets, with the prevailing price on each partial market being different. And the individual sellers are faced not with the general demand curve for a whole class of commodities or for the industry, but with the special demand curve for their own individual product. Price, under such conditions, is no longer beyond their control, and thus Sraffa does not consider the elasticity of demand for their commodities as infinite, either.

A firm can make an inroad into another firm's market only if it increases its selling costs. Firms within their own markets are in a privileged position enjoying advantages similar to those of monopolies.

Earlier, the factors mentioned and regarded by Sraffa as causing imperfections of the market were taken to be merely frictional factors which only delay or disturb the effect of the active forces of the market, which, however, will nevertheless assert themselves in the end. But in Sraffa's view, most of the factors upsetting the unity of the market are not frictions "but are themselves active forces which produce permanent and even cumulative effects."[4] He thinks that "it is necessary,

[3] P. Sraffa: Laws of Returns under Competitive Condition, *The Economic Journal*, December 1926, p. 543.
[4] P. Sraffa: *op. cit.*, p. 542.

therefore, to abandon the path of free competition and turn in the opposite direction, namely, towards monopoly."[5]

Hotelling, following Sraffa, also writes that, contrary to the assumption of the theory of perfect or pure competition, what we encounter in real life is this: "If the purveyor of an article gradually increases his price while his rivals keep theirs fixed, the diminution in volume of his sales will in general take place continuously rather than in the abrupt way which has tacitly been assumed." "Many customers will prefer to trade with him because they live nearer to his store than to the others,... or because his mode of doing business is more to their liking, ... or on account of some difference in service or quality ... . Such circles of customers may be said to make every entrepreneur a monopolist... "[6]

Sraffa and after him Robinson, Chamberlin, Hotelling and Zeuthen, assert that in a real economy pure competition is just an extreme case, and so also is pure monopoly. The actual forms of the market are a mixture of pure competition and monopoly. "Between the perfect competition and monopoly of theory lie the actual cases."[7]

In Robinson's and Chamberlin's representation, competition within an industry is the competition of sellers enjoying a monopolistic position, who are able to differentiate their products from those of other sellers. Such competition is called by Robinson *imperfect competition,* and by Chamberlin *monopolistic competition.*

What do they mean by monopoly? A market stituation in which "monopoly ordinarily means control over the supply, and therefore over the price."[8] "Every individual producer has the monopoly of his own output,"[9] writes Robinson when "...a single producer controls the whole output of such a commodity, the plain man's notion of a monopolist and the logical definition of a monopolist as a single seller coincide..."[10]

Robinson examines what characterizes the monopolistic position of the single seller in imperfect competition. Here, however, she halts her investigation; she does not examine, like Chamberlin, the competition of producers manufacturing the same product, that is, competition within the industry in imperfect competition.

Let us now examine in more detail, relying primarily on Mrs. Robinson's investigations, the determination of equilibrium price under conditions of monopoly.

[5] *Ibid.*
[6] H. Hotelling: Stability and Competition, *The Economic Journal,* 1929, Vol. XXXIX, pp. 41 and 62.
[7] *Ibid.*
[8] E. Chamberlin: *The Theory of Monopolistic Competition,* Cambridge, 1947, p. 7.
[9] J. Robinson: *The Theory of Imperfect Competition,* London, 1954, p. 5.
[10] J. Robinson: *op. cit.,* pp. 5–6.

Chapter 2

PRICE DETERMINATION IN A MONOPOLY SITUATION

TOTAL REVENUE FUNCTION AND MARGINAL REVENUE

A seller enjoying a monopoly situation, differentiating his commodity from the commodities of the other sellers of the industry, is faced in his own market with a demand curve of finite elasticity. Thus, by changing the volume of his output, he is able to change price, which is for him a so-called action parameter.

In seeking to achieve maximum profit, he must reckon, therefore, with the fact that an increase in the quantity produced will decrease the price of his product. Thus in determining the scale of his supply, he must be aware of how his total revenue, i.e. increased quantity multiplied by decreasing price, will develop. His total revenue is the result of two opposed effects, in Stackelberg's[11] terminology of *quantity* and *price effects:* the increase in supply raises, the decrease in price diminishes his total revenue. Whether his total reveneue eventually increases, decreases or stays unchanged, depends on how the percentage increase in the quantity sold is related to the percentage decrease in price, that is, on the elasticity of demand for his product.

It was Marshall who first pointed out that the elasticity of demand changed with price.

Representing the demand function by a straight line on a graph (cf. Figure 2), we find that demand, SP, belongs to the price, $0S$. Reducing price by dp (PR in Figure 2), demand will rise by dq (RP' in the Figure 2). Substituting the corresponding segments of the straight line into the formula of the elasticity of demand, $\dfrac{dq}{q} \cdot \dfrac{p}{dp}$, we obtain $\dfrac{0S}{St}$ as the elasticity of demand.

Setting out from a high price level, and continuously decreasing price, the elasticity of demand will also decrease. While the absolute magnitude of elasticity is greater than unity, money revenue will increase as price decreases, since the quantity sold will rise in a greater proportion as a result of the percentage decrease in price. At the price where elasticity in absolute terms reaches unity, money revenue will remain unaffected by an infinitesimally small change in price. If we further decrease price, the elasticity of demand will drop in absolute terms below unity, and money revenue, too, will decrease.

Representing the curve of total revenue as price multiplied by the corresponding quantity on a graph (Figure 50), the curve will slope up with the decrease in price

---

[11] H. Stackelberg: *Grundlagen der theoretischen Volkswirtschaftslehre,* Bern, 1948, p. 193.

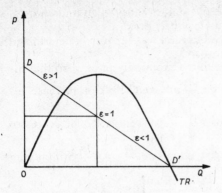

Figure 50

until the elasticity of demand reaches unity, and will be at a maximum at a price where the elasticity of demand equals unity. When price drops below this level, the curve of total revenue will also slope downwards.

Taking into account that with the increase in quantity price will decline, the monopolist striving to maximize his profit cannot expand his output up to the point at which the increasing marginal cost equals price. In this case he would suffer a loss. For if he increases supply by one unit, he thereby decreases the price, as the elasticity of demand for his product is finite. Thus the increment of his revenue cannot be equal to price. He must deduct from it the loss resulting from the lower price at which he must sell the earlier units, too, at the increased output.

Illustrating the above by a simple numerical example, let us assume that in pure competition the firm produces 5 units at 10 dollars each, with a total revenue of 50 dollars, and 6 units at 10 dollars each, with a total revenue of 60 dollars.

Thus, the increment of the firm's revenue resulting from the expansion of output by 1 unit, is 10 dollars.

Suppose now that our firm attains a monopolistic position because, for instance, it is able to differentiate its product from other sellers' products. In this case, the elasticity of demand for its product changes from infinite to finite. Thus, the previous numerical example will be modified in this way: in a monopoly situation, the firm produces 5 units at 10 dollars each, with a total revenue of 50 dollars, and 6 units at 9 dollars each, with a total revenue of 54 dollars.

Thus, its revenue increment is 4, less than price, which is due to the fact that in expanding supply it has to sell the earlier units, too, at a price of 9 instead of 10 dollars.

If it increased its output until marginal cost reached price, 9 dollars, it would lose 5 dollars on the last unit.

The revenue increment different from price has a crucial role to play in determining monopolistic equilibrium. That the two are different was already recognized by Marshall. In his study published in 1930, Harrod determines equilibrium under monopoly given this difference. We first encounter the term *marginal revenue* to denote incremental revenue in Robinson and Chamberlin. This concept expresses the additional revenue accruing to a firm from increasing its output by one unit.

223

In other words, it is the steepness of the curve of total revenue which finds expression in it. In pure competition, marginal revenue equals price.

The size of marginal revenue in a monopoly situation was separately determined by Mrs. Robinson and the Italian Luigi Amoroso.

Suppose the monopolist can sell quantity q at the monopoly price p, so that his total revenue is pq. If now he reduces price by $\dfrac{dp}{p}$ per cent, he can increase his sales by $\dfrac{dq}{q}$ per cent. His total revenue will grow by $\dfrac{dq}{q}$ per cent and will decreases by $\dfrac{dp}{p}$ per cent. The change in his revenue, $d(pq)$, equals $pq\dfrac{dq}{q} - pq\dfrac{dp}{p}$. Simplifying and re-arranging the terms, we get $d(pq) = p\left[dq - \dfrac{q \cdot dp}{p}\right]$.

We obtain marginal revenue by dividing $d(qp)$ by dq:

$$\frac{d(pq)}{dq} = p\left[1 - \frac{q \cdot dp}{p \cdot dq}\right],$$

where $\dfrac{q \cdot dp}{p \cdot dq}$ is the reciprocal of the elasticity of demand. Thus marginal revenue equals price multiplied by $\left[1 - \dfrac{1}{\varepsilon}\right]$.

In Figure 51, representing the demand curve by the line St, and expessing the elasticity of demand at price P as $\dfrac{0S}{St}$, marginal revenue $= 0S\left[1 - \dfrac{St}{0S}\right] = 0S - St$. But $St = BP$, and thus marginal revenue $= 0S - BP = AP - BP = AB$, and is therefore less than price, AP.

This marginal revenue will fall all along as price decreases, expressing that total revenue, until reaching its maximum, rises at a decreasing rate, owing to the decrease in the elasticity of demand. Marginal revenue will be zero at a price where the elasticity of demand drops to unity, and thus total revenue is at a maximum. When price declines further, marginal revenue will fall below zero (Figure 52).

EQUILIBRIUM UNDER MONOPOLY. THE COURNOT POINT

Profit under monopoly is at a maximum when marginal profit equals zero, when revenue increment and cost increment, marginal revenue and marginal cost, are equal. The point at which the marginal revenue curve and the marginal cost curve intersect is called the Cournot point in honour of Cournot, the first to attempt to determine, by means of the demand function, the price level ensuring maximum profit under monopoly conditions. This equilibrium point, however, appears at a lower output level than that which corresponds to the equality of marginal cost and price (Figure 53).

Mrs. Robinson determined price under monopoly by projecting on to the demand curve the quantity given by the point of intersection of the marginal cost curve and the marginal revenue curve.

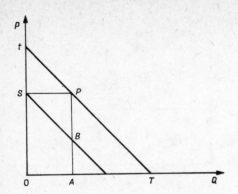

Figure 51

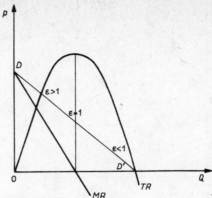

Figure 52

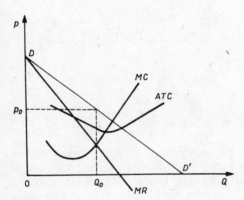

Figure 53

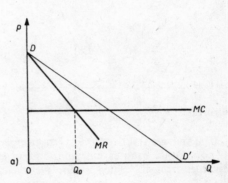

Figure 54a

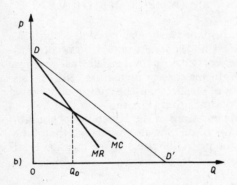

Figure 54b

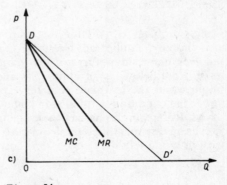

Figure 54c

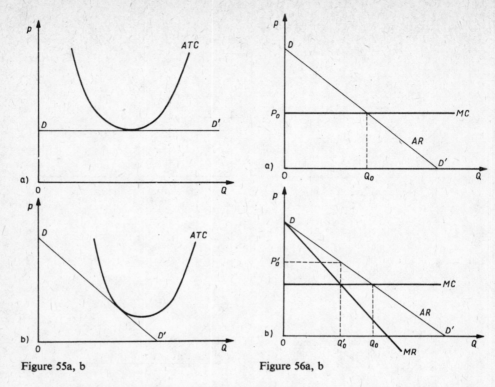

Figure 55a, b   Figure 56a, b

The marginal cost curve in monopoly does not express a supply function, for a monopolist equates marginal cost not to price but to marginal revenue, which diverges from it. "Then a supply curve can no longer be meaningfully or usefully drawn, and cannot be drawn at all...,"[12] writes Shackle in conjunction with monopoly.

SOME DIFFERENCES BETWEEN MONOPOLY AND PURE COMPETITION

Sraffa's problem with diminishing marginal revenue was solved by Mrs. Robinson. In monopoly, equilibrium may be established under conditions of both constant and even increasing returns, if the marginal cost curve cuts the marginal revenue curve 'from below', as in Figure 54a and b. In the case of increasing returns, this requires that the marginal cost curve is more elastic than the marginal revenue curve; the condition is fulfilled in Figure 54b but not in Figure 54c.

Mrs. Robinson emphasizes these changed conditions of the possibility of equilibrium as an essential difference from pure competition. She also points out that if the price in monopoly only covers unit costs, the price line touches the average total

[12] G. L. Shackle: *The Years of High Theory*, Cambridge, 1967, p. 52.

226

cost curve not at its minimum (as under pure competition, see Figure 55a), but at a point on its downward-sloping segment (Figure 55b). Capacity is, then, not utilized optimally in this case.

Mrs. Robinson raises the question of the scale of output and price if a certain commodity, which was formerly produced by competing firms, is monopolized. She assumes that the change affects neither the demand nor the supply curve of the industry. In this case, production under conditions of free competition is, in her view, larger than production under monopoly, and price is lower (see Figures 56a and b).

Mrs. Robinson admits the fact of exploitation in the case of monopoly. The worker cannot get as his wages the marginal productivity of his labour multiplied by the product price, but only the marginal productivity of his labour multiplied by marginal revenue. Illustrating this by a simple example, let us assume that in a firm, under pure competition,

10 workers produce 10 units of product at $10 each: total revenue = $100;
11 workers produce 11 units of product at $10 each: total revenue = $110;
the marginal productivity of labour is 1 unit, money wage is therefore $1 \cdot \$10 = = \$10$.

Under monopoly,
10 workers produce 10 units of product at $10 each: total revenue = $100;
11 workers produce 11 units of product at $9.8 each: total revenue = $107.8;
marginal revenue = $7.8.
Money wage = marginal product multiplied by marginal revenue = $1 \cdot \$7.8$ dollars = $7.8.

Rewards for the services of the other factors of production are obtained similarly.

In the case of a homogeneous and linear production function, the total revenue accruing to the factors of production does not yield the value of total output under conditions of monopoly.

$$L \frac{\partial Q}{\partial L} \cdot p \left[1 - \frac{1}{\varepsilon}\right] + K \frac{\partial Q}{\partial K} \cdot p \left[1 - \frac{1}{\varepsilon}\right] < Qp.$$

The surplus is the entrepreneur's profit. Thus, in monopoly, the firm can realize profit even in an equilibrium position.

If, however, the total revenue of factors equals the price sum of the output, the production function cannot be homogeneous and linear.

Chapter 3

CHAMBERLIN'S THEORY OF MONOPOLISTIC COMPETITION

INTRODUCTION

Simultaneously with Mrs. Robinson, Chamberlin also chose the theory of monopoly, instead of the previously prevalent theory of pure competition, as a starting-point for his value theory. "... it is here that the superiority of approaching the problem through the theory of monopoly rather than through that of competition is at once apparent..."[13] This is because the theory of competition excludes the monopoly elements, while the theory of monopoly presupposes that "... every monopolist faces the competition of substitutes..."[14] It is exactly the investigation of the competitive relationships between sellers in monopolistic positions, and the extension of the examination of the conditions of equilibrium from individual monopolists to the competitive struggle of monopolist rivals which primarily distinguishes his analysis from that of Mrs. Robinson.

Chamberlin reduces the imperfection of the market, the absence of pure competition, to two reasons: (1) the commodity put on the market is not homogeneous, the buyer is not indifferent to the seller's identity. This is , in his view, the source of monopoly; (2) there are few sellers on the market, which—as Triffin emphasizes— may be accounted for by the barriers to entry to the market. The analysis of the latter is completely lacking in Mrs. Robinson's investigations. Chamberlin himself is relatively little concerned with this market situation either, his value theory not being focused on the examination of this question. He is interested in the first place in that form of monopolistic competition in which a large number of sellers put commodities somewhat differentiated from one another on the market, where competition is carried on between them, to use Chamberlin's term, whithin a large group.

He mentions two methods to differentiate products as means which serve similar aims: (1) Changes relating to the nature or quality of the products, new varieties, etc. The advantage derived from them is secured to the firm by patents, licenses and trade marks. He also mentions differences in packaging, and even the geographical distance between the production and marketing locations. (2) Manipulation by expenditure on selling.

Owing to such products differentiation, the markets of individual sellers do not merge as in the case of pure competition, but constitute a network of the particular sellers' connected markets, in each of which the sellers can manipulate prices.

---

[13] E. Chamberlin: *op. cit.*, p. 206.
[14] *Ibid.*

228

Thus, competition exists on three counts, *price changes, changes in the quality of the product and manipulation through selling costs.* It is on these three aspects that Chamberlin examines the conditions of equilibrium, at both the firm and industry or (to use his own term) group level, that is, on the level of the sellers' group.

He generally does not use the concept of industry. In his view, the individual industries can be distinguished only in the case of homogeneous products. He maintains that in the case of sellers offering heterogeneous products it is rather arbitrary to group commodities into particular industries. He is, however, compelled to include commodities in close substitution relationship with one another in separate groups, as their demand-supply relations can be determined unambiguously only if the demand–supply relations of the other commodities belonging to the group are given.

THE CONDITION OF "PRICE EQUILIBRIUM"

Chamberlin determines price equilibrium on the *firm* level like Robinson. In doing so, he disregards the possiblity of changing product quality. Aiming to achieve maximum profit, the firm will supply in equilibrium a quantity at which its marginal cost equals marginal revenue, which is lower than price.

In examining price equilibrium on the *group level,* Chamberlin says he is making "heroic" assumptions. He assumes that consumers' preferences are evenly distributed among particular commodities within the group, and the difference between them is not so great that it could bring about differences in cost. Thus he supposes that the demand and cost curves for each commodity within the group are identical. In the case of this so-called *symmetry assumption,* price is established under conditions of group equilibrium at the same level for each firm. Chamberlin now displays group equilibrium graphically, through one particular firm similar to, and representing, as it were, the other firms (Figure 57).

He distinguishes two sorts of demand curve for the individual firms. *dd'* expresses demand for the product of the firm when, with a change in its price, the price of the products of the other firms within the group remains unchanged. In the case of a large group, the assumption of a *dd'*-type demand curve is, according to Chamberlin, realistic. Demand curve *DD'* reflects the development of demand for the product of the firm under the circumstances of a simultaneous change in product price by all firms within the group. That demand curve is a fractional part of the demand curve for the general class of commodity, and its elasticity is identical with that of the latter; *dd'* is evidently more elastic than *DD',* because the demand for the firm's product increases more if only that firm alone lowers the price of its product and its competitors do not, than if the price reduction is general; or demand decreases more if that firm alone increases the price of its product than if its competitors do the same. The position of *DD'* depends on the sellers' number. The more there are, the more the curve will shift towards the left, the less of the total demand for that kind of product will fall at any given price to one firm, and the less a firm will be able to increase its demand by decreasing the price of its product. If, however, the number of firms decreases, curve *DD'* will shift to the right.

229

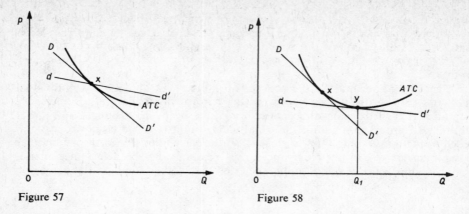

Figure 57   Figure 58

Every firm may increase its profit if it proceeds along curve *dd'*. It need not be afraid of the reaction of its rivals because the increase in its supply will affect their market, owing to their large number, only to a negligible extent. Since every firm is equally interested, in order to increase its profit, in proceeding along curve *dd'*, as a result of their joint action price will decline, and thus *dd'* will also shift downwards along *DD'*.

In Figure 57 *DD'* touches the unit-cost curve at point *x,* and *dd'* will cut it at the point of tangency. At that point price covers only unit cost. *x,* however, is not a lasting equilibrium. This is because any firm moving along *dd'* may earn profit by decreasing price. Every firm expands its supply, decreasing thereby the price of the whole commodity group along *DD'* and *dd'* shifts downwards, finally touching the unit cost curve at point *y* (Figure 58).

However, *y* is not an equilibrium point either, though the *dd'* curve of the individual firms touches the unit-cost curve and thus no firm gains by further decreasing price. It is not an equilibrium point, because if each firm went on expanding its output until the point of tangency of *dd'* and the unit-cost curve, price would generally fall as a result of their concerted behaviour. With this, however, *DD'* instead of *dd'* will be taken into account as the demand curve of their product. Thus, quantity $0Q_1$ represents an exaggerated supply at the point of tangency of the demand curve *dd'*. In our graph (Figure 58), the market is not willing to take from the individual firms quantity $0Q_1$ on the demand curve *DD'* at the price of Q_1y. There are too many firms within the group. Part of them will leave the group as a result of which curve *DD'* shifts to the right. A group equilibrium will come about when *DD'* cuts *dd'* at its point of tangency with the unit-cost curve. Then the supply level along curve *dd'* coincides with the supply level along curve *DD'*, the size of the supplies of the individual firms has been established, and no firm is interested any longer in decreasing price and further expanding its output.

THE CONDITION OF "PRODUCT EQUILIBRIUM"

Let us now look at the problem of product equilibrium within the firm. Since it is now the product which is variable, Chamberlain, in order to examine the effect

230

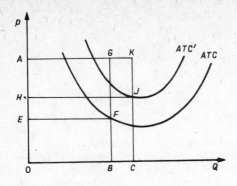

Figure 59

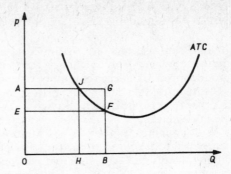

Figure 60

of quality change in isolation, takes price to be constant. If the entrepreneur improves the quality of his product, he can sell more of it, but his production costs will also increase. At a price of $0A$ he was able to sell quantity $0B$, and the size of his profit is represented by the area $EFGA$ (Figure 59). After improving the quality of his product he can sell quantity $0C$ at a price of $0A$, and his profit is $HJKA$. If the latter is larger than the former area, then it pays him to spend more on improving the quality. It is worth-while to increase this cost until the profit reaches its maximum.

In examining the conditions of product equilibrium on the group level, Chamberlin continues to keep up the "heroic" assumptions, and he further supposes that the possibilities of changing the product are equally accessible to everybody. The condition of group equilibrium is in this case, too, that price should cover unit cost for every seller. If a profit is achieved, the inflow of external capital will cause the output of the individual sellers to decrease until price and unit cost are equal. Originally, the firm sold quantity $0B$ at a price of $0A$, and its profit was $EFGA$. After the establishment of new firms, it can sell only quantity $0H$ at a price of $0A$, price being just equal to unit cost HJ (Figure 60).

Taking both price and product to be variable, the firm will choose the combination of them at which profit is at a maximum. For each product line, there exists price at which profit from the quantity sold is maximized. It is the maximum of these maxima which the entrepreneur wishes to achieve. But the rivalry of the outside entrepreneurs will compete away this profit, this being the condition of group equilibrium in the case of variable price and variable product quality, too.

In the case of product equilibrium, the equilibrium point on the group level is reached, as we have seen, on the downward sloping portion of the average total cost curve and not at its minimum. This equilibrium level of unit cost corresponds, under conditions of pure competition, to the minimum of a higher average total cost curve, which, in the case of product equilibrium, means better product quality. In other words, at product equilibrium, under monopolistic competition, a poorer product quality is obtained than under pure competition.

231

THE CONDITION OF EQUILIBRIUM IN THE CASE OF MANIPULATION THROUGH SELLING COSTS

Chamberlin also includes selling costs in his investigations. By his selling costs, the entrepreneur tries to change the demand function for his product, while his production costs affect the supply side.

As quantity sold depends on price, product quality and selling costs, Chamberlin, in order to examine the effect of selling costs in isolation, regards price and product quality as given.

With an increase in selling costs, more and more of a certain quality of product can be sold at a given price. But a given amount of selling costs can be used in different ways and with different efficiency. A commodity may be made popular by making use of a variety of factors promoting sales. Advertisements can be made in magazines, on the radio, etc., window displays and advertising specialists, etc., may be employed for boosting a commodity. Searching for the criteria of the efficient use of selling costs, Chamberlin attempts to apply the technical apparatus used in the theory of production to selling costs, too. He holds the view that the returns to the above factors used for selling diminish if they are increased unilaterally. He points out that in combining these factors the same principle must be applied which also asserts itself in production, when the minimum-cost factor combination is determined by means of isoquants.

The laws of returns, says Chamberlin, also apply to the increase in selling costs: first there are increasing, then constant and finally diminishing returns.

Chamberlin explains increasing returns resulting from increased selling costs by the economies of large-scale operations. Large-scale operations make it possible to establish a more efficient division of labour among those concerned with selling. Specially trained experts, advertising specialists, window dressers, etc. can be employed whose services would not be available at a lower level of advertising costs. He also refers to the suggestive power of repetition, to the fact that the consumer does not change his consumption habits overnight, under the influence of the first appeal of the advertisement. He must be incessantly attacked by advertisements until the commodity concerned evokes his interest.

However, while increasing selling costs, we shall sooner or later face forces working in the direction of diminishing returns. Advertising costs will first conquer the easily accessible buyers. Then, the number of buyers can be increased only by winning over the less easily accessible customers, which will also involve an increase in advertising costs. Later, after consumers have already bought a certain quantity of the commodity in question and want to make further purchases, they will have to renounce other, more and more important goods. They can be persuaded to do so only by a further increase in advertising costs.

Thus, in Chamberlin's representation, the average and marginal costs of advertising are also U-shaped. Their position, the point from which they begin to rise, depends on the nature and price of the product, the competition from substitute products which restrict the market. In his view, the costs affecting the quality of the product and selling costs are closely interrelated. If the quality of the product is improved, less has to be spent on advertising, and conversely, if the quality of the product deteriorates, advertising costs must be increased.

Chamberlin calculates the total cost of a product by adding up production and selling costs. This combined average and marginal cost is also U-shaped in his representations. But it will clearly reach its minimum not at the point where production costs do.

Then he determines by marginal analysis how equilibrium is established on the level of the firm in manipulating through selling costs. He takes price and product as given, and examines how far selling costs have to be increased to ensure maximum profits. Clearly, up to the point where the combined marginal cost reaches the level of marginal revenue.

Taking price and selling costs to be given, the entrepreneur must choose as a next step that version of the product, suggests Chamberlin, which yields maximum profit. Finally, by changing all three factors, price, product and selling cost, the entrepreneur must determine product quality, price and selling cost so that his total profit should be at a maximum.

In Chamberlin's view, in the case of group equilibrium, profit must disappear even if advertising costs are included.

Chapter 4

THE PROBLEMS OF MARKET EQUILIBRIUM IN DUOPOLY

In an intermediate position between monopoly and pure competition lie the cases of duopoly and oligopoly. In analysing monopolistic competition between members of a large group, Chamberlin abandoned one assumption of pure competition theory, that of product and seller homogeneity; in analysing pure duopoly and oligopoly, he abandoned a different assumption, that there exists a large number of sellers.

In duopoly two, or in oligopoly several, big firms are operating in the industry. They regard the economic environment in which they are to operate not as an invariable factor. Each big firm wishing to maximize its profit changes, as Ragnar Frisch points out, a certain number of those economic parameters[15] which characterize the existing market situation, also changing thereby the conditions under which its competitors must maximize their profits. The competitors will react to its step, and thus the market situation will change further. Though each firm is in a position to influence the market by its behaviour, none of them is able to control it completely. The final market situation is, in the last analysis, the result of their combined behaviour. But no firm controls the others' behaviour. Ragnar Frisch stresses that since the profit of each firm also depends on the behaviour of the rest of the firms, all firms must take into account what changes, and of what direction and extent, in the parameters of the other firms will be called forth by changes in their own parameters. Thus, while attempting to optimize his position, every duopolist and oligopolist must reckon with the reaction of his competitor or competitors. Business decisions are closely interlinked, and thus we are faced with an interrelated series of the effects and countereffects of decisions.

While in the case of the market forms discussed so far the individual firms were assumed to control all variables on which the result of their behaviour depended, because neither the actors of pure competition, nor the monopolists, nor the monopolistic competitors in the case of Chamberlin's large group, had to consider the reaction of their rivals, the result of the firm's activity in duopoly or oligopoly

---

[15] It was Ragnar Frisch who first used the term *action parameter* in economic literature. "Let us take a situation with a few polypolists and assume that economic relationships among them are such that each is in a position to choose, at his own discretion, a number of parameters characteristing the general situation. Therefore, we call these parameters action parameters of the various polypolists." See R. Frisch: Monopole, Polypole.—La notion de force dans l'économie, *Nationaløkonomisk Tidsskrift*, Vol. 71, Koppenhagen, 1933. In German translation: *Wettbewerb und Monopol*, Darmstadt, 1968, p. 46.

also depends on variables not controlled by the firm, namely the behaviour of its competitor or competitors.

Does an equilibrium position come about under such conditions? Can a market situation arise in which all participants have achieved the optimum result accessible to them?

According to Ragnar Frisch, what is crucial for the operation of such a mechanism is what the individual firms think their competitors' reactions will be to their moves. Then they formulate their strategies accordingly. Bowley called attention to the necessity to distinguish between various types of policies, and „the list was complemented with other types"[16] by Ragnar Frisch.

Frisch characterizes as an autonomous action the policy in which the individual entrepreneurs in duopoly and oligopoly leave out of account the reaction of their competitors to their own moves and, while trying to maximize their position, behave as if the size of their profits were a function of their own behaviour only.

A similar assumption was made in the examination of duopoly by two French economists, Cournot in the first half and Bertrand in the second half of the last century. Owing to the deficiency of the technical means applied, they had to assume that duopolists ignored their competitors' reactions to their own moves.

Cournot's case of duopoly was demonstrated, with modern tools of analysis, by Stackelberg[17]. Our examination will also be based on his analysis. In investigating duopoly, Stackelberg left Chamberlin's product differentiation out of account. In his theory, duopolists put homogeneous products on the market.

Cournot assumed that each duopolist regarded the other's supply as given, that is, he thought that if he added to his competitor's supply his own profit-maximizing level of supply, his rival would not react to it.

Let us suppose, following Stackelberg, that duopolist A is at first the only supplier on the market. He behaves as if he were a monopolist. His sales curve equals the demand curve of the industry. He supplies that quantity of his product at which marginal cost is equal to marginal revenue. Then Stackelberg examines the quantity supplied by duopolist A if he finds that B has already put on the market his supply of 1, 2, 3 etc. units. In this case A's sales curve will no longer equal the demand curve of the industry, but will shift parallel to it downwards by 1, 2, 3, etc. units. To each of A's sales curves Stackelberg constructs the corresponding marginal revenue curve, and where the marginal revenue curve and A's marginal cost curve intersect, the quantity at the point of intersection will indicate how much A will supply to maximize his profit if he already finds on the market B's supply of 1, 2, 3, etc. units. If we project these quantities supplied by A onto his own sales curve, then the curve joining the points of intersection (C_5–C_0 in the figure) will give A's reaction curve expressing how A will react to the different quantities supplied by B, assuming that B will not change his supply if A adds to it his own profit-maximizing supply.

In Figure 61, $K'(x)$ is A's marginal cost curve, 0, 1, 2, 3, 4, 5 are A's sales curves if B supplies quantities 0, 1, 2, 3, 4, 5.

[16] R. Frisch: *op. cit.,* p. 38.
[17] H. Stackelberg: *op. cit.,* pp. 206–210.

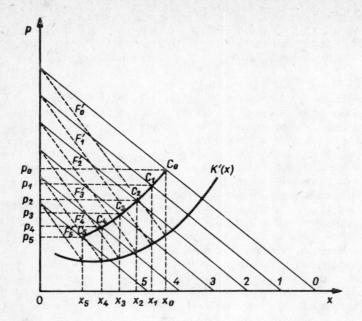

Figure 61

F_0', F_1', F_2', F_3', F_4', F_5' are A's marginal revenue curves for the corresponding sales curves,

C_0, C_1, C_2, C_3, C_4, C_5 are the Cournot points for A, $A's$ supply curve, not in the sense of how much he supplies at different prices, but how much he supplies at B's given supply.

x_0, x_1, x_2, x_3, x_4, x_5 are A's quantities sold,

p_0, p_1, p_2, p_3, p_4, p_5 are the prices on A's and B's shared market.

We can similarly construct on a graph B's reaction curve, too.

Then Stackelberg represents A's and B's reaction curves graphically (Figure 62a,). $0A$ on the x axis shows A's quantity supplied if B's supply is zero, that is, if A is in a monopoly position, $0M$ on axis x expresses that if A supplied quantity $0M$, B would completely withdraw from the market. $0B$ on axis y expresses B's quantity supplied if B were in a monopoly position. $0L$ on axis y expresses B's supply at which A would stop his supply. Point M lies to the right of point A, and point L lies above point B, expressing, as it were, that A's monopoly position offers for B, and B's monopoly position for A, a measure of room for manoeuvre. This is, by the way, the condition for the two reaction curves to cut each other.

The competitive struggle of the duopolists moves the market towards an equilibrium position. This equilibrium position is indicated by the point of intersection of the two reaction curves. At this point the amounts of profit of both parties are simultaneously at a maximum, that is, monopolist A reaches maximum profit with his supply x at a quantity y supplied by B, which B would put on the market to attain maximum profit if he added his own supply to A's supply x. However,

236

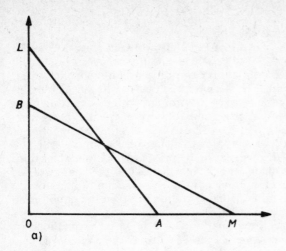

a)

Figure 62a

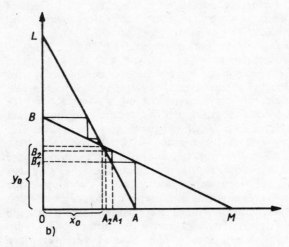

b)

Figure 62b

before an equilibrium position is reached, only one duopolist's profit can be at a maximum, namely the one who adjusts his own supply. Thus, if A supplies initially $0A$, B maximizes his profit by supplying $0B_1$. A must then reduce his supply to $0A_1$, in order to maximize his own profit; in response to this, B increases his supply to $0B_2$ (Figure 62b). In this way, the equilibrium point is approached. The same applies if we start at any other non-equilibrium level of supply.

In Bertrand's representation, duopolist A takes the other party's price policy to be given. In this belief, he cuts the price of his product in order to expand his market. To this duopolist B will react by also reducing the price of his product on the assumption that the price set by *A* will not change further. The difference in prices obviously presupposes the imperfection of the market.

Chamberlin raises the problem of duopoly in the following forms. First he supposes that each of the duopolists forgets about the indirect effect of his action, about his rival's reaction, and imagines that his competitor will not change price if he lowers the price of his own product. In this case, each party will move along his own curve, *dd'*, steadily decreasing the price of his product until *dd'*, shifting more and more downwards, touches the unit-cost curve for both of them. This is Bertrand's case, in which the equilibrium situation comes about as in pure competition It is also possible that each duopolist supposes that the other's supply will not change if he changes his own. But this will cause the price at which the other duopolist has maximized his profit to change, too. He will react to the change in his rival's supply, and in the course of mutual adjustments a definite equilibrium situation will develop assuming an intermediate position between the equilibrium of monopoly and pure competition. This is Cournot's case.

Chamberlin also investigated the situation which arises when each duopolist takes account of his rival's reaction, namely, that if he lowers the price of his product, his competition will do the same. Taking account of behaviour reactions already means a step forward in the theory of duopoly. In this case, the curve *dd'* no longer plays any role, and both duopolists act along curve *DD'*. Each of them knows that his position also depends on his rival's behaviour. Neither will therefore cut the price of his product. The quantity supplied will be such as if a monopolistic agreement had been concluded between them.[18]

Stackelberg enriched the non-Marxian theory of duopoly with the concept of *asymmetric duopoly*. While in Cournot's case the two duopolists adjusted themselves to each other's behaviour, and thus their positions were symmetric, Stackelberg pointed out that one of them might anticipate the other's behaviour as a reaction to his move and would place that amount of his product on the market which, unlike Cournot's case, ensured him maximum profit not before, but after the adjustment of the other party.[19] Stackelberg calls this supply the duopolist's *independence supply*. Thus, in the case of asymmetric duopoly, one party takes the lead and the other adjusts himself. But either may recognize the other's adjustment, compare the independence and dependence positions and choose the one which is more favourable for him. In general, it is the independence position which is more favourable for both. If both want to achieve that position, then a struggle for power without equilibrium will develop between them which, after Bowley, who first examined this case, is called *Bowley's duopoly*. The struggle for taking the lead lasts until one duopolist goes bankrupt or gives up fighting for his independence position. An equilibrium can come about only if one duopolist supplies from an independence, the other from a dependence position. But the equilibrium is very unstable in this case. Sooner or later, the duopolist in a dependence position will make efforts to achieve independence.

Ragnar Frisch tries to express one party's expected reaction to his competitor's or competitors' decisions by the so-called conjectural coefficient or conjectural elasticity. With the attribute "conjectural" Frisch wants to emphasize the expected

[18] E. Chamberlin: *op. cit.*, pp. 30–50.
[19] H. Stackelberg: *op. cit.*, pp. 210–211.

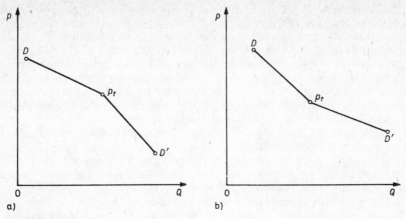

Figure 63a, b

Source: P. M. Sweezy: Demand under Conditions of Oligopoly, *Readings in Price Theory*, Chicago, 1952, pp. 405 and 407.

and not the actual reaction of the firm. This elasticity indicates, for example, the percentage change in parameter i of firm h as an assumed reaction to the percentage change in parameter j of firm k. He assumes as a first step that each firm will act as if any possible change in his rival's action parameter "were a constant function of the change in his own parameter."[20]

In the study cited, Frisch mentions as a more complicated case the one in which the parameters are determined by negotiations, the technique of which is of basic importance from the point of view of the operation of the economic mechanism. Such is the case examined by Zeuthen, "where organizations of employers and workers are opposed to each other..."[21] In Zeuthen's view, under such conditions wages cannot be settled by either party on his own initiative, they can only be determined by negotiations which have a technique of their own. Both parties will pursue a policy which they think will best promote the achievement of their objectives.

The British economists R. L. Hall and C. I. Hitch[22] and the American economist P. M. Sweezy[23] point out in their studies published almost simultaneously in 1939 how certain oligopolies' views on the reaction of their rivals to their price policies influence the shape of their demand curves (sales curves). These demand curves, to use Kaldor's term, are "imagined demand curves" and need not be continuous.

[20] R. Frisch: *op. cit.*, p. 252.
[21] F. Zeuthen: *Problems of Monopoly and Economics Warfare*, London, 1930, Chapter IV, pp. 104–150.
[22] R. L. Hall and C. J. Hitch: Price Theory and Business Behaviour, *Oxford Economic Papers*, May 1939.
[23] P. M. Sweezy: Demand under Conditions of Oligopoly, *The Journal of Political Economy*, Vol. 1939. Reprinted in: *Readings in Price Theory*, Chicago, 1952.

An individual firm may think that if it raises the price of its product above the current price, its rivals will not follow suit and thus it will lose part of its customers. In this case its demand curve, at prices higher then the current price, is elastic, because the demand for its product will vigorously fall as a result of the price rise. If, however, it reduces the price of its product below the current price, it may expect that its rivals will also reduce the price of their products, consequently, the demand for its product will grow only at a relatively slow rate as the price falls. Thus its demand curve will be inealstic at prices lower than the current price (Figure 63a). Both situations are rather frequent during a depression period.

But an oligopoly firm may base its policy on a different assumption. In the period of a creeping inflation or boom, in face of a general price rise, it may think that if it increases the price of its product, its rivals will do the same. Thus the demand for its product will decrease at a relatively slow rate, i.e. its demand curve, at prices higher than the current price, is inelastic. If, however, the firm cuts the price of its product during the period in question, it is justified in expecting that its rivals will not follow suit by reducing their prices. Thus the demand for its product will rise to a relatively great extent. In this case, at prices lower than the current price, its demand curve will be elastic (Figure 63b).

The shape of the demand curve of an oligopoly firm will be similar to this latter case even if it raises its price above the current price, and assumes the position of the price leader,[24] or else, when it decreases the price of its product by a secret discount from the price list so that its rivals are not aware of the price reduction.

These patterns of expected reaction produce a kink at the existing price, in the demand curve for the product of an oligopolist, and the corresponding marginal revenue curve will be discontinuous.[25]

Sweezy draws from the above-mentioned cases the following conclusions for oligopolistic pricing: "... the conditions for short-run equilibrium are not at all precise. It is not possible to apply the condition that marginal cost must equal marginal revenue ... ."

"... it is not permissible to speak of the factors' remunerations being equal to their marginal value productivities."

"... any disturbance which affects only the position of the marginal cost curve may leave the short-run equilibrium of price and output entirely unaffected. Thus, for example, a successful strike for higher wages may be without influence on either price or output."[26]

Hall and Hitch, and others after them, attempt to determine price on the oligopolistic market, and in any other market forms in the framework of which the individual entrepreneurs are price makers, on a basis other than marginal analysis, that is, on the basis of the so-called *full cost principle*.

They think that they can describe the entrepreneur's behaviour more appro-

---

[24] A firm is said to be a price leader when the other oligopolists follow its price policy either because it takes a dominant position, or because the price set by it is rather closely related to changes in market relations.

[25] G. J. Stigler: The Kinky Oligopoly Demand Curve and Rigid Prices, *The Journal of Political Economy*, Vol. 45, 1947. Reprinted in *Readings in Price Theory*, Chicago, 1952, p. 406.

[26] P. M. Sweezy: *op. cit.*, 406.

priately if they present him as one who sets for his products "a price that exceeds average cost by a chosen margin, proportional or absolute."[27]

The full-cost pricing theory is an attempt to make up for the insufficiency of price determination by finding the point of intersection of the marginal cost and marginal revenue curves. However, lacking any basis in value theory, this cannot answer such fundamental questions as to what determines the size of production costs and within it the size of wages, what determines the size of the profit margin, etc. To say that "average cost is reasonably well known",[28] that the firms "know current total cost and current output and can divide the one by the other"[29], does not provide a cost determination. Speight is right in writing that "full cost theory appears ... not a satisfactory general theory of how relative prices and output are *determined*."[30]

The more developed versions of the duopoly theory, which already take into consideration that the maximization of profit by the individual duopolists is dependent not only on their own, but also on the other party's behaviour, continue to apply the same method as in pure competition or in monopoly, where the entrepreneur's profit is a function only of his own behaviour. This method is marginal analysis for the determination of optimal results. To maintain marginal analysis, writers have attempted to make the competitor's reaction appear predictable, that is, to assume it to be known in the target function of a given duopolist.

But how could a duopolist equate his marginal cost with his marginal revenue, when he does not know how much his marginal revenue will become, as its size also depends on the business policy pursued by his competitor? In fact, we cannot suppose our duopolist to know his rival's reaction. This situation may not be characterized simply as a maximization problem. The analysis of the duopolist's and oligopolist's position requires another approach. It was this fact to which attention was also called by the kinky shape of the oligopoly demand curve, discovered by Hall, Hitch and Sweezy. A new approach was attempted by Morgenstern and Neumann when they developed their strategic game theory.

In a work concerned with popularizing game theory, Morgenstern argues that by the time economics emerged as a science, mechanics had already reached a fairly high level in its development, and thus the example and tools of analysis for mathematical economics were provided by mechanics: analysis, differential and integral calculus. Theoretical mathematicians kept away for a long time from economic sciences. They did not find any exciting problems in them, and no significant mathematical theorems emerged in economics for a long time. In analysing economic phenomena, economists made use of the mathematical apparatus evolved in the exploration of natural phenomena. It was in the late 1920s and in the 1930s that a change took place in this field. As pioneers, Morgenstern mentions two mathematicians of Hungarian origin, Abraham Wald and John Neumann. Wald tried to reveal and solve the problems involved in Walras's, Pareto's and Cassel's general equilibrium theory, while Neumann worked out the *theory of strategic games*.

[27] P. J. D. Wiles: *Price, Gost and Output,* Oxford, 1956, pp. 43–44.
[28] P. J. D. Wiles: *op. cit.,* p. 52.
[29] P. J. D. Wiles: *op. cit.,* p. 47.
[30] H. Speight: *Economics,* London, 1960, p. 333.

The theory of gambling, that is of games based merely on chance, such as a game of dice or heads-or-tails, was being developed as early as the 18th century, and this laid the foundation for probability theory. Neumann's strategic game theory, however, is a model of parlour games "whose outcome, unlike gambling, depends not exclusively on mere chance but on the behaviour of the players and, additionally, on a chance component."[31] Every player would like to win as much as possible. His information, however, is often limited. It is a matter of chance what cards are dealt to him. He must contemplate how his fellow players will react to his own moves. The outcome depends on the joint behaviour of all players, and only partly on the behaviour of any individual player. That player behaves rationally who chooses the best of all possibilities available to him. Thus, game theory also elaborated the logic of rational choice, only on assumptions different from those discussed so far.

Business life, too, is full of game situations. The cases of duopoly and oligopoly were so regarded by both founders of game theory, who determined the conditions under which the competition of duopolists and oligopolists yields optimal and stable results.

Game theory does not suppose the duopolists to have a definite idea about the countermeasures to be taken by their rival. It assumes, however, that each of them is familia rwith the other's strategies. He knows the information contained in the table below: how much his profit will be in the various strategy pairs. The players chose their strategies independently of each other, no player knowing in advance the particular variety of strategy which the other players will choose for the given game. Let us further suppose that the sum of the game is zero, the gains made by one player being losses to the other. In this case, it is sufficient to indicate in our model the amount of one party's profits, and we also know the other's profits (or losses); the table gives the profit of A. In our game, neither duopolist wishes to achieve maximum profit, because he knows that his rival may reduce his profit to a minimum. Duopolist A wants to know the amount of the smallest profit he may earn in spite of the efforts to be made by B.. He chooses from the strategies available to him the one which, if B adds to it his own strategy, will yield to him at least the maximum of all minimum profits. He plays a mini-max game.

A \\ B	B_1	B_2	B_3	Row minima
A_1	2	1	3	1
A_2	2	5	2	2
A_3	2	—1	1	—1
Column maxima	2	5	3	

Source: O. Morgenstern: *Spieltheorie und Wirtschaftswissenschaft,* Wien–München, 1963, p. 83.

[31] O. Morgenstern: *Spieltheorie und Wirtschaftswissenschaft,* Wien–München, 1963, p. 77.

In our example, the duopolists have three strategies each available to them. A knows that B will choose strategy B_2 if he chooses strategy A_1, strategy B_1 or B_3 at his A_2, and B_2 at A_3. In this case, A's profit or B's loss will be at a minimum, for in strategy combinations $A_3–B_2$, B will obtain a profit of the size 1. B, however, thinks, no matter which available strategy he chooses, A will add to it that of his own strategies at which he will achieve maximum profit. Thus B will use the strategy which results for A in a minimum of the maximum profits, that is, he plays a maxi-min game.

An equilibrium will be established if the maximum of the row minima equals the minimum of the column maxima: in this case, strategy pair $A_2–B_1$.

A zero-sum game can be solved by linear programming. For one duopolist the dual of finding the best strategy is the determination of the best strategy for the other.

Chapter 5

IN THE PRESENCE OF MONOPOLISTIC ELEMENTS
THE EFFICIENCY CRITERIA OF PURE COMPETITION
NO LONGER APPLY

With the inclusion of monopolistic elements, the picture of capitalism drawn by non-Marxian economics from its model based on pure or perfect competition will change.

It turns out that it is no longer ensured that the consumers spend their incomes so as to achieve maximum satisfaction, since the factors of product differentiation may misinform them about the utility values of commodities and delude them into undesirable purchases, thus misleading them in making their choices. As a consequence, they wrongly estimate the relative marginal utilities of products, so that the coincidence of the estimated marginal rate of substitution and of relative prices does not ensure maximum satisfaction.

The consumer's irrational insistence on buying from the seller he is used to also counteracts maximum satisfaction, because he might buy goods of better quality elsewhere, at the same or even lower prices.

Since product equilibrium is achieved at an inferior product quality in monopolistic competition than in pure competition, the consumer will get poorer quality for the same price, or is compelled to buy the same quality for a higher price.[32]

Making use of product differentiation and of advertising costs in competitive struggle increases the price of products and leads to a waste of resources.[33] In the presence of monopolistic elements the relative prices of products do not ensure an optimal allocation of resources among their different uses. The reward to factors is not equal to their marginal productivity multiplied by product price, but their marginal productivity multiplied by their marginal revenue, which is lower than price. Moreover, since in the presence of monopolistic elements price deviates from marginal revenue differently in the various branches of production, depending on the degree of monopoly in them, identical money incomes may accrue to factors in each productive sector where they are employed, while their marginal productivities multiplied by price, which measures their marginal social significance, are different.[34] The ideal allocation of resources, which would demand that factors should be directed into industries in which marginal productivity multiplied by the price of product is larger, does not materialize. Compared with a perfectly com-

---

[32] E. Chamberlin: *op. cit.*, pp. 99–100.
[33] R. L. Heilbronner: *The Economic Problem*, New Jersey, 1968, p. 516.
[34] J. E. Meade: *An Introduction to Economic Analysis and Policy*, Oxford, 1936, pp. 149–151.

petitive stituation, too much is produced of a commodity for which there is a more elastic demand and whose production is, consequently, less monopolized, and too little of those commodities for which there is a less elastic demand and whose production can therefore be monopolized to a greater extent.[35]

The distortion of demand by a false estimation of the marginal rate of substitution will also lead to an incorrect allocation of resources.

Compared with the situation in pure competition, resources are not efficiently utilized under conditions of monopoly. Equilibrium is established on the downward sloping portion of the unit-cost curve and not at its minimum point.

And since the monopolist restricts his output in such a way that price is kept above marginal costs, part of the resources will remain unutilized.[36] Rigid price in the presence of monopolistic elements "prevent adjustment to an economic change."[37]

Stackelberg points out that the movement of prices in certain varieties of duopoly or oligopoly does not necessarily call forth an appropriate correction to establish market equilibrium. As a result, a permanent disequilibrium comes about, or an economic war causing serious damage, a so-called cut-throat competition, evolves. He emphasizes that in such a case an equilibrium is established "only by means of a price set by the government..., it does not come into being by itself."[38]

[35] J. Robinson, op. cit., p. 318.
[36] F. Machlup: The Political Economy of Monopoly, Baltimore, 1952, p. 73.
[37] M. W. Reder: Studies in the Theory of Welfare Economics, New York, 1949, p. 73.
[38] H. Stackelberg, op. cit., p. 229.

Chapter 6

THE CLASSIFICATION OF MARKET FORMS BY TRIFFIN

Product differentiation, which stimulated Chamberlin to operate with the concept of small and large groups instead of industries, led his disciple, Robert Triffin, to take a further step. Triffin holds that under conditions of monopolistic competition there is no natural boundary whatever by which to isolate certain parts of the economy as industries. Thus we are faced only with sellers who produce products different from those of others. The product of each seller is surrounded by an unbroken chain of substitutes in that each commodity has its more or less close substitute, and these substitutes, too, have their own substitutes. If the price of a commodity rises, some buyers stop buying it and buy something else. Triffin, by eliminating competition between industries, relates the individual firms directly to the general competition of the community of sellers.

Triffin starts from the individual firms in trying to classify the competitive relationships surrounding them. His classification is based on the consideration of how a firm, by changing the price of its product, influences the sales of its rivals' products.

Thus the basis of classification is the cross elasticity of demand. For Triffin, it is not the firm of a particular industry which is in competition with the firms of the same industry or other industries, but one firm with its rivals in general.

Triffin[39] distinguishes three basic cases:

a. If firm j cuts the price of its product slightly and reduces thereby the sales of firm i to zero so as to attract to itself all the customers of firm i, then the cross elasticity of the product of firm j, $\dfrac{\partial q_i}{q_i} : \dfrac{\partial p_j}{p_j}$, is infinite. Both firms supply homogeneous products, and the form of competition between them is: *homogeneous competition*. Firm j may face not only the homogeneous competition of i, but of any number of firms.

b. The other extreme arises when the price cutting of firm j does not affect the sales of firm i, cross elasticity is zero, and there is no competitive relationship whatever between firms j and i. If i's sales are independent of the price policy of any other firm, we are faced with the case of *pure monopoly*.

c. Homogeneous competition and pure monopoly are two extremes. What is

---

[39] R. Triffin: *Monopolistic Competition and General Equilibrium Theory.* Harvard University Press, Cambridge, 1940, pp. 102–105.

generally typical is the case in which firm j, by cutting the price of its product, does influence the sales of firm i without reducing them to zero. The size of cross elasticity is finite. These two firms are in competition with one another, but the struggle between them is not so sharp as in homogeneous competition. The two firms put heterogeneous products on the market, and the form of competitive struggle between them is: *heterogeneous competition.*

Within both homogeneous and heterogeneous competition, Triffin distinguishes two sub-divisions of competition depending on whether firm i, influenced by the price policy of firm j or some of the firms belonging to j, will react with its own *price* and sales policy on the price formation of firm j. Triffin expresses this by the reciprocal of cross elasticity, $\dfrac{\partial p_j}{p_j} : \dfrac{\partial q_i}{q_i}$. What is virtually involved here is the cross flexibility of the price set by firm j. If this indicator is zero, then firm j need not be afraid of the retaliation of firm i. If, however, "... some of these firms j that influence i are themselves affected by the changes in the price–output policy of firm i, this may be expressed in the condition that $\dfrac{q_i \partial p_j}{p_j \partial q_i}$ be also significantly different from zero."[40] In this case, there exists an oligopolistic relationship between i and the firms in question.

Thus, both homogeneous and heterogeneous competition has, depending on the value of cross elasticity, two sub-divisions: *oligopolistic* and *non-oligopolistic* competition.

---

[40] R. Triffin: *op. cit.,* p. 104.

Chapter 7

A CRITIQUE OF THE NON-MARXIAN INTERPRETATION OF MONOPOLY

1. With the inclusion of monopolistic elements in its price theory, non-Marxian economics attempts to bridge the gap, untenable in a period of great economic crisis, between the model of pure or perfect competition and capitalist reality.

Non-Marxian textbooks of political economy usually confine the problem of monopoly to the question of monopoly price. The theory of monopoly price, however, does not analyse at all the essence of modern monopolies.

Monopolies cropped up at every stage of the development of commodity production, while modern monopolies differ in quality from the previous ones. Modern monopoly represents a special stage of capitalist development. Lenin assigned to it its historical place by declaring it to be the highest stage of capitalism,[41] and scientifically analysed its main manifestations.

Most non-Marxian economists, however, see in the monopolies only a certain market form which may occur in any period of the history of commodity production. In non-Marxian economics a fairly widespread interpretation of monopoly maintains that the elasticity of the demand curve for the product of the monopolist is finite, and thus he can pursue an independent price policy, keep price above marginal costs. This interpretation is formal, a definition devoid of all historical elements. It makes the concept of monopoly so broad that it comprises not only monopoly in the Marxist sense of the term, but any firm enjoying, thanks to product differentiation, a privileged position, as well as the formations of pre-capitalistic times with monopoly power, guilds, trading companies endowed with privileges, etc. The formal interpretation of monopolies or duopolies devoid of any historical, social content becomes manifest in the way modern non-Marxian economics evaluates Cournot's work published in 1838 as one which laid the foundations of the theory of monopoly and duopoly. "Cournot," writes Blaug, "not only founded the theory of monopoly but also the theory of duopoly."[42] What could Cournot know in 1838 about the reality of monopoly capitalism? Without analysing the production relations underlying monopoly and duopoly, he wished, in an entirely formal way, to answer the question of how to determine he profit-maximizing price if one or two sellers dominate the market.

---

[41] See: V. I. Lenin: *Imperialism, the Highest Stage of Capitalism,* Selected Works, Vol. V, London, 1944.

[42] M. Blaug: *Economic Theory in Retrospect,* London, 1968, p. 318.

248

Not recognizing the difference between modern monopoly and the monopolies preceding monopoly capitalism, Röpke emphasizes that "we cannot speak of any necessary development tendency…, it is not due to its inherent tendencies that free-competition capitalism changes into monopoly capitalism."[43]

Though Machlup admits that technical progress brings about great economies as a result of large-scale production, yet it would be erroneous, in his view, to deduce from this fact the "technological inevitability of monopoly."[44] At another place he writes that "… the strong element of monopoly prevalent in most industries manufacturing standardized industrial products cannot be said to be unavoidable."[45] He holds the view that the increase in market demand keeps pace with the expansion of the scale of firms, and indeed, the former often increases at an even faster rate. Thus the expansion of the size of firms is easily reconcilable with the fact that a relatively large number of firms produce within the industry. He imagines, therefore, that the firms operating under conditions of free competition expand their size in the course of technical development, a process made possible for them by an appropriate increase in total demand, without their number being necessarily decreased.

This idyllic representation of growth completely leaves out of account that technical progress is being made in a cut-throat competition between the individual capitalist firms. Each tries to make use of a more developed technology to achieve the highest possible profit. The achievement of technical progress, however, cannot be used by each firm of the industry to the same extent. Machlup ignores what Lehmann, a West German economist, formulates in this way: "… very good, good, medium, bad and worse firms meet in the market."[46] The stronger firm possessing more capital has a greater chance to adopt modern technology, to exploit the advantages of large-scale production accompanying technical progress, than a firm short of capital. As a result, the stronger firm becomes still stronger. "A mounting concentration of capitals…", writes Marx about technical progress, "is, therefore, one of its material requirements as well as one if its results."[47] In the course of technical development, the individual capitalist needs an ever greater minimum amount of capital to ensure that the time used up for the production of commodities should be the socially necessary labour time. The capitalist who has not got that minimum of capital, will go down in this struggle, will go bankrupt, or will be absorbed by the larger firms. At the same time, the mightier this minimum of capital needed in particular industries, the more difficult will it be for outside capitals to enter the market.

The inevitable outcome of the concentration and centralization of capital is that a few huge firms in the particular industries will attain a dominant position. "… the difficulty of competition and the tendency towards monopoly arise from the very

43 W. Röpke: *Gesellschaftskrisis der Gegenwart*, Erlenbach–Zürich, 1948, p. 219.
44 F. Machlup: *op. cit.*, p. 51.
45 F. Machlup: *op. cit.*, p. 53.
46 G. Lehmann: *Marktformenlehre und Monopolpolitik*, Duncker und Humblot, Berlin, 1956, p. 166.
47 K. Marx: *Capital*, Vol. III, Moscow, 1962, p. 215.

dimensions of the enterprises ... a score or so of great enterprises can easily arrive at an agreement..."[48]

Let us confront this Marxist–Leninist explanation of the rise of monopoly with Chamberlin's explanation by means of product differentiation.

An improvement in the quality of the product is regarded as technical progress. Though patents ensure exclusive rights and with them lasting super-profit for the firm applying the innovation for a limited period of time, yet this compels the other firms of the industry to catch up, to devise further improvements of the commodity in question. Thus, the patented product is in a competitive struggle with other patented products, and the existence of patents is reconcilable with traditional competition. Chamberlin himself stresses that patents promote competition and stimulate individual initiative. He adds that there are few inventions of a basic importance the patents of which make it possible for particular firms to control the bulk of the production of the industry concerned.

The situation is similar with the other factors of product differentiation such as trade names, trade marks, advertising costs, etc. Competition by means of these factors is reconcilable with the traditional form of competition. The above-mentioned means of product differentiation are *accessible to a large number* of firms involved in the competitive struggle of the industry. Though influencing the buyers' decisions, in that they may stimulate the buyers to pay a higher price for the commodity of a given seller, ensuring thereby a lasting super-profit for him, the amount of that profit is restricted by the competition of other sellers in the industry as well as by the flow of capital between industries. These product-differentiation factors *do not ensure in themselves a dominant position* for their users in the economy.

It should be noted, however, that though the use of the factors of product differentiation in the competitive struggle is easily reconcilable with traditional competition, it is first and foremost under monopoly capitalism that product differentiation comes to play a prominent role. Under conditions of modern capitalism it is no longer price cutting which constitutes the principle means of the competitive struggle. There are already other means available for that purpose, among other things the improvement of the quality of the product. In addition, in the hunt for maximum profit unproductive means of profit-making come more and more into prominence. Selling costs are steadily increasing. The theory of monopolistic competition expresses that the firms themselves shape and formulate the demand for their products, directing and influencing the consumers' decisions. Under such circumstances no consumer sovereignty can exist as succinctly described by Galbraith in Chapters XVII and XVIII of his work *The New Industrial State*.

2. Triffin's classification of competition only formally differs from Chamberlin's. It really reflects the inadequacy of the concept of cross elasticity, or cross flexibility, in determining the market forms.

In homogeneous competition, cross elasticity is infinite because, if firm j cuts the price of its product, then the whole clientele of all firms producing the same product as j will rush to it. This shift of demand in itself, however, does not say anything that would be important from the point of view of classification. The question is whether firm j can satisfy the increased demand. If firm j cannot supply

[48] V. I. Lenin: *op. cit.*, p. 15.

all customers, which is evident in non-oligopolistic homogeneous competition because at a lower price and increasing marginal cost, typical of pure competition, it is unable to satisfy the increased demand, then it increases j's price, and the buyers will return to their original sellers. Thus it turns out that the cross elasticity of j's product is in fact not infinite but zero. In this case, any reaction by its rivals is at the outset out of the question. Consequently, infinite cross elasticity cannot be a characteristic of homogeneous, non-oligopolistic competition. In reality, the magnitude of both cross elasticity and reaction is zero. In that case, however, homogeneous, non-oligopolistic competition does not differ in anything from pure monopoly. On the other hand, in the case of both pure monopoly and homogeneous and heterogeneous non-oligopolistic competition, the rivals' reaction is zero. But the zero value of this coefficient conceals very different features. A pure monopolist does not contemplate his rivals' reaction because his product has only very remote substitutes, while in homogeneous and heterogeneous competition the substitute is a close one, but the effect of the price rise of firm j is divided among so many firms that the reaction is negligible. Thus the zero value of the Triffin reaction includes both the very remote substitution relationship under monopoly and the close substitution relationship in homogeneous and heterogeneous non-oligopolistic competition. The Triffin reaction resolves all difference between the two.[49]

Analysing the competitive relationships of the products of two firms, j and i, with other products, we obtain different cross elasticities for each product both in j and i. How should they be aggregated or averaged, asks Machlup,[50] if we are to decide which firm is in a rather monopolistic and which in a rather competitive position. The Triffin index does not answer this question.

As the non-Marxian theory of market forms approaches the question merely from the angle of price determination, it fails to take account of the fact that both monopoly and duopoly (or oligopoly) are identical formations, the formations of monopoly capitalism. From the point of view of price theory, however, they must be distinguished from one another, since price formation must be explained differently if one single firm or two or more firms have a dominant position in an industry.

Not recognizing the necessity of the emergence of monopolies, some economists imagine that the evils resulting from monopolistic elements can be cured by making the market revert to a purely competitive form. Stackelberg, for example, thinks that the state can freely choose market forms. He writes that "the absence of equilibrium in certain markets can also be eliminated if the state changes the market form. If, for example, by taking appropriate organizational measures it leads the oligopolistic market back to perfect competition... But the state can also create other market forms over which it can better exercise its supervision."[51]

3. As far as price determination under monopoly is concerned, the fact that monopoly price is higher than the price established in pure competition, is higher than social production price, is reflected in the non-Marxian theory of monopoly

---

[49] See: M. Olson and B. McFarland: The Restoration of Pure Monopoly and the Concept of Industry, *Quarterly Journal of Economics*, 1962, No. 4.

[50] F. Machlup: *op. cit.*, pp. 522–523.

[51] H. Stackelberg: *op. cit.*, p. 180.

price by assuming that monopoly price may rise above unit cost, may contain profit. Otherwise, this price theory, too, expresses only the formal conditions of the optimal economy of scarce resources, in the cost function based on the marginal productivity principle and the supply function of factors, and in the demand function derived from marginal utility or from the system of indifference curves, only on the basis of data other than those of pure competition. It merely states that if we know the cost function of the monopolist and the demand function of his product, we can tell how much he must supply in order to maximize his profit.

The determination of monopoly price is virtually a question of determining monopoly profit. This is one of the most complicated problems of political economy which has not been solved up to this day. All that Marxian political economy has managed to achieve in the question of monopoly profit is to reveal its various sources. How does the non-Marxian theory of monopoly price account for monopoly profit? Most authors, it appears, see the source of monopoly profit, quite superficially, in the fact that the monopolist restricts his output relative to demand: increases the scarcity of his product artificially. However, those who admit the existence of exploitation in monopoly, explain it on the basis of the theory of marginal productivity. Just as the model of pure competition makes the essential difference that exists in the position of workers, capitalists and landowners disappear, so also does the model of monopoly. In its representation the monopolist exploits all factors of production, not only the workers, but the capitalists and the landowners, too, since neither the capitalists nor the landowners get as their reward the marginal productivity of capital or land multiplied by the established price, but only their marginal productivity multiplied by marginal revenue, which is lower than price. This exploitation is, however, according to Mrs. Robinson, not necessarily detrimental to the factors of production. In so far as monopolistic marginal revenue is higher than the price in pure competition, the production factors, despite their being exploited, earn higher revenue in monopoly than they would if the market form were pure competition, which, in her view, would render exploitation impossible. "The removal of exploitation may alter both the marginal physical product of labour and the price of the commodity, and we shall find, paradoxical as it may seem, that the removal of exploitation is not always beneficial to the workers concerned."[52]

Though the main source of monopolistic profit is exploitation of the working class, it has, according to the teachings of Marxian economics, other sources, too. Partial economic analyses, however, obstruct the discovery of these sources in non-Marxian price theory.

4. As regards the question of price formation in the case of the product-differentiating factors, we have already emphasized that they do not create a monopoly position for their users, but their use raises an interesting problem of value theory.

The mechanism of equalizing individual values with social values as demonstrated in political economy assumes that the individual sellers within the industry put homogeneous products on the market and, owing to the competitive struggle between producers, a uniform price of that product is established. The use of the

[52] J. Robinson: *The Theory of Imperfect Competition,* London, 1954, p. 283.

product-differentiation factors, however, forms, in the course of competitive struggle, different prices for the products of the various firms within the industry.

How does the law of value work out under such circumstances, when the producers of the industry put differentiated products upon the market, and thus, owing, among other things, to the difference in production costs resulting from different product qualities, no uniform price can be formed?

It must be examined whether, as a criterion of the assertion of the law of value, the flow of capitals under the circumstances of product differentiation creates the average profit rate or whether, as a result of competition within the industry, the firm operating under average technical conditions realizes average profit in the long run: to put it in other words, whether as a result of competition capital working in the particular industries, employed by the firms of these industries, is considered as social average capital.

It appears that the factors of product differentiation alone cannot prevent the industry from taking part in developing an average profit rate. It seems to be unlikely that there should be a substantial difference between industries in utilizing these factors, and thus that individual industries should have permanently an above-average share in social total profit. This is because product differentiation is primarily a means of competition *within* the industry. It is used by the individual firms in the first place to differentiate their products from those of the other sellers of the industry. In so far as the firms of an industry decrease the demand for the products of other industries by means of a more intensive use of product differentiation, and, as a result, most of them realize a profit over and above average profit, this would start a flow of capital from other industries, as was already pointed out by Chamberlin, too. Then the newly-established firms would also try to differentiate their products from those of the other sellers of the industry, which would intensify competition by means of products and selling costs within the industry. If the new firms successfully take up the struggle in this field with the old ones, the individual sellers will be compelled to set the price of their products in such a way that the capital invested in the industry realizes in the long run the same profit as realized by capital invested in other industries. Should it nevertheless occur that a significant part of the firms of the industry are able, despite the sharpening product and selling cost competition, to maintain their favourable position against other industries in respect of product differentiation, that industry will lastingly realize, to the detriment of the other industries, a profit above the average. In this case, the factors of product differentiation counteract the assertion of the law of value.

The use of the factors of product differentiation have a prominent role to play especially in competition within the industry. In this competition, every firm attempts to secure the largest possible share of the profit accruing to the industry by making use of these factors. If the factors of product differentiation were evenly distributed among firms, then even under the circumstances in question, those firms which operate under average technical conditions would realize long-term average profit. If, however, the product-differentiation factors are used by the individual firms with different efficiency, then, assuming an identical level of technical development, more profit will accrue to the firm, which uses these factors in the more efficient way. As regards profits realized, the factors of product differentiation may counterbalance less favourable technical conditions, and the

253

individual firms, depending on the use of these factors, may realize more or less profit than what would have accrued to them as a result of their technical conditions, assuming homogeneous products.

No doubt, the differential use of the factors of product differentiation both among industries and within a particular industry may hinder the law of value from asserting itself in competitive struggle. It may hinder the realization of average profit in both the industries as a whole, and the firms operating under average technical conditions within the industry. It may hinder but do not prevent it, since a competitive struggle is being waged both among industries and among firms within each industry. As a result of this struggle, the profit lastingly realized by the particular industries cannot substantially differ from average profit merely on account of the factors of product differentiation. This competition sets limits to the price manipulations of firms and counteracts any endeavour by a firm with production conditions considerably different from the average for the industry to realize average profit for an appreciably long time. The competitive struggle among firms to catch up with the most advanced ones also goes on under conditions of product differentiation. Anyway, the effect of manipulation using some of the product-differentiation factors, particularly selling costs, advertisements, is rather short-lived and does not ensure their users a favourable position which most of the firms could not sooner or later attein in the competitive struggle. The role of the product-differentiation factors in impeding the assertion of the law of value is substantially less significant than the corresponding role of the monopolies created by the concentration and centralization of capital.

Differentiation between products by firms and their differing prices does not mean that the concept of the industry has entirely lost its significance and has to be thrown overboard by political economy. For Triffin, each commodity faces a wide range of substitutes, and in discarding the concept of the industry, Triffin brings every product into a competitive relationship with the whole commodity world. No doubt, development brings about an ever-increasing range of products, and it is rather difficult to group a new kind of product into a particular industry, or to classify the production of firms turning out different products into different industries. It is also true that in the course of development the boundaries of an industry are changing; the grouping of products by industries reflects the development of science and the productive forces as well as the resulting changes in the social division of labour. Very often, a partial process of manufacturing a kind of product gains a measure of independence, becomes an independent industry, and differences even within one kind of product may assume, through a change in the nature of that product, such proportions that the production of a given sort of a commodity becomes an independent productive sector.

Nevertheless, the concept of an industry should not be dismissed. The degree of substitutability between products of different firms is not the same. Substitution between the products of certain firms is much closer than between the products of other firms, and thus competition between the former firms is much keener. Competition based on a close substitution relationship strongly influences the price of the products of these firms, much more considerably than competition with the products of other firms. Among other things, this relationship, too, may cause certain firms to unite to form an independent industry. It is for similar considerations that Olson and McFarland try to justify the concept of the industry when they argue with Chamberlin by saying that though competition between products can be found everywhere, substitution of every type does not apply to every product at the same time. In their view, a group of firms manufacturing products with no closely competitive substitutes should be called an industry.[53]

Furthermore, a substantial part of tools and equipment used by firms belonging to an industry are similar, as is also the character of the concrete labour used. Competitive struggle between firms of the same industry is also keen on the factor market, which has a significant bearing on the formation of the prices of product manufactured by the industry. Firms belonging to a particular industry jointly enjoy advantages from the increased scale of the industry, the so-called external economies, to use Marshall's term. These circumstances also account for a closer relationship established among firms of a certain group.

[53] M. Olson and B. McFarland: *op. cit.*, p. 622.

Part Four

THE ROLE OF THE TIME FACTOR IN ECONOMIC ANALYSIS

Chapter 1

GENERAL CHARACTERISTICS

Modern non-Marxian theory concentrated its attention for a long time solely on the equilibrium position of the economy. Taking certain conditions as given, such as the available quantities of the factors of production, the taste of the consumers, the level of technical knowledge, it analysed what prices should be established, how much of the different goods should be produced and how much of them consumers should buy for all persons operating in the market, both entrepreneurs and consumers, to attain optimal results. This, in pure competition, is tantamount to the establishment of demand–supply equilibrium in all markets. In an equilibrium situation the false expectations of the economic subjects are corrected, and if the explorations are confined only to the state of equilibrium, it might appear as if the operators in the market acted without any mistakes, with complete prediction. The interrelationships of the capitalist economy, if represented merely in its state of equilibrium established in pure or perfect competition, appear to be in the best possible arrangement. Economic analysis confined to the state of equilibrium fails to reveal that economic processes take place over time, and neglects to demonstrate how that equilibrium came to be established.

In this view the anarchy of capitalist economy, the fact that, owing to the spontaneous mechanisms of the capitalist economy, equilibrium situation is realized only through fluctuations, general crises of overproduction, and the wasteful use of consumers' and producers' goods, is completely lost sight of. It was primarily during the period of the Great Depression that non-Marxian economics came to realize that the spontaneous operation of the price mechanism cannot produce the beneficial effects attributed to it. Non-Marxian economists tried to find an answer to the burning question of why the automatisms of the capitalist economy were unable to cope with its serious ills. We have already dealt with one of the possible answers: it is the presence of monopolistic elements which prevents the ideal functioning of the price mechanism. By way of providing a second answer to it, non-Marxian economists began in the period of the Great Depression to lay special emphasis on economic processes taking place over time, and to regard this as a factor also responsible for the failure of the automatisms of the capitalist economy to nip these ills in the bud. Zwiedineck-Südenhorst emphasizes that with the time factor left out of account, economics "ceases to be laden with problems."[1] "It is almost with an elementary force that the investigation

[1] O. Zwiedineck-Südenhorst: *Subjektivismus in der sozialökonomischen Theorie. Wirtschaftstheorie und Wirtschaftspolitik*, Bern, 1953, p. 20.

of the dynamic processes of the economy bursts forth under the influence of the great economic fluctuations of our time,"[2] wrote Farkas Heller in 1937.

In his studies published in 1929[3] and 1934[4] Rosenstein–Rodan points out that, in the operation of the time factor according to the followers of equilibrium theory, as soon as the equilibrium position is disturbed, the forces acting towards restoring it immediately start operating, and the effect of demand and supply on price and the effect of price on demand and supply begin to make themselves felt at once, with the same velocity of reaction. He emphasizes that in reality it takes some time before these balancing factors begin to operate, and their velocities of reaction are different, too. Therefore, when the equilibrium is disturbed, this state may be a long-lasting one. Consequently, besides examining the equilibrium position, attention should also be paid to what will happen before equilibrium is restored.

The Marshallian short-term equilibrium is already an attempt to study the situation as different from the long-term equilibrium position.

It was this increased attention paid to the time factor which gave rise to a more accurate delimitation of the concepts of statics and dynamics in modern non-Marxian economics.

As far as the interpretation of *statics* and *dynamics* is concerned, there exist two major views in modern non-Marxian economics. The representative of one of them, R. Harrod, points out that his solution "...would provide a definition in the economic field analogous to the division between Statics and Dinamics in physical science."[5] Statics in physics are concerned with the state of rest. An economy in the sense of statics does not mean, according to Harrod, a state of inactivity; economic activity is incessantly being carried on, but it lacks the factors of growth. The size of population, the stock of capital goods, the level of technical knowledge, the taste of the consumers are all given. Thus reproduction is carried on at the same level. The task is to determine relying on these data, the equilibrium quantity and equilibrium price of the products and the equilibrium price of the factors of production.

Dynamics, on the other hand, are concerned with an economy in which the factors of growth are in operation, the scale of output is changing, and an expanded or contracted reproduction is being carried on. The changes analysed by dynamics must, in Harrod's view, be repetitive. The analysis of the effect of once-and-for-all changes is still within the scope of statics. Dynamic exploration is concerned with rates of change, of growth. These rates are the unknowns of the equations to be solved.

The other standpoint accepted by the majority of non-Marxian economists is the one elaborated by Ragnar Frisch. According to his theory, static analysis does not take into account time relationships between economic variables. "...in

[2] F. Heller: *Közgazdasági Lexikon* (Encyclopaedia of Economics), Budapest, 1937, p. 88.

[3] P. Rosenstein-Rodan: Das Zeitmoment in der mathematischen Theorie des wirtschaftlichen Gleichgewichts, *Zeitschrift für Nationalökonomie*, 1929, Vol. I, pp. 129–142.

[4] P. Rosenstein-Rodan: The Role of Time in Economic Theory, *Economics*, 1934, Vol. I, pp. 77–97.

[5] R. Harrod: *Towards a Dynamic Economics*, New York, 1966, p. 3.

such a system, all the variables belong to the same point of time."[6] Dynamic analysis, on the other hand, wishes to give an answer to the question of "...how one situation grows out of the previous one."[7] "In such analyses the magnitudes of certain variables are taken into account at different points of time"[8], and the researchers work with equations which establish relationships between variables belonging to different points of time.

After Frisch, most non-Marxian economists, as opposed to Harrod, mean by statics and dynamics not the nature of the phenomenon examined, but definite *methods of investigation*. They classify the economy, according to its state, as *stationary* or *developing*. A stationary economy lacks the forces of growth, while they are working in a developing one. And, as also pointed out by Schneider, "the stationary and developing phenomena may be subjected to both a static and a dynamic analysis."[9]

Static analysis is a *state analysis* which investigates the economy in equilibrium. Since the values of all variables relate to the same point of time, it assumes that they react infinitely fast to all changes, and hence their reaction velocity is infinitely great.

Representing price, demand and supply relationships in a static way, the demand and supply at the point of time t is a function of price at the point of time t:

$$D_t = f_1(p_t).$$
$$S_t = f_2(p_t).$$

And if the magnitude of any of the the three factors changes, the others will adjust themselves to that change with an infinitely great velocity. Effect and countereffect take place practically at the same time. Using an arrow diagram, the price prevailing at point of time t acts on the demand and supply valid at point of time t, and conversely, the demand and supply at t act immediately on the price at t (see Figure 64).

Static analysis presents a developing economy as a set of equilibrium positions, and the difference between these equilibrium positions expresses the change in one or another of the data underlying them. Schneider emphasizes that in the interest of analytically approaching any change in the interrelated data "only one single datum should of course be changed."[10] The analysis of economic processes by means of collating two particular equilibrium positions is called *comparative statics*. Its drawback is that the data for each equilibrium position should be given separately; their change cannot be derived from the model. Comparative statics is "without regard to the transitional process involved in the adjustment,"[11] that is, it does not express the process of transition from one equilibrium position to another. Thus the static method of analysis is unable to

[6] R. Frisch: Propagation Problems and Impulse Problems in Dynamic Analysis, *Essays in Honour of Gustav Cassel*, London, 1933, p. 172.

[7] R. Frisch: *op. cit.*, p. 171.

[8] *Ibid.*

[9] E. Schneider: *Einführung in die Wirtschaftstheorie*, Vol. II, Tübingen, 1956.

[10] E. Schneider: *op. cit.*, p. 247.

[11] P. A. Samuelson: *Foundations of Economic Analysis*, New York, 1970, p. 8.

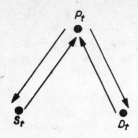

Figure 64

Source: A. E. Ott: *Einführung in die dynamische Wirtschaftstheorie,* Göttingen, 1963, p. 22.

take account of the development of economic processes taking place by means of endogenous forces inherent in the economic system.

As opposed to the state analysis of statics, the dynamic approach is a *process analysis*. In representing the economic processes changing through time, the subsequent states are interconnected in a chainlike fashion. It is sufficient to indicate the data at the beginning, and their further movement can be inferred from the model. This makes an endogenous representation of the economic processes possible. By means of this chainlike interconnection we obtain the sequential, time-dependent development of the values of individual variables, their so-called *time paths*.

Dynamic analysis based on the time factor does not assume the variables to have an infinite velocity of reaction, and takes some of them to react with different velocities to changes in the process of adjustment. It is only by dynamic analysis that relationships can be revealed in which certain magnitudes are dependent upon the development tendencies, the reaction velocities of others, since velocity itself is a magnitude which requires the consideration of two different points of time to be determined. In the dynamic demand function set up by Evans "the demand is ... not merely a function of the price alone, but is stimulated or depressed by the mere fact that the price is rising or falling."[12] Similarly, in his dynamic supply function Evans regards supply as a function not only of the prevailing price, but also of its tendency of development.

Taking account of the different reaction velocities of the variables, the functional relationships for demand, supply and price are no longer related to the same point of time only. Since supply, if we disregard inventory changes, reacts to a change of price with a lag of the production process, the supply at *t* is a function of the price of the previous period:

$$D_t = f_1(p_t)$$
$$S_t = f_2(p_{t-1}).$$

[12] G. C. Evans: *Mathematical Introduction to Economics,* New York–London, 1930, p. 36.

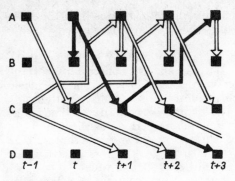

Figure 65

Source: J. Tinbergen: Econometric Business Cycle Research. In: *Readings in Business Cycle Theory*, Philadelphia–Toronto, 1944, p. 63.

Let us illustrate this delayed adjustment by Tinbergen's arrow diagram (Figure 65):

Tinbergen explains the development of an economic process over time by means of four variables, A, B, C and D. By means of arrow diagrams Tinbergen demonstrates how a change in A at time t reacts on other variables at t, or other points of time. He assumes that A reacts on B without a time lag, but on C with a lag of one period, that is $A(t)$ reacts on $C(t+1)$. A change in C reacts on D and A with a lag of two periods. He shows this effect or countereffect by means of arrows. Thus the effect of a change in $A(t)$ is the primary or direct cause of the change in $C(t+1)$, and the secondary or indirect cause of the change in $D(t+3)$. This process will be repeated in the subsequent periods until the structure of the model changes. The arrows can be grouped, in Tinbergen's view, in two ways: (1) according to the variable from which the arrows start out; (2) according to the variable in which they end. The first grouping shows the *complete effect* of a change in one variable on all the others. The other grouping includes *all causes* of changes in one variable. But both groupings describe the same mechanism.

Owing to different reaction velocities, once the equilibrium is disturbed, it is difficult to restore it, or it may even not come about at all. Therefore, dynamics is concerned not only with the analysis of a process taking place under equilibrium conditions, but also with the upsetting of the equilibrium situation, the process taking place under conditions of disequilibrium, changes moving both away from and towards equilibrium.

Comparative dynamics compares two process analyses, which differ from one another owing to the parameters of the model, or the time lags built into it.

Samuelson distinguishes two methods of dynamic analysis: *period* and *rate analysis*.

Period analysis divides the length of time under consideration into consecutive periods of a finite duration. The variables do not change continuously with the time elapsed, but abruptly at the end of the period concerned. They cannot be

263

derived with respect to time. The mathematical apparatus used is the difference equation, which establishes a relationship between a given variable and its difference.

Rate analysis supposes that the variables change continuously over time, that is, they can be derived with respect to time. "...rate analysis concerns itself with flows, with instantaneous rates of change, with speeds..."[13] Its mathematical apparatus is the differential equation which establishes a functional relationship between a variable and its derivative. "The choice between period and rate analysis is usually one of convenience, since by taking periods of short enough duration, we can approximate to rates and can neglect the interrelations within the period."[14]

Samuelson regards the basis of natural logarithm, *e,* as a factor which "...bridges the gap between discrete difference equation analysis and continuous differential equation analysis."[15]

Following his example, let us suppose that somebody deposits one dollar at an interest of 100 per cent per annum with a bank. In a year it will rise to be $1 + 1 = 2$ dollars. If that one dollar yields an interest of 50 per cent semi-annually, then the one dollar inclusive of compound interest will bear $(1 + \frac{1}{2})^2 = 2.25$ dollars by the end of the year. Suppose that the interest is added each time to the deposit n-times a year at a rate of interest of $\frac{1}{n}$ per cent, the original deposit of one dollar will rise, inclusive of compound interest, to $\left(1 + \frac{1}{n}\right)^n$ by the end of the year.

If $n \to \infty$, then $\left(1 + \frac{1}{n}\right)^n$ will approach a limit, 2.71828, which, in Euler's honour, is denoted by e, the initial of his name.

Suppose now that one dollar is deposited not at a rate of 100 per cent, but at r per cent annually, n times a year, for x years. One dollar will increase to $\left(1 + \frac{r}{n}\right)^{nx}$ in x years. Dividing and multiplying the exponent by r, we may write it in the form

$$\left\{\left(1 + \frac{r}{n}\right)^{\frac{n}{r}}\right\}^{xr}.$$

Denoting $\frac{n}{r}$ by m, we obtain the expression

$$\left\{\left(1 + \frac{1}{m}\right)^m\right\}^{xr}$$

[13] P. A. Samuelson: *op. cit.,* p. 359.

[14] P. A. Samuelson: Dynamic Process Analysis. In: *A Survey of Contemporary Economics,* Philadelphia–Toronto, 1949, pp. 354–355.

[15] P. A. Samuelson: *op. cit.,* pp. 359–360.

If $m \to \infty$, $\left(1 + \dfrac{1}{m}\right)^m = e$, then one dollar will increase to e^{xr} at a rate of r per cent in x years with interest computed continuously.

Applying the two kinds of dynamic analysis to the growth of the national income, taking the period to be one year and assuming an annual rate of increase g in the national income, national income Y_0 will increase to $Y_0(1+g)^t$ in t years. Supposing a continuous growth of rate g, Y_0 will become $Y_0 \cdot e^{gt}$ in t years.

Chapter 2

THE ANALYSIS OF PROBLEMS RELATING TO DELAYED ADJUSTMENT BY MEANS OF THE COBWEB THEOREM

How does non-Marxian economics use dynamic analysis in a stationary economy? A stationary economy, as has already been shown, is not characterized by complete rest. Production may oscillate in it, too, but its magnitude is constant in the long run, it has neither a downward-, nor an upward-moving trend. It is, however, possible that the equilibrium position is disturbed in a stationary economy, too, and owing to the different reaction velocities, it takes time for the economy to restore its equilibrium, or it may even move away from a state of equilibrium. We may wish to analyse what will happen when equilibrium is disturbed, that is, in the so-called *transition period*. The determination of what set of prices and quantities demanded and supplied will develop in this period, is, according to Ragnar Frisch's definition, also dynamic analysis.

The gist of the problem, in a Marxist sense, of a delayed adjustment as expressed in the Cobweb Theorem is the following: when a difference develops between demand and supply, an equilibrium position could be restored directly only if the producers knew about the magnitude of the equilibrium price, and took their decisions on the scale of output in that knowledge. Since production requires time, they know only the price prevailing at the beginning of production, but they cannot know the price at which the market is willing to take their commodities when they are ready for marketing. According to the assumption, capitalist entrepreneurs operating independently of each other take their decisions on the volume of output in awareness of the prevailing price, hoping to realize their products at the same price once they are ready for sale.

Since market price invariably deviates from value, that is, from production price, or using the non-Marxian term, from equilibrium price, entrepreneurs decide on the basis of a non-equilibrium price how much they will produce. As a result, they will put a non-equilibrium quantity on the market, which the market will take again at a non-equilibrium price, and entrepreneurs will continue to produce and supply a non-equilibrium quantity. Now the problem arises whether an equilibrium position will be established at all, that is, whether, taking the existing data to be constant, the amplitude of fluctuations will decrease if the equilibrium position is disturbed, so that the economy will be restored to its original state of equilibrium, or a persistent disequilibrium will ensue with fluctuations of a constant or increasing amplitude. In the former case the original equilibrium position was *stable,* in the latter *unstable*.

The foundations of the Cobweb Theorem were laid independently by three authors, the American Henry Schultz, the Dutch Jan Tinbergen and the Italian

266

Umberto Ricci. A substantial contribution to its further development was provided by the American Mordecai Ezekiel. It is primarily on his analysis of the Cobweb Theorem that the discussion here is based.

The fluctuation of demand and supply as expressed in the Cobweb Theorem is also referred to by Marx when he writes that demand and supply are never in equilibrium, and in the course of subsequent oscillations "the result of a deviation in one direction is that it calls forth a deviation in the opposite direction..."[16]

Ezekiel assumes that the supply of the commodities under consideration is completely inelastic in the short run, in other words, that "... the period considered may be taken as so short that the total supply available cannot be changed within the period (as, for example, the supply of cotton or potatoes once the year's crop is harvested)."[17]

He sets out from the assumption that too much of a commodity, quantity Q_1, which is more than the equilibrium quantity, is placed on the market. The market takes this quantity at price p_1, which is lower than the equilibrium price. At this price, entrepreneurs will contract their outputs and, when their product are ready for sale, they will supply Q_2, a quantity smaller than the equilibrium quantity. The market, however, will take this quantity at a higher than equilibrium price, at p_2, which in turn will stimulate entrepreneurs to increase their outputs to a too large quantity, Q_3. As a result, price will fall again below the equilibrium price, to p_3, and so forth. The sets of prices and quantities supplied, p_1, p_2, p_3, etc. and Q_1, Q_2, Q_3, etc. respectively, show how prices and supplies develop in disequilibrium.

In Figure 66, the divergence from their equilibrium values of the non-equilibrium prices and quantities supplied decreases more and more, the cobweb contracts, the market tends to converge to equilibrium. This will be the situation when demand is more elastic than supply. In the reverse case (Figure 67), that is, when supply is more elastic than demand, at the disturbance of equilibrium, prices and quantities supplied will increasingly move away from their equilibrium values, i.e. the cobweb extends.

Deviation from the equilibrium position might continue "...until price fell to absolute zero, or production was completely abandoned, or a limit was reached to available resources (where the elasticity of supply would change) so that production could no longer expand."[18]

If, however, the elasticity of demand equals the elasticity of supply, we obtain fluctuations of a constant amplitude, prices and quantities supplied will deviate from their equilibrium values by identical margins both downwards and upwards. The economy will neither move away from, nor move towards, its equilibrium position (see Figure 68).

Illustrating the above by a numerical example, let the equation of demand be

$$p_t^D = 50 - Q_t, \text{ whence } Q_t = 50 - p_t,$$

[16] K. Marx: *Capital*, Vol. III, Moscow, 1962, p. 186.
[17] M. Ezekiel: The Cobweb Theorem. In: *Readings in Business Cycle Theory*, Philadelphia–Toronto, 1951, p. 426.
[18] M. Ezekiel: *op. cit.*, p. 432.

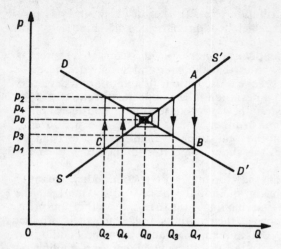

Figure 66

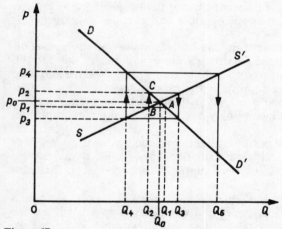

Figure 67

and the equation of supply be

$$p_t^s = \frac{3}{2} \cdot Q_t, \text{ whence } Q_t = \frac{2}{3} p_t.$$

The equilibrium price will develop where the demand for, and the supply of, Q are equal, that is, $\frac{2}{3} p_t = 50 - p_t$, whence $p_t = 30$. The equilibrium magnitude of demand and supply, given a price of 30, will be $50 - 30$, or $\frac{2}{3} \cdot 30 = 20$.

268

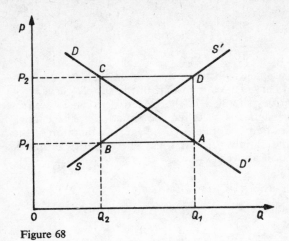

Figure 68

Suppose that a larger than equilibrium quantity, for example 30 units, are put on the market. Demand will take it at a price of 50—30 = 20. At price 20, sellers will next put quantity $\frac{2}{3} \cdot 20 = 13.333$ on the market. Thus, price and supply will have the following values developed over time:

Quantity	Price
30	20
13.333	36.666
24.444	25.555
17.0376	32.9624
.	.
.	.
.	.

The amplitude of fluctuations decreases as the slope of the demand curve is 1, less than the slope of the supply curve, $\frac{3}{2}$.

When our demand equation is

$$p_t^D = 50 - \frac{1}{2} Q_t,$$

and our supply equation

$$p_t^S = \frac{1}{2} Q_t,$$

then the amplitude of the fluctuation is constant, since the slopes of the two curves are equal.

If our demand equation is

$$p_t^D = 38 - Q_t,$$

269

and our supply equation is

$$p_t^s = \frac{9}{10} Q_t,$$

the values of price and quantity supplied will move away from their equilibrium values as the slope of the demand curve is less than that of the supply curve.

The values of prices and quantities supplied in the period between two equilibrium positions are determined by means of difference equations. The change of supply from point of time $t-1$ to point of time t, Q_t-Q_{t-1}, is a function of the difference between the demand and supply price at $t-1$. The quantity supplied, according to the first set of equation above, is

$$Q_t - Q_{t-1} = \frac{2}{3}(p_{t-1}^D - p_{t-1}^s).$$

Substituting the corresponding values for p_{t-1}^D and p_{t-1}^s, we obtain

$$Q_t - Q_{t-1} = \frac{2}{3}\left(50 - Q_{t-1} - \frac{3}{2} Q_{t-1}\right),$$

whence

$$Q_t = -\frac{2}{3} Q_{t-1} + \frac{2}{3} \cdot 50.$$

Thus we obtain a first order non-homogeneous difference equation, the solution of which is

$$Q_t = C(a)^t + \frac{b}{1-a},$$

where $a = -\frac{2}{3}$, $b = \frac{2}{3} \cdot 50$, $C = Q_0 - \frac{b}{1-a}$.

If $Q_0 = 30$, $C = 30 - 20 = 10$,

thus

$$Q_1 = 10\left(-\frac{2}{3}\right) + 20 = 13.333,$$

$$Q_2 = 10\left(-\frac{2}{3}\right)^2 + 20 = 24.444.$$

Let us now also determine the magnitude of price by means of difference equations at the individual points of time.

In equilibrium, demand at point of time t equals supply at point of time t.

$$C\left(-\frac{2}{3}\right)^t + 20 = 50 - p_r,$$

whence $p_t = -C\left(-\frac{2}{3}\right)^t + 30.$

$$p_1 = -10 \cdot -\frac{2}{3} + 30 = 36.666$$

$$p_2 = -10\left(-\frac{2}{3}\right)^2 + 30 = 25.555.$$

Samuelson called attention to the fact that the results obtained by comparative static and dynamic analysis might be contradictory. If, for example, the equilibrium of demand and supply is disturbed, because the demand curve shifts upwards owing to a change in demand relations, in the taste of consumers, which is one of the data of the model, comparative statics will by all means present us with a new equilibrium position which corresponds to the changed conditions. Dynamic analysis, however, which also examines the process of the establishment of equilibrium over time, calls attention to the fact that, depending on the interrelationship of the elasticity of demand and supply, the economy, if market equilibrium is disturbed, may increasingly move away from the equilibrium position (Figure 69).

Samuelson's "correspondence principle" expresses that it is only dynamic analysis which shows whether an equilibrium situation can be restored again after it has been upset, i.e. whether comparative statics concerned with the analysis of

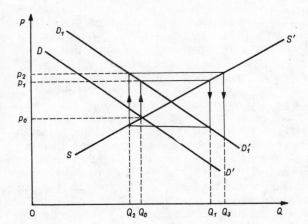

Figure 69

subsequent equilibrium positions can be applied. Samuelson, writing about the correspondence principle, says: "We find ourselves confronted with this paradox: in order for the comparative static analysis to yield fruitful results, we must first develop a theory of dynamics."[19]

From the Cobweb Theorem form of dynamic analysis, Ezekiel draws an important conclusion for the operation of the mechanism of capitalist economy. If prices and quantities do not rapidly converge towards their equilibrium values,

[19] P. A. Samuelson: *Foundations of Economic Analysis*, New York, 1970, pp. 262–263.

then the individual industries producing over the equilibrium point employ too much labour and capital which will remain unused when production falls below the equilibrium point. In this case "... the economic system will never organize all its resources for the most effective use... Even under the conditions of pure competition and static demand and supply, there is thus no 'automatic self-regulating mechanism' which can provide full utilization of resources. Unemployment, excess capacity, and the wasteful use of resources may occur even when all the competitive assumptions are fulfilled."[20]

The method of analysis elaborated taking the time factor into consideration is a major achievement of non-Marxian economics. The technical apparatus evolved may also successfully be applied by Marxist political economy. The problem of whether statics and dynamics are methods of analysis, or just refer to the nature of the phenomenon under examination, is a matter of decision. Frisch, too, distinguishes between stagnant and developing economies, and only the names he gives them are different from those used by Harrod.

It should be noted that the way Marx and Lenin examined the process of expanded reproduction under conditions of equilibrium over several periods by means of their reproduction patterns, a process in which the values of one period are derived from those of the previous one, constitutes a typical process analysis through period analysis. Thus period analysis for the examination of economic variables changing over time was already used by the classics of Marxism.

The differing elasticities of demand and supply as assumed by the Cobweb Theorem are suitable, by the way, to explain at best fluctuations in the production of individual commodities.[21] It would be able to provide an explanation of unemployment, excess capacity, and the wasteful use of resources only if the cobweb cycle were characteristic of a substantial part of the economy. This is what Ezekiel assumes. But the cyclical movement of the capitalist economy is not called forth by the cobweb cycle. Such an explanation divorces the cycles of capitalist reproduction from the relationship between the production of means of production and of consumption goods. In real life, if the production of the means of production shoots ahead of the production of consumer goods, the supply of the latter lags behind the demand for them, and the price level of consumer goods will rise. Though department II expands its output, so long as the dominant role of department I is maintained, incomes will rise, the demand function for consumer goods will shift upwards, and the market will take even the increased supply of consumer goods at increasing prices. Deviation from the equilibrium takes place in the opposite direction if the share of the production of consumer goods increases relative to the production of the means of production. In this view, the disparity between demand and supply increases in a cumulative way both upwards and downwards, unlike the process described by the Cobweb Theorem, where an upward deviation from equilibrium is always interrupted by a downward deviation.

[20] M. Ezekiel: *op. cit.*, p. 442.
[21] The first attempts to utilize the Cobweb Theorem were made in agriculture. The German Hanau applied it to the hog market. An important condition of its applicability is that the magnitude of supply should adjust itself exclusively to the price established at the beginning of the production period, and that it may not be changed during the production process.

272

Chapter 3

THE PERIOD ANALYSIS OF THE STOCKHOLM SCHOOL.
THE ROLE OF EXPECTATIONS

The Stockholm School has evolved a specific kind of dynamic analysis which we shall demonstrate on the basis of the works of Lindahl, Ohlin and Myrdal. Their approach is micro-economic: socio-economic phenomena develop as a result of the interaction of individual behaviours, and thus in exploring them we have to reveal in the first place the motives of the decisions of the economic subjects, and the explanation of the development of economic phenomena over time, of their time-dependent character, must be based on the time dependence of individual decisions. For this purpose they divide the process under examination into consecutive periods, and analysing the decisions of individual economic subjects from period to period, seek to deduce the socio-economic processes from the interaction of many individual steps.

In their view, every individual takes his decision at the beginning of the period. While taking it, he relies on the data of his action. But part of them are data relating to the future. The entrepreneur decides today how much he will produce tomorrow, but his decision is influenced by the expected magnitudes of price, demand, production costs prevalent at the time his product is ready for sale. The individual cannot know, however, the future conditions of his action; he can at most estimate them with more or less accuracy. The estimate of the future conditions of individual actions, the anticipation of the future, that is, *expectation,* plays a prominent role in the dynamic analysis of the Stockholm School. It was first introduced to price theory by Myrdal. Expectation or anticipation "is the calculation of what will happen in the future.... It is these anticipations which determine ... the behaviour of the economic subject...."[22] It is exactly in connection with the introduction of expectations that Lindahl speaks of the economic subject's plans on which his behaviour is based: "... plans are made for the attainment of certain aims (for business firms, for instance, the attainment of maximum net income) and ... they are based on individual expectations concerning future conditions..."[23] "Plans are thus the explicit expression of the economic motives

---

[22] G. Myrdal: *Der Gleichgewichtsbegriff als Instrument der geldtheoretischen Analyse. Beiträge zur Geldtheorie,* Wien, 1933, pp. 394 and 430.
[23] E. Lindahl: *Studies in the Theory of Money and Capital,* London, 1939, p. 36.

of a man, as they become evident of his economic actions."[24] "Plans are regarded as a special sort of expectations."[25]

Thus, the exposition of the motives of individual actions by the representatives of the Stockholm School means the analysis of how the individual plans come into existence. But in a capitalist economy each individual takes his decisions in isolation, independently of the others. Consequently, what they aimed at and what they have actually attained are rather different. This difference finds expression with the economists of the Stockholm School following Myrdal, when they distinguish between *ex-ante* and *ex-post* magnitudes. An *ex-ante* magnitude is what each of the individuals wanted to attain separately. Their exploration is the analysis of the final causes of economic phenomena, of the individuals' motives, or, as Lindahl calls them, of the "psycho-logical causes". At the end of the period, by the time the effect of the decisions has worked itself out, the individual takes account of how his aims have materialized. The magnitude actually achieved is the *ex-post* magnitude. *Ex-post* magnitudes on a social scale are supplied by statistics—writes Baumol—, while *ex-ante* magnitudes can only be ascertained by questioning people about what they intended to achieve by their behaviour in the past.[26] The characteristic feature of equilibrium is, according to the Swedish economists, that the *ex-ante* and *ex-post* magnitudes coincide.

Since the individual behaviours giving rise to economic phenomena are determined by the individuals' expectations and plans, the primary task of dynamic analysis is, according to the Stockholm School, to account for the way these expectations and plans have come about. The expectations are determined partly by non-economic factors. Lindahl assumes that their effect is known to us from period to period. For simplicity's sake, however, these effects may also be left out of account, in which case we obtain a completely endogenous explanation of the economic processes.

Now, according to the theory, individuals adjust their plans at the end of the period by comparing their hopes and the results actually achieved, that is, the *ex-ante* and *ex-post* magnitudes, and the action of the next period will be undertaken on the basis of the new, revised plan. Or, in Ohlin's formulation: "... after a description of actual events during a certain, finished period, and of the differences between these events and the expectations which existed at the beginning of the period, follows an account of those expectations for the future which more or less govern actions during the next period. The registration of events during this second period reveals again that expectations and actions do not all come true, a fact which influences expectations and actions during the third period, etc."[27] It is in a similar way that Lindahl describes how expectations come about: "The retrospective estimate made at t_1 for the same period $t_0 t_1$, may, on the other hand, be supposed to influence his planning for the next period, and is thus of immediate relevance for the explanation of the actions undertaken in that period."[28]

[24] E. Lindahl: *op. cit.,* p. 37.
[25] B. Ohlin: Some Notes on the Stockholm Theory of Savings and Investments. In: *Readings in Business Cycle Theory,* Philadelphia–Toronto, 1951, p. 97.
[26] W. F. Baumol: *Economic Dynamics,* New York–London–Tokyo, 1951, p. 130.
[27] B. Ohlin: *op. cit.,* p. 94.
[28] E. Lindahl: *op. cit.,* pp. 91–92.

Ohlin emphasizes that "... the period is chosen so that he (the individual) does not change his plans until the beginning of the next period."[29]

In this way, the periods are interconnected in a chainlike fashion, the events of one period influence the events of the next one. The actions of one period are directly coupled partly with the *ex-post* values of the previous period, partly with the difference between these *ex-post* and the *ex-ante* values.

The expectations, plans are thus virtually expressions of the relationship between the *ex-ante* magnitudes of a given period and the *ex-post* magnitudes of the previous one. This relationship may be very variable; no generalization in this respect is possible. Hicks made an attempt to specify the possible cases of relationship between the *ex-post* magnitudes of the past and the *ex-ante* magnitudes of the following period. For this purpose he created the concept of the *elasticity of expectations*. "I define the elasticity of a particular person's expectations of the price of commodity x as the ratio of the proportional rise in expected future prices of x to the proportional rise in its current price."[30] He examines how the economic processes develop if the elasticity of the economic subject's expectations is unity, greater than unity, less than unity but greater than zero, or less than zero. Hicks points out that the stability of the system, the restoration of equilibrium, is not ensured at certain values of the elasticity of expectations. Let us assume that at the existing and expected prices both the producer and the consumer have allocated optimally over time in their respective production and consumption plans the resources available to them between the selling and the buying of their commodities both at present and in the future. According to Hicks, the present and the future units of the same commodity have to be regarded as different commodities. The economic units compare the prices and costs prevailing at different points of time by discounting them to the time when they drew up their plans. And the criterion of an optimum situation is similar to the optimum criterion of the static model: the marginal rates of substitution between products must equal the ratio of the present and the future discounted prices in both production and consumption.

Let us assume that the price of a given product has increased by a certain per cent owing to the increased demand for it. Let us suppose that the elasticity of substitution is greater than unity. The agents of the market expect the price of the given commodity to rise in the future at a higher than the current percentage rate. Hicks emphasizes that if the rates of interest can be taken as given, any change in an expected price will change its discounted value in the same proportion. The two of them will always move together, so for the present we can leave the whole matter of discounting out of account. Thus we may say that, as a result of the change, the expected price proportion between the present and the future commodities will change. According to the estimates of the market agents, the price of the future commodity will rise relative to the price of the present commodity. In compliance with the double effect of the price change, both a substitution effect over time and an income effect will evolve. The buyer will bring forward his purchases which were due to be made in the future, and the seller will

[29] B. Ohlin: *op. cit.*, p. 97.
[30] J. R. Hicks: *Value and Capital*, Oxford, 1965, p. 205.

delay his supplies. The income effect will be suppressed by speculation. At present, demand will rise and supply will fall. The originally existing excess demand will increase, the economy will move away from equilibrium. The system is not stable. "A system with elasticities greater than unity, and constant rate of interest, is definitely unstable."[31] In this case, the response of the market agents to price changes is just the opposite to the case in the model which does not reckon with the time factor. At rising prices, supply will decrease and demand increase, because both sellers and buyers expect a still greater price rise in the future. Hicks compares the substitution over time called forth by a change in relative prices to a substitution which, as a result of a change in relative prices, unfolds along the curve of production possibilities.

If the elasticity of expectations equals unity, the market agents will expect the price of a given product to rise in the future at a percentage rate identical with the present one. There is no change in relative prices and there is no substitution over time. There evolves, however, an income effect with an uncertain outcome, and thus the present formation of demand and supply will also be uncertain.

If the elasticity of expectations equals zero, the market agents will expect that the current price rise of the product is only temporary, and its price will, sooner or later, fall back to its original level. A substitution over time will develop, buyers will defer their purchases and sellers will bring forward their sales. The income effect becomes negligible owing to the fact that the price change is taken to be temporary. This value of the elasticity of expectations has a stabilizing effect.

The period analysis as applied by the Swedish economists differs from that of Samuelson. The latter method of analysis refers only to *ex-post* magnitudes, while the approach of the Swedish economists applied both to *ex-ante* magnitudes at the beginning of the period and to *ex-post* magnitudes at its end, that is, they claim to explain the motives of economic actions and through them the development of economic processes by means of *ex-ante* magnitudes.

Lindahl maintains that after the micro-economic analysis of individual actions the examination of macro-economic processes must follow. In order to understand the macro-economic processes, we must know the totality of the plans of the particular period and their changes, those non-economic events which influence the plans and actions as well as the interconnection of actions.

But period analysis based on individual decisions as applied by the Swedish economists is not adequate to reveal the laws governing economic processes, the objective laws that assert themselves through the correction of the plans of the many individuals acting independently of one another. It represents the whole economic process from the side of the individual, and thus what it offers is nothing but the individual reflection of social processes, by the summation of which the analysis wishes to represent the objective social processes. This analysis does not tell us why and in what direction the expectation changes, because it examines the changes in the objective social conditions of action only from the point of view of individual decisions. Though it links expectations to the difference between the *ex-ante* and *ex-post* magnitudes of the previous period, there is no definite relationship between this difference and the changes in expectations, as is also clear from Hick's assumption.

[31] J. R. Hicks: *op. cit.*, p. 255.

No doubt expectations play a role in economic processes as economic laws manifest themselves through conscious human behaviour. Expectations influence economic events primarily in the short run. Owing to the uncertainty of the future, isolated commodity producers may pile up their false computations. As a result, the economy may swing far out of its equilibrium position. Aftalion[32] has pointed out that in the case of inflation, expectations also contribute to the extent to which the prices of the various goods increase. If the price of a commodity is expected to rise substantially in the future, it will be bought in a larger volume in the present, and then its price will really increase more than that of the other commodities.

An important condition for the elimination of inflation, for stabilization, is the favourable formation of expectations. If the public does not trust in stabilization, has no confidence in the new money replacing the old, depreciated one, it will make attempts to get rid of it. This causes the rate of the circulation of money to increase, which exerts the same effect on the price level as if the quantity of money issued had increased. Inflation continues to grow. Or, to quote another example, if the supply of goods is disturbed, if most of the consumers count under the influence of false rumour, on a shortage of certain commodities, and make massive purchases of them, then this shortage will really arise. This is because consumers expected it on a massive scale. Expectations may also influence economic processes in the long run. The more the false expectations of isolated capitalist producers cause the economy to get out of equilibrium, the more this reacts on the rate of growth in the long run.

Expectations are, however, only the subjective manifestations of objective laws. They do not affect the essence of the latter, but do affect the way these laws assert themselves, and influence first of all short-term events. The accumulation of false expectations can disrupt the relative shares of department I and II only up to a certain point. Department I cannot shoot infinitely ahead of department II. In his fundamental work,[33] Péter Erdős has described very succinctly that it is enough for capitalists producing consumer goods to know that, owing to the expansion of department I, significant new capacities will reach the stage of production, for this information to call forth unfavourable expectations in them; as a result they will slow down their increase in production of consumer goods, which is of disastrous consequence for the upswing of the economy. At which stage of the increasing disparity between the two departments the entrepreneurs' optimistic expectation will change into a pessimistic one, is difficult to tell with any measure of accuracy. But it is sure to change sooner or later in a capitalist economy left to itself. By clearing the way for an upswing, an economic crisis will also influence the expectations of entrepreneurs in a definite manner. The differing elasticity of expectations in the situation examined by Aftalion, under conditions of inflation, or the effect of unfavourable expectations under circumstances of panicky purchases of certain commodities, influences only the way in which the law of value works itself out under existing specific conditions.

As regards the assertion of economic laws, the *ex-ante* and *ex-post* method may provide some explanation of the development of short-term economic phenom-

[32] A. Aftalion: *Monnaie, prix et change*, Paris, 1927.
[33] P. Erdős: *Contributions to the Theory of Capitalist Money, Business, Fluctuations and Crises*, Budapest, 1971, p. 382.

ena. If we set out from a given economic situation and are familiar with the behavioural motives of the economic subjects, with the rules governing the social interconnections of their actions, we can find an explanation for the emergence of a concrete situation which will then provide a social framework for further decisions. Of course, with such an explanation supplied, several serious problems relating to aggregation would still arise. Such would be, for example, differences between periods by economic units, and especially the grouping of economic subjects according to their class positions, etc. The serious problem of aggregation is usually evaded by the Swedish economists. Lindahl speaks simply of averaging the individual plans.[34]

Choosing the behaviour of the economic subject as a starting-point of analysis, and introducing expectations, the theory finds itself faced with a complete chaos of uncertainty. True, the prediction of the future is possible also in a socialist economy only within certain limits of accuracy; i.e., the uncertainty factor must be reckoned with in socialist planning, too. But the role of the time factor, the uncertainty concerning changes in the economic processes over time, is of an entirely different character in the capitalist and in the socialist economy. In the theory of non-Marxian economics relating to expectations we have to do with the uncertain expectations of individuals operating in isolation. A number of factors which constitute the object of socialist state planning are entirely outside the scope of control of these individuals. Thus, the uncertainty of the future in the representation of non-Marxian economics is the uncertainty accompanying the anarchy stemming from the private ownership of the means of production. Paulsen calls this the price of human freedom,[35] while Marx sees in it the manifestation of the fact that people are the slaves and not the masters of their own production relations.

[34] E. Lindahl: *op. cit.*, p. 53.
[35] A. Paulsen: *Neue Wirtschaftslehre*, Berlin–Frankfurt, 1954, p. 140.

Part Five

SOME APPLICATIONS OF ECONOMETRICS IN ECONOMIC RESEARCH

Chapter 1

GENERAL CHARACTERISTICS

Econometric research, begun in the 1920s and 1930s, is regarded as an outstanding achievement of non-Marxian economics.

Most economic theories were based on certain premises from which were deduced a large number of relationships formulated in very general terms. (Let it be mentioned in passing that in view of the findings of modern experimental psychology and sociology, and also of direct, empirical observation, the real content of these premises is increasingly criticized even within the limits of non-Marxian thinking.) A good example is Walras's general equilibrium theory, which aims to reveal through logical analysis the relationships between various markets, the interdependence of the markets for consumer goods and the mutual effects which the latter and the markets for production services exert on one another. But the functional relations revealed by Walras are of a completely formal character. They express, for example, that the demand for a given consumer good depends on the price of all consumer goods and the incomes of consumers. But they fail to represent the concrete, quantitative aspect of these functional relationships. "The relevant elasticities, propensities, and other similar constants can conveniently be represented by symbolic letters, say, *a*, or *A* throughout the whole argument and also in the final conclusions. Intricate relationships can thus be set up and studied without any reference to the actual magnitude of the many unknown constants involved in each of them."[1]

It was in the 1920s and 1930s that studies in econometrics began "... to fill the empty boxes of abstract, theoretical argument with actual statistical data..."[2] The term "econometrics" itself stems from Ragnar Frisch: "A new discipline mediating between mathematics, statistics and political economy has been found which, for lack of a better term, we may call *econometrics*."[3] He defines the task of econometrics in a study published as early as the 1920s: "Econometrics aims to subject the abstract laws of the theory of political economy, or pure economics, to an experimental, quantified verification, and to change, as far as possible, pure economics into a science in the strict sense of the word."[4] Tinbergen also defines

---

[1] W. W. Leontief: Econometrics. In: *A Survey of Contemporary Economics*, Philadelphia–Toronto, 1949, p. 390.

[2] *Ibid.*

[3] R. Frisch: Sur un problème d'économie pure, *Norsk Matematisk Forenings Skrifter*, Series I, No. 16, Oslo, 1926. Reprinted in *Metroeconomica*, August 1957, p. 79.

[4] *Ibid.*

econometrics as "statistical observation of theoretically founded concepts"[5], or, alternatively, "mathematical economics working with measured data."[6] Thus, econometrics in this formulation seeks on the one hand to verify the real content of an economic theory by analysing statistical data and on the other to reveal the concrete relationships between economic magnitudes with the aid of data supplied by statistics. Oscar Lange also speaks of econometrics as a discipline trying to express the general, vague laws of economic theory in concrete, quantitative terms by means of mathematical and statistical methods.[7] The emergence of econometrics coincides in time with the rise of monopolies, when "concentration has reached the point at which it is possible to make an approximate estimate of all resources of raw material ... of a country ... An approximate estimate of the capacity of markets is also made, and the combines divide them up among themselves by agreement."[8] All this required econometric research, the knowledge of concrete economic relationships, of the demand elasticities for individual products, of market relations. But the rise of state monopoly capitalism, the endeavour of the state to intervene in economic life, to regulate the economic processes, also called forth econometric research.

Most economic research is impossible without economic theory. The very application of the method of abstraction, the decision on what to single out as important and what as insignificant of the complexity of factors influencing the phenomena examined, cannot be made without theoretical considerations. Thus, econometrics combines statistics, mathematics and economics.

The founders of econometrics were non-Marxian economists who relied in their research activities on the theories of modern non-Marxian economics, a circumstance which determined the scope of their studies and the scientific character of their results.

The forerunners of economic research included the studies in business cycle theory conducted at the Institute for Economic Research at Harvard University; attempts to construct demand curves for certain commodities by means of statistical data (notably by Moore and Schultz); attempts to measure marginal utility (Ragnar Frisch) and to quantify the marginal productivity of labour and capital (Cobb, Douglas).

Of later studies in econometrics, perhaps the most significant is that of W. W. Leontief[9] who tried to work out an approach to "empirical general equilibrium analysis"[10], to examine by so-called input–output analysis the interrelations among the various sectors of the economy. In the input–output table "the entries ... are arranged in a checkerboard fashion, each row and the corresponding column of figures bearing the name of a separate industry—Grain Farming, Steel Works and Rolling Mills, Railroads, and so on. The entries along any one row show the distribution of the total output of the particular industry among all the other branches of the national economy. Thus the figures entered in the "Steel Works

[5] J. Tinbergen: *Econometrics,* New York, 1951, p. 10.
[6] *Ibid.*
[7] O. Lange: *Introduction to Econometrics,* London, 1959, p. 7.
[8] V. I. Lenin: *Imperialism, the Highest Stage of Capitalism,* Selected Works, Vol. V, London, 1944, p. 22.
[9] W. W. Leontief: *The Structure of American Economy,* 1919–1929, Cambridge, Mass., 1941
[10] W. W. Leontief: *Econometrics,* California, 1959, p. 407.

and Rolling Mills" row represent the amounts of the product of this industry directly absorbed by, say, Grain Farming, by the Railroads, by the Automobile Industry, etc.

"The last entry in each row shows the total output of the industry (in this particular example this would be the total output of Steel Works and Rolling Mills), i.e., it represents the sum total of all the other entries along the same row. Government, Households, and Foreign Countries are treated as separate industries, that is, as separate branches of the economy. If read by columns, the same figures show the quantities of the various kinds of inputs absorbed by each individual industry. The Steel Works and Rolling Mills column shows the amount of coal obtained by this industry from Coal Mining, the amount of Transportation received from Railroads, and so on down the column to the amount of labor (labor hours) obtained from the Households, which are also treated as a separate 'Industry.' "[11]

Leontief's input–output table is a modern Tableau Économique with which he tries to show, primarily by means of an empirical analysis of *production,* the interrelationships among economic branches constituting the basis of general equilibrium. Its chief difference from the Walrasian model is that it contains all intermediate products.

[11] W. W. Leontief: *op. cit.,* pp. 407–408.

Chapter 2

RAGNAR FRISCH'S ATTEMPT TO MEASURE THE MARGINAL UTILITY OF MONEY

Already in the 1920s, and then in 1932, Ragnar Frisch tried to find out how the marginal utility of money varies with the change in money income at a fixed price level. Without going into detail in discussing the mathematical–statistical apparatus, we shall merely outline his ideas about the solution of the problem.

Setting out from the fiction of the consumer optimizing his position, Frisch emphasizes that "the fact which enables us to establish a relationship between the abstract theory of pure economics and economic phenomena is … the proportionality of prices and marginal utilities at the point of market equilibrium."[12]

This proportionality of prices and marginal utilities is the marginal utility of money, which is the same for each commodity if the consumer is in an optimum position. While Marshall, relying on Gossen's second law, tried to determine through movements of price the change in the marginal utility of a commodity as a function of its quantity, supposing the marginal utility of money to be constant, Frisch, also relying on Gossen's second law, wanted to quantify the movement of the marginal utility of money as a function of income, supposing the marginal utility of a commodity to be constant. Of the multitude of commodities he chose sugar as the subject of his investigations. He assumed it to be an independent commodity, whose marginal utility is a function of its own quantity only, its marginal utility decreasing as its quantity increases.

By means of an ingenious construction he drew consumption isoquants for sugar. We have encountered isoquants so far in the domain of production. In the theory of production an isoquant shows the combinations of factors of production (inputs) required to produce the same quantity of a particular product. But what does the isoquant express from the point of view of consumption?

If at a given level of the consumer's real income the relative price of sugar, that is the price relative to the general price level, is reduced, the demand for it will rise in accordance with the curve of diminishing marginal utility. According to Frisch, at each level of real income a demand curve can be constructed which shows how consumers increase their demand for sugar as its relative price falls. Similarly, fixing the various relative prices of sugar, we can draw a demand curve for each relative price which shows how the demand for sugar increases with the rise in the consumer's real income. The lower the relative price at a given level of real income, or the higher the real income at a given relative price, the greater will be the demand

---

[12] R. Frisch: *op. cit.*, p. 96.

for sugar. The interrelated values of relative price, real income and quantity demanded together form the consumption surface of our consumer.

In Frisch's theory, for each value of relative price, real income and demand on the consumption surface, the following relationship characterizing the consumer's optimum position can be found: $wf(x) = g(\varrho)$, where w is the reciprocal of the relative price of sugar, $f(x)$ the marginal utility function, ϱ is consumer's real income, and $g(\varrho)$ shows how the marginal utility of money changes with real income. Our equation is essentially the expression of equality between the quotient of the marginal utility of the product and of its relative price, and the marginal utility of money.

In Frisch's view, if we single out, from the multitude of the interrelated values given by the consumption surface of relative price, real income and quantity demanded, those values at which the quantity demanded is the same, we obtain the isoquants of consumption. In principle, an infinite number of isoquants may be constructed, any point on them expressing the same quantity of demand at different combinations of relative price and real income.

Thus, finding along an isoquant the same quantity of the commodity in question, in our case sugar, we must regard, according to Frisch, its marginal utility also as constant for our individual. Our equation will reveal that, if we assume the marginal utility of sugar to be constant, the marginal utility of money will move along the isoquant in a direction opposed to the relative price of sugar, but at the same rate. Since we know the amount of real income attached to the different relative prices of sugar along an isoquant, we can find out, says Frisch, by what percentage the marginal utility of money will change with the percentage movement of real income. It will change with real income in the same proportion as the relative price of sugar.

To express this relationship econometrically, Frisch used the data of a big co-operative in Paris, which kept accurate statistical records of the sales and prices of sugar, the business turnover, the number of members, and the cost-of-living index.

Frisch did not want to construct the individual consumers' isoquants because, as he writes: "... it is not the description of individual elements that matters, but the recognition of certain average properties which are characteristic of the totality of these elements... What is important from the point of view of pure economics is not the knowledge of the decisions of a particular individual constituting part of the given market, but of those of the typical individual."[13] He wished to construct the isoquants of the average, typical consumer.

Frisch examined the data of monthly sugar consumption, the movement of the price of sugar and consumers' real income in the period between June 1920 and December 1922 on the basis of data supplied by the co-operative. He computed the index of the change in the typical individual's monthly money income by dividing the monthly sales of the co-operative by the number of its members. By dividing the index of nominal income by the cost-of-living index, he obtained a ratio which is proportionate to real income, while the price of sugar divided by the cost-of-living index expresses the relative price of sugar.

In the period under examination he selected the data of those months in which

13 R. Frisch: *op. cit.,* p. 97.

per capita sugar consumption was identical. Out of the time series of the quantities concerned and the related prices and real incomes he determined the particular isoquants by the least squares method.

Taking average income and the marginal utility attached to it to be 100 per cent, Frisch found the percentage decrease in the marginal utility of money if income rises above the average, and the percentage increase if income falls below the average.

But there are justifiable doubts about Frisch's procedure. It seems arbitrary that Frisch assumes the constancy of the marginal utility of a given quantity of sugar at different points of time, and that it is only the marginal utility of money that changes. The taste of consumers, the distribution relations and through them the social structure of consumers may change over time. All these factors affect, from the point of view of marginal utility theory, the marginal utility of a given quantity of sugar even in the case of the typical consumer. And a change in the distribution of real income at its given level may also influence the marginal utility of money.

Chapter 3

ATTEMPTS TO FORMULATE THE MACRO-ECONOMIC PRODUCTION FUNCTION IN TERMS OF ECONOMETRICS

THE COBB–DOUGLAS PRODUCTION FUNCTION

The initiators of this procedure, the mathematician Cobb and the economist Douglas, originally wanted to analyse the distribution of the national income between the working and capitalist classes by means of the production function arrived at in their econometric approach, and to verify through it the validity of the principle of marginal productivity.

They thus examined the relationships of production in order to gain insight into the process of income distribution. Since then, the income-distribution aspect of their production function has lost much of its significance, and it is now increasingly used for studying production relationships. Its scope of application is rather wide, and with the emergence of growth theories it has further expanded.

The formula given for the production function, $Q = f(K, L)$, expressed only in general terms that output depended on the quantity of capital and labour used up. Cobb and Douglas wanted to set up a concrete relationship between the scale of output, on the one hand, and the quantity of capital and labour, on the other.

To understand the Cobb–Douglas production function, let us start from the Euler theorem. Douglas himself emphasizes their debt to it. "We were both familiar with the Wicksteed analysis and Cobb was, of course, well versed in the history of the Euler theorem."[14]

According te this theorem,

$$\frac{\partial Q}{\partial L} \cdot L + \frac{\partial Q}{\partial K} \cdot K = Q;$$

and since the production elasticity of capital is

$$\varepsilon_K = \frac{\partial Q}{\partial K} : \frac{Q}{K},$$

and that of labour is

$$\varepsilon_L = \frac{\partial Q}{\partial L} : \frac{Q}{L},$$

[14] P. H. Douglas: Are There Laws of Production? In: *The Theory of Wages*, New York, 1957.

the marginal productivities can be expressed in terms of average productivity:

$$\frac{\partial Q}{\partial K} = \varepsilon_K \frac{Q}{K}; \quad \frac{\partial Q}{\partial L} = \varepsilon_L \frac{Q}{L}.$$

Substituting into the Euler theorem marginal productivities in the form of average productivity multiplied by production elasticity, and denoting the production elasticity of capital by m and the production elasticity of labour by k, we arrive at:

$$\Delta Q = \Delta Lk \frac{Q}{L} + \Delta Km \frac{Q}{K}.$$

Cobb, as mentioned later by Douglas, experimented with a number of functions to express the relationship between Q and the factors K and L. At last he arrived at this one: $Q = bL^k K^m$, where the exponents are production elasticities and b expresses those effects which influence output and which cannot be imputed either to capital or labour separately. The value of Q is obviously influenced not only by K and L, but also by accidental factors, the relationship between Q, K and L being stochastic. It is the effect of these accidental factors which is expressed by b.

According to Douglas, this equation satisfies the requirement of homogeneity and linearity. He and Cobb regarded their production function as such. In this case, the sum total of the exponents equals unity, and the equation may be written in the form: $Q = bK^{1-k}L^k$. The equation further satisfies the requirement that if the value of either L or K equals zero, the scale of output is zero, too.

The establishment of a functional relationship depends on whether the best values can be found for b and the exponents. This Douglas tried to determine by the least squares method, using the time series of labour, capital and output.

Knowing the amounts of the exponents, they claimed to be able also to determine through $k \dfrac{Q}{L}$ and $m \dfrac{Q}{K}$ the marginal productivities of labour and capital.

Douglas analysed the time series of Q, K and L in the American engineering industry on the basis of statistical data available for the 24 years between 1899 and 1922. He assumed that output changed only because the quantities of labour and capital also changed. He therefore left technical progress and also changes in the quality of labour out of account. He was well aware of the inadmissibility of these abstractions, but he defended his procedure by saying that at the time of his investigation he was still unable to quantify these effects, and if he did not leave them out of consideration, he could not arrive at any relationship.[15]

In further assuming that both labour and capital were used with a similar intensity year by year, he also disregarded the cyclical fluctuations of output for the same reason.

He considered only fixed capital, and expressed it just like the quantity of output in terms of dollars of a constant purchasing power; he measured labour by the number of workers employed and in computing the values of b and the exponents, he used indices of Q, L and K, taking the year 1899 as the base year.

[15] P. H. Douglas: *op. cit.*, pp. 125 and 132.

For the determination of b and the production elasticities his approach was the following: if the labour force and the stock of capital grow at different rates, that is, if the capital–labour ratio changes over time, and if we know how output changes with it, then it is possible to determine with the aid of correlation computation how output depends upon labour and capital separately.

Comparing the time series of the labour force, fixed capital and output, Douglas found that during the 24 years the labour force rose by 61 per cent, fixed capital by 331 per cent, and output by 140 per cent.

Assuming the production function to be first degree homogeneous, it is sufficient to compute the value of one exponent only. Thus Douglas operated with only two instead of three time series. Dividing the Cobb–Douglas production function throughout by K, we obtain

$$\frac{Q}{K} = \frac{bL^k K^{1-k}}{K} = b\left(\frac{L}{K}\right)^k.$$

In other words, Douglas tried to set up a relationship between the time series of $\frac{Q}{K}$ and $\frac{L}{K}$.

Taking their logarithms: $(\log Q - \log K) = \log b + k(\log L - \log K)$. Substituting y for $(\log Q - \log K)$, b for $\log b$ and x for $(\log L - \log K)$, we obtain the equation $y = b + kx$, which is nothing else but the equation of the regression line fitted by means of the least squares method among the sets of points $\log \frac{Q}{K}$ and $\log \frac{L}{K}$.

Representing y and x on the logarithmic scale, we find that k is the slope of the regression line which intersects axis $\frac{Q}{K}$ at a distance of b.

Computing the values of b and k, Douglas obtained 1.01 for b and 0.75 for k. He thus formulated the production function for the 24 years examined in the following way:

$$Q = 1.01 \cdot L^{\frac{3}{4}} K^{\frac{1}{4}}.$$

Following Douglas, we can also illustrate the relationship revealed by him by a simple numerical example:

Let $L = 10,000$, $K = 10,000$, then $Q = 10,000^{\frac{3}{4}} \cdot 10,000^{\frac{1}{4}} = 10,000$. In this example, serving only as an illustration, b, a coefficient expressing the effect of the accidental factors, has no role to play.

The exponent of labour shows that if labour is unilaterally increased by 1 per cent, output will grow by $\frac{3}{4}$ per cent, that is, the output of 10,100 units of labour and 10,000 units of capital will be 10,075. Similarly, if capital is increased unilaterally by 1 per cent, that is, if we produce with 10,000 units of labour and 10,100 units of capital, the output will amount to 10,025 units of product.

Douglas computed the marginal productivity of particular factors by dividing the quantity of product multiplied by the production elasticity by the quantity of the factor in question. Thus in our example, we find $\dfrac{0.75 \cdot 10,000}{10,000} = 0.75$ for the marginal productivity of labour and $\dfrac{0.25 \cdot 10,000}{10,000} = 0.25$ for the marginal pro-

ductivity of capital. In this example marginal productivity and production elasticity accidentally coincide, because the average productivity of both labour and capital $= 1$.

Written in the form of the Euler theorem, the relationships will be $0.75 \cdot 10,000 + 0.25 \cdot 10,000 = 10,000$, that is, we obtain the same results as those of the Cobb–Douglas production function.

From the partial derivatives of the Cobb–Douglas production function in respect of labour and capital, we also obtain the value of production elasticity multiplied by average productivity as the marginal productivity of factors:

$$\frac{\partial Q}{\partial L} = bkL^{k-1} K^m.$$

Taking the value of bK^m from the Cobb–Douglas production function, we get $bK^m = \dfrac{Q}{L^k}$. Substituting:

$$\frac{\partial Q}{\partial L} = \frac{Q}{L^k} \cdot kL^{k-1} = k\frac{Q}{L}.$$

Similarly we can derive the marginal productivity of capital also.

With the aid of the formula obtained from statistical data for the marginal productivities of capital and labour, Douglas also made actual computations to find out how the marginal productivities of both factors change over time.

From the Cobb–Douglas production function we can express the dependence of the average productivity of labour on capital per man:

$$\frac{Q}{L} = b\frac{L^k K^{1-k}}{L} = b\left(\frac{K}{L}\right)^{1-k}.$$

Attempts have also been made in Hungary to apply this formula to analysing labour productivity in various industries. The first of these attempts was made by Kálmán Kádas for the Hungarian engineering industry.[16]

Let us now look at the most important characteristics of the Cobb–Douglas function.

One of its basic characteristics is that the elasticity of substitution equals unity, which means that the production elasticities of capital and labour do not change as the capital–labour ratio changes, because the former have been computed as trend values for 24 years.

The marginal rate of substitution expresses in turn the ratio of marginal productivities. Thus, for example, the marginal rate of substitution of capital for

[16] K. Kádas: *Statisztikai Szemle* (Statistical Review), Budapest, August–September 1944.

labour

$$\frac{dK}{dL} = \frac{k\dfrac{Q}{L}}{m\dfrac{Q}{K}} = \frac{kK}{mL}.$$

And, since m and k are constants, trend values, they have been *ipso facto* computed as such, and the percentage change in the ratio of marginal productivities equals the percentage change in capital–labour ratio.

A further characteristic feature of the Cobb–Douglas production function is that it expresses unrestricted substitution between factors in the sense that with a unilateral increase in one factor the value of its marginal productivity, $m\dfrac{Q}{K}$, or $k\dfrac{Q}{L}$, always remains a positive magnitude. Since with the change in relative factor shares m and k are constant and Q, K and L are always positive magnitudes, therefore $m\dfrac{Q}{K}$ and $k\dfrac{Q}{L}$ must also assume positive values. Thus substitution is not limited to a specific domain.

Another characteristic of the Cobb–Douglas production function is that it expresses in a peculiar way *the flexibility of the marginal productivity of factors,* that is, the relationship between the percentage change in the capital–labour ratio and the percentage change in the marginal productivity of factors. If labour increases by 1 per cent relative to capital, its marginal productivity will decrease by the percentage of the exponent of labour, while the marginal productivity of capital will increase by the percentage of the exponent of labour. The situation is the opposite if the amount of capital stock increases by 1 per cent relative to labour.[17]

If capital and labour are increased simultaneously by 1 per cent, output will increase by the $m+k$ power of 1 per cent, $Q = 1.01^{m+k} K^m L^k$. Thus the Cobb-Douglas production function is $m+k$ degree homogeneous, and Douglas supposed only for the sake of the simplicity of computation that the sum of the exponents was 1, and therefore the production function was first degree homogeneous. In this case, the returns to scale are constant. (This should not be mistaken for the characteristic of the function that the elasticity of substitution equals unity. It shows that the change in capital–labour ratio does not affect the magnitudes of the exponents.) If, however, the sum of the exponents is greater or less than unity, this expresses increasing or decreasing returns to scale.

The Cobb–Douglas production function differs from other types of production function in that it does not express how output would change if capital and labour were used with ideal rationality. Q's relation to K and L have been computed on the basis of actual data. And even if we assume that entrepreneurs realize the highest degree of organization in their firms, the anarchy in the capitalist economy does not make it possible to utilize resources optimally on a social scale. Thus the marginal productivities computed with the aid of the Cobb–Douglas

[17] For a mathematical demonstration see P. H. Douglas: *op. cit.,* p. 150.

production function are marginal productivities resulting not from optimal but from actual resource allocation, and cannot therefore be regarded as a yardstick for the optimal allocation of resources.

A CRITIQUE OF THE COBB–DOUGLAS PRODUCTION FUNCTION

In the past few decades, the Cobb–Douglas production function has taken a prominent place among the various production functions. Though originally a production function on the macro-economic level, it has increasingly been used recently to reveal on the firm level too the dependence of output on particular factors of production. Attempts to make use of this function have also been made in socialist economies.

In its original form, however, it is still rather rough. It was designed to reduce the changes in production, even those which are to be attributed to technical progress, merely to quantitative changes in capital and labour. But even at a given level of technical knowledge no unambiguous relationship can exist on a social level between Q, K and L as assumed by macro-economic production functions. Since no programming on a social scale had been made for the optimal allocation of resources before the relationships on a social level between Q, K and L were revealed, the magnitude of Q may be different even with given K and L depending on the sectoral distribution of investments, the degree of capital utilization, etc. The relationships between Q, K and L are also influenced by the economic development of the country, and the age distribution of capital reflecting it. As M. Frankel points out, "enterprises in relatively developed and advanced economies are able to produce more with given inputs of capital and labor than enterprises in relatively underdeveloped economies."[18]

The production elasticities of capital and labour in the Cobb-Douglas production function are constants, while the capital–labour ratio changes over time. In reality they should change; their constancy is based on the fact that they were calculated as trend values for 24 years. In this case, however, the selection of the period under consideration requires utmost circumspection. Care should be taken that it does not contain years in which the economic processes differ essentially from the average path of development.

The results obtained by means of the Cobb–Douglas production function were also biased by the fact that while Douglas included only workers actually employed, he took account of the whole stock of capital, irrespective of its degree of utilization.

To simplify computation, Douglas assumed the production function to be first-degree homogeneous. Thus he only computed one of the exponents, using two time series. He used a two-dimensional regression analysis in order to establish a three-dimensional correlation. This assumption, however, ought to have been proved. Douglas should have sought the correlation among all three time series, i.e. when the changing values of Q are measured on the perpendicular

[18] M. Frankel: The Production Function in Allocation and Growth: A Synthesis, *The American Economic Review*, December 1962, p. 998.

dropped to the K, L plane. The task would now be to choose from among all the planes of the three-dimensional space the one best fitting the set of points. The closest fit is effected here too by the least squares method: it is the minimum of the sum total of the squares of the perpendicular distances between the regression plane and the individual points which has to be found.

Douglas made no attempt to provide evidence using all three times series. If he had attempted this, he would have encountered a serious problem to which Horst Mendershausen, in criticizing the Cobb–Douglas production function, first called attention, viz. the problem of *multicollinearity*. He found that there exists an almost perfect multicollinearity among the three time series. Each pair of the three variables, Q–L, Q–K and L–K, equally shows a high correlation, that is, the three time series are near-collinear. Applied to the Hungarian economy, Kornai and Wellisch[19] demonstrated that capital per head increased exponentially in the course of time, so that a linear relationship exists between the time series of log K and log L, too. Mendershausen states that there exist more than just one linear relationships among the three time series, log Q, log K and log L, and thus "there does not exist one single determinate systematic relation in this set of three variables."[20] Represented on a three-axis graph, the values of log Q, log K and log L over 24 years are found to lie practically on one single line, and thus the regression plane is largely indeterminate.

In his study[21] prepared in association with Bronfenbrenner, Douglas tried to eliminate some of the above difficulties by means of a so-called cross-section analysis. He attempted to find correlations not among time series but among values of Q, K and L existing at a given point of time; starting from the fact that the average capital–labour ratio varies between industries at a given point of time, he tried to find the correlation across industries between the average capital–labour ratio and the corresponding scale of output.

In cross-section analysis the problem of multicollinearity really does not arise, and thus the two exponents can be computed at the same time. There is no need to assume that the production function is first-degree homogeneous. Douglas and Bronfenbrenner thought that in concentrating their analysis on a given point of time they were justified in abstracting from technical progress, and also that they could show through cross-section analysis how the exponents changed from period to period.

In actual fact, however, technical progress cannot be ignored even if the cross-section method is applied, because the level of technical development varies between different branches of production, and thus capital goods representing different levels of technical development are lumped together in a production function

[19] J. Kornai and P. Wellisch: A kalkulatív kamatláb és bértarifa a hosszú lejáratú gazda-ságossági számításokban. Statisztikai vizsgálat és elszámolási elvek (Calculative rate of interest and wage rates in long-term calculations of economic efficiency. Statistical survey and the principles of accounting), *Közgazdasági Szemle*, January 1964.

[20] H. Mendershausen: On the Significance of Professor Douglas' Production Function, *Econometrica*, 1938, Vol. 6, p. 148.

[21] H. Bronfenbrenner and P. H. Douglas: Cross-Section Studies in the Cobb–Douglas Function, *The Journal of Political Economy*, Dec. 1939, Vol. 47, No. 6.

by means of simple summation, which is of course not permissible. The same applies to the way in which the labour force is used. A disadvantage of cross-section analysis as against time-series analysis consists in the fact that the production elasticities existing at a given point of time are of less use for prediction.

Since its inception, the Cobb–Douglas production function has been refined a great deal, it has become more sophisticated. The separation of technical progress was first attempted by Tinbergen in a study published in 1942, and then by Solow in 1957. At first they tried to take account of the effect of technical progress as if it were independent of the age groups of capital and affected all capital goods alike. Thus in much the same way as Douglas and Bronfenbrenner in their cross-section analysis, they included by simple summation capitals of different vintages, representing different levels of technical progress, in one production function. In this approach, technical progress is independent of the increase in capital stock. The modern form of the Cobb–Douglas production function, the vintage model, takes into consideration that technical progress has to be embodied for the most part in new capital goods, and sets up a separate production function for each vintage of them. Account is increasingly taken, in the form of investments, in "human capital", of the effect on the quality and hence the productivity of labour, of expenditure on improvements in skills. Attempts are being made, using the Cobb–Douglas function to measure the effect of expenditure on scientific research, to isolate the effect of technical progress from the scale effect, and also to separate, within the effect of technical progress, the effect of not only embodied and disembodied, but also of neutral and non-neutral technical progress.

But the problem of multicollinearity continues to give trouble in regression analysis.

ATTEMPTS TO COMPUTE THE ELASTICITY OF SUBSTITUTION BY ECONOMETRIC MEANS — THE CES FUNCTION

The value of the elasticity of substitution as assumed in the Cobb–Douglas production function has given rise to heated debates. Arrow, Chenery, Minhas and Solow criticized that basic characteristic of the Cobb–Douglas production function, that the elasticity of substitution, irrespective of technological possibilities, equals unity. But comparing 24 industries of 19 countries they set about computing by cross-section analysis the elasticity of substitution for different industries on an international scale. Since they had available information on the magnitude of capital and its income in only a few countries and industries, the authors made no use of such data at all in their computations. Instead, their basic approach was as follows:

The elasticity of substitution is the relationship between the percentage change in the capital–labour ratio and the percentage change in factor prices. Per capita output, however, is a function of the capital–labour ratio. Instead of the change in capital–labour ratio, the authors chose the change in per capita output, which they related to the change in wages. They tried to determine the relation between the percentage change in per capita net output and wages, that is, the derivative

294

of log $\dfrac{Q}{L}$ with respect to log w, denoted it by b and proved it to be equal, at constant returns to scale, to the elasticity of substitution σ.[22]

Differentiating the Cobb–Douglas production function with respect to labour, we obtain, as has already been shown, the production elasticity of labour multiplied by the average productivity of labour:

$$\frac{\partial Q}{\partial L} = k \frac{Q}{L}.$$

The authors assume that wages equal the marginal productivity of labour, and hence they arrive by substitution at the relationship between wages and output per man:

$$w = k \frac{Q}{L}, \text{ i.e. } \frac{w}{k} = \frac{Q}{L}.$$

The above relationship also reveals the connection between labour per unit of output and the amount of wages:

$$\frac{L}{Q} = \frac{k}{w} = kw^{-1}.$$

Taking the logarithm of the relation between wages and net output per man, or labour per unit of net output, and denoting the exponent of wages by b and substituting $-\log k$ for $\log k$, the authors arrived at the following linear function:

$$\log \frac{Q}{L} = \log k + b \log w,$$

$$\log \frac{L}{Q} = -(\log k + b \log w).$$

As can be seen, b, the positive or negative exponent of wages, expresses the percentage change in output per man, or labour per unit of output, as a function of the percentage change in wages.

Leaving aside the authors' lengthy mathematical demonstration, we can easily illustrate the coincidence of the above percentage change with the elasticity of substitution in the Cobb–Douglas production function.

In this function the elasticity of substitution is, as we have seen, unity. It is also known that in the Cobb–Douglas production function the flexibility of the marginal productivity of labour equals the exponent of capital, that is, using our previous numerical example, 0.25 per cent. Let wages now increase by 0.25 per cent. In this case, capital per man will rise by 1 per cent and output per man by the percentage of the production elasticity of capital, 0.25 per cent, that is, in the same proportion in which wages have increased.

Now the authors determined the elasticity of substitution by applying to each

[22] For a detailed mathematical demonstration see B. S. Minhas: *An International Comparison of Factor Costs and Factor Use*, Amsterdam, 1963, pp. 6–26.

industry on the basis of data for the individual countries the logarithmically linear function derived above, completing it with the error term ε:

$$\log \frac{Q}{L} = \log k + b \log w + \varepsilon.$$

The elasticity of substitution b will be given by the regression coefficient calculated.

As a result of the computation it turned out that the elasticity of substitution deviated from unity; it was least in the manufacture of dairy products, 0.7211, and greatest in non-ferrous metal production, 1.0114. In the other industries it ranged between these values. "... the elasticity of substitution between capital and labour in manufacturing may typically be less than unity."[23]

Instead of the Cobb–Douglas function the authors construct a new production function which is homogeneous, assumes different elasticities of substitution for the various industries, but takes them to be constant since they were obtained as trend values. Hence the name of the function: CES, constant elasticity of substitution. It also occurs in the abbreviation of SMAC, its letters standing for the initials of the authors' name.

The VES function (variable elasticity substitution) set out by Yao-Chi Lu[24] in 1967 abandons the assumption of the constancy of the elasticity of substitution. In this type of production function the elasticity of substitution is a function of the average capital–labour ratio, and changes with it. The regression equation of the VES function is:

$$\log \frac{Q}{L} = \log k + b \cdot \log w + c \cdot \log \frac{K}{L} + \varepsilon.$$

Let us now look at a CES function more closely.

The basic formula of the CES function is $Q = (AK^{-\beta} + \alpha L^{-\beta})^{-\frac{1}{\beta}}$, where β is the *substitution parameter* $= \frac{1}{\sigma} - 1$ and $\sigma = \frac{1}{\beta + 1}$, A is the integration constant and $\alpha = k^{-\frac{1}{b}}$. The CES function contains as an extreme case the Cobb–Douglas production function if $\beta = 0$, in which case $\sigma = 1$, but it also contains the Leontief production function if $\beta = \infty$. In this case $\sigma = 0$.

The marginal productivity of labour and capital is, according to the CES

[23] K. J. Arrow, H. B. Chenery, B. S. Minhas and R. M. Solow: Capital–Labour Substitution and Economic Efficiency, *The Review of Economics and Statistics*, August 1961, p. 246.

[24] Yao-Chi Lu: *Variable Elasticity of Substitution Production Functions. Technical Change and Factor Shares*, Iowa State University, 1967; Yao-Chi Lu and L. B. Fletcher: A Generalization of the CES Function, *Review of Economics and Statistics*, 1968, Vol. 50, pp. 449–452.

function, $\alpha \left(\dfrac{Q}{L}\right)^{\beta+1}$ and $A \left(\dfrac{Q}{K}\right)^{\beta+1}$, respectively. The marginal rate of substitution

$$\frac{p_L}{p_K} = \frac{\alpha}{A} \left(\frac{K}{L}\right)^{\beta+1}, \text{ whence}$$

$$\frac{K}{L} = \left(\frac{A}{\alpha} \cdot \frac{p_L}{p_K}\right)^{\frac{1}{\beta+1}}.$$

The above relationship shows how the factor ratio depends on changes in relative factor prices.

A modified form of the CES function is

$$Q = \gamma \left[\delta K^{-\beta} + (1-\delta) L^{-\beta}\right]^{-\frac{1}{\beta}},$$

where γ, the *efficiency parameter*, shows the combined efficiency of labour and capital. In comparisons between countries, if country x and y use up capital and labour in the same proportion in industry i, $\gamma_{i_x}/\gamma_{i_y}$ expresses the relation of the net products of the two countries in question.

δ is the *distribution parameter*, and $\dfrac{\delta}{1-\delta} = \dfrac{p_K}{p_L} \left(\dfrac{K}{L}\right)^{\frac{1}{\sigma}}$ expresses how the proportion of the incomes of the two countries changes as $\dfrac{K}{L}$ changes. If the value of σ is unity, and the production function is first-degree homogeneous, $1-\delta$ and δ express the production elasticity with respect to labour and capital respectively. In this case, the Cobb–Douglas production function may be written by the parameters of the CES function:

$$Q = \gamma K^{\delta} L^{1-\delta}.$$

It appears that the authors made the same mistake in their computations for which they criticized the Cobb–Douglas production function. They compared the industries in the countries representing the most different levels of technical development, ranging from the USA and Canada to Iran and India, to compute from them elasticities of substitution typical of the technical conditions of production. Criticizing this procedure, Fuchs expresses his doubts when he asks: "... is a single production function appropriate for such a heterogeneous group of countries?"[25] Can it be assumed that, given the same relative factor prices, a particular industry in all countries included in the examination applies, irrespective of its technical development, a production technique requiring the same capital–labour ratio? The authors assumed "that international differences in efficiency affect both inputs equally",[26] or, to put it in another way, that differences in efficiency between countries are *neutral*. While the efficiency parameter varies

25 V. R. Fuchs: Capital–Labour Substitution: A Note, *The Review of Economics and Statistics,* November 1963, p. 437.
26 K. J. Arrow, H. B. Chenery, B. S. Minhas and R. M. Solow: *op. cit.,* p. 233.

from country to country, the distribution and substitution parameters are the same in all countries. Consequently, the isoquants of the same industries in different countries are of the same shape. The difference in technical development is apparent only in so far as the same industries in different countries produce different quantities of products with the same inputs of capital and labour, that is, identical isoquants express different quantities of products in different countries. But the differing efficiency of factors does not affect the magnitude of the elasticity of substitution.

In one of his studies Leontief emphasizes that countries with different development levels differ from one another primarily in respect of their labour productivity. Even an economically less developed country can buy more efficient capital equipment. What he considers as a bottleneck is in the first place skilled labour.[27] Therefore, the marginal rate of substitution cannot be the same even at a given capital–labour ratio in the same industry of different countries. But then the shape of the isoquant constructed for the same industry of different countries cannot be the same either. Thus, the efficiency parameter is not neutral.

In so far, however, as there is a difference also in respect of the level of technical development between the industries in different countries under consideration, it will not leave the substitution relations unchanged either. The greater the degree of mechanization and automation in a given industry, the more limitational is the relation between factors, the greater is the steepness of the isoquants and less is the elasticity of substitution.[28]

[27] Cf. W. W. Leontief: Domestic Production and Foreign Trade: the American Capital Position Re-examined. Reprinted in: *International Trade*, Penguin Books, 1969, pp. 127–128.
[28] H. Frisch: Die CES-Funktion, *Zeitschrift für Nationalökonomie*, 1964, Fasc. 3, p. 441.

Part Six

THE PROBLEM OF UNITING HISTORY AND LOGIC IN NON-MARXIAN ECONOMICS

Chapter 1

INTRODUCTION

The problem of uniting history and logic, which non-Marxian economics has not solved up to this day, reflects the limitation arising from the bourgeois class position. W. Eucken writes that all significant economic schools have grasped just one aspect of the economic problem: they have either tried to discover laws, or to reveal the historical character of economic phenonema.[1]

Modern non-Marxian economics in trying to discover economic laws, sets out from the assumption that the economic subject tries to optimize his position on the basis of existing data, and wishes to maximize his advantage with the least possible inputs. The theory examines what economic relationships evolve as a result, or as a summation, of the actions of the large number of isolated individuals. By reducing the individual's economic behaviour to the above motive, these theories divorce economic phenomena from non-economic social phenomena, and limit the task of the economist merely to the analysis of the former, since "it is only in these phenomena that necessity in the sense of economic theory finds expression."[2] By this very abstraction, however, they exclude the examination of the social framework of the economy from the scope of economic research. Unlike Marxian political economy, according to which in the context of social relations it is production relations which constitute the essential element determining economic processes, non-Marxian economics holds the view that the economic system has been shaped by a number of factors whose analysis goes beyond economics. Such are, among others, the state, the legal system, morals, habits, the culture of the population, etc. As Stackelberg writes: "Economy is carried on within the framework of the system of the state and of definite social and legal organizations. These are superimposed on the economy, are *data*, neither the result nor the subject of the economic process."[3] Non-Marxian theories searching

---

[1] W. Eucken: *Nationalökonomie wozu?* 4th unchanged edition, Düsseldorf–München, 1961, pp. 21–22.

[2] H. Stackelberg: *Grundlagen der theoretischen Volkswirtschaftslehre*, Bern, 1948, pp. 11–12.

[3] H. Stackelberg: *op. cit.*, p. 11.

for economic laws regarded the economic order merely as data of the model and were unable to explain its historical changes in an endogenous way. Thus the processes taking place under the existing economic system lost their historical character. It is the unhistorical nature of non-Marxian economic theory to which Eucken refers when talking about economists who wish to reveal laws in the economy without making any historical approach to economic phenomena, and claim the absolute nature of the economic reality of their age.

Chapter 2

THE VIEWPOINT OF THE GERMAN HISTORICAL SCHOOL

The unhistorical approach of the subjective tendencies evolving in economic literature since the 1870s is sharply criticized by the *new German historical school*. It emphasizes the significance of historical change in economic processes, as against relationships deduced by assuming that actions are directed by unchanging motives. "... national economy ... is subjected to change just as individual economies, private or public, ...", writes Bücher, "and any economic phenomenon is at the same time a historical–cultural phenomenon, too ... and the law governing its movement is not of an absolute nature, is not valid for all times and states of culture. Therefore, the task of science with respect to the economy is to deduce it [i.e. the economic process—A. M.] genetically."[4] Schmoller, a leading personality of the new German historical school, also stresses that economic phenomena change with historical periods and can be explained only in their context. He does not recognize, however, what determines the incessant changes in economic phenomena. He is unable to find a cause in the changing economy which, though changing itself and therefore not devoid of development, has a relative constancy within the historical period concerned and causes economic phenomena to recur. He tries to apply the historical method in economics by reducing economic phenomena to all those factors which, according to the non-Marxian view constitute the economic order of the period under consideration, and whose examination the theories aimed at establishing lawful relationships wish to exclude from the domain of economics. By rejecting the method of abstraction, Schmoller takes a neo-Kantian stand on the laws of economic life. But the neo-Kantian approach appears in a specific form in his theory.

According to Windelband, one of the leading exponents of neo-Kantian philosophy, "... in exploring reality, empirical sciences seek either the general in the form of laws of nature, or the specific in a historically determined form... The former are the natural sciences, and the latter the historical sciences... If we want to insist on established terms, we may speak of confronting the disciplines of natural and historical sciences..."[5] But how do neo-Kantians justify the absence of recurring events in history? Virtually like Kant, namely, that "the ultimate and innermost essence of personality resists fragmentation by universal categories,

[4] K. Bücher: *Die Entstehung der Volkswirtschaft*, Tübingen, 1901, pp. 101–102.
[5] W. Windelband: *Preludiumok* (Preludes), Budapest, (No date) pp. 120–121.

and this inconceivable thing appears to our consciousness as the feeling of the indeterminateness of our being, of the freedom of the individual."[6]

Schmoller holds that the neo-Kantian view which regards historical, social and economic phenomena as unique, individual ones is exaggerated. He claims the possibility to make generalizations from observing individual economic phenomena. Schmoller does not deny that there are internal relationships in economic life, that there are laws governing it. But since he rejects the method of abstraction, he understands the general as a concept including all factors, both those regarded as essential from a Marxian point of view, and the non-essential ones alike. Thus he is unable to get hold of the inner relationships, the laws governing economic life. He refers to the complexity and diverging nature of the factors involved. In economic life "a whole set of causal complexes confront each other, each having its own specific nature and requiring an individual scientific treatment"[7] ranging from individual psychology to the comparative history of morals and law.

Thus the analysis of economic life calls for the knowledge and method of various disciplines. The exploration of social phenomena is made particularly difficult by the fact that most of the causes working in the economy are of a spiritual, moral nature, and we have practically no scientific psychology of peoples and countries available.[8] It is exactly the complexity of causal relationships which underlines the individual character of social phenomena and explains why "we do not, cannot have any general law governing the activity of economic forces..."[9] "We have available merely tentative attempts, hypothetical propositions and teleological views concerning the development of the economic relations of humanity."[10]

Schmoller was unable to create a theoretical system based upon the unity of history and logic, and arrived only at collecting data in his scientific activity. Eucken cites Schmoller's introductory words to the hundredth booklet containing data collected by him. They faithfuly reflect the failure of his efforts: "No single booklet constitutes a contribution to the theory of national economy. My opponents will say: because I underestimate theory; my answer is: because I overestimate it."[11]

[6] W. Windelband: *op. cit.*, p. 313.
[7] G. Schmoller: *Grundriss der allgemeinen Volkswirtschaftslehre I*, München–Leipzig, 1923, p. 109.
[8] G. Schmoller: *op. cit.*, 109.
[9] G. Schmoller: *op. cit.*, p. 110.
[10] *Ibid.*
[11] Quoted by W. Eucken: *Die Grundlagen der Nationalökonomie*, Jena, 1941, p. 44.

Chapter 3

THE VIEWPOINT OF THE SOCIO-LEGAL SCHOOL

It is the social character of economic phenomena which is emphasized by the representatives of the *socio-legal school,* too. They also reject as unhistorical the starting-point of the economists searching for laws, the fiction of the individual wishing to optimize his position. Like the followers of the historical school, they abandon the view which regards the social framework of the economy as given for economic investigation. They pay attention precisely to discovering the essence of the historically changing economic system. But, owing to an incorrect interpretation of the economic system, they did not recognize the historically determined nature of individual economic systems and did not come to realize what laws govern economic life. Moreover, the two most prominent representatives of the socio-legal school to be discussed here even denied the existence of economic laws.

One of them, Stolzmann, attacks his non-Marxian fellow economists for ignoring in their investigations the social forms of the economy. "It is absolutely impermissible and incorrect to regard capital, according to the still prevailing view, merely as a produced means of production, and to transfer the laws of the significance, rise and growth of capital indiscriminately and uncritically ... to the natural means of production..."[12]

But what does Stolzmann mean by the social character of economic categories? His view is typically neo-Kantian. There are, in his opinion, two sides to each economic category, a purely *economic* and a *social* side. By the purely economic side of economic categories he in effect understands that aspect in which man's relation to nature manifests itself. The purely economic side belongs to material reality, is subordinated to the law of causality. But Stolzmann believes that the social implications of economic categories are not subject to the law of causality. In his view, the social framework of the economy "originates in man's social nature, the historically changing laws of co-existence and co-operation as well as in the established power and legal relations which man as a *being having free will* [italics are mine—A. M.] sets for himself..."[13] Stolzmann maintains that the social order of the economy has been created by man of his own free will in the interest of achieving certain aims. No laws can be discovered in its emergence, nor in the processes taking place in the individual economic systems. In this way,

---

[12] R. Stolzmann: *Die soziale Kategorie in der Volkswirtschaftslehre,* Berlin, 1896, p. 258.
[13] *Ibid.*

Stolzmann makes a sharp distinction between production and production relations. Necessity is dominant in the field of production, while freedom is dominant in the domain of the economy.

A view similar to Stolzmann's is also adopted by R. Stammler, another prominent representative of the socio-legal school. He criticizes any economic investigation setting out from the individual: people have never produced like Robinson Crusoe, but always in close association with one another. And the form of co-operation has changed over time, as have economic categories, too. But the existing economic order always depends, as he thinks, on the prevailing system of law, since economic co-operation among people is regulated by law. "Any exposition on land-rent, wage rates, interest on capital or entrepreneurial profit depends, just as all teachings concerning money, credit, price formation or any other departments of economic research, on the existence of a concrete system of law."[14]

Owing to the confusion of the base and superstructure, Stammler cannot recognize the determined character of the order of law. In a neo-Kantian fashion he regards the system of law, and through it the economic system, too, as a product of human free will, which strives to achieve certain ideals and objectives.

Stammler is incapable of reconciling freedom with necessity, the law of causality with human aims. Human actions are either determined, and in that case we cannot speak, he thinks, of conscious actions, of free will; or people act consciously and freely, in which case it makes no sense to speak of the lawful development of society and the assertion of the law of causality in economic life. Social phenomena have either their own causes, and in that case it is senseless, according to Stammler, to speak of objectives, or people are pursuing certain aims, and then the law of causality has no validity.

This metaphysical view is also apparent when he criticizes Marx for regarding social development as a process following strict laws, and still speaking of will, aims, party: "besides his exclusively causal approach he introduced a new, second viewpoint for social movements: namely, will, the pursuit of aims, in addition to the exact recognition of causal relationships."[15] If nothing else were involved than a causally determined development in which all people's actions are absolutely involved, then it would be impossible to speak of aspirations, desires and will. "It is impossible to found a party which wants purposefully to promote the advance and incidence of an exactly computable lunar eclipse."[16]

Does the law of causality really exclude the setting of aims and does necessity really prevent conscious human action? Those who maintain that it does, would divorce history from human activity and regard the working of the laws of social development as the working of mechanical laws, an accusation levelled by Stammler at Marxism. But Marxism does not deny that people can set aims for themselves, does not deny the significance of will and conscious action. But

[14] R. Stammler: *Wirtschaft und Recht nach der materialistischen Geschichtsauffussung*, Leipzig, 1906, p. 185.
[15] R. Stammler: *op. cit.*, p. 423.
[16] R. Stammler: *op. cit.*, pp. 423–424.

people's consciousness and will are determined by their class positions, and they can set only such social aims to themselves whose conditions have already matured, which stem from the existing production relations, and whose progressive character is determined by the extent to which they coincide with the objective tasks facing the development of society. If the aims correspond to the objective, necessary processes, then people's endeavours do promote the realization of these processes and, if they do not, they impede it. Stammler, however, seeks the aims of society outside the world of experience, in the domain of metaphysics. It is left to the free will of the members of society whether they want to put these aims into effect or not. By this Stammler denies that causal relationships can work in the economy.

Chapter 4

EUCKEN'S ATTEMPT TO RESOLVE THE "GREAT ANTINOMY" IN A HISTORICAL AND LOGICAL APPROACH TO ECONOMIC PHENOMENA

Among recent attempts to realize the unity of history and logic, mention should be made of the work of W. Eucken (died 1950), the leading personality of German neo-liberalism. His influence is still very significant in the Federal Republic of Germany. The book in which he attempted to solve the problem concerned already reached its 4th edition in 1961.

Eucken emphasizes that "the forms in which man carries on his economic activity are steadily changing."[17] Therefore, economics "has to be both a theoretical and historical science."[18]

The way for Eucken's efforts was cleared by the emergence of the modern theory of market forms. It was this theory which directed his attention to the fact that economic relationships change with market forms. Eucken applied this recognition to historical development.

Unlike the followers of the German historical school, he excludes from economic investigations the data of economic action, among them the forms of "legal and social organization" comprising traditional order, laws, habits, the spirit people are imbued with; "theoretical explanation ends in actual data of the economy as a whole."[19] Thus he applies the method of abstraction in a similar fashion as those modern non-Marxian economists who try to discover economic laws. Economic relationships also evolve in his theory through the behaviour of economic subjects trying to optimize their results. The principle of economic efficiency runs through the history of mankind as an eternal principle typical of the behaviour of the economic subject. It is exactly the assertion of this principle which ensures, in his view, the possibility of setting up a theory for each period. The historical character of the theory finds expression in his approach in the recognition that the conditions for attaining optimal results, the data of economical action, vary from period to period. By his so-called pointedly emphatic (*pointierend hervorhebende*) abstraction Eucken tries to characterize the various historical-economic systems as combinations of universal common elements.

Depending on whether the economic processes evolve as a result of central decisions or decisions made by economic units, plants or households, he "discovers" two elementary forms, *ideal types,* of the economic systems: centrally

---

[17] W. Eucken: *Nationalökonomie wozu?* Düsseldorf–München, 1961, p. 19.
[18] W. Eucken: *op. cit.,* p. 23.
[19] W. Eucken: *Die Grundlagen der Nationalökonomie,* Jena, 1941, p. 189.

directed economy and market economy. The forms of the centrally directed economy are small in number. Such is, for example, the closed family economy, which may be accounted for even by a single man, but such is the state-managed economy, too. What they have in common is that the economic plan encompasses the economic activity of the community as a whole. It only considers the data of economic activity relating to the entire economy. These are: the needs of the members of the community, the factors of production available to the community, technical knowledge, the legal and social organization of the community.

Economics has to concern itself, in Eucken's view, primarily with market economy characterized by a multitude of market forms. He distinguishes 25 forms of market. In a market economy, decisions are decentralized; the plans of the economic subjects are partial plans comprising only part of the whole economic process and match therefore only partly the data pertaining to the economy as a whole. In drawing up their plans, the individual economies, unlike centrally directed economies, have to take into account the behaviour of the other economic subjects.

Now the concrete, historically established economic systems are combinations of the various manifestations of the ideal types: of the individual market forms, and of the forms of the centrally directed economy. A German peasant economy as operated in 1938 is, according to Eucken, a simple, centrally directed economy in so far as it produces for its own consumption. Simultaneously, it is producing for the market, and is thereby a member of the market economy. But the state regulates the output of certain products centrally, and in this respect the peasant economy is also part of the whole, centrally directed economy.

The unity of history and logic is affected, according to Eucken, first by stating the combination of the various ideal types of which the concrete historical-economic system under consideration is composed, and the way in which they are fitted together; then the dominant form has to be found; finally, the corresponding theory deduced form the behaviour of the rationally acting individual has to be adjusted accordingly.

Representing the concrete economic system as a combination of individual market forms and forms of central direction, Eucken criticizes those representatives of the German historical school who wished to grasp the general or typical by establishing economic stages in the economy of individual periods. His criticism was aimed first of all at Bücher's periodization. According to this theory, the peoples of Central and Western Europe have gone through three stages of economic development: family economy, urban economy and national economy. Eucken criticizes Bücher not because his periodization, owing to the superficial application of abstraction, did not express the essential features of the economy of the individual periods of time, but because he tried to select a certain general characteristic from the complex social relations of the particular periods, and wanted to force economic forms displaying a great variety over time into one single concept. In the Middle Ages, for example, economic activity was carried on, according to Eucken, in the most different forms. How can they be included in one single economic form, in the form of urban economy, says Eucken, in a reproachful comment on Bücher.

But he regards capitalism as an empty concept, too, and the edge of his critique is here directed against Marx. The concept of capitalism, says Eucken, cannot express the basic characteristic of the modern system of economy, since the economic order called capitalism is so varied and different from country to country; and what Marxists now call capitalist economy has gone through so many changes in the course of history that it cannot be covered by one single concept.

Did Eucken solve the problem of uniting history and logic? No, he did not. He concludes by stating how the ideal types combine in the different historical–economic systems. We are, however, not given an answer to the question of what laws determine the rise of and change in the combinations of ideal types in the course of history. In his analysis the laws governing their combinations and the changes in economic systems are brought about by a whole set of causes, changes in historical, spiritual, religious, legal and political factors as well as in data pertaining to the economy as a whole, whose investigation outgrows the scope of economics. Eucken himself acknowledges that the theory cannot explain exactly why a particular centrally directed economy or a particular market form has come into being. The failure of his method of analysis to go beyond the statement of data and to reveal the essence of the economic system is well characterized by his statement that though according to the teaching of history there is a close interrelationship between the development of technology and the social and legal organizations, we are unable to reveal that relationship, both being data for economic research.[20]

In the application of the method of pointedly emphatic abstraction, the rejection of generalizing abstraction and the representation of the different historical–economic systems as a synthesis of common elements, Eucken uses the argument that economic life has special categories, commodity, money, etc., which extend over several methods of production. But by excluding the investigation of social relations underlying market forms and central direction from economic research, he ignores the content of the elementary forms which vary according to economic systems. He does not recognize that there are different production relations behind the ideal type of the market economy, and that the commodity expressed other production relations in a slave-holding society than, for example, in capitalism. A centrally directed economy may also cover different production relations.

Because his investigation abstracts from any social content, Eucken's attempt to look at things historically turns into a completely unhistorical approach. For instance, all difference disappears in it between modern monopolies and the formations enjoying monopoly positions in the pre-capitalistic period. "If in a medieval town three glaziers appear, who have concluded no agreement among themselves, then an oligopoly situation obtains there ... it is on the basis of our theoretical knowledge of present-day monopoly that we can get to know very thoroughly," says Eucken, "the effects of the monopolies in imperial Rome, in the late Middle Ages, or in 18th century Germany."[21] Again Eucken's concept of a centrally directed economy can apply to direction both by a monopoly capitalist state and by a socialist state and, what is more, this elementary economic form materialized most clearly in his view in the 15th century Inca state.

Marx picked out of the complexity of social relations the determining factor, production relations, and reduced the historical changes in economic systems to changes in production relations. Commodity production, or to use Eucken's

<hr>

20 W. Eucken: *op. cit.*, p. 190.
21 W. Eucken: *op. cit.*, p. 124.

terminology, market economy, becomes general under capitalism. The sphere of commodity exchange also extends to the labour force. This increasing predominance of commodity production is not just a possible combination of elementary economic forms which, in respect of its origin, is a combination outside the scope of economic research, but is a necessary stage in the development of production relations, and is as such of a historical, transitory character. The national features in capitalistic development do not affect the essence of capitalist production relations: the capitalist ownership of the means of production, the system based on the exploitation of wage labour, the irreconcilable contradiction between the capitalist and working classes. These are not affected even by changes taking place within the capitalist system, the replacement of traditional competitive capitalism by monopoly capitalism. On the contrary, the rise of monopoly capitalism itself can only be explained by a scientific analysis of capitalist production relations. It is not the Marxian abstraction of capitalism, but Eucken's abstractions which are devoid of content and, as we have seen, ahistorical too.

Eucken's approach is typical of those non-Marxian economists in general who search for laws in the economy: to reveal how the economic system under consideration came about, exceeds, in their view, the scope of economic research, whose task is merely to examine what is taking place within the system concerned.

Part Seven

DETERMINATION OF THE PRICE LEVEL—ATTEMPTS TO FIT MONEY INTO THE EQUILIBRIUM THEORY

Chapter 1

INTRODUCTION

In trying to determine prices, equilibrium theory left the monetary aspect out of account. Its representatives maintained that money was a "veil", concealing actual relationships. Ignoring money, they tried to determine relative prices. But obviously they had to determine the price level, too: "... it was necessary to determine the multiplicative factor by means of which the relative prices can be converted into absolute money prices."[1] They regarded the determination of the price level as a task of monetary theory. For a long time, however, they treated monetary theory and price theory proper, the theory of determining relative prices, in complete separation from one another. There slowly evolved the requirement to fit monetary theory into the theory of relative prices, and, further, to integrate monetary theory and price theory proper, that is, to relate the monetary and real processes to each other, or, as Patinkin emphasized, to apply in both fields "the same analytical techniques" in constructing the demand functions.

[1] G. Myrdal: Der Gleichgewichtsbegriff als Instrument der geldtheoretischen Analyse. In: *Beiträge zur Geldtheorie*, Vienna, 1933, p. 372.

Chapter 2

THE DETERMINATION OF THE PRICE LEVEL
IN IRVING FISHER'S THEORY

STATEMENT OF THE THEORY

One of the universally known attempts to determine the price level was made by Fisher. In the preface to his book dealing with the problem he writes: "The contentions of this book are at bottom simply a restatement and amplification of the old 'quantity theory of money'."[2]

In his famous equation of exchange he equates the total value of goods sold with that of the money exchanged for them. "The equation thus has a money and a goods side,"[3] he writes. "The money side is the total money paid, and may be considered as the product of the quantity money multiplied by its rapidity of circulation. The goods side is made up of the products of quantities of goods exchanged multiplied by their respective prices."[4]

Written in an equation form: $MV = TP$, where M is the total amount of money, V is its velocity of circulation, and thus MV is total demand; T is the volume of transactions made, which may be taken in a simplified form to be the volume of production, P is the price level and TP the price sum of the goods sold.

The equation of exchange in this form is a common tautology: the total value of the goods sold necessarily equals the total value of goods bought. This does not provide any causal explanation, but merely expresses that M, V, T and P mutually influence each other.

Fisher tries to transform his equation of exchange into a theory of exchange, which already contains a causal relationship concerning price formation.

He holds the view that "one of *the normal effects of an increase in the quantity of money is an exactly proportional increase in the general level of prices*."[5] The levels of V and T are, he maintains, independent of any change in the quantity of money; consequently, the latter affects only the price level, and in proportion to the change. Thus any change in the quantity of money causes a change in the price level.

It should be noted that Fisher is already aware of the necessity of distinguishing between the immediate and the later effects of changes in the quantity of money. Along with the examination of equilibrium situations he also considers the transition period between equilibrium positions. "If the quantity of money were suddenly doubled, the effect of the change would not be the same at first as later."[6] At first,

---

[2] I. Fischer: *The Purchasing Power of Money*, New York, 1912, p. VII.
[3] I. Fisher: *op. cit.*, p. 17.
[4] *Ibid.*
[5] I. Fisher: *op. cit.*, p. 157.
[6] I. Fisher: *op. cit.*, p. 55.

the rise in prices induces the buyers to get rid of their depreciated money, and thus the change in the quantity of money temporarily influences the circulation velocity of money. At the same time, the rising prices lead to increased profit and thereby simulate production to expand. In this way changes in the quantity of money also affect at first the volume of production. "They are like temporary increases..."[7] Once the effect of the change in the quantity of money has fully unfolded, the new equilibrium price level corresponding to the increased quantity of money will be proportional only to the quantity of money; the velocity of circulation and the volume of production will fall back to their original levels. In determining the level of prices Fisher thus compares two equilibrium positions, before and after the increase in the quantity of money. He skips the transition period: his method of examination is basically comparative statics.

He asserts that the price level is lastingly affected not only by changes in the quantity of money, but also by changes in the velocity of circulation, or in the volume of production. These changes may increase or neutralize the effect exercised on the price level by the changes in the quantity of money. But the change in the velocity of circulation or of the volume of production extending beyond the transition period is no longer the result of changes in the quantity of money, but of other causes as well. Their analysis, as he maintains, goes beyond the scope of price theory.

Following Fisher, other economists also wish to transform the equation of exchange into a causal theory, by assuming that the velocity of circulation of money is constant in the short run, depending only on institutional factors, paying habits, etc., which change only very slowly. In the short run, the volume of production is also constant: society produces as much as it is able to produce with the available production factors under full employment and at the given level of technical knowledge.

With the velocity of circulation of money and the volume of production being constant, the price level changes in proportion to the money stock.

A CRITIQUE OF THE THEORY

Fisher's equation, like the other formulas set up in modern non-Marxian economics to determine the price level, seeks a law of the level of prices measured in terms of paper money having no intrinsic value. No doubt, the price level measured in terms of paper money does indeed have a law of its own. This law, however, remains undiscovered if the researcher is satisfied with expressing merely a surface relationship, namely that the level of prices equals the ratio of total demand, MV, to the volume of goods supplied, T. From this we cannot deduce any law governing the relationship of total demand to total supply.

Marx grouped the output of aggregate social capital into two broad classes (departments): means of production and consumption goods. Each department supplies its products partly for itself, partly for the other department, and demands

[7] I. Fisher: *op. cit.*, p. 64.

at the same time its own products and those of the other department. It is on the relationship of the two departments that the actual state of the trade cycle, the ratio of total demand to total supply, depends. If department I shoots ahead of department II, total demand will exceed total supply, and the level of prices will increase. The opposite happens if the production of department I contracts relatively to the production of department II. Thus we can see that the internal relationship underlying the ratio of total demand to total supply, and through it the level of prices, is the law governing the reproduction of aggregate social capital. The price level increases in Fisher because the quantity of money in circulation has increased and through it total demand, which increasingly exceeds the constant volume of total production. Fisher, however, does not examine the alternative case, of crucial importance from the point of view of the price level, namely that the primary cause of price rises should be sought in changes arising not from the money but from the goods side. If we disregard money issued by the government independently of the money requirements of reproduction, the relationship set up by Fisher is exactly the reverse in real life: the money stock increases because total demand has increased, because more and more money is needed to effect reproduction. In non-Marxian literature Erich Schneider, among others, criticizes the Fisherian version of price theory, because it ignores changes arising from the goods side. "The causal relationship considered by the quantity theory of money starts from changes in the money supply and arrives through changes in effective demand at changes in the prices of goods. The quantity theory of money is unable to deal with the reverse case, when the change in effective demand induces a change in the quantity of money supplied, when, for example, an increase in effective demand may lead to an increase in the money stock."[8]

Fisher's global statement of total demand does not deal, among other things, with the fact that the two main constituents of total demand, the demand for means of production and for consumer goods, are governed by different laws. Knowledge of total demand presupposes knowledge of its constituents as subjected to the reproduction of aggregate social capital. In non-Marxian literature it was first Wicksell and later Keynes who, in examining the movement of total demand, tried to analyse total demand broken down into its consituent parts, instead of in a global way as hitherto in non-Marxian literature.

By the way, non-Marxian criticism also stresses that the increase in total demand is certain to lead to an increase in the price level only if production cannot be increased because, at the given level of technical knowledge, full employment has already been realized.

Non-Marxian criticism also finds fault with Fisher's equation claiming to determine the price level because it completely abandons the procedure adopted by equilibrium theory for determining the prices of individual goods and through them relative prices. Equilibrium theory constructs demand and supply curves for each good as a function of price, in order to determine the equilibrium price.

[8] E. Schneider: *Einführung in die Wirtschaftstheorie*, Vol. III, Tübingen, 1957, p. 213.

And it always builds the demand and supply curves on the behaviour of sellers and buyers who wish to optimize their positions in given circumstances. Fisher's formula, however, claims to determine the price level not on the basis of demand and supply curves, and thereby on the basis of people's optimization decisions, but simply by means of the available stock of money. This procedure of Fisher's disrupts the unity of non-Marxian price theory. In connection with such attempts Forstmann justly remarks that "monetary theory—along with credit theory—was (and still largely is) a branch of political economy leading a more or less independent life of its own outside general economic theories."[9]

[9] A. Forstmann: *Volkswirtschaftliche Theorie des Geldes*, Vol. II, Berlin, 1955, p. 2.

Chapter 3

THE CASH-BALANCE APPROACH

STATEMENT OF THE THEORY

The cash-balance approach is a peculiar version of the quantity theory of money. Since its elaboration is primarily due to the economists of the Cambridge School, Marshall, Pigou and Robertson, it is often referred to as the Cambridge version of the quantity theory of money. This version rejects the view that the price level is simply a function of the quantity of money. Instead they argue that the price level, i.e. the exchange value of money, is based, like relative prices on human decisions, on the relationship between the demand for money, as traced back to human decisions, and the supply of money.

In order to arrive at the cash-balance approach, let us set out from Fisher's equation of exchange. In the equation V expresses the number of times that a unit of money is used for transacting business during a given period. Solving Fisher's equation for M, we obtain:

$$M = \frac{1}{V} PT.$$

$\frac{1}{V}$ shows the ratio of the available quantity of money to the total exchange of goods, to PT. If, for example, $V = 10$, the unit of money changes hand 10 times during a given period, and $\frac{1}{V}$ expresses that the amount of money needed to effect business transactions is $\frac{1}{10}$ of the total exchange.

But the total stock of money available to society, in the cash-balance approach is held as cash by the economic subjects at any given moment. Thus the total quantity of money held by them is always equal to the total quantity of money available to society. But equality is not the same as equilibrium. According to the theory, if individuals do not wish to keep the money held, but to pass it on, they increase thereby the demand for goods. If, on the other hand, they want to increase the quantity of money held, they have to sell goods, which will increase their supply.

The cash-balance approach is based on the assumption that people want to hold as much money as is available to society. This quantity of money is, on the analogy of holding any stocks, an average magnitude, the quantity of money people want to hold on average over a certain period of time. Its actual amount steadily changes during that period. It is this average quantity of money desired to be held that the cash-balance approach calls the demand for money. But why do people want to hold a certain cash balance? What useful service accrues to them from holding cash? The followers of the theory argue that "A large command of resources in the form of currency renders their business easy and smooth, and puts them at an advantage in bargaining."[10] "It will be readily granted that the ordinary person likes to keep to his hand a little pool of money, partly for the sake of convenience in conducting the ordinary business of life, and partly as a margin to fall back on in unforeseen contingencies."[11] In other words, the reason for holding a certain amount of money is, on the one hand, that the incomes and payments of economic subjects do not coincide in time, and, on the other, that unforeseen expenses may arise. The economic subject "may thus be said ... to exercise a 'demand' for the money ..."[12] in the form of his desire to hold cash balances. Keynes calls this demand for money "transactions demand". (More about this will be found in the section on Keynes's theory of interest in Part Eight.)

Our investigations relating to price theory have included so far only the marginal utility of money income, i.e. the utility of goods that can be bought for the last unit of money. Now we are concerned with the marginal utility of a service that money held can render for the economic subject. It is, according to the cash-balance theory, for this service that money is demanded.

This demand for money is for an amount of money with a definite purchasing power: "... it can be expressed in terms of the real things ... the purchase of which he [i.e. the economic subject—A.M.] forgoes in order to enjoy instead the practical convenience and peace of mind yielded him by his pool of money."[13]

In recent literature, Don Patinkin designates the real value of money held by individuals, that is, "the purchasing power over commodities which these holdings represent", by the term "real balances".[14]

As a first approximation, this demand for money is then regarded as a function of real income, that is, as a function of the purchasing power of money income, and is expressed as a certain proportion of it. Keynes explicitly regards the transactions demand as a function of real income.

Marshall, Pigou and Robertson make the amount of cash holdings dependent, in addition to real income, on incomes deriving from the fruitful use of money. The individual compares, in their view, the benefits of holding money with those arising from its profitable investment, and takes his decision, on the basis of the principle of equal advantage, on holding either a smaller or larger proportion of his real income in money form. "By instinct and experience he balances the benefit against the loss of a large holding."[15] According to Pigou, the amount of money held depends, at a given level of real income, on "... how much non-material benefit is yielded by the marginal unit of given quantities of real resources held

[10] A. Marshall: *Money, Credit and Commerce*, London, 1929, p. 45.
[11] D. H. Robertson: *Money*, Cambridge, 1959, p. 28.
[12] *Ibid.*
[13] D. H. Robertson: *op. cit.*, p. 29.
[14] D. Patinkin: *Money, Interest and Prices*, Evanston – New York, 1956, pp. 19–20.
[15] A. Marshall: *op. cit.*, pp. 46–47.

in the form of money."[16] Robertson writes that "... the magnitude of the demand for money, like that of the demand for bread, turns out to be the result of a process of individual weighing-up of competing advantages at the margin..."[17]

In examining the early variants of the cash-balance approach, let us assume that individuals want to hold on average a certain k proportion of their real incomes as a cash balance. By representing the demand for money as a certain proportion of real income, Fisher's T, the sum of transactions carried out within a given period, is replaced, in the course of determining the price level, by real income, y, and the velocity of circulation of money, V, by the income velocity of money, or its reciprocal, the proportion of real income held as cash, which Marshall denotes by k,

$$M = kPy.$$

The real income figuring in the cash-balance approach is smaller than T in Fisher's exchange equation, that is, in the transactions approach, which contains not only final but also intermediate transactions, the entrepreneurs, purchases from one another, the exchange of already existing real assets. The cash-balance approach, however, takes into account only the values added by individual transactions. Thus the velocity of circulation of incomes, $\frac{1}{k}$, is clearly not identical with V in Fisher's formula. Fisher's version emphasizes that money circulates, while the cash-balance approach stresses that money is held. "... our concern is with the utility of *holding* money, not with that of *spending* it. This is the concept implicit in all cash-balance approaches... ."[18] "... there must be something which can serve as a temporary abode of purchasing power in\the interim between sale and purchase. This is the aspect of money emphasized in the cash-balance approach."[19]

It is the price level on which the money amount of real balances, i.e. the nominal balance, kyP, depends. If the price level decreases, the real balance is expressed in less money, and if it increases, in more money.

The followers of the cash-balance theory regard the quantity of money as an exogenous datum of the model. Thus, if the equilibrium of the demand for and the supply of money is disturbed, the demand for money adjusts itself, in their view, to the actual supply of money. This will require a change in one or more of the variables—k or P or y—for monetary equilibrium to be restored.

Let us see what mechanism restores the disturbed equilibrium of the demand for and the supply of money. Let us assume that people want to hold a smaller proportion of their real income, that k decreases and the demand for money is less than its supply. The nominal stock of money is determined by financial authorities or institutions. The holders of money are unable to change this stock, but they can influence the real value of their cash balance. This is possible because with a decrease in real money that they wish to hold, the real balance held by individuals

[16] A. C. Pigou: *The Veil of Money*, London, 1949, p. 77.
[17] D. H. Robertson: *op. cit.*, pp. 36–37.
[18] D. Patinkin: *op. cit.*, p. 63.
[19] U. Friedman: A Theoretical Framework of Monetary Analysis. *The Journal of Political Economy*, 1970, No. 2, p. 200.

is greater than necessary, its marginal utility diminishes, and thus the benefit gained by its holding is less than the advantage forgone. People, therefore, decrease their nominal cash balances by increasing their expenditures. But this does not change the nominal stock of money to be held. Even if some people succeed in diminishing their nominal cash balances, this is possible only because they are transferred to others. But with expenditures growing, money income and with it the price level will rise, and finally the amount of real money drops to the desired level, and monetary equilibrium is established. If y is given, then the ratio of M to Y, k, or its inverse, the income velocity of money, is determined by the quantity of real money. By wishing to change, at the given level of real income, the stock of real money to be held, people change the ratio of the flow of income to the stock of money.

Let us illustrate this statement by a numerical example.

Let y be 100, k $\frac{1}{4}$, and M 1,000. In this case, the demand for real money will be in equilibrium with the available stock of real money at a price level of 40.

$$1,000 = \frac{1}{4} \cdot 40 \cdot 100.$$

Assume that people want to diminish the ratio of their stock of real money to be held in their real income to $\frac{1}{5}$. At a price level of 40, they want to hold only 800 units of money, and spend the excess stock of money (200 units). But then, at unchanged real income, the price level will rise, the quantity of real money demanded will correspond to the available stock of real money at a price level of 50.

$$1,000 = \tfrac{1}{5} \cdot 50 \cdot 100.$$

And since, as a result of the rise in the price level, nominal income has increased from $40 \cdot 100 = 4,000$ to $50 \cdot 100 = 5,000$, k has decreased from

$$k = \frac{1,000}{4,000} \frac{M}{Y} = \frac{1}{4} \text{ to } \frac{1,000}{5,000} \frac{M}{Y} = \tfrac{1}{5}.$$

The case is the reverse if people want to hold a larger proportion of their real income as real cash balance. They diminish their money expenditures in order to increase their nominal stock of money. As a result of the decrease in money expenditures, the price level will fall, the purchasing power of the stock money held and with it the real stock of money will grow, until finally it reaches equilibrium with the quantity of real money demanded.

So far we have discussed cases when, with a given quantity of money, monetary equilibrium was disturbed, owing to a change in the demand for money. But the followers of the theory suppose that changes in the demand for money, in the desired real balances, tend to proceed slowly, and that substantial changes are likely to occur more frequently in the supply of nominal balances, and it is primarily the latter that upset the monetary equilibrium. In this case, taking real income to be given, the purchasing power of the changed stock of money will decrease or increase through the above-discussed mechanism, as a result of the rise or fall in the price level until the demand for and the supply of money is in equilibrium.

In the view of the earlier followers of the cash-balance approach "the change in the nominal quantity of money need not alter any of the 'real factors' on which k and y ultimately depend"[20], and thus "in the final full equilibrium, the adjustment will, in general, be entirely in P ..."[21] And the cash-balance approach tries to deduce the price level from the ratio of the demand for a stock of money with unchanged purchasing power, ky, to the supply of money, M. "The price level of money value, therefore is primarily determined by exactly the same two factors as determine the value of any other thing, namely, the conditions of demand for it, and the quantity of it available."[22] Friedman, too, points out: "the cash-balances approach fits in more readily with the general Marshallian demand–supply apparatus than does the transactions approach."[23]

Don Patinkin calls the effect derived from a change in the real value of cash held by individuals and affecting the demand-supply relations of commodities the *real-balance effect*. "This is the real-balance which measures in Patinkin the effect on the demand for goods derived, *ceteris paribus*, from the change in real value of the initial stock of money held."[24] This effect had already been examined by Pigou, too, and so Patinkin justly refers to it as the Pigou effect. Later we shall return to the Pigou effect when discussing Keynes's theoretical system.

Don Patinkin complements Hicks's theory concerning the double effect of price change by this third effect, which makes itself felt when the economic subject also holds a cash balance. In his view, a change in the prices of particular goods elicits three effects in the demand of the individual for various goods, namely (1) the *substitution effect* as a result of changes in relative prices; (2) the *income effect* caused by changes in real income; and (3) the *real-balance effect* resulting from changes in the price of goods affecting the price level and altering thereby the purchasing power of cash holdings.[25] The real-balance effect shatters the principle of homogeneity. It turns out that the demand for particular goods also depends on the price level as a change in it alters the purchasing power of cash balances and through it the demand for individual goods. This effect is left out of account in the models which regard money only as a measure of price, which is thus not worthwhile to hold since it has no independent utility in this capacity. According to the representatives of the theory, if availability of cash balances is supposed, the price level will be determined by their existence. Given a too low price level, part of the cash balances will become superfluous, and if they are spent, the price level will rise. If, on the other hand, the price level is too high, the economic agents will replenish the insufficient cash balances and therefore reduce the spendings, which in turn lower the price level.

We shall see later that recently non-Marxian economists have attached great importance to the cash-balance effect in promoting full employment. So far we have regarded the level of real income as given in the formula expressing the

[20] M. Friedman: The Demand for Money: Some Theoretical and Empirical Results. In: M. Friedman: *The Optimum Quantity of Money and Other Essays*, Chicago, 1969, p. 116.
[21] *Ibid.*
[22] D. H. Robertson: *op. cit.*, p. 29.
[23] M. Friedman: A Theoretical Framework of Monetary Analysis, *The Journal of Political Economy*, 1970, No. 2, p. 201.
[24] H. Möller: Die "Geldillusion" als Problem der nationalökonomischen Theorie, *Jahrbücher für Nationalökonomie und Statistik*, January 1971, p. 19.
[25] D. Patinkin: *op. cit.*, p. 21.

equilibrium of the demand for and the supply of money. Let us assume now that there does exist unemployment. Under the pressure of the unemployed, money wages and hence the price level will fall. The purchasing power of cash holdings will increase, by which part of them becomes superfluous and as such will be spent. Aggregate demand, output and employment will rise. But given a larger scale of output and a higher level of real income, a larger cash balance is needed, and now the equilibrium between the demand for and the supply of money will be restored by increasing output. Real money increasing as a result of decreasing money wages and price level may also reduce the rate of interest. Decreasing interest rate stimulates both investment and consumer demand, and the fall in money wages may increase employment, according to the latest followers of the theory, through these channels, too.

In today's inflationary circumstances, non-Marxian economics no longer refers to the real-balance effect caused by declining price level. But the followers of the theory continue to emphasize that the real-balance effect also arises when an increase in the quantity of money is not immediately followed by a rise in the price level. In this case, a larger quantity of money, at the earlier lower prices, represents a larger purchasing power and hence a larger quantity of real money, too. It leads to the formation of excess money reserves, whose spending increases aggregate demand.

The old quantity theory of money was "strictly an explanation of what determines the price level,"[26] while its present-day version is "essentially a theory of income determination."[27] This new version of the quantity theory of money will be the subject of our investigations, when analysing Friedman's theory, following the discussion of Keynes's system.

A CRITIQUE OF THE CASH-BALANCE APPROACH

We shall criticize the modern theory of the demand for money by discussing Friedman's views. We are going to give here a critique of the earlier versions of the cash-balance approach.

While criticizing the cash-balance approach, Don Patinkin points out that it has not succeeded in finding a relationship between the monetary and the real spheres, and has failed to integrate money and price theory, and thus the dichotomy expressing the separation of the two spheres continues to exist. In its price level formula, the cash-balance approach, says Don Patinkin, tries to determine the new equilibrium stituation brought about by changes in the stock of money, that is, it compares equilibrium positions. However, he continues, the effect of a change in the quantity of money on the real sphere can only be captured in the transition period between the two equilibrium positions. This effect ceases to work as soon as

[26] L. S. Ritter: The Role of Money in Keynesian Theory. Reprinted in *Readings in Macroeconomics, Theory, Evidence, and Policy,* (ed.: N. F. Keiser) Prentice-Hall, Inc., Englewood Cliffs, N. 7., 1970, p. 161.
[27] *Ibid.*

the equilibrium position is established. It is "... precisely this dynamic analysis which was not integrated into the cash-balance tradition of Marshall, Pigou, Keynes and Robertson..."[28]

Don Patinkin is right in saying that price theory must also analyse the formation of the price level during the transition period between the two equilibrium positions when the equilibrium of the economy is upset. But he blames the cash-balance approach for failing to disclose how changes in the quantity of money affect the real sphere in the transition period. On the other hand, the Marxian critique of the cash-balance approach points out that it does not disclose that changes in the price level invariably reflect, except for the period of rapid-rate inflation, the reproduction process, the changes in the relationship between the two departments of social production. It is simply impossible to disclose this law, which is manifested in the movement of the price level, without investigating the transition period.

In Marxist theory, it is the movement of reproduction which is of basic importance in the relationship between financial processes and reproduction, though Marx himself does not deny that financial processes have a bearing on real processes. Actually, all variables in the formula set up by the followers of the cash-balance approach, which expresses the equilibrium between the demand for and the supply of money, follow the movement of reproduction. But what does a change in the stock of money depend on? It may change for reasons other than economic activity, for example, when the state resorts to increasing the issue of money to cover its defense expenditures. Such an increase in the quantity of money starts an inflationary process and raises the price level. But if we want to provide a fully endogenous explanation of changes in the price level, we have to assume that the quantity of money changes exclusively for economic reasons. It increases or decreases in relation to an initial period depending on whether reproduction needs a greater or lesser quantity of money. The movement of reproduction also affects the duration of the transition between money expenditure and money revenue, i.e. how long on average, money is held by the economic subjects, or in other words, what is the circulation velocity of money income. And the movement of reproduction is also manifested in changes in the level of real income and thus in the price level, too.

A basic deficiency of the view held by the followers of the cash-balance theory is apparent in the fact that they examine changes in the price level divorced from the reproduction process, and analyse them only in the monetary sphere.

This shortcoming of the cash-balance approach was also pointed out by Keynes, saying that even if the quantity and the circulation velocity of money are assumed to be unchanged, the price level may still change if the amount of savings diverges from the costs of new investments, or, translated into the language of Marxian political economy, if the proportion between production of capital goods and consumer goods changes.[29] In making the real-balance effect dependent on the movement of reproduction, and not the other way round, i.e. in making the movement of reproduction a function of the real-balance effect, it appears to be un-

[28] D. Patinkin: *op. cit.*, p. 100.
[29] See J. M. Keynes: *A Treatise on Money*, London, 1933, Chapter X.

likely that a price fall, for example in a slump period, would induce people, by causing an increase in the purchasing power of cash-balances, to increase their spendings.

And now we have arrived at a further deficiency of the cash-balance approach. According to it, cash holdings are active money, a medium of exchange. However, the recognition is missing that money is also held as a store of wealth in its Marxian sense, or as a "hoard" in its Keynesian interpretation. In a crisis period, cash balances set free as a result of price reduction, and held originally for transaction purposes, need not be spent on buying commodities or securities; people may hold them also as a hoard. Then, with a decrease in P, k grows, and the increase in the stock of real money will have no effect on aggregate demand.

According to the cash-balance approach, monetary equilibrium disturbed as a result of an increase in M, at given y and k, will be restored by a change in P. If, however, we start from the determining character of the reproduction process, we shall be faced with the opposite relationship: a change in the total price of commodities requires a greater or lesser quantity of money, and the quantity of money will increase or decrease accordingly. In this case, the quantity of money is an endogenous variable of the model, and the supply of money adjusts to the changes in the demand for money.

Chapter 4

WICKSELL'S EXPLANATION OF CHANGES IN THE PRICE LEVEL

WICKSELL'S ATTEMPT TO INTEGRATE MONEY THEORY AND PRICE THEORY

A significant contribution to the non-Marxian explanation of changes in the price level was made by the Swedish economist Knut Wicksell. His research activity covered a great many fields of economics, yet he achieved his greatest success, as generally admitted, in monetary theory. His investigations were furthet developed by his followers, notably Lindahl and Myrdal, in the 1930. It is his followers who are usually referred to as the *Stockholm School* of economics.

With regard to the problem under discussion, we refer mainly to two works by Wicksell, *Geldzins and Güterpreise* (Jena, 1898) (first published in English in 1936 under the title *Interest and Prices*) and Volume II of his *Vorlesungen über National-ökonomie* (Jena, 1922) (published in English in 1935 under the title *Lectures on Political Economy*).

According to Wicksell, changes in the price level have to be explained in the same way as those in the prices of other goods. Just as the price of goods changes if the demand for them diverges from their supply, so the price level, too, alters because aggregate demand deviates from aggregate supply. "Every rise or fall in the price of a particular commodity presupposes a disturbance of the equilibrium between the supply of and the demand for that commodity ... What is true *in this respect* of each commodity separately must doubtless be true of all commodities collectively. A general rise in prices is therefore only conceivable on the supposition that the general demand has for some reason become, or is expected to become, greater than the supply ... Any theory for money worthy of the name must be able to show how and why the monetary or pecuniary demand for goods exceeds or falls short of the supply of goods in given conditions."[30]

General equilibrium theory, in trying to determine equilibrium price proportions, is unable to account for this fact. The theory of relative prices rests on the assumption that the supply of a good creates demand for other goods, that total demand always equals total supply. Contrary to Say's Law, Wicksell maintains that the exchange of goods always takes place through the medium of the exchange of goods for money and of the exchange of money for goods, and total demand may diverge from total supply. This has, by the way, proved to be true of the other price-level theories discussed so far. In Fisher, for example, the increase in the quantity of money would raise total demand, MV, above PT if the price level did not change. Thus the price level has to increase. In the cash-balance approach the

---

[30] K. Wicksell: *Lectures on Political Economy*, Vol. II, London, 1935, pp. 159–160.

increase in the supply of money raises the cash holdings of individuals above the desired levels. Surplus cash balances are diminished and, as a result, total demand will exceed total supply, and the price level will increase. Wicksell wanted to go beyond such merely monetary explanations and find an answer to the question of how the increased quantity of money comes into circulation, or why the quantity of money in circulation decreases and what changes in the real process, in turn altering the price level, are brought about by changes in the monetary sphere. He thinks that all this is required in order to fit money into general equilibrium theory and, further, that the demand for and supply of money are represented as a function of certain price phenomena.

The versions of the quantity theory of money hitherto discussed also admitted that changes in the quantity of money caused changes in the real sphere. Since this effect extends, in their view, only to the transition period, while the theories in question concentrated rather on the investigation of the equilibrium position, they devoted but little attention to the effect of changes in the amount of money on real processes. Wicksell, however, emphasizes that his theory is concerned in the first place with the transition period: "... here, however, we are concerned with precisely what occurs, *in the first place,* with the middle link in the final exchange of one good against another, which is formed by the demand of money for goods and the supply of goods against money."[31]

Wicksell regards his contribution as a further development of the quantity theory of money. In order to show the impact of the quantity of money on the price level through changes in the real processes, he divides net social production into two classes: the production of *consumer goods* and *investment goods*. However, the incomes deriving from production are partly spent on purchasing *consumer goods,* and are partly *saved*. He further assumes a closed credit economy: credit money is created in close relation to real processes, and its withdrawal from exchange is likewise connected with their termination.

He regards savings, the part of the money income not consumed, basically as a function of the rate of interest: "... *ceteris paribus,* the rate of interest exercises a determining influence on the volume of savings..."[32] Since any money income is backed by a corresponding amount of commodity value, the saving of part of the income means, according to Wicksell, that production factors are released from the sphere of consumer goods to be used in the production of investment goods. "The accumulation of capital consists in the resolve of those who save to abstain from the consumption of a part of their income in the immediate future. Owing to their diminished demand, or cessation of demand, for consumer goods, the labour and land which would otherwise have been required in their production is set free for the creation of fixed capital for future production and consumption..."[33]

Entrepreneurs obtain the production factors released through saving and needed for investment by borrowing the consumers' money income saved and deposited with banks.

[31] *Ibid.*
[32] K. Wicksell: *op. cit.,* p. 205.
[33] K. Wicksell: *op. cit.,* pp. 192–193.

What stimulates entrepreneurs to borrow money for investment, and how far are they willing to go in making investments or in raising loans? In his investments, the entrepreneur is guided by the expected profits of newly formed capitals, the anticipated marginal productivity of investment. The expectations which play such an important role in the theories of Swedish economists were already important factors in economic processes for Wicksell, too. If the expected yield of capital is larger than the market rate of interest at which the entrepreneur can get credit from the banks, he will increase his investments, will change to a more roundabout, i.e. more capital-intensive production technique; this will increase the demand for credit, and through it the demand for factors of production needed for investment, until the expected marginal productivity of capital drops to the level of the market rate of interest.

For the establishment of monetary equilibrium between the demand for and supply of credit, assuming that the banks are satisfied with their role as mediators of credit offering only their clients' savings, Wicksell provides the following explanation:

Let us assume that the expected return on capital increases relative to the market rate of interest. The demand for loan capital will increase and exceed the supply of credit. As a result, the interest rate on loan capital will rise. Then consumers will increase their savings, entrepreneurs will slightly cut their investments, and in the market of loan capital "a new equilibrium is reached at a slightly higher rate of interest."[34] Thus it is the movement of the interest rate which brings about equilibrium between saving and investment, between the supply of and the demand for credit.

Wicksell mentions three characteristics of the monetary equilibrium thus established:

1. In monetary equilibrium the market rate of interest corresponds to the expected marginal productivity of newly created capitals. He calls this rate of interest the *natural* or *normal rate of interest*. It is exactly the natural rate of interest which links the real sphere with the monetary sphere in Wicksell's theory. The natural rate of interest is determined by a real magnitude, the marginal productivity of capital, and the market rate of interest in the credit market tends to come into equilibrium with natural rate.

2. With the natural rate of interest, the demand for loan capital to be invested just corresponds to the supply of loan capital; investments and savings are in equilibrium. Wicksell sets up demand and supply functions for credit money as a function of the rate of interest, similar to those of equilibrium theory for goods as a function for their prices. The supply of credit increases, and the demand for it decreases, as the rate of interest rises.

The saving–investment equilibrium reflects in Wicksell basically the equilibrium of reproduction: entrepreneurs wish to produce the quantity of capital goods, which they can produce with the available factors at the intended level of saving, and those employed in the production of consumer goods and new capital goods

[34] K. Wicksell: *op. cit.*, p. 193.

create, with their incomes, a demand for consumption goods which can be met at established prices. "Equilibrium between the demand for and the supply of saving," writes Lindahl in characterizing Wicksell's monetary equilibrium, "evidently implies equilibrium in respect to the demand and supply of consumption goods during the period."[35] Denoting national income by Y, if investment I is in equilibrium with saving S, the demand for consumer goods, $Y—S$, is in equilibrium with the supply of consumer goods, $Y—I$. Thus monetary equilibrium reflects the equilibrium of reproduction.

3. In monetary equilibrium money is *neutral* with respect to price formation, that is, if the banks extend credit only within the limits of saving, the interest mechanism brings about monetary equilibrium. The total demand for goods cannot lastingly differ from the total supply of goods, for if banks put into circulation purchasing power only to the extent to which saving withdraws it from circulation, the money side does not affect the price level, "so that wages and price will remain unchanged."[36] In monetary equilibrium economic relationships are established as in non-money, i.e. barter economies.

Davidson criticized Wicksell on the grounds that of the three conditions only the first two are consistent with one another. But the fulfilment of the first two conditions does not mean at all that the price level is stable. Technical discoveries which increase the marginal productivity of capital increase the volume of products placed on the market. If in order to maintain monetary equilibrium, the market rate of interest is raised to the increased level of the natural rate of interest, with the quantity of money being unchanged, the price level, despite the existence of monetary equilibrium, will have to decrease owing to increased productivity.

It was Wicksell's unprecise statement which enabled Davidson to criticize him. For what Wicksell maintains is that in the position of monetary equilibrium the price level is not influenced by effects from the money side. This, however, does not exclude changes in the price level due to real causes, for example, as a result of technical discoveries. But Wicksell seeks to support his statement under conditions of developing technology and growing labour productivity.

THE DISTURBANCE OF MONETARY EQUILIBRIUM UPSETS THE EQUILIBRIUM OF REPRODUCTION

In Wicksell's view, the monetary side begins to bring pressure to bear upon the real processes, and total demand for goods begins to diverge lastingly from the total supply of goods, when the banks extend credits for investment in excess of savings. He characterizes investment as an activity through which output will expand in the future only, while the demand for raw materials, labour and hence consumption goods increases already in the present.[37] In other words, investment creates demand in the present without simultaneously increasing the available supply. On the other hand, those who save, sell more than they buy.

[35] E. Lindahl: *Studies in the Theory of Money and Capital*, London, 1939, p. 250.
[36] K. Wicksell: *op. cit.*, p. 193.
[37] K. Wicksell: *op. cit.*, p. 199.

If entrepreneurs want to invest more than society wants to save, and obtain the necessary investment credit from the banks, the total demand for goods will exceed their total supply.

Wicksell notices that the modern banking system greatly increases the amount of credit that can be extended separately by the individual banks. "Banks are not, like private persons, restricted in their lending to their own funds or even to the means placed at their disposal by savings."[38] Under the modern system, banks "... possess a fund for loans which is always elastic, and on certain assumptions, inexhaustible ... the banks can always satisfy any demand whatever for loans, and at rates of interest however long, at least as far as the internal market is concerned."[39]

What happens under such circumstances if monetary equilibrium is upset? The disturbance of equilibrium is caused, Wicksell assumes, by external factors. He mentions that certain factors, among them technical progress, raise the marginal productivity of capital and thereby increase the natural rate of interest above the market rate. Seldom do banks take the initiative and decrease the market rate, for reasons external to the model, below the natural rate of interest.

The higher natural rate of interest induces entrepreneurs to adopt more roundabout, more capital-intensive techniques. They wish to increase their investments, and therefore increase their demand for credit. At the same time, saving has not increased because the market rate of interest, which stimulates saving, has not changed. The intention to invest, owing to the divergence of the two rates of interest, exceeds the intention to save; the demand for credit is greater than its supply. If banks granted credit only within the limits of saving, the increased demand for credit would raise the market rate of interest to the level of the natural rate of interest, and thereby keep investment within the limits of saving, and total demand to the level of total supply. But the elastic credit supply of the modern banking system satisfies even increased credit demands at a lower than natural rate of interest by extending credit over and above the level of saving. It thereby prevents the interest mechanism from restoring the disturbed monetary equilibrium, and a lasting divergence develops between the two rates of interest, investment lastingly exceeds saving and, as a result, total demand will lastingly rise above total supply.

What will be the consequence according to Wicksell?

Entrepreneurs want to employ more original factors in the production of capital goods than are made available to them by savings. Wicksell regards full employment as the normal state of a capitalist economy. "... we are entitled to assume," he writes, "that all productive forces are already fully employed..."[40] For lack of surplus production factors, entrepreneurs, in order to make investments in excess of savings, attempt to attract factors from the production of consumption goods by promising them higher incomes. "... increased monetary demand principally takes the form or rivalry between employers for labour, raw material and natural facilities."[41] In this way, money incomes grow, and the vertical structure of production changes. The production of the means of production increases, and so do the number and incomes of those employed in it, those who create more consumer

---

[38] K. Wicksell: *op. cit.*, p. 194.
[39] *Ibid.*
[40] K. Wicksell: *op. cit.*, p. 195.
[41] *Ibid.*

demand in the present, without putting products on the market. However, the quantity of factors participating in the production of consumer goods decreases, and so does production itself. The demand for consumption goods exceeds their supply, and the price level of consumption goods increases.

Owing to his interpretation of changes in the price level of consumption goods, Wicksell is regarded as one of the first representatives of the *income theory of money:* the increased amount of money affects the price level of consumption goods by the fact that it first becomes income, and income in its turn is the source of the demand for consumption goods. Thus the ratio between the proportion of income spent on satisfying the demand for consumption goods and their supply, determines the price level of consumption goods.

Lindahl,[42] following Wicksell, gives the same formula for the price level of consumption goods. According to his formula, that part of the national income which is not saved, and appears therefore as consumption demand, $Y(1-s)$, always equals the volume of consumption goods sold multiplied by the price level, QP.

$$\text{Hence } P = \frac{Y(1-s)}{Q}.$$

The *external impulse* affecting the economy, the impulse which has increased the marginal productivity of capital and thus the natural rate of interest, together with the *passivity of banks,* which is shown by the fact that they are in no hurry to raise the market rate of interest to the level of the natural interest rate, brings about, through the interaction of the demand for consumption and investment goods, the self-reinforcing, *cumulative process* of prosperity. The yield from investments, and thus the natural interest rate, too, are now derived from causes *internal* to the system. The rising price level of consumption goods evokes optimistic expectations in entrepreneurs. "When prices have been rising steadily for some time, entrepreneurs will begin to reckon on the basis not merely of the prices already attained, but of a further rise in prices."[43] With the rising prices of consumption goods the profit expectations of investments become more and more favourable, for the latter depend, in the last analysis, on the demand for consumption goods. The movement of the natural rate of interest and its divergence from the market rate of interest are now completely linked with a change in prices. With rising prices of consumption goods and at an unchanged market rate of interest, entrepreneurs increase their investments. The luring away of factors from the production of consumption goods into that of producer goods continues, the vertical structure of production shifts more and more in favour of the latter, and, owing to the changing ratio between the two departments, the demand for consumption goods increasingly surpasses their supply, the price level of consumption goods rises, which in turn increases the profit expectations of investments, and increases the natural rate of interest.

This is the essence of the cumulative process. This investment boom lasts as long as the natural rate of interest exceeds the market rate.

Though the banks may grant credits for investment purposes beyond the level of

42 E. Lindahl: *op. cit.,* p. 142.
43 K. Wicksell: *Interest and Prices,* London, 1936, p. 96.

savings desired by society, the production of investment goods, says Wicksell, can only increase as a result of actual savings. For factors to be transferred from the production of consumer goods to that of investment goods, society has to curtail consumption. And if voluntary saving does not prove sufficient, an additional compulsory reduction of consumption must take place. The form this takes is that those strata whose incomes do not increase, or increase at a rate lower than the price level of consumption goods, are compelled to reduce their consumption, and provide so-called *forced saving*. Saving desired by society, plus the forced saving resulting from the rise in consumer goods prices, make an increase in investment possible in Wicksell's model.

The increase in the production of investment goods at the expense of consumption goods, and thus the process of upswing and the rise in the price level, is ended, according to Wicksell, by the fact that, owing to rising prices and increasing transactions, bank reserves begin to be depleted as a result of satisfying the increased demand for credit, and the issue of banknotes begins to exceed its legal limits. As Wicksell remarks, "the technical discoveries", giving rise to the increase in the natural rate of interest, "have not brought them [i.e. the banks, A. M.] any additional supplies of money..."[44] Banks are eventually compelled to raise the market rate of interest to an adequate extent. By raising the market rate of interest to the level of the natural rate, the demand for consumption goods drops to their supply level, investment will be in equilibrium with the amount of saving desired by society at the increased rate of interest, monetary equilibrium will be established, and the price level will settle at a constant level. But the new equilibrium price level will be higher than the earlier one: "... everything is in equilibrium at a higher level of money prices, wages and rents,"[45] writes Wicksell.

The cumulative process will take place in the reverse direction if the natural rate of interest falls below the market rate. This is the situation if "... the natural rate falls, ... while the market rate is maintained at its previous level."[46] Wicksell did not elaborate the process of a fall in the price level in anything like so detailed a way as that of price rises: he only outlines the process. Wicksell explains in his *Interest and Prices* the divergence of the two rates of interest by the fact that after the banks increase the market rate, the investments made at the earlier artificially low market rate mature, and thus "... the natural rate falls as a result of the accumulation of real capital..."[47] below the market rate.

Entrepreneurs decrease the output of the means of production and the demand for factors needed for it. As a result, the reward of the original factors will decline. A smaller quantity of total money wages and total money rent will be set against an unchanged quantity of consumption goods. Consequently, the price of consumption goods will decrease. This, in turn, reacting on the manufacture of the means of production, will further decrease it, and, as a result, the demand for consumption goods will further decline. Now the cumulative process will work itself out in a downward direction. But for Wicksell, the movement of factor prices ensures full employment even in a slump cycle, and thus the volume of production

[44] K. Wicksell: *Lectures on Political Economy*, Vol. II, p. 207.
[45] K. Wicksell: *Interest and Prices*, London, 1936, p. 147.
[46] K. Wicksell: *op. cit.*, p. 150.
[47] *Ibid.*

will not change even in that case: "... the whole activity will be maintained at its former level."[48]

Wicksell characterizes the boom period by a large-scale increase in the production of fixed capital; while in depression, entrepreneurs "will not venture the capital which is now being accumulated in such a fixed form."[49] The amount of consumption goods in total production increases relative to the production of the means of production. Lindahl gives this interpretation of Wicksell's not a very clear expositon: "... the output of consumption goods for each period is greater than it was to begin with, the capital of the community will by degrees be diminished."[50] Depression will be brought to an end either by new technical progress increasing the marginal productivity of capital, that is, the natural rate of interest, or by banks decreasing the market rate. Banks are sooner or later compelled to do the latter, because with the contraction of the money requirements of investments, surplus money will flow back to the banks, which have to pay a high rate of interest on it, but are unable to lend it at such a high rate.

The workings of the modern banking system, as is clear for Wicksell, prevent the interest mechanism from performing its role in maintaining the equilibrium of saving and investment and thereby of reproduction. By adjusting the market rate to the natural rate only with a time lag, the banks continually maintain the disturbance of equilibrium, and bring about a rise or a fall in the price level.

However, the function of the interest mechanism in bringing saving and investment into line will eventually, even if indirectly, assert itself. In Wicksell's view, it is precisely the movement of the price level which establishes, through its impact on bank reserves, the relationship between the market rate and the natural rate of interest in the modern banking system, and adjusts the market rate to the natural rate. For a rise in the price level, by decreasing reserves, compels the banks sooner or later to raise the market rate to the natural rate, while a fall in the price level compels them to decrease the market rate because of the increase in bank reserves.

Wicksell's analysis was further refined by Lindahl and Myrdal. Lindahl's contribution consisted mainly in introducing the various expectations of entrepreneurs and, further, in examining the process outlined by Wicksell under full and underemployment, under conditions when the factors cannot be transferred from one department to the other, or when productivity changes only in the production of either capital goods or consumption goods. Myrdal complemented Wicksell's analysis by the introduction of his *ex-ante* and *ex-post-analysis* already discussed in Part Four.

A CRITIQUE OF WICKSELL'S THEORY

What progress was made by Wicksell in the determination of the price level compared with the theories discussed so far? This progress consists in the fact that Wicksell, in seeking an explanation of changes in the price level, deals with *the*

---

[48] K. Wicksell: *op. cit.,* p. 149.
[49] K. Wicksell: *Lectures on Political Economy,* Vol. II, p. 212.
[50] E. Lindahl: *op. cit.,* p. 184.

process of reproduction. He recognizes that what is behind investment in excess of saving is an increase in the production of investment goods relative to the production of consumption goods. This accounts for the fact that total demand for consumption goods exceeds their total supply. The price level decreases, however, if the production of investment goods contracts relative to the production of consumption goods. The cumulative process described by Wicksell reflects the mutually reinforcing or weakening effect of the two departments. In his theory, the relation of the movement of the price level to cyclical changes is consciously recognized: "Our conclusion is therefore that the changes in the purchasing power of money caused by credit are under existing conditions certainly ultimately bound up with industrial fluctuations..."[51] He also associates profit expectations with reproduction in pointing out that any profit expectations following the first external impulse are usually dependent on the relationship between the production of investment and consumption goods.

Wicksell's theory of the determination of the price level is at the same time a trade-cycle theory. Ragnar Frisch considers Wicksell as the first representative of a type of trade-cycle theory which is based on showing how an external impulse affecting the economy is transformed in the course of propagation into a cyclical movement. The trade-cycle theory outlined by Wicksell was to be further developed by his Swedish followers, Lindahl and Myrdal, and by the Austrians Hayek and Mises.

Lindahl's price formula based on the Wicksellian conception also presents changes in the price level as a function of reproduction. If the market rate of interest declines, the share of investment goods in total production will grow, and consequently the relative output of consumption goods will decrease. For the expansion of the output of investment goods entrepreneurs get the necessary credits and, following the regrouping of factors, Y will increase. An increase in Y expands consumer demand, but a fall in the market rate will also increase it by diminishing savings made from incomes. The price level of consumption goods will rise. This price level will, however, decline if the banks raise the market rate of interest.

Wicksell's explanation of changes in the price level differs from that given by the cash-balance approach. The latter explains changes in the price level simply by changes in the ratio of the available quantity of money to the amount of money desired to be held. Wicksell, however, goes deeper, and derives changes in the price level from cyclical changes, from changes in the relation between the production of means of production and consumption goods.

But he distorts his correct recognition of the dependence of the price level on reproduction by making the banks responsible for cyclical changes in reproduction, for cyclical movements in the price level. This explanation fits in with his attempt to develop further the quantity theory of money on the basis of his analysis of the price level.

In his theory, an economic upswing, a large-scale increase in the production of fixed capitals, is due to technical progress as an external impulse, while depression is caused by the fact that there are no technical discoveries which are "sufficiently

---

[51] K. Wicksell: *op. cit.,* p. 211.

336

tested, or promise a profit in excess of the margin of risk attaching to all new enterprises..."[52] If banks adjusted the rate of interest to the profit rate on capital, to the natural rate of interest, both in prosperity and in depression, increasing it during the former and decreasing during the latter period, the price level would remain the same, and "presumably the real element of the crisis would be eliminated."[53] In other words, Wicksell believes that the interest or discount policy of the central bank is equally able to stop and reverse both the inflationary and deflationary processes. Since, however, the banks adjust the market rate to the natural-rate only with a lag, under the pressure of changes in bank reserves, they disrupt the proportion of the two departments, causing thereby a rise or fall in the price level.

Wicksell, however, reversed the true order of the causal relationships. If the production of the means of production, and within them of fixed capitals, increases in relation to the production of consumption goods, and as a result the price level increases, or if the process of prosperity is interrupted by a depression, in which the output of the means of production, of fixed capitals, contracts relative to the output of consumption goods so that the price level declines, then this cannot be explained by credit considerations. On the contrary, the demand for and the supply of credit, the changes in the rate of interest, are a function of the process of reproduction. The termination of a boom period is not caused by the lack of credit. It is the boom which widens the possibilities of granting credits, because production itself is expanding, and the reflux of capitals is unhindered. Consequently, *commercial* credit, which Marx holds to be the basis of the credit system, expands on an immense scale. Commercial credit is the basis for issuing banknotes, and the issue of banknotes provides the basis for increasing deposit money.[54] "This rapid development of loan capital is, therefore ... a consequence of the development of the reproduction process..."[55] Only when reproduction is interrupted, and the realization of goods comes up against difficulties, when bills of exchange cannot be cashed but have to be prolonged, only then is commercial credit extended by capitalists to each other taking part in the reproduction process, bound to rely to an increasing extent on bank credit. The sharpening of contradictions, the increasing difficulties of reproduction bring forth an increase in the demand for bank credit which finally leads to a depletion of bank reserves, and the tightening of bank credit. Wicksell's illusion is succinctly characterized by Marx's following lines: "In a system of production, where the entire continuity of the reproduction process rests upon credit, a crisis must obviously occur—a tremendous rush for means of payment—when credit suddenly ceases and only cash payments have validity. At first glance, therefore, the whole crisis seems to be merely a credit and money crisis. And in fact, it is only a question of the convertibility of bills of exchange into money. But the majority of these bills represent actual sales and purchases, whose extension far beyond the needs of society is, after all, the basis of the whole crisis."[56] And from the fact that at the beginning

[52] K. Wicksell: *op. cit.*, p. 212.
[53] *Ibid.*
[54] P. Erdős: *Contributions to the Theory of Capitalist Money, Business Fluctuations and Crises,* Budapest, 1971, p. 72.
[55] K. Marx: *Capital,* Vol. III, Moscow, 1962, p. 491.
[56] K. Marx: *op. cit.*, p. 478.

of recovery, exactly because of the previous cut-back of reproduction, there was ample credit available and the market rate was low, it would be incorrect to conclude, as Wicksell does, that it was the low rate of interest and the ample availability of credit which started off the process of recovery.

The idea underlying Wicksell's faulty conception consists in the assumption that it is the rate of interest that regulates saving and investment and thus the proportion of consumption goods to investment goods within the national income, and if the banking system hinders the free operation of the interest mechanism, then it causes a long-term disequilibrium of reproduction, bringing about a boom or a slump. This basic role attributed to the rate of interest was to be severely criticized in non-Marxian economics by Keynes.

Lindahl's formula for the explanation of the price level of consumption goods is also based upon Wicksell's faulty conception. Lindahl thinks that if saving and thus the demand for consumption goods are entirely a function of the interest rate, then, in order to determine the price level of consumption goods, he has only to set the total demand for consumption goods against their total supply. But consumer demand cannot be explained independently of class relations, on the basis of a sort of general consumer psychology. The consumer demand of the working class obeys laws entirely different from those governing the demand of the capitalist class.

The consumption of the two classes can all the less be summed, as both act differently on the price level of consumer goods. The quantity of the money wage paid out to the working class flows entirely to the product market. On the other hand, the consumption outlays of capitalists are in themselves indeterminate, as they are relatively independent of the capitalists' incomes. They act on the price level of consumer goods by their volume. Therefore, in determining the price level of consumer goods, the Hungarian economist Péter Erdős sets the money wages paid out to the working class against the quantity of consumer goods left out of the consumption of the capitalist class.

On the other hand, if we regarded the demand for consumption goods as a function of the rate of interest, the price level would lose its relative stability, since in this case consumer demand and through it the price level of consumption goods would react to any change in the rate of interest. Keynes sees the basis of the relative stability of the price level in the relative rigidity of money wages.

Wicksell, like other non-Marxian economists of his time, is confident that the movement of factor prices ensures full employment. Therefore, cyclical fluctuations appear in his system in a peculiar way. The volume of production is unchanged in the period of boom and slump alike, and only the structure of production and the price level are subject to changes.

Finally it must be noted that the vicious circle regarding the measurability of capital appears in a peculiar light in the Wicksellian conception, which attributes such a great significance to the marginal productivity of capital. Marginal productivity theory can explain the marginal productivity of capital and the natural rate of interest only in terms of market prices. The market rate of interest should be adjusted to the natural rate thus defined.

However, any change in the market rate of interest relative to the natural rate causes a price change and through it a change in the natural rate of interest, itself.

Part Eight

THE KEYNESIAN TURNING-POINT IN NON-MARXIAN ECONOMICS

Chapter 1

INTRODUCTION

The central questions of pre-Keynesian neo-classical economics were the theories of value, price and income distribution. The representatives of this school endeavoured to answer the question of what price proportions have to be established if the economic subjects, with the data of the model, want to make optimum use of the resources available to them. As these economists see it, it is the undisturbed functioning of the price mechanism that ensures this ideal result. In such a model there cannot be persistent general unemployment, because the free play of the wage mechanism adjusts demand to supply also on the labour market. And the operation of the price mechanism also ensures that the expenditure of society on consumption and investment always equals total costs (including normal profit) of the amount of the goods produced at full employment. In this model, claiming to prove the effective functioning of the capitalist economy left to itself, there is no room for state economic intervention.

In the period of the Great Depression, such theories could no longer be maintained. They sharply contradicted reality and were unable to answer the serious question facing the bourgeoisie of how to get out of the economic crisis, whose depth had been unprecedented in the history of capitalism, of how significantly to reduce unemployment which was assuming threatening dimensions, and jeopardizing the very existence of capitalism. This is how Joan Robinson writes about the first crisis of economics: "The first crisis arose from the breakdown of a theory which could not account for the level of employment."[1] The immense shock inflicted on the capitalist system compelled non-Marxian economics to turn to the burning questions of the time and find an explanation of the serious ills of the economy. In answering these questions, non-Marxian economics referred, among other things, to the presence of monopolies and to the time requirement of the economic processes. These explanations, however, did not create a new theoretical system which could have been confronted with the old one and which, as the ideology of state monopoly capitalism, would have organically included the economic intervention of the state, or would have provided a support for it.

It was Keynes who succeeded in fulfilling this social demand of the bourgeoisie in the most satisfactory manner. Keynes asserted that the only measure that could be used to pass judgement on what he called classical economic theory was the question of whether it was capable of serving as a theoretical support to solve

[1] J. Robinson: The Second Crisis of Economic Theory, *The American Economic Review*, May 1972, p. 6.

the economic problems of the real world. His critique of the classical theory, writes Keynes, does not refer primarily to its logical deficiencies. The root of its shortcomings lies in the fact that "its tacit assumptions are seldom or never satisfied...[2]; consequently, it cannot show how to cure the grave problems of the capitalist economy.

As generally accepted by those economists called "classical" by Keynes and "neo-classical" by American economists (the latter a term now in common use in non-Marxian literature), the undisturbed play of the price mechanism performs a *double* function. It regulates, *on the one hand,* how much of each good should be produced and how the factors should be combined to minimize production costs and, further, how the volume of the goods thus produced should be distributed among the owners of the individual factors. *On the other hand,* however, it also provides for full employment with aggregate demand being in line with aggregate supply, ensuring thereby the market for the volume of output produced at full employment. Keynes accepted only the first of the two functions ascribed to the price mechanism and rejected the second. "It is in determining the volume, not the direction of actual employment that the existing system has broken down."[3]

Out of a capitalist economy represented by neo-classical economists as a world in which views on the future are reliable and not subject to changes, Keynes takes us into a world of uncertainties, a world in which people act under the impact of ideas relating to an uncertain future. Thus there is no room in it for an automatic mechanism which turns the economy in the direction of a state of full employment. The high degree of uncertainty about the profit expectations of investments makes it unlikely for Keynes that changes in the rate of interest within the scope of reality could significantly affect investment activity and create the volume of investment needed for full employment. But the uncertain future, in the form of uncertainty about changes in the future market of bonds, also prevents the movement of the rate of interest from keeping pace wit h a fall in the marginal efficiency of capital. Moreover, as a result of the views on future changes in the interest rate, it may get stuck at a level which is unfavourable for the realization of full employment. Keynes emphasizes that "the evidence indicates that full, or even approximately full, employment is of rare and short-lived occurrence."[4]

The fact that the representatives of the neo-classical view believe in automatic adjustment assuring full employment, and that Keynes rejects it, is reflected in their theoretical systems: in the neo-classical model the system reacts to changes in aggregate demand with price changes, with the levels of output and employment remaining unchanged at full employment, whilst in Keynes's system the reaction takes place in the volume of output and employment, and prices vary only in that a change in production causes marginal costs to change.

By rejecting automatic full employment, an assumption contradicting reality, Keynes invalidates neo-classical price theory. In equilibrium, under conditions of perfect competition, prices have to equal marginal costs, which, in the neo-classical interpretation, presupposes that the factors are rewarded according to

[2] J. M. Keynes: *The General Theory of Employment, Interest and Money,* London, 1936, p. 378.
[3] J. M. Keynes: *op. cit.,* p. 379.
[4] J. M. Keynes: *op. cit.,* pp. 249–250.

their marginal productivity. The marginal productivity of factors, however, can only be determined if the number of workers employed at a given stock of capital is known. Neo-classical theory assumed that employment was full. "The theory of value, the theory of allocation of resources," writes Shackle, "assumes full employment".[5] If, however, the price mechanism does not ensure full employment, the marginal productivity of factors, and hence production costs and prices, become indeterminate, and thus the validity of neo-classical price theory sustains a severe shock. Therefore, an answer had to be found to the question of what determines the volume of employment, if no automatic adjustment exists in a capitalist economy to provide for full employment.

It is for this reason that Keynes suggested the division of economics into two parts. One part would be " 'the Theory of the Individual Industry of Firm' and of the rewards and the distribution between different uses of a *given* quantity of resources"[6], and the other part "the Theory of Output and Employment as a *whole*..."[7]. The problems of price theory and income distribution continue to be examined, as a rule, on a micro-economic basis. These problems, however, are subordinated to the theory of aggregate output, of aggregate employment, which requires analysis to be made on a macro-economic basis.

The shattering of confidence in the effectiveness of automatic adjustment processes in a capitalist economy directed Keynes's attention to the functioning of the economic system as a whole. "Keynes clearly recognized that the price theory of his day did not, and could not, explain employment," write Brunner and Meltzer. "Two alternatives were available: one a reformulation of price theory, the other a framework that separated macro- and microtheory. Keynes chose the latter..."[8]

The paving of the way for state economic intervention also makes it necessary for the macro-economic approach to come to the fore. And Keynes recognizes that what is achieved at a social level is something entirely different from what people want individually: what is valid at the micro-level, often turns into its opposite at the social level. "The world is *not* so governed from above that private and social interest always coincide... It is *not* a correct deduction from the Principles of Economics that enlightened self-interest always operates in the public interest. Nor is it true that self-interest generally *is* enlightened; more often individuals acting separately to promote their own ends are too ignorant or too weak to attain even these."[9]

Since no automatic adjustment exists in a capitalist economy to eliminate involuntary unemployment, a high level of employment must—according to Keynes—be ensured by economic policy measures. But by what kind of economic policy measures?

In the USA, in the 1920s, it was assumed, as Samuelson writes[10], that the Federal

5 G. L. S. Shackle: *The Years of High Theory*, Cambridge, 1967, p. 146.

6 J. M. Keynes: *op. cit.*, p. 283.

7 *Ibid*.

8 K. Brunner and A. H. Meltzer: Friedman's Monetary Theory, *Journal of Political Economy*, Sept/Oct. 1972, p. 840.

9 J. M. Keynes: *Essays in Persuasion*, London, 1931, p. 312.

10 See P. A. Samuelson: *Economics*, McGraw-Hill Inc., New York, 1973, p. 328.

Reserve system had learnt for ever how to curb business cycles by monetary means.

A similar conclusion can also be drawn from those varieties of the quantity theory of money as were predominant in Keynes's time. Though the quantity theory was originally created with a view to determining the price level, it can, as is believed today, also be regarded as a theory of the determination of the level of nominal national income. Consequently, "income is what it is because a certain amount of money is available and because this money is being spent at a certain rate."[11] Out of the two components of aggregate demand interpreted as MV, V is, according to the earlier representatives of the quantity theory, an institutional datum; aggregate demand and thus nominal national income, too, can be altered by changing M.

Then the Great Depression ruined the idea that business cycles can be eliminated merely by monetary policy measures. Keynes does not believe that the cumulative process of a declining output and increasing unemployment can be stopped by such measures. In his theory of money and interest he points out that while M is changing, a change in V is fairly uncertain and indeed, a reduction in V may also compensate for an increase in M, in which case monetary policy becomes absolutely ineffective. In Keynes, monetary policy is a necessary but not sufficient condition for increasing aggregate demand, national income and employment.

Instead of monetary policy, Keynes places emphasis *on fiscal policy*. In determining aggregate demand, and employment, Keynes ascribes a crucial role to investment. And if private investment is insufficient to ensure the aggregate demand necessary for full employment, then fiscal policy must create the necessary demand by government expenditure. According to Keynes, the national income is, through the multiplier effect, a more reliable function of investment than, given an uncertain V, of M.

In the period of the Great Depression, the British Conservative Government attacked the view that employment could be increased by increasing state outlays.

It was, essentially, the idea of budgetary equilibrium which lay behind such arguments, the idea that government expenditure, like that of private individuals, must stay within the limits of its revenue, and cannot, without the risk of inflation, transgress the level of intended social saving with its investments. If the government, in order to diminish unemployment, creates public-works opportunities and increases its outlays, it must either increase taxes or raise more credit. But the increased tax burden and the higher interest rate caused by the growing state demand for credit discourage private investments, reduces the consumer demand of the heavily taxed households, and thus it is doubtful whether public works will increase aggregate demand and employment. Seeking a solution to the problem of unemployment by economic policy measures, Keynes came to establish a number of theoretical innovations. Thus, in opposition to the orthodox view, he emphasized that it was investment that determined the magnitude of saving: government expenditure, together with private investments, increased in a situation of unemployment the national income through the multiplier effect to such an extent that intended saving effected from national income eventually equalled

[11] W. Fellner: Employment Theory and Business Cycles. In: *A Survey of Contemporary Economics*, Philadelphia–Toronto, 1948, p. 51.

the intended investment of the private sector plus government expenditure. It appeared that the government, unlike private individuals, might spend, in a situation of unemployment, over and above its revenue. National income, increased as a result of government expenditure, would ensure backing for its outlays afterwards, when the government withdrew, by taxation, such a proportion of national income which would not have materialized if such government expenditure had not been made.

Preparing the theoretical basis for state economic policy, Keynes's work brought about a change in non-Marxian economics in another respect also. Robbins was still of the opinion that "economic analysis is wertfrei in the Weber sense,"[12] i.e. economics has to be an objective science which only endeavours to explore the relationship between given ends and the available resources, or to reveal the economic connections based on them without advocating or fighting particular objectives of economic policy, or passing judgement on the existing social relations. It used to be a widespread view in economics that so long as there was no unit of measurement to compare utilities between individuals, it was impossible to take up a scientifically founded position on the effect that a certain economic policy and economic system exercised upon the welfare of individuals. Scitovsky writes in this regard that a student may have learnt at the university what the difference is between perfect competition and monopoly, between protectionism and free trade and between inflation and price stability, but he has seldom been given value judgements on them.[13] As a result of the shock which the Great Depression inflicted on capitalist economy, the view of bourgeois theoreticians has changed. The choice between prosperity and depression, high and low national income, high and low level of employment, or the acceptance of their realization have become so unambiguous that these activities do not require the commensurability of utilities. Paving the way theoretically for state economic intervention, Keynes passes judgement on the capitalist system left to itself, and takes sides with a definite economic policy. "The outstanding faults of the economic society in which we live are its failure to provide for full employment and its arbitrary and inequitable distribution of wealth and incomes."[14] "... I believe that there is social and psychological justification for significant inequalities of incomes and wealth, but not for such large disparities as exist to-day."[15] "I conceive... that a somewhat comprehensive socialisation of investment will prove the only means of securing an approximation to full employment..."[16]

Under the conditions of state economic intervention, modern non-Marxian economic science, primarily under the influence of Keynes, gives up its objectivity in evaluating the basic processes of capitalist economy as regards the aims of economic policy.

[12] L. Robbins: *The Nature and Significance of Economic Science*, London, 1932, p. 126.
[13] See T. Scitovsky: The State of Welfare Economics, *The American Economic Review*, 1961, p. 305.
[14] J. M. Keynes: *The General Theory of Employment, Interest and Money*, p. 372.
[15] J. M. Keynes: *op. cit.*, p. 374.
[16] J. M. Keynes: *op. cit.*, p. 378.

Chapter 2

THE OUTLINES OF KEYNES'S EMPLOYMENT THEORY

In the period following the Great Depression, Keynes rejects those neo-classical assumptions which contradict reality, among them the assumption that automatic adjustment operating in a capitalist economy provides for full employment, ensures adequate aggregate demand for the amount of the goods produced at full employment; he seeks to answer the question on what the volume of aggregate demand and the volume of employment depend.

Keynes examines the question of employment in the short run. Like the neo-classical price models in static equilibrium, his theory takes the level of technical knowledge, the quantity of the available factors of production, consumer tastes and the way in which income is distributed as given, and looks for the determinants of the amount of the available labour in employment. In the short run, at the given level of technical knowledge employment increases or decreases with output, and thus "the amount of employment associated with a given capital equipment will be a satisfactory index of the amount of resultant output..."[17] Besides determining employment, Keynes also attempts to determine the equilibrium level of net output, of national income. Consequently, his employment theory is at the same time an *income analysis,* too.

The framework of Keynesian employment theory or income analysis is simple. It is constructed on the analogy of Marshall's price theory. Each level of employment, of the production of national income has its own aggregate costs, which are practically identical with factor costs for Keynes, too. Entrepreneurs are willing, as a rule, to employ a certain amount of labour, to maintain the production of national income at a certain level if they hope that the expected proceeds will cover their total costs including normal profits. The proceeds so expected are the *aggregate supply price* of the level of employment or national income concerned, and Keynes denotes it by Z. And the aggregate supply function expresses how the aggregate supply price changes with changes in employment, in output.

Economists following and explaining Keynes usually represent the aggregate supply function by a straight line drawn at an angle of 45°. They plot expected aggregate demand and aggregate income on the y-axis, and aggregate costs at the different levels of employment or national income including normal profits, on the x-axis.

The aggregate supply function represented by a straight line drawn at an angle

17 J. M. Keynes: *op. cit.,* p. 41.

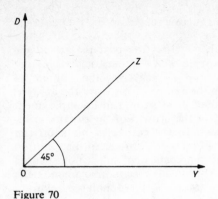

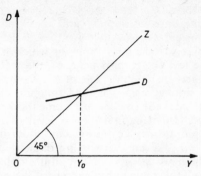

Figure 70   Figure 71

of 45° expresses that entrepreneurs are willing to maintain any level of employment or national income only if they expect aggregate demand to equal the aggregate costs of the employment, i.e. production of the national income in question, plus normal profit.

To each level of employment or the national income Keynes also attaches an *aggregate demand price,* which, using his notation, is *D*. This is the amount of aggregate demand or aggregate proceeds that entrepreneurs expect at a certain level of employment, of the national income. The aggregate demand function connects the aggregate demand price with the different levels of employment or the national income. The form of the aggregate demand function in Figure 71, of function *D*, will be explained later on.

In the theory of neo-classical economists, accepting Say's dogma, aggregate demand and supply prices coincide at each level of employment, of the national income. In this case, as Keynes put it, "... the competition between entrepreneurs would always lead to an expansion of employment up to the point at which the supply of output as a whole ceases to be elastic, i.e. where a further increase in the value of effective demand will no longer be accomplished by any increase in output. Evidently, this amounts to the same thing as full employment."[18] Keynes, however, who criticizes Say's dogma, wishes to demonstrate that aggregate demand and supply prices coincide only at one single level of employment or national income, which is the level of full employment only in exceptionally favourable cases, and is usually lower than that.

To determine the equilibrium level of employment, Keynes borrows from neo-classical price theory the principle of profit maximization. Entrepreneurs increase employment and output as long as the amount of their profits increases. And the amount of their profits increases as long as the aggregate demand price exceeds the aggregate supply price. The amount of profit will be at a maximum at a volume of employment and output at which the aggregate demand and supply functions intersect. Keynes calls the value that the aggregate demand price assumes at the point of intersection *effective demand.*

[18] J. M. Keynes: *op. cit.,* p. 26.

347

Keynes asserts that the aggregate supply function depends on the physical conditions of supply, and that "the aggregate supply function... involves few considerations which are not already familiar."[19] "It is the part played by the aggregate demand function which has been overlooked."[20] Yet, in his opinion, the level of employment, of the national income, depends on the volume of aggregate demand. Therefore, Keynes places in the *centre* of his work the analysis of the aggregate demand function. The explanation of short-run unemployment excludes the impact of technical development, of the growth of the organic composition of capital on the level of employment. In the course of his short-run explorations, Keynes concentrates attention on finding an answer to the question of why, given the existing data, that level of aggregate demand is not ensured which would give rise to full employment. Approaching economic phenomena from the angle of *realization, of the market,* he establishes, as we shall see, relationships quite different from those of neo-classical economists.

Keynes does not interpret aggregate demand as MV. As Hansen points out, "those who are accustomed to look at the matter trough the MV glasses, find it very dfficult to conceive of any problem of inadequate Aggregate Demand."[21] Given the global aspect of demand, it appears that if there is no demand for one good, there there will be a demand for another.

In the MV approach, the market-governing role of investment gets lost. Instead of a global representation of aggregate demand, Keynes distinguishes between two elements constituting aggregate demand: consumption and investment, C and I. In his theory, the level of employment, of the national income, adjusts itself to aggregate demand determined by consumption outlays and investment outlays. "The decisions to consume and the decisions to invest between them determine incomes."[22]

It should be noted at the outset that if the aggregate demand is composed of C and I, Keynes cannot represent the aggregate demand price as a function of employment since, as we shall see, he can connect consumption, but not investment, with employment, with the national income.

The sum of consumption demand and investment, as money outlays, determine in Keynes's theory *nominal income,* the amount of net output, of real income expressed in terms of money. Since, however, employment can be full, in Keynes' view, only in exceptionally favourable circumstances, the growth in nominal income is accompanied by changes in net output, in real income. "... except in conditions of full employment, there will be an increase of real income as well as of money-income."[23] Thus C, I and Y alike may be interpreted as real and nominal magnitudes. This is an essential difference between the view held by Keynes and that of the representatives of the quantity theory of money. With the latter, the determination of the price level is based precisely on the difference between nominal and real incomes. From the point of view of price determination they took the volume of real income to be an exogenous datum, a magnitude at full employ-

[19] J. M. Keynes: *op. cit.,* p. 89.
[20] *Ibid.*
[21] See A. H. Hansen: *A Guide to Keynes,* London, 1953, p. 26.
[22] J. M. Keynes: *op. cit.,* p. 64.
[23] J. M. Keynes: *op. cit.,* p. 82.

ment. They maintained that if aggregate income changes, it is the price level that has to change, and nominal income adjusts itself through the price level to changes in demand, leaving real income, the volume of output, unchanged.

Since, according to Keynes, output and employment move together with changes in aggregate demand and nominal income, he wishes to determine the levels of employment, output and real income by nominal income divided by the wage unit, i.e. the money wage per unit of labour assumed to be constant. "... we shall measure changes in current output by reference to the number of men employed (whether to satisfy consumer or to produce fresh capital equipment)."[24]

Keynes's model assumes the *money wage* to be an *exogenous datum* which changes rather slowly. It changes slowly because workers are, in Keynes's opinion, slaves to the money illusion, and resist, through their trade unions, the entrepreneurs' attempt to cut their money wages, but no trade union is willing to stage a strike whenever, with money wages being unchanged, real wages decline owing to a rise in living costs. The assumption of the Keynesian model that money wages constitute a datum, shows that Keynes does not attribute a governing role to flexible wages. Owing to the rigidity of money wages, the price level too is relatively rigid in the Keynesian model. When demand changes, the price level can change at most to the extent to which marginal costs are increasing with the rise in output.

We can speak about the rigidity of money wages only in the sense that workers really resist any attempt to cut their money wages. But precisely the inflationary tendencies today provide the evidence that the workers are far from being slaves to the money illusion. They demand and by fighting for it, often succeed in getting a wage index tied to the price index. They pay attention not only to changes in money wages but also to the movement of the price level.

In the following we shall examine, following Keynes, the determinants of the amount of consumption demand and investment. For both elements of aggregate demand Keynes establishes functional relationships different from those set up by neo-classical economics. Thus the Keynesian theory provides at the same time the basis for a critique of Say's dogma, which assumes that aggregate demand grows in line with an increase in aggregate supply.

[24] J. M. Keynes: *op. cit.*, p. 44

Chapter 3

KEYNES'S THEORY OF AGGREGATE DEMAND

CONSUMER DEMAND

Neo-classical economists supposed that the available resources were fully utilized, and thus the volume of the national income was constant in the short run, with the quantities of factors and technical knowledge being given. They directed their attention to the way in which consumers distribute their *given incomes* optimally between their present and future needs, that is, to the proportion which they spend on consumption and that which they save. And they came to the conclusion that this depends on the level of the rate of interest. Keynes, on the other hand, points out that the automatic adjustment processes of the capitalist economy do not provide for full employment. The volume of employment and with it of the national income too change in the short run even with the above factors being constant. Essentially, he is concerned with the question of how consumption, or saving, changes with the national income.

The representatives of neo-classical economics tried to determine, on the basis of the rational choice of the consumer, the division of the given income between consumption and saving. Keynes, however, sees it as the manifestation of consumer psychology, and thereby attempts to explain how consumption or saving changes with income. "The psychology of the community is such that when aggregate real income is increased aggregate consumption is increased, but not by so much as income."[25] Or "... when real income increases ... the community will wish to consume a gradually diminishing proportion of it."[26] Expressed in terms of mathematics, $\dfrac{dC}{dY}$, the marginal propensity to consume, i.e. the increment of consumption as a proportion of an infinitesimally small increase in income, falls as income rises. And since saving is income minus consumption, similarly, saving too is a function of income. This functional relationship between consumption, or saving, on the one hand, and income, on the other, the Keynesian consumption function, or as it came to be called later, the *absolute income hypothesis,* plays a central part in Keynes's theoretical system. It is on the basis of this function that he tries to determine in what proportion investment expands the market and through it the national income. As he puts it in a study written later: "This psychological law was of the utmost importance in the development of my

[25] J. M. Keynes: *op. cit.,* p. 27.
[26] J. M. Keynes: *op. cit.,* p. 120.

350

own thought, and it is, I think, absolutely fundamental to the theory of effective demand..."[27]

He explains the lag of consumer demand behind the growth of the national income partly by lagged adjustment. In the short run, there is not enough time for consumption habits to adjust themselves to the changed conditions. "For a man's habitual standard of life has the first claim on his income, and he is apt to save the difference which discovers itself between his actual income and the expense of his habitual standard..."[28] The lag, however, does not establish any real functional relationship between consumption, or saving, and income. Therefore, Keynes investigates in detail what factors affect the propensity to consume, what proportion of their income people spend on consumption. He distinguishes objective and subjective factors.

Among the objective factors he mentions the change in the difference between income and net income. The more of the income is set aside as sinking funds or depreciation allowances, the less is left for consumption. On the other hand, the windfall changes in capital-values not allowed for in calculating net income, increase the consumption expenditures out of the income. Here Keynes makes reference to the wealth effect which plays such an important role in contemporary non-Marxian economics, the effect that a rise in asset values, whether it be the consequence of an increase in the marginal efficiency of capital, or of a decrease in the rate of interest, raises the propensity to consume out of current income. In present-day non-Marxian literature, great significance is attached, besides the substitution and income effects of a change in the rate of interest, to its effect on wealth. Of these effects, Keynes ascribes a certain significance to the wealth effect in respect of consumption demand or saving.[29]

Among the subjective factors affecting the propensity to consume, or stimulating the individual to refrain from spending his income, are included in Keynes's system the provision of funds for emergencies, old age, the education of children, the pleasure of a sense of independence and of the awareness of being able to do things, though without a clear idea or definite intention of specific action, the securing of the manoeuvring basis for carrying out speculative or business plans, the intention to leave an inheritance, mere avarice, etc.

Keynes stresses that "the subjective factors... are unlikely to undergo a material change over a short period of time except in abnormal revolutionary circumstances,"[30] "whilst the short-period influence of changes in the rate of interest and the other objective factors is often of secondary importance..."[31] Thus "the propensity to consume is a fairly stable function..."[32] and "short-period changes in consumption largely depend on changes in the rate at which income (measured in wage units) is being earned and not on changes in the propensity to consume out of a given income."[33]

[27] J. M. Keynes: The General Theory, *The New Economics*, London, 1963, p. 190.
[28] J. M. Keynes: *The General Theory of Employment, Interest and Money*, p. 97.
[29] J. M. Keynes: *op. cit.*, p. 94.
[30] J. M. Keynes: *op. cit.*, p. 91.
[31] J. M. Keynes: *op. cit.*, p. 110.
[32] J. M. Keynes: *op. cit.*, p. 96.
[33] J. M. Keynes: *op. cit.*, p. 110.

Consumption demand has in Keynes's system a double role: as one element of aggregate income, it *determines* the volume of the national income, but it is also *dependent on it*.

Making consumption outlays and saving dependent on the volume of real income, Keynes explains the lag of consumption demand behind the increase in the national income, referring this time to consumer psychology, as follows: "... the satisfaction of the immediate primary needs of a man and his family is usually a stronger motive than the motives towards accumulation."[34] Therefore, people belonging to a lower income groups spend their full incomes on buying consumer goods. At a particular level of income, "when a margin of comfort has been attained...,"[35] a new desire arises in the consumer: the desire to save, which, with the increase in real income, grows at an ever faster rate. Keynes interprets saving, as also reflected by the subjective factors giving rise to it, differently from neo-classical economics. "... the act of saving implies, not a substitution for present consumption of some specific additional consumption... but a desire for 'wealth' as such, that is for a potentiality of consuming an unspecified article at an unspecified time."[36]

Keynes thinks that with a stable function between income and consumption outlays it is possible to predict how much, at the different levels of the national income, people want to spend on consumption and how much they want to save.

Does such an interrelationship as established by Keynes really exist between the levels of consumption and saving, on the one hand, and changes in income, on the other? This question has also been widely debated in non-Marxian literature. Keynes treats the consumption and saving of the capitalist and working classes under one heading. He attempts to disclose the factors affecting aggregate consumption and aggregate saving *in general,* irrespective of class relations. In reality, most savings stem from firms that are compelled to save by the competitive struggle, the hunt for profit, by their endeavour to maintain or even expand their market shares, and not by some sort of consumer psychology. As soon as we assume that a substantial proportion of saving is not consumer saving, it becomes impossible to make the level of saving, merely by means of consumer psychology, dependent on the national income. But then the amount of the multiplier, interpreted as the reciprocal of the marginal propensity to save, also becomes indeterminate, and so does the level of national income attached to the given level of investment.

The firms' decisions on the level of their savings cannot be explained by a kind of consumer psychology. Now the question arises if the consumer psychology as defined by Keynes can be applied to consumer behaviour in general. It is also impossible to establish a general principle in respect of the consumer's decision on spending a certain proportion of his income, a principle which is independent of his position in society and stems from a kind of consumer nature. It is impossible to give the motives for saving, regardless of class relations.

Among the motives enumerated by Keynes as affecting the propensity to consume in general, we can hardly find a few which can be supposed to give rise to

[34] J. M. Keynes: *op. cit.,* p. 97.
[35] *Ibid.*
[36] J. M. Keynes: *op. cit.,* p. 211.

saving in the Keynesian sense also within the working class. The worker will not and cannot save to enjoy the pleasure of a sense of independence, or to set aside reserves for manoeuvering or speculative purposes. Keynes's consumption function is designed to explain the consumption of the different social classes in conformity with different laws on a uniform basis, by means of an abstract consumer psychology. In reality, the consumption of the working class and the capitalist class as well as their incomes from which they cover their consumption, are governed by different laws. In Keynes's time, the savings of the working class were insignificant. The working class spent its total income, as a rule, on buying consumer goods. Therefore, in order to find out how its consumption demand changes, we ought to know about the short- and long-term movement of its wages. The consumption of the capitalist class is rather inelastic. It does not fall with a fall in profit, and grows just slightly when the profit rises. The laws governing the volume and the changes of capitalist consumption are still not sufficiently known to us; however, the Keynesian consumption function seems to be generally observable in the short-term changes of consumption outlays made out of profits. The Keynesian propensity to consume in fact reflects in a vulgar way that the capitalist intends to get the highest possible income not in order to consume still more, but to increase his *abstract wealth* in the greatest possible degree. Therefore, unlike the neo-classical economists, Keynes stresses that saving does not include the desire for future consumption, and this is why he fails to represent in his theory the rational distribution of income between the satisfaction of present and future needs. Then, in Keynes's model, the consumer makes profitable use of his income saved either by buying securities or, if he deems the future to be unfavourable, by keeping it in cash. But he tries to explain the desire for the acquisition of abstract wealth by consumer psychology.

Explaining the relationship between national income and consumption demand by a consumer psychology interpreted apart from social relations, Keynes finds that the inadequacy of consumer demand is primarily the consequence of the low propensity of society to consume: within the existing framework of distribution relations the members of society will not consume enough. But differences in class relations break through the consumer psychology constructed by Keynes. The marginal propensity to consume is lower in the capitalist than in the working class. Therefore, Keynes too refers to the possibility of raising the level of consumer demand out of a given national income through the redistribution of incomes.

Samuelson[37] calls attention to the statistical difficulties in constructing a social consumption function.

Kuznets was the first to examine the long-run relationship between consumption demand and national income. It has turned out, however, that consumption changes with national income in the long run differently from how Keynes assumed it did in the short run. Kuznets's calculations (see his "Proposition of Capital Formations to National Product" in: *The American Economic Review,* Papers and Proceedings, XLII, May 1952, pp 507–526) revealed that average propensity to consume was practically constant in the long run, though real income increased substantially.

[37] See P. A. Samuelson: *Economics,* McGraw-Hill Inc., New York, 1973, pp. 217–218.

ATTEMPTS TO RECONCILE THE SHORT- AND LONG-RUN CONSUMPTION FUNCTIONS

In the macro-economic theory of consumption, one of the central problems has been posed in the post-war period by the reconciliation of the short-run consumption function formulated by Keynes with the long-term consumption function revealed by Kuznets.

One of the attempts to solve the problem is the *relative income* hypothesis. Summarizing the ideas of its representatives, we can outline the following picture. The individual adjusts himself in his consumption habits to the members of his own social stratum. He competes with them, and seeks steadily to achieve the highest possible income. And if he succeeds in reaching a higher living-standard, he sticks to it even if his income has fallen off.

Duesenberry now tried to connect the short- and long-term consumption functions with one another in the following manner. In his view, consumers adjust their short-run consumption outlays, owing to the cyclical fluctuations of incomes, to the highest income level reached at the top of the boom. Once they are accustomed to that higher living standard, they refuse to cut their consumption even if their income drops in depression. As their income declines, their consumption will change as a result of a double effect. They insist, on the one hand, on the living standard reached at the highest level of their income, while the fall in their income tends to restrict their consumption. This will result in a slower rate of decrease in consumption than in income, and consumers will choose to cut their savings. J. S. Duesenberry calls this effect the "ratchet effect". (See his *Income, Saving* and *Theory of Consumer Behaviour*, Cambridge [Mass.], 1949.) With the decrease of income from Y_0^1, the highest level reached in the short-run cyclical fluctuation, to Y_1, consumption demand will move along the curve C_s^1. Therefore, according to Duesenberry, short-term consumption is a function of the current and the highest income level reached before,

$$C_s = f\left(\frac{Y_1}{Y_0^1}\right).$$

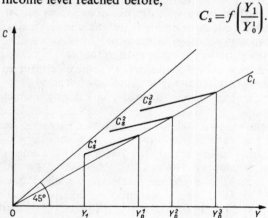

Figure 72

Represented in the system of co-ordinates:
When now income rises again from Y_1 to Y_0^1, consumption will move to its

earlier highest level along the same short-term path. With this reasoning, it appears, Duesenberry supported the Keynesian assumption. Then, when income has risen again to the highest level reached earlier and approaches the highest level of the following cycle, Y_0^2, consumption will rise along its long-term trend, i. e. with a more or less unchanged ratio. The earlier highest income will no longer exercise an effect on the volume of consumption. To the income Y_0^2 we can also construct a short-term consumption function just as to the highest income levels of the following cycles, to Y_0^3, Y_0^4, etc.

Y_0^1, Y_0^2, Y_0^3, etc. represent the long-term trends of changes in the national income. C_l is the long-term trend of consumption outlays which expresses that consumption changes over a long-term period in an unchanged proportion to the rise in income.

In connection with the long-term growth of consumption, Modigliani refers, among other things, to the fact that with technical progress new products and new services emerge which, with the increase in income, raise the desire to buy.[38]

By distinguishing between *permanent income* or *consumption* and *measured income* or *consumption,* Friedman also attempts to reconcile the short-term consumption function with the long-term one. Measured income and measured consumption are actual income and actual consumption, while permanent income is average income with which consumers may reckon on average over a long-term period. Friedman represents it as the weighted average of measured incomes, and states that the more remote a given income, the lesser is its weight in averaging; and the sum of weights equals unity. According to his so-called *permanent income hypothesis,* consumers plan their expenditure not on the basis of their actual but on that of their permanent income. The consumption outlays thus incurred are permanent consumption outlays. Permanent consumption outlays represent a constant proportion of permanent income. This proportion, says Friedman, "does not depend on the size of permanent income but does depend on other variables..."[39] and thus may vary from consumer to consumer. From among these variables let us isolate wealth, which plays such a pronounced role in contemporary consumption theory. The explorations relating to the effect of wealth upon consumption strengthened, writes Katona, after the Second World War. In many countries war expenses were financed, at least partly, by selling government bonds. "This raised the amount of liquid wealth available to the people ..., incentives to save were supposed to weaken with an increase in wealth. The richer the family, the smaller the need to add to its wealth ... Many economists thereupon postulated that given unchanged income, the greater the liquid assets, the larger the proportion of income spent."[40]

The difference between actual and permanent income or consumption is a *transitory* component of income or consumption. The transitory component reflects the effect of factors which the consumer regards as chance or random as well as errors of measurement. Friedman stresses that "... the transitory components

[38] See F. Modigliani: Fluctuations in the Saving–Income Ratio. In: *Readings in Macroeconomics* (Ed. by N. F. Keiser), Prentice Hall Inc., Englewood Cliffs, New Jersey, 1970, p. 66.

[39] M. Friedman: *A Theory of Consumption Function,* Princeton, 1957, p. 221.

[40] G. Katona: *The Mass Consumption Society,* New York–San Francisco–Toronto–London, McGraw Hill Book Company, 1964, pp. 213–214.

of consumption and income can be taken to be incorrelated with the corresponding permanent components and with each other; there are an essential part of the hypothesis presented in this monograph."[41] As he says, a short-term increase in consumer income by an unforeseeable quantity results in a rise in the proportion of saving. Conversely, when the consumer experiences a transitory decrement of income, it nonetheless adjusts consumption to permanent income, financing any excess over measured income by drawing down assets or increasing liabilities. "The transitory components of income shop up primarily in changes in the consumer unit's assets and liabilities, that is, in his measured saving."[42] While, therefore, the long-term relationship between permanent income and permanent consumption is constant, the case is different in the relationship between measured income and measured consumption: "the ratio of consumption to income declines as measured income increases..."[43]

It is further argued in the permanent income hypothesis that consumption may also be influenced by the transitory element, but only indirectly, through the wealth effect, and as long "as it alters wealth."[44]

Close to Friedman's permanent income hypothesis is the so-called *life-cycle hypothesis of savings* of Modigliani, Brumberg and Ando. In a jointly written article, Modigliani and Brumberg state that they wish to replace Keynes's "mysterious psyhcological law with the principle that men are disposed as a rule and on average to be forward-looking animals."[45] According to their theory, the major purpose of the individual's savings is to ensure reserves for himself in case of substantial changes in his income, including changes that may typically occur during his life cycle, notably at retirement, less systematic short-term fluctuations of his income, and emergencies. In each period of his active life he strives, even in the case of a decline in his income or of retirement, to maintain the same standard of living which he had ensured for himself on average in the period in question. Hence, there exists no close relationship between the consumption of a short period and the income of the same period. "The rate of consumption in any period is a facet of a plan which extends over the balance of the individual's life, while the income accruing within the same period is but one element which contributes to the shaping of such a plan."[46] His saving in a given period is proportionate to the accustomed level of his income in that period, i.e. proportionate only on average to the consumer's basic earning capacity in the given period. This statement is analogous to the one made by Friedman, namely, that the relationship between permanent income and permanent consumption is constant.

But what will happen when the current income unexpectedly rises above the earlier accustomed level? Saving will rise either because the consumer deems that the change is only transitory, or because he expects that the increase in his

[41] M. Friedman: *op. cit.*, p. 222.

[42] M. Friedman: *op. cit.*, p. 221.

[43] M. Friedman: *op. cit.*, p. 223.

[44] M. R. Dorly: Postwar U. S. Consumption, Consumers Expenditures and Saving, *The American Review*, May 1975, p. 218.

[45] F. Modigliani and R. Brumberg: Utility Analysis and the Consumption Function: An Interpretation of Cross-Section Data. In: *Post-Keynesian Economics*, (Ed. by K. K. Kurihara), New Brunswick, 1954, p. 430.

[46] F. Modigliani and R. Brumberg: *op. cit.*, p. 392.

income will be a steady one, and in this case his assets are "too low to enable the household to live for the rest of its expected life on a scale commensurate with the new level of income..."[47] He will increase the stock of his assets by increasing his savings. Otherwise, when his income decreases, he will cut his savings or consume his accumulated wealth, i.e. he will carry out dissaving in order to fulfil his optimal consumption plan which is in accordance with the new situation.

The life-cycle hypothesis of savings allows the transitory component of income a certain slight degree of direct effect on current consumption, and in this respect it somewhat differs from Friedman's theory.

The elasticity of consumption with respect to income is also a function of the consumer's age. This elasticity decreases with age. According to Modigliani and Brumberg, if the consumer deems the increase in his current income to be permanent, then in his more advanced age he has to make great efforts to increase his savings, and through them his wealth, if he is to enjoy a higher income in retirement. Young people, however, when their income increases to a permanently higher level, tend to spend more on consumption because of the greater number of years over which the higher level of income will be received.

With respect to the attempts further to develop the consumption function, we must make the same objection as we have made with respect to the Keynesian saving function. The followers of the theory think that by analysing consumer behaviour they can account for changes in saving; however, most of the savings are made not upon consumer considerations but exclusively on business considerations. As regards the business savings of the capitalist class, it can hardly be stated that the richer the family, the lesser its claim to increase its wealth. And even if most people strive to create a reserve fund to ensure themselves against possible falls in income, or against unforeseeable expenses, yet, as Katona remarks, "many people in their forties and fifties appear to have given some thought, often considerable thought, to the questions of what they will do and how they will find the means to satisfy their needs during retirement."[48]

Moreover, the theories of consumer behaviour as discussed above are trying to disclose characteristics of a general consumer behaviour which is independent of class relations. Non-Marxian critique too is aware of the inadequacy of assuming indiscriminately identical preferences concerning present and future consumption for families with lower and higher incomes alike. "... it is also of crucial importance for saving habits whether what is involved is wage or profit income."[49] Life-cycle saving does not occur with every social stratum and, in addition, also depends on the prevailing social relations and institutions, on the fact, for example, how developed in a given society national insurance is. Further, for the allocation of the transitory part of income to consumption or saving, or to buying capital assets, the social position of the consumer is of vital importance. Obviously, the way in which a worker and a capitalist uses his unexpected income is different. Criticizing Friedman's theory, Bodkin refers to the jump in consumer demand caused by the once for all rent paid to American veterans in 1950. The American veterans spent this unexpected rise in their income almost completely on buying consumer goods.[50]

[47] F. Modigliani and R. Brumberg: *op. cit.*, p. 407.
[48] G. Katona: *op. cit.*, p. 188.
[49] K. Oppenländer: *Die moderne Wachstumstheorie*, Berlin–München, 1963, p. 109.
[50] See R. Bodkin: Windfall Income and Consumption, *The American Economic Review*, 1959, Vol. 49.

Chapter 4

INVESTMENT

Investment has a central role to play in Keynes's theoretical system. "The *General Theory* devotes a whole Book to the Inducement to Invest," writes Shackle.[51] At the important points, Keynes regards demand for investment as the basic element of aggregate demand. As a result of investment, aggregate demand and within it the demand for consumer goods grow, and so does employment, too. "... increased employment for investment must necessarily stimulate the industries producing for consumption and thus lead to a total increase of employment which is a multiple of the primary employment required by the investment itself."[52]

"... the expectation of an increased excess of Investment over Saving... will induce entrepreneurs to increase employment and output."[53]

The central role of investment in Keynes reflects a real relationship, namely, that at the macro-level surplus value is embodied primarily in investment goods and is realized therefore by the entrepreneurs' investments. Consequently, it is investment demand that stimulates capitalist production.

What does Keynes understand by investment? "... current investment is equal to the value of that part of current output which is not consumed..."[54] "Investment... consists of fixed capital, working capital or liquid capital..."[55] Keynes's definition of investment also subsumes under the concept of investment unintended changes in inventories, and this is precisely which Keynes means by liquid capital. With investment thus interpreted, we must emphasize that it is only the intended investment of the capitalist class which realizes surplus value. True, that part of the national income which is piled up in the form of unsold inventories in the entrepreneurs' warehouses *is* surplus value, too in that it is an amount of value created by labour but never enjoyed by the working class, yet it is not realized surplus value.

What in Keynes stimulates investment? In making their investment decisions, entrepreneurs compare the capitalized market value of investment goods with their supply price or more exactly, with their replacement cost. Capitalized market value is the value discounted at the current rate of interest of the expected net yields of

[51] G. L. Shackle: Keynes and Today's Establishment in Economic Theory: A View, *The Journal of Economic Literature*, June 1973, p. 516.

[52] J. M. Keynes: *The General Theory of Employment, Interest and Money*, p. 118.

[53] J. M. Keynes: *op. cit.*, p. 78.

[54] J. M. Keynes: *op. cit.*, p. 63.

[55] J. M. Keynes: *op. cit.*, p. 75.

capital. If this net value exceeds the supply price of the capital good, it is profitable to invest. Put another way, looking at the motive stimulating investment, Keynes maintains that we must find the discount rate which equates the expected net yields of capital with the supply price of the capital good in question. Keynes calls this discount rate, i.e. the rate of the expected net return over the supply price of the capital good, *marginal efficiency of capital*. He borrowed the concept from Irving Fisher. The marginal efficiency of capital differs from the marginal productivity of capital as commonly interpreted. According to Keynes, economists generally represent the marginal productivity of capital in a static way, basing it on the current return on capital, while they describe the net present value as capitalized current return. In other words, they assumed that the prospective return on capital equalled the yield of capital in the present, "... there is no changing future to influence the present...",[56] that is, the entrepreneur made his investments in the expectation of certain profits. Using the concept of the marginal efficiency of capital, Keynes wanted to show that since investment takes place over time and is completed in the future, the entrepreneur's investment decisions are governed by uncertain expectations of prospective yields. "The outstanding fact is the precariousness of the basis of knowledge on which our estimates of prospective yield have to be made. Our knowledge of the factors which will govern the yield of an investment some years hence is usually very slight and often negligible."[57] The uncertainty of the future influences the present in Keynes mainly through the marginal efficiency of capital. The investment decisions are made difficult not only by the uncertain expectations of prospective yields, but also by the frequent changes in these expectations over time, since they cannot be checked before the investments are completed. The uncertainty and variability concerning the prospective yields of investment are, according to Keynes, increased by the growing role of the Stock Exchange in investment decisions. There are people who spend large sums on new establishments only to sell them at the Stock Exchange. Certain investments are governed not by the real expectations of professional entrepreneurs but rather by those of speculators. And Keynes points to the increasing danger that with the further refinement of the organization of investment markets, speculation will get the advantage over realistic investments. Thus in a capitalist economy left to itself, the volume of investment is "subject to the vagaries of the marginal efficiency of capital as determined by the private judgement of individuals ignorant or speculative..."[58]

In Keynes's view, in the course of continuous investment "the marginal efficiency... of capital will diminish...;"[59] thus he takes over from marginal productivity theory the principle of diminishing returns, which means that the entrepreneur will invest until the marginal efficiency of capital falls to the level of the rate of interest. Thus in his system investment is a function of the marginal efficiency of capital and of the rate of interest.

In the chapters of his *General Theory* on interest Keynes mentions the uncertainty and instability of the marginal efficiency of capital and the long-term inflexibility

56 J. M. Keynes: *op. cit.*, p. 145.
57 J. M. Keynes: *op. cit.*, p. 149.
58 J. M. Keynes: *op. cit.*, pp. 324–325.
59 J. M. Keynes: *op. cit.*, p. 136.

of the interest rate as factors preventing investment from attaining a level needed to establish full employment. According to Leijonhufvud, Keynes does not believe in the efficiency of monetary policy because of the inflexibility of the long-term rate of interest.[60] In the *General Theory*, however, we can also find statements to the effect that even flexibility of the rate of interest could not offset the un-favourable state of the marginal efficiency of capital and in this case monetary policy alone, on account of the interest-inelasticity of investment, is not effective. "... during the downward phase," he writes, "... the schedule of the marginal efficiency of capital may fall so low that it can scarcely be corrected, so as to secure a satisfactory rate of new investment, by any practicable reduction in the rate of interest."[61] In another place: "... the collapse in the marginal efficiency of capital may be so complete that no practicable reduction in the rate of interest will be enough."[62] The rate of interest exercises "... in normal circumstances, a great though not a decisive, influence on the rate of investment."[63] "... the fluctuations in the market estimation of the marginal efficiency of different types of capital... will be too great to be offset by any practicable changes in the rate of interest."[64] He explains the trade cycle, unlike Wicksell, not by the fact that the banks adjust the market interest rate to the natural interest rate belatedly. He simply asserts that "the Trade Cycle is best regarded... as being occasioned by a cyclical change in the marginal efficiency of capital..."[65]

There can be no doubt about it that with unchanged profit prospects a low level of the rate of interest may stimulate investment. But in a phase of depression, when profit expectations steadily deteriorate, and the danger arises that entre-preneurs will not only not realize any profit on their investments but not even recover their costs, monetary policy cannot, even with a flexible rate of interest, bring the decline to a halt and start a recovery. If we follow the Keynesian train of thought against the assumption that monetary policy is able to realize full employment given a flexible rate of interest, we can say that if the marginal efficiency of capital is low at the very outset, then in the course of continuous investment, the marginal efficiency of capital will reach even a rate of interest reduced by monetary policy at a much lower level of investment than that needed to achieve full employment.

Keynes analyses the role of investment in the short run and takes into account only the income-increasing effect of investment, namely how investment outlays can also expand consumption. This gave rise to criticisms raised first by Domar. It should be noted, however, that Keynes becomes occasionally aware of the fact that completed investments increase serious troubles in capitalist economy. Thus he mentions that in the developed capitalist economies the propensity to consume is low, and therefore a great many investments are needed to compensate for the loss in aggregate demand from savings. With the investments completed, however, the accumulated stock of capital is growing, which worsens profit expectations:

[60] See A. Leijonhufvud: *On Keynesian Economics and the Economics of Keynes*, New York–London–Toronto, 1968, p. 42.
[61] J. M. Keynes: *op. cit.*, pp. 319–320.
[62] J. M. Keynes: *op. cit.*, p. 316.
[63] J. M. Keynes: *op. cit.*, p. 164.
[64] J. M. Keynes: *op. cit.*, p. 164.
[65] J. M. Keynes: *op. cit.*, p. 313.

"Not only is the marginal propensity to consume weaker in a wealthy community, but, owing to its accumulation of capital being already larger, the opportunities for further investment are less attractive...,"[66] and thus it becomes ever more difficult to find new investment opportunities. As if forestalling Domar, he asserts that "... each time we secure to-day's equilibrium by increased investment, we are aggravating the difficulty of securing equilibrium tomorrow,"[67] and full of anxiety for the future, he raises the question of what will happen when the stock of capital is so large that demand will be saturated. This question—says Keynes— has been raised so far only in connection with public investments. " 'What will you do', it is asked, 'when you have built all the houses and roads and town halls and electric grids and water supplies and so forth which the stationary population of the future can be expected to require?' "[68] In Keynes's opinion, however, "... the same difficulty applies to private investment and to industrial expansion."[69] In actual fact, however, since in the course of economic development population and with it wants too are increasing, no danger exists that investments will reach a stage when the needs of the population are all satisfied. Keynes may have come to this conclusion when, having realized the capacity-expanding effect of investments, he gave up the assumption that the volume of capital stock was a datum, while continuing to maintain unchanged the other data of his model such as consumers' needs, population, the level of technical knowledge, distribution relations, etc.

When completed, the investments come into conflict with the capitalists' profit interests. With the utilization of increased capacities, the supply of consumer goods would grow. And since consumer goods embody surplus value on the macro-level only to a small extent, the lion's share of demand in the market of consumer goods being represented, owing to its very size, by the working class, the increase in the supply of consumer goods, unless it is offset by increased investment, diminishes the rate of realized surplus value, decreasing the profit margin realized in the product price. If, however, in order to avoid that, entrepreneurs do not fully utilize the increased capacities, investments will be discouraged. This is the Marxist explanation of the problem raised by Keynes of why capital accumulation, increased as a result of investments completed earlier, deteriorates the profit expectations of further investments. The recognition that increased capital accumulation, as a consequence of earlier, completed investments, diminishes the rate of realized profit and reduces expected profits, induces Keynes to distinguish between produced and realized profit when he asserts: "if capital becomes less scarce, the excess yield will diminish, without its having become less productive—at least, in the physical sense."[70] On the other hand, it compels him to adopt a very superficial interpretation of the source of profit. He sees the source of profit simply in the scarcity of capital goods. "... the only reason why an asset offers a prospect of yielding during its life services having an aggregate value greater than its initial supply price is because it is scarce..."[71]

[66] J. M. Keynes: *op. cit.*, p. 31.
[67] J. M. Keynes: *op. cit.*, p. 105.
[68] J. M. Keynes: *op. cit.*, p. 106.
[69] *Ibid.*
[70] J. M. Keynes: *op. cit.*, p. 213.
[71] *Ibid.*

Profit expectations, the assessment of how future effective demand will change in response to future supply, are completely indeterminate in Keynes. He classes the marginal efficiency of capital among the independent variables of his theoretical system. In this way, he involuntarily adopts the point of view of individual capitalists who are not in a position to control the expected profit on their investments. Thus the view he adopts on the question of expectations lags far behind the approach taken by the Swedish economists who attempt at least to fit expectations as determinable factors into their theoretical systems. Shackle blames Keynes because in his system the "expectations do not rest on anything solid, determinable, demonstrable."[72]

But if investments are so greatly dependent on a number of unpredictable elements of the economic system, on exogenous factors, then no stable investment function can be constructed. Consequently, the point of intersection of the aggregate demand and supply curves cannot be unambiguous, apart from the difficulties arising from the construction of the consumption function, due to the instability of the investment function. Depending on changes in the entrepreneurs' profit expectations, we may get different points of intersection.

In connection with Keynes's investment theory, we still have to add that he does not consistently stand by his statement that investment demand constitutes the decisive element of aggregate demand. Occasionally, he appears to defend the position that the low level of investment demand could be offset by increasing consumer demand. "If it is impracticable," he writes, "materially to increase investment, obviously there is no means of securing a higher level of employment except by increasing consumption."[73]

KEYNES'S REPRESENTATION OF THE RELATIONSHIP BETWEEN SAVING AND INVESTMENT

In Keynes's view, each individual is supposed to be free to make savings irrespective of his own or other people's investments. But society as a whole can, in his view, save neither more nor less than what entrepreneurs wish to invest. This view is opposed to that of the neo-classical school, and makes Say's dogma untenable. It was a postulate of the neo-classical model that saving automatically becomes investment, and thus demand grows together with output. In contradistinction, Mrs. Robinson stresses that "if saving directly caused investment, it would be very difficult to see how unemployment could possibly occur."[74]

For Keynes, saving alone cannot create investment. Approaching the relationships from the aspect of realization, of demand, he came to the conclusion that in order to save, we have first to realize the income made, which in turn necessitates an appropriate demand. The demand needed to realize intended saving is created by investment. Consequently, if there is no sufficiently strong inducement to invest, the intended saving of society cannot come into being. This follows from the simple

[72] G. L. Shackle: Keynes and Today's Establishment in Economic Theory, *The Journal of Economic Literature*, June 1972, p. 516.

[73] J. M. Keynes: *op. cit.*, p. 325.

[74] J. Robinson: *Introduction to the Theory of Employment*, London, 1937, p. 14.

fact that "… there cannot be a buyer without a seller or a seller without a buyer."[75] He who saves, will buy less than he sells. Obviously, everybody cannot save all at the same time. Some people can afford to sell more than they buy, because there are people who buy more than they sell. Those individuals, for example, who spend not only the money they received for their commodities sold but also their earlier savings, make it possible for others to save. But in this case society cannot save anything, since the savings of individuals are offset at a social level by the dissavings of others, i.e. the spending of earlier savings. Investment creates a demand until it is completed, without the investors taking commodities to the market. Investment makes it possible for certain individuals in society to sell more than they buy, that is, for saving to be effected also on a social plane. Should society wish to save more than it invests, total demand will be less than the volume of net output, and the income of certain people will therefore decrease, they will save less than the level they intended to reach, and the social volume of saving will drop to the level of investment. "Every such attempt to save more [in relation to investment—A. M.] by reducing consumption will so affect incomes that the attempt necessarily defeats itself."[76]

Neo-classical economics maintains that increased saving will appear through the network of credit as increased credit supply, which in turn, by reducing the rate of interest, will stimulate investment; it will be clear from the above that this reasoning is incorrect. Without appropriate investment, intended saving cannot materialize.

Nor can society save less than it invests. Otherwise, it would want to consume more than the amount of consumer goods offered for sale, and the rising price of consumer goods would reduce consumer demand to the volume of supply, and raise effective saving thereby to the level of investment. "… the extent of effective saving is necessarily determined by the scale of investment…"[77]

Thus saving is always *equal* to investment for Keynes, who defined both of them as being parts of the national income not used for private consumption. Society does not require commodities for consumption purposes to the extent of saving and thus he regards the commodity not consumed as investment. What is invested, however, cannot be consumed from the national income, it must therefore be saved.

From the constant equality of saving and investment follows the problem of how saving can nevertheless deviate from investment in Keynesian analysis: how he can assert that unemployment takes place because investment is seldom stimulated to reach the level of savings which society wishes to make out of its income at full employment.

The solution to the problem was provided by the Swedish economists who, by analogy with price theory, distinguished, in respect of saving and investment, between *equality* and *equilibrium*. In the market, demand and supply are always equal in the sense that total sales and total purchases are always equal. But demand and supply are not always in equilibrium. It is obvious—to use the Marxist terminology—that if demand is equated with supply by a price which is either higher

[75] J. M. Keynes: *op. cit.*, p. 85.
[76] J. M. Keynes: *op. cit.*, p. 84.
[77] J. M. Keynes: *op. cit.*, p. 375.

or lower than the social production price, equality does not mean equilibrium. It does not mean equilibrium because a market price differing from social production price stimulates an increase or a decrease in output.

Similarly, saving and investment, according to the Swedish economists, are always equal, but not always in equilibrium. The members of society may have wished to save more or less at the given level of the national income than the entrepreneurs' intended investment. In this case, despite their equality, there is no equilibrium between saving and investment. Keynes does not make any distinction between them. In demonstrating the equality of saving and investment he either points out their actual equality, or refers to their being in equilibrium. The merging of equality with equilibrium follows in Keynes from the fact that his method of analysis is that of comparative statics. He focuses on equilibrium positions and skips the intermediate positions. In order to demonstrate the difference between equality and equilibrium, the Swedish economists—in much the same way as in respect of demand and supply—also distinguish, in relation to saving and investment, between *ex-ante* and *ex-post* magnitudes. *Ex-ante* saving and investment are the intended volume of saving and investment, and *ex-post* saving and investment are actually materialized saving and investment. Hence saving and investment are always equal *ex-post,* but it is not sure that they are equal magnitudes *ex-ante,* too. *Ex-post* saving and investment contain unintended as well as intended saving and investment.

The question is how the Swedish economists demonstrate the equality of *ex-post* saving and investment by introducing the concept of unintended saving and investment. Their approach is of a double nature. With a given level of national income, if there is a difference between intended saving and intended investment (or between aggregate demand price and aggregate supply price), then either the price level or the volume of inventories may be treated as variable.

Let us examine the first case. If, at a given level of national income, the entrepreneurs' intended investment exceeds society's intended saving, then society wishes to spend more than the total cost of national income including normal profit. It is the rise in the price level which restricts consumption to the limits of output, and equates demand with supply. As a result of a rise in the price level, entrepreneurs will realize a profit which is larger than the expected one. "The business man who, after the closing of his accounts, finds that he has had a larger net income than he expected and that therefore the surplus over and above his consumption is greater than his planned savings, had provided 'unintentional savings' which are equal to this extra surplus."[78] Contrarily, if, at a given level of the national income, the entrepreneurs' intended investment lags behind society's intended saving, and thus society wishes to spend less than the aggregate supply price of the national income, the price level will fall, which will ensure the realization of the whole quantity of output, equating demand with supply. The resulting consequences have already been dealt with. The entrepreneurs' income will fall below the expected level, and their actual saving will lag behind their planned saving. Because of this unintended dissaving, the actual, *ex-post* saving of society will be equal to intended investment.

---

[78] B. Ohlin: Some Notes on the Stockholm Theory of Savings and Investment. In: *Readings in Business Cycle Theory,* Philadelphia–Toronto, 1951, p. 101.

The fall of actual saving to the level of intended investment means that the Swedish economists assumed that intended investment always materialized, and a deviation was possible only between *ex-ante* and *ex-post* saving in the form of unintended saving.

The *ex-post* equality of saving and investment appears to be different if, at a given level of the national income, when there is a deviation between intended saving and intended investment (and thus between the aggregate demand price and the aggregate supply price), supply adapts through changes in inventories to the amount which society intends to spend. Such a case may arise, for example, if monopolies fix the price. In this case, when consumer demand and investment together do not reach the volume of the national income already produced, that is, part of the national income is not consumed by society and entrepreneurs themselves do not want to invest it either, then society may not save more in money than investment, but the unconsumed part of real income which piles up as unsaleable stock in the entrepreneurs' warehouses will increase their inventories. This increase in inventories is not intended investment. Intended investment below intended saving has now produced unintentional investment, and the sum of intended and unintended investment, i.e. *ex-post* investment, is equal to intended saving. If, however, at a given level of the national income, intended investment exceeds intended saving, the aggregate demand price surpasses supply price, "... the increase in sales ... has been attended by a contraction in stocks...,"[79] without any price rise, "... the result will... be an unintentional disinvestment..."[80] and the difference between intended and unintended investment will result in *ex-post* investment equal to intended saving.

In the cases now discussed intended saving materializes, and intended investment is not realized, in that entrepreneurs wish to invest more or less than the unconsumed quantity of the real income.

With unintended investment included, it turns out that the Keynesian proposition according to which the volume of investment determines the volume of saving, applies to intended investment. Keynes does not know the concepts of unintended saving and investment. As has already been mentioned, his explorations are directed towards equilibrium positions, and in such positions no unintended investment and unintended saving can occur.

Examining further the relation of investment to saving in Keynes, we find that the approach to the problem is determined by breaking away from the neo-classical view, which maintains that the automatic adjustments of the capitalist economy ensure that aggregate demand grows together with aggregate supply, and full employment is realized. The confrontation of the state of the economy under full and underemployment runs through his whole work. He maintains that those theses of economics which are valid at full employment lose their validity at underemployment. He calls neo-classical economics *Euclidean* economics, since they set up their propositions under the assumption of full employment. Keynes wishes to create a *general* theoretical system in the sense that "... we need... to work out

[79] E. Lindahl: *Studies in the Theory of Money and Capital*, London, 1939, p. 132.
[80] *Ibid.*

the behaviour of a system in which involuntary unemployment in the strict sense is possible."[81]

He agrees with neo-classical economics in the assumption that at full employment investment can be increased without inflation only if society increases its savings, i.e. decreases its consumption. "... in conditions of full employment a low propensity to consume is conducive to the growth of capital."[82] If in conditions of full employment intended investment exceeded intended saving, the aggregate demand in excess of aggregate supply would cause inflation. "When full employment is reached, any attempt to increase investment still further will set up a tendency in money-prices to rise without limit; i.e. we shall have reached a state of true inflation."[83] But in this case too the proposition will remain valid, namely, that investment enables savings to be made, and society has always to save as much as the amount of intended investment.

At underemployment, however, "... up to the point where full employment prevails, the growth of capital depends not at all on a low propensity to consume..."[84] Investment, and with it consumer demand, may grow without any danger of inflation arising. If, however, in conditions of underemployment, society's intended saving increases, this will decrease the demand for consumer goods and will not stimulate but discourage investment. Thereby "... the act of saving will not merely depress the price of consumption-goods and leave the efficiency of existing capital unaffected, but may actually tend to depress the latter also. In this event it may reduce present investment-demand as well as present consumption-demand."[85]

The Keynesian statement that intended saving does not automatically change into intended investment, undermined the attempt of neo-classical reasoning to prove the necessity of unequal income distribution. The neo-classical view held that large-scale inequalities in distribution relations were favourable for the economy as they increased the volume of saving. If, however, intended saving, given full employment, exceeds the volume of intended investment—and this is what Keynes holds to be the source of the serious ills of advanced capitalist countries—it is not the wealth but the poverty of society, i.e. unemployment, which grows. Translating Keynes's statements into Marxist terminology, if the spendings of the capitalist class do not reach the level of the surplus value produced, then part of it remains unrealized, which will in turn exercise an unfavourable impact on output.

[81] J. M. Keynes: *op. cit.*, p. 17.
[82] J. M. Keynes: *op. cit.*, p. 373.
[83] J. M. Keynes: *op. cit.*, pp. 118–119.
[84] J. M. Keynes: *op. cit.*, pp. 372–373.
[85] J. M. Keynes: *op. cit.*, p. 210.

Chapter 5

THE DETERMINATION OF THE EQUILIBRIUM LEVEL OF NATIONAL INCOME—THE MULTIPLIER EFFECT

According to Keynes, saving in a non-Euclidean economy is not a real condition of investment. For investment to increase, saving need not release factors of production from the sphere of production for consumer goods as they are available in excess quantities. By utilizing excess factors, the output of investment goods can be increased without curbing the output of consumer goods.

But those engaged in the production of investment goods wish now that income accrues to them to devote part of their income to buying consumer goods. Since their own products cannot be consumed, society has to provide through its savings the consumer goods they need. As a result of raising the level of investment above the level of saving, the output of investment goods and the number of those employed in the investment-goods industries will in the Keynesian model just as in that of Wicksell's rise out of proportion to the output of consumer goods and to the number of workers employed in them. Consumer demand will exceed the supply of consumer goods. But in Keynes's non-Euclidean world it is possible for consumer goods output to be increased. As output increases, incomes and the savings designed to be made from them are also increasing. Thus investment itself, given partial employment, will create, through the increase in the national income, a corresponding intended saving. "... the savings which result from this decision are just as genuine as any other savings."[86] As a result of the adjustment of the output of consumer goods to increased demand, the required proportions will be established in the distribution of the labour force between industries producing consumer goods and investment goods.

This process, represented by a numerical example, takes place in the following manner. Let the size of the national income be 1,000, and of intended investment and intended saving therefrom 300 and 200, respectively. Thus the savings ratio will be $\frac{1}{5}$. Employment is partial, the labour force needed for investment exceeding intended saving is available, and thus the 300 units of investment can be realized. At a national income of 1,000, society would like to spend 800 on buying consumer goods, but their supply is only 700. Savings and investment are equal *ex-post,* since society, given a national income of 1,000, is unable to consume more than 700; it has to save 300, or, if inventories are decreased by 100, actual investment will be 100 less than intended investment, i.e. just equal to saving. Demand exceeding supply by 100, or the decrease of 100 in inventories, stimulates entre-

[86] J. M. Keynes: *op. cit.,* p. 83.

367

preneurs to increase the output of consumer goods. Since employment is partial, on Keynesian assumption, output can be expanded. Thus entrepreneurs will increase the production and the supply of consumer goods by 100. Yet the demand for and the supply of consumer goods will not be in equilibrium because, as the output of consumer goods rises, employment in the production of consumer goods, and hence incomes and consumer demand, will also increase. Incomes, according to Keynes, have also risen by 100, $\frac{4}{5}$ of which society wishes to devote to buying consumer goods. Even though the supply of consumer goods has increased from 700 to 800, the demand for them has also risen from 800 to 880. The output and supply of consumer goods will be further increased by 80, but as a result of the additional income, consumer demand will also rise by 64. "Thus their [the community's— A. M.] effort to consume a part of their increased incomes will stimulate output..."[87]

The Keynesian problem is this: to what extent must output be expanded so that community should wish to devote an amount of the national income thus produced to buying consumer goods equal to their supply, that is, so that the supply of consumer goods should catch up with the demand for them. Or, put another way, to what extent should output be increased so that society should desire to save as much of the national income thus produced as entrepreneurs wish to invest.

At a $\frac{1}{5}$ propensity to save society wishes to devote $\frac{4}{5}$ of the national income to buying consumer goods. Thus, in equilibrium, $\frac{4}{5} Y$ must be equal to the supply of consumer goods, $Y—I$.

$$\frac{4}{5}Y = Y—I,$$

$$Y\left(1—\frac{4}{5}\right) = I,$$

$$Y = \frac{1}{1—\frac{4}{5}} \cdot I.$$

$1—\frac{4}{5}$ is the savings ratio, and therefore

$$Y = \frac{1}{s} \cdot I.$$

The same solution can also be reached as follows: Y has already been determined as $C+I$.

Let us express C as $(1—s)Y$. Substituting: $(1—s)Y+I = Y$. From which $sY = I$, and thus $I\frac{1}{s} = Y$. From the equation $C+I = Y$ we can now deduce the equation

$$I\frac{1}{s} = Y.$$

[87] J. M. Keynes: *op. cit.*, p. 117.

Keynes determines the equilibrium level of the national income by multiplying the amount of intended investment by the reciprocal of the savings ratio. In our example $Y = 300 \cdot 5 = 1,500$.

Out of 1,500 national income society wishes to spend 1,200 on buying consumer goods, and their supply is also $1,200 = 1,500—300$. Or, out of 1,500 national income society wishes to save 300 at a savings ratio of $\dfrac{1}{5}$, the same quantity as entrepreneurs intend to invest. Thus 1,500 is the equilibrium level of the national income. Along with it, aggregate demand and aggregate supply, intended saving and intended investment are also in equilibrium. Or, if the task is to determine the increment of the national income, then intended investment, assuming 1,000 national income, will exceed intended saving by 100, $\Delta I = 100; 100 \cdot \dfrac{1}{s} = 500$.

When the national income is increased by 500, out of this increment of income society wishes to save 100, which makes intended saving equal to intended investment.

The reciprocal of the savings ratio by which investment, or the increment in investment, has to be multiplied in order to obtain the equilibrium level of the national income, or the increment in the national income needed to reach the equilibrium level, is called the *multiplier*. In essence, the multiplier effect expresses in Keynes that if intended saving and intended investment differ from each other, it is intended saving that has to be adjusted to intended investment. But at a given savings ratio or marginal savings ratio, intended saving is a function of the amount of the national income. Thus the adjustment of intended saving to intended investment can only take place through changes in the national income. "The multiplier tells us by how much their employment has to be increased to yield an increase in real income sufficient to induce them to do the necessary extra saving..."[88]

Keynes concerns himself primarily with the investment multiplier, but it appears that he also touches upon the problem of the employment multiplier: "... increased employment for investment must ... lead to a total increase of employment which is a multiple of the primary employment required by the investment itself."[89]

Keynes raises the question of what will happen when intended investment exceeds intended saving in conditions of full employment. After full employment is reached, intended investment in excess of intended saving can no longer result in an increase in output but will lead to inflation.[90]

When intended saving exceeds intended investment, the multiplier effect will realize the equilibrium between them through a decrease in output, national income and employment. Let us assume that full employment is reached at 1,500 national income, the social savings ratio is $\frac{1}{5}$, and the amount of saving is 300. Entrepreneurs, however, want to invest only 200. The national income has to fall to 1,000, and with it employment too, for the two intentions to be in equilibrium.

The mechanism is entirely different from that described by the neo-classical economists. It may be clear from what has been set out above, what the decisive

[88] J. M. Keynes: *op. cit.*, p. 117.
[89] J. M. Keynes: *op. cit.*, p. 118.
[90] See J. M. Keynes: *op. cit.*, pp. 118–119.

difference is between the views held by Keynes and the neo-classical economists. In the neo-classical model, in the case of a deviation, it is the movement of the interest rate which equalizes the intended saving of society and the intended investment of entrepreneurs and through it aggregate demand and aggregate supply. But the equilibrium between aggregate demand and aggregate supply is reached at full employment, because changes in wages prevent employment from decreasing if there is a deviation between aggregate demand and aggregate supply. When an equilibrium position is reached, the only change is in the division of aggregate demand and aggregate supply into the demand for and the supply of consumer goods and investment goods respectively. Thus in the neo-classical model the multiplier effect is missing. In Wicksell, owing to the credit policy of banks, investment can lastingly deviate from saving, aggregate demand from aggregate supply. But total employment will be maintained even in the cumulative process. Cyclical movements will take place not in output, in employment, but in *price*. In Keynes, in the case of a deviation between intended saving and intended investment, and through it between aggregate demand and aggregate supply, since in his system the wage mechanism does not ensure full employment, it is national income that has to decrease or increase, except for the extreme case when intended investment exceeds intended saving at full employment. In Keynes, it is the *change in output, employment, national income* that brings about, through the multiplier effect, an equality between intended saving and intended investment and thereby between the aggregate demand price and the aggregate supply price. As a result of the working of the multiplier effect, equilibrium of intended saving and intended investment can be established in the goods market even in conditions of underemployment. This implies that *the demand for and the supply of commodities can be in equilibrium without an equilibrium on the labour market*. This is quite inconceivable in the neo-classical model. The pressure of the unemployed decreases wages, entrepreneurs increase employment and output and the supply of commodities cannot therefore stop expanding as long as unemployment exists.

Owing to the multiplier effect, the relationship between saving and the rate of interest appears in Keynes to be just the contrary of what it is in the neo-classical model. In the neo-classical model, saving is stimulated by a rise in the interest rate, and discouraged by a fall. In Keynes's model, however, intended saving adjusts itself, through the multiplier effect, to intended investment. Taking the profit prospects to be constant, a fall in the interest rate stimulates investment, and, as a result of the increase in the national income, intended saving must grow. A rise in the rate of interest, however, by discouraging investment, leads to a decrease in national income and through it in saving.

Going further into this difference between Keynes and the neo-classical economists, we must mention that, irrespective of whether employment is full or not, saving does not constitute a condition of credit supply and hence of investment financing. The modern banking system is not simply a credit-granting institution. Exploring the modern banking system, Schneider asserts that it is not savings that banks grant as credits. "Increased saving is therefore not an indispensable condition of granting new credits."[91] "New credits are granted not from occasionally

_____

[91] E. Schneider: *Einführung in die Weltwirtschaftstheorie*, III, Tübingen, 1957, p. 60.

available amounts of money, but from new giro money created by the bank itself."[92] If in a non-Euclidean economy entrepreneurs receive bank credits in excess of the amount of intended saving, there is no need to assume that a Wicksellian cumulative process will set in. As has already been mentioned, an investment exceeding intended saving creates ın the non-Euclidean world of Keynes an intended saving which is equal to investment.

IS THE SAVING–INVESTMENT EQUILIBRIUM A CONDITION OF THE EQUILIBRIUM OF REPRODUCTION?

As we have already seen, in the determination of the equilibrium level of output (employment) the question of the saving–investment equilibrium plays a crucial role in the Keynesian system: those who save and those who invest are different, and the two intentions are not co-ordinated, since consumer saving is a function of the national income, and the investments of entrepreneurs depend on profit expectations and on the interest rate.

Does the equilibrium of saving and investment, as a central question of the Keynesian model, really reflect a sort of equilibrium condition for the process of capitalist reproduction?

It does reflect it, even if not in the form presented by Keynes. According to him, society as a whole effects saving. In Marx's reproduction schemes it is the capitalist alone who saves part of the surplus value. And in Marx's presentation, the capitalist invests the whole of the surplus value saved. It appears that intended saving and intended investment always coincide in Marx.

In reality, however, the two intentions are not co-ordinated in the Marxian reproduction theory either. They may deviate from one another. Marx points out that the individual capitalists have to store up part of the surplus value designed to be invested in money form over several periods of the reproduction process until it reaches the necessary level. But surplus value not spent will decrease total demand. The problem continues to exist even if the capitalist raises the amount of money needed for investment in the form of credits. In this event, he has to save part of the surplus value to repay his credits. In Marx, it constitutes the equilibrium condition of reproduction that those capitalists who, owing to their past savings, are carrying out an actual expansion of reproduction, shall invest an amount equal to that part of the realized surplus value which other capitalists have set aside in the form of money. Assuming the equality of selling and buying, Marx announces that it is investments made by certain capitalists that enable others to store up part of their surplus value in money form. "Money is withdrawn from circulation and stored up as a hoard by selling commodities without subsequent buying. If this operation is therefore conceived as a general process, it seems inexplicable where the buyers are to come from, since in that process everybody would want to sell in order to hoard, and none would want to buy. And it must be conceived generally, since every individual capital may be in the process of accumulation."[93] And Marx's answer is this: "Some are still in the stage of hoarding, and sell without

[92] *Ibid.*
[93] K. Marx: *Capital*, Vol. II, Moscow, 1957, p. 491.

buying; the others are on the point of actual expansion of reproduction, and buy without selling."[94] In Marx's presentation, contrary to Keynes's, the investments of individual capitalists make saving possible not for the members of society in general, but enable other capitalists to pile up in money form part of the surplus value designed to be invested.

But there is no guarantee in Marx either that those capitalists who wish to use their savings from the surplus value for the expansion of reproduction will invest to the same extent to which other capitalists want to save part of the surplus value for the purpose of an investment to be made at a later point of time. Given a deviation of the two intentions, the equilibrium of reproduction will be upset. If the capitalists of department I sell more to the capitalists of department II than they buy from them, part of the commodities of department II will remain unsold. "Formation of virtual additional money-capital in class I (hence under-consumption from the point of view of II); the piling up of commodity supplies in class II which cannot be reconverted into productive capital (hence relative over-production in II); surplus of money-capital in I and reproduction deficit in II."[95]

Later, in conditions of monopoly capitalism, a substantial part of saving is effected by parasitic, coupon-clipping capitalists, while investments are made by entrepreneurs. Their intentions are likewise not co-ordinated.

If depreciation is in excess of replacement, this also constitutes a fall in the purchasing power in much the same way as saving exceeding investment. Marx regarded the equilibrium of depreciation and replacement also as a condition of proportionate reproduction. Here again the problem arises out of the fact that with those capitalists who are now replacing the whole of their capital assets, the volume of replacement coincides only occasionally with the money set aside by other capitalists for such replacements as are due to be made later.[96] When, however, the two deviate from one another, the equilibrium of demand and supply will be upset. The question also occurs in Keynes when he points out that depreciation is equalled by replacement only in a stationary economy. In a dynamic economy, however, the stock of capital is quickly expanding. "In the United States" this "... had led to the setting up of sinking funds and depreciation allowances in respect of the plant which did not need replacement..."[97]

Thus in an expanding economy the increase in the replacement funds exceeds the increase in replacements due to be made. Keynes raises a real problem which was to be elaborated later in more detail by Domar. Thus the new investments ought to equal not only the savings certain capitalists wish to effect for new investments to be made at a later point of time, but also part of the sinking funds in excess of replacement. The volume of such funds had increased, writes Keynes, "by 1929... on so huge a scale that an enormous volume of entirely new investment was required merely to absorb these financial provisions; and it became almost hopeless to find still more new investment on a sufficient scale to provide for such new saving as a wealthy community in full employment would be disposed to set aside. This factor alone was probably sufficient to cause a slump."[98] "The

[94] K. Marx: *op. cit.*, p. 523.
[95] K. Marx: *op. cit.*, p. 503.
[96] See K. Marx: *op. cit.*, pp. 457–466.
[97] J. M. Keynes: *op. cit.*, p. 100.
[98] *Ibid.*

372

deduction for entrepreneurs' repairs, maintenance, depreciation and depletion remained at a high figure even at the bottom of the slump,"[99] he writes in another place.

All this is the abstract requirement of reproduction. What real problem of the capitalist economy of his time did Keynes wish to express by the saving–investment mechanism?

Keynes holds that with national income increasing, consumer demand will increase only at a slower pace; therefore, for aggregate demand to grow together with aggregate output, the ratio of investment to the national income should grow. But, in his view, the investment ratio seldom rises to a level which would correspond to full employment.

Let us approach the problem of capitalist economy, as reflected in the Keynesian system, from a Marxist point of view. In a model of pure capitalism, assuming only industrial capitalists and productive workers, and leaving unproductive workers or substantial state expenditures as well as foreign trade out of account, we divide national income into wages and profits. Let us suppose that the working class spends its wages fully on buying consumer goods. Let us now narrow down the Keynesian problem to the question of profit realization. Under the conditions introduced by us, the profit is realized by the expenses of the capitalist class, that is, by the capitalists' outlays on consumption and investment. "... the wages of new workers cannot be s, nor can they be profit. The same applies to the pay rise of the workers already employed. Since the capitalist class gets its profit through its purchases exceeding its costs, the wages paid out to new workers are neither s, nor profit, they are the same kind of cost as the usual wage bill, or the wage increment paid out to the already employed workers."[100]

The profit-realization capacity of the capitalist class depends primarily on the volume of investment. But investments serve eventually to increase the productive capacity of the consumer-goods industries, and this new capacity is available for production over a long period. Even if investments are made repeatedly at the same level, the capacity for producing consumer goods will steadily expand; but with increasing investments, they will grow at an increasing rate. If they are fully utilized, the output of consumer goods will rise vigorously. It is, however, a fact of experience that the rate at which the consumption of the capitalist class grows will be smaller. The basic reason for this fact is, in the long run, the process of capital concentration and centralization disclosed by Marx, as a result of which the social product assumes the form of the productive capital of a relatively ever smaller number of capitalists. The consumer demand of the capitalist class represents, in the course of capitalist development, an ever smaller proportion of aggregate consumption demand. According to Weintraub: "... even in the United States, about 90 per cent of consumption purchases are made by wage and salary earners; in other countries the percentage runs even higher."[101]

With the full utilization of steadily expanding capacities for producing consumer

[99] J. M. Keynes: *op. cit.*, p. 104.

[100] T. Erdős: Még egyszer a profitnagyságról (Once more on the magnitude of profits), *Közgazdasági Szemle*, April 1979, pp. 480–481.

[101] S. Weintraub: Cost Inflation and the State of Economic Theory—Comment, *The Economic Journal*, June 1974, p. 381.

goods, an ever smaller percentage of the increasing quantity of consumer goods therefore embodies surplus value, and an ever larger proportion of that quantity has to serve as wages and salaries if the mass of consumer goods produced is to be realized. The increase in the output of consumer goods, unless investment increases with it adequately, decreases the share of the capitalist class in national income, decreases the surplus of price over the cost of production, the profit margin, or as Péter Erdős calls it, the profit ratio.[102] Since in the Erdős-formula of the profit ratio it is the ratio of surplus value which constitutes the decisive element, changes in the profit ratio reflect changes in the rate of the surplus value. Let us examine, making use again of the formula constructed by Erdős for the rate of surplus value, how it would be possible to maintain a constant rate of surplus value, and hence profit ratio, as the output of consumer goods increases.

Erdős attempts to capture the rate of surplus value through the proportion of the volume of such goods expressed in terms of value in which surplus value and real wages are embodied. Hence $\dfrac{S}{V} = \dfrac{S_c + S_k}{C - S_k}$, where S_c is net investment, S_k the consumption of the capitalist class, C the total output of consumer goods and $C - S_k$ the amount of consumer goods produced accruing as real wages to the working class.

When earlier investments reach maturity, the supply of consumer goods, C, will grow. Since, however, in our model extending over a longer period of capitalist development S_k rises at a smaller rate than C, for $\dfrac{S}{V}$ and through it for the profit ratio to remain unchanged, S_c ought to increase at a greater rate, i.e. the ratio of investment to the national income ought steadily to rise at such a rate that the increase in the volume of surplus value keeps pace with the value of the increasing quantity of consumer goods available to the workers. It would be conceivable *in abstracto* also to keep $\dfrac{S}{V}$ at an unchanged level in the case of full utilization of consumer goods capacities if S_c and S_k grew at the same rate as C. In this case, the ratio of investment to the national income would remain constant. But we have dismissed this possibility by pointing out that in the course of capitalist development the increase in S_k lags behind the increase in C.

It is impossible to increase the investment ratio infinitely only to maintain $\dfrac{S}{V}$ at an unchanged level as it expands the capacities for producing consumer goods to such an extent that the unfavourable effect of the increased capacities on $\dfrac{S}{V}$, or through it on the profit ratio, must sooner or later inevitably prevail. The accelerator effect (to be discussed later in detail), i.e. the effect in our case of an increased output of consumer goods on stimulating investment, will assert itself only if the expansion of the output of consumer goods does not decrease the profit ratio.

If the individual capitalists are able to manipulate prices—and this is the case when monopoly or oligopoly prevails and, further, when certain sellers of the

[102] P. Erdős: *Contributions...*, p. 234.

374

industry can distinguish their products from those of the other sellers of the industry—they strive to maintain prices even at an increasing productive capacity of consumer goods in order to maintain the profit ratio. They do it by not fully utilizing the increased capacity. This will result in the long run in a slow increase in the output of consumer goods. This slow increase does not require a fast expansion of productive capacities; thus investment too will experience a slow growth, giving rise to a long-term decrease in the profit ratio with unemployment growing due to an insufficient investment activity. In the long run, it is of course not only the profit ratio but the profit rate too which will decrease. It will decrease for one thing because the increase in S_c does not offset the relative lag of S_k. It will decrease because of the increase in the organic composition of capital.[103]

Let us illustrate the case in point by a numerical example: Let $S_c = 200$, $S_k = 200$, $C = 1,000$. In this case, the magnitude of surplus value will be 400. The quantity of the consumer goods at the disposal of the workers is 800, thus $\dfrac{S}{V} = \dfrac{400}{800} = 50$ per cent. For simplicity's sake let the profit ratio be the rate of surplus value. The national income $C + S_c = 1,200$. The ratio of investment to the national income is $\dfrac{200}{1,200} = 16.666$ per cent.

If the efficiency of investment is $\frac{1}{2}$, 200 units of investment will result in an increase of 100 in the capacity of producing consumer goods. In the case of a full utilization of capacity, the output of consumer goods must rise to 1,100. Let us assume that S_k increases at a smaller rate, from 200 to 210. For a 50 per cent rate of surplus value to be maintained, 235 S_c are needed. In this case, the magnitude of surplus value is $210 + 235 = 445$, and the ratio of investment to national income has increased to $\dfrac{235}{1,335} = 17.6$ per cent.

Let us assume, however, that S_c has not increased but remained at 200. With 200 S_c and 210 S_k, capitalists have to decrease C to 1,030 in order to maintain the 50 per cent rate of surplus value and through it the prevailing profit ratio. The amount of surplus value is then 410, the portion accruing to the working class out of the quantity of consumer goods produced is $1,030 - 210 = 820$, thus $\dfrac{S}{V} = \dfrac{410}{820} = 50$ per cent.

If there is full employment, given a national income of 1,335, and capitalists are willing to produce such a quantity of the national income only if they can simultaneously maintain their 50 per cent rate of surplus value, or the existing magnitude of the profit ratio, they need to obtain 445 units of surplus value. In this event, out of 1,100 units of C, 890 will be the consumption of the working class and 210 the consumption of the capitalist class. But let us suppose that S_c is only 200. Full employment cannot be achieved, since in full employment 445 units of surplus value produced at a 50 per cent rate of surplus value cannot be realized. The quantity of surplus value produced in excess of S_k is, to use the Keynesian, or more exactly the post-Keynesian terminology, intended saving. The unrealizability of the surplus value produced at full employment could be expressed in post-Keynesian language in this way: out of the surplus value produced at full employment the capitalist class wants to save more than it wants to invest, $445 - 210 = 235$, and this is more than 200 units of investment. The consequence, as we have seen, is that in order to maintain the profit ratio, capitalists will decrease the output of consumer goods to 1,030.

When we asked, approaching the problem from a Marxian point of view, which ill of capitalist society Keynes wanted to illustrate by his saving–investment mechanism, we focused our attention on the realization not of national income but of surplus value, since gaining surplus value is the driving force of capitalist

[103] P. Erdős: Reálbér és értéktörvény a kapitalizmusban (Real wages and the law of value under capitalism), *Közgazdasági Szemle*, Budapest, December 1974, pp. 1380–1382.

economic activity. That the capitalist class does not spend the whole surplus value produced may also be formulated, as we have seen, in this way: the difference between the surplus value produced and the consumption of the capitalist class exceeds the amount of investment. Yet Marxian political economy shows the movement in aggregate demand, the market-expanding effect of investment, not through the saving–investment mechanism, because the difference between the surplus value produced and capitalist consumer demand cannot be regarded as a saving based primarily on consumer psychology. As we have already pointed out, savings out of surplus value are savings made in the first place for business considerations. And the capitalist, if the business prospects are favourable, strives to invest as much as possible. This endeavour of his is not restricted by the amount of his profit realized since he can finance his investments out of credits, too. And even if it happens to occur, as Marx himself points out in Volume II of *Capital,* that the endeavour of certain capitalists to set aside part of their realized profit as an investment fund exceeds the actual investments of other capitalists, an occurrence which may upset the equilibrium of aggregate demand and aggregate supply, this might be the manifestation of a slump, which results in a drop in the realized profit of the capitalist class. And in this case it is not intended saving stemming from consumer psychology and representing an allegedly reliable function of income which clashes with intended investment. Hence, it has no sense to express the inadequacy of the demand needed to reach full employment by Keynes's saving–investment mechanism. We have simply stated that under capitalist conditions there seldom occurs such an amount of $S_c + S_k$ as is needed to realize a surplus value produced at full employment and unchanged $\dfrac{S}{V}$, and have tried to explain why S_c and S_k are insufficient to realize, at an unchanged profit margin, the surplus value produced under full employment.

The endeavour to maintain the profit ratio would be a possible means to explain a characteristic of the Keynesian theoretical system often discussed in non-Marxian literature, namely, that it is primarily output and not prices that react to changes in demand. To a fall in demand entrepreneurs react not with a decrease in prices but with a decrease in output, and if demand increases, then they will increase, at least as a first reaction, output and not prices, not the profit ratio.

It is a contradiction of the capitalist economy left to itself that from the point of view of the profit of the capitalist class it would be desirable to increase investment activity vigorously. At the same time, the capacities increased as a result of completed investments affect the profit ratio or even the profit rate unfavourably, because of the long-term decreasing share of the capitalist class in aggregate consumer demand. This fact leads to a slowdown in the increase in consumer-goods output and to investments being too low from the point of view of full employment. This insufficiency of investments made in the capitalist economy is expressed by Keynes when he criticizes Hobson for placing emphasis on the excessive savings and the correspondingly great investments of the capitalist class when, in Keynes's view, this is the lesser problem. The main problem is that there are seldom as many new investments as the savings society wishes to make at full employment.[104]

[104] J. M. Keynes: *op. cit.,* p. 370.

376

Finally, mention must also be made of the reality-content of the multiplier effect. The employment multiplier was already introduced before Keynes into the literature of economics by Kahn in 1931. He pointed out that if the state ensured by public works a certain number of employment opportunities, then aggregate employment would increase by a multiple of the initial amount of employment. Workers employed in public works and thus receiving income, would increase their consumption. In spheres where their incomes flowed, output would be increased, and additional workers would be employed. The demand of these workers would stimulate further employment. A similar effect, though opposite in direction, can also be found in Marx. The circumstance that workers were ousted from production by machines, "that they were 'freed' by the machinery from the means of production, changed them from buyers into non-buyers. Hence a lessened demand for those commodities ..., ... the labourers employed in the production of necessary means of subsistence are in their turn 'freed' from a part of their wages ... machinery throws workers on the streets, not only in that branch of production in which it is introduced, but also in those branches in which it is not introduced."[105]

Keynes explored, however, by the investment multiplier the effect of a *given* level of investment on the expansion of the demand for and the output of consumer goods. He therefore availed himself of two assumptions: first, that there was enough surplus labour to increase the output of consumer goods and, second, that the output of consumer goods could be increased by the means of production already available, and thus did not require additional investment. He thereby pointed to the relationship already formulated by the classics of Marxism, namely, that in a capitalist economy the production of the means of production, and within them specifically the production of fixed capital, calls forth an expansion of the market and thus also increases the demand for consumer goods.

How could the Keynesian investment multiplier be represented in terms of the Marxian two-department scheme?

To do this, let us assume that the consumption of capitalists is a constant proportion of surplus value.

In the course of this representation a difficulty arises from the fact that Keynes operated with a magnitude net of intermediate goods, i.e. with national income, while Marx is concerned with social annual product also containing intermediate goods. Further, in the Marxian scheme, the capital advanced is completely used up in one production period, and capitalists make use of the amount saved from the surplus value realized in one production period for the expansion of their capital in that very period. Thus the Keynesian problem in the form that some capitalists want to save more or less from surplus value than other capitalists wish to invest, cannot emerge at all.

Let us now upset the equilibrium existing between the two departments. If department I shoots ahead of department II, it will demand more consumer goods than is supplied by department II. Thus a situation arises which is similar to the case of intended investment exceeding intended saving. Though entrepreneurs

---

[105] K. Marx: *Capital,* Vol. I, Moscow, 1954, p. 440.

in both departments necessarily invest as much from surplus value as they save from it, yet, as a result of the disproportion between the two departments, investment interpreted as the difference between national income and the supply of consumer goods, exceeds saving interpreted in the Keynesian way as the difference between national income and the demand for consumer goods.

$$s_1 + v_1 + s_2 + v_2 - \left(c_2 + v_2 + s_2 {\nearrow s_{2c} \atop \to s_{2v} \atop \searrow s_{2k}} \right) > s_1 + v_1 + s_2 + v_2 - (v_1 + v_2 + s_{1v} + s_{2v} + s_{1k} + s_{2k}).$$

By cancelling, we obtain the inequality expressing the disproportion between the two departments:

$$v_1 + s_{1v} + s_{1k} > c_2 + s_{2c}.$$

We must note, however, that the excess investment thus obtained is gross excess investment, because we have made our computation with the full value of the combined output of the two sectors, including replacement for the means of production already used up. And saving in our model is also gross saving since it contains, in addition to the provision for net investment, the depreciation allowance, too. The excessive increase in department I means an excessive increase in the production of capital goods not only for new investments but also for replacements.

How is equilibrium established between the demand for and the supply of consumer goods, and through it between the two departments? Let us, following Keynes, fix the output of department I, which makes it possible for an equilibrium position to be established in our example by the output of department II catching up with it.

Owing to the more rapid growth of department I, entrepreneurs producing consumer goods will increase their output to the extent of $v_1 + s_{1v} + s_{1k} - (c_2 + s_{2c})$. Let us now assume, following Keynes again, that the output of department I is not yet matured in the period under consideration. Thus the capitalists of department II will expand their output by utilizing their excess capacities with the result that the difference between $v_1 + s_{1v} + s_{1k}$ and $c_2 + s_{2c}$ enables them to save to the extent of the sum of part values $\Delta c_2 + \Delta s_{2c}$. But their output has not yet come into equilibrium with the demand for consumer goods. Because, as output increases, incomes in department II and with them the demand for consumer goods will rise by $\Delta v_2 + \Delta s_{2v} + \Delta s_{2k}$. What department I can get out of the increment of output is only an amount of consumer goods corresponding to the value of $\Delta c_2 + \Delta s_{2c}$. In order to satisfy the remaining consumer demand of department I, the entrepreneurs of department II will further expand their output in the above way with the result that the consumer demand of department II will continue to rise. Will the supply of consumer goods catch up with the demand for them? This is what Keynes also investigated in analysing the size of the multiplier effect. The Marxist answer is this: supply will catch up with demand because, as the output of consumer goods increases, their supply will grow at a faster rate than their demand. The demand for and the supply of consumer goods, i.e. department I and department II, will reach equilibrium when the capitalists of department II expand the output of consumer goods until, by the gradual increase in consumer goods, the series of part values $\Delta c_2 + \Delta s_{2c}$ satisfy the uncovered

378

consumer demand, $v_1 + s_{1v} + s_{1k} - (c_2 + s_{2c})$, of department I. Those engaged in department I consume what department II itself does not wish to use out of its own products. Although the total output of department II is bought out of incomes, not all earnings become income for the capitalists of department II. It is from these earnings that they have to replace the means of production used up, c_2. They pass on part of their products included in c_2 to those engaged in department I in exchange for means of production. And they also pass on consumer goods included in s_{2c} in order to buy new investment goods. The equilibrium between the two departments, which was upset by department I shooting ahead, will be restored when department II has increased its output to such an extent that its share designed to replace worn-out means of production and to make new investments is just equal to the consumer demand of department I, or, in other words, $\Delta c_2 + \Delta s_{2c}$ is just equal to the excess demand of department I for consumer goods.

In the Marxian scheme, operating with gross magnitudes containing aggregation it is $c + s_c$, which means leakage, i.e. saving, of the Keynesian model: that part of the aggregate output of the individual departments whose value is not used by the department in question for private consumption. We can also determine by how much department II has to increase its total output to satisfy the increased consumer demand of department I: Since department II consumes v_2, $s_2 v_2$ and $s_2 k_2$ out of its own output, and thus passes only $c_2 + s_2 c_2$ on to department I, therefore it has to increase its output as many times the initial excess demand of department I as its own output exceeds $c_2 + s_2 c_2$, the portion it has not consumed, i.e. savings in the Keynesian sense.

If, however, we want to find out the increase in value in department II as a result of the adjustment process, i.e. of the growth in national income—and it is this approach which is nearer to the Keynesian view operating with net magnitudes—, then we must isolate s_{2c} from the gross investment $c_2 + s_{2c}$, which department I intends to pass on to department II. In this case, the multiplier effect express the increase in the national income produced in department II if it is to satisfy the excess consumer demand of department I also by consumer goods embodied in s_{2c}. Now $\dfrac{s_c}{v+s}$ means the savings ratio in both departments, which coincides with the investment ratio since, according to the assumption of the Marxian model, part of the surplus value accumulated in the production period is spent entirely on buying means of production in the period in question.

And in our Marxian model Δs_{2c} multiplied by $\dfrac{v_2 + s_2}{s_{2c}}$ expresses the increase in new value in department II in the adjustment process. Similarly, the opposite process could also be shown when as a consequence of the contraction of department I, it is gross saving which exceeds investment with the result that the output of department II will be cut.

The representation of the multiplier effect in Marx's two-department scheme demonstrates that in the case of department I shooting ahead, department II must really increase its output by a multiple of the missing consumer goods if it is to catch up with the increased consumer demand of department I. At the same time, it also demonstrates the limitations of the multiplier effect.

Saving in the Keynesian sense is made, according to the Marxian scheme, out of surplus value. Thus saving ought to be related to surplus value and not to national income. However, what is characteristic of saving out of surplus value is not that it is made for consumer considerations, but for business purposes, for accumulation. Saving of this type cannot be brought, on the basis of a sort of consumer psychology, into a function-like relationship with the income of the capitalist class. But the greater the proportion in the adjustment process, of surplus value not used for the personal consumption of the capitalists of department II, the more products of department II are transferred to department I, i.e. the greater is $c_2 + s_{2c}$ relative to $c_2 + v_2 + s_2$. This ratio, however, is, owing to the indeterminate character of the ratio of savings made by the capitalists of department II, indeterminate, too.

As department II catches up with department I, the ratio of $c_2 + s_{2c}$ to $c_2 + v_2 + s_2$ is affected by the circumstance how the organic composition of capital changes in the process. Since in the catching-up process real wages rise, this will stimulate entrepreneurs to introduce more capital-intensive techniques. As a result, department II will now be able, by slightly increasing its output, to reach the consumer demand of department I.

In the catching-up process, the rate of surplus value, s/v changes, i.e. it falls. This will influence both the consumer demand in department I and the ratio of $c_2 + s_{2c}$ to $c_2 + v_2 + s_2$ in department II. This effect of changes in distribution relations on the multiplier was also referred to by Keynes: "... the multiplier will be influenced by the way in which the new income resulting from the increased effective demand is distributed between different classes of consumers."[106] And, since the extent of changes that may occur in the catching-up process cannot be predicted, this fact adds to the difficulty in estimating the market-expanding effect of consumer goods via the ratio of $c_2 + s_{2c}$ to $c_2 + v_2 + s_2$.

Non-Marxian economists have also come to realize the shortcomings of Keynes's multiplier theory. His critics have pointed out that various circumstances may complicate and indeed hinder the functioning of the multiplier effect. Thus, among other things, we cannot know how entrepreneurs will respond with their output to an increase in demand. If they anticipate a further increase in demand, and wish to maintain a constant proportion between their inventories and increasing demand, they will step up their output in excess of increased demand. Or they may satisfy increased demand even without stepping up their output, simply by cutting their excess inventories. Monopolies react to an increase in demand by raising prices and not by stepping up output. In the first case, a multiplier effect greater than expected will manifest itself, while in the two latter cases no multiplier effect will be experienced.

Keynes investigated the multiplier effect by the method of comparative statics. He assumed that intended saving and intended investment would come into equilibrium independently of time. Keynes's followers, dissolving the rigidity of comparative statics, try to represent the multiplier effect dynamically, that is,

[106] J. M. Keynes: *op. cit.*, pp. 298–299.

with a time dimension, so as to trace the change over time of the new equilibrium level of national income if intended investment exceeds intended saving, or the other way round. In this case, however, there is the problem of finding out the time that is needed for the multiplier effect fully to unfold in the process of its switching from one productive branch to another, i.e. the time needed for the new equilibrium level to be established, the length of the transitional period. It would be necessary to know this time period in order to plan state investments designed to stimulate demand.

In the multiplier effect Keynes examined the spill-over effect of a once-and-for-all investment on aggregate demand (aggregate output). For this reason he assumed that the increased demand for consumer goods could be met by utilizing existing excess capacities, that is, without making new investments. But increased demand obviously creates a favourable climate for investment, and the further intensification of investment activity will in turn expand the market and increase employment. The multiplier effect can only be studied as embedded in the whole process of capitalist reproduction. Its magnitude depends on a number of unpredictable, unassessable factors. Non-Marxian critiques also maintain that a complete model expressing the formation of economic processes must be used if the market-expanding effect is to be represented. In Keynes's formula, as Ackley notes, the multiplier effect holds true "... only as a first approximation, under ideal conditions."[107] In Ackley's view, so many limiting factors are required for national income to increase by the reciprocal of the marginal propensity to save that the real processes definitely do not unfold in compliance with the Keynesian formula. Ackley is right in saying that "... the multiplier theory is of little practical use in planning."[108] Similarly, Smithies also holds that it is impossible to squeeze the market-expanding effect into one single formula.[109]

We have characterized the multiplier effect as an effect working in the direction of restoring the disrupted equilibrium of reproduction. Instead of investigating the equilibrium of reproduction, the equilibrium of the two departments, Keynes centres his attention on the question of whether there will be as large an amount of consumer demand plus investment as the national income produced, whether there will be an intended investment corresponding to intended saving from national income. By means of the Keynesian scheme, however, the structure of supply can also be captured. Since I is to Keynes net capital formation, provided the magnitude of intended investment is known, we will also know the supply of consumer goods from national income, $Y-I$. Such a division of national income between the supply of consumer goods and investment captures national income at a time when the exchange between departments has essentially taken place, when it has already been embodied in consumer goods and new capital goods. The new part values $v_1+s_{1v}+s_{1k}$, which are embodied in means of production, have been exchanged for consumer goods supplied in the values c_2+s_{2c}. Thus national income is embodied, instead of in means of production to the value of $v_1+s_{1v}+s_{1k}+s_{1c}$ and consumer goods to the value of $v_2+s_{2v}+s_{2k}+s_{2c}$, in consumer goods to the

[107] G. Ackley: The Multiplier Time Period: Money, Inventories and Flexibility, *The American Economic Review*, June 1951, p. 368.
[108] *Ibid.*
[109] A. Smithies: The Multiplier, *The American Economic Review*, 1948, p. 305.

value of $c_2 + v_2 + s_2$ and investment goods to the value of $s_{1c} + s_{2c}$. This representation of the supply side, besides containing net magnitudes only, does not correspond to the division by Marx of social production between the two departments because intended investment also contains a part of the consumer goods produced, the part which increases the stock of inventories. The supply of consumer goods, Y less intended investment, is thus less than the output of department II by the portion designed to increase the inventory stocks. The equilibrium examined by Keynes is basically market equilibrium, the equilibrium between aggregate demand and aggregate supply. Keynes does not go into the deeper problem of the equilibrium of reproduction, the equilibrium between department I and II, which constitutes the basis of market equilibrium.

The catching up of department II with department I as represented in our example does not mean a stable equilibrium. The disproportionately great weight of department I in total output makes the demand for consumer goods exceed their supply. In department II realized profit is increasing. The relative growth of the output of department II, its approximation to equilibrium, diminishes the rate of realized profit, weakens the boom and plunges the economy into a crisis. In reality, the equilibrium of the two departments is established through a general overproduction crisis.

Let us represent the Keynesian multiplier effect within the Marxian two-department scheme by a concrete example, under simplified conditions, when the organic composition of capital, the distribution relations and the division of surplus value are unchanged.

Let the initial output of department I and II be:

$$1,500c_1 + 1,500v_1 + 1,500s_1 \begin{array}{l} \nearrow 300s_{1c} \\ \rightarrow 300s_{1v} \\ \searrow 900s_{1k} \end{array}$$

$$1,500c_2 + 1,500v_2 + 1,500s_2 \begin{array}{l} \nearrow 300s_{2c} \\ \rightarrow 300s_{2v} \\ \searrow 900s_{2k} \end{array}$$

Department I demands consumer goods to the value of 2,700, and department II supplies them to it only to the value of 1,800. Hence the excess demand of department I is 900. Investment in the Keynesian sense = 6,000 (national income)—4,500 (aggregate supply of consumer goods) = 1,500.

Saving in the Keynesian sense = 6,000 (national income)—5,400 (aggregate demand for consumer goods) = 600. Investment exceeds saving by 900. Excess investment over saving consists partly of replacement investment and partly of means of production for net investment.

Department II expands output until the supply of consumer goods is in equilibrium with the demand for them. Let us now see by how much department II has to increase its output, through the multiplier effect, to reach the equilibrium position.

Let us compute the multiplier first as a relationship between gross magnitudes. Since $c_2 + s_{2c}$ is 0.4 times the total output of department II, $c_2 + v_2 + s_2$, hence the multiplier is 2.5.

With the data of the model, department II has to increase its output by $900 \times 2.5 = 2,250$ so as to satisfy both its own consumer demand, which increases as a result of the catching-up process, and the consumer demand of department I.

In an equilibrium position, the output of department II is

$$2,250c_2 + 2,250v_2 + 2,250s_2 \begin{array}{l} \nearrow 450s_{2c} \\ \rightarrow 450s_{2v} \\ \searrow 1,350s_{2k} \end{array}$$

382

In an equilibrium position department II supplies to department I consumer goods to the value of 2,700, 900 more than their initial value. From 900 surplus income it sets aside $750\Delta c_2$ as a depreciation allowance and $150\Delta s_2 c$ as an investment fund.

Applying the multiplier only to the relation of new investment to national income, we obtain 10 for the value of the multiplier.

Consequently, the national income produced in department II must increase in equilibrium by 10 times $\Delta s_2 c$, that is, by $150 \times 10 = 1,500$, compared with its initial value. In our example, this value has increased from 3,000 to 4,500.

Let us assume that in the catching-up process department II has increased the organic composition of capital. Thus department II may come into equilibrium with department I, for example at the following magnitudes and composition:

$$2,400c_2 + 1,500v_2 + 1,500s_2 \begin{array}{l} \nearrow 300s_{2c} \\ \rightarrow 187.5s_{2v} \\ \searrow 1,021.5s_{2k} \end{array}$$

The output of department II, owing to the increase in the organic composition of capital, rose only to 5,400 instead of 6,750, and new value only to 3,000 instead of 4,500.

Similarly, it can also be shown how the equilibrium amount of the output of department II is influenced by the fact that income distribution relations are bound to change in the catching-up process.

Chapter 6

KEYNES'S THEORY OF MONEY AND INTEREST

The Keynesian proposition that a capitalist economy left to itself cannot guarantee a growth in aggregate demand in line with aggregate output, nor an amount of aggregate demand needed to provide full employment, must also be reflected in his theory of money.

Keynes vigorously emphasizes the special role that money plays in the world of commodities. In a model which is designed to show that in a capitalist economy full employment can rarely materialize, because aggregate demand rarely reaches a level at which the output produced under full employment could be exchanged for money at a cost price including normal profit, the significance of money in respect of commodities will of course increase.

In what exactly does Keynes see the special role of money? In the fact that it has a high degree of liquidity, while its cost of holding is negligible. In explaining Keynes' theory, Mrs. Robinson writes as follows: "The two qualities—certainty of future value and easy marketability—blend together in the quality of liquidity."[110]

How did money emerge from the world of commodities and how did it achieve such a high degree of liquidity? Marx examines in detail how, as a result of the basic conctradiction of commodity production, namely, the contradiction between the social and private character of labour, the particular use-values of commodities prevented the free movement of their value; how it became necessary, with the development of commodity production, for a form of motion to come into being for that contradiction; how a commodity was singled out of the world of commodities, a commodity which, as money, assumed a general use-value, with the result that its use-value did not prevent the free movement of its value. With the emergence of money, commodities are exchanged for it, and thus their values gain independence in the form of money; they are divorced from their use-values, which allow them but limited movement, and now move on freely as money. With money coming into existence, the world of commodities is divided into two parts: money as the embodiment of value, and all other commodities as use-values. Thus the intrinsic contradiction inherent in the commodity, the contradiction between value and use-value, appears with the emergence of money as an external contradiction between money and all the other commodities. And Marx emphasizes that one commodity can be in a state of direct exchangeability, because all the other

[110] J. Robinson, *The Accumulation of Capital*, London, 1956, p. 30.

commodities are excluded from it. Money as an independent value also becomes the object of independent ambitions. There are people who sell goods in order to obtain money and accumulate it as "hoards".

Instead of explaining the special position of money arising from social relations, Keynes simply refers to the fact that two essential qualities are needed for an object to prove its liquidity and serve as money. While real capital assets, with the exception of land, can be reproduced, the supply of money is rigid because, when the demand for it increases, individual entrepreneurs cannot increase its output at will, and if its exchange value increases, there is no tendency for it to be substituted by another factor either. "The attribute of 'liquidity' is by no means independent of the presence of these two characteristics. For it is unlikely that an asset of which the supply can be easily increased or the desire for which can be easily diverted by a change in relative prices, will possess the attribute of 'liquidity' in the minds of owners of wealth."[111] Keynes stresses that, owing to the special position of money, contracts and thus wage contracts too are fixed in money. In Keynes's view, however, wages measured in money terms have a higher stability than real wages, because wage-commodities can be freely reproduced. "... wages, when fixed in terms of it [i.e. in money—A. M.] tend to be sticky."[112] The relative rigidity of money wages increases in turn the stability of money value, the liquidity of money. A high degree of liquidity enables money to play its role as a store of value.

In neo-classical economics prior to Keynes, money also had a double role: as a medium of exchange and as a store of value. In the earlier theories of the demand for money, money was held under the transactions motive, and partly for precautionary considerations, in order to cover unforeseen expenses. In the latter case, money was held as a store of value. But the significance of this role of money was not investigated by the neo-classical economists. It was not investigated because in the world as pictured by them uncertainty did not play any role. In an economy in which the future can be predicted with a high degree of certainty, it would be senseless to store wealth in money form instead of investing it profitably.

In the Keynesian theory, however, uncertainty has a basic function. In making his decisions, economic man cannot possibly reckon with his expectations always coming true. Keynes holds that in a world of uncertainty money as a store of value has an important role to play.

By emphasizing the function of money as a store of value, Keynes "reinforced the shift of emphasis from the transactions version of the quantity equation to the cash balance version."[113]

Keynes traces the demand for money back to three motives: (1) the transactions motive, that is, the need for cash to transact personal or business exchanges; (2) the precautionary motive, that is, holding money with a view to having cash available for unforeseen contingencies requiring immediate payment, and, further, to settle debts fixed in money and due to be repaid in the future; (3) the speculative motive.

---

111 J. M. Keynes: *op. cit.*, p. 241.
112 J. M. Keynes: *op. cit.*, p. 233.
113 M. Friedman: A Theoretical Framework of Monetary Analysis, *Journal of Political Economy,* March/April, 1970, p. 212.

According to Keynes, the amount of money needed to satisfy the transactions motive and the precautionary motive, depends, in normal circumstances, on the general level of activity of the economic system and the level of money income. Keynes groups the two varieties of holding money in cash together under the term liquidity preference, L_1. The demand for money, L_1, is not too sensitive to changes in the rate of interest, only to the extent that it influences the level of national income. In the old cash-balance theory these two needs were the source of the demand for money, and the amount of money desired was a function of national income.

Keynes complements the old cash-balance theory with the demand for money arising from the speculative motive. The speculative demand for money is one of the cornerstones of Keynes's theoretical system. Money for speculative purposes is demanded in its quality as a store of value. Though money for precautionary purposes is also held in its function as a store of value, the two demands for money are determined by different factors and that is why Keynes distinguishes between them. It is primarily the speculative motive which for Keynes is involved in holding money as "hoards", and the new element in the Keynesian interpretation of monetary equilibrium consists in its attempt to examine on what the amount of *ex-ante* hoards depends.

What in Keynes is the source of the speculative demand for money? It is, on the one hand, the fact that some people wish to hold their wealth in money because they are afraid that wealth held in another form will lose its value in the future and thus they will suffer a loss, their wealth will diminish. On the other hand, people demand money for speculative purposes if they think that prices will fall in the bond market, and thus it is worthwhile to hold a stock of money in readiness to buy bonds if their price has fallen to a low enough level. And while the money held under the precautionary motive is a function of economic activity, of national income, Keynes represents the speculative demand for money as a function of the rate of interest.

Keynes wishes to create an interest-rate theory different from that of the neo-classical school, which he can use in his critique of Say's dogma. Neo-classical economists saw the interest of rate as a real phenomenon, the expression of the marginal productivity of capital, of the marginal disutility of saving, or of the "time preference" of the public. And movements in the interest rate establish equilibrium between intended saving and intended investment, at the point of intersection of the saving and investment functions. Thus the mechanism of the interest rate ensures that what society does not spend on personal consumption from the national income produced at full employment becomes investment.

For Keynes, saving is a function not of the rate of interest but of national income. For equilibrium to be established, the intended saving of society adjusts itself through the multiplier effect, through changes in national income, to the level of intended investment. Therefore, in Keynes's view, there exists no definite natural rate of interest at the point of intersection of the saving and investment functions; the equilibrium between saving and investment can materialize at any level of the interest rate, from which he infers that several natural rates of interest are possible. Thus the equilibrium of saving and investment does not tell us anything about the level of the rate of interest until the level of national income is known. Keynes determines the level of the interest rate not through the saving and investment functions, but, as we shall see, through the relationship between the interest-sensitive speculative demand for money and the amount of money available for speculative purposes.

Let us now look more closely at the speculative demand function for money or, to use Keynes's term, at the liquidity function L_2.

A household is faced, according to Keynes, with two decisions. First, it must decide how much to save from its income. Second, it must decide in what form to hold its wealth saved. It may hold it, according to Keynes, either in bonds or other assets, or else in money form, too.[114] As we shall see later, it was particularly important for Keynes to demonstrate that the demand for money was interest-elastic. However, he was able to do so only while relying on the speculative behaviour of the "bears". It appears that with the inclusion of bearish speculation Keynes distinguished only two forms of holding assets depending on to what extent the present value of an asset is interest-elastic. These are: money and its alternative, long-term bonds, expected to yield fixed interest.

In the case of bonds with fixed interest rates there exists, according to Keynes, a two-sided relation between their rate of interest and rate of exchange. The higher the exchange rate of a bond promising a fixed rate of interest on its nominal value, the lower its current interest rate, or, the lower the exchange rate of the bond in question, the higher its current interest rate. At the same time, the exchange rate of fixed-interest bonds also depends on the current market rate of interest. Their exchange rate will rise if the current market rate of interest falls, and will drop if the current market rate increases. This impact of changes in the interest rate on the exchange rate of securities is but insignificant for fixed-interest, short-term bonds, thus their present exchange rate is not interest-elastic, but this impact is very significant in the case of fixed-interest, long-term bonds, whose present exchange rate, however, is highly interest-elastic. It appears that Keynes treats the assets held in short-term bonds as money. Keynes interprets money, according to Leijonhufvud, in a rather flexible way. If the discussion of the problem in question requires, he finds it permissible for the concept of money also to include assets that do not have one or another function he attributes to money. And in fact, at one point in his *General Theory* Keynes writes that "we can draw the line between money and debts at whatever point it is most convenient for handling a particular problem. For example, we can treat as *money* any command over general purchasing power which the owner has not parted with for a period in excess of three months, and as *debt* what cannot be recovered for a longer period than this..."[115] In another place he characterizes the holding of wealth in money form by saying that it "... yields little or no interest..."[116]

Friedman, too holds the view that the Keynesian alternatives to money in its broader sense, as an asset, are bonds and other fixed-interest securities. He writes that the Keynesian analysis is "concentrated on the relation between money, on the one hand, and bonds or other fixed-interest securities, on the other."[117] Hicks is

114 See J. M. Keynes: *op. cit.*, p. 200.
115 J. M. Keynes: *op. cit.*, p. 189.
116 J. M. Keynes: *op. cit.*, p. 168.
117 M. Friedman: Post-War Trends in Monetary Theory and Policy. In: *The Optimum Quantity of Money and Other Essays,* Chicago, 1969, p. 70.

also of the opinion that for Keynes "the only choice that is open is a choice between holding money and holding bonds."[118] The Keynesian interest rate, writes Hicks at another place, is "... the rate of interest of long-term government bonds."[119]

According to Leijonhufvud, however, Keynes's alternative to money in its broader sense, as a form of holding wealth, is all non-money assets. This interpretation is based on Keynes's determination of the present price of capital goods. Keynes determined it, as we have seen, in a way similar to the present exchange rate of securities, as the discounted value of expected yields at the prevailing rate of interest. And since, according to Leijonhufvud, Keynes always assumed a given state of long-term expectations, in order to ensure the determination of short-term equilibrium, the assets with otherwise changing yields, for example, the current prices of shares or real capital assets, too, changed only if the rate of interest changed.

In reality, the Keynesian alternative to holding wealth in money form is holding fixed-interest bonds, more exactly long-term bonds. Leijonhufvud's broad interpretation of the alternative forms of holding wealth in money form would contradict the Keynesian concept. That is because in this case monetary stimulation, an increase in the quantity of money, would move, through open-market operations, from the bond market to the market of real capital assets; it would directly stimulate investment (output), which in turn would imply that monetary policy alone was enough to ensure the high level of output (employment). Davidson also asserts in one of his studies that Keynes would reject such an interpretation of his theory.[120] For Keynes, an increase in the quantity of money through open-market operations affects output only through changes in the rate of interest. Thus it appears that we can give a correct account of Keynes's position on the problem in question if we confront money in its broad interpretation, that is to say, also including short-term securities, with long-term bonds as an alternative form of holding wealth. It is the long-term movement of the rate of interest that Keynes is interested in. Increased investment suggested as a remedy against unemployment calls for a decrease in the long-term rate of interest.

In the case of the speculative demand for money, the only intelligible explanation of individuals trying to use money as holding wealth is, according to Keynes, the "... *uncertainty* as to the future course of the rate of interest..."[121] On the basis of past experience and of the present state of expectations concerning future monetary policy, people have a certain idea about the safe level of the rate of interest. These ideas vary from individual to individual, and have no absolute reliance on the real state of affairs. In Keynes's view, changes in the current market rate of interest need not call forth a corresponding change in the expected future rate of interest. Expectations concerning the future rate of interest are inelastic for Keynes. Those who think that the current rate of interest is lower than they expect the likely rate to be in the future will want to convert their bond holdings to money to avoid losses from a decline in the market price of bonds; or they do not spend their

[118] J. R. Hicks: *The Crisis in Keynesian Economics,* Oxford, 1974, p. 35.
[119] J. R. Hicks: *op. cit.,* p. 38.
[120] See P. Davidson: A Keynesian View of Friedman's Theoretical Framework for Monetary Analysis, *Journal of Political Economy,* 1972, Vol. 80, pp. 878–879.
[121] J. M. Keynes: *op. cit.,* p. 201.

money holdings on buying bonds if they think that in the future they can buy them at a lower price. Therefore, money for speculative purposes will be demanded by those who judge the future in a pessimistic way and expect a rise in the interest rate and a fall in market prices, that is, who speculate on a slump. But some people will speculate on a fall in the future rate of interest relative to the current one, that is, on a rise in market prices, on a boom. They will want to buy securities or borrow short-term money to buy debts of longer term. For Keynes, it is speculation about the future uncertainty of the rate of interest which brings about the interest-elasticity of the demand for money. And the lower the present rate of interest, the more individuals will be afraid that the future rate of interest will rise and security prices will fall, that is, the more speculators will join the "bear brigade", the more of them will seek to get rid of their securities and hold their wealth in money as, according to their calculations, even a small expected fall in security prices will annihilate not only the interest yield on their claims, but will also decrease their wealth held in the form of bonds. At the same time, those who hold their wealth in money, have to sacrifice but a small interest income for the security that their wealth will not depreciate, and thus the opportunity cost of holding cash is low.

Thus, depending on expectations, to any rate of interest there belongs for Keynes a certain demand for money on the part of the "bears", or a certain supply of money on the part of the "bulls". With the rate of interest changing, the relation between the "bears" and the "bulls" will shift, and the rate of interest will be stabilized at a level at "which the sales of the 'bears' and the purchases of the 'bulls' are balanced."[122] Or, formulated in a different way, "... the rate of interest and the price of bonds have to be fixed at the level at which the desire on the part of certain individuals to hold cash (because at that level they feel 'bearish' of the future of bonds) is exactly equal to the amount of cash available for the speculative motive."

Those economists who, following Keynes, represent the speculative demand curve of money diagrammatically as a function of the rate of interest, proceed in the following way: the demand for money is made up of the amount of money that existing money-holders wish to retain as a store of wealth, rather than purchase bonds, plus the amount which, at the given interest rate, bond-holders wish to obtain by selling bonds.[123] The equilibrium level of the rate of interest is then that level at which the demand for money thus obtained will be equal to the amount of money available for speculative purposes, M_2, which is nothing else but the total quantity of money available to society, M, minus the quantity of money needed to satisfy the demand for money for transactions and precautionary purposes, M_1.

The lower the rate of interest, the more elastic for Keynes will be the curve of the speculative demand for money, because the more rapidly 'bulls' change into 'bears', the more the quantity of money available for speculative purposes will have to grow for the rate of interest to decrease in the same degree. Then, at a certain rate of interest the interest-elasticity of the function of the speculative demand

[122] J. M. Keynes: *op. cit.*, p. 170.
[123] See G. Haberler: *Prosperity and Depression,* 3rd ed., Geneva, 1941, p. 210; or E. Schneider: *Einführung in die Wirtschaftstheorie,* Tübingen, 1957, Vol. III, pp. 80–81.

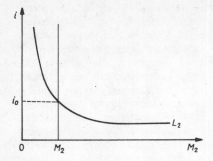

Figure 73

for money will become almost infinite in the sense that "almost everyone prefers cash to holding a debt which yields so low a rate of interest."[124] Keynes's followers speak of a *liquidity trap*. The speculative demand for money absorbs all money without affecting the rate of interest.

In Keynes, the rate of interest only brings the speculative demand for money into line with the quantity of money available for such purposes; it does not directly influence the demand for money under the transactions and precautionary motives. If these are added to the speculative demand for money, and the amount of money needed to satisfy the demand for money under the transactions and precautionary motives is added to the money available for speculative purposes, then this will leave the level of the rate of interest unaffected. The function of the demand for money has shifted by the same amount as the amount of money supplied.

Keynes asserts that in discussing the speculative demand for money a distinction must be made between such changes in the interest rate as are caused by changes in the supply of money available for the satisfaction of the speculative demand for money without any change in the L_2 function, on the one hand, and those changes, on the other hand, which stem primarily from the fact that as a result of a different judgement of the future, the L_2 function itself has been modified. When the L_2 function shifts at a given M_2, the rate of interest suffers an almost abrupt change. The collapse of the marginal efficiency of capital shifts the L_2 function and increases the rate of interest in Keynes, since it increases uncertainty about the future.[125]

With a given L_2 function, if the quantity of money available for speculative purposes increases, excess money will be spent on buying bonds. The price of bonds will increase, and the rate of interest will decrease. Those 'bulls' who find that the current rate of interest has fallen below the expected safe level, will join the 'bear brigade' and offer their stocks for sale in exchange for money to hold their wealth in. But the monetary equilibrium will not necessarily be restored simply by a decrease in the interest rate. This is because a lower rate of interest may stimulate investment as a result of which national income will rise, together with the demand for money, L_1. The quantity of money needed to satisfy that demand will be raised

[124] J. M. Keynes: *op. cit.*, p. 207.
[125] See J. M. Keynes: *op. cit.*, p. 316.

390

by issuing bonds yielding a higher interest, and thus a portion of the increased amount of money will be withdrawn from speculative uses. And monetary equilibrium will be restored when national income and the rate of interest reach a level at which the increased quantity of money is demanded in its entirety partly for transactions and precautionary, partly for speculative purposes.

In the earlier varieties of the cash-balance theory, whenever monetary equilibrium was upset because, for example, the quantity of money had increased, the surplus quantity of money was spent, directly increasing thereby aggregate demand and through it national income in terms of money. The disturbance of monetary equilibrium, as a result of the increased quantity of money, may affect national income for Keynes, too, and a change in national income may also be a condition for establishing monetary equilibrium. Since, however, owing to the uncertainty of the future, money is also demanded, in Keynes's view, as a store of wealth, depending on the rate of interest, monetary equilibrium is tied to certain specific values not only of national income but also of the rate of interest. While in the case of interest-inelastic investment only the rate of interest changes as a function of the increased quantity of money, but national income remains unchanged, in the liquidity trap both national income and the rate of interest remain unchanged as the quantity of money changes.

By introducing the speculative demand for money and by bringing interest-elasticity to the fore, Keynes wants to show, *first,* how monetary policy can influence the level of the interest rate. Those economists who determined the rate of interest by real factors denied that monetary policy could exercise a lasting influence on the level of the rate of interest and affect its equilibrium level. Such a view is also held, by the way, by today's monetarists, among them Friedman, and this position was also taken by Wicksell, whose theory we have already discussed. By issuing credits over and above savings, the central bank can drive down the level of the rate of interest. But in Wicksell this fall in the rate of interest upsets the monetary equilibrium and through it the equilibrium of reproduction. Since, in his view, full employment is ensured, production cannot be augmented, and the increase in the quantity of money raises the price level. Then the unfolding inflationary process compels the banks, sooner or later, to raise the market rate of interest. As has already been mentioned, it is the movement of the price level which adjusts the market rate of interest to the natural rate, while monetary policy is unable to influence the level of the natural rate of interest since the increase in the quantity of money affects neither the time preference of the public nor the marginal productivity of capital.

According to Keynes, who regards full employment only as an exceptional state, intended saving adjusts itself to increasing investment through the rise in national income. By reducing the rate of interest, the banks may stimulate investment and through it the production of national income. They may bring about a new equilibrium position by an appropriate equilibrium rate of interest.

Keynes maintains that it is exactly the interest-elasticity of the speculative demand for money that makes open-market operations possible: the fact that, under normal conditions, the banking system is always able to buy or sell bonds, because even by a slight change in the rate of interest the banks can induce some people to buy bonds or sell them in exchange for cash. Thus the banking system can change the quantity of money through open-market operations. But it can also thereby

391

modify the L_2 function and bring about changes in the expectations concerning the future monetary policy of the central bank or the government.

Secondly, by introducing the speculative demand for money, Keynes also wants to indicate the limitations of monetary policy. Reference has already been made to the fact that, according to Keynes, investment does not necessarily respond to a drop in the rate of interest. And the efficiency of monetary policy is also impeded by the behaviour of the "bears." If the central bank buys bonds through its open-market operations, it thereby forces up their prices; the rate of interest will fall, the "bear brigade" will grow, and some of the "bulls" will become "bears." The supply of bonds will grow, which slows down their price rise and the fall in the rate of interest. As a result, the rate of interest "does not fall in response to an increase in its quantity to anything approaching the extent to which the yield from other types of assets falls when their quantity is comparably increased."[126]

"Bear" speculation is, according to Keynes, particularly harmful because the public conventionally expects a long-term rate of interest to be at too high a level from the point of view of full employment. The actual rate of interest, too, remains unchanged at a relatively high level. This is because as soon as the actual market rate of interest falls below the future long-term rate expected by most of the public, people will dump such a large quantity of bonds on the market that the rate of interest will rise, as a result of the drop in the exchange rate, towards the expected level. Consequently, the long-run rate of interest develops, according to Keynes, at a level that is expected by the majority of the public: "Any level of interest which is accepted with sufficient conviction as *likely* to be durable will be durable...."[127] "... the current market interest rate ... is largely determined by the rate that is expected to prevail over a longer period..."[128] And the long-run rate of interest expected by the greater part of the public is "the most stable, and the least easily shifted, element in our contemporary economy..."[129]

Now the formation of the effective demand necessary to realize full employment is impeded in Keynes by the fact that "... a conventional and fairly stable long-term rate of interest is combined with a fickle and highly unstable marginal efficiency of capital..."[130]

Given an infinite interest-elasticity of the speculative demand-for-money function, monetary policy becomes completely ineffective.

Expressing with the help of Irving Fisher's formula of the quantity theory of money the limitations set on monetary policy by the behaviour of the "bears", we can say that with M increasing through open-market operations, the fall in the rate of interest increases the speculative demand for money. The rise in the speculative demand for money impedes in turn an appropriate fall in the rate of interest and thereby hinders an increase in investment and national income. Thus the effect of an increase in M is absorbed partly by a fall in V. The situation is similar in the case when the interest-elasticity of investment is low, given a fall in the rate of interest resulting from an increase in M, national income increases but

[126] J. M. Keynes: *op. cit.,* p. 233.

[127] J. M. Keynes: *op. cit.,* p. 203.

[128] M. Friedman: A Monetary Theory of Nominal Income, *Journal of Political Economy* March–April 1971, p. 326.

[129] J. M. Keynes: *op. cit.,* p. 309.

[130] J. M. Keynes: *op. cit.,* p. 304

slightly, and therefore V has to fall. But the change in V, as a result of a rise in M, is a function of interest expectations, and hence uncertain. Therefore, the formation of aggregate demand through an increased quantity of money is in Keynes an inappropriate economic policy measure. The effect of the speculative demand for money on slowing down falls in the rate of interest is strengthened by the circumstance that "... a large increase in the quantity of money may cause such uncertainty about the future that liquidity-preference due to the security-motive may be strengthened..."[131] and the L_2 function is shifted. And if the speculative demand for money is infinitely interest-elastic, the effect of an increase in M is completely counterbalanced by the fall in V.

Keynes holds that the speculative demand for money is harmful because it *hampers* the fall in the rate of interest and thereby the growth of investment, and is directed at the same time towards something that cannot be produced, thus *preventing* aggregate demand from growing together with aggregate supply, and full employment from being realized.

Owing to the above-mentioned limitations of monetary policy Keynes writes that "... it seems unlikely that the influence of the banking policy on the rate of interest will be sufficient by itself to determine an optimum rate of investment,"[132] and therefore monetary policy has to be supplemented by budgetary policy.

A CRITIQUE OF THE KEYNESIAN THEORY OF INTEREST

The theory of the speculative demand for money is one of the pillars of Keynes's theoretical system. Keynes wished to create, on the one hand, a theory of interest in which the interest mechanism does not perform the function attributed to it by neo-classical economics, i.e. does not regulate saving and investment and ensure an equilibrium between them. On the other hand, he wished to show how monetary policy can, by changing the quantity of money, persistently influence the rate of interest and through it the level of national income and employment. At the same time, Keynes also wanted to call attention with his theory of money to the limitations of monetary policy, to the very fact that the speculative demand for money of the "bears" hampers the endeavour of the central bank to force down the rate of interest by open-market operations, and prevents the rate of interest from falling to the level needed for full employment.

Evaluating Keynes's theory of interest from the viewpoint of Marxist political economy, we agree with his statement that it is possible to influence the rate of interest through monetary policy, and hence the levels of investment, employment and output. As Marx puts it "the average rate of interest prevailing in a certain country—as distinct from the continually fluctuating market rates—cannot be determined by any law. In this sphere there is no such thing as a natural rate of interest..."[133] and thus it can be formed by the credit policy of the central bank.

But we cannot accept the explanation of interest given by Keynes, namely his

---

131 J. M. Keynes: *op. cit.*, p. 172.
132 J. M. Keynes: *op. cit.*, p. 378.
133 K. Marx: *Capital*, Vol. III, Moscow, 1962, p. 355.

statement that interest is entirely a financial, psychological factor, the price for giving up liquidity, and that it brings the speculative demand for money into equilibrium with the quantity of money available for speculative purposes.

The rate of interest is by no means "the reward for parting with liquidity..."[134] Hoarding, the insistence on holding wealth in money cannot be looked upon as typical of capitalist economy. As Marx puts it "... money ... may be converted into capital on the basis of capitalist production, and may thereby be increasing value."[135] Marx's answer to the question of what the money-capitalist" rcnounces" for the period of time for which he lends his money, expresses the essence of the capitalist mode of production, namely, that he renounces the use-value of his capital, that is, its capacity of producing average profit.[136] Marx emphasizes that the capitalist entrepreneur wants to derive profit even from the money accumulated temporarily as treasure. "The eagerness to utilize this surplus-value accumulating as virtual money-capital for purpose of deriving profits or revenue from it finds its object accomplished in the credit system and 'papers'."[137]

No doubt, an increase in the rate of interest diminishes the price of long-term bonds. Already Marx wrote about this as follows: "... a rise in interest implies a fall in the price of securities..."[138] Those bond-holders who expect the rate of interest to rise, try to get rid of their bonds. Yet they do it not in order to hold their wealth in money, but in another, safer but still profitable form. In the case of shares, for example, in boom periods, the effect of a rising rate of interest on decreasing share prices is outweighed for a long time by the effect of rising dividends on increasing share prices. Under such circumstances, it is worthwhile to hold one's wealth in shares instead of in long-term bonds. As Hansen puts it: "in the expansion phase, there is a shift from bonds to equities..."[139]

No doubt, asset-holders endeavour to hold their wealth in a safe rather than a less safe form. This does not mean, however, an insistence on money, merely an exchange of one profitable asset for another, for a safer and more profitable one. But if they hold an equity instead of a long-term bond because they expect the rate of interest to rise, then in this case it is not the demand for money but the demand for equities which is interest-elastic.

If a speculator, taken in the narrower sense, holds cash, he does it merely in order better to utilize a favourable opportunity to buy depreciated securities more cheaply and to get thereby a higher rate of return, or to obtain a capital gain by selling his securities later, at a higher price. He sacrificed the interest for the period in which he held his wealth in cash not for greater safety, but in the hope of an expected higher interest revenue or capital gain. In his computations he compares these expectations with the interest revenue sacrificed and takes his decision on whether to defer buying securities or rather buy them immediately. Incidentally, a "bear" need not let the money needed to buy securities lie idle even in the short

134 J. M. Keynes: *op. cit.*, p. 167.
135 K. Marx: *op. cit.*, p. 332.
136 K. Marx: *op. cit.*, p. 345.
137 K. Marx: *Capital*, Vol. II, Moscow, 1957, p. 498.
138 K. Marx: *Capital*, Vol. III, Moscow, 1962, p. 354.
139 A. Hansen: *A Guide to Keynes*, London, 1953, p. 138

run. "... even if he is bearish ... he will switch not into money, but into bills."[140] In Keynes, however, short-term bonds, owing to the interest-inelasticity of their price, come under one heading with money in its strict sense in the L_2 function, and thus he has no possibility of representing an asset-holder's choice between money in its strict sense and short-term bonds.

In Keynes, a bearish speculation is set off when the market rate of interest falls below what is believed to be the safe long-term rate of interest. Marx also distinguishes the market rate of interest from the average rate of interest, which is the average of the interest rate across the cycle, in line with the cyclical movement of capitalist reproduction. According to Marx, the average rate of interest is relatively constant in the long run. He sees its cause in the relative constancy of the general profit rate. "... its relative constancy [i.e. of the general rate of profit—A. M.] is revealed precisely in this more or less constant nature of the average, of common rate of interest."[141] In Keynes, however, the durability of expectations concerning the long-term rate of interest is devoid of any objective foundation.

The endeavour to sell bonds when their price is rising and hence the rate of interest is falling, may also be explained if we do not assume that a fall in their price is expected. We only need to assume that the asset-holder wishes to exchange his asset yielding a decreasing interest for another asset with a higher yield, which will compensate him also for the loss of capital gain on the asset sold whose price was rising.

Besides rejecting the Keynesian view that interest is the price of giving up liquidity, we cannot accept another proposition of his either, namely, that if the expansion of output requires a larger sum of money, operating capitalists can get hold of this money only if they induce money owners, to give up liquidity by paying them a higher rate of interest. Entrepreneurs raise the necessary amount of money primarily from banks. Banks demand interest not as a reward for renouncing liquidity. Being business undertakings, they seek to reach an average rate of profit on their capital, and try therefore to satisfy the demand for credit of individuals and institutions which can be relied upon to repay the credits granted to them.

In open-market operations it is not only the speculative motive, the fear of a fall in the price of assets that stimulates wealth-holders to sell their long-term bonds. They may offer them for sale also because they are obliged to make payments, because they need money for their business undertakings, because they wish to hold their wealth in more profitable securities, or banks may offer their long-term bonds for sale because they want to acquire notes issued by the central bank in order to extend loans. We can read in Samuelson's *Economics* that since 1953 "the Federal Reserve authorities have decided to limit themselves to open-market operations in short-term government bills..."[142] Short-term government bonds, however, do not constitute, according to the Keynesian theory, the object of speculations, while they may be the object of selling and buying in open-market operations.

Interest as the price of renouncing liquidity for Keynes is, according to Hicks a risk-premium.[143] The degree of risk in fact influences the level of the rate of

[140] J. M. Hicks: *The Crisis in Keynesian Economics*, Oxford, 1974, p. 45.
[141] K. Marx: *Capital*, Vol. III, Moscow, 1962, p. 358.
[142] P. A. Samuelson: *Economics*, New York–Toronto–London, 1961, p. 363.
[143] J. R. Hicks: *Value and Capital*, Oxford, 1965, p. 164.

interest. Marx's remark on the larger profit of more hazardous undertakings "... that investments of capital in lines exposed to greater hazards... are compensated by higher prices"[144] also refers to higher interest rates set in credit transactions involving greater risks. But just as profit cannot be regarded as a reward for the risks of undertakings, in the same way, interest cannot be considered either as a premium for the risk-taking involved in making loans. Samuelson reminds us of this when writing that "... it would be a mistake... if it were thought that uncertainty and liquidity differentials are the *sine qua non* for the existence of a rate of interest."[145]

And how could the rate of interest be determined in a certain world in which the Keynesian propensity to hoard, the liquidity function L_2, is missing? According to Hicks, the true nature of interest can be revealed if we find a reason for the existence of pure interest, that is, for the rate of interest on bills of such a short term that the possibility of having to rediscount is ruled out.[146] By mentioning this problem, Hicks wants to emphasize that the existence of interest cannot be explained merely by referring to risk. But the solution offered by him is not acceptable either. In his opinion, "the level of the rate of interest measures the trouble involved in investing funds..."[147]

Marx does not explain the fact that a long rate of interest is usually higher than a short rate by the greater risk involved. In this connection he writes "... that the rate of profit is not only determined by the relation of profit made in one single turnover to advanced capital-value, but also by the length of this period of turnover..."[148] This circumstance appears in connection with interest-bearing capital in such a way "that a definite interest is paid to the lender for a definite time span."[149]

Nor does Marx determine the rate of interest through the relationship between the demand for and the supply of money. In his system "... the relation between the supply of loanable capital on the one side, and the demand for it on the other, decides the market level of interest at any given time."[150] He regards as a decisive element of the demand for loanable capital "... the demand of industrial capitalists for money-capital"[151], which is determined "by conditions of actual production".[152] And in Marx the banking system does not increase the supply of loanable capital at will, regardless of capitalist reproduction as a whole, irrespective of the actual position of the business cycle. For Marx the movement of the rate of interest basically reflects the evolution of reproduction. By the way, Hansen's comments on the Keynesian theoretical system also reveal that the Keynesian propensity to hoard is a function of the reproduction process. "... the propensity to hoard is lowest in the recovery and the early stage of expansion and highest in the crisis

[144] K. Marx: *Capital,* Vol. III, Moscow, 1962, p. 206.
[145] P. A. Samuelson: *Foundations of Economic Analysis,* Cambridge, Harvard University Press, 1947, p. 122.
[146] J. R. Hicks: *Value and Capital,* Oxford, 1965, p. 164.
[147] J. R. Hicks: *op. cit.,* p. 165.
[148] K. Marx: *Capital,* Vol. III, Moscow, 1962, p. 350.
[149] *Ibid.*
[150] K. Marx: *op. cit.,* p. 359.
[151] K. Marx: *op. cit.,* p. 410.
[152] *Ibid.*

phase."[153] Thus the level of the rate of interest cannot be regarded, even on a Keynesian theoretical basis, as a merely financial, psychological phenomenon. The dependence of the rate of interest on reproduction becomes manifest in Keynes in another way also. Assuming a given quantity of money and a given L_2 function, the level of national income determines, according to Keynes, how much money will be left to satisfy the speculative demand for money, and hence how high will be the rate of interest. In actual fact, the rate of interest is decisively influenced by the supply of securities offered by those who want to obtain money for production purposes, who offer long-term bonds for sale not because they are afraid of their falling price and demand money, nor because holding it in cash ensures safety and convenience, but because they want to spend it in the interests of reproduction. In Keynes, however, the L_1 money-demand function is not interest-elastic, and therefore Keynes does not take it into account in determining the equilibrium level of the rate of interest.

It must be noted, however, that even if we do not accept Keynes's view that the level of the rate of interest is determined by the relation between the speculative demand for money and the supply of money, we must still admit that the interest rate is undoubtedly affected by speculative behaviour. It is affected by such behaviour that speculators demand credit and thereby increase the demand for loans when they want to buy securities whose price is expected to rise; the rate of interest is also affected by the speculators buying and selling bonds in great quantities. By selling long-term bonds and buying short-term securities instead, the "bears" change the relation between short and long rates of interest. Hicks pointed out how strongly the bearish behaviour of speculators countered in England the government's attempt to reduce the rate of interest on long-term bonds by open-market operations. "How powerful such speculation can be was demonstrated practically, in England, soon after Keynes died. The Attlee government attempted to hold the long-term rate of government securities down to 3 per cent; but their patience was exhausted before that of the speculators."[154]

The insistence, as emphasized by Keynes, on money as the safest form of holding wealth is typical under capitalist conditions only if people expect a general fall in the price of securities. "As a picture of reality, this model becomes most nearly justifiable in periods of depression when also liquidity preference comes nearest to being an operative factor in its own right."[155] It becomes absolutely clear in a period of depression how impermissible it is to regard short-term bonds as money in its strict sense. At that time, even short-term bonds, except for short-term government bills, experience a massive drop in price not because the rate of interest is increasing but because they represent unsaleable commodities, and thus they cannot be redeemed at maturity.

Otherwise, the massive demand for money in times of depression cannot be represented as a function of the rate of interest. Securities yielding variable earnings, e.g. shares, lose in value not only as a result of a rise in the rate of interest, but "... as a result of the decrease in revenues for which it constitutes drafts..."[156]

153 A. Hansen: *op. cit.,* p. 139.
154 J. R. Hicks: *The Crisis in Keynesian Economics,* Oxford, 1974, p. 36.
155 J. A. Schumpeter: *Ten Great Economists,* London, 1966, p. 283.
156 K. Marx: *Capital,* Vol. III, Moscow, 1962, p. 482.

The demand for money by shareholders is a function not only of the increase in the rate of interest, but also of the decrease in dividends. In a slump period, however, not only security-holders want to keep their wealth in a safe form, but also productive capitalists. Under conditions of an overall fall in prices, they prefer to hold their money reserves earmarked for expanding or replacing their stock of capital rather than to spend them. This attempt by entrepreneurs to hold money definitely conflicts with its representation as a function of the rate of interest. Marxist political economy does not define the price of real capital assets as a capitalized return.

Chapter 7

POST-KEYNESIAN MICRO-THEORY
OF THE DEMAND FOR MONEY

The Keynesian theory of the demand for money was criticized from several view-points even by Keynes's followers. Thus it was criticized, among other things, because Keynes tried to explain the interest-elasticity of the demand for money by the heavily debated speculative motive. To demonstrate the interest-elasticity of the demand for money, some economists referred to the interest-elasticity of the transactions demand instead of the speculative demand for money. Why could people not hold their transactions balances, too, they asked, in profitable assets until payments fell due? According to Tobin, a relationship must be found between average cash holding, or average bond holding, and the interest rate, on the assumption that the individual divides the total transactions balances between cash and bonds in such a way that he maximizes his interest earnings, net of transactions cost.[157] The switch of cash into profitable assets and the sale of these assets if payments fall due involve costs. "The minimum broker's fee is what makes it unprofitable to take cash out of investments in frequent small driblets..."[158] It is worthwhile buying bonds if they can be held long enough so that interest earnings exceed the transactions costs incurred when selling and buying them. With an increase in the interest rate the optimal balance of idle cash decreases, because it becomes more economical to withdraw cash from investments even more frequently and in driblets whenever this becomes necessary with payments falling due. Thus transactions balances can be held longer in bonds and, consequently, the average investment holding will grow.

Even at an unchanged rate of interest it is possible to increase the number of withdrawals if the amount of money withdrawn increases. Namely, the greater this amount, the smaller will be the broker's fee in relative terms. Thus the number of optimum withdrawals grows with the volume of transactions. When the volume of transactions per firm increases, optimum cash balances will grow too, but at a lesser rate than the volume of transactions payments.

And with the increase in the volume of transactions, writes Tobin, the range of values of the interest rate for which the demand for cash is sensitive to the interest rate will grow too. "... large transactors may be quite sensitive to the interest

---

[157] See J. Tobin: The Interest-elasticity of Transactions Demand for Cash, *The Review of Economics and Statistics*, August 1956, p. 242.

[158] W. J. Baumol: *Economic Theory and Operations Analysis*, Englewood Cliff, New Jersey, 1961, p. 244.

rate."[159] Smaller transactors, however, do not find it worthwhile holding their transactions balances in assets other than cash. Then, as the volume of transactions rises, the number of optimum withdrawals will increase even at a lower interest rate, and the share of cash in the necessary transactions balances will decrease even at a lower rate of interest. As Baumol puts it: "... if firms are efficient profit maximizers, Keynes was probably wrong in playing down the influence of the interest rate in the transactions demand for cash."[160]

Baumol tries to determine the size of the optimum cash inventory on the analogy of optimum product inventories. In this sense he writes that "inventory theory and monetary theory can learn from one another."[161]

Thus, in order to represent the interest-elasticity of the demand for money, he substitutes the inventory theory of demand for speculative demand. In this way, certain post-Keynesian economists attempted to set up a functional relationship between the demand for money and the interest rate. But this shifts attention away from substitution, as a result of changes in the interest rate, between long-term securities and money (broadly interpreted so as to include also short-term securities), in the direction of substitution between short-term securities and money proper. Keynesian speculative demand for money is based on the assumption that a change in the rate of interest influences the price of long-term securities strongly, but that of short-term securities to a negligible extent. Thus the transactions and precautionary demand for money, for whose satisfaction necessary funds are held either in cash or short-term securities interpreted as money in its broad sense, are not interest-elastic. Baumol and others, however, examine how people decide, depending on the level of the interest rate, on an optimum division of their transactions balances between money and short-term securities.

These economists present a modified function for the demand for money, with which, they argue, it is possible to determine the establishment of monetary equilibrium, the interest-elasticity of demand for money, and all the effects that Keynes attempted to point out by introducing the concept of speculative demand for money. In the 1973 edition of Samuelson's *Economics,* open-market operations by the central bank influence the level of the rate of interest already through the demand for cash inventories; the liquidity trap, too, appears in this function at an adequately low level of the interest rate. At a low interest rate, transactions and precautionary balances are held in cash rather than in securities, not because of anxiety about a future decrease in security prices, but simply because at a low rate of interest it is not economical to undertake to pay the transactions costs stemming from the buying and selling of securities. Tobin also emphasizes that for the demonstration of the interest-elasticity of money demand it is not necessary to assume uncertainty concerning the future level of the interest rate: "Even if there were unanimity and certainty that prevailing interest rates would continue unchanged indefinitely, so that no motive for holding cash other than transactions requirements existed, the demand for cash would depend inversely on the rate of interest.

[159] J. Tobin: The Interest-elasticity of Transactions Demand for Cash, *The Review of Economics and Statistics,* August 1956, p. 246.
[160] W. J. Baumol: *Economic Theory and Operations Analysis,* Englewood Cliff, New Jersey, 1961, p. 244.
[161] See W. J. Baumol: The Transactions Demand for Cash: an Inventory Theoretic Approach, *The Quarterly Journal of Economics,* November 1952, p. 545.

The reason is simply the cost of transactions between cash and interest-bearing assets."[162]

Evaluating the post-Keynesian theory of the demand for money as set out above, we may regard as realistic the assumption of the theory that productive capitalists do not want to let even the money reserves needed to maintain the continuity of production lie idle, and attempt instead to use them profitably until payments fall due, and grant credits to one another from the money released temporarily. Thus this new version of the theory of the demand for money also represents—to use a Marxist term—so-called commercial credit. And we may agree that a high interest rate stimulates the economic use of cash balances.

But the background to the optimum utilization of cash is also provided in the short run by the level of reproduction. In times of depression, the interest rate is low, but this does not stimulate investment, and national income will not grow. On the contrary, it will contract, and the demand for transactions balances will decrease. The demand for transactions cash will also decrease, even though the low rate of interest may increase the share of the cash in the transactions balances. Under such circumstances, despite an increase in the quantity of money, owing to open-market operations, people are reluctant to hold the increased quantity of money for transactions purposes even at a low rate of interest. Surplus money will be accumulated at the banks as unintended surplus reserves.

Under recovery, however, investment will grow even at a high rate of interest, and a similar growth will be experienced in national income, transactions balances, and optimal cash balances, too, though the share of the latter in transactions balances will decrease owing to the higher level of the interest rate.

The amount of the necessary transactions balances is a function of reproduction. With an increase in transactions balances the demand for transactions cash will grow, and with their decrease it will fall. The level of the interest rate exercises a direct effect at best on the form of holding a given magnitude of transactions balances. Leijonhufvud is right in saying that "it is not evident that the interest-elasticity of the demand for cash balances will be as quantitatively significant as it appears in the Baumol–Tobin framework."[163]

Let us finish our critique of Keynesian and post-Keynesian interest-rate theories by saying that even non-Marxian economists raise the objection that those who attempt to explain the short-term rate of interest by transactions costs and the long-term rate by the inconvenience and risk incidental to giving up liquidity, focus their attention on the choice between money and near money, or on money in its broad sense and long-term bonds, and lose sight of the process of production taking place in the background.[164] Though the non-Marxian critique connects the rate of interest with production in a way which cannot be accepted by Marxian economics, it is right in stating that the interest rate cannot be explained independently of production. As Marx puts it, "... qualitatively speaking, interest is surplus-value..."[165]

[162] J. Tobin: The Interest-elasticity of Transactions Demand for Cash, *The Review of Economics and Statistics*, August 1956, p. 241.

[163] A. Leijonhufvud: *On Keynesian Economics and the Economics of Keynes*, New York–London–Toronto, 1968, p. 358.

[164] A. Leijonhufvud: *op. cit.*, p. 359.

[165] K. Marx: *Capital*, Vol. III, Moscow, 1962, p. 369.

Chapter 8

HICKS'S AND HANSEN'S ATTEMPTS TO DETERMINE THE RATE OF INTEREST AND NATIONAL INCOME SIMULTANEOUSLY BY MEANS OF THE *IS* AND *LM* CURVES

In criticizing the view of neo-classical economics, Keynes asserts that until we know the magnitude of national income, the equilibrium between investment and saving tells us nothing about the level of the rate of interest. In fact, it is no surprise, because the supply and demand functions for saving, i. e., the investment function are not independent of each other. If a new investment opportunity shifts the investment function upwards, national income will grow, and the saving function will shift, too.

Hansen, however, points out that with his theory of interest Keynes himself, too, uses a circular argument. With a given quantity of money and a given liquidity preference function, Keynes wants to determine the interest rate by the amount of money available for speculative purposes. But it is on the level of national income that the amount of speculative money supply depends. The higher the national income with a given quantity of money, the less is the amount of money available for speculation, and the higher the rate of interest. The level of national income depends in its turn on the level of investment which, without the interest rate being known, is indeterminate; so is, consequently, the level of national income, too. Keynes did not realize this contradiction. In determining the rate of interest he assumed the level of national income as given; while he regarded the rate of interest as constant in determining the equilibrium level of national income.

Hicks[166] and later Hansen[167] tried to evade the vicious circle that can be found in both the neo-classical and the Keynesian interest theories by determining the rate of interest and national income simultaneously. The equilibrium of the real sphere is expressed by the equation $Y = C + I$, and the equilibrium of the monetary sphere by the equation $M = L_1 + L_2$, where $C = f_1(Y)$, $I = f(r, i)$, $L_1 = f_2(Y)$ and $L_2 = f(i)$. Both equations contain two unknowns, Y and i. The solution of the two simultaneous equations will also determine, according to Hicks and Hansen, the values of Y and i.

Their method is represented graphically according to H. G. Johnson.[168] First, they constructed the saving function $S = f(Y)$ (Figure 74a), then the investment function $I = f(r, i)$. Taking r, the independent variable of the system, as given, investment appears to be a function of the rate of interest only (Figure 74b).

[166] J. R. Hicks: *A Contribution to the Theory of Trade Cycle*, Oxford, 1950, Chapter XI, pp. 136–154.

[167] A. Hansen: *A Guide to Keynes*, McGraw-Hill Publishing Company Ltd., New York–London–Toronto, 1953, pp. 144–146.

[168] H. G. Johnson: *Money Trade and Economic Growth*, London, 1962.

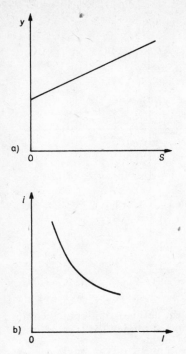

a)

b)

Figure 74a, b

By combining the two curves, those of investment and saving, they constructed the *IS* curve, that is, the investment–saving curve, which expresses the level of national income at each of the various levels of the rate of interest (Figure 75).

If the rate of interest is high, then, according to the investment function, the amount of intended investment is small. Therefore, in equilibrium, the level of intended saving adjusted to intended investment must be low too; so also, according to the saving function, is the equilibrium level of national income. By similar reasoning they pointed out that, given a low rate of interest, the equilibrium level of national income must be high. According to Hansen, neo-classical economics determined by the saving and investment functions not the equilibrium level of the rate of interest, but only the *IS* curve.

The *IS* curve expresses the equilibrium of intended saving and intended investment for the different coordinate values of the rate of interest and national income. But the curve itself does not tell us at what values of the rate of interest and national income the actual equilibrium is established. For this to be known, the particular rate of interest must, as a datum, be included in the model.

As a next step, Hicks and Hansen determined the value of the rate of interest. They represent the function of the speculative demand for money in the upper

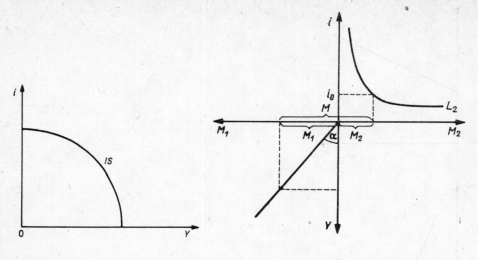

Figure 75   Figure 76

right-hand corner of the diagram (see Figure 76), the level of national income
on the negative section of the y-axis and the demand for money for transactions
purposes on the negative section of the x-axis. The tangent of the angle α, $\dfrac{M_1}{Y}$,
expresses the ratio of national income to the quantity of money required, and
shows, with the help of α, how much of a given total money supply is tied up by the
demand for money under the transactions motive at the different levels of national
income. Deducting the quantity of money thus tied up, M_1, from the total quantity
of money, they obtain the quantity of money available for speculative purposes,
M_2. Representing this on the positive section of the x-axis, they get the equilibrium
level of the rate of interest for each level of the national income. It will be clear
from Figure 76 that, at a given total money supply and a given $\dfrac{M_1}{Y}$ ratio, the
smaller the national income, the lower is the equilibrium rate of interest owing to
the increasing quantity of money available for speculative purposes.

Hicks and Hansen then constructed the LM curve, as shown in Figure 77, i.e.
the curve of the demand for and the supply of money, which expresses those
interconnected values of the rate of interest and of national income at which aggregate demand for money is just in equilibrium with money supply.

In Hansen's opinion, what is determined by Keynes's interest theory, the relationship of the speculative demand for money to the supply of money available
for speculative purposes, is not the equilibrium level of the rate of interest, but only
the LM curve. By the Keynesian method the actual equilibrium level of the rate of
interest can only be determined if the supply of money available for speculative
purposes is known, which in turn presupposes knowledge of the level of national

404

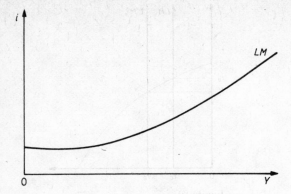

Figure 77

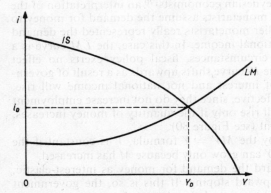

Figure 78

income. Consequently, in order to determine the equilibrium level of the rate of interest, the level of national income must be included as a datum in the model.

Hicks and Hansen thought that the point of intersection of the *IS* and *LM* curves provided the equilibrium level of the rate of interest and national income (see Figure 78). At an interest rate thus obtained, entrepreneurs wish to invest, in compliance with the investment function, as much as society wishes to save out of national income thus obtained, in accordance with the saving function. On the other hand, assuming a given supply of money, the national income and the rate of interest will be such that the supply of money available for speculative purposes exactly equals the speculative demand for money.

In the dispute between monetarists and neo-Keynesians, in the course of which "neo-Keynesians believe that *both* monetary and fiscal policies affect nominal

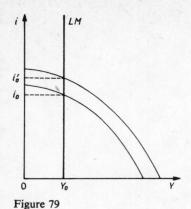

Figure 79

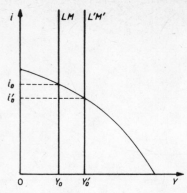

Figure 80

income, and monetarists believe that only monetary policies do so,"[169] both sides make use of the *IS* and *LM* curves for illustrating their respective views.

We can often encounter in neo-Keynesian economists[170] an interpretation of the monetarist view according to which monetarists assume the demand for money to be completely interest-inelastic. Earlier monetarists really represented the demand for money only as a function of national income. In this case, the *LM* curve is a vertical straight line. Under such circumstances, fiscal policy exerts no effect whatsoever on national income. If the *IS* curve shifts upwards as a result of government expenditures, only the rate of interest and not national income will rise. The outlays on public works are ineffective, since they do not increase employment (see Figure 79). National income will rise only if the quantity of money increases, when the *LM* curve shifts to the right (see Figure 80).

Expressing the monetarist view by the $MV = Y$ formula, V is constant if the *LM* curve is a vertical straight line. Y can grow only because M has increased.

Keynes's followers, however, regard the demand for money as interest-elastic, and assume the *LM* curve to be upward sloping. If this is so, the government expenditures can increase national income and thereby employment even at the given quantity of money. Needing part of the existing quantity of money, the government raises the rate of interest. The higher rate of interest releases part of the quantity of money used as a store of wealth, which in turn makes it possible to finance public works without withdrawing the quantity of money needed for it entirely from private investment.

Expressing the above by the formula $MV = Y$, and taking M to be given, the interest rate increased by government expenditures decreases the speculative demand for money, raises the circulation velocity of money, and, as a result, both MV and Y will rise.

Present-day monetary economists admit that the *LM* curve is interest-elastic, that changes in the quantity of money affect V. While admitting this, they want to

[169] J. Tobin: Friedman's Theoretical Framework, *Journal of Political Economy*, 1972, Vol. 80. p. 852.

[170] See, among others, J. Tobin: *op. cit.*, p. 853.

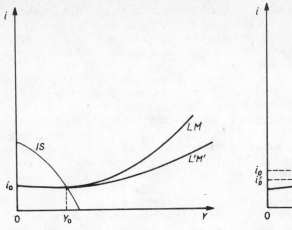

Figure 81

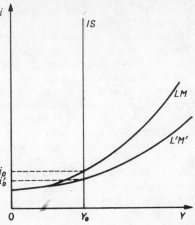

Figure 82

prove the priority of monetary policy over fiscal policy and argue that if M does not change in line with government expenditures because, for example, they are financed from borrowings from the public, the government demand for credit will raise the rate of interest and thereby diminish private investment. In the case of an interest-elastic demand for money, total investment will grow but, owing to the decrease in private investment, by a lesser margin than the growth in government expenditures. Consequently, national income will rise but relatively slightly.

If, however, government expenditures are financed by creating money, with M rising, the LM curve will shift downwards and national income will increase significantly.

According to Friedman, if government expenditures increase in a given year and fall back later to their original level, then, provided the quantity of money has not changed, IS curve will shift downwards to resume later its original position, and real and nominal income will increase for a year to fall back afterwards to its original value. On the other hand, if the transitory, one-year increase in government expenditures is financed by creating money, the LM curve will shift downwards and stay there afterwards, too, and the IS curve will resume its original position. In this case, given an unchanged price level, both real and nominal income will stabilize at a higher level. If, however, the price level eventually rises, real income will fall to its original level, but nominal income will stay at its higher level. Thus "the monetary effect is 'alchemy of much deeper significance' than the fiscal effect."[171]

However, all this only shows that fiscal policy has to be combined with monetary policy, but it does not prove the priority of monetary policy over fiscal policy.

[171] M. Friedman: Comments on the Critics, *Journal of Political Economy*, 1972, Vol. 80. p. 916.

The increase in the quantity of money in itself does not necessarily mean a rise in total demand. On the contrary, it is exactly fiscal policy that makes it possible for the increased quantity of money to appear as greater demand and as a result of the rise in the price level, for nominal income to stabilize at a higher level even after a decrease in government expenditures.

The Keynesian arguments relating to the limits of monetary policy are also valid in respect to Friedman. Keynes's objections expressed by means of the *IS* and *LM* curves may be summed up like this no matter that the quantity of money increases and curve *LM* shifts downwards, national income will not change if we are in the liquidity trap. This section of curve *LM* is a straight line, and the growth in the quantity of money leaves the position of this section unchanged. Neither will it change, if as a result of the increased quantity of money, investment is interest-inelastic, i.e. if curve *IS* is a vertical straight line. The increased quantity of money will not raise total demand in either case (see Figures 81 and 82).

We shall see later that according to Keynes's critics the automatisms of the capitalist economy ensure full employment even in the case of the infinite interest elasticity of the demand for money or in the case of the interest-inelasticity of the investment function, through the various wealth effects which shift the *IS* curve upwards or, in the case of the interest-inelastic investment function, to the right, because the consumers save a smaller proportion of their incomes. We shall also deal in greater detail with the uncertainty of the wealth effect later.

Chapter 9

THE LABOUR MARKET IN KEYNES

Keynes rejects the neo-classical view which maintains that under unemployment a fall in money wages creates an equilibrium between the demand for and the supply of labour.

In his theory, employment depends on aggregate demand, and the equilibrium level of employment is established at the point of intersection of the aggregate demand and supply functions.

Does a decrease in money wages increase the demand for labour, asks Keynes?

A fall in money wages decreases production costs, diminishing the aggregate supply price. Neo-classical economists focused their attention only on that fact, and ignored the effect of a fall in money wages on demand. Under such circumstances they came to the conclusion that a fall in money wages, by increasing entrepreneurial profit, stimulates increased employment. The neglect of the effect of a decline in money wages on demand, says Keynes, can be accepted only at the firm or industry level. But this effect has to be reckoned with at a social level. In Keynes's view, the level of employment, as a result of a fall in money wage rates, depends on how a decrease in money wages, through its effect on the propensity to consume, on the function of the marginal efficiency of capital, or on the rate of interest, affects aggregate demand. Will the aggregate demand function intersect the aggregate supply schedule at a higher or lower level of employment? Employment will grow if, with decreasing nominal wages, aggregate demand measured in money terms remains the same as it was, or does not fall at least to the same extent as nominal wages.

Keynes thinks that it is really impossible to tell how the money wage rate affects aggregate demand and through it employment. In some conditions it will exercise a favourable, in others an unfavourable effect on them.

Let us examine some of the more important possibilities mentioned by Keynes.

If, with a fall in money wages, prices decrease to a lesser extent because the incomes of other factors constituting marginal cost have not declined, then the real income of the latter will grow to the detriment of the workers' real income. The result is likely to be a fall in the propensity to consume and through it a decline in consumer demand and employment.

However, by decreasing production costs, a fall in money wages may favour exports with a resulting growth of employment.

If entrepreneurs think that the fall in money wage rates is only transitory, and expect a rise in money wages in the future, then this may give rise to favourable profit expectations on their part and induce them to take advantage of the opportunity offered by the lower money wage rates, to step up their current investments and thereby employment. But if they think that wage rates will fall still lower, they will tend to defer their investments since the marginal efficiency of capital will fall "if current costs of production are thought to be higher than they will be later on..."[172]

A fall in prices due to declining money wages may increase the tax burdens of some of the indebted entrepreneurs up to insolvency, seriously affecting investment as a result.

With decreasing money wages, the entrepreneurs' demand for money for transactions purposes will fall, and out of the given quantity of money available to the economy more will be assigned to speculative uses; the demand for bonds and therefore their prices will rise, and the rate of interest will fall. Given a fixed supply of money, the effect of declining money wages on the rate of interest will, according to Keynes, be the same as if, with unchanged money wages, the quantity of money had increased. This effect of money wage cuts is what the literature of economics calls the *Keynes-effect*.

A declining interest rate may stimulate investment. If, however, profit expectations, i.e. the marginal efficiency of capital are unfavourable, a fall in the rate of interest will not stimulate investment: the investment function will be completely interest-elastic. Equally absent will be the stimulating effect of declining money wage rates on investment, if the schedule of the speculative demand for money is infinitely interest-elastic. In this case, people will not use the money released from the transactions reserve for buying securities, but will prefer to hold their wealth as money. Now the fall in money wages will have no appreciable effect on the level of the rate of interest.

In the last analysis, Keynes comes to this conclusion: "There is, therefore, no ground for the belief that a flexible wage policy is capable of maintaining a state of continuous full employment..."[173] By so saying, he relieves the working class of the responsibility for unemployment. The ultimate cause of unemployment is not wages kept at a high level by organized labour. "It is not very plausible to assert that unemployment in the United States in 1932 was due either to labour obstinately refusing to accept a reduction of money-wages, or to its obstinately demanding a real wage beyond what the productivity of the economic machine was capable of furnishing."[174] Just on the contrary, the chief result of an economic policy designed to cut nominal wages "... would be to cause a great instability of prices, so violent perhaps as to make business calculations futile in an economic society functioning after the manner of that in which we live..."[175]

Even if we accept Keynes's reasoning with reservations, we must admit that he is right in saying that a cut in money wages is not an adequate means to eliminate unemployment.

Despite Keynes's arguments Pigou insists on his view that under unemployment the economy cannot reach equilibrium and that flexible wage rates ensure full

172 J. M. Keynes: *The General Theory of Employment, Interest and Money*, p. 317.
173 J. M. Keynes: *op. cit.*, p. 267.
174 J. M. Keynes: *op. cit.*, p. 9.
175 J. M. Keynes: *op. cit.*, p. 269.

410

employment. In his work published in 1944,[176] Pigou refers to a mechanism which, in conditions of unemployment, would increase consumption demand as a result of a decline in money wages. The increase in consumption demand would take place not through investments, nor through the multiplier effect; it would thus come into force even if investment is interest-inelastic, or the speculative demand for money is infinitely interest-elastic. The so-called *Pigou* or *real-balance effect* expresses that, when money wages decline under the pressure of unemployment, the price level falls, with the consequence that the real value of money assets will grow. According to the so-called *real financial effect,* related to the former, a reduction in money wages leads to the growth of the real value of nominally fixed non-money claims. The owners of these assets, becoming richer, will spend a greater proportion of their incomes on consumption. As the demand for consumer goods increases, entrepreneurs will expand the output of consumer goods and increase employment. "There always exists a sufficiently low price level such that if expected to continue indefinitely, it will generate full employment,"[177] writes Don Patinkin. The Keynes-effect may also stimulate consumption demand because the reduction of money wages, through an increase in the quantity of real-money assets, decreases the rate of interest, which in turn raises the price of securities, and this growth of assets also stimulates consumption.

As a matter of fact, however, modern money is credit money. And even if, owing to the declining price level, the wealth of money owners or creditors grows, the burden of debtors will also increase. This is, among other things, how Keynes argues against the Pigou effect.[178] More recently, however, under the influence of Gurley and Shaw,[179] a distinction is made between inside money and outside money. Inside money is credit money, while outside money is fiat paper money, government bonds. And since the government, unlike private debtors, does not reduce its outlays if its debts increase, then, according to a recently accepted view, the Pigou and the real financial effect can freely unfold on the basis of outside money.

The so-called wealth effects, already mentioned, are theoretically conceivable, but they stimulate the growth of output only in so far as they increase the total profit of the capitalist class. An increase in consumption through the wealth effects would be of interest primarily in the case of the working class due to its volume. But the consumption outlays of the working class made out of wages do not increase the profit of the capitalist class, while its savings decrease the profit. This is so because the sum of money that is returned to the capitalist class through the purchases of the working class is in this case smaller than what the capitalists have advanced to the workers in the form of wages. If, as a result of the wealth effect, the working class saves a smaller proportion of its wages, the loss of the capitalist class decreases and its profit becomes greater than what it gained at a larger saving ratio of the working class. At the time the *General Theory* was published, the savings of the working class were insignificant, and thus its assets held in money and bonds were also negligible. On the other hand, the wealth

176 See A. C. Pigou: *Lapses from Full Employment,* Bloomington, 1944, p. 22.
177 D. Patinkin: Price Stability and Full Employment. In: *Readings in Monetary Theory,* New York, 1951, p. 271.
178 J. M. Keynes: *op. cit.,* p. 264.
179 J. G. Gurley and E. S. Shaw: *Money in the Theory of Finance,* Washington, 1960.

effect is unlikely to increase the consumption of the capitalist class significantly, except, perhaps, the consumption of small capitalists. But the circumstances of a slump may counteract this effect. During such a period, workers and capitalists alike will probably take care not to react to a rise in their real assets by increasing their consumption outlays. And under unfavourable cyclical conditions a possible rise in consumption demand is unlikely to stimulate investment, this important profit component. During a slump there is ample idle capacity, and thus the increased demand for consumer goods may be satisfied even without any new investments.

We have already discussed Keynes's view about the effect of the reduction of money wages on investment. This effect is unfavourable if entrepreneurs expect a further fall in money wages. This is the situation in a period of depression. And the fall in the rate of interest accompanying the reduction of money wages is not sure to stimulate investment. Incidentally, in connection with the consumption-expanding influence of the Keynes-effect, it is worth noting that even though a decreasing rate of interest does have a bearing on the prices of securities with variable yields, these depend not only on the interest rate but also on their yields. And in slump conditions, when unemployment is large and dividends are low, this circumstance counteracts the effect of a low interest rate on security prices.

Making the level of employment dependent on aggregate demand, Keynes constructs a causal relationship opposed to that constructed by neo-classical economics. He accepts the proposition of neo-classical economics that entrepreneurs reach maximum profit at a level of employment at which the workers' real wage rates are equal to the marginal productivity of labour. He also accepts the assumption of the neo-classical school that at a given level of technical knowledge and of capital stock, if employment increases, then the marginal productivity of labour will diminish. In neo-classical economics, however, decreasing money wages, and the resulting decrease in the real wage, stimulated the expansion of employment. By contrast, the Keynesian causal relationship is this: if aggregate demand increases, employment will increase with it and, as a result, the marginal productivity of labour will decrease, causing real wages also to decrease. In the neo-classical model, the reduction of real wage rates through a cut in money wages is the cause of an increase in employment, while in Keynes the reduction of real wages is the consequence of increasing employment.

By pointing out that the effect of a cut in money wages on aggregate demand and through it on employment cannot be predicted, Keynes refutes from another angle the neo-classical assertion that unemployment was caused by the workers' rigid insistence on a given rate of money wages, thereby impeding the reduction of real wage rates needed to maintain full employment. According to the neo-classical view, the bargain between workers and employers refers to the level of real wages. Though the amount of wages is stipulated in money terms, the formation of money wages reflects the movement of real wages. According to this view, decreasing money wages coincide, at least in the short run, with decreasing real wages. Keynes, however, holds the view that the bargain concluded in money terms between workers and employers cannot determine the level of real wages throughout the economy. It all depends on how a decrease in money wages affects the level of aggregate demand. In so far as it decreases aggregate demand and employment, the marginal productivity of labour, and hence real wages, will increase. The reduction of money wages will cause a decrease in real wages too, if it leads to a rise in aggregate demand and employment, and thus to a fall in the marginal productivity of labour.

Keynes accepts the neo-classical statement that the equilibrium level of real wages equals the marginal productivity of labour. But it follows from the inverse causal sequence that he must reject the neo-classical view, that the equilibrium level of real wage rates expresses, from the supply side of labour, the marginal disutility of the given level of employment. This postulate is based, in Keynes's view, on the assumption that the workers themselves can stipulate the wage rates for which they are prepared to work. For Keynes, however, the level of employment, the marginal productivity of labour and real wages depend, irrespective of the workers' will, on the level of aggregate demand. Real wages established in dependence on aggregate demand need not equal at all the marginal disutility of employment at the existing level of aggregate demand. If aggregate demand is less than is necessary for full employment, given a relatively low level of employment, the marginal productivity of labour will be relatively high, and the corresponding real wages will exceed the marginal disutility of the given level of employment. Given such a high rate of real wages, labour supplied will be more than effective demand makes it possible to employ. It is only at full employment that, according to Keynes, real wages coincide with the marginal disutility of labour. In conditions of full employment, real wages corresponding to the marginal productivity of labour are established at a level which expresses the marginal disutility of this employment, which means that as many workers are employed as are ready to take up work at the given level of real wages.

Since the effect that the level of money wage rates, agreed upon in the labour contract, exerts on real wages cannot be assessed in advance, Keynes thinks that the bargain between workers and capitalists refers to nominal and not to real wages. "Now ordinary experience tells us, beyond doubt, that a situation where labour stipulates (within limits) for a money wage rather than a real wage, so far from being a mere possibility, is the normal case."[180] "They [the workers—A. M.] resist reductions of money wages, ... even though the existing real equivalent of these wages exceeds the marginal disutility of the existing employment..."[181] But, Keynes thinks, labour supply is usually not reduced on the labour market if, given unchanged money wages, wage goods become costlier, and thus real wages decrease. "They [the workers—A. M.] do not raise the obstacle to any increase in aggregate employment which is attributed to them by the classical school."[182]

From the point of view of price stability, Keynes attributes a great significance to the fact that workers insist on a certain level of money wages. In his system, marginal cost is a basic component of money wages. If, under unemployment, the money wage were allowed to fall freely, the price level would lose its stability altogether, and money could not perform its function as a measure of value. "In fact," he writes, "we must have some factor, the value of which in terms of money is, if not fixed, at least sticky, to give us any stability of values in a monetary system."[183]

180 J. M. Keynes: *op. cit.*, p. 9.
181 J. M. Keynes: *op. cit.*, p. 14.
182 J. M. Keynes: *op. cit.*, pp. 14–15.
183 J. M. Keynes: *op. cit.*, p. 304.

Keynes's statements concerning the labour market logically follow from the basic propositions of his theoretical system. If employment depends on aggregate demand, a change in money wages can affect employment only through a change in aggregate demand. But this effect cannot be assessed in advance, and thus a change in money wages need not express a change in real wages.

We must agree with Keynes when he says that money and real wages move differently, though his arguments, based virtually on the principle of marginal productivity, are not acceptable to Marxist economists. Péter Erdős expresses the Marxist view when he says that "the level of money wages... does not at all determine that of the real wages."[184] Similarly, through a Marxist approach, he concluded that "the relative stability of the price level can be secured only by the relative stability of the sum of money wages, or wages level."[185]

Keynes's statement that real wages have to decline with a rise in employment, because the marginal productivity of labour decreases, is based on the theory of marginal productivity. In this form his statement is incompatible with the political economy of Marxism. But does the movement in an opposite direction of employment and real wages reflect to any extent the reality of capitalism? Yes, it does, but not as Keynes explains it. It is commonly known that in a capitalist economy the market expands and employment grows as a result of an increase in the production of the means of production. An upswing in the cycle of capitalist reproduction is caused by the fact that the production of the means of production runs ahead of the production of consumer goods. Employment grows in department II, but it grows to an even greater extent in department I. As a result, the products of those employed in department II are demanded by too many, and, if we leave aside technical developments, real wages have to decline. Even though in a slump period output and employment decrease alike in both sectors of social production, the production of the means of production falls to a greater degree than that of consumer goods. The number of people demanding the products of department II will sharply decrease, and, though the impoverishment of the working class reaches its peak in times of depression, the real wages of those who are fortunate enough to be employed will rise.

According to Keynes, who rejects the assumption of full employment, aggregate demand and aggregate supply may be in equilibrium on the market of commodities even under unemployment. For reasons other than those of Keynes, Marx also holds that the movement of wages does not ensure full employment on the labour market. On the market of commodities, as Marx puts it, demand and supply are equated on average over a reproduction cycle. On the labour market, however, they need not be equated.

As we have already mentioned, the inflationary phenomena of today produce precisely the evidence disproving Keynes's assumption that workers were slaves to the money illusion. Workers are not fighting only for higher money wages: they also keep an eye on the movement of their real wage rates. Their successful fights for sliding wage scales tied to the price level shows that they are very much concerned about their real wages.

[184] P. Erdős: *Contributions to the Theory of Capitalist Money, Business Fluctuations and Crises*, Budapest, 1971, p. 204.
[185] P. Erdős: *op. cit.*, p. 155.

When Keynes stresses that in conditions of underemployment real wages are in excess of the marginal disutility of employment, he is prejudiced by his view that an increase in employment through an increase in aggregate demand is associated with a decreasing marginal productivity of labour. Therefore, real wages have to fall as employment increases. If he admitted that real wages always corresponded to the marginal disutility of employment, he would not be able to prove the employment-expanding effect of an increase in aggregate demand under decreasing returns. Hansen, commenting on Keynes, also objects to the evidence based on the law of diminishing returns. "Keynes was a little too hasty in assuming that modern industry always operates under conditions of increasing marginal cost."[186]

In his representation of the labour market, Keynes doubtless assumes a more realistic position than the neo-classical economists. But however great his efforts to correct neo-classical wage theory, the too does not go any further than stating that wages, even under unemployment, have necessarily to equal the marginal product of labour.

[186] A. Hansen: *A Guide to Keynes,* New York–London–Toronto, 1953, p. 21.

Chapter 10

A SUMMARY APPRAISAL OF THE KEYNESIAN THEORY

In his model of an unregulated economy, Keynes, in the conditions of the Great Depression, tries to explain why the free functioning of the price mechanism does not ensure full employment, and why it does not ensure the demand needed to absorb the output produced under full employment. For an effective working of the capitalist economy he regards the economic intervention of the state as indispensable. The picture he draws of a capitalist economy is more realistic than the one drawn by neo-classical economics. He finds the ultimate cause of unemployment in the inadequacy of investment activity.

We have attempted to give a Marxist explanation of the problems raised by Keynes. We have also tried to show how the conflict between a type of production subordinated to profit interest on the one hand, and the living standard of masses on the other, prevents an adequate increase in output, investment and employment and that, as a result, a capitalist economy made up only of industrial capitalists and productive workers is threatened by the danger of stagnation.

Keynes asserts, however, that the independent variables which lead to the serious problems inherent, as he has shown, in the capitalist economy "... consist of (1) three fundamental psychological factors, namely the psychological propensity to consume, the psychological attitude to liquidity and the psychological expectation of future yield from capital assets, (2) the wage-unit as determined by the bargains reached between employers and employed and (3) the quantity of money as determined by the action of the central bank..."[187] Under such an approach, he treats the problems of the capitalism of his age in isolation from the prevailing social relations, and presents them occasionally as problems existing across all economic systems. "... there has been a chronic tendency throughout human history for the propensity to save to be stronger than the inducement to invest. The weakness of the inducement to invest has been at all times the key to the economic problem... The desire of the individual to augment his personal wealth by abstaining from consumption has usually been stronger than the inducement to the entrepreneur to augment the national wealth by employing labour on the construction of durable assets."[188]

He directs his attack only on one specific form of capital, on interest-bearing capital. In the interest of saving the capitalist system, he thinks that it is desirable

---

[187] J. M. Keynes: *op. cit.*, pp. 246–247.
[188] J. M. Keynes: *op. cit.*, pp. 347–348.

to sacrifice interest-bearing capital. Full employment requires a high level of investment, and leads to a large-scale increase in capital stock, such that the marginal efficiency of capital dwindles to an insignificant value. This would make it necessary to abolish interest. The removal of interest would not, according to Keynes, have any serious economic consequences because, as we have seen, the rate of interest is not a stimulant of saving in this system. What Keynes desires is "the euthanasia of the rentier."[189] He is far from understanding the essence of capitalism. He regards "… the rentier aspect of capitalism as a transitional phase."[190] He thinks that in a reformed type of capitalism entrepreneurs would be rewarded only in return for their exercising the function of capital, enjoying that reward as a compensation for taking risks, for exercising their skills, judgement and supervision, but not for owning capital. In other words, the return on capital as property would cease. Keynes, too, is slave to an illusion; as if the yield of working capital stemmed exclusively from those transactions or functions which capitalists as entrepreneurs perform in the reproduction process, and as if their incomes were independent of capital ownership. The cessation of interest would in fact mean that profit would accrue to the entrepreneur only, without it being divided between him and the creditor of capital. But the basis of the appropriation of profit would continue to be the capitalist ownership of the means of production. Production subordinated to the acquisition of surplus value would continue to survive with all its consequences.

The essence of the economic policy suggested by Keynes is that the government should interfere in the capitalist economy; it should increase the elements of effective demand, stimulate consumer demand and private investment and supplement insufficient private investment by increasing government expenditures. "… it indicates the vital importance of establishing certain central controls in matters which are now left in the main to individual initiative… The State will have to exercise a guiding influence on the propensity to consume… I conceive, therefore, that a somewhat comprehensive socialisation of investment will prove the only means of securing an approximation to full employment…"[191] Neo-classical economists wished to minimize the amount of government expenditure, whether financed by taxes, state debentures or the issue of money. Government outlays give rise in a Euclidean economy to inflation, to a withdrawal of resources from productive uses and to their utilization for unproductive purposes. In Keynes's non-Euclidean economy, however, government expenditures ensure job opportunities for the unemployed and generate increased production. They thereby create, through the multiplier effect, their own financial funds. "… any level of private investment and Budget deficit will always produce an equal amount of saving to finance these two items… there will always be such an increase in incomes as to create an increase in savings equal to the increase in Budget deficit."[192]

Keynes lays stress, as we have seen, on supplementing private investment by government investment in order to provide for full employment. Thus aggregate

[189] J. M. Keynes: *op. cit.*, p. 376.
[190] *Ibid.*
[191] J. M. Keynes: *op. cit.*, pp. 377–378.
[192] M. Kalecki: Three Ways to Full Employment. In: B. Blackwell (ed.): *The Economics of Full Employment*, Oxford, 1944, p. 41.

demand, $C+I+G$, where G means, using the notation of Keynes's followers, government outlays, can be increased by increasing G to the extent required by full employment.

The arguments in support of an increase in government expenditures and the socialization of investments mean that some followers of Keynes admit that fluctuations in investments, and thus in unemployment too, are caused by the subordination of investments to the profit motive. Thus Joan Robinson writes that government investments "... are not subject to the profit motive in the same direct way as private investment, and do not necessarily follow the same rhythm... Public works therefore act to some extent as a counterweight to the fluctuations in investment undertaken by profit-seeking entrepreneurs."[193]

Government expenditures are for the most part unproductive outlays which generate demand without increasing supply. Unproductive outlays also include arms expenditures. The British economist Strachey asserts that it is always easier for the state of a capitalist country to have credits voted for armaments because armaments are the only state activity in whose increase citizens do not see a danger from the left.[194]

The government siphons off and uses surplus value in the sense that both the investment goods and consumption goods made use of by the government have been produced by productive workers without their getting the countervalue for them. The excess labour of the working class also constitutes the source of tax receipts, which is therefore surplus value. "The state *takes* a part of the surplus value of the capitalists, but only such part as exists because the state takes it (and then spends it) ..."[195]

Although the source of government outlay is surplus value, they are made not at the expense of the profit of the capitalist class, not even if they were financed entirely by taxes imposed on profit. It is an actual fact that profit taxation does not compel the capitalist class to cut its expense. It maintains the previous volume of its consumption even after paying the taxes, drawing, at worst, on its savings, and need not decrease even its investments, since they can be financed from credits. If, however, profit tax does not diminish the consumption and investment outlays of the capitalist class, the amount of their realized profit will not decrease either. Government expenditures increase the amount of gross profit. At the same time, they increase, like capitalist investments, demand by a multiple of their amount, and stimulate the expansion of output.

But the increase in output and employment through government expenditures is a consequence of the fact that part of the working class is employed in an unproductive way, and part of the quantity of products produced is used unproductively. Keynes points out that if political or practical difficulties prevent labour from being used for productive purposes for providing for full employment, e.g. by building houses, then even absolutely senseless or useless expenditure proves a better solution than nothing. "Pyramid-building, earthquakes, even wars may serve to increase wealth..."[196] "If the Treasury were to fill old bottles

[193] J. Robinson: *Introduction to the Theory of Employment*, London, 1937, pp. 32 and 37.
[194] See J. Strachey: *Contemporary Capitalism*, London, 1956.
[195] P. Erdős: *Wages, Profit, Taxation. Studies on Controversial Issues of the Political Economy of Capitalism*, Akadémiai Kiadó, Budapest, 1982, Chapter XXIII.
[196] J. M. Keynes: *op. cit.*, p. 129.

with banknotes, bury them at suitable depths in disused coalmines which are then filled up to the surface with town rubbish, and leave it to private enterprise on well-tried principles of *laissez-faire* to dig the notes up again... there need be no more unemployment and, with the help of the repercussions, the real income of the community, and its capital wealth also, would probably become a good deal greater than it actually is."[197]

But senseless, useless spendings mean a waste of the productive forces. Keynes involuntarily passes judgement on the capitalist economic system when he regards even such expenditures as favourable for reaching a higher level of employment.

[197] J. M. Keynes: *op. cit.*, p. 129.

Chapter 11

KALDOR'S ATTEMPT TO CREATE A DISTRIBUTION THEORY ON A KEYNESIAN AS DISTINCT FROM A MARGINAL PRODUCTIVITY BASIS

Keynes accepted marginal productivity theory at least as an instrument to determine the size of real wages. In the past two decades, however, economists of the Cambridge School have launched a vigourous attack against the explanation of the process of income distribution by the principle of marginal productivity. Mrs. Robinson set against the theory of marginal productivity the problems relating to the measurability of capital, while in the 1960s Sraffa, Garignani and Pasinetti tried to refute the marginal productivity theory by referring to the "reswitching of technique". In 1955 Kaldor built on the theoretical basis of the Keynesian system a distribution theory[198] which was independent of the marginal productivity principle and was later to be complemented by Pasinetti.

Kaldor raised the question of income distribution at the macro-level, and attempted to determine the respective shares of wages and profits in national income. Then he built his income-distribution theory into his growth theory.

As is commonly known, Keynes, unlike neo-classical economists, holds that savers are at the mercy of investors. Society has to save as much as entrepreneurs wish to invest. And since the volume of saving on a social scale depends, at a given propensity to save, on national income, national income has to change so as to enable society to save as much as investors wish to invest. Then aggregate demand and aggregate supply are in equilibrium.

Kaldor points out that the multiplier principle can be used in two alternative ways. With given distribution relations, it can be used for the determination of the level of employment or output, but, with a given level of employment or output, it can also be used to determine the relation between prices and wages and, through it, income distribution. The multiplier principle was invented for the purpose of an employment theory, and Kaldor attempts to develop it into a distribution theory. It is for this reason that he makes a distinction between the capitalist and working classes' propensities to save. He regards them as the independent variables of his income-distribution theory. He assumes full employment, and thus intended saving and intended investment are not harmonized in his system by a change in national income. If intended saving and intended investment differ from one another, then the *relations of income distribution,* the respective shares of the capitalist and working classes in national income,

[198] N. Kaldor: Alternative Theories of Distribution. In: *Essays on Value and Distribution,* London, 1960, pp. 209–236.

must be changed so that, given their propensities to save, they want to save as much as the volume of the entrepreneurs' intended investment. Thus in Kaldor it is a change in income distribution relations that is to bring about, within the given volume of the national income, the equilibrium between saving and investment, and through it the equilibrium of aggregate demand and aggregate supply. "... in any given situation there must be some division of the product between wages and profits which makes the total demand for commodities equal to the total supply."[199]

He represents this mechanism as follows:

If intended investment exceeds intended saving, then the demand for consumer goods will exceed their supply. The price level of consumer goods will rise. Since in the capitalist system there exists no mechanism which could adjust the increase in nominal wages to the increase in the price level of consumer goods, real wages and thus the share of the working class in national income will decrease. The share of the capitalist class, however, will rise until intended saving is in equilibrium with intended investment, and aggregate demand with aggregate supply. Conversely, if intended saving exceeds intended investment, the demand for consumer goods will fall behind their supply. Then prices will fall relatively to the wage level, the real wages of the working class will increase, and so will their share in national income. Consumer demand will grow. While in Keynes unemployment results if intended investment is lower than intended saving at full employment, Kaldor asserts that, assuming flexible prices or rather flexible profit margins, "the system is thus stable at full employment."[200]

In his view, these two uses of the multiplier principle are not incompatible. The employment theory built upon the multiplier principle is a short-run theory, and the distribution theory based thereon is a long-run one.

Kaldor introduces the following relationship between the investment ratio and the profit ratio.

He sets out from the basic Keynesian relationship: $I = S$. He divides S between saving effected from wages and from profits, and thus

$$I = s_w W + s_c P, \text{ and since } W = Y - P,$$

$$I = s_w Y + (s_c - s_w) P, \text{ hence}$$

$$\frac{P}{Y} = \frac{1}{s_c - s_w} \cdot \frac{I}{Y} - \frac{s_w}{s_c - s_w}.$$

The profit rate can be determined in a similar way:

$$\frac{P}{K} = \frac{1}{s_c - s_w} \cdot \frac{I}{K} - \frac{s_w}{s_c - s_w} \cdot \frac{Y}{K}.$$

[199] N. Kaldor: Capitalist Evolution in the Light of Economics. In: *Essays on Economic Stability and Growth*, London, 1960, p. 250.

[200] N. Kaldor: Alternative Theories of Distribution. In: *Essays on Value and Distribution*, London, 1960, p. 230.

The mathematical formula given for $\dfrac{P}{Y}$ and $\dfrac{P}{K}$ is valid if these conditions are met:

$$s_w < \frac{I}{Y}, \; s_c > \frac{I}{Y}.$$

At given s_c and s_w, the share of profits in national income and thus the profit rate are the greater, the higher the ratio of investment to national income. At a given investment ratio, the profit share and the profit rate are the smaller, the larger, at a given s_w, is propensity to save of the capitalist class. In the limiting case when $s_w = 0$, the sum total of profit equals the consumption and investment of the capitalist class. Then the Keynesian parable about the widow's cruse holds true: a decrease in s_c, that is, a rise in the capitalists' consumption increases total profit by the same amount.

The multiplier effect cannot be applied, according to Kaldor, to explaining income distribution if real wages are at the subsistence level. And this was the situation in the first stage of capitalist evolution. In this case, profit is the surplus of national income over and above the subsistence wage bill, i.e. a residual, which implies that the saving made out of it is available for investment purposes, and the classical reaction mechanism will prevail. The size of saving available for investment will determine the volume of investment, and not the other way round. Output will be limited by the available capital and not by labour. The system does not ensure full employment because saving made from profit interpreted as surplus over the subsistence wage level is not certain to be sufficient to maintain the investment necessary for full employment. The situation is reversed in a more advanced stage of capitalism. As soon as wages rise above the subsistence level, profit will not be a residual, but the share of wages "equalling the difference between production and the share of profits as determined in a 'Keynesian' manner, by the propensities to invest and to save."[201]

Let us illustrate Kaldor's statements by a simple numerical example. Let the length of a worker's working day be 10 hours, and assume that 5 hours are needed to ensure subsistence wages. In this case, the rate of surplus value will be 100 per cent, half the national income will accrue to the working class as wages and the other half will fall to the capitalist class as profit. We assume that only the capitalist class makes savings from profits, and the savings ratio is 50 per cent. In this case, the investment ratio, $\dfrac{I}{Y}$, will be 25 per cent. Should the maintenance of full employment require a 30 per cent investment ratio, this cannot materialize because in this case the wages ratio would be only 40 per cent, which in turn cannot ensure subsistence wages. Investment is limited in this case by saving made from the surplus over the subsistence wage bill, i.e. from profit as a residual.

Let the quantity of labour necessary to produce the subsistence wage now be reduced, because of rapid growth of the productivity of labour, to 3 hours. The wages ratio cannot remain 30 per cent, nor can the profit ratio remain 70 per cent. At a 70 per cent profit ratio the saving of the capitalist class would be 35 per cent of output, which would exceed the 30 per cent invest-

[201] N. Kaldor: A Model of Economic Growth, London, 1960, p. 295.

ment ratio necessary for full employment. Aggregate demand would fall below aggregate supply, the price-level would decrease relative to money wages, real wages would grow over and above the subsistence wage level until the equilibrium between aggregate demand and aggregate supply comes about at a 60 per cent profit ratio and a 40 per cent wage ratio.

An inflexible profit margin prevents the mechanism from bringing about the 60 and 40 per cent respective shares. If the capitalist class insisted on a 70 per cent profit ratio, aggregate demand would lag behind aggregate supply, inducing entrepreneurs to decrease output, and now the multiplier effect would operate not through a change in distribution relations but through a decrease in production and employment.

Let now compare with Kaldor's model the approach attempted by the Marxist economist Péter Erdős, with respect to the way he reveals the laws underlying long-term changes in real wages. The comparison will show which of Kaldor's statements can be accepted as valid from a Marxist point of view, and at what points the Marxist explanation appears to be different from Kaldor's view.

Erdős emphasizes that "the mechanism which regulates the prices of other commodities is ineffective in respect to the real price of labour—the exchange rate between consumer goods and money wages."[202] Therefore, in order to demonstrate the laws governing the long-term formation of real wages, he deems it appropriate to regard the level of real wages as the residue of national income, and reveals those laws which regulate the movement of surplus value. Knowing these relationships, at least as regards the main tendencies, he can find out the nature of the laws governing the level of real wages.

Erdős, as has been shown, approximates surplus value in a peculiar way. In a model assuming only productive workers and industrial capitalists, surplus value, writes Erdős, is divided between the consumption fund and the accumulation fund of capitalists; he conceives of surplus value as their sum total. Thus the volume of surplus value, S, equals $S_c + S_k$. He takes S_v into account as a value merged with the wages fund V.

In the amount of surplus value, $S_c + S_k$, the term S_k is rather stable in size, changing only slowly and to a small extent. In turn, the volume of accumulation, S_c, is a highly variable magnitude. Thus a change in surplus value depends mainly on accumulation, and Erdős also attempts to explain the trend of real wages by the long-term formation of accumulation.

The relative shares of the incomes of the two social classes are expressed in Erdős by the already discussed rate of surplus value. $\dfrac{S_c + S_k}{C - S_k}$. In the course of capitalist development, changes in the magnitudes included in the formula also help to explain the movement of the ratio of surplus value to national income, i.e. Kaldor's profit ratio.

Erdős's formula to the rate of surplus value also clarifies that, assuming S_c to be unchanged, with a stable consumption of the capitalist class an increase in the output of consumer goods, C, increases the share of the working class in national income and decreases that of the capitalist class, but an increase in S_c, at unchanged C and S_k values, increases the relative share of the capitalist class and decreases the relative share of the working class. In other words, making use of

202 P. Erdős: Reálbér és értéktörvény a kapitalizmusban (Real wages and the law of value under capitalism), *Közgazdasági Szemle*, Dec. 1974, p. 1374.

the Marxian two-sector scheme for the explanation of relative shares, the greater the weight of department I in total output, the greater the ratio of profits to national income and *vice versa*.

A real element, therefore, in Kaldor's distribution theory is the fact that he makes the division of national income between profits and wages (at a given ratio of the worker and capitalist classes' propensity to save) dependent on the size of the investment ratio. And, in order to reveal the laws governing the long-term movement of wages, Erdős also, when examining the factors influencing the movement of surplus value, regards wages as a residual value. He does this not on the grounds that wages were regulated by different laws in the more advanced and the earlier stages of capitalism, but because he thinks that in this way the role played by the law of value in regulating real wages can be better revealed.

Kaldor is right in asserting that wages cannot be regarded as a residual if they do not outstrip the subsistence level. We cannot agree, however, with his statement that Marx determined labour wages by the subsistence level. For Marx, it is the reproduction costs of labour power that determine the value of labour, and real wages thus interpreted will rise in the course of capitalist development. Marx criticized Smith and Ricardo for determining wages as minimum costs of living. And while in Kaldor the investment ratio determines changes in the relative shares of classes through the multiplier effect in such a way that aggregate demand and aggregate supply come into equilibrium at full employment, Erdős approximates the determination of changes both in relative shares and in S_c on the basis of the conflict of interests between the capitalist and the working classes. In Erdős's view, as has been shown, the share of profits in national income grows with the investment ratio. But sooner or later investments will mature, which in turn increases the capacity of the consumer-goods industries. If the increased capacity were fully utilized, the rather inelastic consumption of capitalists, S_k, would not keep pace with the increase in C, the supply of consumer goods. Thus the increase in C lowers $\dfrac{S}{V}$, diminishes the profit share and increases the wages share in national income. In order to maintain the profit margin unchanged in the price of their product, capitalists do not fully exploit the increased capacity and slow down the growth in C. This circumstance in turn does not stimulate S_c to the extent to which the maintaining of $\dfrac{S}{V}$ at an unchanged level would require an increase in S_c.

Though in Erdős's model of pure capitalism the share of wages in national income increases in the long run, but because the rate of increase in the output of consumer goods is slowed down in view of the increasing productivity of labour, real wages will also rise slowly, and unemployment will grow. The subordination of production to profit interests has come into conflict with the interests of the masses, which in turn demand that the output of consumer goods be increased. Thus we cannot assume that full employment is ensured in the long run.

The multiplier principle presents the effect that the investment ratio exerts on the determination of the relative shares of classes from the viewpoint of market equilibrium between aggregate demand and aggregate supply, and does not penetrate into the depth of class conflicts which determine the movement of market processes.

In the explanation of income distribution based on the multiplier principle, the difference between the situation of the working and capitalist classes, which accounts for their different incomes, is reflected as a difference between the propensities to save of the working and capitalist classes. The difference between the two is a precondition for the validity of the model. Its analysis, however, stops at a point where the disclosure of essential interrelationships should follow: the difference between the propensities to save of the two classes ought to be traced back to their positions in production relations. If the propensity to save varies between classes, its explanation must obviously lie in class relations. True, under the influence of the criticism of his theory by neo-classical economists, Kaldor attempts to explain the greater propensity to save of the capitalist class. He refers to the pressure of competition, to the fact that the competitiveness of each firm depends on the size of its market share which it seeks to keep up and, indeed, to enlarge in the market-expanding process. All this requires a substantial amount of saving.[203] The great saving, however, which competition compels capitalists to make, already presupposes a greater income of the capitalist class. Thus Kaldor's determination of the shares of wages and profits in national income already supposes the existence of a system of income distribution under which the capitalist class can save a greater share of its income than the working class.

An attempt to complement Kaldor's theory of income distribution was undertaken by another Cambridge economist, Pasinetti. In his view, Kaldor leaves out of account one important point: if workers make savings, they also wish to invest them, hence, they receive a profit on their savings. Thus workers also have their share in total profits. It is for this reason that in Kaldor the distribution of national income between workers and capitalists is not the same as its distribution between wages and profits. Pasinetti complements Kaldor's theory of income distribution by also including in his explanation the share of the working class in total profits. He points out that, within the limits of the validity of Kaldor's income-distribution theory, "... workers' propensity to save, though influencing the distribution of income between capitalists and workers..., does not influence the distribution of income between profits and wages... Nor does it have any influence whatsoever on the rate of profit..."[204] Both are only a function of the capitalists' savings ratio.

The neo-classical economists Samuelson and Modigliani[205] attacked the Pasinetti-version of Kaldor's theory of income distribution. They have pointed out that under steady-state growth, if workers become thrifty and s_w increases, the workers' share in profits will steadily increase, and their capital stock will represent an ever greater proportion of total capital stock. And then, as the workers' propensity to save reaches, or exceeds, the profit share in national income multiplied by the capitalists' savings propensity, we shall arrive at the dual of Pasinetti's theory of income distribution.

[203] N. Kaldor: Marginal Productivity and the Macro-Economic Theories of Distribution. In: *The Review of Economic Studies*, October 1966, p. 310.

[204] L. L. Pasinetti: Rate of Profit and Income Distribution in the Rate of Economic Growth. In: *The Review of Economic Studies*, October, 1962, p. 272.

[205] See P. A. Samuelson and F. Modigliani: The Pasinetti Paradox in Neo-classical and More General Models. In: *The Review of Economic Studies*, 1966, pp. 269–301.

But the amount of s_w, given a steady-state growth, cannot reach this magnitude in Pasinetti's model. This is because his model is based on the Keynesian assumption that investment determines savings, and "profits should be determined by the need to generate sufficient savings to finance investment."[206] If $s_w \gtreqless s_c \dfrac{P}{Y}$, then, in Pasinetti's model, either unemployment, i.e. insufficient demand, will develop, or profits must become negative.

Samuelson and Modigliani, in their turn, focus attention on the case when $s_w \gtreqless s_c \dfrac{P}{Y}$. As Kaldor puts it, they conjure up a Walrasian world "in which all savings get invested somehow, without disturbing full employment..."[207] In this world, the excess of the savings ratio over the investment ratio forces down the rate of interest and stimulates investment. Hence, the magnitude of capital per head and the capital–output ratio will rise. And this rise will correspond to the extent of the increase in the savings ratio, and thus the rate of growth will not change. Steady-state growth, assuming full employment, will continue unchanged, but capitalists will no longer have their share in profits. Exactly for this reason, the rate of profit, the capital–output ratio, and the distribution of income between profits and wages are now completely independent of the capitalists' propensity to save, of s_c. The capital–output ratio, in steady-state growth, depends only on the rate of growth and on the workers' propensity to save, and equals $\dfrac{s_w}{n}$, where n is the equilibrium rate of growth. It is not dependent on the shape of the production function. The rate of profit, the share of profit in national income, the size of capital per head and the volume of output per head depend on s_w, n and the shape of the production function, respectively.

Let us illustrate what we have set forth above by a simple example. Let our production function be of a Cobb–Douglas type. Assume that the production elasticity of capital is 0.4, and the production elasticity of labour is 0.6. Let s_c and s_w be 0.25 and 0.05, respectively. Since $s_w < s_c \dfrac{P}{Y}$, the rate of profit, and the profit share in national income, does not depend on s_w. The share of savings in national income equals in this case $s_c \cdot \dfrac{P}{Y}$, and amounts, with the data of our model, to 10 per cent. Assume a growth rate of 10 per cent, which, if we disregard technical progress, expresses the growth rate of population. In this case the capital–output ratio, $\dfrac{s}{n} = 1$. Let us assume that, in a given period of time, along the steady-state growth path, the magnitude of national income is 1,000. Then the magnitude of the stock of capital will be 1,000, too. Out of a national income of 1,000, 40 per cent, i.e. 400, will be earnings on capital, profit, and 60 per cent, i.e. 600, will be wages. Not only do the production elasticities, which we take as data of our model, express this proportion of income distribution, but $\dfrac{1}{s_c} \cdot \dfrac{I}{Y}$ also determines the share

[206] N. Kaldor: Marginal Productivity and the Macroeconomic Theories of Distribution. Comment on Samuelson and Modigliani. In: *The Review of Economic Studies*, October 1966, p. 311.

[207] N. Kaldor: *op. cit.*, p. 312.

of profits in national income: $4 \cdot 0.1 = 40$ per cent. The marginal productivity of capital, $\frac{P}{K}$, equals the production elasticity of capital multiplied by the average productivity of capital, that is, 0.4. Or, to put it another way: $\frac{P}{K} = \frac{1}{s_c} \cdot \frac{I}{K}$, where $\frac{I}{K}$ is the growth rate of capital, which, in the case of steady-state growth, equals the growth rate of national income, n, and thus $\frac{1}{0.25} \cdot 0.1$ will also give us 0.4. If we assume that the labour force employed in the period in question is 1,000, then capital per head, $\frac{K}{L} = 1$. With the help of s_w and s_c it is possible to calculate the capitalists' and workers' shares in a profit of 400. The volumes of profits accruing to capitalists and workers will be $P_c = 250$ and $P_w = 150$, respectively. Hence, at a profit rate of 40 per cent, out of society's capital of 1,000, 625 belongs to capitalists and 375 to workers. And since the savings of capitalists, $S_c = 0.25 \cdot 250 = 62.5$, and the savings of workers, $S_w = 0.05(150 + 600) = 37.5$, the capital stock of the two classes will also grow at a rate of $n = 10$ per cent.

Let s_w rise in the growth process to 0.08, so that it will still remain below the critical 10 per cent. With our Cobb–Douglas type of production function, out of the national income higher by 10 per cent at 1,100, 40 and 60 per cent, or 440 and 660 in absolute terms, will continue to be profits and wages respectively.

But how is the 440 profit now distributed between capitalists and workers? At the values of $s_c = 0.25$ and $s_w = 0.08$, P_c and P_w will be, in round figures, 130 and 310, respectively, while $S_c = 32.5$ and $S_w = 77.6$.

The capital stock of the capitalist class, $\frac{32.5}{625}$, will grow by less than 10 per cent and that of the working class, $\frac{77.6}{375}$, will rise by more than 10 per cent. But the values of $\frac{K}{Y}, \frac{K}{L}, \frac{P}{Y}, \frac{P}{K}$ will remain unchanged.

Let s_w now rise in the growth process to the critical 10 per cent. In this case $s_w Y = s_c P$, whence $s_w = s_c \frac{P}{Y}$. Since under the conditions of steady-state growth, Y has grown from 1,100 to 1,210, and so has the capital stock, then out of a national income of 1,210, assuming a 0.4 production elasticity of capital, the respective shares of profits and wages will be 484 and 726. It is easy to calculate that now the entire profit of 484 will accrue to the working class, as $P_c = 0$. But the values of $\frac{K}{Y}, \frac{K}{L}, \frac{P}{Y}, \frac{P}{K}$ will remain unchanged.

But at the critical, more than 10 per cent, value of s_w, when e.g. $s_w = 0.12$, $\frac{K}{Y}$ will rise to $\frac{s_w}{n} = \frac{0.12}{0.1} = 1.2$. Thus $\frac{K}{Y}$ depends only on s_w and n. At a national income of 1,210 and at a 12 per cent value of s_w, the volume of capital stock is 1,450. And capital per head will also rise from 1 to 1.2. At the same time, the marginal productivity of capital will decrease from 0.4 to $0.4 \frac{Y}{K}$, that is, to 0.333. The total volume of profits will accrue again to the working class, and the value of P_c will invariably remain 0.

The criticism brought up against the Kaldor–Pasinetti model by neo-classical economists has been rejected both by those authors and by Joan Robinson, who pointed out that the neo-classical critique is based on a presentation of the saving–investment relationship which is entirely different from that in the Kaldor–Pasinetti model. What in fact that critique took advantage of was that Kaldor and Pasinetti have failed to analyse the question of how the difference between the capitalists' and workers' propensity to save arises from their different social positions, of how as a result entirely different objectives are served by the savings of the capitalist and the working classes. Modigliani's and Samuelson's argument is an ingenious but empty logical play in which they assume that the workers' propensity to save may take on a magnitude at which the economic power of the capitalist class is broken, or, as Kaldor notices: the end to which the capitalist class will be put "is not a violent revolution à la Marx, but the cosy world of Harrod, Domar and Solow, where there is only a single savings propensity applicable to the economy..."[208]

The process presented by Samuelson and Modigliani, in which the share of the working class in total profits will increase, contradicts the reality of capitalism. We agree with Kaldor's answer, which is at the same time a correction of Pasinetti's viewpoint, namely, that the net savings of wage and salary earners "is not... an indication of the savings available for the acquisition of business capital or for lending to the business sector, since a large part of it goes to finance personal investment in consumer durables."[209] If, on the other hand, a large part of the savings of the working class does not serve accumulation purposes, then they cannot regularly receive either interest or profit on them.

[208] N. Kaldor: *op. cit.*, p. 311.
[209] N. Kaldor: *op. cit.*, p. 312.

Part Nine

GROWTH THEORIES
IN NON-MARXIAN ECONOMICS

Chapter 1

INTRODUCTION

The best economists of the progressive bourgeoisie fought against obsolete production relations which impeded economic development, and devoted a prominent place in their works to examining the long-term problems of economic growth. Then, with the decline of early classical economics, questions of economic growth were increasingly pushed into the background. The direction of economic research began to change. For about half a century, from the 1870s on, non-Marxian economic research was concentrated on the problem of how the available scarce resources should be used optimally to attain a given aim. This was the problem of the bourgeoisie having already come to power and striving to adapt itself to the existing order in the most rational way. As a result, the exploration of problems relating to long-term economic growth was replaced by research concerned with the phenomena of the short period, and economics came to be dominated by statics. "As the static analysis came to be refined and perfected by the use of the marginal concept and by mathematical expression" writes Harrod, "the dynamic analysis fell out of view."[1]

In the period following the Second World War, however, the questions of economic growth came again into prominence in non-Marxian economics. One of the reasons lay in the economic competition of the two social systems. As E. James writes: "In a world like ours, divided by two ideologies, the communist and the capitalist, is it not the crucial problem that we would like to know if capitalism is capable of developing, surviving and improving?"[2] Also the increasing degree of economic intervention by the state made it necessary to determine the main factors of growth, the conditions of equilibrium of a growing economy. The fact that with the disintegration of the colonial system a number of countries chose to follow the course of independent development also helped to direct attention to the problems of economic growth.

This work is not intended to provide a detailed analysis of the models concerned with the problems of economic growth of the developing countries; it merely examines the models set up by their initiators for the developed capitalist economy.

Non-Marxian growth theories operating with abstract models and assuming a developed capitalist economy have, as regards their theoretical basis, two fundamental types: one which is based on the Keynesian system and the other, the so-called neo-classical growth model.

---

[1] R. Harrod: *Towards a Dynamic Economics*, New York, 1966, p. 15.
[2] E. James: *Histoire de la pensée économique au XXe siècle*. Vol. II, Paris, 1955, p. 577.

Both are built upon a certain idea of equilibrium growth. They are intended, in the first place, to reveal relationships which hold in the growth process under equilibrium conditions, but the characteristics of growth in the transition period, growth deviating from the path of equilibrium, are also examined.

The analysis of growth under conditions of equilibrium raised the question of the interpretation of dynamic equilibrium.

Non-Marxian economics interprets static equilibrium, not unlike the concept of mechanical equilibrium, as a state of rest, a state of the economy in which change is in nobody's interest, since everybody has attained, under the existing data, the optimal results available to him. But this interpretation of equilibrium cannot be applied to a growing economy, for, under conditions of economic growth, economic subjects are invariably striving to change the given situation, are increasing production and the stock of capital. Harrod was the first to give a definition of dynamic equilibrium, which has been widely adopted in non-Marxian economics up to this day. In much the same way as non-Marxian theory interpreted static equilibrium, Harrod too attempts to approach dynamic equilibrium from the subjective side, relying on the satisfaction of the economic subject. According to this view, we may speak of dynamic equilibrium when a growth rate has developed which entrepreneurs are no longer interested in changing, because at this rate of growth their expectations have come true, that is, what has happened is broadly what they expected when taking their decisions. Just as static equilibrium is characterized by the constancy of certain values, so Harrod's idea of a dynamic equilibrium is also marked by the constancy of definite growth rates. Growth *at a constant rate,* at which production, the stock of capital, the labour force, technical progress grow over time, and indeed, as we shall see, production and the stock of capital increase at the same rate, came to be called later, following Mrs. Robinson, the *golden age,* referring to the fact that such a process "represents a mythical state of affairs not likely to obtain in any actual economy."[3] The fiction of the golden growth path plays an important role in neo-classical growth theories. By its assumption, attempts are made to solve certain tasks of optimization under the circumstances of economic growth, to determine the efficient growth path.

[3] J. Robinson: *The Accumulation of Capital,* London, 1956, p. 99.

Chapter 2

GROWTH MODELS BUILT UPON A KEYNESIAN THEORETICAL BASIS

GENERAL CHARACTERISTICS

The American Domar and the British Harrod, the first two representatives of modern non-Marxian growth theories after the Second World War, built their growth models upon Keynesian theory. In compliance with the questions raised by Keynes, both treated as a central problem the issue whether there will be an adequate aggregate demand for the increased quantity of products in the course of economic growth. Following Keynes, they held the view that the market would expand as a result of investments. Investment plays a significant role in Keynesian growth models. In attempting to reveal the investment function, some theoreticians adopting the Keynesian approach distinguished two sorts of investment: *autonomous and induced investment*. The names stem from Hicks, who first used these terms in his trade-cycle theory published in 1950. But the concept of this distinction dates back to Harrod's growth theory, which appeared in 1948.

Autonomous investment, as is indicated by its name, is the independent variable of the growth model. It cannot be deduced from the theoretical system, as it is not due to national income or aggregate demand determined by the Keynesian model, but to factors which are exogeneous to the model.

Hicks distinguishes three groups of factors giving rise to autonomous investment. He classifies government expenditures as belonging to the first group. Decisions on government expenditures cannot be deduced from the model as they are not determined directly by aggregate demand or aggregate output. To the second group belong investments induced by technical progress. The stimulating effect exerted by technical progress on investment was already mentioned by Marx: "With the development of the productive forces, the number of spheres of production is also steadily increasing, thus creating possibilities for capital investment which previously did not exist at all."[4] Such investments may also appear to be autonomous as they have not been induced by changes in output. Finally, Hicks also classifies among autonomous investments long-term investments whose products mature only in the distant future, and thus the expectations that entrepreneurs have in mind in respect to future demand when making their investment decisions cannot be deduced from the demand or output as determined by the model for the period of the investment decision.

The singling out of part of the investments as autonomous expresses that entrepreneurs make their investments to satisfy an uncertain future demand, and the

---

[4] K. Marx: *Theorien über den Mehrwert*, 2. Teil, Dietz Verlag, Berlin, 1959, p. 536.

longer the investment period, the more uncertain the future market appears. It further expresses a characteristic of capitalist reproduction, namely that the production of capital goods, and within it primarily the production of fixed assets, may increase in relative independence from the production of consumer goods. Thus entrepreneurs will increase their investments under the pressure of the compulsion to accumulate, even if they take into consideration that they will probably not be able to make full use of the increased capacity. They will increase them because having greater capacity at their disposal ensures for them greater economic power in the competitive struggle. The treatment of part of the investments as autonomous reflects, in addition to the relative independence of the production of capital goods, that especially investments made in the capital-goods industries are justifiable through the demand for consumer goods, but only indirectly, through transmissions.

A capitalist economy turns from a slump into a boom precisely through the increased production of capital goods, and within it primarily the increased production of fixed capital; and the demand for consumer goods also grows because of the increased production of capital goods, and then reacts on investment. Hansen, Hicks and others stress that autonomous investment gives rise to the growth process: "the entire boom depends fundamentally upon the vitality of autonomous investment."[5]

The relative independence of the production of fixed capital and its role in a boom period in economic growth does not mean that it can completely be divorced from the demand for and the production of consumer goods. The final aim of investments is the promotion of the production of consumption goods. Thus autonomous investment, even though it is not caused by a change in the demand existing at the time of the investment decision, must be justifiable, in so far as it expands productive capacity, by means of demand at the time of maturity. We cannot therefore accept the views of those authors who represent autonomous investment as not needing to be justified by an increase in demand or output. This could only be maintained by assuming that autonomous investment does not increase productive capacity at all. In general, the treatment of autonomous investment as an independent variable, its inclusion in the model as an exogeneous datum, is not permissible: it would leave the fundamental factor of Keynesian growth models unexplained.

The other variety of investment, induced investment, can be deduced from the model built upon a Keynesian basis, because it is determined by certain variables of the model. On the question of what determines induced investment, the views held in non-Marxian economics are divided. According to Samuelson, Hansen and others, it is a function of the change in the demand for consumer goods. The increase in the demand for consumer goods leads to an increase in their production, which in turn makes investment necessary. J. M. Clark, however, makes induced investment dependent upon the demand for finished products, stressing

[5] A. Hansen: *Business Cycles and National Income*, New York, 1951, p. 193.

that the increase in the demand for capital goods also requires new investment, in that it stimulates an expansion of the output of capital goods.[6]

A change in the demand for finished products leads to a change in production, and some economists, Hicks and Harrod among others, regard the change in production as the independent variable in the investment function. In this connection, increased production is accompanied by an excessive utilization of existing productive capacity. The entrepreneur invests in order to ensure optimal capacity for continuous production with minimal average cost. In this view, it is the difference between actual and optimal capacity which stimulates investment. Since this difference depends on changes in production, the investment function in this form too remains a function of production, that is, of a change in output.

How does induced investment depend, then, upon demand or production?

THE ACCELERATOR EFFECT

This relationship is expressed by what J. M. Clark called the *acceleration principle*. Acceleration is a concept borrowed from physics. Acceleration means a change over time of a time-dimensional factor, of velocity, the second derivative of the distance covered with respect to time. There are *factors of a time dimension* in the economy, too, such as income, output, demand, etc. Their magnitudes are related to a certain duration of time, and thus we speak of annual, monthly incomes, output, demand, etc., in contrast to *stock magnitudes*, which are related to certain points of time, for example national wealth, the number of population, etc. Induced investment depends on changes over time of these time-dimensional factors, upon their positive or negative increments, that is, their acceleration. "...the demand for new construction or enlargement of stocks depends upon whether or not the sales of the finished product are growing... If demand be treated as a rate of speed at which goods are taken off the market, maintenance varies roughly with the speed, but new construction depends upon the acceleration."[7] It depends upon acceleration, more exactly upon the acceleration of demand created by autonomous investment. Clark made use of the acceleration principle in his examination of business cycles. He wished to find an answer to the question of why the output and price of capital goods show a greater fluctuation during business cycles than the output and price of consumer goods.

The accelerator effect applies to investment in fixed capital, while it affects circulating capital only in inventory investment.

Let us first see in a simple numerical example how investment in fixed capital changes as a result of the accelerator effect. Let the capital–output ratio, that is the quantity of capital needed to produce one unit of output, be 1. In this case, the magnitude of total capital will be equal in the course of the increase in demand or production to the size of demand or production. Let the life of a machine be 10 years, that is, it is replaced after ten years of use.

[6] J. M. Clark: Business Acceleration and the Law of Demand: a Technical Factor in Economic Cycles, *Journal of Political Economy*, March 1917. Reprinted in: *Readings in Business Cycle Theory*, Philadelphia–Toronto, 1944, p. 238.

[7] *Ibid.*

Period	1	2	3	4	5	6	7	8
Demand (production)	1,000	1,000	1,100	1,200	1,300	1,500	1,800	1,900
Stock of capital	1,000	1,000	1,100	1,200	1,300	1,500	1,800	1,900
New investment	—	—	100	100	100	200	300	100
Replacement	100	100	100	100	100	100	100	100

In the first and second periods, demand does not increase and investment is confined to replacement only. In the third period, demand increases by 10 per cent, capital stock also has to increase by 10 per cent. Another 100 units of capital are needed, and the magnitude of new investment is 100. Total investment grows by 100 per cent. This new capital of 100 units operates in the productive process for 10 years, so that its replacement does not have to be taken into account in our model extending over 8 periods. In the 4th period too, 100 more units of capital are needed, new investments being again 100. As this numerical example reveals, the induced investment in capital stock of a period is proportional to changes in the demand or production, of the same or the immediately preceding periods. The factor of proportion is the capital–output ratio. And the percentage change in demand or production brings about a higher percentage change in investment. The reason for it lies in the fact that even though capital stock changes in the same proportion as demand or production has changed, since capital stock is greater than the output of capital goods, the percentage change in the latter is greater than that of the stock of capital or consumption goods.

The accelerator effect may be expressed in a formula, in the form of period analysis:

$$I_{\text{ind}} = v\varDelta Y,$$

where v is the capital–output ratio and I_{ind} is induced investment; expressed in the form of rate analysis:

$$I_{\text{ind}} = v \cdot \frac{dY}{dt}.$$

In the view of some non-Marxian economists, an equation which links up investment with the future growth of production does not express any accelerator effect. The relationship $I_{\text{ind}}(t) = v(Y_{t+1} - Y_t)$ does not express the effect of the growth of production on investment, but the capacity-expanding effect of investment.

Our numerical example clearly illustrates a characteristic of the accelerator effect. For induced investment to remain at the same level, production (demand) has to increase by the same increment, or at the same rate. Induced investment will grow only if the increment or growth rate of production increases. If production grows, but the increment or rate of growth decreases, then induced investment will drop in absolute terms. The more the magnitude of the capital coefficient exceeds unity, the more intensively the change in production will make itself felt in induced investment. Owing to this characteristic of the accelerator effect, non-Marxian economists ascribe an important role to it in cyclical fluctuations. The multiplier in itself has a stabilizing role. It promotes the establishment of the equilibrium

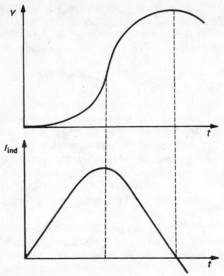

Figure 83

level of national income. The accelerator effect, however, added to that of the multiplier, may trigger off an oscillation around the equilibrium value of national income.

Assume that total demand or production increases as a function of time first at an increasing, then at a decreasing rate, and finally reaches its maximum. Following changes in total demand or production, induced investment grows as long as total demand or production grows at an increasing rate. If it grows at a decreasing rate, induced investment will decline in absolute terms, after reaching its maximum when demand or production turns from changing at an increasing to changing at a decreasing rate, that is, the maximum of induced investment lies at a point of inflexion. Its level will be zero when demand or production reaches its maximum value.

Let us represent this on a graph (see Figure 83).

In the relationship between demand or production and induced investment we are dealing with the so-called *lead* phenomenon, in which the effect in its tendency of change preceedes the cause. The change in demand or production as a cause gives rise to induced investment as an effect, but investment reaches its maximum earlier than the cause bringing about that change.

In contrast to induced investment, replacement depends upon the absolute magnitude of demand or production: $I_r = f(Y)$, or $I_r = f(D)$. If owing to the insufficiency of aggregate demand only part of the available capital stock is used, part of the worn-out capital goods will not be replaced, so that replacement will decrease with a fall in demand and increase with a rise in demand. Thus replacement will also increase beyond the inflexion point of the curve representing changes

437

in total demand or production, until total demand or production reaches its maximum, and may thereby offset the decrease in induced investment beyond the inflexion point. The smaller the share of replacement within gross investment, the more violent the fluctuation in gross investment caused by changes in demand or production.

In inventory investment the accelerator effect makes itself felt in the following way:

Entrepreneurs, in order to ensure the undisturbed process of reproduction, hold inventories in a certain percentage proportion to their sales. Inventory investment would remain at a constant level if sales increased by the same increment, at the same rate of growth. For inventory investment to grow, sales must increase at an increasing rate. If sales increase, but at a decreasing rate, then the absolute amount of inventory investment will-fall back. Consequently, inventory investment reacts to an increase in sales in much the same way as investment in fixed capital to an increase in demand (production). And inventory investment also changes to a higher degree than sales.

Hansen points out that the further a given productive branch lies from the final consumer, the more strongly it will feel the fluctuations in final consumer demand, owing to the accelerator effect in inventory investment. If the sales of the final product have increased, retailers will increase their inventories, and place larger orders relative to increased demand with wholesalers. Likewise, wholesalers wish to build up their inventories and buy more from the manufacturers of the final product than retailers have ordered from them. Manufacturers of finished products wish to fill up their inventories of semi-finished products, and buy more-of them than is necessary to produce the quantity ordered from them by wholesalers. Manufacturers of semi-finished products in turn will buy more raw materials from primary producers than ordered by manufacturers of finished products to produce semi-finished goods. Thus a small fluctuation in the trade in final consumer demand will cause an ever greater fluctuation the more closely we approach the production of raw materials through the superimposed stages of production.[8]

In modern non-Marxian business-cycle theory a great significance is attached to the circumstance that the accelerator effect, if production decreases in absolute volume, is restricted with respect to investment in fixed capital. Making use of our numerical example: if the amount of demand is 1,000 at a capital–output ratio of one, 1,000 units of equipment are necessary to satisfy demand with an optimal use of equipment. If demand drops to 900, the necessary stock of capital will be 900, too. Since the life of a machine is 10 years, the natural wear and tear of the capital stock is 10 per cent per annum. Now capital stock will be reduced from 1,000 to the necessary level of 900 in accordance with the accelerator effect by not carrying out the 10 per cent replacement falling due, and therefore 100 units of capital will be used up completely. But if demand falls from 1,000 not to 900 but to 800, capital stock can only be reduced by 100, even though the accelerator effect would call for a reduction by 200. In the case of a decrease in demand (production), the accelerator effect is restricted by the fact that capital stock can be diminished only to the extent to which the otherwise necessary replacement is not carried out.

[8] A. Hansen: *op. cit.*, p. 185.

438

Evaluating the acceleration theory of non-Marxian economics, let us examine how it reflects reality.

The accelerator effect expresses that the increase in production sooner or later makes investment necessary, because without investment, production can be expanded to a certain limit only. The excessive use of available equipment is not economical in the long run. The accelerator effect further expresses a characteristic of fixed capital, namely that it serves several production periods, and thus it is the increment in output which requires investment in fixed capital. Originally, the acceleration principle was evolved in connection with investment in fixed capital. This relationship between the increase in investment in fixed capital and production can also be found in Marx: "A continuous expansion in the branches of industry which use these machines is required in order to keep this capital employed [i.e. in machine building—A. M.] and merely to reproduce it annually. (An ever greater expansion is required if he himself accumulates.) Thus *even the mere reproduction of the capital invested in this sphere* requires continuous accumulation in the remaining spheres of production."[9]

But the relationship between the increase in investment and production (demand) varies violently, being not nearly as close as supposed by the first formulators of the acceleration principle, who thought that the percentage change in capital stock always corresponds to the percentage change in demand (production). It depends in fact partly on technical, partly on socio-economic factors. We can say in general that anything that affects the capital–output ratio of an industry, or society as a whole, will also influence the accelerator effect in that industry, or society as a whole. Technical advance, changes in the production processes will also cause the relationship between the increase in production and investment to alter. The fact that the notion of capacity is rather broad, and output may be increased to a significant extent even with the existing equipment, also contributes to making the relationship between the increase in production and investment very unstable. And it will also vary because of technical innovations which, owing to investments sharply expanding capacity, can only be adopted independently of whether the increase in production or demand justifies such an expansion of productive capacity. Generally, a difficulty is caused in the working of the acceleration principle by the indivisiblity of capital goods. In the case of indivisible factors of production even a slight change in demand may induce a large investment. There is also a loose relationship between the increase in demand and those investments wich are made by firms with a view to increasing their economic power. The magnitude of the accelerator effect may also be influenced by the business cycle. The more idle capacities exist in a given economy, the less an increase in demand makes new investments necessary. The entrepreneurs' attitudes also influence the size of the accelerator effect. The increase in demand is irrelevant if entrepreneurs deem it to be temporary; they will not invest, but attempt instead to satisfy increased demand by making a more intensive use of their existing equipment. The acceleration principle in its strict formulation further presupposes that entrepreneurs expect demand to rise at just the same rate in the future as it did in the past, that is, that the elasticity of their expectations is unity. The principle of acceleration further

[9] K. Marx: *op. cit.*, p. 481.

assumes that profits are a function of demand only. Tinbergen, who tries to approach the acceleration principle statistically, distinguishes the effect of sales upon investment from the effect of profits upon investment. As a result of his econometric computations, he concludes that there exist industries in which a correlation can be found between profit and investment, but not between sales and investment. All this reflects that sales and profits do not always move in the same direction.

The size of the accelerator effect may also be changed on the macro-economic level, by changes in the structure of demand and, subsequently, in the relations between sectors, even if total demand has not changed. If demand shifts away from the product of an industry in which the capital–output ratio is relatively small, or in which there are significant idle capacities, towards the product of an industry where the capital–output ratio is relatively high, or where there is hardly any idle capacity, investment will grow. This may also happen in the case when the capital–output ratio is the same in both industries, or the size of unused capacity is the same, too if the increase in the investment in one industry is not offset by the decrease in capital stock in that industry for whose product the demand has fallen. This is the case when the necessary decrease in capital stock exceeds the amount of the necessary replacement.

In addition to the factors already mentioned we might continue at will the list of those which cause the relationship between the increase in demand and investment to be a loose one.

The acceleration principle in its less strict formulation does not assert that any change in demand induces an increase in investment in the proportion of this change multiplied by the capital–output ratio. It only maintains that there is correlation between the changes. All this goes to show that though the theory of acceleration does contribute to the explanation of investment decisions, it is in itself far from being able to provide an explanation of investment. This is also supported by the statistical explorations made by Tinbergen. He examined three industries, railways, cotton-weaving and shipping. He found that only the reaction of railways reasonably approached the acceleration principle, obviously because railways are obliged to transport any goods consigned. Summarizing his findings, Tinbergen came to the conclusion that "... the acceleration principle cannot help very much in the explanation of the details in real investment fluctuations... As a rather poor principle with the chief object of explaining the tendency to more intensive fluctuations in durable goods production, it remains of value; but the tendency seems to be half as large as would be expected."[10]

The analysis of the relationship between changes in demand (production) and investment raises the question of whether it is justifiable to divide investment into autonomous and induced investment. In real fact, any investment, in so far as it puts goods on the market, has, sooner or later, to be justifiable by demand, primarily by demand for consumer goods, and in this sense all investment is induced investment. A difference appears at most in the fact that investments made in the production of consumer goods have to be justified directly by the demand for consumer goods, while investments in the production of capital goods, particularly in the sector of the production of capital goods for the capital-goods industries,

[10] J. Tinbergen: *Econometrics*, Philadelphia, 1951, p. 229.

440

are justified only through transmissions. At the same time, owing to the key role of the production of capital goods, especially of fixed capital, the market for consumer goods expands primarily through investments in the production of capital goods. This circumstance also singificantly contributes to the fact that a substantial part of the latter appears as autonomous investment in relation to investment made in the production of consumer goods.

It is, by the way, absolutely arbitrary to separate investments caused by changes in demand from those which are aimed at incorporating technical progress. Investments stimulated by current demand may incorporate all achievements of the latest technical advance. There is no Chinese wall either between investments induced by current demand or investments stimulated by profit prospects going beyond those expected of former investments. In the case of the former, entrepreneurs also take into account more remote profit prospects, but expectations underlying long-run investment decisions may also be influenced by changes in demand.

Let us now investigate in detail the individual growth models built upon the Keynesian theoretical basis.

DOMAR'S GROWTH THEORY

Statement of the theory

Domar developed his growth theory while criticizing the one-sidedness of Keynes's system and further improving some of his views. In determining the equilibrium growth rate, Domar assumes full employment and a full utilization of productive capacity. He maintains that the same growth rate ensures both full employment and the full use of productive capacity. The latter can be measured, in his view, by means of either of two approaches. We either multiply the existing labour force by the average productivity of labour, or we multiply capital stock by the average efficiency of capital. Domar chooses the latter approach, since by means of the increase in capital stock not only can the expansion of productive capacity be approximated, but also the expansion of the market. Thus he accepts the central idea of Keynesian theory that the market expands in the wake of investments. Building his growth model entirely upon changes in investment, he leaves out of his model the increase in the labour force. In his model he finds no criterion for full employment other than that which comes about when demand ensures the full use of capacity.

Domar sees the deficiency of Keynesian theory in the following terms.

In Keynes's view, full employment is ensured when entrepreneurs wish to make an investment corresponding to the intended saving from national income produced at full employment. This size of investment creates, through the multiplier effect, a total demand which is identical with national income produced at full employment. Full employment, according to the logic of the Keynesian theory, will continue to exist as long as entrepreneurs keep total investment at this level. Domar recognizes that the Keynesian train of thought takes into account only the market-expanding effect of investment, namely the fact that while the production of investment goods is going on, investment *increases* only *demand*. Confining his investigation to the short period only, Keynes ignored that as soon as the investment goods have been produced, they increase the production possibilities, that is, *productive capacity*. He further ignored the problem that if entrepreneurs sustain social aggregate investment at the same level, investments, as soon as they are matured, will keep on increasing the productive capacity of society, while the size of total demand remains unchanged. If yesterday's investment ensured the total demand needed fully to utilize capacity and thereby full employment, the same size of investment today will call forth a demand smaller than needed for full-capacity utilization, full employment cannot materialize, and excess capacity will hinder any further investment.

Let us illustrate the above by a simple numerical example. If national income at full employment was 1,000 at the beginning of our investigation, and the desired size of saving from this source was 200, then 200 units of intended investment will give rise, through the multiplier effect, to the demand needed to realize a level of national income ensuring full employment. The savings ratio, s, is $\frac{1}{5}$ in our example, and thus the multiplier is $\frac{1}{s} = 5$. An investment of 200 causes, then, a demand of 1,000. The 200-unit investment, however, when it has reached maturity, will increase productive capacity. Let us suppose that the efficiency of investment —Domar denotes it by σ—is $\frac{1}{2}$, and thus investment, if it remains at the 200 level, will increase capacity, once it reaches maturity, always by 100. Thus the original productive capacity increases from 1,000 to 1,100, 1,200, etc. over time; total demand, however, will remain unchanged at the 1,000 level as the size of investment has not changed. Output adjusting itself to demand will not grow into the increased capacity, and thus part of it will remain unused and unemployment will rise. A solution could be found if in the period when investments mature additional demand were created for the excess capacity. When the 200-unit investment matures and increases productive possibilities by 100, an additional demand of 100 would be needed. But what creates it? In Domar's view, it is the additional investment made in the period of maturity of the previous 200-unit investment which, before reaching maturity, expands the market by 100 owing to the multiplier effect, that is, by the same amount by which the previous investment expanded capacity at its maturity. In our example, the multiplier is 5, and thus 20 units of additional investment will ensure 100 units of additional demand in the period of the maturity of the 200 units of investment, so that at that time the entrepreneurs should invest already a total of 220 units. If the 220 units of investment also mature, capacity will grow by another 110 units, and now already 22 units of additional investment, altogether 242 units of investment, will ensure that total demand corresponds to increased capacity, that is, that full employment is sustained. Domar stresses that investment is today a cure for economic ills, because it creates demand for increased capacity, but it is at the same time a source of even greater future troubles in that, once matured, it further increases capacity. An investment which is sufficient today will make more and more investments necessary tomorrow.[11]

The problem of equilibrium growth arises in Domar's theory in the form that

[11] E. D. Domar: Expansion and Employment, *The American Economic Review*, March 1947, p. 49.

a growth rate of investment must be found at which its double effect, the market- and capacity-expanding effects, are in equilibrium.

If investment I increases capacity by $I \cdot \sigma$, an additional investment is needed which creates, through the multiplier effect, an additional demand of $\Delta I \cdot \dfrac{1}{s}$, that is,

$$I \cdot \sigma = \Delta I \cdot \frac{1}{s}.$$

The adequate demand for increased capacity being ensured at this growth rate of investment, total output will grow so as to use total capacity. The equilibrium rate of growth of investment is thus

$$\frac{\Delta I}{I} = s \cdot \sigma.^{12}$$

If investment grows at this rate, capacity, output and market will grow together, ensuring full-capacity utilization at full employment. At a rate greater than that, the increase in demand will exceed the increase in capacity. At a growth rate smaller than that, it is the increase in capacity that exceeds increased demand.

There is no symmetry, says Domar, between the two effects of investment. Even with investment increasing, while the size of investment is positive, capacity will grow. For demand to grow, however, investment has to rise in relation to the previous period.[13]

A critique of Domar's theory

In Domar's growth model, as we have seen, it is the increase in investment which determines the growth process of the economy. Investment causes the productive capacity of society to grow, but it is again investment which calls forth the demand needed to exploit that capacity. At an increase ensuring full-capacity utilization, output also grows at a rate of $s \cdot \sigma$. Domar's equilibrium growth will be maintained as long as s and σ do not change over time.

Can the equilibrium rate of growth be expressed by $s \cdot \sigma$?

Let us examine the question by means of Marx's scheme representing the re- lationships of expanded reproduction under equilibrium conditions. To simplify computations, let us suppose that the organic composition of capital is the same in both departments, and that the magnitudes of c, v and s are also identical within both departments.

Period I, department I:
$$1,000c + 1,000v + 1,000s; \text{ utilization of } s:$$

$$400\ s_c$$
$$400\ s_v$$
$$200\ s_k$$

12 E. D. Domar: *op. cit.*, p. 41.
13 E. D. Domar: *op. cit.*, p. 40.

department II:

$$1{,}142.85c + 1{,}142.85v + 1{,}142.85s; \text{ utilization of } s:$$

457.14 s_c
457.14 s_v
228.87 s_k

Period II, department I:

$$1{,}400c + 1{,}400v + 1{,}400s; \text{ utilization of } s:$$

560 s_c
560 s_v
280 s_k

department II:

$$1{,}600c + 1{,}600v + 1{,}600s; \text{ utilization of } s:$$

640 s_c
640 s_v
320 s_k

Period III, department I:

$$1{,}960c + 1{,}960v + 1{,}960s; \text{ utilization of } s:$$

784 s_c
784 s_v
392 s_k

department II:

$$2{,}240c + 2{,}240v + 2{,}240s; \text{ utilization of } s:$$

896 s_c
896 s_v
448 s_k

By means of these tables it is possible to demonstrate how the demand for consumer goods surpasses their supply if department I runs ahead of department II, and it can also be shown that the faster growth of the production of consumer goods in comparison to the means of production is the indication of a bad business cycle.

In the Marxian model, the efficiency of capital or investment, $(v+s):c = 2$, and the proportion of national income set aside for saving—saving interpreted in the Keynesian sense, meaning by it only the part of the surplus value intended to be spent on means of production—is 20 per cent. The growth rate of national income, $s \cdot \sigma = 40$ per cent. And indeed, the size of national income in the subsequent periods increases by 40 per cent, rising from 4,285.75 to 6,000, and from 6,000 to 8,400. And investment also grows at the same rate, taking the value of σ to be constant, namely from 857.14 to 1,200, and from 1,200 to 1,680. From the fact that national income increases from one period to another by investment multiplied by the efficiency of investment, that is, by $\Delta Y = I \cdot \sigma$, while investment is equal to the saved part of national income, $I = sY$, the rate of growth set up by Domar can be deduced. This is because on the basis of the above relationship

$$\Delta Y = sY\sigma, \text{ whence } \frac{\Delta Y}{Y} = s \cdot \sigma.$$

Domar's determination of the equilibrium growth rate expresses, therefore, a real relationship that can also be deduced from Marx's scheme. It expresses —approaching the increase in output from the side of investment—that if investment grows, the quantity of use-value embodying national income and measured at unchanged prices will also rise owing to the efficiency of investment. And since investment is a certain proportion of national income, the growth rate will depend

444

upon the proportion of national income, or within it of the surplus value, serving the expansion of the production of capital goods, and upon the efficiency of capital goods.

In Marx's scheme, however, it is capitalists who save and invest; both saving and investment are stimulated by the profit motive, which in turn depends on class relations. If department I runs ahead of department II, the increase in real wages will lag behind the increase in the productivity of labour, and the realized profit of capitalists will grow, which stimulated them again to further investments. The situation is just the opposite if the weight of department II increases in relation to department I. Thus the similarity between Domar's and Marx's model is only a formal one, since the latter is built upon Marx's surplus value and reproduction theory.

In his growth model, Domar raises the old problem which Keynes held, in contrast to Hobson, to be of less importance: Does investment not go beyond the limits of the market? And is there a sufficient market for matured investment, for the increased supply of consumer goods? The market would be ensured if department I went on expanding production, that is, if capitalists continued their investment activities at an appropriate rate.

But as soon as investments have matured, they act unfavourably upon the trade cycle and deteriorate the profit prospects. And yet, what stimulates capitalists to maintain their investment activities at an unchanged rate? Domar fails to answer this question. He only sets up the abstract conditions of equilibrium growth, but missing in his model are those forces which govern the actual growth rate in a capitalist economy. He does not give any investment function, does not tell us on what factors investment depends in a capitalist economy. Without any representation of forces giving rise to the growth process, the question of the existence and stability of equilibrium growth does not even arise in his model. The way in which he refers to it[14] is merely intended to provide a theoretical support for the economic policy of the state. He wishes to give an answer to the question of what growth rate it would be desirable for the state to establish, and by influencing what factors it would be possible to create that equilibrium growth rate.

In criticizing Domar's model, mention should also be made of the deficiency that in the case of growth at an even rate σ is constant over time, and thus the model does not express the effect of technical progress. The constancy of σ implies that either there is no technical advance in the course of economic growth, or that capital per head and output per head increase at the same rate. He does not discuss the character of technical progress, and thus from the unchanged magnitude of σ the conclusion may be drawn that Domar's growth model does not explicitly take into account technical progress when attempting to determine the equilibrium rate of growth. By building the determination of the equilibrium rate of growth solely upon the growth rate of investment, Domar's model does not take into consideration the increase in employment either. That is the reason why he was compelled to interpret the criterion of full employment in a roundabout way, as a realization of full-capacity utilization.

[14] E. D. Domar: *op. cit.*, p. 55.

HARROD'S GROWTH THEORY

Another pioneer of modern non-Marxian growth theories based upon Keynesian foundations, Harrod, tried to complement growth theory with an *investment function*. In his model, investment is called forth, through the accelerator effect, by the increase in national income, and through it in consumer demand. "New capital is required in relation to new output... it is the new capital required to sustain the output which will satisfy the demands for consumption arising out of consumers' marginal addition to income."[15]

The equilibrium rate of growth, G_w

Harrod's growth model is built upon the interaction of the multiplier and accelerator effects. The increase in consumer demand or in national income induces investment through the accelerator effect, and investment increases total income through the multiplier effect. If national income rises at an equilibrium rate G_w, it calls forth, through the accelerator effect, as much investment as creates, through the multiplier effect, a total demand equal to the national income of the period in question. Thus at a rate of G_w the intention to save and invest are just in equilibrium, and total demand grows with total output. This is why Harrod calls this rate G_w, the warranted rate of growth, since growth at such a rate guarantees the equilibrium of these magnitudes.

Harrod's G_w rate of growth can now be deduced by either of two approaches.

We may start out from the assumption of Keynes's theory that at an equilibrium rate of growth the intentions to save and invest are in equilibrium, that is,

$I_{\text{ex-ante}} = S_{\text{ex-ante}}.$

On the basis of the accelerator effect,

$I_{\text{ex-ante}} = C_r \Delta Y,$

where C_r is the capital–output ratio at equilibrium growth, while

$S_{\text{ex-ante}} = sY.$

At an equilibrium of the intentions to save and invest

$$C_r \Delta Y = sY, \text{ whence}$$

$$\frac{\Delta Y}{Y} = \frac{s}{C_r}.$$

But Harrod's equilibrium growth rate can also be derived from the Keynesian equation for the determination of national income:

$$Y = C + I,$$
$$C = cY,$$
$$I = C_r \Delta Y,$$
$$Y = cY + C_r \Delta Y.$$

[15] R. Harrod: *op. cit.*, p. 83.

Collecting the Y terms and factorizing them:

$$Y(1-c) = C_r \Delta Y, \text{ whence}$$

$$\frac{\Delta Y}{Y} = \frac{1-c}{C_r}.$$

$1-c = s$, and thus we have obtained the same formula for the determination of the equilibrium rate of growth which we derived on the basis of the equilibrium of the intentions to save and invest.

Yet the two approaches are not identical. They give the same solution to the determination of the value of G_w if at the time when total expenditure is in equilibrium with national income, the intentions to save and invest are also in equilibrium. But the two kinds of equilibrium, as we shall soon see, do not always coincide.

Since $\dfrac{1}{C_r} = \dfrac{Y}{K}$, which is Domar's σ, Harrod's formula also expresses the equilibrium rate of growth as the product of the savings ratio and the efficiency of capital. But the formal difference between the two formulae also refers to their difference in content. Domar's formula contains, in addition to the savings ratio, the efficiency of capital, because Domar builds his growth theory on the assumption that investment causes productive capacity to grow, and demand created by investment ensures that production grows to utilize fully the increased capacity. In Harrod's formula we can also find the capital–output ratio, in addition to the savings ratio. But he builds into his growth model an investment function, investment being stimulated by the increase in production through the accelerator effect, whose size in turn depends on the capital–output ratio.

Refining Harrod's formula, Hamberg,[16] Ott[17] and others pointed out that the basic formula needs a slight modification depending on to what points of time the values of the variables are to be related.

If $I_t = C_r(Y_t - Y_{t-1})$ and $S_t = sY_t$, then we obtain the following equation for the equilibrium rate of growth:

$$G_w = \frac{s}{C_r - s}.$$

Let us now illustrate Harrod's G_w by a numerical example on the basis of the formula expressing the time relation of the variables by $\dfrac{s}{C_r - s}$. Let s be 20 per cent, and C_r, 2.2; this gives rise to the following changes in the variables:

---

[16] D. Hamberg: *Economic Growth*, New York, 1956. (See the chapters on built-in lags.)
[17] A. Ott: *Einführung in die dynamische Wirtschaftstheorie*, Göttingen, 1965, p. 214.

	t		$t+1$		$t+2$		$t+3$
Y	1,000		1,100		1,210		1,331
S			220		242		266.2
ΔY		100		110		121	
I			220		242		266.2
$C+I$			1,100		1,210		1,331

At a growth rate of $G_w = 10$ per cent, the increment in output gives rise, through the accelerator effect, to investment of the amount of 220, 242 and 266.2 respectively, which, through the multiplier effect—the multiplier being 5 in our example—brings about a demand equal to output. Looking at the fundamental characteristic of growth at the rate of G_w from another aspect, we find that the difference between national income and saving, consumer demand, plus investment achieved through the accelerator effect, yields the size of national income produced over any period.

What, in Harrod's view stimulates entrepreneurs to invest? Why does the increase achieved in the past in national income induce investment? Harrod assumes that the initial demand relations were such that they stimulated entrepreneurs to utilize their productive capacity to a greater than normal extent. They invest in order to restore the normal utilization of capacity. The increased demand caused by this investment ensures a market for the output produced by the excessive utilization of capacity. Experiencing that their earlier decisions on production have been justified by demand, they wish to expand production at the same rate as they did in the past, which will again be possible only if they utilize the capacity increased by investment to a greater than normal extent. Their endeavour to restore normal capacity induces them to further investment, which again ensures market for increased output. As Harrod writes, "... perhaps C_r should be deemed to have a value slightly slower than the required amount of capital, lower, that is, by the amount necessary to keep producers moving forward on the line of advance."[18]

With a growth at the rate G_w, output and the stock of capital will increase at the same rate. According to Harrod, a capitalist economy does not have any automatism which could ensure that growth takes place at the rate of G_w, but should the rate of G_w accidentally develop, it will be sustained until s and C_r have changed in the course of growth. It will be sustained, since entrepreneurs are interested in maintaining the established growth rate of G_w because they see their expectations justified at this rate, which ensures that total demand increases parallel with total output. Consequently, they wish to expand their output at the rate G_w. "There is a line of advance," he writes, "which, if adhered to, would leave producers content with what they had done."[19] "I define G_w as that over-all rate of advance which, if executed, will leave entrepreneurs in a state of mind in which they are prepared to carry on a similar advance."[20]

[18] R. Harrod: op. cit., p. 86.
[19] Ibid.
[20] R. Harrod: op. cit., p. 82.

448

As far as the constancy of s and C in the growth process is concerned, s, as the savings ratio of the national income, will change as a result of changes in distribution relations. For s to remain constant in the growth process, distribution relations must not change.

As for the constancy over time of C_r, it depends, according to Harrod, on the fulfilment of two conditions.

1. The rate of interest cannot change in the growth process. At a constant level of technical knowledge "with interest constant, the requirement for capital will grow at the same rate as the population,"[21] that is, capital per head will remain unchanged. At the given level of technical knowledge, a change in the rate of interest calls forth the substitution effect by stimulating entrepreneurs to adopt more or less capital-intensive productive methods, so that C_r, the equilibrium capital–output ratio, will change.

2. If the rate of interest is constant, the neutrality of technical advance is, according to Harrod, the second condition for the capital–output ratio to remain unchanged in the course of economic growth. A widely accepted classification of technical progress in non-Marxian economics was given by Harrod himself. In classifying technical progress he takes the rate of interest to be constant, to eliminate thereby the substitution effect in the change in the capital–output ratio. Given a constant rate of interest, the capital–output ratio can change in his theory only as a result of technical progress. We can speak of *neutral technical progress, in Harrod's sense,* only if it does not affect the capital–output ratio at an unchanged interest rate. *Capital-using* technical advance at unchanged rate of interest increases the capital–output ratio, and *capital-saving* technical advance decreases it.

The British economist Meade illustrates Harrod's neutral technical progress, following the train of thought of neo-classical theory, in the following diagrammatical way[22] (see Figure 84).

Prior to technical progress, production is carried on along the F_1 production function with capital per head of $0K_1$. At that $0K_1$, the marginal productivity of capital is the slope of the tangent drawn to curve F_1 at point P_1. This expresses, in a neo-classical sense, the size of the rate of interest. In the course of technical progress this production function will shift upwards. For the interest rate to remain unchanged even after technical progress, capital per head must be increased, in Meade's view, until the marginal productivity of capital increased by technical progress falls back along the new F_2 curve, as a result of the substitution effect, to the old level, that is, until the tangent drawn to the new curve becomes parallel to the tangent drawn to the old curve. Assume now that this occurs at the capital per head of $0K_2$, at point P_2 on curve F_2. If points P_1 and P_2 lie on the same ray starting out from the origin, then not only the marginal productivity of capital, but the capital–output ratio too, will be identical at points P_1 and P_2 respectively. This is because the tangent of the angle formed by the ray and the X axis is $\dfrac{Y}{K}$,

[21] R. Harrod: *op. cit.*, p. 22.
[22] J. E. Meade: *A Neo-Classical Theory of Economic Growth,* Revised new ed., London, 1965, p. 57.

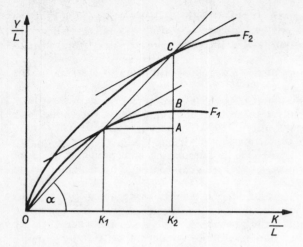

Figure 84

that is, the "average productivity" of capital, and if this is identical at points P_1 and P_2, then its reciprocal $\dfrac{K}{Y}$, that is, the capital–output ratio, is also identical.

If, however, the marginal productivity and the "average productivity" of capital do not change in the course of technical progress, their quotient, the production elasticity of capital, does not change either. Assuming a first-order homogeneous production function—this is what neo-classical growth theories suppose in determining the equilibrium rate of growth—technical progress also leaves the production elasticity of labour unaffected. Thus, approaching the Harrodian interpretation of neutral technical progress from a neo-classical viewpoint, we may derive as a further characteristic that it has no bearing on the production elasticity of either capital or labour. Since in neo-classical theory production elasticities express the relative shares of social classes in national income, neutral technical progress in Harrod's sense does not change the income-distribution relations either. In this way, the first condition of a constant-rate growth is also fulfilled: the savings ratio, s, remains constant in the equilibrium growth process.

However, if neutral technical progress does not affect the capital–output ratio, that is, the average productivity of capital, in what does the effect of technical progress manifest itself in Harrod at a G_w rate of growth?

One of the deficiencies of Harrod's definition of G_w is exactly the fact that, in much the same way as Domar's formula, it does not express the effect of technical progress. Still, it does express it implicitly. Harrod's neutral technical progress raises labour productivity. Its effect as interpreted by non-Marxian economics is the same as would be achieved if the number of efficient workers had grown, that is, as if the quantity of output increased in the course of technical progress could also have been attained without technical progress, merely by employing a larger

450

labour force. This is called in modern non-Marxian growth theory *labour-augmenting* technical progress. It is expressed by the neo-classical production function as follows: $Y = f[A(t)L, K]$, where $A(t)$, the multiplier expressing technical progress, shows how many times output rises in the course of technical progress, while capital per head is increased by such an amount that the marginal productivity of capital falls back to the previous level. It is by this $A(t)$ that the actual number of the labour force has to be multiplied in order to obtain the number of the efficient labour force.

Let us illustrate the above by a numerical example. Assume that 100 workers produce 100 units of output with 100 units of capital. With the development of technology let us increase the stock of capital by an amount which ensures that its marginal productivity remains at an unchanged level. Assuming neutral technical progress, the capital–output ratio also remains unchanged. After introducing new production techniques, 100 workers will produce 120 units of output with 120 units of capital. The multiplier expressing technical progress, $A(t)$, is 1.2 in our example. The amount of output has increased 1.2 times after the adoption of technical innovations. The same volume of output could have been achieved without technical progress if 120 workers had produced with 120 units of capital. Thus, as a result of technical progress, 100 workers perform the work of a labour force of 120, 100 workers counting as 120 efficient workers.

The G and G_n rates of growth

In addition to the G_w rate of growth, Harrod distinguishes two more rates of growth.

G is the actual rate of growth. $G = \dfrac{s}{C}$, where C is the actual capital–output ratio. G may differ from G_w as "G is a quantity determined from time to time by trial and error, by the collective trials and errors of vast numbers of people."[23]

If the actual growth rate, G, differs from G_w, there is no mechanism foreseen by Harrod which could adjust G to G_w. On the contrary, in the case of a deviation, G moves more and more away from G_w. In other words, Harrod's G_w has no stability.

If $G > G_w$, the actual growth rate induces investment higher than intended saving. Total demand, that is, consumer demand plus investment, exceeds output. Illustrating this process by a numerical example: if G is 15 per cent, Y will rise from 1,000 to 1,150. Society wishes to save 230 out of that 1,150, consequently, the amount of consumer demand will increase to 920. The increment of output, 150, will induce 330 units of investment at a capital–output ratio of 2.2. Thus total demand, $920 + 330 = 1,250$, will exceed 1,150, the size of output. This stimulates entrepreneurs to increase further the actual rate of growth, as a result of which G will increasingly rise above G_w, intended investment will more and more surpass intended saving, total demand will outstrip total supply. "Whenever G exceeds G_w, there will be a tendency for a boom to develop..."[24] Since now $\dfrac{s}{C} > \dfrac{s}{C_r}$,

23 R. Harrod: *op. cit.*, p. 86.
24 R. Harrod: *op. cit.*, p. 88.

the actual capital–output ratio will be smaller than the equilibrium one, because, owing to the vigorous increase in demand, the equipment is overutilized, inventories are run down, and less capital is used to produce a unit of output.

The situation is just the opposite if $G < G_w$. In this case a growth rate lower than the equilibrium rate induces less investment than intended saving, and the sum of consumer demand and investment yields a demand which is smaller than output. Let the rate lower than the equilibrium growth rate be 5 per cent. In this case, Y will rise from 1,000 to 1,050. The amount of intended saving out of 1,050 national income is 210. Consumer demand is 840. The increment of output, 50, will produce an investment of 110 at a capital–output ratio of 2.2. The sum of consumer demand and investment is 950, and thus total demand lags behind the 1,050 size of total output. This stimulates entrepreneurs to further decrease the rate of growth. G will increasingly fall below G_w, intended investment will drop more and more below intended saving, and total demand will increasingly lag behind total supply. G falling below G_w is an indication that the process of decline has set in.

If $\dfrac{s}{C} < \dfrac{s}{C_r}$, the actual capital–output ratio will be greater than the equilibrium ratio. This is because part of the capacity is underutilized, inventories are increasing, and more and more capital falls to a unit of output.

We have arrived at the so-called *Harrod paradox*. If $G > G_w$, total demand will increasingly outstrip total output, production proves more and more insufficient relative to demand, because it has been developed at too high a rate. If $G < G_w$, total demand will increasingly lag behind the increase in total output. Total output is too large relative to demand, because the latter has increased at too low a rate.

Harrod's third rate of growth is the natural rate of growth, G_n. This is the highest rate of growth that can be sustained in the long run, "... the rate of advance which the increase of population and technological improvements allow."[25] Output, however, may also rise temporarily at a higher than G_n rate. G may be temporarily greater than G_n when there exists unemployment. In this case, employment may, as a result of the unemployed getting job opportunities, increase to a greater extent than would be made possible by the natural increase of the working population. But with full employment being realized, G may not be greater than G_n.

If, however, $G_n > G_w$, it means that even though total demand and total supply increase in step with one another in the course of economic growth, employment is nevertheless not full. This is the dynamization of the Keynesian proposition according to which the economy may come into equilibrium even at underemployment. And while in Keynes a capitalist economy has no automatism which could ensure full employment, there is in Harrod no automatism of a capitalist economy to ensure the G_n rate of growth.

Some critical comments on Harrod's growth model

Criticizing Harrod's growth model, his demonstration of booms and slumps, we have to point out at the outset that though Harrod wanted to dynamize Keynes's

[25] R. Harrod: *op. cit.*, p. 87.

theory, his investment function set up, by means of the accelerator effect, a causal relationship which is opposed to that of Keynes. Keynes correctly recognized that market in a capitalist economy expands primarily as a result of investment. Though the market-expanding effect of investment is part of Harrod's growth theory, investment is induced, according to his theory, by the increase in production, more exactly in the production of consumer goods following the increased demand for consumer goods.

By associating the multiplier effect with the accelerator effect, Harrod attempts to expand his growth theory to a theory of the trade cycle. It is obvious, however, that the development of booms cannot be explained by the increase in the output of consumer goods. Harrod's starting-point is that the capacity for producing consumer goods is overutilized at the outset. If the utilization of capacity were normal, that is, "if C_r were precisely equal to requirements, they [i.e. producers— A. M.] might lapse into a stationary condition."[26]

And now, depending on the degree of the overutilization of capacity, that is, on the quantity of investment required to restore the normal utilization of capacity, demand will run ahead of production or lag behind or rise in balance with it in the course of growth. It is, according to Harrod, the excessive increase in output in relation to existing capacity which gives rise to investment, through the accelerator effect, and also justifies it.

But how did the initial conditions come into existence which induced entrepreneurs to increase the production of consumer goods over and above the normal utilization of capacity? According to Marx "... a crisis always forms the starting-point of large new investments."[27] Crises will be followed by massive replacements of fixed capital assets. Owing to these massive replacements, the production of the means of production runs ahead of the production of consumer goods. The demand for consumer goods outstrips their supply. In producing consumer goods, entrepreneurs strive to adjust to increased consumer demand by an increasingly intensive utilization of capacity. It is here that Harrod's explanation of growth, of boom, begins, and not with the upswing in the production of fixed capital.

Following the course of Marxist thinking, we may state that the massive replacement of fixed capital usually has a capacity-expanding effect too, since old machines have to be replaced by better ones. But the renewal of fixed capital is primarily of a capacity-maintaining character. At the same time, the replacement of fixed capital will abruptly raise consumer demand, and stimulate net investment, too. And, with the elapse of time, the share of net investment has to grow within the volume of total investment, because the massive replacement of worn-out fixed capital will sooner or later come to an end. These, however, when matured, will have an unambiguously capacity-expanding effect. Until the investments mature, as also pointed out by Domar, demand will be expanded, improving thereby the business cycle, but if the capacity of producing consumer goods is expanded as maturity is reached, investments will be detrimental to the business cycle,[28] because if these

26 R. Harrod: *op. cit.*, p. 86.
27 K. Marx: *Capital*, Vol. II, Moscow, 1957, p. 186.
28 For a detailed Marxist description of the process see P. Erdős: *Contributions to Theory of Capitalist Money, Business Fluctuations and Crises*, Budapest, 1971, pp. 364–387.

expanded capacities are to be employed fully, real wages have to grow, or else the large quantities of consumer goods offered for sale cannot be realized. Increasing real wages, however, diminish real profit, and thus increased output clashes with the profit interest, and the boom comes to an end. It is interesting to note that Harrod, while writing about recovery from a crisis, remarks that in a crisis "... the old machines or other fixed equipment need not be replaced at the end of their working life owing to reduced output... The actual reduction of capital stock becomes greater than what is convenient... But sooner or later the requirements for replacements must become positive, if any output at all is to be maintained.... This will arrest the downward movement and turn it into an upward one."[29] This correct recognition, however, is just a fraction in his train of thought, and Harrod does not build it organically into his theory of the trade cycle. He does not show how the process of massive replacements lead to an increased demand for consumer goods.

However, if we set out from the production of consumer goods, we cannot account for cyclical changes in capitalist reproduction, for the unfolding and halt of the boom and the recovery from crisis. Concerning the development of booms, Harrod speaks simply of the collective mistake of entrepreneurs who have expanded the output of consumer goods in excess of existing capacity, which induces them to investments which raise demand above output. The excessive expansion of the market gives rise to optimism in entrepreneurs stimulating them to increase output at an even faster rate. In other words, it is, according to Harrod, the optimism generated by a collective mistake of entrepreneurs which maintains the upswing and further fosters the entrepreneurs' optimism.

If, however, in making their decisions entrepreneurs happened collectively to hit upon the rate of G_w, the justification of their decisions gives rise to expectations which cause them to keep on increasing their production at a G_w rate.

But such expectations about the growth process being maintained are without any firm foundations in Harrod. If entrepreneurs have by chance excessively expanded the output of consumer goods, what stimulates them to further investments? Why do they suppose that there is a lasting market ensured for the quantity of output produced by the overutilization of capacity, and that it is worthwhile expanding the capacity by making investments? However, starting out from an increased production of capital goods does provide an explanation for the entrepreneurs' optimism: consumer demand for the products of department I lastingly exceeds the supply by department II for department I, which nourishes the entrepreneurs' optimism and stimulates their investment activities. And if in making their decisions entrepreneurs accidentally hit upon the G_w rate, it does not follow from this at all that they will expand their output at the same rate in the subsequent period, too. Here again, Harrod assumes, quite unaccountably, entrepreneurs to have definite expectations. Entrepreneurs, however, may strive for a time to sustain their increased output at an unchanged rate, but they also may, encouraged by their previous investments becoming justified, increase their output in the subsequent period at a much higher rate than required by the G_w rate of growth. What is characteristic of capitalist reality is not an even, but an uneven kind of

[29] R. Harrod: *op. cit.*, p. 91.

development. Capitalist anarchy makes it absolutely impossible for an even development process to materialize. The growth process is realized on the basis of decisions made by a large number of entrepreneurs independent of one another. None of them knows the business plans of the others, while the income of each firm depends upon the expenditure of the others. Each is compelled to act in the present in reliance on speculation about the future. There is no firm basis for his investment decisions. Since all entrepreneurs invest for an uncertain future, they are bound to make mistakes which have to be corrected in the period to follow. Harrod's contented capitalist who evenly develops his production does not exist in real life.

The investigation of the Marxian scheme of expanded reproduction shows that quite special values of the production of departments I and II are needed for a constant rate of equilibrium growth to be derived in a completely abstract form.

How can the break in a boom be explained on the basis of Harrod's approach? In his view, a boom may last infinitely; it has no impediment inherent in the system. By investments making possible the normal utilization of capacity, entrepreneurs may create a demand exceeding output, which, by boosting their optimism, induces them to further expand their output, and keep a steady boom going. The maturing of investment goods has no detrimental effect, for Harrod, on the boom, on the contrary, it may stimulate an even greater increase in production, and further improve the trade cycle. Starting from the overutilization of capacity in the production of consumer goods, Harrod attempts to account for the breaking of the upward trend in business in the following way. In the course of the upward trend, total demand increasingly exceeds total output, which stimulates entrepreneurs to increase the actual rate of production. While growing, G will slowly catch up with and even surpass G_n. But the growth of G is accompanied by the increase in G_w. While the growth of demand increasingly surpasses supply, entrepreneurs will realize more and more profit. The increase in realized profit will induce entrepreneurs to make added savings. Harrod maintains that "even if saving as a fraction of income is fairly steady in the long run, it is not likely to be so in the short run."[30] In a boom period, "companies are likely to save a large fraction of short-period increases of net receipts."[31] In order to induce a degree of investment needed to equalize this, it is necessary to increase output at a higher and higher growth rate, as a result of which G_w, following though not reaching the growth of G in the upswing, will also rise, catching up with and even outstripping G_n. As soon as full employment is realized, G may no longer be greater than G_n, but will drop to its level and will thereby fall below G_w. However, a G smaller than G_w is already an indication that the boom has come to an end and a slump has set in. A G_w surpassing G_n after full employment has been realized means that society saves so much of the national income that, for inducing an investment large enough to equalize it, a growth rate would be needed which the factors determining the natural rate of growth, such as population increase and technical progress, would not make possible.

Illustrating the above by a numerical example, let us suppose that G_n is 20 per cent, and full employment has just been attained. National income can increase from 1,000 to 1,200 only.

30 R. Harrod: *op. cit.*, p. 89.
31 *Ibid.*

At 1,200, however, owing to the excessive increase in profit, 50 per cent of the national income, that is, 600 is saved instead of the earlier 20 per cent. A 20 per cent rate of growth of income, however, induces an investment of $200 \cdot 2.2 = 440$. For an equilibrium of total demand and total supply to be established, a greater rate of growth would be needed, of a degree which induces an investment of 600. Such a size of Gw, however, is not feasible since full employment has been attained. Total demand will lag behind the increase in total output, and the upward business trend will be broken.

It is a case held to be typical by Keynes: full employment cannot be maintained, because there is no possibility of making profitable investments of an amount which would be equal to socially intended saving out of the national income produced at full employment.

It was Harrod who introduced into non-Marxian economics the idea that a boom ends because increasing output hits the ceiling of full employment. It is not the system which sets up internal barriers to an upswing, it is not capitalist production relations which prevent the continuous growth of production from lasting infinitely, but the G_n rate, which is an external datum of the Harrodian model. The factors determining its magnitude, natural population growth and technical progress, cannot be deduced from the model. We shall discuss this problem further below when dealing with Hick's trade-cycle theory.

Continuing the discussion of the problems raised by Harrod's growth model, we wish to refer to non-Marxian criticism pointing to the fact that in determining the G_w rate Harrod left lags out of account. In his theory, both saving and investment depend on the given magnitude of national income or its change in the current period. It is only by this assumption that he can maintain the equilibrium of saving and investment in his growth model. The critique, however, points out that if we assume that the consumption of the current period, and thereby also the saving of the current period, is a function of the income of the past period (or of past periods), then saving even in an equilibrium-growth economy cannot be in equilibrium with investment. Though total demand corresponds to total output, $C + I = Y$, the amount of the income used, $C + S$, must necessarily lag behind the magnitude of the newly created income, behind $C + I$. The two can only coincide if current income were equal to the national income of the past period. But then no economic growth would exist. If, under conditions of economic growth, there is a lag in consumer expenditures, the intention to invest must exceed the intention to save. Saving and investment may have only an *ex-post* equality. It is precisely the surplus of intended investment over intended saving which shows by what amount national income has grown from one period to another. In the above case, the approaches from $I_{\text{ex-ante}} = S_{\text{ex-ante}}$, and from $C + I = Y$ do not yield the same result for G_w. If we set out from the approach $I_{\text{ex-ante}} = S_{\text{ex-ante}}$, the two intentions will be in equilibrium in the growth process in so far as intended investment at the point of time t is just equal to intended saving at that point of time, but total demand, $C + I$, will be smaller than the national income produced. However, at a G_w, computed by means of the approach $C + I = Y$, $C + I$ corresponds to the amount of total output, but the intention to invest will deviate from the intention to save. In the former case we are faced with the paradoxical situation that at the equilibrium of the intention to save and of the intention to invest a non-intended investment appears, while in the latter case there is a non-intended saving.

Harrod, following Keynes, represents saving as a function of national income. The model does not reveal that saving is made primarily from profit, and the

456

saving made by the working class is negligible. Harrod does not show what role class relations, the relative shares of classes in national income, play in the growth process even in the form in which Kaldor did, when he made a distinction between the propensity to save of the working class and the capitalist class, pointing to the effect that the increase in investment exercises on the process of income distribution.

HICKS'S TRADE-CYCLE THEORY

The Hicksian model of growth at a constant rate

Hicks published his work *A Contribution to the Theory of the Trade Cycle* in 1950, a work which non-Marxian economists called the most ingenious and most original trade-cycle theory of the post-war period. According to Haberler, "since the appearance of the 'General Theory' no work on economics has met with such a violent response as Hicks's study."[32] Though these lines were written by Haberler in 1955, it is beyond doubt that Hicks's trade-cycle theory has been a major focus of interest within non-Marxian economics up to this day.

In order to come to grips with his ideas, let us first construct the Hicksian model of steady-state growth, or, as Hicks calls it, "Regularly Progressive Economy". This Keynes-type theory is based on the interaction of the multiplier and accelerator effects.

Harrod's model too is built upon the interaction of the multiplier and the accelerator effects. But Harrod, as Allen states, includes no lags in his model, which is why his theory has "no oscillatory feature."[33] It has no such feature because by leaving lags out of account he could not set up a higher-degree difference equation whose solution would have provided him with a model of the movement of production diverging from equilibrium growth. Hicks, however, wanted to set up a dynamic theory in the sense of Ragnar Frisch, "in which we consider the magnitudes of certain variables at different points of time..."[34] and in which the equations comprise the values of variables related to different points of time.

According to Allen, with the introduction of lags it is convenient to assume that the intentions to consume and invest are always realized, that the divergence o intended from realized magnitude appears in savings only.[35] Hicks's trade-cycle theory is based upon this assumption. In his theory, consumers may consume to the limit of their intentions, while the investments of entrepreneurs are also realized to the extent to which they were originally desired. No non-intended investment can develop in the form of an increase or decrease in inventories.

Building lags into his trade-cycle model, Hicks assumes that in any t period people spend on consumption a certain proportion of their incomes obtained in the previous period: $C_t = cY_{t-1}$. With this, he wants to substitute for the Keynesian

[32] G. Haberler: *Prosperität und Depression*, Tübingen–Zürich, 1955, p. 538.
[33] R. G. D. Allen: *Mathematical Economics*, London, 1965, p. 69.
[34] J. R. Hicks: *A Contribution to the Theory of the Trade Cycle*, Oxford, 1950, p. 10
[35] R. G. D. Allen: *op. cit.*, pp. 78–79.

consumption or savings function another functional relationship. In his view, even if we cannot say with certainty that the Keynesian consumption or savings function is wrong, we have no convincing arguments either to prove that it is correct. Hicks looks with suspicion at the statistical foundation of the Keynesian propensity to consume, too. He holds that for lack of sufficient information it is better to consider the saved proportion of income to be independent of national income.

Hicks thinks that his consumption function has the same stabilizing effect as the Keynesian propensity to consume. By the propensity to consume Keynes wanted to explain why the demand for consumer goods fluctuates in trade cycles to a lesser extent than investment. Propensity to consume curbs, in his view, the upturn of the economy, in that with increasing incomes consumer demand rises to a lesser extent, damping the decline by decreasing consumer demand to a lesser degree than income. According to Hicks, the same effect can also be captured by building lags into the consumption function. In a boom period, the excessive increase in consumer demand is counteracted because, according to the assumption of the model, the source of consumer spending on purchasing consumer goods is the lower income of the previous period. In a period of depression, however, the fall in consumer demand is mitigated by the fact that the source of consumer demand is now the higher income of the previous period.

Induced investment is caused in Hicks by a change in national income realized two periods earlier:

$I_t^{ind} = v(Y_{t-1} - Y_{t-2})$, where v is what Hicks calls the investment coefficient.

In addition to induced investment, Hicks also introduces into his model autonomous investment whose growth rate is an exogeneous datum of the model, and the absolute magnitude of autonomous investment is also given at any point of time.

National income at a point of time t is for Hicks, no matter whether growth has taken place at an equilibrium rate or at a rate deviating from it, the sum total of consumer expenditure and of induced and autonomous investment outlays:

$$Y_t = cY_{t-1} + v(Y_{t-1} - Y_{t-2}) + I_t^{aut}.$$

Hicks points out that the assumption that the intention to consume and the intention to invest are always realized, and thus total demand increases together with total supply, will lead in a growth economy, owing to the lag of consumer expenditure or intended saving, to the consequence that actual saving as a difference between national income and consumer expenditure exceeds the magnitude of intended saving. Our equation set up for Y_t only expresses the equality of intended investment and *ex-post* saving.

In Hicks's model, the growth rate of Y depends upon the growth rate of autonomous investment. "It is the rate of growth of autonomous investment which determines the equilibrium rate of growth of the whole system..."[36] Manifested in it is the Keynesian effect, the central role of investment, the determination of national income by investment through the multiplier. But since autonomous investment is of an exogenous nature, and therefore its growth rate cannot be

[36] J. R. Hicks: *op. cit.*, p. 61.

458

derived from the model, the Hicksian model also expresses that it is Y that has to adapt itself in its growth to the rate of autonomous investment. For Y to grow at a constant rate, autonomous investment must increase at a constant rate over time. And since the growth rate of autonomous investment is an exogeneous datum of the system, Hicks assumes that this rate remains constant over time. He calls the equilibrium growth rate of Y that rate which coincides with the constant rate of growth of autonomous investment. If we also know the absolute amount of autonomous investment, the magnitude of Y is also determined in any period. While in the Harrodian model autonomous investment was an alien body, in the Hicksian model, though also built upon the interaction of the multiplier and the accelerator effects, the rate of growth is governed by the growth of autonomous investment, and it is the amount of autonomous investment which determines the magnitude of Y. For this purpose, Hicks had to extend the concept of the multi-plier to a *super-multiplier*. This expresses the values which Y has to take on in the individual periods, with a given magnitude and growth rate of autonomous in-vestment, to correspond to total demand, determined by autonomous investment, the induced investment made possible by national income growing at the rate of autonomous investment, and consumer expenditure made from the national in-come of the previous period growing at that rate. In other words, it shows what values Y has to take on in the individual periods for the amount of induced invest-ment thus brought about and the amount of autonomous investment as an exo-genous datum jointly to equal *ex-post* saving, over and above the amount of consumer expenditure left over from the national income in question. "The level of output (in each period and therefore in all periods) must be such as will engender an amount of saving, and an amount of induced investment equal to saving when the given autonomous investment is taken into account."[37] The super-multiplier differs from the simple multiplier in that the former contains, in addition to the effect of autonomous investment, the effect of induced investment, too.

For the derivation of the super-multiplier we have to start from the equality of saving and investment: $S_t = I_t^{\text{ind}} + I_t^{\text{aut}}$. In this case, saving is an *ex-post* magni-tude. Hicks also writes the above equation as the equality of their ratio related to Y:

$$\frac{S_t}{Y_t} = \frac{I_t^{\text{ind}}}{Y_t} + \frac{I_t^{\text{aut}}}{Y_t}; \text{ hence } \frac{I_t^{\text{aut}}}{Y_t} = \frac{S_t}{Y_t} - \frac{I_t^{\text{ind}}}{Y_t}.$$

S is a rate constant over time of Y in the case of steady-state growth and Hicks expresses that proportion in terms of the rate of growth:

$$\frac{S_t}{Y_t} = \frac{Y_t - cY_{t-1}}{Y_t} = \frac{Y_0(1+g)^t - cY_0(1+g)^{t-1}}{Y_0(1+g)^t} = \frac{(1+g)^t - c(1+g)^{t-1}}{(1+g)^t} = 1 - \frac{c}{1+g},$$

where g is the constant growth rate of output, equal to that of autonomous invest-ment.

At the same time, it is possible to express the relationship of induced investment to Y in terms of the growth rate, a relationship which remains constant during the

---

[37] *Ibid.*

growth process:

$$\frac{I_t^{ind}}{Y_t} = \frac{v(Y_{t-1} - Y_{t-2})}{Y_t} = \frac{v[Y_{t-2}(1+g) - Y_{t-2}]}{Y_{t-2}(1+g)^2} = \frac{v[Y_{t-2}(1+g-1)]}{Y_{t-2}(1+g)^2} = \frac{vg}{(1+g)^2}.$$

If there were no autonomous investment, the growth rate of national income would bring $\dfrac{I^{ind}}{Y}$ and $\dfrac{S}{Y}$ into balance at each point of time. In other words, it would be necessary to determine that growth rate of national income which would keep both ratios in balance. Since autonomous investment does exist, the growth rate of Y, and through it $\dfrac{I^{ind}}{Y}$ and $\dfrac{S}{Y}$, are determined by the growth rate of autonomous investment. Because of the existence of autonomous investment, the two ratios cannot be in balance with one another.

$$\frac{S}{Y} - \frac{I^{ind}}{Y}$$

gives the ratio of autonomous investment to national income, which is therefore determined by its own growth rate, and through it is determined the super-multiplier, which expresses the ratio of Y to autonomous investment.

On the basis of the relationships demonstrated for $\dfrac{S}{Y}$ and $\dfrac{I^{ind}}{Y}$,

$$\frac{I_t^{aut}}{Y_t} = 1 - \frac{c}{1+g} - \frac{vg}{(1+g)^2},$$

whence

$$Y_t = I_t^{aut} \frac{1}{1 - \dfrac{c}{1+g} - \dfrac{vg}{(1+g)^2}},$$

that is, national income is $\dfrac{1}{1 - \dfrac{c}{1+g} - \dfrac{vg}{(1+g)^2}}$ times the amount of autonomous investment.

This is the super-multiplier, whose magnitude, at a constant c and v, depends on the growth rate of autonomous investment, g.

The above relationships may be expressed by a numerical example in the following way: Let the growth rate of autonomous investment be 10 per cent; then, assuming equilibrium growth, Y will also grow by 10 per cent. If 80.8181 per cent of the income of the previous period is devoted to consumption, the proportion of saving to current national income will be $1 - \dfrac{0.808\,181}{1.1} = 26.529$ per cent. Current induced investment is called forth by an increase in national income realized two periods earlier. If the investment coefficient is 2, $\dfrac{I_t^{ind}}{Y_t} = \dfrac{2 \times 0.1}{(1.1)^2} = 16.529$ per cent, and thus $\dfrac{I_t^{aut}}{Y_t} = 10$ per cent. Hence $Y_t = \dfrac{I_t^{aut}}{0.1}$.

460

The super-multiplier is 10, that is, national income is ten times the amount of autonomous investment. Let autonomous investment be 100 at the point of time t_1. Knowing the growth rate of autonomous investment (in our example 10 per cent), the consumption ratio, and the investment coefficient in relation to induced investment, the time series of consumption, induced investment and national income along the equilibrium path are determined.

Time	t_1	t_2	t_3	t_4	t_5
I^{aut}	100	110	121	133.1	146.41
Y	1,000	1,100	1,210	1,331	1,464.1
ΔY		100	110	121	133.i
I^{ind}			200	220	242
Total investment			321	353.1	388.41
C			889	977.9	1,075.69
$C+I$			1.210	1,331	1,464.1

The 10 per cent growth rate of autonomous investment determines the growth rate of output, while the amount of autonomous investment settles the quantity of output through the super-multiplier, the quantity and growth rate of output determine the amount of induced investment and the quantity of output multiplied by the consumption ratio yields the amount of consumer expenditure in the subsequent period.

The explanation of the cyclical movement of reproduction

Marxian political economy finds the material basis for periodical crises in the periodical replacement and expansion of fixed capital. In explaining the periodicity of reproduction Marx presupposes its cyclical nature. The first cyclical crisis leads on to the others. Marx did not wish to answer the question of how the first cyclical crisis came about. Another approach to the problem is taken by those non-Marxian growth theoreticians who wish to extend their theory to a trade-cycle theory. Hicks, like Harrod, starts from a steady-state rate growth process in which replacements are proportionately spread over time, and examines how the divergence of actual development from the equilibrium growth changes into a cyclical movement. "... since we want to show how the cycle arises, it is natural to begin from a state of affairs in which there is no cycle."[38] We are faced practically with the problem which Ragnar Frisch called "impulse and propagation": how the external shock affecting the economy which may come, for example, from technical progress—this is what Frisch calls "impulse"—is transformed in its propagation through the mechanisms of the economic system into a cyclical movement. This transformation is carried out in Hicks by the interaction of the accelerator and the multiplier effects. "The theory of the multiplier and the theory of the accelerator are the two sides of the theory of the fluctuations, just as the theory of demand and the theory of supply are the two sides of the theory of value."[39]

In Hicks's trade-cycle model autonomous investments grow at a constant g rate. Using a semi-logarithmic scale, Hicks represents output or investment by its logarithms on the y axis, and time on the x axis. Autonomous investment is

[38] J. R. Hicks: *op. cit.*, pp. 96–97.
[39] J. R. Hicks: *op. cit.*, p. 38.

shown in Figure 85 by the straight line AA, the angle of which is the rate of growth g. Autonomous investment determines by means of the super-multiplier the equilibrium path of output, EE. Output grows at the same g rate as autonomous investment, and thus the straight lines EE and AA are parallel to each other. It is above the EE equilibrium path that the "ceiling of full employment", FF, lies, that is, the path of growth at full employment, Harrod's G_n. In Hicks, the equilibrium path EE does not necessarily imply full employment; he assumes, like Harrod, that equilibrium growth may also occur at underemployment. In his model, the ceiling of full employment grows approximately at a g rate, too, and thus FF is also parallel to both AA and EE.

Hicks assumes that output grows initially at an equilibrium rate along EE. But some disturbing circumstance, an impulse in the sense used by Frisch, moves it away from the equilibrium path. Such a circumstance disturbing equilibrium growth may be a temporary running ahead of autonomous investment caused by technical progress, after which the former falls back to its constant-rate path, AA. This temporary oscillatory movement of autonomous investment above the equilibrium growth rate also raises the growth of induced investment and output above their equilibrium rate. These, however, need not return to their equilibrium path even after autonomous investment has relapsed to the equilibrium growth rate. The interaction of the multiplier and the accelerator effects may change their initial movement away from the equilibrium rate into a cyclical movement.

Now the question arises whether output in deviating from its equilibrium path fluctuates around it at an increasing, decreasing or constant amplitude, or approaches it or moves away from it without any oscillations. All this depends for Hicks, following from the key role of investments, upon the movement of induced investment: only upon induced investment, as it is its movement only which Hicks can deduce from the model, for autonomous investment grows, on his assumption, at a constant rate independently of the phases of reproduction. By contrast, induced investment changes in his theory in dependence on the extent of the accelerator effect. That is why Hicks characterizes changes in reproduction through the value of the investment coefficient.

Those domains of the value of the investment coefficient, within which output performs one or the other above-mentioned specific movements following a deviation from the dynamic equilibrium path, are derived by Hicks, expressing them mathematically in terms of savings ratios, in the following way:

Denoting national income moving along the equilibrium path by $\overline{Y}$, $\overline{Y}_t =$
$$= c\overline{Y}_{t-1} + v(\overline{Y}_{t-1} - \overline{Y}_{t-2}) + I_t^{\text{aut}}.$$ Thus Hicks determines the national income at the point of time t by a second-order difference equations, as cyclical deviations from the equilibrium growth rate can only occur in the case of complex roots, and complex roots are possibly only in the case of quadratic or higher-degree equations.

He determines the amount of national income changing along the non-equilibrium path at the point of time t in a similar way. Its amount will be different from the level determined by autonomous investment at the point of time t and by the super-multiplier:

$$Y_t = cY_{t-1} + v(Y_{t-1} - Y_{t-2}) + I_t^{\text{aut}}.$$

Since the intention to consume and the intention to invest are always realized in the Hicksian system, output automatically adjusts itself to the established demand, which, owing to the inclusion of lags, is a function of the past growth rate and the volume of output. Thus the cyclical movement of reproduction does not appear in the difference between demand and supply, but in the changes in the degree of employment of the existing productive capacities.

The actual amount of current national income is linked by the same relationship with the national incomes of past periods which associates the national incomes lying on the equilibrium path with one another.[40] Autonomous investment, the consumption ratio and the investment coefficient are identical on both paths. This made it possible for Hicks to determine by subtraction the difference between actual national income and national income growing along the equilibrium path, that is, y.

$$y_t = Y_t - \overline{Y}_t,$$

wherefrom

$$Y_t - \overline{Y}_t = c \cdot Y_{t-1} + v(Y_{t-1} - Y_{t-2}) + I_t^{\text{aut}} - [c\overline{Y}_{t-1} + v(\overline{Y}_{t-1} - \overline{Y}_{t-2}) + I_t^{\text{aut}}] =$$
$$= c(Y_{t-1} - \overline{Y}_{t-1}) + v[(Y_{t-1} - \overline{Y}_{t-1}) - (Y_{t-2} - \overline{Y}_{t-2})].$$

Thus

$$y_t = cy_{t-1} + v(y_{t-1} - y_{t-2}).$$

Substituting $1 - s$ for c and reducing the equation to 0, we obtain: $y_t - (1-s)y_{t-1} - v(y_{t-1} - y_{t-2}) = 0$. Solving the quadratic homogeneous difference equation obtained for the deviation, we get, according to Hicks, the changes in the deviation over time and thereby the answer to the question why $\overline{Y}$ fluctuates around Y if a factor moves national income away from its equilibrium path.

In order to solve the difference equation, let us write λ^t for y_t. Then we obtain the following auxiliary equation: $\lambda^t - (1-s)\lambda^{t-1} - \lambda^{t-2} = 0$.
Re-arranging the equation, we are left with: $\lambda^t - (1-s+v)\lambda^{t-1} + v\lambda^{t-2} = 0$.
Dividing the equation by λ^{t-2} throughout, we reduce it to a quadratic equation and obtain the characteristic form of the difference equation:

$$\lambda^2 - (1-s+v)\lambda + v = 0.$$

The roots of the equation satisfy the original difference equation, too, and thus provide the value sought. The solution of our characteristic equation is

$$\lambda_{1,2} = \frac{1-s+v \pm \sqrt{(1-s+v)^2 - 4v}}{2}.$$

The character of the deviation from the equilibrium path depends on the sign and magnitude of the roots as shown by the discriminant $(1-s+v)^2 - 4v$. The magnitude of the roots will, therefore, change according to the values of v and s. If the discriminant is positive, that is, $(1-s+v)^2 > 4v$, the equation has two different real roots. Transforming the inequality, we obtain $v < (1-\sqrt{s})^2$, and $v > (1+\sqrt{s})^2$, respectively.

If $v < (1-\sqrt{s})^2$, both roots will lie between 0 and $+1$, the values of the successive deviation from the equilibrium path will decrease, and national income will move, without any fluctuation, towards its equilibrium path. If $v > (1+\sqrt{s})^2$, both roots will lie between 1 and $+\infty$, the successive values of deviation from the equilibrium path will increase, and national income will move, without any fluctuation, away from the equilibrium value.

The situation is similar if the discriminant is 0, when both roots of our equation are real and identical. In the case of $v = (1-\sqrt{s})^2$, the actual amount of national income will approach the

---

[40] J. R. Hicks: *op. cit.*, p. 85.

equilibrium path without any fluctuation. If, on the other hand, $v = (1+\sqrt{s})^2$, it will move away from it without any fluctuation.

If the discriminant is negative, that is, $(1-s+v)^2 < 4v$, there are no real roots. The quadratic equation has two conjugate complex roots. In this case, national income in deviating from the equilibrium path performs a cyclical motion.

In the case of complex roots, the value of v lies between these limits:

$$(1-\sqrt{s})^2 < v < (1+\sqrt{s})^2.$$

The roots:

$$\lambda_1 = \frac{1-s+v+\sqrt{4v-(1-s+v)^2}i}{2} \text{ and}$$

$$\lambda_2 = \frac{1-s+v-\sqrt{4v-(1-s+v)^2}i}{2}, \text{ respectively.}$$

In the case of conjugate complex roots the general solution of quadratic difference equations is, writing the complex numbers in trigonometric forms:

$$y_t = C_1\lambda_1 + C_2\lambda_2 = r^t C_1(\cos \varphi t + i \sin \varphi t) + C_2(\cos \varphi t - i \sin \varphi t),$$

where C_1 and C_2 are constants determined by the initial conditions, and r is the absolute value, the modulus, of the complex number. Writing A for $C_1 + C_2$ and B for $(C_1 - C_2)i$, we obtain:

$$y_t = r^t(A \cos \varphi t + B \sin \varphi t).$$

$A \cos \varphi + B \sin \varphi$ is a linear combination of the sine and cosine functions.

The sum of the two periodic functions in the brackets provides again a periodic function. Since the value of the modulus is always greater than 0, there are three possibilities depending on the magnitude of the modulus:

1. $r = 1$. Multiplying the periodic function by 1, the amplitude of fluctuation will remain constant.

2. $r > 1$. In this case, r^t will grow with time; the periodic function has to be multiplied by ever higher values, and the amplitude of fluctuation will increase.

3. $r < 1$. In this case, the value of r^t will decrease over time; the periodic function has to be multiplied by ever smaller values, and the amplitude of fluctuation will decrease.

Determining the value of the modulus by the formula $r^2 = x^2 + y^2$,

$$r = \frac{\sqrt{(1-s+v)^2 + 4v - (1-s+v)^2}}{2} = \sqrt{v}.$$

Thus, if $v = 1$, the modulus will also be 1, if $v > 1$, the amplitude of fluctuation will grow, if $v < 1$, the amplitude of fluctuation will fall.

Now, expressing the value of v in terms of the magnitude of the savings ratio, we can distinguish the three cases from one another in the following way:

1. $(1-\sqrt{s})^2 < v < 1$.
2. $(1-\sqrt{s})^2 < v = 1 < (1+\sqrt{s})^2$
3. $1 < v < (1+\sqrt{s})^2$.

In Hicks's model only v influences the pattern of change of national income as it deviates from its equilibrium path. The value of s is relevant only in the determination of that domain of the values of v within which national income performs a cyclical motion.

Those economists who maintain that a certain external shock affecting the capitalist economy is transformed by the accelerator and multiplier effects into a cyclical motion, at certain values of the investment coefficient, are faced with the following difficulties. If the value of the investment coefficient is such that the amplitude of the fluctuations declines, the cyclical motion will eventually cease. But then how can the cyclical nature of reproduction still survive in a capitalist economy? According to Ragnar Frisch, external, erratic shocks are needed whenever the initial motion begins to lose its cyclical character and to change into an even development. It is the temporarily arising, erratic shocks which, changing into a cyclical motion owing to the interaction of the accelerator and multiplier effects, maintain the cyclical nature of capitalist reproduction. But in this case, the cycles no longer have their continuity: from a cyclical motion once started no further cyclical motions can be derived, since both were started by external, accidental factors, which always appear, strangely enough, only if the fluctuations are about to cease. Hicks holds such an explanation to be insufficient. If the values of the investment coefficient are instead greater than 1, but less than $(1+\sqrt{s})^2$, fluctuations of an increasing amplitude will come about following a single disruption of equilibrium growth. In a boom period, output would more and more vigorously exceed the equilibrium value, and in a slump period, it would fall deeper and deeper below it. Such a motion would eventually upset the whole economic system. It cannot provide a sufficient explanation for cyclical movements. However, a perpetual cyclical motion may develop from a single deviation from equilibrium growth if the value of the investment coefficient is 1. The amplitude of fluctuation is constant, and no external shocks are needed to maintain the cyclical character of motion. Hicks is right in criticizing this view when he points out that it is hardly conceivable that cyclical fluctuations occur in real life simply because the investment coefficient has remained constant at this particular value for two centuries.[41]

He sees the possibility of a solution in assuming a magnitude of the investment coefficient at which the deviation of production from the equilibrium path generates a level of induced investment capable of further increasing the deviation, that is, when output as a result of the interaction of the multiplier and accelerator effects, moves away from the equilibrium path without any fluctuations, or with fluctuations of an increasing amplitude. But this movement away has its limits. At a growth rate higher than the equilibrium rate, output will eventually hit the ceiling of full employment, FF at a certain point (in Figure 85, point P_1). Now it can grow only at a rate not higher than that of the ceiling. But it can move along the ceiling of full employment only if the accelerator effect appears belatedly, that is, if induced investment is brought about by the growth of national income of past periods increasing at a higher rate. Moving along the ceiling, sooner or later the time will come when investment is induced by output growing along the ceiling, that is, at a rate g lower than that of the previous periods. However, at an output growth-rate g, induced investment, together with the given, steadily increasing autonomous investment, after a single fluctuation can only ensure the development of output at an equilibrium rate along the EE path. At a certain point, output will rebound from the FF, to the EE path. Once, however, a decline sets in, it must

[41] J. R. Hicks: *op. cit.*, p. 89.

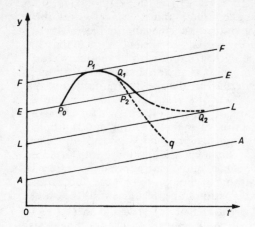

Figure 85

continue. Nothing can stop output at the equilibrium path once it begins to fall. Suppose that output reaches the equilibrium path at point P_2. It must continue to fall since the change in induced investment is determined by this fall.

If the accelerator effect were to assert itself in the same way in the case of falling as it does in the case of rising output, then, given an output fluctuation of increasing amplitude, output would perhaps fall further below EE than it was above it. In this case, the path of fall is indicated by P_1q. But the assertion of the accelerator effect is also limited in a downward direction. A fall in output will generate a negative induced investment only to the extent of the depreciation of the capital stock. As soon as in the course of the output decline negative induced investment has reached this magnitude, it will no longer depend on changes in output. Hicks asserts that this investment will virtually cease to be an induced one. Now total investment equals autonomous investment less a constant expressing the worn-out but not renewed part of the capital stock. This, according to Hicks, would mean the same as if the line AA representing autonomous investment had shifted downwards, parallel to itself. Thus he argues that the accelerator effect no longer operates, being replaced by the downward adjustment of autonomous investment.

Now he characterizes the crisis in this formulation: autonomous investment drops below its normal level, while induced investment equals 0. Under such circumstances output moves along the equilibrium path LL lying below EE, which is determined, in the absence of the accelerator effect, through the simple multiplier by autonomous investment less depreciation. Q_1Q_2 shows the way in which output drops to the equilibrium path LL. This lies above the Q_1q path created by the accelerator effect asserting itself without any disturbance, expressing, as it were, that the limitation of the accelerator effect delays the fall in output. And while Q_1q may fall infinitely, movement along Q_1Q_2 is limited, the crisis has its floor.

Hicks eliminated the accelerator effect from the period of crisis in order to explain the escape from it. In a crisis, there is only autonomous investment below its normal level, which continues to grow at a rate of g. Output grows with it, as

466

a result of the multiplier effect, along the path *LL*. However, as soon as excess capital has been used up, this will again set the accelerator effect in motion, and with induced investment coming into being, a super-multiplier will take again the place of the simple multiplier, and the equilibrium growth path of output will be again *EE* instead of *LL*. Output will grow towards the *EE* path, but on reaching it, cannot stop because its rate was higher than *g,* so that the upswing will continue until output reaches the ceiling *FF*.

It follows from the above that the scope of cyclical reproduction has its limits even in the case of fluctuations of an increasing amplitude, or of a continuous deviation from the equilibrium path. As soon as output deviating from the equilibrium path reaches the lower or upper limit, it will rebound from it. In a boom period, full employment means the upper limit of the increase in output, while in a slump period autonomous investment increasing at a steady rate even in a crisis prevents the fall in output through its multiplier effect. Samuelson appropriately called this type of cycle theory a billiard-table theory.[42]

An evaluation of the Hicksian trade-cycle theory

Let us approach Hicks's trade-cycle theory from a Marxian viewpoint.

1. In the abstract, the various movements of output as represented by Hicks can also be demonstrated by the Marxian two-department scheme if the Hicksian delays are built into it, if the value of the investment coefficient is taken to be within the limits set by him, and if the proportion of the national income of the previous period spent by the capitalist class on personal consumption in the current period is assumed to be constant. In order to represent these movements, not even the concept of autonomous investment has to be applied. The simple upward deviation in autonomous investment can be expressed in the Marxian scheme like this: department I of social production has run ahead of department II, and thus the boom period has set in.

It is really true that an infinite growth may evolve in capitalist economy at certain values of the investment coefficient—growth that comes to an end only when reaching the ceiling of full employment?

The cyclical movement of capitalist reproduction reflects the movements of the opportunities of capital to gain profit. Approaching the question from a Marxian angle we may say that the profit share in national income, and through it in product price, develops in the Hicksian model according to how the shares of autonomous investment, induced investment and the consumption of the capitalist class change in national income in the course of the reproduction process. The simple upward deviation in autonomous investment increases the profit share, and the maintenance of the situation favourable for capital after the rate of autonomous investment has fallen back, depends for Hicks on whether induced investment is able to counterbalance the unfavourable effect of the fall in the rate of autonomous investment. In Hicks's system, the greater than equilibrium growth rate of national income will

---

[42] P. A. Samuelson: *Foundations of Economic Analysis,* Harvard, 1947, p. 340.

be maintained at certain values of the investment coefficient even after the rate of autonomous investment has dropped to its original level. The high growth rate of production induces large-scale investments. Large investments, in turn, by substantially expanding the market, maintain a greater than equilibrium rate of growth. Though at the accelerate growth rate of national income the proportion of autonomous investment to national income will fall, yet the share of induced investment will rise, and thus, on the assumptions of the Hicksian model, the profit share in national income will continue to increase and the boom process will go on.

In reality, however, the consumption of the capitalist class grows at a slower rate than the output of consumer goods. The existing demand for consumer goods and their supply, which in the Hicksian model adjusts itself to demand, constitute a constant proportion of the national income of the previous period. In a dynamic economy, this proportion, owing to the Hicksian delay, decreases, in the current national income, but the share of the consumption of the capitalist class steadily falls even within this proportion, and a steadily larger ratio of the consumer goods produced will accrue as wage goods to the working class. For the profit share not to decrease in the increasingly growing national income, the share of induced investment ought to rise to offset the fall not only in the share of autonomous investment but also in the proportion of national income used for the personal consumption of the capitalist class.

For Hicks, the aim of investments is to restore the normal state of productive capacities excessively utilized by the great increase in output. Since, however, any productive investment increases in the last analysis the capacities of consumer-goods production, and an ever smaller proportion of the growing supply of consumer goods embodies surplus value and an ever greater proportion of that supply increases the real wage bill, this fact does not stimulate an increase in investments, on the contrary, it stimulates entrepreneurs to abstrain from fully utilizing the existing capacities of consumer-goods production. The accelerator effect stimulates investment only if the investment climate is favourable. If, however, the expending output of consumer goods worsens the profit prospects of capital, increased output will not encourage investors. The boom period will break not because the ceiling of full employment is reached, but because a further expansion of output would change the distribution relations in favour of labour and to the disadvantage of capital, and would therefore come more and more into conflict with the profit motive. Hicks, like Keynes, examines consumer demand only in its totality, neglecting the analysis of its constituents, viz. the consumer demand of the capitalist and the working class, although this would have been needed for the explanation of the cyclical movement of reproduction and the break in the upswing.

2. Reference must also be made to the role of autonomous investment which is a determining element of economic growth in the Hicksian model. Its acceleration starts the upswing, and its steady-state growth helps to get out of the crisis situation. But autonomous investment is an exogenous datum in his model. He does not examine its nature, does not explore on what its growth depends. It is independent, for Hicks, of cyclical changes, increases demand without increasing productive capacities. Government investments serving unproductive goals might be regarded as best approaching autonomous investments in the Hicksian sense. But post-Keynesian economics also classifies long-term private capital investments as autonomous, even though they serve productive purposes, because they have

been elicited not by the existing growth of demand or output. But capacity-expanding long-term investments subjected to profit interests are not independent of cyclical movements. If the profit prospects are unfavourable, this type of autonomous investment too is discouraged, its rate cannot remain constant irrespective of the trade cycle. Or, autonomous investment, in so far as it increases productive capacities, is bound, on maturing, to have a bearing on the trade cycle, in exerting a harmful effect on it.

3. In explaining the cyclical nature of reproduction, the Hicksian approach, namely that he starts out from the process of equilibrium growth, is not superior to the Marxian one. In explaining the trade cycles, Marx presupposes the cyclical nature of capitalist reproduction from the very outset. This being given, it is the crisis itself which clears the way for a new upswing, and the massive renewal of capital assets neglected in the slump period marks the beginning of the boom. Hicks, however, bases his explanation of the escape from a crisis situation on the steady-state growth of autonomous investment which also continues in the slump period, and explains the emergence of a boom by referring to another external factor, the unexpected increase in autonomous investment. While the Marxian model explains the breaking of the upswing by the profit opportunities of capital becoming unfavourable as a result of the maturing of new investments, Hicks refers here too to an exogeneous factor, the attainment of the ceiling of full employment. To put it another way, in the so-called billiard-table theory both the lower and upper limits of the cyclical fluctuation of reproduction are exogeneous data.

4. A further critical comment on the Hicksian trade-cycle theory should also be mentioned here. In his theory, the equilibrium growth rate is given from the very outset by the growth rate of autonomous investment. The interaction of the multiplier and the accelerator effects causes fluctuations only around this trend of growth. That is, Hicks applies cyclical changes to the growth process "from outside", so that they do not affect the growth rate. In reality, however, a development trend free from cyclical fluctuations is different from non-cyclical development. The more significant the cyclical fluctuations, the more they influence the rate of growth.

Chapter 3

NEO-CLASSICAL GROWTH MODELS

GENERAL CHARACTERISTICS.
FACTORS INFLUENCING THE RATE OF GROWTH

In the past one and a half decades, neo-classical growth theories have made significant headway within non-Marxian growth theories. This too is the consequence of a strengthening economic state intervention as was the rise of the Keynesian system in the 1930s. In those years Keynes shattered the belief upheld by non-Marxian economics that the automatisms of a free capitalist economy do not allow economic troubles to arise, since they ensure that total demand grows with total supply and that they realize full employment. Keynes wanted to provide with his theory an ideological support for economic state intervention. More recently, on the basis of fully realized state monopoly capitalism, voices even more optimistic than that of Keynes begin to make themselves heard in non-Marxian economics. Under the conditions of state intervention, some non-Marxian economists begin to trust again in the beneficial effects of capitalist economic mechanisms. In neo-classical growth theories, in questions relating to economic growth, more and more basic propositions of orthodox economics criticized by Keynes begin to crop up again, intermingled with certain Keynesian elements. It is interesting, by the way, that Keynes predicted in his *General Theory* that in the case of successful state intervention neo-classical tenets might regain their validity: "... if our central controls succeed in establishing an aggregate volume of output corresponding to full employment as nearly as is practicable, the classical theory comes into its own again from this point onwards."[43]

The American R. Solow, one of the initiators and the most significant representative of neo-classical growth theory, criticizes Harrod, because, relying on Keynesian traditions, he holds the view that in a capitalist economy there is no mechanism which could make it possible for G_n to arise. By contrast, Solow maintains that "... the real return to factors will adjust to bring about full employment of labour and capital,"[44] that is to say, the substitutability of factors, the movement of factor prices determined by marginal productivities, ensures the equilibrium of the demand for and the supply of factors and thus the bringing about of G_n. The neo-classical growth model also postulates the equilibrium of intended investment and saving at full employment, and thus total demand growing with total output, i.e. the adjustment of G to G_w. The mechanism, however, which should ensure harmony

[43] J. M. Keynes: *The General Theory of Employment, Interest and Money*, London, 1936, pp. 378–379.

[44] R. Solow: A Contribution to the Theory of Economic Growth, *The Quarterly Journal of Economics*, February 1956, p. 68.

470

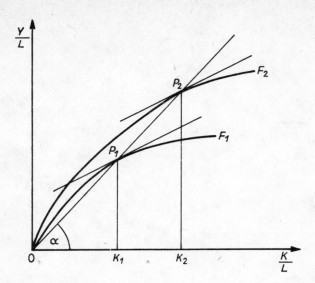

Figure 86

between G and G_w is not specified by the neo-classical growth models, and in their study written on growth models in general, Hahn and Matthews express their doubts that the initiators of the neo-classical growth models have really solved the problem of the stability of G_w.[45]

Assuming that the mechanisms of the capitalist economy bring about full employment and the equilibrium of aggregate demand and aggregate supply, the representatives of the neo-classical model approach the question of growth exclusively from the side of *supply*. They rely on the theory of production as elaborated by modern non-Marxian economics, and their growth model is virtually a dynamized production function. It is by dynamizing the production function that they seek to determine the rate of growth.

Let us write, following Solow, the general formula of the production function built upon the substitutability of factors, including the effect of technical progress:

$Q = f(K, L, t)$, where t is the effect of technical progress as a function of time. It is by taking the differential of the production function with respect to time that the growth rate Q is obtained from the growth rates of K and L and technical progress.

The growth rate of Q is influenced not only by the rate, but also by the character of technical progress. In classifying technical progress Meade, a representative of the neo-classical approach, criticizes Harrod's procedure. He says that the constancy of the rate of interest interpreted as the marginal productivity of capital presupposes the growth of capital per head in the classification of technical pro-

[45] F. H. Hahn–R. C. O. Matthews: The Theory of Economic Growth: A Survey, *The Economic Journal*, December 1964, p. 790.

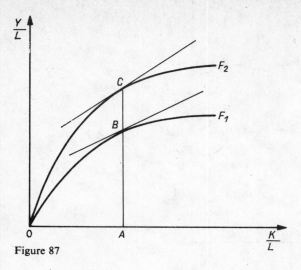

Figure 87

gress. Thus the effect attributed by Harrod exclusively to technical progress also contains the substitution effect, the movement along the given production function.[46]

According to Harrod, as a result of technical progress, per capita production has increased, as shown in Figure 86, by AC. Meade, however, who criticizes Harrod's theory from the viewpoint of marginal-productivity theory, points out that technical progress has increased per capita production only by BC. AB should be imputed to the substitution effect. The movement of capital per head from $0K_1$ to $0K_2$ would have raised per capita production by AB even without technical progress.

Neo-classical growth theory tries to classify technical progress without taking the substitution effect into account. Its representatives adopt the classification set up by Hicks as early as 1932. In examining the effect of technical progress, Hicks regards the capital–labour ratio as given. He considers technical progress as neutral if, given a certain capital–labour ratio, it increases the marginal productivity of both capital and labour by the same percentage. Thus neutral technical progress leaves unchanged the relative marginal productivities of factors, and thereby the marginal rate of substitution between them, i.e. the substitution relationship.

Meade represented Hicksian neutral technical progress diagrammatically in the following way[47] (see Figure 87).

At an unchanged capital–labour ratio, output per head has increased, as a result of technical progress, from AB to AC. Consequently, the effect attributable to technical progress is BC. The growth rate of output per head achieved by technical progress is BC/AB. Technical progress is neutral in the Hicksian sense if the mar-

[46] J. E. Meade: *A Neo-Classical Theory of Economic Growth,* Revised, new edition, London, 1965, pp. 55–60.
[47] J. E. Meade: *op. cit.,* pp. 23–24.

472

ginal productivity of capital increases at the rate of technical progress. This implies that AC is as many times greater than AB as the marginal productivity of capital at the point C is greater than the marginal productivity of capital at B, that is, the same number of times as the slope of the tangent drawn to the curve at the point C is greater than the slope of the tangent drawn to the curve at B. Since at given capital and labour magnitudes the marginal productivity of capital increases in the course of technical progress at the same rate as the volume of output, the average productivity of capital will also grow at the same rate. Thus neutral technical progress in the Hicksian sense does not affect the production elasticity of capital. Assuming that the production function is first-degree homogeneous, technical progress does not affect the production elasticity of labour either, and the marginal productivity of labour increases at the same rate as its average productivity, that is, at a rate which is identical with that of the marginal productivity of capital. And since in neo-classical theory production elasticities express the relative shares of classes in national income, neutral technical progress also leaves the distribution relations unchanged. Neutral technical progress as defined by Harrod left the same magnitude unaffected, but at an increased capital per head. It is the Cobb–Douglas production function by which both interpretations of neutral technical progress can be expressed. This is because in this production function, as is well known, the elasticity of substitution is 1, and thus the effect of substitution leaves the production elasticities unchanged. With this production function it is possible, therefore, to demonstrate both Hicks-neutral technical progress, which leaves the production elasticities unaffected at a given capital–labour ratio, and Harrod-neutral technical progress, which leaves them unchanged as capital per head increases. It is primarily for this property that the Cobb–Douglas production function is a favourite tool of expression in neo-classical growth theories.

In the case of Hicksian neutral technical progress, the production function may be written in this particular way: $Q = A(t)f(K, L)$, where factor $A(t)$ is the measure of the shift of the production function taking place as a result of technical progress at a given capital–labour ratio, and where it, as a multiplier, expresses that technical progress increases capital and labour productivity to the same extent. In the case of the so-called multiplicative function thus obtained, if at the same time the elasticity of substitution between factors is 1, the effect of technical progress can entirely be imputed to each of the factors by increasing the relative amount of the other until its average productivity remains unchanged in the course of technical progress. This change in the ratio of factors does not affect the production elasticity of factors when the elasticity of substitution is unity.

The neutrality of technical progress in Hicks's interpretation assumes that the production function is first-degree homogeneous. Non-Marxian economists point out that "the whole scheme breaks down when the underlying production functions do not obey constant returns to scale."[48] In this case, the marginal productivity of the factors also depends on their absolute amounts. In so far as technical progress, which stimulates an increase in production, is accompanied by a scale effect, the latter, in changing the optimal factor combination, will change the substitution relations even if the amounts of the factors increase at unchanged rates.

[48] M. Blaug: *Economic Theory in Retrospect*, London, 1968, p. 475.

The definition of Hicksian neutral technical progress logically leads to an interpretation of non-neutral technical progress. At an unchanged capital–labour ratio "labour-saving inventions increase the marginal product of capital more than they increase the marginal product of labour; capital-saving inventions increase the marginal product of labour more than that of capital."[49]

Dividing the total derivative with respect to time of the $Q = A(t)f(K, L)$ production function by Q, Solow derived for the growth rate of Q in the case of neutral technical inventions the following formula:

$$\frac{dQ}{Q} = \frac{dA}{A} + \varepsilon_k \frac{dK}{K} + \varepsilon_L \frac{dL}{L}.$$

The growth rate of the production function equals the rate of technical progress plus the growth rate of the individual factors multiplied by their production elasticities. A relationship similar to Solow's for the rate of growth was also obtained by the British economist Meade.

In contrast to most of the post-Keynesian growth theories, Solow's model determines the rate of growth completely by means of factors influencing production. He fails to take into account the effect of increased demand upon the increase in production.

Solow and most neo-classical growth theorists regard the rate of technical progress and the growth rate of population as exogeneous data of the model, as magnitudes that cannot be influenced by economic means, and assume, therefore, that both remain unchanged through time.

Non-neutral technical inventions change the production function, and thus we obtain for the rate of growth the following formula:

$$\frac{dQ}{Q} = \frac{1}{f}\frac{\partial f}{\partial t} + \varepsilon_K \frac{dK}{K} + \varepsilon_L \frac{dL}{L}.$$

If technical inventions are not neutral, they do not leave the production elasticities unchanged.

According to Meade, the character of technical inventions influence the rate of growth in the following way: it affects the growth rate favourably if it increases the significance of the factor growing at the fastest rate at the margin. If, for example, the rate of capital accumulation is faster than the growth rate of population, and technical inventions are of the capital-using type, the rate of growth will increase. Conversely, technical inventions will raise the rate of growth less if they increase the significance of the factor which grows at a relatively slower rate.

If the various factors grow at different rates, the rate of growth is also affected by the elasticity of substitution. If it is greater than 1, the production elasticity of the factor which grows at a faster rate will increase, and, as a result, the growth rate will increase, too; but the production elasticity of the less rapidly growing factor will increase if the elasticity of substitution is less than 1, leading to a slower growth rate.

If both factors grow at the same rate, the growth rate is independent of the

[49] J. R. Hicks: *The Theory of Wages*, New York, 1948, pp. 121–122.

elasticity of substitution. It was Meade who pointed out that the growth rate will also change favourably if the character of technical inventions and the substitution relation between the factors of production are such that the shares in national income change to the benefit of those who save most. This causes capital accumulation to speed up, which in turn increases the rate of production, according to the formula given for the rate of growth.

SOLOW'S ATTEMPT TO REDUCE THE RATE OF GROWTH OF PER CAPITA OUTPUT TO TWO COMPONENTS AND TO CONSTRUCT AN AGGREGATE PRODUCTION FUNCTION BY STATISTICAL MEANS

Starting from his expression for the growth rate and relying on statistics of American industry, Solow[50] attempted to separate from one another the effect of technical progress and the substitutions effect, and to construct on this basis an aggregate production function.

Assuming a homogeneous and linear production function, he expresses the production elasticity of labour as $1—\varepsilon_k$, and thus the growth rate as

$$\frac{dQ}{Q} = \frac{dA}{A} + \varepsilon_k \frac{dK}{K} + (1—\varepsilon_k)\frac{dL}{L}.$$

Rearranging the equation, we obtain:

$$\frac{dQ}{Q} - \frac{dL}{L} = \frac{dA}{A} + \varepsilon_k \left(\frac{dK}{K} - \frac{dL}{L}\right).$$

$\frac{dQ}{Q} - \frac{dL}{L}$ expresses by how much the growth rate of production exceeds the growth rate of the labour force employed, which is the growth rate of per capita output q.

$\frac{dK}{K} - \frac{dL}{L}$ on the other hand, indicates the amount by which capital stock increases faster than the population employed, that is, expresses the growth rate of k, capital per head. Thus

$$\frac{dq}{q} = \frac{dA}{A} + \varepsilon_K \frac{dk}{k}.$$

From this it follows that the growth rate of output per head is made up of two effects, $\frac{dA}{A}$, the effect of technical progress, and $\varepsilon_K \frac{dk}{k}$, the effect of substitution.

[50] R. Solow: Technical Change in the Aggregate Production Function, *The Review of Economics and Statistics*, Vol. XXXIX, 1957.

$\dfrac{dA}{A}$ expresses the percentage shift of the production function, and $\varepsilon_K \dfrac{dk}{k}$ is the movement along the given production function.

The rate of technical progress:

$$\frac{dA}{A} = \frac{dq}{q} - \varepsilon_K \frac{dk}{k}.$$

Solow maintains that if we know the growth rate of production and capital per head and the partial production elasticity of capital, the rate of technical progress can be found out statistically. The data needed for this were those of the industry of the USA between 1909 and 1949.

Instead of $\dfrac{dq}{q}$ and $\dfrac{dk}{k}$, he made use of the annual changes

$$\frac{\Delta q}{q} \text{ and } \frac{\Delta k}{k}.$$

He decreased the data available for the stock of capital in proportion to the level of unemployment in order to obtain the amount of the capital stock used up. For capital and output per head he took capital and output per man-hour. As a result of his investigations, he found that output per man-hour nearly doubled during 40 years. About $\frac{1}{8}$ of the total increase was attributable to the rise in capital per man-hour, that is, to the effect of substitution, while $\frac{7}{8}$ was due to technical inventions. He further found that the time series $\dfrac{\Delta A}{A}$ did not correlate with the change in capital per man-hour, and consequently, technical progress could be regarded as neutral.

Computing the annual rate of technical progress and knowing the annual rate of change of q and k, Solow argued that neutral technical progress made it possible for him to construct an aggregate production function. He started from $Q = A(t)f(K, L)$, the production function applying in the case of neutral technical progress. If the return to scale is constant, both sides of the equations may be divided by L:

$$\frac{Q}{L} = A(t)f\left(\frac{K}{L}, 1\right), \text{ i.e., } q = A(t)f(k, 1).$$

q cannot be directly represented as a function of k, because the change in q over time reflects not only a change in k, but also the effect of technical progress. Thus the interrelated changes in q and k do not yield different points on one curve, but each value of q would lie on a different curve, shifted as a result of technical progress. Solow, therefore, filters out the effect of technical progress from q. The ratio q to $A(t)$ expresses only the effect of substitution, how production per man-hour changes, at a given level of technical knowledge, with a change in k.

Thus the relationship sought between $\dfrac{q}{A(t)}$ and k is the following:

$$\frac{q}{A(t)} = f(k, 1).$$

He computes $A(t)$, the annual amount of technical progress by means of the annual rate of change in the technical level, $\dfrac{\varDelta A}{A}$. He assumes the level of technical progress in the initial year of his investigations, 1909, to be $1 : A(1909) = 1$. The effect of technical progress between two periods can be expressed as follows:

$$A(t+1) = A(t) \left[1 + \frac{\varDelta A(t)}{A(t)}\right].$$

Knowing the amount of $A(t)$, Solow draws the set of points corresponding to the values $\dfrac{q}{A(t)}$ attached to the different values of k, and seeks the curve most closely fitting them, which represents the aggregate production function in the period of investigation.

We shall give a detailed critique of neo-classical growth theory further below. This theory has developed a great deal during the past 10 years, and seeks to eliminate several deficiencies of the first neo-classical growth models. But Solow's statements as set forth above on the effects of technical progress and substitution have often been referred to ever since by a great many economists. Now we only wish to answer the question of whether Solow really succeeded in determining the amount of these two effects in the USA. Did he really succeed in constructing an aggregate production function?

$\dfrac{\varDelta q}{q}$ and $\dfrac{\varDelta k}{k}$ can be determined by statistical means. Now the expression of the rate of technical progress only depends on whether Solow managed to compute the production elasticity of capital.

Since the work of Douglas, attempts have been made to derive the production elasticities of factors from time series or cross sections by means of regression analysis. But several objections have been made to applying regression analysis to time series. We have already referred to the critique by Mendershausen, who pointed out that capital and labour correlate not only with production, but also with one another. Obviously, capital, labour and technical progress also correlate with one another. Solow tried to evade the difficulties of regression analysis in a peculiar way. He did not determine the production elasticity of capital by regression analysis. He simply assumed that the production elasticity of capital was equal to the share of capital in national income, and multiplied the growth rate of capital per head by the relative share of capital in national income.

Non-Marxian critiques emphasize that by making these assumptions Solow presupposes that the factors are rewarded in real life according to their marginal productivities, whereas increasing returns to scale and monopoly make it impossible at the very outset. Marxian political economy does not accept the explanation of income distribution built upon marginal productivity theory. Thus the difference between the growth rate of output per head and the growth rate of capital per man-hour multiplied by the relative share of capital in national income cannot express the growth rate of technical progress. In fact it is no surprise that Solow found no correlation between the growth rate of technical progress thus obtained and the growth rate of capital per man-hour.

On account of his incorrect approach to determining the production elasticity of capital, we cannot accept Solow's estimate of how much of the increase in output per man-hour can be attributed to the effect of technical progress, and how much to the substitution effect. Also unacceptable is his attempt to construct an aggregate production function.

In any case, the procedure recommended by him claims to be able to separate the effect of technical progress from that of substitution only in the case of neutral technical progress. But Solow's evidence of the neutrality of technical progress is devoid, as has been shown, of any acceptable foundation.

If we look at the time series computed by Solow of the growth rate of technical progress, the very figures make the success of his attempt very doubtful. In particular, it is striking that there are also negative amounts among them. Hogan is right when he says that "while it is true that one can have a decline in the value of the stock of capital, it is not the same thing to postulate a fall in the stock of technical knowledge. Once acquired, it is difficult to see how this stock can be destroyed."[51]

THE GOLDEN-AGE GROWTH

As we have already pointed out, most non-Marxian growth models, whether Keynesian or neo-classical, assume technical development and population growth to be exogenous data of the system, and postulate for them constant rates of change over time. If in the neo-classical growth theory technical progress is in addition neutral, that is, if it does not affect the production elasticities at a given capital–labour ratio, and the elasticity of substitution between factors is 1, then a change in the capital–labour ratio and the resulting substitution effect does not influence production elasticities either at the given level of technical knowledge; and if, further, the savings ratio of national income is also constant, then the economy tends to develop towards growth at a steady rate, in the course of which production and capital stock grow at a constant and identical rate. This steady-state growth, a specific interpretation of dynamic equilibrium at full employment, which is assumed in the neo-classical model, is what Mrs. Robinson called *the golden age*. In golden-age growth, Harrod's G_w coincides with G, but at the same time the available resources are fully exploited and thus G_w coincides with G_n, too. This growth rate, which never occurs in real life, performs the role of a measure of analysis in neo-classical growth theories. It is in starting from and relating to this growth rate that the process of growth taking place in a different way, under different conditions, is being examined. By assuming a golden-age growth, these theories also seek to solve certain optimization problems in a growing economy.

[51] W. P. Hogan: Technical Progress and the Production Functions. *The Review of Economics and Statistics*, November 1958, p. 40.

478

Let us derive the golden-age growth rate relying primarily on Weizsäcker[52] and Meade[53].

We start from the formula set up by Solow for the growth rate of Q:

$$\frac{dQ}{Q} = \frac{dA}{A} + \varepsilon_K \frac{dK}{K} + (1-\varepsilon_K)\frac{dL}{L}.$$

In a golden age

$$\frac{dK}{K} = \frac{dQ}{Q}.$$

Substituting:

$$\frac{dQ}{Q} = \frac{dA}{A} + \varepsilon_K \frac{dQ}{Q} + (1-\varepsilon_K)\frac{dL}{L}.$$

Solving the equation for $\frac{dQ}{Q}$ and denoting $\frac{dA}{A}$ by μ, we obtain:

$$\frac{dQ}{Q} = \frac{\mu}{1-\varepsilon_K} + \frac{dL}{L}.$$

Since in golden-age growth Q and K increase at the same rate, $\frac{K}{Q}$ is constant over time. But at an unchanged production elasticity of capital the marginal productivity of capital is also constant in the growth process. Technical progress only increases the productivity of labour, while capital per head and output per man grow at the rate of $\frac{\mu}{1-\varepsilon_k}$; hence technical progress in the golden-age type of growth is *labour-augmenting*, neutral in Harrod's sense: the marginal productivity of capital is constant, and so is the "average productivity" of capital, while labour productivity increases. Now the static production function ought to be multiplied by $A(t) = (1+\mu)$ to obtain the amount of output increased as a result of technical progress at given K and L, or, if we fully impute the effect of technical progress to labour, the actual labour force should be multiplied by $\left(1+\frac{\mu}{1-\varepsilon_K}\right)$ to obtain the number of efficient workers. This is because, with technical progress at a rate of μ, output increases in the same proportion as if the labour force had increased $\left(1+\frac{\mu}{1-\varepsilon_K}\right)$-fold without technical progress.

Yet the nature of technical progress is not fully identical with neutrality as interpreted by Harrod. Harrod's concept, seen from a neo-classical aspect, does not separate the substitution effect from the effect of technical progress, but includes it, since the criterion of classification is whether technical progress, given the constancy of the rate of interest, affects the capital–output ratio or not. The neo-classical growth model, on the other hand, classifies technical progress

[52] C. Ch. Weizsäcker: *Wachstum, Zins und optimale Investitionsquote*, Basel, 1962, p. 47.
[53] J. E. Meade: *op. cit.*, p. 35.

according to how it affects, at a constant capital–labour ratio, the marginal productivity of factors. In the neo-classical growth model the capital–output ratio remains unchanged in the golden-age type of growth not because of the neutrality of technical progress, but as a result of the substitution effect.

In the golden-age type of growth technical progress is neutral in the Harrodian and at the same time in the Hicksian sense, too. The two can materialize at the same time only because the elasticity of substitution is 1, and hence the rate of increase in capital per head does not change the production elasticities.

The golden-age rate of growth of Q can be interpreted as Harrod's G_n. And since in a golden age $G_n = G_w$, therefore $G_n = \dfrac{s}{C_r}$. According to the representatives of the theory, if s and G_n are known, the capital–output ratio is also known: $C_r = \dfrac{s}{G_n}$. And since ε_K is also known, the golden-age marginal productivity of capital, the golden-age profit rate is also determined:

$$\frac{\partial Q}{\partial K} = \varepsilon_K \frac{Q}{K} = \varepsilon_K \frac{1}{C_r}.$$

Let us now examine the golden-age growth rate. For the convenience of analysis let us leave out of account population growth, taking the labour force to be constant. If the stock of capital is constant too, no golden-age growth is possible, and production will grow, in compliance with Solow's basic formula, at a rate of $\dfrac{dA}{A} = \mu$. If now we assume μ to be 10 per cent, output will grow, at a given capital stock and labour force, by 10 per cent, and so will output per unit of capital too, though it ought to be constant in a golden-age growth. Thus the effect of technical progress increasing the average productivity of capital has to be counterbalanced. This is performed in the neo-classical model by the substitution effect. Let capital stock also increase by 10 per cent. If the production elasticity of capital is $\frac{1}{2}$, the growth rate will be $\mu + \varepsilon_K \cdot \dfrac{dK}{K} = 15$ per cent. Capital per head will grow by 10 per cent, and output per head by 15 per cent. The increase in capital per head by 10 per cent will raise output per head only by 5 per cent. The inclusion of the substitution effect gives rise to decreasing returns. Now the growth rate of the stock of capital and thereby capital per head has to be increased until the substitution effect offsets the effect of technical progress expanding the average productivity of capital. If capital stock increases by 20 per cent, output will also rise by 20 per cent, and thus we have arrived at the golden-age path of growth. Capital per head increases

$$\frac{\mu}{1 - \varepsilon_K} = \frac{10}{\frac{1}{2}} = 20 \text{ per cent},$$

output per head also increases by 20 per cent, and the average productivity

480

of capital does not change in the growth process. Golden-age growth may be characterized by saying that under its circumstances the effect of technical progress is counterbalanced by the substitution effect in such a way that the average productivity of capital, the capital–output ratio, remains constant in the growth process, while output per head increases at the same rate as capital per head.

The factor $\dfrac{1}{1-\varepsilon_K}$ expresses that capital per head has to increase by $\dfrac{1}{1-\varepsilon_K}$ —times the rate of technical progress to offset the effect of technical progress increasing the average productivity of capital. If it grows at a rate lower than that, for example by 10 instead of 20 per cent, then the effect of technical progress, as has been shown, will be stronger than the substitution effect. If capital grows by a greater percentage than the golden-age rate, for example by 30 instead of 20 per cent, the rate of growth will be 25 per cent, and the substitution effect will exceed the effect of technical progress. The average productivity of capital and its marginal productivity will decline. The less is ε_K, the slower is the growth rate of capital per head at which the two effects will reach equilibrium, because with the increase in the amount of capital per head the principle of decreasing returns will come all the more rigorously into effect. The greater is ε_K, the more it will counteract the principle of decreasing returns, and for the two effects to reach equilibrium, the higher the necessary growth rate of capital per head.

The increase in the stock of capital cannot have a bearing upon the golden-age growth rate. Its amount depends only on the rate of technical progress, the rate of population growth and the production elasticity of capital. μ and $\dfrac{dL}{L}$ are exogenous data for the model and not controllable magnitudes. In the case of neutral technical progress and a unitary value of σ constituting a condition for a golden-age type of growth, ε_K does not change either over time. By changing the savings ratio, the golden-age rate cannot be changed. With this we have arrived at a viewpoint diametrically opposed to the post-Keynesian theories, at least to most of them. In Harrod, the equilibrium rate of growth, G_w, depended basically on the savings ratio, and investments played a prominent role in the Harrod–Domar growth models already discussed. In the neo-classical models, however, the golden-age growth rate is completely independent of the savings ratio, and the increase in capital stock is completely missing in the formula of the golden-age growth rate. In a golden-age type of growth "the higher investments of the economy, ... their effect upon the growth rate are completely counterbalanced by the lower productivity of capital goods,"[54] writes Weizsäcker, one of the first representatives of neo-classical growth theory. It will be remembered that Harrod too made his G_n dependent only on technical progress and the rate of population growth, but did not examine it more closely. He was interested mainly in exploring G_w.

The increase in the savings ratio makes growth deviate from its golden-age path. To use Harrod's terms, G_w deviates from G_n. But a golden-age type of growth is *stable*, assert the representatives of the theory. If the growth rate deviates from it, the mechanism making it return to the golden-age rate will come into

[54] C. Ch. Weizsäcker: *op. cit.*, p. 18.

effect and equates G_w to G_n. Solow criticized Harrod, among other things, because he confronted G_w and G_n, saying that in a capitalist economy there exists no mechanism to co-ordinate them.

Let us assume that the economy developed at a golden-age rate. Then stock of capital also increased at a golden-age rate:

$$\frac{dK}{K} = \frac{\mu}{1-\varepsilon_K} + \frac{dL}{L}.$$

Since the increment of capital stock, dK, is the same as investment, and in the neo-classical model this is in equilibrium with savings from national income, herefore

$$\frac{dK}{K} = \frac{I}{K} = \frac{sQ}{K} = G_n$$

and

$$\frac{sQ}{K} = \frac{s}{\dfrac{K}{Q}}.$$

If now the savings ratio is increased[55], $\dfrac{sQ}{K}$ will surpass G_n and capital stock will increase more than at a golden-age rate. For this reason, the increase in output will also deviate from the golden-age rate, changing in compliance with the formula $\mu + \varepsilon_K \dfrac{dK}{K} + \varepsilon_L \dfrac{dL}{L}$. We have seen however, that if the growth rate of capital exceeds the golden-age rate, the substitution effect with the resulting decreasing returns will surpass the effect of technical progress on expanding the average productivity of capital. The marginal and average productivity of capital cannot remain unchanged as they are in the case of a golden-age growth, but will decrease. And since $\dfrac{dK}{K} = \dfrac{sQ}{K}$, the decrease in $\dfrac{Q}{K}$ will slow down the growth rate of capital, causing, according to Solow's formula for $\dfrac{dQ}{Q}$, the growth rate of Q also to decline. As long as $\dfrac{dK}{K} > G_n$, the decrease in the average productivity of capital, $\dfrac{Q}{K}$, will slow down he rate of increase in capital and through it in output, until eventually both drop, n mutual interaction, to their golden-age amounts. Thus the increase in the savings ratio influences the growth rate only in the period of deviation from the golden-age path, but does not affect the golden age rate itself.

Approaching the question from another side, we find that $G_w = G_n$ along the

55 J. E. Meade: *op. cit.*, pp. 42–43.

golden-age path, and thus $G_n = \dfrac{s}{C_r}$. In the golden age the average productivity of capital is constant, and therefore its reciprocal, C_r, is constant, too. And since G_n, the golden-age rate, is an exogenous datum of the model, because μ and $\dfrac{dL}{L}$, at a constant ε_K, cannot be derived from the model either, a definite C_r is therefore attached to given G_n and s values along the golden-age path. If s increases, the denominator of the fraction will also increase, and G_w will temporarily exceed G_n. Then, as we have already mentioned, as a result of the substitution effect, the average productivity of capital, $\dfrac{Q}{K}$, will decrease, and therefore the capital–output ratio, $\dfrac{K}{Q}$, will rise. As the formula $G_n = \dfrac{s}{C_r}$ will clearly show, if s increases at a given G_n, C_r also has to rise until it counterbalances the effect of the increase in s on the rate of growth. The change in the capital–output ratio ensures *through the substitution effect* in the neo-classical growth model that in the case of a disturbance G_w adjusts itself to G_n.

The mechanism ensuring harmony between G_w and G_n in the neo-classical growth model operates similarly if the savings ratio declines.

No golden-age growth can occur if technical progress is not neutral. If the rate of technical progress does not change over time, and the nature of technical progress is for example capital-using, i.e. increases the production elasticity of capital, the growth rate will increase through time, provided the stock of capital increases at a faster rate than the labour force. It was Mrs. Robinson who called attention to the fact that steady-state growth can materialize even in the case of non-neutral technical progress, but then the rate of technical progress cannot remain unchanged through time.[56]

OPTIMUM RATE OF THE INVESTMENT RATIO AND THE GOLDEN RULE OF ACCUMULATION

The golden-age growth rate is determined, as has been shown, by the growth rate of technical progress and population at constant production elasticities. Both are exogenous data of the model, hence the golden-age rate itself is an exogenous datum. With an increase in the savings ratio growth will temporarily rise above its golden-age rate but, owing to the substitution effect, it will slowly return to that rate. Thus an increase in the savings ratio does not affect the golden-age rate, but increases capital per head and output per head, the latter at a lesser rate than the former. In this way, it decreases the efficiency of capital and increases the capital–output ratio. Thus in the neo-classical growth model a golden-age growth path is attached to each savings ratio. These paths are logarithmically parallel to each other. Along each of these paths, output and capital grow at the same G_n rate, and capital per head and output per head increase at the same

[56] J. Robinson: Equilibrium Growth Models, *The American Economic Review*, June 1961.

$\dfrac{\mu}{1-\varepsilon_L}$ rate. These golden-age growth paths, however, differ from each other in level. The greater the savings ratio, the more will be the amount of capital per head and output per head along the golden-age path belonging to that savings ratio, at a given point of time, though the latter will grow at a lesser rate than capital per head, and thus the smaller the efficiency of capital, the greater the capital–output ratio.

All this can be illustrated with fictitious figures in the table below:

s	$\dfrac{K}{L}$	$\dfrac{Y}{L}$	C_r	$G_n = \dfrac{s}{C_r}$	S	C
20 per cent	200	100	2	10 per cent	20	80
25 per cent	300	120	2.5	10 per cent	30	90
30 per cent	400	133	3	10 per cent	40	93
35 per cent	500	143	3.5	10 per cent	50	93
40 per cent	600	150	4	10 per cent	60	90

The table fixes the values of the golden-age paths belonging to the different savings ratios in cross-section, at given points of time.

The question is now what proportion of national income society should save if changes in the savings ratio do not affect the rate of growth. The answer to this question was given simultaneously by several non-Marxian economists, such as Phelps, Allais, Joan Robinson, Swan and Weizsäcker: that savings ratio which ensures maximum consumption.

The methods discussed so far of determining the optimization conditions assumed static circumstances: the number of population, the amount of capital stock, the level of technical knowledge, etc., all were supposed to be given. Harrod characterized marginal analysis as a completely static method: "Dynamics did not give such scope to the marginal analysis."[57]

But the question of optimization, of optimal growth, was also raised within the theory of growth. In an early article attracting little attention at the time, von Neumann examined the existence and characteristics of the paths of a balanced growth taking place at the highest possible rate of growth.[58] Ramsey, in another study written in 1928 and also stirring little interest at the time, regarded the maximization of utility with respect to consumption as a task which has to be solved by an appropriate investment policy.[59] Dorfman, Samuelson and Solow[60] examined the case in which an economy sets out from a historically given stock of capital, K_0, and wants to attain a K_T stock of capital in a finite T time horizon. Or, as Hicks characterizes the so-called *turn-pike theory* concerned with the above problem: "... the theory of the optimum path when the terminal stock, at the end of a given period, is the sole maximand."[61]

[57] R. Harrod: *Towards a Dynamic Economics*, New York, 1966, p. 15.
[58] J. von Neumann: Über ein ökonomisches Gleichungssystem und eine Verallgemeinerung des Browerschen Fixpunktsatzes. In: *Ergebnisse eines mathematischen Seminars*, Wien, 1938.
[59] F. P. Ramsey: A Mathematical Theory of Savings, *The Economic Journal*, December 1928.
[60] R. Dorfman, P. A. Samuelson and R. Solow: *Linear Programming and Economic Analysis*, New York–Toronto–London, 1958, pp. 309–345.
[61] J. Hicks: *Capital and Growth*, Oxford, 1965, p. 208.

We are concerned with the attempts of the representatives of the neo-classical growth model to utilize marginal analysis for optimization within an infinite time horizon—or, in Phelps's words, in a non-limited golden age, which is infinite, at least in retrospect,—under conditions of a growing economy when resources are changing over time. Under conditions of a growing economy they try to answer the question of how national income should be divided between consumption and saving or investment in an optimal way.

The application of marginal analysis to production supposes that with a change in factor proportions, for example with an increase in capital per head, the increment of output—at least after reaching a certain capital–labour ratio—will become smaller and smaller. But capital per head and output per head grow along golden-age paths at the same rate, and thus marginal analysis cannot be applied. If, however, we proceed at any point of time from one golden-age path to another cross-sectionnally, we have to regard the level of technical knowledge as given, and with the increase in the savings ratio capital per head and output per head will grow, though the latter at a smaller rate. Thus at a given point of time a concave production function can be constructed between the golden-age growth paths, a function which shows the effect of the growth of capital per head at the given level of technical knowledge.

Now the maximum amount of consumption can be determined—following Phelps's procedure[62]—in the following way:

Let us change at a given point of time from a golden-age path belonging to a low savings ratio to a golden-age path attached to a higher savings ratio. As a result of the increase in the savings ratio, capital per head will rise by ΔK, and output per head by $\Delta K \dfrac{\partial Q}{\partial K}$. But all the increment of the output per head cannot be consumed. A fraction of it must be accumulated to ensure a further rise of the increased stock of capital at a golden-age, that is, at a G_n rate. Out of $\Delta K \dfrac{\partial Q}{\partial K}$ the amount $G_n \Delta K$ has to be saved. Only the rest can be consumed. Therefore, as a result of the increase of capital per head by ΔK, the increment of consumption, $\Delta C = \Delta K \dfrac{\partial Q}{\partial K} - G_n \Delta K$. Let us now choose the golden-age paths belonging to an ever greater savings ratio in such a way that by changing from one growth path to another capital per head should always grow by ΔK. The marginal productivity of capital will fall, and so will the increment of output per man, $\Delta K \dfrac{\partial Q}{\partial K}$, but its part assigned to accumulation will not change as both G_n, and the increment of capital, ΔK, are constant. The positive and negative terms come closer to one another. But as long as their difference, ΔC, is positive, the amount of consumption will rise. The amount of consumption will reach its maximum at a savings ratio at which the marginal productivity of capital, owing to the increase in capital

[62] E. S. Phelps: The Golden Rule of Accumulation: A Fable for Growthman, *The American Economic Review*, September 1961, pp. 638–643.

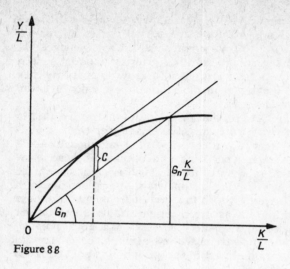

Figure 8 8

per man, drops to an amount at which the increment of consumption $\Delta C = 0$. In this case $\Delta K \dfrac{\partial Q}{\partial K} = G_n \Delta K$. Simplifying by ΔK, we obtain: $\dfrac{\partial Q}{\partial K} = G_n$. At the optimum rate of investment, that is, at one which ensures maximum consumption, capital per head is so large that the *marginal productivity of capital equals the golden-age rate of growth*. This is one of the characteristics of the growth path ensuring maximum consumption. Represented diagrammatically (see Figure 88): the line starting from the origin shows how much of the amount of output per head

must be accumulated for capital to grow at a G_n rate. Obviously this is $G_n \dfrac{K}{L}$.

The slope of the line is equal to the rate of growth: $G_n \dfrac{K}{L} : \dfrac{K}{L} = G_n$. The amount

of consumption will be at its maximum when the tangent drawn to the production function, whose slope is the marginal productivity of capital, is parallel to the

line with a slope of G_n. In this case, the slopes of both will coincide, $G_n = \dfrac{\partial Q}{\partial K}$.

The golden-age path at which the amount of consumption is at a maximum, has a dominant position relative to the other golden-age paths. Though consumption also grows at a G_n rate along all golden-age paths, but since the paths do not intersect, the dominant path retains its advantage over the other paths all along the growth process. Phelps suggests that all generations are likely to choose this path and the corresponding investment ratio in the course of human history. If the economy has saved less than the optimum rate of investment, it has to reduce its current consumption so that in the long run society may consume a maximum amount compared with other golden-age growth paths. In so far as society saved more than the optimum rate of investment, the decrease in the savings ratio increases both current and future consumption.

486

Phelps determines the optimal investment ratio ensuring maximum consumption in the following way:

He multiplies both sides of the equation

$$\frac{\partial Q}{\partial K} = G_n$$

by the capital–output ratio:

$$\frac{\partial Q}{\partial K} \cdot \frac{K}{Q} = G_n \frac{K}{Q}.$$

$G_n \cdot K$ is the increment of capital stock increasing at a G_n rate or, in other words, investment.

In the neo-classical model, however, the investment ratio equals the savings ratio, $\frac{S}{Q} = s$. Thus the right side of the equation means the savings ratio, while its left side,

$$\frac{\partial Q}{\partial K} \cdot \frac{Q}{K},$$

is the production elasticity of capital. Hence, for the amount of consumption to be at a maximum in the growth process, it is necessary to save a proportion of the national income which is equal to the production elasticity of capital. This proposition is kown in neo-classical growth theory as the *golden rule of accumulation*[63], first formulated by the American Phelps. The equality of the savings ratio and the partial production elasticity of capital, along with the equality of the marginal productivity of capital and of the rate of growth, is another characteristic of the path ensuring maximum consumption, or, as we might call it now, of the *golden-rule path*.

To the dominant golden-age path only one capital–output ratio is attached. Its amount is easy to determine. Since along the golden-age path $G_n = \frac{s}{C_r}$, $C_r = \frac{s}{G_n}$. Along the dominant path $s = \varepsilon_k$. Thus the capital–output ratio of the dominant path $C_r = \frac{\varepsilon_K}{G_n}$.

Phelps pointed out that the existence of the path ensuring maximum consumption is not necessarily tied to neo-classical co ditions, namely to strict concavity, positive marginal productivity and double differentiability. It is also valid in the case of Leontief's production function.[64] Phelps thinks that it is Leontief's production function with its rigid capital–labour ratio which might serve as the basis of the Harrod–Domar growth theory. Both of them held the view, following Keynes, that in a capitalist economy it is not certain that a change in nominal wages relative to the interest rate will lead to a change in the capital–labour ratio.

---

63 E. S. Phelps: *op. cit.*, p. 273.
64 E. S. Phelps: Second Essay on the Golden Rule of Accumulation, *The American Economic Review*, September 1965.

According to Leontief's production function, the amount of consumption at a given point of time

$$C_t = \min \left(\frac{K_t}{a_K}, \frac{L_t}{a_L} \right) - G_n K_t.$$

At the outset Phelps assumes that there is unemployment, the amount of capital available is not sufficient to realize full employment, and, leaving technical progress out of account, capital grows at the same rate as the working population. In this case, the initially existing unemployment will continue to remain. Since in Leontief's production function the capital–output ratio is fixed, production grows at the same rate as capital increases, and so will consumption too, since the accumulation share of production, $G_n K$, will rise now at the same rate as production. Continuously increasing the initial stock of capital, we obtain, until full employment is reached, a higher and higher growth path at a G_n rate of growth with ever higher levels of output and consumption because the level of employment also continues to rise. By increasing the initial stock of capital, the levels of output and consumption may be stepped up as long as employment can be expanded, in other words, until full employment is reached. In the Domar–Harrod model it is the growth path at full employment which is dominant as compared with the others, the growth of the economy along this path ensuring the maximum of consumption. If the initial stock of capital is increased higher than necessary to ensure full employment, production no longer expands, accumulation, however, rises owing to the increase in capital stock, and consumption decreases compared with the growth path at full employment.

Capital stock along the dominant path is proportional to labour as expressed in the production function, $K:L = a_K:a_L$, which means that the stock of capital is equal to $L \dfrac{a_K}{a_L}$ at any point of time.

Let us represent the maximization of consumption diagrammatically according to Leontief's production function (see Figure 89).

A golden-rule growth path is possible only in the case of a golden-age type of growth when capital and output grow at the same and constant rate, and thus the average productivity of capital does not change over time, and technical progress increases only the productivity of labour or, put another way, is of the labour-augmenting type. But Phelps attributes a heuristic significance to the golden-rule path. Starting from it as a yardstick, he tries to demonstrate that even if development is not of the golden-age type, there is a critical path which, from the viewpoint of consumption, has the same normative significance as the golden-rule path which assumes a golden-age growth. He emphasizes that if technical progress is partly or fully capital-augmenting (when in the course of economic development the substitution effect does not offset the expanding effect of technical progress upon the average productivity of capital, which means that the average productivity of capital also increases in the growth process and thus capital and output cannot grow at the same rate), or if the rate of population growth and technical progress are not constant over time, in which case of course no golden-age growth can occur, even then we may, by increasing the savings ratio, reach a growth path which will result, compared with the other growth

488

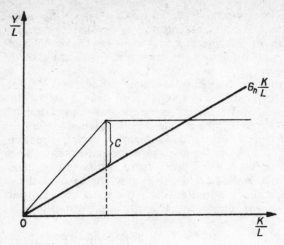

Figure 89

paths attached to other savings ratios and at least in a certain period, in a greater, but never in a smaller amount of consumption.

EMBODIED TECHNICAL PROGRESS AND THE VINTAGE MODEL

In the first neo-classical models, for example Solow's early model or Meade's model, any capital good, old and new alike, equally partakes of technical progress.

In his study published in 1960 Solow comes to realize that this idea contradicts the everyday observation that "… many if not most innovations need to be embodied in new kinds of durable equipment before they can be made effective."[65] "I assume," he says, "that new technology can be introduced into the production process only through gross investment in new plant and equipment."[66] He distinguishes two types, *non-embodied and embodied technical progress.*

Non-embodied technical progress means the perfection of the organization and operation of production factors, independently of their nature. Its utilization does not require any investment. The representatives of neo-classical growth theory begin to stress that only non-embodied technical progress affects capital stock as a whole, and thus capital goods can be regarded as homogeneous only from the point of view of non-embodied technical progress.

Embodied technical progress, however, affects only capital goods of the latest vintage. According to this assumption, any capital good represents the latest technology when it comes into being, but does not take part in further technical development. Solow emphasizes that "… embodied technological progress is by

[65] R. Solow: Investment and Technical Progress. In: *Mathematical Methods in the Social Sciences,* California, 1960, pp. 89–104.
[66] R. Solow: Technical Progress, Capital Formation and Economic Growth, *The American Economic Review,* Papers and Proceedings, LII, May 1962. pp. 765–786.

a substantial margin the more important kind."[67] In its further stage of development, neo-classical theory sees the vehicle of technical progress in investments, more exactly in *gross investments*, since replacement, too, is closely connected with technical progress. Net investments figuring in earlier neo-classical growth models are replaced by gross investments.

According to the traditional theory, if already available labour and capital can replace one another, unemployment and surplus capital cannot exist. The introduction of the concept of embodied technical progress makes us aware of the fact that once a plant has been equipped, the change-over to a labour-intensive technique in the case of unemployment, or the adoption of a capital-intensive technology in the case of surplus capital, are far less simple processes than those represented in the model assuming the easy malleability of capital goods. The replacement of existing capital stock embodied in concrete goods by a stock of capital embodying a different technology adopting itself better to the changed factor supply, can only take place slowly, mostly by the gradual renewal of the old capital stock.

Distinguishing between the two types of technical progress and denoting the rate of embodied technical progress by λ and that of non-embodied technical progress by μ, Phelps's formula of the rate of golden-age growth is modified as follows:

$$G_n = \frac{\lambda + \mu}{1 - \varepsilon_k} + \frac{dL}{L}.$$

Given a constant savings ratio, $\frac{dK}{K}$ also adjusts itself to $\frac{dY}{Y}$.

Since however, each vintage of capital is of a different efficiency, capital stock cannot be represented as a homogeneous magnitude expressing an identical level of technical knowledge. The efficiency of the capital stock is also influenced by its mean age. The equilibrium mean age of capital depends, *on the one hand,* on the rate of depreciation. Phelps assumes that capital goods depreciate exponentially at the rate δ per annum. The equilibrium mean age of capital is, *on the other hand,* dependent on the equilibrium rate of output, to which the growth rate of capital adjusts itself along the equilibrium path. Each vintage of capital has increased at a G_n rate, its proportion to total capital stock remains constant in equilibrium growth. Phelps emphasizes that the mean age of capital does not depend on the savings ratio, because both δ and G_n are independent of s. If the savings ratio increases, the weight of capital of the latest vintage will temporarily grow within the total stock of capital, and this will decrease the mean age of capital. But the new equipment is becoming more and more obsolete over time, which increases the weight of obsolete machinery, and the mean age of capital slowly rises to its earlier equilibrium level. The persistent reduction of the mean age by increasing the savings ratio requires a steady increase in the latter. However, this is not a practicable way of decreasing the mean age.

Since in the case of embodied technical progress each vintage of capital re-

[67] *Ibid.*

presents different levels of technical progress, for each vintage a separate production function should be set up.

The Cobb–Douglas type of production function set up for the output of products produced with capital of vintage v at the point of time t is:

$$Q_v(t) = B_0 e^{\lambda v} K_v^m(t) L_v^{1-m}(t),$$

where B_0 is the level of technical progress at the point of time t_0.

Owing to their different degrees of efficiency, capital goods of different vintages cannot be aggregated by a simple summation to yield total social capital. They have to be weighted according to their degrees of efficiency.

With this in view, Solow imputes the effect of technical progress entirely to capital. If $\sigma = 1$, and technical progress is neutral in the Hicksian sense, then the effect of technical progress may entirely be imputed either to capital or labour. And thus we have arrived at the interpretation of neutral technical progress in Solow's sense, which is the reverse image of Harrod's neutrality. Technical progress is neutral in Solow's view if, given constant wages, it does not affect the labour coefficient, the average productivity of labour. It only affects the efficiency of capital and is, therefore, *capital-augmenting*. It has no bearing on the production elasticity of labour, nor, assuming a first-degree homogeneous production function, on the production elasticity of capital.

By how much does technical progress increase the efficiency of capital?

In much the same way as he computed the growth rate of labour productivity in the case of Harrod's neutral technical progress, Phelps also determined the growth rate of the efficiency of new capital goods, which is: $\dfrac{\lambda}{1-\varepsilon_L}$. Or, if we also take into account the effect of non-embodied technical progress, the efficiency of each capital good increases at the rate $\dfrac{\mu}{1-\varepsilon_L}$, and that of new capital goods at the rate $\dfrac{\mu+\lambda}{1-\varepsilon_L}$.

In summing them, capitals of different vintages have to be treated as $\left(1 + \dfrac{\lambda}{1-\varepsilon_L}\right)$ —times the capital goods of the previous vintage.

And the amount of efficient capital available to society is

$$J_t = \int_{-\infty}^{t} e^{\frac{\lambda}{1-\varepsilon_L}} K_v(t)\, dv,$$

while aggregate production function is

$$Q_t = J_t^m L_t^k.$$

Phelps emphasizes that "the fact that capitals of different vintages get different technical weights is immaterial in the determination of the exponential equilibrium growth rate."[68]

The introduction of embodied technical progress constitutes a step forward in the direction of relating to each other the factors determining the rate of growth, represented hitherto in isolation. More recently, attempts have also been made within the neo-classical growth model to show the effect on production of investments in improving the quality of labour.

Balogh and Streeten emphasize the necessity of separating these investments "from investment in physical capital."[69] Schultz points out that between 1900 and 1956 "educational costs also rose about three and a half times as rapidly as did the gross formation of physical capital in dollars."[70] He further emphasizes the significance of investments to improve the quality of labour: "Some growth of course can be had from the increase in more conventional capital even though the labor that is available is lacking both in skill and knowledge. But the rate of growth will be seriously limited."[71] On the basis of his investigations in the field of agriculture, Griliches stresses the significance of the qualification of the labour force: "The education of the farm labour force is again a 'significant' variable, entering the equation with a coefficient which is not significantly different from that of the labor variable."[72]

Arrow calls attention to the fact that investments embodying the effect of technical progress significantly increase, by amassing production experiences, the quality of live labour. This recognition means one more step towards integrating the factors of growth. "I would like to suggest here an endogenous theory of the changes in knowledge...,"[73] writes Arrow. The development of technical knowledge manifests itself in his theory not only in producing newer and newer capital goods, but also in increasing the production experiences of workers operating them. In this *"learning-by-doing"* theory he correctly emphasizes that learning takes place not only in educational and research institutions but in production, too, as its by-product. The introduction of new machines requires the workers to gain more knowledge, which in turn leads to higher productivity. Krelle constructs the elasticity of labour quality with respect to capital equipment, which indicates by what percentage the quality of labour changes with 1 per cent change in capital per head.[74] Arrow points out that even without new investments the quality of labour increases as a result of the fact that a worker gains more and more production experience in performing his work even with unchanged capital

[68] E. S. Phelps: The New View of Investment: A Neo-Classical Analysis, *The Quarterly Journal of Economics*, 1962, No. 4, p. 556.

[69] Th. Balogh and P. Streeten: The Coefficient of Ignorance, *Bulletin of the Oxford University Institute of Economics and Statistics*, May, 1963, pp. 99–107.

[70] T. W. Schultz: Investment in Human Capital, *The American Economic Review*, March 1961, p. 11.

[71] T. W. Schultz: *op. cit.*, p. 16.

[72] Z. Griliches: Research Expenditures, Education and the Aggregate Agricultural Production Function, *The American Economic Review*, December 1964, pp. 961–974.

[73] K. Arrow: The Economic Implications of Learning by Doing, *The Review of Economic Studies*, June 1962, p. 155.

[74] W. Krelle: Beeinflussbarkeit und Grenzen des Wirtschaftswachstums, *Jahrbücher für Nationaökonomie und Statistik*, Aug. 1965, pp. 3–27.

492

equipment. The *Horndal effect,* so called by Lundberg, expresses exactly that in the Horndal Iron Works in Sweden output per man-hour increased by an annual average of 2 per cent for 15 years even without new investments, that is, without any significant changes in the production methods. This continually increasing performance was the result of knowledge gained by experience.[75]

THE THEORY OF INDUCED TECHNICAL PROGRESS AS THE ALTERNATIVE NEO-CLASSICAL THEORY OF EQUILIBRIUM GROWTH

In addition to the fact that neo-classical growth theory has already taken into account embodied technical progress in recent years, a further important change can now be observed in that theory. "It has typically been assumed in the neo-classical growth model literature that technical change is exogenous, though this is presumably not the case in real life,"[76] writes Conlisk. They assumed it to be exogenously given in total amount and exogenously given in bias (capital-saving, labour-saving). More recently, attempts can be found in neo-classical growth models which resolve both assumptions. The first of these attempts was aimed, while continuing to take the amount of technical progress as given, to handle the nature of technical advance as an endogenous variable in the growth model. The initiators of models of this kind refer to Hicks's already mentioned work, *The Theory of Wages,* in which the author distinguishes between autonomous inventions regarded as exogenous data and induced inventions, "those inventions which are the result of a change in the relative prices of the factors... We shall expect, in practice, all or nearly all inventions to be labour-saving."[77]

In his work on the questions of economic growth, published in 1956, Fellner attributes a basic importance to induced technical innovations. "Approximate adjustment of the character of improvements to existing resource scarcities suggests the existence of a mechanism which tends to induce the required type of improvement."[78] He expounds the same idea in two of his more recent articles on the question one published in 1961,[79] the other in 1969[80]. Corry, too, characterizes induced technical progress as "a direct response to what are loosely called technical bottlenecks."[81]

Fellner emphasizes that the handling of the character of innovations as an endogenous variable reflects the fact that in the post-war period expenditures on scientific research and development have grown tremendously.[82]

[75] K. Arrow: *op. cit.,* p. 156.
[76] J. Conlisk: The Neoclassical Growth Model with Endogenously Positioned Technical Change Frontier, *The Economic Journal,* June 1969, p. 348.
[77] J. R. Hicks: *The Theory of Wages,* New York, 1948, p. 125.
[78] W. Fellner: *Trends and Cycles in Economic Activity,* New York, 1956, p. 220.
[79] W. Fellner: Two Propositions in the Theory of Induced Innovations, *The Economic Journal,* June 1961.
[80] W. Fellner: Profit Maximization, Utility Maximization and the Rate and Direction of Innovation, *The American Economic Review,* May 1969.
[81] B. A. Corry: The Role of Technological Innovation in the Theories of Income Distribution, *The American Economic Review,* May 1966, p. 40.
[82] W. Fellner: Profit Maximization, Utility Maximization and the Rate and Direction of Innovation, *The American Economic Review,* May 1969, p. 24.

The inclusion of induced technical innovations in the neo-classical growth model was hindered by the interpretation of technical progress as neutral, because it presupposes that the relative scarcity of one factor does not affect technical progress.

More recently, several authors, among them Fellner, Kennedy and Samuelson, began to find an answer to the question of whether the relative shares of classes in national income can remain constant in the long run, or whether the production elasticities can be constant, if we abandon the assumption of the unitary elasticity of substitution and neutral technical progress.

Let the stock of capital grow at a higher rate than the labour force. If the elasticity of substitution $\sigma < 1$, then, according to the neo-classical growth model, the relative share of the working class in the national income will increase in the course of growth, the production elasticity of labour will grow, and the relative share of the capitalist class will decrease, together with the production elasticity of capital. The situation will be reversed if the value of σ is greater than unity. Samuelson provides the proof that in the case of a steady growth of the capital–labour ratio, long-run equilibrium of constant relative shares will exist, independently of the value of σ if "the induced technical change is relatively labour-augmenting in comparison with capital augmentation."[83] This happens when labour is augmented in relation to capital to the same extent to which the growth rate of capital surpasses the growth rate of labour. Then "the ratio of capital (in efficiency units) to labour (in efficiency units) remains constant in the growth process."[84] In this case technical progress is neutral in Kennedy's sense: it counterbalances, at an exponentially increasing capital–labour ratio, the substitution effect which influences the relative shares of capital and labour and the production elasticity, and creates such circumstances as if the value of σ continues to be unity throughout the growth process.

Let us illustrate the above by a numerical example:

Let the stock of capital and the size of the labour force be 1,000 each at a point of time of t_1, and the production elasticity and marginal productivity of capital and labour 0.5 each. In this case, if the production function is first-degree homogeneous, the volume of production will be 1,000.

Let now the stock of capital grow by 20, and the labour force by 10 per cent. Thus the rate of growth of the stock of capital will exceed that of the labour force by 10 per cent.

The amount of the stock of capital at the consecutive points of time will be 1,200, 1,440, etc.

The size of the labour force will be 1,100, 1,210, etc. at the corresponding points of time.

[83] P. A. Samuelson: A Theory of Induced Innovation along Kennedy-Weizsäcker Lines, *The Review of Economics and Statistics*, November 1965, p. 348.
[84] P. A. Samuelson: *op. cit.*, p. 356.

In this case the long-run equilibrium of constant relative shares requires that the marginal productivity of labour should increase by 10 per cent more than that of capital. If the marginal productivity of capital increases by 10 per cent, that is, if its value is 0.55, 0.605, etc. at the consecutive points of time, then the marginal productivity of labour must assume the following values: 0.6, 0.72, etc.

In this case the contribution of capital and labour to the quantity of the product produced will be at the consecutive points of time as follows: $1,200 \cdot 0.55 = 660$, $1,440 \cdot 0.605 = 871.2$ etc. and $1,100 \cdot 0.6 = 660$, $1,210 \cdot 0.72 = 871.2$ etc. And the efficient capital–labour ratio will assume the following magnitude in the growth process: $\dfrac{1,200 \cdot 1.1}{1,100 \cdot 1.2}$, $\dfrac{1,440 \cdot 1.1^2}{1,210 \cdot 1.2^2}$, etc.

The capital–labour ratio will therefore be constant in terms of efficiency units in the course of equilibrium growth, and so will be the production elasticity of capital and labour, or, according to neo-classical theory, the relative shares of capital and labour.

But through what mechanism does induced technical progress ensure the constancy of the relative shares of capital and labour, or the constancy of their production elasticities in equilibrium growth?

Hicks examined that question on the macro-economic level. If the stock of capital increases at a higher rate than the labour force, it will raise, according to him, the relative share of labour at the given level of technical knowledge and at a less than unitary value of the elasticity of substitution, and it will also increase the production elasticity of labour compared to that of capital; thus it will stimulate labour-saving technical innovations. This type of technical invention increases the marginal productivity of capital more than that of labour, raises the rate of interest more than wages, and counteracts thereby the increase in the relative share of labour. If, however, the value of the elasticity of substitution is greater than unity, then the marginal productivity of labour has to be increased, by capital-saving inventions, more than the marginal productivity of capital, and wages have to be raised more than the rate of interest.

Hicks, however, did not examine, says Fellner, through what mechanism changes in the macro-economic resource position of an economy stimulate the individual firms to effect a corresponding bias in innovations. Kennedy was among the first to demonstrate the working of a mechanism which, by means of the entrepreneurs' choice among the differing possibilities of innovation, keeps the relative shares of labour and capital in the national income, or their production elasticities, at constant levels in the process of economic growth.

While, however, "macroeconomically seen, the changing ratio of input supplies (changing K/L ratio), may be regarded as a given datum, and this changing ratio leads to a changing ratio of input prices,"[85] micro-economically, these input prices are data for the individual entrepreneur. He cannot change them by changing the character of the innovation. His decisions are confined to utilizing an appropriate innovation, decreasing the amount of the more expensive factor needed to produce a unit of output, and changing thereby the proportion between the amounts of factors needed to produce a unit of product. Thus Hicks provided

[85] W. Fellner: Empirical Support for the Theory of Induced Innovation, *The Quarterly Journal of Economics*, November 1971, p. 580.

no solution for the entrepreneur when he suggested that, on the macro-economic level and given an elasticity of substitution less than unity, the increase in the marginal productivity of labour should be held back relative to the growth of the marginal productivity of capital by labour-saving innovation. This would result, at given factor prices, in just the opposite effect. The amount of labour needed for producing a unit of product would increase in relation to the quantity of capital per a unit of product, and the weight of the cost of labour in unit cost would not decline but rather rise. Therefore, as we shall see, a new form of technical innovation appears in Kennedy's model.

To demonstrate the entrepreneur's choice among the different innovation possibilities, Kennedy constructs, on the analogy of the curve of production possibilities (transformation curve), the *innovation possibility frontier*. The production possibility curve expresses what combination of the two products the entrepreneur is able to produce with the available capital and labour by the efficient utilization of factors. The innovation possibility frontier, however, expresses what innovation possibilities are available to the entrepreneur with a given amount of resources for research and development: by what q per cent he can reduce the capital necessary to produce a unit of output if he decreases labour needed for the production of a unit of output by a certain p per cent. In other words, $p = f_1(q)$ and $q = f_2(p)$, or $\varphi(p, q) = 0$.

The slope of the innovation possibility frontier, $\dfrac{dq}{dp}$, "expresses at any point a marginal trade-off rate; i.e. the marginal opportunity cost of additional labour-augmentation in terms of the capital-augmentation that must be sacrificed to obtain a small additional unit of labour-augmentation."[86] Like the transformation curve, the innovation possibility frontier is assumed to be concave to the origin. "The greater the reduction in the labour required to produce a unit of output, the smaller will be the possible reduction in capital required."[87]

The effect of technical progress divided between the increase in the productivity of labour and capital is given by Beckmann and Sato in their article[88] classifying technical progress in the following dynamic production function:

$$Q = f[A(t)K, B(t)L].$$

In this case they speak of a new form of technical progress, called *factor-augmenting* technical progress, which has the same effect as if both capital and labour had increased without technical progress, capital by a factor $A(t) = (1+p)$, and labour by a factor $B(t) = (1+q)$.

This factor-augmenting technical progress is at the same time factor-saving technical progress, as it decreases the capital or labour required to produce a unit of output. If $\sigma = 1$, the effect of technical progress could fully be imputed either to one or to the other factor. In Harrod's neutral technical progress only p in-

[86] W. Fellner: Profit Maximization, Utility Maximization and the Rate and Direction of Innovation, *The American Economic Review*, May 1966, p. 30.

[87] C. Kennedy: Induced Bias in Innovation and the Theory of Distribution, *The Economic Journal*, September 1964, p. 544.

[88] M. J. Beckmann and R. Sato: Aggregate Production Function and Types of Technical Progress. A Statistical Analysis, *The American Economic Review*, May 1969, p. 29.

creases, in Solow's only q. In the Cobb–Douglas production function, however, technical progress cannot unambiguously be divided into its labour- and capital-augmenting components.

Now the question arises, which point of the curve of innovation possibility the entrepreneur chooses, on the basis of what considerations he decides the proportional increase in the productivity of labour and capital with the resources available to him for research and development, or the percentage reduction in labour or capital needed to produce a unit of output; in other words "... whether the bias [in technical change—A.M.] is itself induced by economic considerations."[89]

Let us assume, following Kennedy, that technical progress takes place only in the production of consumer goods using two factors, capital and labour, and the production function is first-degree homogeneous. Let us denote the labour cost needed to produce a unit of output by L, capital cost by C. Let $\dfrac{L}{L+C}$, the share of labour cost in total costs, be λ, and $\dfrac{C}{L+C}$, the share of capital cost, γ.

Let technical progress reduce the labour required to produce a unit of product by p per cent, and the capital needed to produce a unit of output by q per cent. At given factor prices the cost of a unit of output decreases by $r = \lambda p + \gamma q$ per cent. For Kennedy, the entrepreneur decides entirely on the basis of economic considerations which to choose from among the different innovations. He wants to maximize r, the measure of cost reduction. Therefore, he will try to find labour-saving innovations if the relative share of labour cost is greater than that of capital cost, that is, if $\lambda > \gamma$, or he will seek capital-saving innovations if the relative share of capital exceeds the relative share of labour cost, if $\gamma > \lambda$. In the former case, he will move along the curve as long as $dp\lambda > dq\gamma$, that is, it is worthwhile for him to increase the productivity of labour at the expense of increasing the efficiency of capital. Since in the continuous increase in labour productivity the increase in the efficiency of capital has to be sacrificed to an increasing extent, $dp\lambda$ will eventually be equal to $dq\gamma$, that is, $\dfrac{dq}{dp} = \dfrac{\lambda}{\gamma}$. Thus the measure of cost reduction will reach its maximum when the slope of the curve equals the ratio of the relative shares of capital cost and labour cost.

In his study on induced technical progress Samuelson determines this point diagrammatically as follows (Figure 90).

He constructs the budget-line expressing the relationship $r = \lambda p + \gamma q$. This line indicates what combinations of labour-saving and capital-saving innovations will lead to the same percentage reduction of the unit cost of output. And the point of intersection of the budget-line and the axes expresses what percentage of reduction is needed for total costs to decrease by a given r per cent, if only

[89] K. J. Arrow: Classificatory Notes on the Production and Transmission of Technical Knowledge, *The American Economic Review*, May 1969, p. 29.

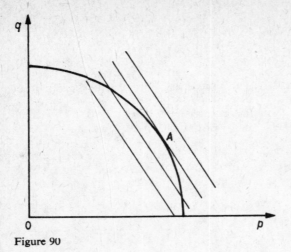

Figure 90

labour cost or only capital cost is reduced unilaterally. This percentage is obviously $\frac{r}{\lambda}$ in the case of labour, and $\frac{r}{\gamma}$ per cent in the case of capital.

Let us illustrate the above by a numerical example.

Let the quantity of labour per unit of output be 10, and the quantity of capital 80. If the wage of one worker is 4 dollars and the cost of using a unit of capital is 2 dollars, then the labour cost per unit of output is 40 dollars and capital cost is 160 dollars. Total cost is therefore 200 dollars. In this case λ, the share of labour cost in total costs, is 20 per cent, while γ, the share of capital cost in total costs, is 80 per cent. If the entrepreneur reduces labour cost per unit of output by 10 per cent and capital cost per unit of output by 12.5 per cent, the new labour coefficient will be 9, and the new capital coefficient will be 70. Given unchanged factor prices, labour cost will fall to 36 dollars, capital cost to 140 dollars, and thus the new total cost will be 176 dollars, by 12 per cent less than the original total cost $(r = 12$ per cent $= 0.1 \cdot 20$ per cent $+ 0.125 \cdot 80$ per cent).

Had the entrepreneur wanted to achieve the 12 per cent reduction of total cost only by decreasing labour cost, then, assuming unchanged wage rates, he ought to have reduced the quantity of labour per unit of output by 12 per cent: 20 per cent = 60 per cent. In this case, the labour coefficient would have been 4 instead of 10, and labour cost per unit of output 16 dollars instead of 40 dollars. The new total cost, 176 dollars, is really 12 per cent less than the original value.

If, however, the entrepreneur had wanted to achieve the 12 per cent reduction of total cost by decreasing only capital cost, then he ought to have reduced the quantity of capital per unit of output by 12 per cent: 80 per cent = 15 per cent, that is, from 80 to 68. Thereby, the capital cost per unit of output would have fallen from 160 dollars to 136 dollars. And the lower total cost would have been again 40 dollars + 136 dollars = 176 dollars.

Thus the slope of the budget-line is $\frac{\lambda}{\gamma}$. Budget-lines must be constructed for the different amounts of r. Where the innovation possibility frontier touches the budget-line, the point of tangency expresses what combination of labour-saving and capital-saving innovations the entrepreneur should choose within the scope of his possibilities, by what per cent he should decrease labour and capital required to produce a unit of output to achieve a maximum reduction of total costs.

498

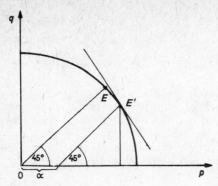

Figure 91

According to Kennedy[90], λ and γ express not only the relative shares of labour and capital in total costs, but also the relative shares of the working and capitalist classes in national income. Thus they also express, according to the logic of the neo-classical theoretical system, the production elasticities of labour and capital.

But the equilibrium point determined by Kennedy is valid only in the short run and does not express the equilibrium requirement of a growing economy.

Samuelson tries to build Kennedy's innovation possibility frontier into the neo-classical growth model, taking into account that during the growth process the capital stock as well as the labour force increase and, depending on the difference between their growth rates, the ratio of marginal productivities and the ratio of incomes also change, and so do relative shares. Samuelson tries to present the already discussed relationship by making use of Kennedy's trade-off frontier; namely, how the individual entrepreneurs must manipulate the various innovation possibilities in the course of economic growth when the increase in capital stock surpasses that of the labour force by α per cent, so that the relative shares in national income remain unchanged. By means of the Kennedy frontier it can also be demonstrated that technical progress tends to be biased in a labour-saving or a labour-augmenting direction.

First he assumes that capital and labour grow at the same rate on the social level and thus growth will not effect the substitution relations. For the relative shares of the classes and the production elasticities of capital and labour to remain constant, the point of tangency of the budget-line and the innovation possibility frontier of individual entrepreneurs has to lie at the point of intersection of the frontier and the line drawn from the origin at an angle of 45°. In this case, at the point of tangency E, $p = q$, the proportionate rate of capital augmentation and the proportionate rate of labour augmentation are identical. Under such circumstances, as Samuelson emphasizes, "the induced inventions will have become neutral in the 1932 sense of Hicks, augmenting both factors at the same percentage rate."[91]

[90] C. Kennedy: *op. cit.*, p. 545.
[91] P. A. Samuelson: *op. cit.*, p. 346.

Let us assume that the capital–labour ratio increases at a steady rate of α, that is $\dfrac{dK}{K} - \dfrac{dL}{L} = \alpha$. Samuelson determines the proportionate rate of capital augmentation and that of labour augmentation for individual entrepreneurs in this case diagrammatically as shown in Figure 91.

Starting from the origin, Samuelson plots the distance α on the positive section of the p-axis of the graph. Then he draws a straight line at an angle of 45° from the point thus obtained. At the point of intersection of the line drawn at an angle of 45° and the innovation possibility frontier, the rate of labour-saving innovation will obviously be greater by α than the rate of capital-saving innovation. The slope of the curve expresses at the point of intersection the equilibrium rate of relative shares, $\dfrac{\lambda}{\gamma}$.

The figure, he writes, shows how neutral equilibrium in the Hicksian sense shifts to South-East, towards labour augmenting or labour saving if the stock of capital increases at a rate α per cent higher than that of the labour force. The figure also shows that at the new equilibrium point E' the share of labour has increased and that of the faster growing capital stock has decreased. This then stimulates the entrepreneurs to increase the productivity of labour more than the productivity of capital. And if the productivity of labour increases α times faster than that of capital, the share of labour will not continue to rise and that of capital will not continue to fall, and the shares expressed by the new equilibrium point will get stabilized in the growth process. And, as Fellner writes, "the assumed concavity to the origin of the innovation possibility frontier assures that the firms will gradually move to a point ... where the innovations are just enough labour-saving to offset the labour-share-increasing effect of the rising physical capital–labour ratio."[92]

Samuelson pointed out that the long-run equilibrium of constant relative shares established as a result of the adequate rates of labour-augmenting and capital-augmenting innovations will remain stable if $\sigma < 1$. Let us assume that no equilibrium could be established, because the induced labour-augmenting character of the innovational process was not able fully to offset the labour-share-increasing effect of the growth of the K/L ratio. Capital–labour ratio, measured in efficiency units, could not fall to a level needed to keep the relative shares at constant levels.

Consequently, the relative share of labour will increase. Micro-economically, entrepreneurs react to this by reducing the share of labour cost in total costs, that is, increase the rate of labour augmenting, or of labour saving, and divert the economy in the direction of equilibrium. If, however, equilibrium could not be established because the rate of labour augmentation is too high, then the ratio of efficient capital decreases relative to labour measured in efficiency units more than what is needed to keep the relative shares at constant levels; in this case, when the value of σ is less than unity, the relative share of capital will increase. Now the forces working in the direction of equilibrium will come into operation again. Entrepreneurs try to force down the weight of capital cost within the firm, and increase the rate of capital augmenting or saving.

92 W. Fellner: *op. cit.*, p. 31.

500

At the same time, the economy as a whole moves away from long-run equilibrium if capital in efficiency units increases or decreases relative to labour in efficiency units, and the value of σ is greater than unity. In the first case, the relative share of capital will increase. Entrepreneurs will now raise the rate of capital augmenting to force down the weight of increased capital cost in total costs. Thus they will further increase at the macro-level the capital–labour ratio in efficiency units. If, however, this ratio decreases, because the rate of labour augmenting is too high, thereby causing the relative share of labour to increase at a value of σ greater than unity, entrepreneurs will step up the rate of labour augmenting in order to decrease the weight of labour cost in total costs. The capital–labour ratio in efficiency units will continue to fall, and the economy will move away from long-run equilibrium.

But Samuelson does not believe that technical progress is *ipso facto* of a labour-saving character. At minimum-cost equilibrium, all factors are equally cheap and efficient marginally, because the same output increment falls to the last dollar of their utilization costs. Thus the entrepreneur is not interested in expending more effort to reduce one dollar of expenditure than another. Then an induced invention has no systematic bias, the entrepreneur is interested in increasing the productivity of each factor at an equal rate, that is, the induced technical progress is neutral in the Hicksian sense, and the change in the relative shares depends upon the drift of exogenous technical changes and upon the change of factor proportions.

An appraisal of the theory

The explanation by induced technical progress of equilibrium growth taking place under unchanged relative shares of classes significantly differs from the golden-age model of growth discussed so far. Earlier, in constructing the golden-age model, it was assumed that technical progress was neutral in so far as it did not affect the production elasticities and the relative shares of classes in national income, and the value of the elasticity of substitution equalled unity. Under such conditions of golden-age growth, the substitution effect offsets the capital-efficiency-increasing effect of technical progress. By taking into account induced technical progress, the adherents of the theory give up the assumption of neutral technical progress. "Recently, ... the device of a technical change frontier [the function of innovation possibilities—A.M.] has been used to relax the Harrod neutrality assumption."[93] For economic considerations, entrepreneurs themselves decide on the character of technical innovations. And the theory also abandons the assumption that the substitution elasticity equals unity. In a steady-state growth constructed under such conditions, it is not the substitution effect which offsets the effect of technical progress, but on the contrary, the character of technical progress is chosen in a way that offsets the substitution effect. Harrod's neutrality in this representation is the result of economic considerations, and not an assumption made for the sake of convenience.

[93] J. Conlisk: Nonconstant Returns to Scale and the Technical Change Frontier, *The Quarterly Journal of Economics*, August 1971, p. 483.

In a recently published study Fellner enumerates the possibilities resulting from the theory[94]:

a. Neither the rising capital–labour ratios of Western economies, nor the character of inventive activities tend to change the income distribution based on the principle of marginal productivity. The model may assume the unitary value of substitution elasticity under neutral technical progress.

b. Increasing capital–labour ratios tend to raise the relative share of the working class, but the character of technical progress tends to reduce it. In the model a less than unitary substitution elasticity may be included with labour-saving technical progress in the Hicksian sense.

c. Increasing capital–labour ratios tend to reduce the relative share of the working class, while the character of technical progress tends to raise it. The model may assume that the elasticity of substitution is greater than unity, and the character of technical progress is capital-saving in the Hicksian sense.

That the growth model takes into account labour-saving, that is, induced technical progress, is compatible with the view held by Marxist political economy, too: the more expensive is labour, the more important it is to decrease labour cost by labour-saving technical innovations. Capital-saving technical innovations also play an important role in Marx. This, by the way, has also been pointed out by Blaug.[95] Marx deals with innovations of this kind in the chapter on "Economy in the employment of constant capital" of Vol. III of his *Capital*, evaluating them as factors raising the profit rate and counteracting its declining tendency. At the same time he points out that economy in the utilization of constant capital originates in part from the effectiveness of large-scale production, "from the social nature of labour."[96] This aspect of the question is dealt with in non-Marxian literature in connection with the economies of scale. On the other hand, says Marx, "savings made in capital expenditures in one line of industry is due to the fact that the productive power of labour has increased in another,"[97] the one which supplies its means of production. Thus, what appears in one industry as a capital-saving technical innovation, is in fact the result of a labour-saving technical development in another productive branch. The American Marxian economist Gillman points out, under the circumstances of modern capitalism, the capital-saving effect of instrumentation and automation.[98]

Besides reflecting a real process, the introduction of induced technical progress into the neo-classical growth model raises, in addition to the "reswitching" problem, another serious question in connection with the theory of marginal productivity. If the relative increase in wages induces labour-saving technical progress, and also gives rise to the substitution effect, how can the shift of the production function be distinguished from movement along the production function? And this separation is of basic importance from the viewpoint of the theory of marginal productivity since the calculation of the marginal productivity

[94] W. Fellner: Empirical Support for Induced Innovations, *The Quarterly Journal of Economics*, November 1971, pp. 580–581.

[95] M. Blaug: *Economic Theory in Retrospect*, London, 1968, pp. 252–253.

[96] K. Marx: *Capital*, Vol. III, Moscow, 1962, p. 79.

[97] K. Marx: *op. cit.*, p. 81.

[98] See J. A. Gillman: *The Falling Rate of Profit*, London, 1957, pp. 77–78 and 139–144.

of factors presupposes that it is possible to measure the increment of output at the given level of technical knowledge resulting solely from a change in the proportions between factors. The construction of the production function takes into account the possibility of separating the two effects. This serious problem for marginal productivity theory, which is connected with the intertwining of the two effects under the consideration of induced technical progress, has also been pointed out by non-Marxian economists. Corry emphasizes that with labour-saving technical progress induced by a change in factor prices "... statistical difficulties of distinguishing the effects of innovation from the effects of substitution"[99] arise. The same difficulty is also referred to by Kennedy and Thirlwall in their study summarizing the latest non-Marxian theories concerning technical innovation. "At the empirical level, if not also in principle, the basic difficulty is that of distinguishing between movements along a given production function and shifts in the production function."[100]

With the introduction of induced technical progress it turns out that technical innovations and the capital–labour ratio are closely interrelated. In his growth theory, Kaldor breaks away, as we shall see, from the procedure which distinguishes the effect of technical progress from the substitution effect. His technical progress function unites both effects.

By taking into account the effect of induced technical progress, the theory gives up the assumption of unitary substitution elasticity. Most neo-classical growth models, however, are based on the assumption that technical progress is neutral in the Hicksian sense, and the elasticity of substitution is unity. Recent models, as Kennedy and Thirlwall point out, overestimate the contribution of capital to growth, and underestimate the role of technical progress, if the elasticity of substitution is really less than unity. When then σ changes together with the change in capital–labour ratio, the growth model, by taking the value of σ to be constant, attributes to technical progress such changes in growth as are consequences of changes in resulting from shifts in factor proportions.[101]

As to Kennedy's model assuming induced technical progress, non-Marxian critiques doubt whether induced technical progress is able to stabilize the proportions of labour costs and capital costs, and thereby the relative shares of the working and capitalist classes in the national income. Fellner holds it to be "premature" to ascribe this effect to induced technical progress. Instead, he merely speaks of "a counteracting tendency generated by innovational biases in economies in which labour is getting scarce relative to capital."[102] Thus he does not believe that induced technical progress is capable of keeping incomes at their equilibrium level, but maintains that by preventing narrow bottlenecks from coming about, it is a factor working in the direction of equilibrium.

Did neo-classical theory make any progress in determining the relative shares of classes by introducing induced technical progress? Those models which assume

[99] B. A. Corry: The Role of Technological Innovation in the Theories of Income Distribution, *The American Economic Review*, May 1966, p. 40.

[100] C. Kennedy and A. P. Thirlwall: Technical Progress. A Survey, *The Economic Journal*, March 1972, p. 20.

[101] C. Kennedy and A. P. Thirlwall: *op. cit.*, pp. 23–25.

[102] W. Fellner: Profit Maximization, Utility Maximization and the Rate and Direction of Innovation, *The American Economic Review*, May 1966, p. 31.

that the elasticity of substitution is unitary and technical progress is neutral in the Hicksian sense, take relative shares to be given at the outset, and these shares remain constant in these models throughout the whole growth process. By accepting induced technical progress, neo-classical growth theory rejects the assumption of neutral technical progress and unitary substitution elasticity. By doing so, it approaches reality, but is unable, as also shown by the possibilities listed by Fellner, to provide, even from its own theoretical basis, an unambiguous ˉexplanation of how distribution relations change in the course of the growth process. If, for example, an answer were to be given to the question why the share of the working class in the national income rises with the increase in the capital–labour ratio, the theory may say that it grows because technical progress is neutral in the Hicksian sense, and the elasticity of substitution is less than unity; but it would be completely in accordance with the logical foundations of the theory if the answer were that it grows because the character of innovations is capital-saving in the Hicksian sense, and the elasticity of substitution is equal to or greater than unity.

The theory of marginal productivity is the income-distribution theory of non-Marxian economics. A distribution theory should express the laws which determine the distribution of the national income between classes. Thus it must contain laws which express the inherent, substantial relationships of processes and determine their necessary development. Hence, the theory is expected to give a generalized description of the phenomena in the field under consideration, to disclose how and in what direction these processes develop in the present, and to make possible scientific prediction. These criteria of science, however, are not met by the theory of marginal productivity. As Corry remarks: "... the neoclassical approach does not in general predict the course of relative shares."[103] All that it says is that it depends on the growth rate of factor supply, the elasticity of substitution, the character of technical progress and differences in capital intensity. Blaug, too, comes to the conclusion that "no determinate theory of relative shares in the presence of technical progress has yet emerged"[104] within the theory of marginal productivity.

THE AMOUNT OF TECHNICAL CHANGE TREATED AS AN ENDOGENOUS VARIABLE

As has already been mentioned, neo-classical growth models regard the amount of technical change in general as an exogenous variable. In this representation technical progress is a kind of manna falling from heaven without mankind having to make any special effort. Even embodied technical progress, which becomes effective by means of investments, was treated by the theory as externally given. "The vintage approach," write Hahn and Matthews, "does not necessarily involve any departure from the assumption that technical progress takes place at an externally given rate. The difference from the orthodox approach is merely that the manna of technical progress falls only on the latest machines."[105]

[103] B. A. Corry: *op. cit.*, p. 39.

[104] M. Blaug: *Economic Theory in Retrospect*, London, 1968, p. 446.

[105] F. H. Hahn and R. C. O. Matthews: The Theory of Economic Growth: a Survey, *The Economic Journal*, December 1964, pp. 837–838.

This treatment of technical progress, writes Arrow, is "basically a confession of ignorance."[106] Being unaware of its exact interrelationships, writes Schmookler, the followers of the theory did not take technical progress into account as a dependent variable.[107] Considering it as a dependent variable is aggravated by the fact that the investigations into the efficiency of investments made in scientific research and vocational training are as yet in their infancy. "These expenditures have for long been recalcitrant to theoretical treatment..."[108] "We are still a long way", writes Solow, "from having any quantitative estimate of the pay-off to society of resources devoted to research, education, and improvements in allocative efficiency."[109] Such investigations are aggravated, among other things, by the significant time-lag existing between the investments in research and the training of qualified labour on the one hand, and the manifestation of economically profitable results on the other, and, further, by the fact that these results are spread over a long period of time. And later economists began really to think that technical progress is primarily not an economic phenomenon, "that its causes lay in other domains of human behaviour and therefore should in principle be treated in the same way as earthquakes."[110] Thus the golden-age, or natural rate of growth, too was viewed as a non-malleable, exogenous datum of the model. "... any economy has to live, after all, at such a rate which was destined for it by nature."[111] More recently, however, we can increasingly come across the view that technical progress, though it contains exogenous elements, has a predominantly endogenous character. "It is only a minimal fraction [viz. in technical progress—A.M.] that can be imputed to the simple brain-wave of a mind not equipped with resources."[112] Arrow says that "... a view of economic growth that depends so heavily on an exogenous variable... is hardly intellectually satisfactory."[113] As we have seen, he also attempted to represent changes in the worker's production experience, which is part of technical progress, as an endogenous process. The coming into prominence of induced technical progress is an attempt to represent it as a factor that can be manipulated in respect of its direction. Under the conditions of scientific–technical revolution, attempts have also been made within the neo-classical growth model to treat the amount of technical change as an endogenous variable, to establish a functional relationship between the amount of technical change and spendings on the development of technical know-how and the improvement of vocational training. This finds expression in the statements that "the creation of new knowledge is increasingly becoming a particular eco-

[106] K. J. Arrow: The Economic Implications of Learning by Doing, *The Review of Economic Studies*, June 1962, p. 155.

[107] J. S. Schmookler: Technological Change and Economic Theory, *The American Economic Review*, May 1965, p. 335.

[108] T. Balogh. and P. P. Streeten: The Coefficient of Ignorance, *Bulletin of the Oxford University Institute of Economics and Statistics*, May 1963, p. 99.

[109] R. M. Solow: Technical Progress, Capital Formation and Economic Growth, *The American Economic Review*, May 1962, p. 86.

[110] J. S. Schmookler: *op. cit.*, p. 335.

[111] G. Bombach: Von der Neoklassik zur modernen Wachstums- und Verteilungstheorie, *Schweizerische Zeitschrift für Volkswirtschaft und Statistik*, September 1964, p. 431.

[112] W. Krelle: Beeinflussbarkeit und Grenzen des Wirtschaftswachstums, *Jahrbücher für Nationalökonomie und Statistik*, August 1965, p. 7.

[113] K. J. Arrow: *op. cit.*, p. 155.

nomic branch."[114] "... the production of new technology is itself an economic activity."[115] "Inventions are produced within the system. An invention is viewed as a new process of production."[116]

In addition to capital and labour, Weizsäcker complements the Cobb–Douglas production function by a new input element, expenditures of technical development, by R. Its exponent, c, expresses the measure of contribution of these expenditures to production. Production function is in this case no longer homogeneous and linear, the sum of the exponents need not be 1.[117]

In the next section we are going to examine more closely Eltis's attempts[118] to treat the amount of technical change as an endogenous variable of the model.

While in one of his studies Phelps attempts to prove[119] that golden-age growth is also possible by including in the model technical progress as a dependent variable, Eltis's conclusions mean in fact the negation of neo-classical ideas concerning the golden-age path in the case of endogenous technical progress.

Let us have a look now at Eltis's model.

Eltis's model

Eltis holds the view that "it is clear from almost all approaches to what determines an economy's equilibrium rate of growth that the rate of technical progress has a dominant influence upon it."[120] What factors influence the rate of technical progress? This is the question he explores in his paper to be discussed below. He establishes a relationship between the rate of technical progress and total costs required to realize it.

The function RR as represented in his model (see Figure 92) "shows the amount entrepreneurs expect to have to spend on research and development *per annum* in order to discover how to produce capital equipment which will permit reductions in unit costs of production with new equipment at various proportional annual rates."[121]

X is the amount of annual expenditures of research and development, m the annual percentage decrease in unit costs of production.

Curve RR cuts the perpendicular axis in its positive section as, according to Eltis, it is rational to assume that first a minimum sum has to be assigned to research and development before any appreciable result can be achieved. It is further rational to suppose in the functional relationship expressed in RR "that a high annual rate of cost reduction will be more expensive than a low rate, and

[114] W. A. Jöhr: Gedanken über die Wirtschaft in hundert Jahren, *Schweizerische Zeitschrift für Volkswirtschaft und Statistik,* September 1964, p. 385.

[115] J. S. Schmookler: *op. cit.,* p. 335.

[116] W. D. Nordhaus: Theory of Innovation. An Economic Theory of Technological Change, *The American Economic Review,* May 1969, p. 19.

[117] C. Ch. Weizsäcker: *Wachstum, Zins und optimale Investitionsquote,* Basel, 1962, p. 66.

[118] W. A. Eltis: The Determination of the Rate of Technical Progress, *The Economic Journal,* September 1971, pp. 502–524.

[119] See E. S. Phelps: Models of Technical Progress and the Golden Rule of Research, *The Review of Economic Studies,* April 1966, pp. 133–145.

[120] W. A. Eltis: *op. cit.,* p. 502.

[121] W. A. Eltis: *op. cit.,* p. 503.

that beyond a certain point it will become increasingly expensive to reduce cost at a higher proportional rate."[122] Making such assumptions, the curve RR will slope upwards at an increasing rate.

Eltis does not accept the principle of diminishing returns in the field of research and development as he maintains that all discovery serves as a starting-point for further discoveries. He explains the increasing slopeness of the curve RR by the fact that costs rise at a growing rate, while the rate of technical progress grows by the same percentage only because entrepreneurs want to achieve an increasingly higher rate of development within a given period of time, say, a year.

Eltis tries to answer the question how much it is worthwhile for entrepreneurs to spend on research and development per annum, by referring to the entrepreneurs' profit-maximizing behaviour. He thinks that it may be assumed that "the development of capital equipment which permits production with unit costs which are lower than they otherwise would be by a proportion of m ... will allow the firm responsible for these developments to charge a price for the equipment it markets... which is higher than it otherwise would be by a proportion of $u \cdot m$ (here u is a constant)."[123] And, for simplicity's sakes he assumes that the extra profit expected to be achieved in realization will also rise by a $u \cdot m$ per cent, that is, that entrepreneurs may hope to get twice as much extra profit after selling a piece of equipment which reduces the production costs by 10 per cent than by selling one which reduces the costs only by 5 per cent.

If an entrepreneur is able to sell equipment to the annual value of I, and makes a discovery which cuts costs by m, he may expect to realize an annual I times

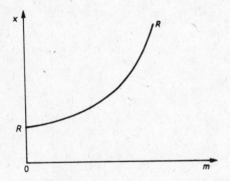

Figure 92

$u \cdot m$ extra profit. According to this assumption, he may get twice as much extra profit by a particular cost reduction if investment doubles in the economy, and thus he is able to sell twice as much equipment. In this way, the extra profit that can be realized from successful research and development is proportionate, on the one hand, to the proportionate cost reduction made possible by develop-

[122] *Ibid.*
[123] W. A. Eltis: *op. cit.*, p. 506.

507

ment, and, on the other, to the expected sales of equipment. This extra profit of the size I times $u \cdot m$ is represented in Figure 93 by the line DD starting from the origin with a slope of $u \cdot I$. If the sales of equipment increase twofold, threefold, etc., always new DD lines must be drawn with a twofold, threefold, etc. slope. And the entrepreneur maximizing his profit with a given DD will increase his research and development expenditures up to the point at which "the extra profits obtained from the development of superior capital equipment exceed the cost of developing such equipment by the greatest possible amount...,"[124] and this will be the case when the gap between DD and RR is at a maximum, that is, where the tangent drawn to RR becomes parallel to DD, when $\dfrac{dX}{dm}$ equals $I \cdot u$. The larger the market for investment goods and the steeper DD, the farther to the right will shift the point of tangency of the curve RR and of the tangent parallel to it, and the larger amounts entrepreneurs will be ready to spend on research and development, the greater will be the rate of technical development. Eltis is of the opinion that the growth in employment is also accompanied by increasing investment, and this also exercises a favourable effect on the rate of technical progress.

The results obtained so far have been based on the assumption that entrepreneurs undertaking research and development seek to maximize their profit. The profit thus realized will be a lasting one if there is no free entry into research and development.

Equilibrium within an industry, however, supposing undisturbed competition, does not tolerate super-normal profits. If entry is free, firms will always enter where DD is above RR, consequently the slope of DD will decline. The entry of extra firms will continue until DD touches RR. In this case, abnormal profits

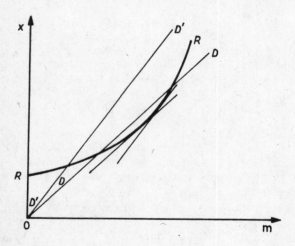

Figure 93

124 W. A. Eltis: *op. cit.*, 507.

508

earned by research and development will disappear. This point of tangency, says Eltis, is independent of the investment rate of the economy, since we can obtain it by drawing from the origin, a tangent to RR, and thus it will simply be a function of RR. "This means that any connection between aggregate investment and the distance along RR, which it pays firms to choose, will completely disappear..."[125]

Eltis, on the other hand, wants to prove that a higher rate of investment increases technical progress. Therefore he finds that the argument that the point of tangency of DD and RR is the final equilibrium position, is not a strong one. In the case of free entry it is more realistic, he thinks, to assume that the equilibrium has come to be established from the right-hand point of intersection of DD and RR. Extra profit will disappear here, too, and thus this field of activity does not attract other firms, while firms operating there are better off "in terms of market share, size and aggregate profits."[126] If, however, there is no fear of entry and, according to Eltis, in a modern economy this is just as realistic as the former one, equilibrium will come about, as has already been shown, at the maximum amount of extra profit. In both cases it is evident that the shift of DD as a result of brisker investment activity will also change the equilibrium position, and thus the rate of technical progress depends on the size of the savings ratio.

The relation $m_r = A_r + B_r s$ expresses in Eltis how the rate of technical progress depends on the market for investment goods, or on the investment or savings ratios determining the size of that market. m_r is the rate of technical progress attributable to research and development, and A_r and B_r are constants expressing the character of the relationship. If $A_r < 0$, then m_r will change at a lower rate than s, if $A_r > 0$, it will change at a higher rate than s.

But in his view the rate of technical progress also depends on exogenous elements: $m = A + Bs$. m without any index is the rate of total technical progress generated by exogenous elements and investment. $A = A_e + A_r$, where A_e expresses the effect of the exogenous elements on m, while A_r is an endogenous element, a constant expressing the dependence of the rate of technical progress on investment. $B = B_r + B_z$, where both B_r and B_z are endogenous elements. B_r expresses, as we have seen, the dependence of the rate of technical progress upon the volume of investment, while B_z expresses the effect of the increase in vocational training, in learning, upon technical progress, and this effect is, in Eltis's view, proportional to the savings and investment ratio, respectively. If $B = 0$, then $m = A$, and technical progress is completely exogenous (in this case A_r contained in A is not taken account of as m is not dependent on s). If, however, $A = 0$, technical progress is entirely of an endogenous character, a function of investment. The function of technical progress is situated in reality, according to Eltis, between these two extreme values.

Eltis's model is an attempt to construct in the most general terms a function-relationship between technical progress and certain exogenous and endogenous variables. Economics is still in its infancy in giving a concrete formulation of this relationship. Eltis is undoubtedly right in saying that the expansion of the market stimulates technical progress, but a concrete relationship in this respect is far from

125 W. A. Eltis: *op. cit.*, pp. 508–509.
126 W. A. Eltis: *op. cit.*, p. 509.

being worked out. It is unlikely that the *RR* function does not change in technical development, that technical progress does not affect the costs of technical development.

From Eltis's model, however, just because it treats technical progress partly as an endogenous variable, depending on the size of the market of investment goods or the amount of employment, peculiarities opposed to the characteristics of the golden-age path can be derived, despite the vague character of the relationships inherent in the model.

1. Let us assume that national income increases and the savings or investment ratios are constant. In this case investment increases with the national income, the slope of curve *DD* will be greater and greater, and, at a given *RR* function, the point of equilibrium continually shifts to the right, as a result of which the rate of technical progress will steadily rise until the *RR* curve becomes vertical. In this case, no steady rate of growth is possible until the *RR* curve becomes perpendicular.

2. If in two economies the *RR* functions are identical, and so are the rates of employment, but the savings or investment ratio is larger in the one than in the other, "... the economy with a higher share of investment will have faster technical progress, and a faster equilibrium rate of growth."[127] Treating technical progress as an endogenous variable, Eltis comes to a conclusion diametrically opposed to the view presented by most of the neo-classical growth models: the equilibrium rate of growth is not independent of the savings and investment ratios, it can be influenced by their changes. Conlisk, who also regarded technical progress as an endogenous variable, came to a similar conclusion in his model based on neo-classical foundations: "... the equilibrium growth rate of the model is found to increase with the increase in the rate of saving. This is in strong contrast to the models cited in the first paragraph (and to neo-classical growth models in general), which predict that the equilibrium growth rate of an economy will be unaffected by a change in the savings rate."[128] In Eltis, by the way, steady growth will be a possibility with no tendency for *DD* to shift in relation to *RR* as economic growth takes place. Then there will be particular equilibrium points where *DD* and *RR* are parallel and where they intersect.

3. If in two economies the *RR* functions are identical, and so are the savings and investment ratios, but the level of employment is higher in one than in the other, investment will be greater at the higher level of employment, and thus the slope of the *DD* curve will be steeper, and consequently the rate of technical progress will be greater, too. Given a steadily growing employment, *DD* continuously increases with employment, the equilibrium point, at which *RR*, taken to be constant, and *DD* become parallel to one another, shifts steadily to the right, and the rate of technical progress keeps increasing. In Eltis's opinion, no steady-state growth can exist unless those sectors of the economy in which the rate of technical progres can be influenced by research and development expenditures

[127] W. A. Eltis: *op. cit.*, p. 513.

[128] J. Conlisk: The Neoclassical Growth Model with Endogenously Positioned Technical Change Frontier, *The Economic Journal*, June 1969, p. 348.

are so insignificant compared with the economy as a whole that their effect can be ignored.

4. Eltis's model rejects the basic feature typical of the golden age, that the capital-efficiency-expanding effect of technical progress is offset by the substitution effect, that, to put it differently, the capital–output ratio should increase by the same rate as does the savings ratio.

The natural rate of growth $G_n = m+n$, (to use Eltis's symbols), where m is the rate of technical progress and n the growth rate of population. Substituting the relation set up by Eltis for m into the formula given for the growth rate, we obtain: $G_n = A+n+Bs$. As already known, the equilibrium capital–output ratio

$$C_r = \frac{s}{G_n}, \text{ that is, } = \frac{s}{A+n+Bs}.$$

Since the rate of technical progress is partly endogenous, if s is doubled, C_r will not grow twofold, that is, the effect of technical progress on expanding the efficiency of capital will not be offset by the substitution effect. If now technical progress is completely endogenous, and the growth rate of population is 0, the change in s will have no effect whatever on the capital–output ratio.

SOME CRITICAL REMARKS ON NEO-CLASSICAL GROWTH THEORIES

1. Having surveyed the development of the neo-classical growth models we come to the conclusion that its representatives, in trying to trace the rate of growth to its components, take an increasingly wider scale of influencing factors into account. Compared with Solow's 1956 version, this approach has undergone a significant change during the past two decades. Part of the deficiencies of the earlier models, as they were revealed during the further development of the theory, have been eliminated by the initiators of the theory themselves. Certain recent varieties, however, which have been created within the system, abandon the rigid assumptions of the greater part of the neo-classical growth models, and undermine thereby their basic principles.

The representatives of the neo-classical growth models are right when they rank technical progress first of all factors affecting the rate of growth. They make interesting attempts to distinguish the effect of embodied from non-embodied technical progress, as well as the effect of the expenditures on scientific research and the improvement of skilled manpower on the rate of technical progress. They correctly point out that as a result of the investment rate only a temporary shift takes place in the age-distribution of capital stock in favour of the latest vintage of equipment, and thus the increase in the rate of investment, at least through the age-distribution of the stock of capital, can only temporarily influence the rate of technical progress. Of interest also is Eltis's investigation into how the increase in the demand for investment goods stimulates technical development. Real-life interconnections are studied in the attempts to show, by means of induced technical progress, how the increase in the share of wages in total costs shifts technical progress towards labour-saving innovations, how entrepreneurs try to reduce capital costs too in the value of product by applying capital-saving technical innovations.

Placing emphasis, in contrast to Harrod and Domar, on the effect of technical progress, the neo-classical growth models call attention to the fact that an increase in the savings ratio provides only limited possibilities to raise the rate of growth.

2. A basic shortcoming of the neo-classical growth models, however, lies in the fact that they examine the quantitative, technical aspect of the growth process, but do not analyse it from the viewpoint of the influence of those social relations on the growth process in the framework of which growth takes place. By assuming neutral technical progress not to affect income distribution relations, or by seeking to find the conditions for the long-run equilibrium of constant relative shares, the neo-classical models obstruct the exploration of the effect of production relations upon economic growth, at least by the effect upon it of distribution relations. Reference to the interconnection between growth and production relations can be found at most in the form of the effect of the savings ratio changing with the change in distribution relations on the rate of growth.

In general, the neglect of any analysis of the dependence of growth on social relations, whether existing social relations support or impede the growth process, is a common deficiency of non-Marxian growth models—excepting those growth models which are concerned with the problems of the economically underdeveloped countries.

In the abstract growth schemes many basic problems of real economic growth are missing. Some of them are pointed to by Mrs. Robinson. She denies that poverty will disappear with the increase in social wealth, and therefore the problem of poverty need not be studied. On the contrary, says Mrs. Robinson, the majority of population, considerably more than 50 per cent, live below a decent standard, however, high the absolute level of their consumption. According to her, a decent acceptable standard of life is somewhere the average that society can provide.

Technical progress, Mrs. Robinson goes on in enumerating the serious problems accompanying growth, "alters the composition of the labour force, making more places for educated workers and fewer for uneducated, but opportunities to acquire qualifications are kept ... for those families who have them already. As growth goes on at the top, more and more families are thrown out at the bottom."[129] These problems are also discussed by Galbraith in Chapter XXI of his work *The New Industrial State*.

Mrs. Robinson also mentions the serious problem of the pollution of the environment as a result of growth, a fact that the growth models also fail to discuss.

Let us add to the above deficiencies the claim of neo-classical growth model that the mechanisms of the capitalist economy ensure economic growth fully utilizing the results of technical progress and the available stock of capital and labour. This obviously contradicts reality. We have already pointed out and, in criticizing Kaldor's growth model, we shall repeatedly emphasize that in a capitalist economy left to itself no steady-state growth can exist for a longer period of time. This economy is bound to be exposed to the danger of stagnation.

---

[129] J. Robinson: The Second Crisis of Economic Theory, *The American Economic Review*, May 1972, p. 7.

3. Let us now explore some specific features of neo-classical growth models in some detail.

In trying to find the conditions of dynamic equilibrium, these models divorce the effect of technical progress from the substitution effect. Neutral technical progress in the Hicksian sense presupposes from the outset that technical progress does not affect factor proportions, that their changes are independent of technical progress. If technical progress were not neutral, this would change the substitution relationship between capital and labour, and thereby the production elasticities of capital and labour. The constancy of the latter, however, is a precondition for dynamic equilibrium. In the case of neutral technical progress in the Hicksian sense, just as of any model ignoring technical progress, substitution arises only if changes occur in the relative scarcities of factors. The capital–labour ratio changes only because in a growth process, which is also influenced by technical progress, national income rises, and its rate exceeds that of the increase in labour force, and thus, assuming the savings ratio to be constant, capital stock will also rise at a higher rate than the labour force. Consequently, it is not technical progress but simply the quantitative increase in capital that causes the capital–labour ratio to increase. Technical progress has at best the effect that, as a result of changes in factor proportions, the marginal productivity of the relatively increased factor will begin to fall from a higher level, which in turn makes it possible to go a long way in substituting capital for labour without the marginal or average productivity of capital falling below the level attained along the golden-age path.

In the neo-classical growth model, assuming Hicks's neutral technical progress, the substitution effect is taken to be equivalent to the effect of technical progress. Along the golden-age path, the latter's effect on the efficiency of capital is always counterbalanced by the substitution effect. Krelle emphasizes that if technical progress is not neutral, then, "apart from a few uninteresting cases, there is no constant equilibrium growth rate at all."[130] The two effects are separated from one another even in the vintage model, since that model also presupposes that technical progress does not affect, under equilibrium conditions, the capital–labour ratio. "I am assuming", writes Solow with respect to the vintage model, "that factor proportions are freely variable throughout the life of the equipment."[131] The same golden-age rate can materialize, depending on the savings ratio, at the most different capital–labour ratios in the vintage model, too. The inclusion of induced technical progress merely serves the aim to eliminate, by manipulating the direction of technical progress, the unfavourable substitution effect on an increase, independent of technical progress, in the capital–labour ratio.

At the same time, the assumption of neutral technical progress has also the advantage that it will not change production elasticities. These changes would give rise to serious difficulties in the growth model since "there is hardly anything possible except conjecture about how the exponents, m and $1-m$, change over time."[132] Obviously, it was these advantageous characteristics that Solow had

[130] W. Krelle: *op. cit.*, p. 20.

[131] R. Solow: Investment and Technical Progress. In: *Mathematical Methods in the Social Sciences*, Stanford, California, 1960, p. 89.

[132] A. Ott: Produktionsfunktion, technischer Fortschritt und Wirtschaftswachstum. In: *Einkommensverteilung und technischer Fortschritt*, Berlin, Duncker-Humblot, 1959, p. 190.

in mind when writing about the assumption of neutrality of technical progress in his growth model: "there is not much evidence for or against this assumption; since it is a great convenience, it will be adopted without comment."[133]

It is on this separation of the substitution effect from the effect of technical progress that the assumption is based that by changing the savings or investment ratio, capital per head, and through it the capital coefficient too, can be changed at will. It is exactly this relationship between the savings or investment ratio and capital per head or the capital coefficient, which ensures the stability of the neo-classical growth model, the adjustment of G_w to G_n. If the savings ratio decreases, the growth rate of the stock of capital falls below the growth rate of output, capital per head will, independently of technical development, decrease and the capital coefficient will fall until dynamic equilibrium is restored. The opposite process will take place if the savings ratio rises.

Let us examine to what extent the basic assumptions of the neo-classical growth models and the statements based on them are realistic. Is the assumption of neutral technical progress not affecting the substitution relations between capital and labour a realistic one? Can it be accepted that the substitution effect counterbalances the effect that technical progress exerts on increasing the efficiency of capital? Can the capital–labour ratio be altered at will even without technical progress, merely by an increase in the savings ratio? To what extent is the growth rate independent of the savings ratio? The clarification of these questions is of crucial importance for the appraisal of the neo-classical growth model.

The representatives of the neo-classical growth models are right in saying that if full employment is ensured in the economy and the workers are always supplied with adequate, up-to-date equipment which corresponds to the given level of development of technical knowledge, then the highest growth rate that can be lastingly maintained depends on the rate of technical progress and on the growth rate of the labour force. This view is shared, by the way, also by Harrod who accepts the basic elements of the Keynesian theoretical system. However, full employment of the available labour force supplied with the latest equipment in all fields of production is a mere ideal assumption which has never been realized and which contradicts the law of unequal development; furthermore, there exists no mechanism for its realization.

The neo-classical growth models presuppose that at a given level of technical knowledge the entrepreneurs can avail themselves of various techniques for the production of any product with various capital–labour ratios, with different per capita output, with different capital–output ratios, and they choose that one from among them with which they can produce their products with minimum costs at the given factor prices. Thus the substitution effect may also assert itself without the development of technical knowledge. This assumption has given rise to disputes among non-Marxian economists. They have raised the objection that the increased growth in capital per head presupposes new inventiveness and new production experiences on the part of workers, and expresses therefore a different level of technical knowledge. It is this intertwining of technical progress and of the substitution effect that induced Kaldor, among others, to discard the production function and to con-

[133] R. Solow: *op. cit.*, p. 141.

struct instead the technical progress function. Theory has never clarified what is meant by the assertion that the various production techniques represent the given level of technical knowledge.

Let us suppose, however, that the production techniques out of which entrepreneurs can choose represent the same level of technical progress. In this case it can be assumed that a change in relative factor prices has an effect on the technique the entrepreneurs wish to adopt. But the capital-absorbing capacity of the economy depends on technical progress, that is, technical progress sets limits to the possibility of changing capital per head and determines the scope of functioning of the substitution effect. Consequently, the substitution effect is not independent of technical progress which is, therefore, not neutral. Or, as Aukrust writes, "there is much less possibility than generally assumed"[134] to increase the capital–labour ratio at the given level of technical progress. If capital per head is too high and its magnitude exceeds the quantity that can be absorbed by technical progress, part of the capital will remain unutilized. Then the substitution effect can no longer function with respect to this part of the capital. The opposite case, a discretional decrease in the capital–labour ratio, though conceivable *in abstracto,* leads "to such methods as were already in use earlier, and have therefore no future in the long run."[135]

Let us assume full employment and that all workers are supplied with up-to-date equipment. Hence, the economy develops at a natural growth rate determined by the rate of technical progress and by the growth rate of the working population. If the savings ratio rises, the rate of growth cannot increase. For society to use the increased quantity of capital, it has to transfer to a higher level of growth at the given growth rate. As a result, the capital–output ratio will change. Thus, by changing the savings ratio, the capital–output ratio can be altered through the substitution effect. But the limits within which it can be altered are set by the level of technical knowledge, in the same way as the level of growth society can reach at a given point of time by means of changing the savings ratio is also determined by the level of technical knowledge.

By increasing the savings ratio it is of course also possible to act upon the rate of growth if the capital stock in the economy is not sufficient to supply, at full employment, the working population with up-to-date equipment which corresponds to the existing level of technical knowledge.

The impact of the changing of the savings ratio on the capital–output ratio is only interesting in the context of the given level of technical knowledge which in turn limits the sphere of that impact.

The historical tendency of the development of the capital–output ratio depends on technical progress decisively. And for a given growth rate to materialize, a smaller or larger proportion of national income, depending on the development trend of the capital–output ratio, has to be saved. In this approach we have turned our attention from the substitution effect to technical progress. It is a basic characteristic of the relationship between the savings ratio and the capital–output ratio that whenever the latter changes as a result of technical progress, that range

---

[134] Cited in K. Oppenländer: *Die moderne Wachstumstheorie,* Berlin, Duncker-Humblot, 1963, p. 220.
[135] C. Ch. Weizsäcker: *op. cit.,* p. 60.

of the savings ratio in which the capital–output ratio can be manipulated has to be shifted in the interest of maintaining the existing growth rate.

If technical progress increases the capital–output ratio, then, for the growth rate G_n to be maintained, either the savings ratio has to be increased along any given growth path or, at an unchanged savings ratio, a lower-level growth path has to be chosen. If at the given level of technical knowledge this is no longer possible, only a part of the workers can be supplied with up-to-date equipment, while, for the lack of such equipment, the rest of them cannot be employed. Thus the substitution effect cannot come into force.

If, however, technical progress diminishes the capital–output ratio, then, for the growth rate G_n to be maintained, either the savings ratio has to be decreased along the individual growth paths or a higher-level growth path has to be chosen. If at the existing level of technical knowledge this is no longer possible, part of the capital stock will remain idle. So the substitution effect cannot again come into force, this time with respect to the capital left idle.

If technical progress does not affect the capital–output ratio, then, for the given growth rate G_n to be maintained, the savings ratio need not be changed. If we increase or decrease it, then a higher- or a lower-level growth path will have to be chosen, but, as has already been mentioned, this is only possible within the limits set by technical progress.

We have made the capital–output ratio dependent basically upon technical progress and, to a lesser extent, upon the production technique chosen at the given level of technical progress, as if expressing thereby the fact that the working of the substitution effect is limited by technical progress. In reality, however, the development of the capital–output ratio, though depending, as regards its historical tendency, on technical progress, is a much more complex process. The capital–output ratio is always the resultant of several factors. Completely untenable is the view held by the advocates of neo-classical growth theory that along the golden-age path the capital–output ratio is merely a monotonous function of the savings ratio: it increases when the savings ratio rises, and decreases when it declines. Even at a given savings ratio, the capital–output ratio may change, depending, among other things, on the structure of investments. Even non-Marxian economists emphasize that a theory of capital–output ratio would be needed to determine the growth rate.

4. Let us now examine the question of the optimal investment ratio. Does it contain any rational elements?

At the given level of technical knowledge, depending on which of the available production technique entrepreneurs in the different branches of production choose, the level of net output per man will be different. If it were possible to construct a social production function by which the amount of output per man could be revealed at the various values of the capital–labour ratio and at the given level of technical development, then it would also be possible to find out what proportion of these amounts of output per man should be accumulated to ensure a given growth rate, and what would be the capital–labour ratio whose corresponding accumulation proportion would maximize the volume of consumption.

But let us scrutinize the neo-classical theory of the optimal investment ratio.

Entrepreneurs seek to earn maximum profit and choose, with this in view, the appropriate production technique at the given level of technical knowledge.

A production method, however, in which entrepreneurs maximize the volume of their profits, absolutely need not ensure also a maximum volume of consumption.

According to the neo-classical price theory, the creation of equilibrium equally ensures, within the scope of existing production possibilities, maximum profit for entrepreneurs and a maximum amount of subjectively interpreted utility for consumers. In neo-classical theory, both maxima can be reached simultaneously in the case of a subjectively interpreted utility concept, but no reference can be found as to whether the maximum volume of consumption can be reconciled with the maximum volume of profit. Studies conducted in this field ought to have revealed how the endeavour to gain maximum profit conflicts with the interest of the consuming masses. By the way, whichever growth path entrepreneurs should choose in a capitalist economy, lasting unemployment and idle capital make it impossible from the very outset to keep production at a level which ensures the maximum volume of consumer goods.

According to neo-classical growth models, capital per man and output per man will increase along the golden-age path corresponding to the different savings ratios at identical and steady rates, technical progress will not affect the substitution relations, and thus the savings ratio which ensured the maximum volume of consumption at a given point of time will also ensure it at any other point of time along the corresponding growth path.

Having supposed that the historical development tendency of the capital–output ratio decisively depends on technical progress, if in the course of growth technical progress increases or decreases the capital–output ratio, society can only maintain the existing rate of growth if it changes the savings ratio or if it chooses a lower- or higher-level growth path. But in this case the maximum consumption belonging to the existing growth rate can only be ensured if the optimal investment ratio changes. However, as the representatives of the theory emphasize, a very long time is needed before the economy adjusts itself to the growth path which corresponds to the changed savings ratio. R. Sato writes that "... the adjustment process in the neo-classical system of variable proportions takes place only at an extremely slow rate."[136] Already the long adjustment process prevents the realization of an optimum investment ratio from becoming a realistic objective of economic policy.

Krelle points out that, precisely owing to the long adjustment period, not only the laws of equilibrium growth but also those of the transitory period have to be explored.[137]

The problems related to the measurement of capital may also cause difficulties in the neo-classical growth model. Proceeding from one growth path to another, capital per head will grow at a given point of time, and the rate of interest, which measures the rate of return to capital, will fall. As long as in the process of its fall the interest rate has not reached the golden-age rate of growth, the adjustment to

[136] R. Sato: The Harrod-Domar Model *vs* Neo-classical Growth Model, *The Economic Journal*, June 1964, p. 387.

[137] Cf. W. Krelle, *op. cit.*

517

a higher-level growth path, which represents a lower interest rate, will increase per capita consumption. Taking into account the impact that a fall in the interest rate exerts on the evaluation of capital goods, it is not sure, as shown above, that a growth path with a lower rate of interest means greater capital per head. Thus, a fall in the interest rate which is higher than the golden-age growth rate does not necessarily increase per capita consumption either. And if, at an interest rate equal to the golden-age rate of growth, the system has a switch point, then two techniques belong to this rate of interest, each with a different capital–labour ratio and, consequently, with different per capita consumptions.

Chapter 4

KALDOR'S GROWTH THEORY

STATEMENT OF THE THEORY

Kaldor's model occupies a specific place among the various growth theories. Kaldor, just as the neo-classical theoreticians of growth, attempts to prove the existence of golden-age growth and to demonstrate its stability. He also assumes that the golden-age growth rate is independent of the savings ratio. But all this he derives from the Keynesian theory by means of an expression peculiar to it: "The present model is based on Keynesian techniques of analysis..."[138] In expounding his growth model, Kaldor criticizes the neo-classical growth model, its theoretical foundations. His objectives, too, are different from those of neo-classical growth models. The adherents of these models did not generally claim real-life representation. Phelps, for example, emphasized that the assumptions of his model very rarely occurred in reality. By contrast, Kaldor intended to find an explanation, by means of his equilibrium growth theory, for the phenomenon which, as he says, can long be observed in the advanced capitalist countries, namely, that the capital–output ratio does not change in the growth process, and development leaves the relative shares of the working and capitalist classes in national income unchanged. Thus Kaldor constructed his growth model with a view to explaining this real process.

The Keynesian character of his model manifests itself primarily in the fact that it is investment which plays the active role in it, while saving is assigned a passive role in that it merely adjusts itself to magnitude of investment. But unlike Keynes's *General Theory,* he uses the saving–investment mechanism for the determination not of national income but of distribution relations. Therefore, going beyond Keynes, Kaldor distinguishes between the propensity to save of the capitalist and working classes. As has already been mentioned, he regards Keynes's under-employment equilibrium as a short-run phenomenon which is inconsistent with the long-run equilibrium of a growing economy. Without assuming full employment, he would have been unable to construct his distribution theory. He points out that saving, at full employment, adjusts itself to changes in investment not through changes in national income. At a given level of output and employment, the amount of saving adjusts itself in his theory to changes in investment through changes in distribution. Since the propensity to save is greater for the capitalist class than for the working class, if the intention to invest

---

[138] N. Kaldor: A Model of Economic Growth. In: *Essays on Economic Stability and Growth,* London, 1960, p. 261.

519

surpasses the intention to save, then relative shares will shift in favour of profit and to the detriment of wages until intended saving, at a given level of propensity to save for the capitalist and working classes, catch with intended investment. Conversely, if the propensity to save is greater than the propensity to invest, relative shares have to change in favour of wages and to the detriment of profit for intended saving to drop to the level of intended investment. Supposing, for simplicity's sake, that investment is made out of profit, that is, if we ignore the savings of the working class, an assumption which corresponds to the reality of capitalism, then the relative share of profit in national income can be determined, according to Kaldor, in the following way:

At the equilibrium of saving and investment

$$\frac{I}{Y} = \frac{s_c P}{Y},$$

whence

$$\frac{P}{Y} = \frac{I}{Y} \cdot \frac{1}{s_c}.$$

that is, the relative share of profit in national income is the product of the investment ratio and the reciprocal of the propensity to save for the capitalist class as a specific multiplier. At a given s_c, the greater the investment ratio, the greater the relative share of profit in national income, and vice versa.

In the neo-classical model, the movement of the rate of interest ensured that all saving should become investment, and thus total demand should grow with total output. In this view, saving rather than investment was to be the determinant. For Kaldor, who asserts the active role of investment, changes in the distribution relations ensure the equilibrium of total demand and total supply through the equilibrium of saving and investment. According to this view, G and G_w cannot persistently deviate from one another. If investment shoots ahead of saving, a change in the overall savings ratio creates their equilibrium through a change in distribution. Kaldor indeed argues with Harrod that even with constant savings propensities for the capitalist and working classes and a constant capital–output ratio, G_w may have different values depending on the level at which changes in distribution form an average propensity to save for the community as a whole.

He also asserts the equality of G_w and G_n as the economy develops, in his view, along the golden-age path.

Determining income distribution by the saving-investment mechanism, by the multiplier effect, he rejects marginal productivity theory, which constitutes the foundation and ensures the stability of the neo-classical model.

He rejects not only the determination of incomes by means of the marginal productivities of factors, but also the neo-classical production function as a whole. Within the neo-classical production function, the dependence of output on the contribution of individual factors is shown by the increment of output which is obtained—under the exclusion of technical progress—by increasing the individual factors unilaterally by an infinitely small unit. And the representatives of neo-classical growth theory accepting the Hicksian classification try to determine the effect of technical progress by the increase in the marginal productivities of factors under the exclusion of the substitution effect, i.e. at a given capital–labour ratio. The separation of these two effects, the effects of substitution and

520

technical progress, plays a basic role in the neo-classical growth model. According to Kaldor, however, it is "arbitrary and artificial" to distinguish the effect of the increase in capital per head at the given level of technical knowledge, that is, movement along the given production, from the effect of technical progress at a given capital–labour ratio as expressed by the shift of the production function. He maintains that the increase in capital per head inevitably leads to the introduction of superior techniques, "which require 'inventiveness' of some kind, though these need not necessarily represent the application of basically new principles or ideas."[139] On the other hand, "most, though not all, technical innovations which are capable of raising the productivity of labour require the use of more capital per man—more elaborate equipment and/or more mechanical power."[140] In his model, it is exactly by means of the increase in capital per man that the development of technical knowledge can be exploited. Owing to this close interrelationship between technical progress and capital accumulation, the separation of their effects on growth is, in his view, unacceptable.

Kaldor's growth model is based, instead of upon the neo-classical production function, upon the *technical progress function,* which no longer contains the assumption that the increase in output per man is due partly to technical progress, partly to the increase in capital per head. He assumes instead a single relationship between the increase in capital and productivity which includes the effect of both factors. It shows at what rate the productivity of labour increases as the rate of capital accumulation enabling the increasingly greater utilization of the current stream of inventions grows. He assumes that the growth of productivity takes place at a certain rate which is maintained even at an unchanged amount of capital per head, because certain innovations make the increase in productivity possible even without additional investments. Therefore, the technical progress function does not start from the origin but from a point somewhat above it. A rate of growth greater than that already depends on the growth rate of the capital stock. There is, however, according to Kaldor, "some maximum beyond which the rate of growth in productivity could not be raised, however fast capital is being accumulated".[141] Hence the TT' curve is likely to be convex upwards and flattens out altogether beyond a certain point (see Figure 94).

If the rate of capital accumulation is less than would be required for the current stream of inventions to be exploited up to the point at which the growth rates of capital and output are equal, the capital–output ratio will decline with the growth rate of accumulation. To the right of point P, however, the growth rate of accumulation exceeds that of output, and the capital–output ratio rises. As we shall see, the mechanisms presented by Kaldor move the economy towards that point of the TT' function at which capital per head increases at the same rate as output per head, the capital–output ratio is constant over time and technical progress is neutral. This point is situated on the TT' curve, where the line drawn from the origin at the angle of 45° cuts it, that is, at the point P. Whether the capital–output ratio will be rising or falling, that is, whether the character of

[139] N. Kaldor: *op. cit.,* p. 264.
[140] N. Kaldor: *op. cit.,* pp. 264–265.
[141] N. Kaldor: *op. cit.,* p. 266.

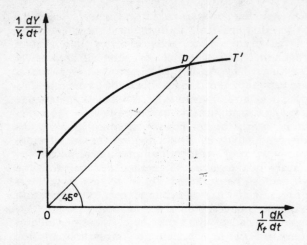

Figure 94

inventions is capital-saving or labour-saving, depends, according to Kaldor, "not on the technical nature of the inventions, but simply on the relationship between the flow of new ideas ... and the rate of capital accumulation."[142]

Taking population to be constant, the growth rate of output for Kaldor is

$$\frac{Y_{t+1} - Y_t}{Y_t} = \alpha'' + \beta'' \frac{I}{K},$$

where α'' is the effect of technical progress not dependent, and β'' the effect of technical progress dependent on the growth rate of capital per head.

The height of the curve TT' expresses the technical dynamism of society, the extent to which it is able to invent, and to which its producers are able to break away from traditional methods and introduce new techniques of production. A burst of new inventions shifts the TT' curve upwards, while a drying up in the flow of ideas pushes it downwards. In the first case there is a fall, in the second a rise in the capital–output ratio.

Steady-state growth requires that the rate of technical progress should be constant over time.

It depends, according to Kaldor, on technical dynamism to what extent society is able to absorb capital. In a society where technical change is insignificant, and producers are reluctant to adopt new techniques, the rate of capital accumulation is necessarily low. It influences, however, the rate at which society is capable of exploiting new techniques.

In Kaldor, technical progress materializes as a result of investment, and therefore, the investment function is closely related to the technical progress function.

[142] N. Kaldor: *op. cit.*, p. 267.

Kaldor has often modified the investment function, but he always chooses it in such a way that the investments, once they have got under way, reinforce themselves and channel the economy towards the golden-age path.

Investment in his model is, on the one hand, a function of the growth rate of output through the accelerator effect. "The model assumes that investment is primarily *induced* by the growth in production itself."[143] Entrepreneurs, according to Kaldor's assumption, expect, when making their investment decisions, that output will grow at the same rate in the future as it increased in the past. Since, at a constant rate of profit, they want to maintain a constant relationship between output and capital stock, if they expect that the profit rate will be the same as it is in the present, they will increase capital stock at the same rate at which production has increased over the last period. By doing so, they raise the actual amount of accumulation to the desired level. On the other hand, investment depends for Kaldor also on changes in the rate of profit. He maintains that, owing to the uncertainty and risk of the future, entrepreneurs prefer such investments whose return takes less time, and make investments with slow returns only if the profit prospects are more favourable. In so far as the profit rate increases, they are ready to increase capital at a rate higher than the one at which output expanded in the past. Thus, the relationship between capital and output is also an increasing function of the expected profit rate.

Once investment is started, output will rise in its wake, and, as has been shown, at a higher rate than that of the increase in capital stock until the golden-age path is reached, and thus output per unit of capital will grow. If, however, entrepreneurs expect that both the profit rate and the rate of growth of output will remain unchanged in the future, they will adjust the increase in capital stock to the growth rate of output. As a result, owing to the more intensive exploitation of technical progress ensured by the higher rate of increase in capital stock, output will rise at a still higher rate. In this representation, investment has a double role: by making use of the results of technical progress it gives rise to the increased growth of output, and at the same time, it is the consequence of increased output, and thus virtually reinforces itself.

As long as, owing to the utilization of the achievements of technical progress, output increases more than capital stock, the accelerator effect will also raise the growth rate of capital stock. Moving along the curve of technical progress, however, we shall come, as the rate of capital stock increases, across a point at which output increases only at the rate of the increase in capital stock. The accelerator effect adjusting the growth rate of capital stock to the growth rate of output will no longer increase the growth rate of capital stock, and output and capital accumulation will now rise at the same rate. The economy has embarked upon the golden-age growth path.

In the neo-classical growth model it was through saving or investment constituting a constant proportion of output, that the rate of increase in capital stock adjusted itself to the growth rate of output, while in Kaldor's model this adjustment takes place through the accelerator effect generated by, and proportionate to,

[143] N. Kaldor and J. A. Mirrlees: A New Model of Economic Growth, *The Review of Economic Studies*, June 1962, p. 175.

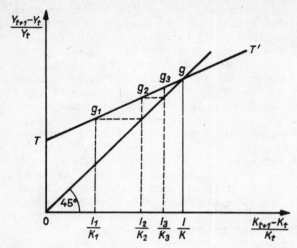

Figure 95

the growth rate of output. The representation of adjustment, however, is similar in both cases. While adjusting itself to the rate of output, the growth rate of capital stock exercises an influence on it. It does this in the neo-classical model by generating the substitution effect, in Kaldor's model by making the exploitation of technical progress possible. In the adjustment process the capital–output ratio changes in both models, in the former as a result of the substitution effect, in the latter as a result of technical progress. In Kaldor's model, however, the savings ratio will also change in the adjustment owing to a change in $\dfrac{I}{Y}$, while in the neo-classical model it is constant. It is typical of Kaldor's model that while the growth rate of capital stock and output, adjusting themselves to one another, direct the economy towards the golden age, both the savings ratio and the capital–output ratio change in the adjustment process.

In Figure 95 a certain initial growth rate of $\dfrac{I_1}{K_1}$ of capital stock increased output at a g_1 rate. Expecting that output will continue to rise at a g_1 rate in the future too, consequently, that the already established capital–output ratio will not change, entrepreneurs will also raise the rate of capital accumulation to g_1. Now output will expand at g_2, a higher rate than g_1. Entrepreneurs will now regard this rate as a lasting one, and will raise capital stock at a g_2 rate, too, as a result of which output will increase at g_3, a rate higher than g_2. Increasing the rate of output and adjusting to it the growth rate of capital stock, the latter will eventually reach the growth rate of output at point g.

Kaldor emphasizes this self-reinforcing effect of investments also when he attributes to them a dual role in respect of the profit rate. Through the saving–investment mechanism profit increases as a result of investments. The increase in profit in turn stimulates investment. This means that once investment is made,

524

it will increase the profit rate until the golden age is reached, which will react on investment and stimulate it in addition to the accelerator effect. The profit rate may be expressed as the product of the profit ratio and the efficiency of capital:

$$\frac{P}{K} = \frac{P}{K} \cdot \frac{Y}{Y} = \frac{P}{Y} \cdot \frac{Y}{K}.$$

The efficiency of capital, $\frac{Y}{K}$ will rise until the attainment of the golden age, because Y grows at a higher rate than K. Thus the increase in the profit rate depends on how the profit share develops. If we take the savings ratio of the working class to be 0, then, as has already been shown, it will be equal to $\frac{I}{Y} \cdot \frac{1}{s_c}$. Since in his view s_c is constant over time, the increase in $\frac{P}{Y}$ depends on the increase in $\frac{I}{Y}$. And $\frac{I}{Y}$ will also grow until the golden age is attained.

According to Kaldor's investment function, $\frac{I}{Y}$ depends, if the profit rate is taken to be constant, on the growth rate of output through the accelerator effect:

$$\frac{I_1}{Y_1} = \frac{Y_1 - Y_0}{Y_0} \cdot \frac{K_1}{Y_1}.$$

And the rise in the growth rate of output more than offsets, until the attainment of the golden age, the fall in the capital–output ratio, so that $\frac{I}{Y}$ will rise and through it the profit rate too, speeding up thereby the attainment of the golden-age growth rate.

Through the accelerator effect and changes in the profit rate Kaldor demonstrates the stability of the golden-age path also in the opposite case, that is, at a growth rate higher than the golden-age rate. In this case capital stock grows at a higher rate than output, and the accelerator effect decreases the growth rate of capital to the level of the growth rate of output, as a result of which, until the attainment of the golden age, output will grow at a lower rate than capital. A fall in the profit rate also influences the decrease in the accumulation rate.

On the golden-age path, capital and output grow at an identical and constant rate in Kaldor's model, too, and thus the capital–output ratio does not change over time. The profit ratio and the investment ratio are constant, and consequently the shares of wages and profit in national income. The profit rate does not change either. Thus Kaldor explains the stability of the capital–output ratio and the relative shares of profit and wages in the national income, as documented by bourgeois statistics in recent years, in such a way that the mechanisms described by him direct the economy towards the golden-age path. Since in the golden age the rates of capital stock and output are identical, therefore

$$\frac{dY}{Y} = \alpha'' + \beta'' \frac{dY}{Y} = \frac{\alpha''}{1 - \beta''}.$$

The golden-age rate is independent of the savings ratio for Kaldor, too. At a constant level of the working population it only depends on technical progress, but if we abandon the assumption of a constant population, it depends on the growth rate of the working population and technical progress. It corresponds, therefore, to the Harrodian G_n. And the growth rate of capital stock could be expressed in this way:

$$\frac{I}{Y} = \frac{I}{Y} \cdot \frac{K}{K} = \frac{I}{K} \cdot \frac{K}{Y},$$

where $\dfrac{I}{Y}$ is the savings ratio, $\dfrac{I}{K}$ the growth rate of capital, and $\dfrac{K}{Y}$ the capital–output ratio, or more exactly, at the equilibrium of saving and investment, the Harrodian C_r. After substitution we obtain the following relationship: $s = \dfrac{I}{K} \cdot C_r.$

From this the growth rate of capital stock $\dfrac{I}{K} = \dfrac{s}{C_r}$, which is Harrod's G_w. Thus, along the golden-age path, $\dfrac{I}{K} = \dfrac{dY}{Y}$, that is, $\dfrac{dY}{Y} = \dfrac{s}{C_r}$, which means that G_w and G_n are equal as in Kaldor's model, too.

Some of the conclusions of Kaldor's growth model are similar to the findings of the neo-classical growth model, with the difference that he arrived at similar results by following the Keynesian approach.

Equally conspicuous is the similarity between Kaldor's technical progress function and the vintage model. In both models a great part of technical progress can be made use of in production only as a result of investment, and in both theories output depends not only on the amount of accumulated capital, but also on its composition. But the vintage model is also a production function in the neo-classical sense, and thus the effect of technical progress is still separated from the substitution effect. It was for that reason that separate production functions had to be set up for the individual vintages. The close interrelationship between technical progress and accumulation will be revealed only if we take into account the long series of successive vintages. For Kaldor, the two effects are not separated from one another. Thus the relationship between technical progress and accumulation is expressed by one single function, the technical progress function. But Kaldor had also learnt from the vintage model. In the first version of the technical progress function capital per head still increased. In his 1962 model he already modified this view. Now the technical progress function applies only to the growth rate of the labour productivity of workers operating newly introduced machines and further, not to the growth rate of capital per worker, but only to the growth rate of investment per worker. More exactly, it only applies to the rate of gross investment, since renewal too is closely connected with technical progress.

SOME CRITICAL COMMENTS ON KALDOR'S GROWTH MODEL

At the time of its appearance, in 1957, Kaldor's growth model was definitely superior to the earlier versions of the neo-classical growth models, which rigidly separated the effect of technical progress from investments. Moreover, it is superior to the present-day versions, too, in so far as it entirely subordinates the substitution effect to the effect of technical progress. It is exactly because of the inseparable relationship between the effects of technical progress and substitution that we cannot find in this model the series of golden-age paths attached to the different amounts of the savings ratio. Therefore, only one golden-age path can exist for Kaldor at the given rate of technical progress.

Kennedy points out the similarity between Kaldor's technical progress function and his own innovation possibility function. Kaldor relates the percentage change in capital per head to the percentage change in output per head. From these two variables it is possible to derive the percentage change in output per unit of capital, and we obtain the percentage change in the efficiency of capital along the technical progress function at a certain percentage change in labour productivity. "... if the technical progress function is known, the innovation possibility function can be derived from it."[144]

In Kaldor's technical progress function, as clearly revealed by Mrs. Robinson in her comment on Kaldor's model, a peculiar succession appears as regards the character of technical progress: "At low rates of growth, there is a capital-saving bias in the succession of techniques and at the high rates, a capital-using bias; there is a regular succession of degrees of bias, first less capital-saving and then more capital-using, corresponding to higher and higher rates of accumulation. At one rate of growth neutral progress obtains."[145]

Without the peculiar form of the technical progress function and without the peculiar succession in utilizing innovations, Kaldor would not have been able to prove its golden-age stability, to demonstrate G_w catching up with G_n, the constancy of the capital–output ratio in the growth process.

Kaldor, however, approaches the changes taking place in capital–output ratio only from the aspect that the capital-absorbing capacity of the economy depends on technical progress. What is completely lacking in his theory is a historical approach which could have disclosed that in the course of its historical development an increase in the capital–output ratio is characteristic of the period in which the transition from manual work to machine work took place. In a more recent stage of development, however, there is a tendency for the capital–output ratio to be stabilized, and indeed to decrease. The reason for it is to be sought, among other things, in the fact that while earlier production changed over from manual work to machine production, in the following stage of development of technology, machines, or production processes using machines, have been improved. Kaldor, however, asserts that changes in the capital–output ratio over time, the character of technical progress, depends not on the character of inventions but on the rela-

---

[144] C. Kennedy: Induced Bias in Innovation and the Theory of Distribution, *The Economic Journal*, September 1969, p. 547.

[145] J. Robinson: *Essays in the Theory of Economic Growth*, London, 1962, p. 117.

tionship between the flow of new ideas and the rate of capital accumulation. In this representation, the rise or fall in the capital–output ratio is not a consequence of the historical development of the productive forces. In any stage of the development of the productive forces the capital–output ratio may decrease if the accumulation rate is low, and may increase if the accumulation rate is high.

But Kaldor is aware of the historical changes in the capital–output ratio, too. "In this first stage of capitalism ... the capital–output ratio ... will show a steady increase..."[146] He attempts to find an explanation for the increase in the capital–output ratio in conformity with the theoretical foundations of his model. In the early stage of capitalism productivity of labour is low. Thus, though in this period the worker's nominal wages hardly surpass the subsistence level, the surplus over the subsistence wage makes only very limited investment possible. It is lower than that required by the accelerator effect and the existing level of the profit rate. As a result of inadequate investment, actual capital cannot come into line with desired capital even at the point of intersection of the ray starting out from the origin at a 45° angle and of the TT' curve, that is, where capital stock and output grow at the same rate. For this it would be necessary for the rate of accumulation to go beyond the point of intersection, where the capital–output is already rising.

What is historical in this explanation of the increase in the capital–output ratio is not the peculiarities of technical progress characteristic of this stage of development, but the circumstance that in the early stage of capitalism labour productivity is low; hence the volume of profit, and thus the size of investment made out of this profit are low, too.

In connection with the technical progress function mention must also be made of the fact that the reference to technical dynamism really only touches the surface of the problems. Why does technical knowledge develop more in one society than in another? Why can one economy make a better use of technical achievements than another, what prevents that economy from doing it? Reference to differences in technical dynamism does not take us any nearer to the solution. Shell succinctly characterizes the formal character of technical dynamism in not going beyond general pronouncements. "The technical progress function is an eclectic amalgam summarizing basic technical and institutional forces in a free enterprise economy."[147] It is obviously more convenient simply to refer to one concept including a number of the most different factors than to examine more closely how the existing social relations influence a country's technical development.

Let us now critically investigate how investments change in the growth process in Kaldor's view.

In his model, it is the growth of national income which gives rise to investment, and investment, in turn, incorporating technical progress, triggers off an even higher rate of increase in national income, which further increases investment. Progress towards the golden-age path helps to increase the profit rate, too. Kaldor stresses the interrelationship between changes in profit rate and investment.

[146] N. Kaldor: *op. cit.*, p. 259.
[147] K. Shell: Toward a Theory of Inventive Activity and Capital Accumulation, *The American Economic Review*, May 1966, p. 62.

If the investment ratio increases within national income, this will increase, given a constant s_c, not only the profit share but also the profit rate. An increasing profit rate, however, will stimulate greater investment, and further increase the anyway growing investment ratio.

We get a different picture of the capitalist growth process if we take into account that the consumption of the capitalist class, in the course of expanding output, is a rather inelastic magnitude able to change slowly, only to an insignificant extent. Even at an unchanged profit share in Kaldor's sense, s_c rises in the growth process, consumer goods embody an ever smaller proportion of the surplus value, and in order to keep the profit share at an unchanged level, the investment ratio has to increase. But the result of an investment activity increasing at a rapid and ever accelerating rate can hardly be other than the expansion of capacities serving the output of consumer goods. For this to take place continually, the capacities have to be fully utilized, and the output of consumer goods has to be stepped up at an increasing rate. In this case, given the inelastic consumption of the capitalist class, a larger and larger proportion of the increasing volume of consumer goods would fall to the share of the working class, increasing its real wages.

Thus, while Kaldor asserts that the increase in output induces investment through the accelerator effect, and that the growth of output increasing until the golden-age path is reached stimulates even greater investment through the increase in the profit share and profit rate, our critique questions Kaldor's statement that, with the increasing share of the working class in the volume of consumer goods produced, investment will grow at a high enough rate for the profit share not to change. The increase in this relative share of the working class decreases the share of the capitalist class in national income, worsens its profit prospects. Why, under such circumstances, should the capitalist class increase investment to such an extent as would be needed to maintain the profit share at an unchanged level? It appears likely that capitalist entrepreneurs would not fully utilize the matured capacities. This, however, impedes investment at a time when the task of keeping the relative share of the capitalist class at an unchanged level requires the expansion of investments at an increasing rate.

If we assume nevertheless a rising long-term trend of development, then its path will be such as outlined by the Hungarian P. Erdős in his model assuming only the existence of industrial capitalists and productive workers.[148]

According to his model, it appears most likely that the output of consumer goods will grow at a slow and increasingly slower rate. But its growth at a slow and an even increasingly slower rate does not require a rapid increase in productive capacities. The accumulation ratio can only be low, because a high accumulation ratio is accompanied by a rapid expansion of capacities. Investment activity does not grow sufficiently enough to offset the causes leading to a decrease in the profit share. In the course of the process here outlined, the profit rate also tends to decline. It declines because the relative lag of the consumption of the capitalist class is not counterbalanced by an adequate increase in investments. A further reason for its decline is, as already noted by Marx, that the volume and value

---

[148] P. Erdős: Reálbér és értéktörvény a kapitalizmusban (Real wages and the law of value under capitalism), *Közgazdasági Szemle*, December 1974, pp. 1380–1382.

of capital stock per man increase. The increase in the productivity of labour and the retarding effect of the development of production combine to result in the growth of unemployment. Erdős asserts, however, that it was only after the great economic crisis of the 1930s that non-Marxian economists of the western world were afraid of the danger of secular stagnation represented in this model. Since that time the crisis-sensitivity of the capitalist economy has decreased. This is due primarily to structural changes in the capitalist economy, among them mainly to the immense expansion of the state sector. The Marxist analysis of this process is dealt with by several studies.[149]

However, the long-run growth of the capitalist economy continues to pose serious problems. The danger of secular stagnation is replaced by the danger of runaway inflation and a concomitant economic chaos.

[149] The most detailed analysis is provided by Péter Erdős in his work *Wages, Profit, Taxation. Studies on Controversial Issues of the Political Economy of Capitalism,* Akadémiai Kiadó, Budapest, 1982.

Part Ten

THE THEORETICAL REFLECTION OF THE PROBLEMS OF INFLATION AND UNEMPLOYMENT IN CONTEMPORARY NON-MARXIAN ECONOMICS

Chapter 1

THE PHILLIPS CURVE DOCTRINE

THE POST-KEYNESIAN EXPLANATION OF THE MOVEMENT
OF MONEY WAGES AND OF INFLATION

Along with the three basic psychological factors, Keynes also regards occasionally "the wage-unit as determined by the bargains reached between employers and employed"[1] as an independent variable. By taking the money wage to be unchanged, he strives to transform the nominal magnitudes into real magnitudes.

However, in the inflationary economy of our days, post-Keynesian economics can no longer treat money wages as an invariable factor. With respect to money wages, Meltzer[2] states that the equation which would make it possible to determine the changing money wages is missing from the Keynesian model.

But in his *General Theory* Keynes does not always regard money wages as invariable. In the chapter on money wages he presents them as a function of demand. It is likely, he writes, that a rise in effective demand will increase the wage-unit (i.e. the wage payed for a unit of work done), because in that case the entrepreneurs are less reluctant to yield to the workers' pressure to raise their money wages.[3] Thus, "the wage-unit may tend to rise before full employment has been reached..."[4] In another place of the *General Theory,* however, Keynes emphasizes that wages are rigid downwards. It was on the basis of these analyses that in 1958 Phillips tried to give an explanation of inflation, which came to receive general interest for years after its appearance. He held the view that the movement of money wages had to be explained in the same way as that of prices, that is, through changes in the demand–supply relationship. He expressed the changes in the relationship between demand and supply on the labour market by the percentage change of unemployment. He examined with econometric means the relation between the rate of change of money wage rates and the change in the percentage level of unemployment. Thus in his model the percentage level of unemployment is the independent variable, and the rate of change of money wage rates the dependent variable. On examining the relationship over a period of more than half a century, he has recognized that the rate of change of money wage rates depends not only on the percentage level of unemployment, expressing the relationship between demand and supply on the labour market, but also on the changes in the demand for labour and thus in unemployment as well: "...in a year

---

[1] See J. M. Keynes: *The General Theory of Employment, Interest and Money,* London, 1936, p. 247.
[2] See A.H. Meltzer: On Keynes's General Theory, *Journal of Economic Literature,* March 1981, p. 57.
[3] See J.M. Keynes: *op. cit.,* pp. 300–301.
[4] J.M. Keynes: *op. cit.,* p. 300.

of rising business activity with the demand for labour increasing and the percentage level of unemployment decreasing, employers will be bidding more vigorously for the services of labour than they would be in a year during which the average percentage unemployment was the same but the demand for labour was not increasing."[5]

In order to represent diagrammatically the relationship between the rate of change of money wage rates and the percentage level of unemployment, however, he takes the average of the rates of change of money wage rates corresponding to the same percentage level of unemployment. According to his estimate, the relationship between the growth rate of money wage rates and the percentage level of unemployment can best be demonstrated by the figures of the period between 1861 and 1913. It was for this reason that he chose them to construct the curve named after him. In this graphical representation he indicated the average values of the rates of change of money wage rates when unemployment moved between 0 and 2, 2 and 3, 3 and 4, 4 and 5, 5 and 7, 7 and 11 per cent. Then to the points thus obtained he constructed a curve best fitting them. Phillips emphasizes that each interval includes years in which unemployment was increasing and years in which it was decreasing, but averaging cancelled out the effect of the changes in unemployment on the rate of change of money wage rates. According to Phillips, the averaging of the observed rates of increase results, at the various levels of employment, in such a rate of increase of money wage rates which could be related to the indicated level of unemployment "if unemployment were held constant at that level."[6]

The curve Phillips constructed by his statistical approach (Figure 96) expresses an inverse relationship between the rate of change of money wage rates and the percentage of unemployment. In explaining the shape of the curve, he asserts that at a low level of unemployment, which expresses a high demand for labour, the percentage rise of money wage rates is great, since employers bid the wage rates up quite rapidly. If, however, a high level of unemployment prevails, which reflects a low demand for labour, then wage rates fall but very slowly, because workers are reluctant to offer their services at less than the prevailing rates. And Phillips states: "The relation between unemployment and the rate of change of wage rates is therefore likely to be highly non-linear."[7]

During the period 1861–1913 there were six and a half fairly regular business cycles with an average period of about eight years. Phillips drew for each phase of the business cycle the actual rate of change of money wage rates in the curve which he constructed on the basis of the average rate of change of money wage rates associated with the various percentages of unemployment. Thus he obtained an anti-clockwise loop configuration (see Figure 97), as unemployment moved through a cycle, which shows that "there is also a clear tendency for the rate of change of money wage rates at any given level of unemployment to be above the average for that level of unemployment when unemployment is decreasing during the upswing of the trade cycle and to be below the average for that level of unemployment when unemployment is increasing during the downswing of the trade

---

[5] A.W. Phillips: The Relation between Unemployment and Rate of Change of Money Wage Rates in the United Kingdom, 1861–1957, *Economica*, November 1958, p. 283.

[6] A.W. Phillips: *op. cit.*, p. 290.

[7] A.W. Phillips: *op. cit.*, p. 283.

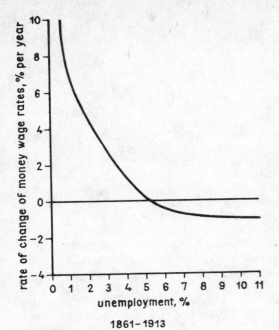

Figure 96

1861–1913

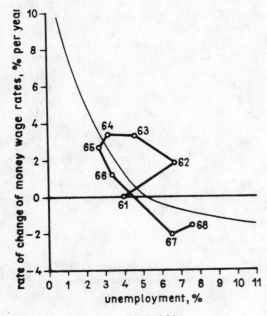

Figure 97

1861–1868

535

cycle."[8] This "loop" expresses in general that the rate of change of money wage rates changes without the simultaneous change of the percentage level of unemployment.

How does now Phillips explain the inflationary process in the light of the relationship he has revealed? Let us illustrate his idea with an example borrowed from him.

Suppose that the productivity of labour rises steadily at a rate of 2 per cent per annum, and aggregate demand also rises in such a way that the percentage level of unemployment remains unchanged, i.e. 2 per cent. Let us further assume that at this level of unemployment wage rates are rising by 3 per cent annually. In this case, for the shares of classes in national income to remain unchanged, the price level must rise by 1 per cent annually. Then real wages will increase at the same rate as the productivity of labour. A continuous inflation will emerge, because the steady growth of aggregate demand stabilizes unemployment at such a percentage level at which money wages increase at a higher rate than labour productivity. Thus inflation itself is the result of the rise in aggregate demand. The adjustment of wages to a 1 per cent price rise has no effect on the inflationary process. If we set out from the assumption that money wage rates increase at the rate of labour productivity, that is, by 2 per cent annually, then the price level would not change because of the rise of money wage rates. If increased demand raises the price level by 1 per cent annually and workers, in order to ensure that their real wage rates continue to increase at the rate of labour productivity, raise the rate of increase of their money wage rates to 3 per cent per annum, then we obtain the same inflationary process. Demand on the labour market increases the growth rate of money wage rates by the same percentage by which the workers would increase it, owing to the rise in the price level caused by increased demand. The increase in money wage rates is but a reflection of increased demand.

Phillips regards cost-push inflation, i.e. a rise in the price level caused by increases in costs due to exogenous factors, as an exceptional case only. He regards the increase in import prices as a factor which, owing to the rise in the cost of living, would raise the rate of increase of money wage rates above the growth rate of labour productivity and would cause inflation thereby. In the period 1861–1913, which he chose for his analysis, he found that import prices had only an insignificant effect on the rate of increase of money wage rates, and thus the figures of this period "represent the 'demand pull' element in wage adjustment."[9]

In connection with the relationship expressed by the Phillips curve, an answer has had to be found to the question of why inflation is possible when demand and supply are in equilibrium on the labour market, and thus full employment is reached, and, what is more, even before it is achieved. Keynes admitted this possibility only in one place of his *General Theory*. This question was examined in greater detail, among others, by Tobin.

Tobin examines the labour market not as an aggregate but as heterogeneous markets. In these markets there is steady disequilibrium. The patterns of demand and technology are changing continuously. In some markets there is excess supply, that is, there is unemployment, in others there is excess demand, which takes the

[8] A.W. Phillips: *op. cit.*, p. 290.
[9] A.W. Phillips: *op. cit.*, p. 298.

form of unfilled vacancies. Even if workers' information about the market were perfect, there would exist a structural disparity between the two. The skill of the unemployed worker does not make it possible for him to take up a new job in another field of production. Thus it is possible for unemployment and labour shortage to exist side by side.

On a labour market where excess demand prevails, money wage rates will steeply rise, while on other labour markets where there is excess supply, money wage rates will not, or only slowly, decrease. Thus, even though employment is full in the sense of equality of vacancies and unemployment, the rise in wage rates in the excess-demand markets will surpass the fall in wage rates in the excess-supply markets, and money wage rates will rise even in spite of the global equilibrium of demand and supply on the labour market. "The economy", says Tobin, "is in perpetual sectoral disequilibrium—even when it has settled into a stochastic macro-equilibrium."[10] In his opinion, zero-inflation requires that there should be more unemployed than new vacancies.

The Phillips curve shows a trade-off between inflation and unemployment. If unemployment is reduced, then this always causes increasing inflation. According to the Phillips curve, modern inflation is caused by a growing demand for labour and a concomitant increase in employment. This sort of inflation may already occur when there is still unemployment. If, however, price stability is to be ensured, this can only be bought, as was also referred to by Tobin, by means of a certain degree of unemployment. Stable prices can only be established at that percentage level of unemployment to which the same rate of increase of money wage rates pertains as is the rate at which labour productivity increases. The stability of money wage rates requires an even higher level of unemployment.

According to the Keynesian interpretation of trade-off, there exists involuntary unemployment in the economy, and consequently employment can be increased by enlarging demand. But the enlargement of demand for labour increases the rate of increase of money wage rates, and, at a certain percentage level of unemployment, it causes inflation. Tobin characterizes the Phillips curve as "the post-war analogue of Keynesian wage and employment theory."[11]

CRITICAL COMMENTS

The Phillips curve doctrine connects the change in nominal magnitudes with the change in real magnitudes: as a result of the change in nominal demand, changes ensue not only in money wages and the price level, but also lasting changes occur in output, employment and unemployment. Such a connection can only exist in the case of involuntary unemployment. The new anti-Keynesian views do not recognize—at least in the long run—the impact of nominal demand on the magnitude of employment because their representatives deny the existence of involuntary unemployment. In their opinion, if nominal demand increases, its effect in the long run appears as an increase in the price level and in money wage, and therefore real demand does not increase, and neither can employment and output

[10] J. Tobin: Inflation and Unemployment, *The American Economic Review*, March 1972, p. 11.
[11] J. Tobin: *op. cit.*, p. 4.

grow. However, in the case of involuntary unemployment assumed by the Phillips curve doctrine, it depends on the percentage magnitude of unemployment as to what extent the money wage rates and to what extent the price level increases. A high percentage level of unemployment is accompanied by a relatively low percentage increase in money wage rates and the price level. When now nominal demand rises, it may occur that the price level and the money wage rates increase only to such an extent that the growth of real demand exceeds the growth rate of production. Entrepreneurs will raise output, employment will rise.

In the evaluation of the Phillips curve doctrine it must be pointed out that it contains a statistically observed correspondence between the percentage level of unemployment and the growth rate of money wage rates for a period when the gold standard still existed and the state budget was balanced. At a relatively stable price level, the inflationary expectations were not yet built into the process of setting prices and wages. During the past few decades, however, inflation has persisted. And since prices and wages are usually set in advance for a relatively long period, the rate of inflation is also reckoned with in advance. But in this case, the given percentage level of unemployment, depending on the expected inflation, is accompanied by different rates of increase in money wage rates and in inflation. Thus, the position of the Phillips curve, depending on the expected inflation, will also be different. Many of the non-Marxian critics of the doctrine have also called attention to this fact.

Lipsey, Archibald and others also pointed out that since money wage rates increase more in a market with excess demand than they decrease in a market with excess supply, the growth rate of money wage rates may also change at a given percentage of unemployment if there is a change in its dispersion among the markets. "Observed rate of increase of money wage rates will be higher for given unemployment when the dispersion of unemployment is higher than when it is low."[12] Thus, the Phillips curve "may be shifted by changing the dispersion of unemployment."[13] Therefore, says Lipsey, if we wish to predict the rate of change of money wage rates, we must know not only the level of unemployment, but its dispersion among the markets as well. If, at a given percentage level of unemployment, the inequality of its dispersion among the markets changes considerably, then, at that given percentage level of unemployment, the rate of change of money wage rates will change with it.

The increasing strength of the trade unions also affects the position of the Phillips curve. The unions "might, for example, cause a faster increase of wages in response to excess demand and a slower fall in response to excess supply than would otherwise occur",[14] which means that the Phillips curve may be influenced by the distribution of industries among strongly unionized and poorly unionized and non-unionized industries, respectively. In Lipsey's view, a stable trade-off between unemployment and the growth rate of money wage rates could only exist if the influence of the unions remained relatively stable over time.

[12] G. C. Archibald: The Phillips Curve and the Distribution of Unemployment, *The American Economic Review*, May 1969, p. 126.

[13] G. C. Archibald: *op. cit.*, p. 125.

[14] R.G. Lipsey: The Relation between Unemployment and the Rate of Change of Money Wage Rates in the United Kingdom, 1862–1957: A Further Analysis, *Economica*, February 1960, p. 17.

In his study on the Phillips curve, Desai expresses his doubts that the numerical relationship as constructed by Phillips when averaging the money wage rates of the years between 1861 and 1913 in order to eliminate their cyclical movements, could also be used for a later period of capitalist development. Because this would, in his opinion, presuppose that unemployment fluctuates with the same amplitude in each cycle and that the length of the individual cycles is equal. If, however, the cycles were irregular and of an unequal amplitude, there would be a large variance between the average obtained and the true average desired, and "in this sense the Phillips procedure will be inefficient."[15] Namely, in this case, the rate of increase in money wage rates would also be influenced, at the given level of unemployment, despite averaging, by the rate of change in unemployment. Desai emphasizes that the cyclical pattern of the 19th century data is very suitable for Phillips's averaging procedure. For the periods 1914–1947 and 1947–1971, however, he finds that "the shape of the Phillips curve did not remain unchanged from period to period"[16] and, he thinks, it would be futile to attempt, merely out of *a priori* considerations, to deduce a single shape for the Phillips curve.

Writing on the transitory lay-off of workers in the industry of the United States, Feldstein[17] points out that a part of those workers on lay-off who had good jobs and enjoyed higher wages, expect that they will be recalled by their companies and so they do not search for new jobs; hence, they do not increase supply on the labour market. Therefore, the divergence between demand and supply does not express the full size of unemployment.

The question arises whether a trade-off between inflation and unemployment can really exist. Our answer is yes, but not for the same reason as maintained by the advocates of the Phillips curve doctrine. The developed capitalist countries have been characterized in the past few years by the increase of the non-productive sector and within it by the greater weight of the state sector. The strengthening of the non-productive sector exerts a favourable effect on employment in the productive sector. It is a manifestation of the contradictory nature of social production subordinated to profit interest that part of the products of the productive workers has to be used in the capitalist economy in a non-productive way in order to realize the surplus value produced and attain a high level of employment. But the expenditures of the non-productive sector have an inflationary impact, namely, they create demand without supplying commodities to the market. The consumer expenditures of the non-productive sector may also raise the price level of consumer goods if the wages of those employed in the non-productive sector are financed by taxes. The turnover tax does not diminish nominal income, but its spending increases nominal demand. Profit tax does not diminish the expenditure of the capitalist class, but increases demand. And when all factors acting upon the price level are taken into account,[18] it will turn out that demand-pull inflation

[15] M. Desai: The Phillips Curve: A Revisionist Interpretation, *Economica*, February 1975, p. 5.

[16] M. Desai: *op. cit.*, p. 16.

[17] M.S. Feldstein: The Importance of Temporary Layoffs: An Empirical Analysis, *Brookings Papers on Economic Activity*, 1975/3.

[18] See P. Erdős and F. Molnár: *Infláció és válságok a hetvenes évek amerikai gazdaságában* (Inflation and crises in the US economy of the 1970s), Közgazdasági és Jogi Könyvkiadó, Budapest, 1982, pp. 72–73.

will ensue not only when the growth rate in the money wages of workers employed in the productive sector exceeds the growth rate of the productivity of labour, but may also occur when the rate of the former lags behind that of the latter while the rate of increase of expenditures secured from state revenues or from deficit significantly rises, or also when taxes imposed on wages, or the workers' savings decrease at a high rate. Thus the Marxist explanation also shows that the rate of inflation may be different even at a given percentage rate of unemployment.

The method suggested by the Phillips curve doctrine to cure inflation is held to be unacceptable even by some non-Marxian authors, because this method is designed to weaken the workers' struggle by increasing unemployment and by aggravating their poverty. This panacea enhances social tensions and may become dangerous to capitalist society. Phillips wished to complement Keynes's theoretical system with the determination of money-wage changes; the theory of Keynes who wanted to lower the level of unemployment by economic policy measures. Under the conditions of inflation, the two conflicting economic policy objectives led Phillips to arrive at an economic policy recommendation which was contrary to that of Keynes. He wished to remedy inflation by unemployment.

The Keynes-inspired Phillips curve was in the forefront of interest in non-Marxian economic literature for over a decade. Then in the 1970s it came to be ignored completely. A new phenomenon began to unfold in the capitalist economies, viz. the process of stagflation. With the growth of inflation, unemployment also increased and thus the trade-off between unemployment and inflation ceased. Under such circumstances, the recommendation of an economic policy to cure inflation by unemployment became senseless. This meant a complete bankruptcy of the Phillips curve. Stagflation called attention to the explanation of inflation by means of costs, and the theory of cost-push inflation experienced its revival in non-Marxian economic literature.

Chapter 2

FRIEDMAN'S MONETARIST COUNTER-REVOLUTION

THE MAIN CHARACTERISTICS OF THE ECONOMY OF THE
UNITED STATES AFTER THE SECOND WORLD WAR

After the Second World War significant structural changes took place in the major capitalist countries. The author of this book wishes to illustrate them on the example of the United States.[19] The weight of services increased in the economy. More than 60 per cent of the active labour force worked in that sphere. And the demand for services is less crisis-sensitive. The share of the government in national income experienced a considerable growth. Government expenditures were not subordinated to the profit motive and were, therefore, not subjected to the cyclical fluctuations of the economy. The built-in stabilizers were operating, the system of unemployment benefits became extended and as a result of the structural changes, the crisis-sensitivity of the capitalist economy diminished. Economic recessions were often elicited by an erroneous economic policy in this period.

Aggregate demand and employment had reached a high level by the end of the 1960s. Within unemployment as a whole, the share of unemployment induced by the lack of demand diminished and, as a result of the scientific-technological revolution, the ratio of technological-structural unemployment increased. Economic cycles were no longer of a classical character. The role of fixed-capital investment and of replacement in the formation of cycles diminished, while the role of durables increased. And since owing to consumer credit, the demand for them is interest-elastic, the responsibility of monetary policy for the creation of cycles grew.

The theoretical model of present-day capitalist economy had to take account of the savings of the wage- and salary-earners and of the economic implications of the fluctuations in these savings.

However, along with the above-mentioned structural changes, the process of inflation also began to unfold. Owing to the applied oligopolistic price formation, a significant part of nominal aggregate demand enhanced by government expenditure became absorbed not by the growth of production and employment but by the rise in the price level. Then demand-induced inflation slowly changed into endogenous cost-push inflation. Namely, inflation alters the income distribution relations by shifting the incomes from the poorer to the richer population.[20] "In

---

[19] See P. Erdős and F. Molnár: *Infláció és válságok a hetvenes évek amerikai gazdaságában* (Inflation and crises in the US economy of the 1970s), Közgazdasági és Jogi Könyvkiadó, Budapest, 1982.

[20] See P. Davidson: Post-Keynesian Economics: Solving the Crisis in Economic Theory. In: *The Crisis of Economic Theory*, London, 1981.

this phase, the inflation is no longer due to excess demand-pull, but rather to what may be labeled endogenous cost-push..."[21]

Under the condition of a long-lasting inflation, when the inflationary expectations have already become persistent and demand-pull and cost-push inflation intertwined, the inflationary process gets more and more out of the control of the government. The conflict between the two basic economic policy objectives: how to ensure simultaneously both a high level of employment and the stability of the price level, appears to be an unsolved and increasingly serious problem.

As a result of the unsolved problems, contemporary capitalist economy has come again to face a crisis. However, in present-day economic literature more and more authors write on the crisis of Keynesianism which occupied a dominant position in economics until quite recently. It was the strengthening of inflation which undermined trust in it. Keynes's theory reflected the characteristics of capitalism of his time, but could not describe the peculiarities of present-day capitalism. The Keynesian economic policy mitigated unemployment, but could not provide any remedy to solve the serious current problems of capitalist eonomy, especially to fight inflation. Johnson[22] emphasized that it was primarily the acceleration of the inflationary process that brought about the monetary counter-revolution, which was directed not only against the Keynesian theoretical system and its economic policy, but against all state regulation of the economy, making state intervention in the economy responsible for the serious troubles of capitalist economy. The harmful consequences of the abortive government economic policy measures also underpinned this anti-Keynesian fight.

As counter-theories to Keynesianism, various neo-classical tendencies came into being. Paradoxically, it was the relatively favourable capitalist development after the Second World War, ensuing from the increased economic role of the state, which reinforced trust in the effectiveness of the automatisms of the capitalist economy. Many non-Marxian economists who lost their faith in Keynesianism also joined the neo-classical school.

The disputes of the 1930s experience a revival in our days. At that time, it was the crisis of the capitalist economy that led to the crisis of neo-classical economics, while today it is the correctness and applicability of Keynesian economic policy and theory and the efficiency of state economic policy that are queried.

The key issue of the dispute today is invariably the question whether capitalism is a viable system, whether its automatisms can control its arising ills. The Keynesian answer was a negative one: the economic difficulties can only be overcome with the help of the state. By contrast, the answer of the neo-classical economists, becoming more and more militant under the present-day conditions, is opposed to the Keynesian answer. They see the principal source of economic ills in state economic policy. In their opinion, the economic activity of the government only disturbs the stable operation of the real processes of the capitalist economy. Some of them even hold the view that is was the incorrect economic policy of the government that could be made responsible also for the economic crises of the

[21] F. Modigliani: Rediscovery of Money—Discussion, *The American Economic Review*, May 1975, p. 180.
[22] See H.G. Johnson: The Keynesian Revolution and the Monetarist Counter-Revolution, *The American Economic Review*, May 1971, p. 8.

past. Under state monopoly capitalism, the principle of economic freedom typical of pre-monopoly capitalism has revived in an anachronistic way.

Characterizing the opposed viewpoints of the disputing parties, Barro writes: "The interpretation of the Great Depression is a key matter dividing policy activist from nonactivist. The activist view is that the Great Depression was a symptom of an inherently unstable private economy... The alternative view is that the Great Depression was in large part a product of governmental mistakes; specifically, the inept monetary policy of the Federal Reserve. Further, the governmental interventions associated with the New Deal, including the volume of public expenditures and direct price regulations, retarded the recovery of the economy..."[23]

The monetarist counter-revolution began with Friedman's study published in 1956.[24]

FRIEDMAN'S PRINCIPAL STATEMENTS

Earlier, writes Friedman, the view prevailed that money was an utterly passive magnitude which responded to other economic forces, but had only negligible independent influence.[25] By contrast, Friedman emphasizes that changes in the stock of money have a serious impact on economic processes. Since money "is so pervasive, when it gets out of order, it throws a monkey wrench into the operation of all the other machines. The Great Contraction is the most dramatic example but not the only one."[26] He demonstrates by econometric analysis that changes in the supply of money had generally preceded the great turning-points of cyclical movement, upturn and downturn, in economic history. However, in cases when changes in nominal income only followed the changes in the money stock, the latter was the cause and the former the effect.

By assigning such a great role to money in the economic processes, Friedman emphasizes the significance of monetary policy as compared to fiscal policy.

He interprets monetary policy in a specific way; he criticizes the view, held by Keynesianists, according to which the behaviour of the rate of interest is a substantial criterion for the evaluation of the efficiency of monetary policy. In his view, there is a two-edged relation between the volume of money and the rate of interest. As we shall see later, a change in monetary growth affects the interest rate first in one and then in the opposite direction. Thus "interest rates are a highly misleading guide in monetary policy."[27] Monetary policy is important not because of its impact on the rate of interest, but because of its impact on the quantity of money: "... central bankers should look rather at the quantity of money"[28], as "... there

---

[23] R.J. Barro: Second Thoughts on Keynesian Economics, *The American Economic Review*, May 1979, p. 57.

[24] M. Friedman: The Quantity Theory of Money: A Restatement. In: M. Friedman (ed.): *Studies in the Quantity Theory of Money*, Chicago, 1956.

[25] M. Friedman: Rediscovery of Money—Discussion, *The American Economic Review*, May 1975, p. 176.

[26] M. Friedman: The Role of Monetary Policy, *The American Economic Review*, March 1968, p. 12.

[27] M. Friedman: *The Counter-Revolution in Monetary Theory*, The Institute of Economic Affairs, Westminster, 1970, p. 25.

[28] M. Friedman: *The Counter-Revolution...*, op. cit., p. 18.

is a consistent relation between the rate of growth of the quantity of money and the rate of growth of the nominal income."[29]

Friedman distinguishes between monetary and credit policy. In his view, this highly important distinction has so far been much neglected. By credit policy he understands "... the effect of the actions of monetary authorities on rates of interest, terms of lending, the ease with which people can borrow, and conditions in the credit market."[30] By contrast, he defines monetary policy as "the effect of the actions of monetary authorities on the stock of money..."[31]

To illustrate the effect of monetary and fiscal policy, he separates them, as he says, for analytical considerations. He interprets fiscal policy *per se* as the change in budgetary expenditures or in the tax rate at a given quantity of money.[32]

If budgetary expenditures are financed from taxes, then the government spends the sum that the tax-payers would spend. When government expenditures are financed from credits borrowed from the public, then the public can spend less or lend less to others. It is uncertain in both cases whether nominal demand will grow as a result of budgetary expenditures. In Friedman's view, this depends on as to who has the greater propensity to spend: those from whom the money needed for covering government expenditures was withdrawn, or those into whose possession it came as income. With reference to the so-called *crowding-out effect,* monetarist authors are trying to prove that fiscal policy in itself has no effect on nominal aggregate demand. They hold the view that government expenditures as a whole are crowding out private spendings. Friedman's argumentation shows a great resemblance to that of the economists of the 1930s.

Nor does a change in the tax rate alter nominal demand with a given quantity of money, says Friedman. With unchanged government expenditures, a rise in the tax rate does not diminish nominal demand. All what happens is merely that government expenditures formerly financed by credits from the public will be covered from tax revenues. Thus the money taken up formerly as government credits will now remain with the public for its own spendings or for private lending, and nominal demand will not diminish. With a similar argumentation it could also be proved that nominal demand will not even rise if the tax rate is diminished. Then the government is bound to finance its spendings from credits taken up from the public, which, as a result, can spend less and extend less credit for private purposes.[33]

If, however, government expenditures are financed from additional money issues, then the government does not withdraw money from the population in the form of taxes or credits and so nominal demand will grow. Thus, according to Friedman, the demand-increasing effect of government expenditures depends on the method of financing, and so does the multiplier effect of these expenditures, too. Therefore, this multiplier effect does not in itself provide any information on the market-expanding effect of investments, of government outlays. And the method

[29] M. Friedman: *The Counter-Revolution...,* op. cit., p. 12.

[30] M. Friedman: Post-War Trends in Monetary Theory and Policy. In: *The Optimum Quantity of Money and Other Essays,* Chicago, 1970, p. 75.

[31] *Ibid.*

[32] See M. Friedman: *The Counter-Revolution...,* op. cit., p. 18.

[33] See M. Friedman: Comments on the Critics, *Journal of Political Economy,* 1972, No. 5, pp. 914–915.

of financing already belongs to the monetary sphere. Thus nominal demand increases not as a result of government spendings, but as a result of the growth of the quantity of money. The change in nominal demand depends on changes in the quantity of money. Therefore, it is the cyclical movement of the quantity of money and not that of investments or of state spendings that elicits the disturbances, the upswings and downswings of economic life.[34]

If the quantity of money and nominal demand change, the price level will, according to Friedman, also change with them. It will increase if the quantity of money and nominal demand grow, and will decrease if the quantity of money and nominal demand diminish. Thus real demand can be neither too abundant nor too insufficient. It just corresponds to the quantity of output. In Keynes, if the propensity to save exceeded, at full employment, the magnitude of investment, it resulted in insufficient aggregate demand, involuntary unemployment. In Friedman, if society wishes to save too much and, consequently, the demand for commodities is too low, the price level will fall, the purchasing power of the money stock will rise and real demand will stay at its earlier level.

Prices which are flexible both upwards and downwards also clear the individual markets (the paradigm of market-clearing). Thus the real variables, viz. output, employment, real wage and real interest rate, are established at their equilibrium values, are exposed to the impact of real factors only, and they may assume any nominal magnitudes. Thus changes in the quantity of money do not effect real magnitudes, i.e. money is *neutral* with respect to real processes. The homogeneity postulate prevails, that is, a given magnitude of either real demand or real supply may persist at any price level, it is only a function of relative prices. In Friedman, the real sphere is stable. Involuntary unemployment stemming from demand shortage cannot exist. Labour demand and supply depend on real wages. Those who are willing to take up work at the existing real wage rates, can find job opportunities.

Certain types of unemployment, however, may persistently exist also in Friedman's view, as the actual market is not identical with the Walrasian ideal market. Actual market relations are hard to survey, market conditions are subject to fast and unexpected changes, information on vacancies and labour availabilities is costly, and professional and geographical mobility in the case of changing demand and supply relations is also expensive. Thus there exists with Friedman a *natural* or equlibrium rate of unemployment[35] (natural-rate hypothesis). Unlike the irrational unemployment in the Keynesian model, this is voluntary and is the result of a rational decision. At the existing real wages, the worker, also taking account of the costs of information and mobility, chooses the most suitable one of the possibilities available to him: instead of taking up a job, he chooses unemployment with the unemployment benefit and the advantage of leisure.[36] This is an equilibrium magnitude which depends only on real factors. It can be influenced persistently neither by fiscal nor by monetary policy. If, at given real wage rates, unemployment could be reduced by economic policy measures persistently,

[34] M. Friedman: Money and Business Cycles. In: *The Optimum Quantity of Money and Other Essays,* Chicago, 1970, pp. 234–235.

[35] M. Friedman: The Role of Monetary Policy, *op. cit.,* p. 9.

[36] M. Friedman: Nobel Lecture: Inflation and Unemployment, *Journal of Political Economy,* 1977, No. 2, p. 459.

then Friedman should acknowledge that unemployment has been involuntary.

As has been shown, the effect of fiscal policy without monetary policy is, according to Friedman, uncertain, while monetary policy is, also without fiscal policy, certain to act on nominal demand. Friedman characterizes monetary policy *per se,* separated from fiscal policy, as the changing of the quantity of money while government expenditures and taxation are left unchanged.[37] The task of monetary policy is in Friedman not the adjustment of the interest rate, but the regulation of nominal demand through changing the quantity of money, that is, the insurance that the monetary sphere should not disturb the real sphere of the economy which is developing along the equilibrium path, but should secure a stable framework for it. He maintains that monetary policy is the only effective instrument of control.[38]

Friedman presents the demand-increasing effect of pure monetary policy, when a change in the quantity of money is not due to a sales or a credit transaction, through open-market operations.[39]

Through offering high prices, the central bank buys bonds from the commercial banks or from the public. Because of the high prices offered, they are willing to sell their stocks. As a result, the composition of their balance-sheet will undergo a change. The quantity of bonds will decrease and the quantity of money will increase among their assets. And since the price level has temporarily not changed, the quantity of real money will increase. In the Keynesian model, it is not necessary to spend the increased stock of money. In this model, it is owing to the uncertainty of the future that, over and above the transaction motive, a specific function of money, money as a store of value, has come to play an important role. People, who because of certain events begin to worry about the future, may find that the benefit of holding money may exceed the advantages of holding other assets. The uncertainty of the future as presented by Keynes cannot be found in Friedman's theory. Erroneous expections are adjusted in his system in an error-learning process, and therefore money is not the safest one to play the role of the store of value. Although he regards money, like Keynes, as an asset, he blurs the distinction between money as an asset with its specific role and the other assets. In his theory, money and the other assets, among them reproducible assets, too, are good substitutes for one another. He criticizes Keynes for the narrow interpretation of the balance-sheet.[40] Owing to the specific position of money among the assets, Keynes pays concentrated attention only to the substitution relation between money and the promise for future money, i.e., long-term fixed-interest bonds, while Friedman focuses attention on the substitution relation between money and a wide range of assets. In Friedman's system, if there is too much money among the assets, the utility of holding money diminishes, and it is advisable to use part of this money for buying more profitable assets. Excess money stock is spent not only on buying financial but also real assets. Thus excess money stock becomes, through the so-called portfolio balance effect, direct nominal demand. It is from this aspect that he evaluates the real-balance effect revealed by Pigou and Haberler. According to this effect, in the case of a fall in the price level, people spend their excess cash, i.e. the amount which is larger than they

[37] M. Friedman: *The Counter-Revolution...,* op. cit., p. 18.
[38] M. Friedman: *The Counter-Revolution...,* op. cit., p. 26.
[39] M. Friedman: Money and Business Cycles, *op. cit.,* p. 230.
[40] M. Friedman: Comments on the Critics, *op. cit.,* p. 230.

desire to hold and which is increased in its purchasing power, directly on buying commodities.[41] Friedman also mentions that monetary theory is part of the *theory of wealth*.[42] Through investments stimulated by a depressed interest rate resulting from the growth in the quantity of money, the rise in nominal demand constitutes in his theory only a slight proportion of the increase in aggregate demand.

At flexible prices, however, the growth in nominal demand is not accompanied by a rise in real demand. The increase in the quantity of money does not bear upon the real sphere, only upon nominal magnitudes such as the price level, money wages, nominal interest rate, nominal national income, that is, upon the price sum of real national income. Emphasizing that "there is a close relation between changes in the quantity of money and the subsequent course of national income"[43], Friedman tries to determine the nominal national income through the quantity of money.

THE DETERMINATION OF NOMINAL NATIONAL INCOME
IN FRIEDMAN'S THEORY

In Keynes, national income adjusts itself to the magnitude of aggregate demand which is determined by expenditures. Assuming a rigid price level, the consumption and investment expenditures, or the latter through the multiplier effect, determine the magnitude of not only the nominal but also of the real national income.

Nominal national income adjusts itself also in Friedman, to nominal aggregate demand, but he does not determine the magnitude of the latter by expenditures, because, in his view, as we have seen, spendings are sure to increase nominal aggregate demand only if the quantity of money rises. Therefore, nominal aggregate demand is in his theory the product of the quantity of money and of the velocity of circulation.

In earlier quantity theories of money, the velocity of circulation was an institutional datum. In Keynes, the velocity of circulation is not unchanged, but its movement is uncertain due to the instability of liquidity preference. In Friedman, the velocity of circulation is also a changeable, but determined magnitude, and its movement is predictable. It is determined by factors which specify the quantity of money people wish to hold for a longer period of time on average, that is, by the magnitude of their demand for money. Even at a given quantity of money, nominal aggregate demand is greater if the velocity of circulation is higher, because people want to hold a smaller proportion of their wealth in money form. An opposing situation develops if, at a given quantity of money, the desire to hold money increases.

In Friedman's view, the demand for money and the velocity of circulation are a stable function of a few key variables. The behaviour of the velocity of circulation can be explained by the function of the demand for money. He also emphasizes

[41] M. Friedman: Post-War Trends ..., *op. cit.*, p. 72.
[42] M. Friedman: Post-War Trends..., *op. cit.*, p. 73.
[43] M. Friedman: *The Counter-Revolution* ..., op. cit., p. 27.

35*

that the modern quantity theory of money is a *theory of the demand for money*.[44] And he sets the stable function of the demand for money against Keynes's unstable liquidity preference, by which, according to Keynes, the interpretation of aggregate demand as the product of the quantity of money and of the velocity of circulation becomes questionable.

Since the velocity of circulation is in Friedman a determined magnitude and its movement predictable, if the quantity of money increases and this increase is predictable, then the product of the quantity of money and of the velocity of circulation is also determined and its increase is also predictable, that is, the function of money to store wealth does not impair the efficiency of monetary policy.

Trying to construct a stable function for the demand for money, Friedman maintains that the demand for money with a given purchasing power, that is, the demand for real money, depends primarily on the magnitude of real wealth. But since adequate information for assessing total wealth is rarely available, he holds it to be more expedient to work with permanent real income than with wealth.

Friedman transferred the concept of permanent real income from his theory of consumer behaviour into the theory of the demand function of money. According to the so-called permanent-income hypothesis, the consumer makes his demand for consumer goods not only on the basis of his current but also on that of his average real income which is valid for a longer period of time. To determine the length of that period, Friedman goes back from the present into the past as long as he finds a correlation between past income and present consumption demand. He estimates that permanent real income is the average of the real incomes of some 2.5 to 3 years. In averaging, the actual real incomes at the respective points of time have to be taken into account by weighting them according to the degree of correlation. The greatest weight, 0.33, is assigned to current real income and, proceeding towards the past, the weights decrease exponentially and their sum equals 1.[45]

Thus the demand for money, like the demand for consumer goods, is also in Friedman a function of permanent real income. On the basis of US data for the period 1870 to 1954 he found that, given a 1 percent increase in permanent real income, the demand for real money grew by 1.81 per cent, and thus the income velocity decreased by 0.81 per cent.[46]

The expected development of permanent real national income can be extrapolated from its present-day development, taking into account the estimated long-term trend of growth.[47] In this way, the demand for real money, or the secular behaviour of the velocity of money, the movement of the so-called *permanent velocity,* can also be judged.

Now, if we can also assess the expected growth rate of the quantity of money, the movement of permanent nominal income can also be assessed.

Keynes tried to determine the equilibrium level of national income by the saving-

[44] M. Friedman: The Quantity Theory of Money: A Restatement. In: M. Friedman (ed.): *Studies in the Quantity Theory of Money,* Chicago, 1956.

[45] M. Friedman: *A Theory of Consumption Function,* Princeton, 1957, pp. 142–147.

[46] M. Friedman: The Demand for Money: Some Theoretical and Empirical Results. In: *The Optimum Quantity of Money and Other Essays,* p. 13.

[47] M. Friedman: Money and Business Cycles ..., *op. cit.,* p. 224.

investment mechanism. As long as intended investment exceeds intended saving, aggregate demand will be higher than the magnitude of the national income produced. The production of national income is increased and, as its function, the magnitude of intended saving will grow with it. And at the equilibrium level of national income, saving and investment, and through them aggregate demand and aggregate supply, will come into equilibrium with one another.

In Friedman's view, if the quantity of money increases, it will exceed, at the prevailing price level, the quantity of money demanded, i.e. the quantity designed to be held. Excess money is spent and nominal demand will rise. But those to whom this money flows do not wish to hold it either and they also spend it. How will then an equilibrium be established between the demand for and the supply of money on the one hand and, through them, between the aggregate demand for and the aggregate supply of commodities on the other? In this theory, owing to the increase in nominal aggregate demand, the price level will rise, the purchasing power of the increased quantity of money, i.e. the supplied quantity of real money, will fall and will eventually reach an equilibrium with the quantity of real money demanded and designed to be held.

In a stationary economy it is the product of the existing permanent real income and of this price level which provides that magnitude of the permanent nominal income at which an equilibrium comes about between the available quantity of nominal money and the demand for it. In a growing economy, permanent nominal income has to rise at a rate which ensures that the demand for money absorbs its increasing quantity. And if the growth rate of the quantity of money rises, which does not effect either the growth rate of permanent real income nor, as a consequence, the velocity of circulation, then the price level and, through it, permanent nominal income have to rise at a faster rate. In other words, since the velocity of circulation is basically dependent on real forces, it has no key role to play in the acceleration of inflation. Friedman maintains that at a stable demand function of money, the change in the quantity of money and the change in permanent nominal income are closely correlated. Or vice versa: if the change in the quantity of money and the change in permanent nominal income are correlated, a stable demand function of money must prevail.

Now we shall illustrate what we have said above by Friedman's numerical examples:[48] Let the growth rate of permanent real income, α_y, be 2 per cent. If permanent real income elasticity of the demand for money, $\delta = 3/2$, that is, if permanent real income grows by 1 per cent, the demand for money at unchanged price level, the so-called demand for real money, will rise by 1.5 per cent.

The growth rate of the demand for money, $\delta\alpha_y$, is 3 per cent in our example. If the quantity of money rises by an annual 4 per cent, that is, if $\alpha_M = 4$ per cent, the growth rate of money supply will exceed the growth rate of the demand for money, the excess money will be spent on purchases, the price level will rise by $\alpha_M - \delta\alpha_y = 1$ per cent, hence $\alpha_p = 1$ per cent. Then the growth rate of real money demand, $\delta\alpha_y$, has come into equilibrium with the growth rate of real money supply, $\alpha_M - \alpha_p$. The growth rate of nominal permanent national income equals the growth rate of permanent real income plus the growth rate of the price level, $\alpha_y + \alpha_p$. This is 3 per cent in our example. At the 3 per cent growth rate of nominal

48 M. Friedman: Money and Business Cycles..., *op. cit.*, p. 229.

permanent national income, the rate of money demand, $\delta\alpha_y + \alpha_p$, equals the rate of money supply, α_M. If the growth rate of the quantity of money rises to 10 per cent, the growth rate of the price level will increase to 7 per cent, and that of nominal permanent national income to 9 per cent.

What the change in permanent velocity cannot explain with permanent real income, can be traced back, says Friedman, to changes in the rates of returns on other assets that could be held instead of money. From among these alternative assets, this study wishes to deal with only two.

As to the effect of the change in the interest rate of bonds on the demand for money and, through it, on the velocity of circulation, Friedman writes that it has evolved in the theoretically expected direction. Money demand diminished when the interest rate rose, and it increased at a diminishing rate of interest, but it is "too small to be statistically significant".[49] In Keynes, the demand for money as a store of wealth is heavily interest-elastic. At a given quantity of money, it is the rise in the rate of interest that sets free part of the cash balances, tied up originally for wealth-holding purposes, for government spending or investments. Thereby it increases the velocity of money. Friedman's analysis reveals the insignificance of that part of the given quantity of money which is untied through the increase in the velocity of money caused by the rise in the interest rate.

In his view, it is the return increased by the inflationary price rise of real assets included in the balance-sheet that exerts a more significant effect on both the demand for money and the velocity of money. And in hyper-inflationary times, as was the case e.g. in Hungary in 1945–46, it is the effect of the expected rate of inflation on the velocity of circulation that becomes dominant in the function of the demand for money. Its role at such times is greater than that of permanent real incomes—points out Friedman relying on Cagan's study.[50]

For the quantity of money to remain neutral, for its change not to act on the real processes of the economy, that is, for the real variables to move along their equilibrium paths, and for the price mechanism to fulfil its market-clearing function, it is necessary, according to Friedman, that people be able to recognize the new price level adjusted to the change in the quantity of money and thereby in nominal aggregate demand, that is, that they reckon with its movement in advance, in order to adjust to it when making their economic decisions. In short, inflation or deflation should be anticipated. And all what is required is, according to Friedman, that the issue of money should take place at an even rate (i.e. the so-called fixed monetary growth rule).[51] In this case, the rate of change of the price level will remain stable over time, too, which means that the anticipated rate of inflation or deflation can be taken into account in the contracts, money wages and nominal interest rates can be established accordingly, and everything in the economy will develop in a way as if it were free from inflation or deflation.

[49] M. Friedman: The Demand for Money ..., *op. cit.*, p. 113.
[50] See Ph. Cagan: The Monetary Dynamics of Hyperinflation. In: M. Friedman (ed.): *Studies in the Quantity Theory of Money and Other Essays*, pp. 25–117.
[51] See M. Friedman: The Role of Monetary Policy, *op. cit.*, pp. 16–17.

THE EFFECT OF UNANTICIPATED INFLATION

What will happen if the quantity of money increases unexpectedly, because the government, as in Friedman's example, wants to depress unemployment below its natural rate, and to achieve this it covers its spendings by issuing money? Nominal aggregate demand and the price level will rise. If the entrepreneurs knew that inflation was general, they would not increase their production, since not only the price of their products but also their costs have risen while their real profit has remained unchanged. Neither would the workers enhance the offer of their labour power, as not only their money wages but also the price level have risen, and thus their real wages have not changed. Since, however, the agents of the market take notice of the inflation with a time lag, and the Walrasian auctioneer is missing in Friedman's model, their information is initially imperfect. Friedman, relying in his study published in 1977 on Lucas's distinction between price level and local price, points out that the entrepreneurs cannot recognize for a time whether the price level has increased owing to the increase in nominal aggregate demand, or the relative prices have altered as a result of the change in the structure of demand. First they think that they are faced only with a change in relative prices and it is only the demand for and the price of the product they turn out that have changed. They are willing to offer the workers higher money wages to acquire the necessary labour force. But money wages cannot grow to such an extent as the price of their product, because, in accordance with the logic of the marginal productivity theory, entrepreneurs will increase employment only if the wage rates of their workers have diminished relative to the product they produce. But the workers are only willing to increase the offer of their labour power if their real wages increase. Friedman tries to resolve this dilemma by assuming that although the workers take notice of the rise in their money wages, they compare these not to the price of the product produced by them but to the general price level which, owing to their deficient information, they suppose to be unchanged. Thus, although their real wages have in fact diminished, the workers believe that their real wages have increased. That is, real wage rates simultaneously grow *ex ante* for the employees and fall *ex post* for the employers. Therefore, those workers who at the existing real wage rates are the representatives of natural unemployment are now willing to supply their labour. As a result of an increase in government spending, production and employment are temporarily rising.

However, the false expectations, as a result of a learning process, slowly undergo an adjustment. The workers come to recognize that the price level has increased and they adjust the growth rate of their money wages to the actual rate of inflation. Real wage rates rise to their original level. Those workers who at this real wage rate refused to take up work, withdraw again from the labour market, and unemployment will reach its natural rate. As the real wage rate rises to its original level, entrepreneurs decrease their output to the initial level. State intervention disrupted only the equilibrium of economic life. The initial upswing is first followed by the contraction of output and employment, by a recession and then finally all real variables assume their original equilibrium values. Government intervention proves to be completely ineffective in the long run, and it only increases the rate of inflation. In the short run, however, it disrupts the equilibrium of real economy.

551

The temporary disequilibrium presented by Friedman is based on Cagan's *adaptive expectations* hypothesis.[52] According to this hypothesis, in forming their expectations, people mechanically project the weighted average of actual past inflation rates into the future.

Although the recent past is represented in averaging by a greater weight than the more remote one, expectations are anyway always based on past experience. Thus the government is able to mislead people by changing its economic policy in the meantime. It also follows from this hypothesis that the agents of the market recognize the actual rate of inflation only in the course of a learning process.

According to the adaptive expectations hypothesis, unemployment can *persistently* be forced below its natural rate only if the central bank steadily accelerates the rate of inflation and steadily diverts thereby the actual rate from its expected rate. Thus it continually misleads the agents of the market as regards the actual rate of inflation. Friedman calls this method of decreasing unemployment accelerationism.[53] And the higher the rate of inflation that the workers expect to ensue, the greater inflation is needed to depress unemployment below its natural rate.

In the course of decreasing the quantity of money, a process evolves which goes in a direction opposite to the one just outlined. At decreasing nominal demand, the fall in the price level would establish an equilibrium between real demand and the volume of output if people were adequately informed about the general character and the rate of deflation. However, the enterprises first believe that the demand for and the price of only their product have decreased. They cut their demand for labour, and money wages fall. For a time, the workers do not recognize the general fall in the price level and suppose that their real wages have also fallen. They will leave their jobs and as a result unemployment rises above its natural rate. And its rise will last until the agents of the market recognize the general character and the actual rate of deflation. Thus increasing unemployment is only a consequence of the fact that the market was unable to provide adequate information for insuring the formation of true expectations in the course of an unexpected fall in aggregate demand.

With Friedman, in the case of unanticipated inflation, the change in the quantity of money and nominal demand elicits not only a change in prices, but temporarily, also a quantitative adjustment. Namely, there is a change in the magnitude of both output and employment. This means that, though temporary, a trade-off between inflation and unemployment can also be found in Friedman. However, in Friedman the causal relationship shows a direction opposite to that in Phillips. It is not the fall in unemployment that elicits inflation but inflation brings about the fall in unemployment. It is not the price level that adjusts to the growth of money wages, but the growth rate of money wages adjusts to the actual rate of inflation. In Phillips until the growth rate of the price level reaches the growth rate of money wages, real wages grow faster than the rate of labour productivity, and then the growth rate of real wages falls to the growth rate of the productivity of labour. This, however, does not diminish the supply of labour, does not increase unemployment, as the Keynesian model acknowledges the existence of involuntary unemployment. In Friedman, however, as long as the growth rate of the money

[52] See Ph. Cagan: *op. cit.*, pp. 37–39.
[53] See M. Friedman: Nobel Lecture ..., *op. cit.*, p. 459.

wage does not adjust itself to the growth rate of the price level, the actual real wage grows at a slower rate than labour productivity. As soon as the expected rate of inflation catches up with the actual rate of inflation, real wage rises at the rate of the productivity of labour, the expected growth rate of real wage diminishes, the demand for and the supply of labour fall, and unemployment rises to its natural rate. Thus the loop in the presentation of the natural-rate hypothesis is clockwise.

Thus the neo-classical Phillips curve expresses in Friedman not the growth rate of money wages as a function of the percentage change of unemployment, but the change in the supply of labour as a function of the actual movements of money wages and of the price level expected by the worker, that is, as a function of the imagined real wage. Thus the fluctuation of employment is the result of the workers' voluntary choice on a labour market which would be cleared spontaneously if the workers' expectations concerning the price level were not erroneous.

In the long run, when inflation already becomes anticipated, complete adjustment will only take place in the price level. Thus the Phillips curve in Friedman is in the long run a vertical straight line. And thereby in the long run the homogeneity postulate comes into force. As with the growth of the quantity of money its purchasing power has not increased, neither has aggregate real demand. The growth of the quantity of money becomes neutral with respect to real processes.

It must have been the recognition of the inflationary process and of its consideration in economic calculations by the public at large that made Friedman realize that this fact offers a possibility of attacking Keynes's theory of interest. Friedman emphasizes that in the course of the price rise which follows the growth of the quantity of money, the nominal interest rate also increases. In order to demonstrate this, he borrows Irving Fisher's distinction between real and nominal interest rates. The nominal rate of interest is made up of two components: the real rate of interest and the magnitude of the price level.[54] He criticizes Keynes's theory of interest by referring to the rise in the nominal rate of interest in the present-day inflationary period: how can, under the conditions of inflation, the interest rate be determined by means of the liquidity preference diagram, on one axis of which the magnitude of the interest rate, while on the other the quantity of money are given. The decreasing rate of interest at the time when the quantity of money increases, as pointed out by Keynes, is only temporary in Friedman's view. As soon as, owing to the growth of the quantity of money, the inflationary process has evolved and people usually reckon with the price rises, a relationship opposed to the Keynesian one will emerge. With the growth of the money stock, nominal interest rate will also rise. "... high interest rates mean that money has been easy in the sense of increasing rapidly, and low interest rates, that money has been tight in the sense of increasing slowly..."[55]

Since expectations in Friedman slowly adjust themselves to reality, the Keynesian uncertainty cannot be found in his model, and thus the specific role of money that Keynes could only explain by referring to uncertainty is missing from it.

In the natural-rate hypothesis, which assumes flexible prices, there is no place for cost-push inflation. As long as the quantity of money is constant, there is no

[54] See M. Friedman: A Monetary Theory of Nominal Income, *Journal of Political Economy*, 1971, No. 2, p. 326.

[55] M. Friedman: *op. cit.*, p. 335.

possibility for the price level and for the general level of money wages to rise, the pressure through cost cannot prevail. What the wage struggles of the trade unions can attain, is only a redistribution of money wages.

The unanticipated growth of the quantity of money pushes output, temporarily, above its value belonging to the equilibrium path, while the price level is also rising. As a result, in the course of an upswing the velocity of circulation rises temporarily above its permanent value. According to Friedman, this formation of the actual velocity of circulation also constitutes part of the movement along the stable function of the demand for money. If the quantity of money increases, permanent nominal income, as has been shown, has to rise so that the increased nominal demand for money belonging to it could absorb the growth in the money stock. But permanent nominal income increases through actual nominal income. For permanent nominal income to reach its appropriate level, the rise in actual nominal income must be greater, since in permanent income calculations, actual income has a weight of less than 1. Applying the weight of 0.33 used by Friedman, actual income has to increase by three times the permanent income. Accordingly, the actual velocity of circulation has to exceed the permanent one as many times as actual nominal income is greater than permanent nominal income. A similar relation can be shown to exist if the quantity of money falls.

By distinguishing actual from permanent velocity of circulation and disclosing their relationship, Friedman tries to resolve the contradiction in his model, namely, that the permanent velocity of circulation decreases with the growth of permanent income and increases with a fall in permanent income, whereas the actual velocity of circulation rises together with the increase in actual income in the case of an upswing and decreases together with the fall in actual income in the case of a downswing.

By finding an explanation of why actual nominal national income and velocity of circulation move in the short run in the same direction, Friedman makes use of the weaknesses of Keynes's argumentation and launches an attack against him. The Keynesian criticism of the monetarist interpretation of aggregate demand as MV cannot be accepted, as in the case of an upswing with the rise in the quantity of money, the velocity of circulation also rises (and does not fall)[56]. Really, the Keynesian argumentation did not reckon with cyclical changes in the capitalist economy, and this can be maintained even in the Keynesian logical system only in the case of unchanged profit expectations. In an upswing, however, profit expectations are steadily improving, and thus the slow-down of the fall in the interest rate resulting from the growth in the quantity of money, as pointed out by Keynes, need not decelerate investments and through them the rise in national income.

AN ATTEMPT TO ANSWER SOME PROBLEMS RAISED BY MONETARISM

What can a mere change in the quantity of money be expected to achieve? Does it increase or decrease nominal aggregate income? Can it elicit an upswing or a crisis? Has its effect increased in contemporary capitalism? Are the changes in the quantity of money and in nominal national income really correlated?

[56] See M. Friedman: The Demand for Money ..., op. cit., p. 138.

A great part of the quantity of money, in contemporary capitalism too, enters into circulation to satisfy the money requirements of the circulation of commodities, to realize the price sum of commodities. This is, primarily, why Friedman found a correlation between the change in the quantity of money and the movement of nominal national income in both the long and the short run. In this context, however, it was not the quantity of money that, together with the velocity of circulation, determined the magnitude of nominal national income, but it was the price sum of commodities that determined the quantity of money to be put into circulation at the existing velocity.[57] Under the conditions of cost-push inflation this relationship is especially obvious. If the rate of monetary expansion does not adjust to the cost pressure, output and with it employment will fall. By making use of Friedman's data, Kaldor proves that it was not due to the scarcity of money that the Great Depression emerged or deepened to such an extent. He points out that the quantity of money in the United States "increased and not decreased, throughout the Great Contraction".[58] The supply of money, however, did really decrease. It decreased because the banks were cautious enough to increase their liquidity, and it also decreased as a "consequence of an insufficient demand for loans—of the horse *refusing* to drink..."[59]

For similar considerations, non-Marxian economists criticize also that statement by Friedman that an upswing is due to an increase in the quantity of money because it precedes the increase in output. Davidson and Weintraub refer to the fact that if entrepreneurs expect an increase in sales, they increase their equipment and inventories and "...are likely to borrow in advance of the event... If the Monetary Authority acquiesces by providing the finance required, then the statistical series will show the money supply increase as *preceding* the output increase."[60]

Another part of the increased quantity of money does not serve the needs of the circulation of commodities, as it is designed to finance government expenditures through which it directly appears as nominal demand. As such, it may increase partly the price level, partly the output, but in either case it increases nominal national income. According to Friedman, government expenditures were able to increase nominal national income because they were financed by issuing money, and thus nominal national income was raised by the growth of the quantity of money. We must agree with Friedman when he states that the effect of government expenditures on increasing nominal demand depends on the method of financing. But it is not that the government spends more because the quantity of money increases, but that the quantity of money increases because the government wishes to spend more. It was not the monetary policy that gave rise to fiscal policy, but it was fiscal policy that stimulated monetary policy to issue larger quantities of money.

And when due to the fluctuations in government or private expenditures the quantity of money fluctuates, the cyclical changes are not the consequence of the fluctuations in the quantity of money but of those in state or private spendings.

[57] N. Kaldor: New Monetarism, *Lloyds Bank Review*, March 1970, p. 16.
[58] N. Kaldor: *op. cit.*, p. 13.
[59] N. Kaldor: *op. cit.*, p. 14.
[60] P. Davidson and S. Weintraub: Money as Cause and Effect, *The Economic Journal*, December 1973, p. 1118.

Another part of the quantity of money is transmitted to the commercial banks or to the public exclusively through monetary policy, by open-market operations. This might be the quantity of money that could exert the effect outlined by Friedman. Those who have sold bonds, that is, income-yielding assets to the central bank, wish to place the money thus obtained in a profitable way. In the course of this process, the composition of their wealth changes, and the resulting effect may transgress the framework of the portfolio, may elicit nominal demand for reproducible goods and may thus stimulate their output.

Especially in inflationary times, when the function of money as a store of wealth becomes weaker, the economic agents try to spend the money obtained through open-market operations (or otherwise) by investing it in assets of a more stable value. In the case of unanticipated inflation, as we can read in Grosseschmidt's work,[61] it is worthwhile investing money in real rather than in financial assets, because the price of the former changes with inflation, while financial assets can keep pace with the price level only through the interest rate. However, the rise in nominal interest rate lags behind the rise in the price level and thus real interest rate declines. In inflationary times, investments by enterprises, banks and the public in real assets or inventories are considered to be promising that inflation will offer gains or at least preserve the value of the real asset. Fellner writes: "The most important shift that occurred in the structure of American household wealth in the inflationary period following the year 1965 was a change in the proportion between the value of net financial assets and the value of real assets."[62] Under inflationary circumstances, Friedman's criticism of Keynes's statement appears to be justified, namely, that when analysing the function of money as a store of wealth, Keynes paid attention only to the substitution relation between money and government bonds and neglected the substitution relation between money and other assets.

However, even under inflationary conditions, the economic agents will be reluctant to invest the money they obtained through open-market operations in reproducible assets if they expect an unfavourable cyclical change during which the realization of real assets held as wealth is impossible, except on unfavourable terms. That is, they are faced with the danger of suffering losses or losing their liquidity. "... no commodity accumulation whatsoever can offer the same security as is ensured in the world of stable prices by money or demands on fix sums which can be recovered practically without any risk."[63] In other words, neither in inflationary periods can commodities fulfil the wealth storing function of money of a stable value. Under such circumstances, it may appear to be preferable to invest excess money in safe, profitable securities that are easy to realize. But then the effect of monetary policy on restructuring the balance-sheet does not go beyond the framework of the portfolio, does not increase nominal demand for reproducible

[61] See B. Grosseschmidt: *Kritik der postkeynesianischen Stabilitätspolitik*. Duncker and Humblot, Berlin, 1976, p. 107.

[62] W. Fellner: Piaci reakciók az inflációs irányzatra: változások az amerikai magánháztartások vagyonának összetételében és a vállalatok mérleghelyzetében (Market reactions to the inflationary trend: changes in the structure of American private households and in the balance-sheet position of enterprises). In: Á. Schmidt and E. Kemenes (eds.): *Változások, váltások és válságok a gazdaságban* (Changes, transitions and crises in the economy). Tanulmányok Varga István emlékezetére (Studies in the memory of István Varga), Budapest, 1982, p. 86.

[63] W. Fellner: *op. cit.*, p. 93.

goods and does not give rise to demand-pull inflation. And a monetary equilibrium may arise in such a way that, through the increase in security prices, the "rates of return on financial assets adjust themselves in such a manner as to make people content to hold the larger stock of money."[64]

It is a function of the business cycle how wealth holders change the structure of the balance-sheet as a result of the growth in the quantity of money, whether they buy only financial assets or also reproducible assets and what combination of securities they realize within the financial assets. In Friedman, however, it is exactly the spending of the increased quantity of money on financial and real assets that changes their rate of returns and leads to cyclical fluctuations.

As regards the effect of the quantity of money on the formation of nominal demand, Friedman's statement is only a half-truth: the increase in nominal demand, especially if the velocity of circulation, as Friedman asserts, falls in the long run, presupposes an increase in the money stock. However, a mere quantitative growth in the money stock does not necessarily increase nominal demand for reproducible assets. Therefore, though nominal aggregate demand can be expressed as the product of the quantity and of the velocity of circulation of money, this approach does not show what factors are responsible for the growth in aggregate demand. Friedman's statement is superficial compared to Keynes's who approached aggregate demand through expenditures, by which he clarified how the market expanded through investments and how it expanded if the income-distribution relations were changed in favour of the poor and to the detriment of the rich.

We may argue similarly against the statements made by Friedman concerning the change in the tax rate. If at an unchanged money stock and unchanged government expenditures the tax rate rises, the quantity of money released as a result of the decreasing loans raised by the government is not necessarily spent on the purchase of commodities and therefore it is not ensured that aggregate demand will not decline.

In connection with the long-term movement of the velocity of circulation disclosed by Friedman, let us see what Samuelson says about it. In his view, the velocity of circulation showed, historically, a falling trend in the long run. In the past few years, however, the velocity of circulation has generally increased as a result of inflation, high nominal interest rates, through the use of computers, credit cards and as a result of the improved methods of planning the money stock.[65] That is, no unambiguous functional relationship can be established between the velocity of circulation and permanent real income. In other words, the expected movement of permanent real income does not provide a safe basis on which to assess the velocity of circulation.

In Friedman, through upsetting the equilibrium of the balance-sheet, the rise in the stock of money directly increases nominal aggregate income. Many, mainly post-Keynesian authors, however, maintain the view that the mere increase of the quantity of money can only exert an impact on nominal aggregate demand indirectly, through the interest rate. But they present this impact on a much broader scale than Keynes, also taking into account, among other things, the various

64 F.H. Hahn: Professor Friedman's Views on Money, *Economica*, February 1971.
65 See P.A. Samuelson: *Economics*, New York, 1973, Chapter 15, p. 75.

wealth effects: "... just about every component of aggregate demand ... responds to interest rates...", writes Modigliani.[66] The lesson that can be drawn from this is that the effect of the change in the money stock, which asserts itself through the interest rate and acts on the growth of nominal demand, is also a function of the cyclical movement. It is uncertain to what extent monetary policy can increase nominal demand, and this effect may become especially uncertain under the circumstances of a high-rate inflation, which aggravates the economic calculations of the entrepreneurs. More certain than this is the effect of monetary restrictions. The experiences of the 1970s in the United States, for example, show that monetary restrictions did not stop inflation, but through creating a tense situation in the credit market, they contributed to a lessening in output, primarily through a fall in construction.[67]

We can argue in a similar way against Friedman's idea that with a given quantity of money no cost-push inflation is possible. If, with the same quantity of money, the price level rises because the costs have increased, output and employment will decrease. Thus inflation may unfold also at a given quantity of money. In Friedman, however, at least in the case of anticipated inflation, output and employment cannot fall, since full employment is ensured.

As regards the effect of monetary policy, we can state that it may help to give rise to a good and even more to a bad cyclical change, but it is just one of the factors inducing cyclical movement. Cycles are formed as the joint resultant of these factors. It may occur that in this process, the effect of monetary policy becomes the strongest or that, from among the many effects, it is just the effect of monetary policy that makes the balance-arm sway. The upswing-inducing effect of monetary policy is more vigorous in such a period when the other factors acting upon cyclical movements ensure a relatively more even economic development and when the less crisis-sensitive sectors have a significant weight in the economy (as, e.g., the service and the state sector). But monetary policy has always been able to attain this effect only in conjunction with the other factors.

Out of the factors forming cyclical changes, Friedman one-sidedly selects the monetary factor and presents its effect independently of the cyclical situation. In his theory, it is exactly the unexpected change in the quantity of money that gives rise to cyclical fluctuations. And from the fact that in the capitalist economy of our time the role of monetary factors in forming cyclical changes has increased, he comes to the conclusion that the earlier cycles, among them the great economic depression of 1929–1933, were also elicited by monetary factors.

IS THE GOVERNMENT REALLY UNABLE TO INFLUENCE EMPLOYMENT AND OUTPUT?

In this respect, Friedman's statements are based on two neo-classical assumptions of his model: (1) economic agents optimize their positions; (2) the free play of prices clears all markets. In this case, unemployment means an optimum sit-

[66] F. Modigliani: Rediscovery of Money—Discussion, *The American Economic Rewiew*, May 1975, p. 181.
[67] See P. Erdős and F. Molnár: *op. cit.*, pp. 224 and 226.

uation for the worker, chosen voluntarily. Unemployment can only have a natural rate.

According to Friedman's positive economics,[68] it is demanded from a theoretical system that the conclusions derived from its hypotheses should correspond to reality. If this requirement is met, its hypotheses are justified even if they might happen to appear incorrect. Friedman's interest is concentrated on which assumptions provide a better result in forecasting the effects of economic policy.

According to post-Keynesian economics, the keeping down of unemployment is accompanied by inflation. That is, the lower the percentage level of unemployment, the higher the rate of inflation. Friedman, however, emphasizes that on the basis of his assumption he can explain how a wide variety of inflation rates may belong to a given percentage of unemployment; furthermore, he also explains that, contrary to the Keynesian assumption, the worker is interested not only in the magnitude of his money wage, but also in that of his real wage. Namely, as soon as he recognizes that his real wage has decreased, he adjusts the growth rate of his money wage to the rate of inflation. According to Keynes, monetary policy can permanently decrease the nominal interest rate by increasing the quantity of money. In Friedman's view, the increase in the quantity of money, by causing inflation, gives rise to an opposite effect: after a transitory fall, the nominal rate of interest will rise, as soon as inflation becomes anticipated.

At the same time, the natural-rate hypothesis does contradict the facts. Non-Marxian criticism also points out that, taking unemployment as voluntary, it is unlikely that the enormous fluctuations of employment in the period of the Great Depression in 1929–1933 were a consequence of the workers' erroneous information.[69] According to Sargent[70], who is a defender of the natural-rate hypothesis, it was the natural rate of unemployment that shifted in that period. Modigliani justly ridicules that statement by saying that in that case the great unemployment "… was a severe attack of contagious laziness."[71] And despite that large-scale unemployment, no accelerating rate of the fall of the price level could be experienced which, according to Friedman, regularly ensues to adjust the false expectations of the workers and to restore thereby the natural rate of unemployment. This, at the same time, also proves that prices and wages have no downward flexibility.

Anyway, the mechanism described by Friedman would not have been able to decrease the excessive growth of unemployment even at flexible prices and money wages. As Gerfin points out[72], in the period of a persistently high-rate unemployment, the skills of the unemployed workers become morally obsolete, as they can neither preserve nor further develop them in the work process. Thus, the unemployment caused originally by a demand shortage, will turn into and

[68] See M. Friedman: The Methodology of Positive Economics. In: *Essays in Positive Economics*, Chicago, 1953.

[69] See R. J. Gordon: Recent Developments in the Theory of Inflation and Unemployment, *Journal of Monetary Economics*, 1976, No. 1, pp. 196–197.

[70] See T. I. Sargent: A Classical Macroeconomic Model for the United States, *Journal of Political Economy*, April 1976, pp. 207–237.

[71] F. Modigliani: The Monetarist Controversy or, Should We Forsake Stabilisation Policies? *The American Economic Rewiew*, March 1977, p. 6.

[72] See H. Gerfin: Informationsprobleme des Arbeitsmarktes, *Kyklos*, 1982, Vol. 35, Fasc. 3, pp. 425–427.

persist as structural unemployment. But this fate will be assigned to Friedman's voluntarily unemployed workers, too, if they are unemployed for a longer period; because after a certain time, even if they wanted to, they would not be able to find suitable jobs for themselves.

As soon as we suppose that there does exist involuntary unemployment, economic policy may prove efficient in increasing employment. Those models which, unlike the paradigm of market-clearing, set out from the assumption that prices are sluggish, sticky and do not clear the market, and thus not all of the unemployed people become unemployed voluntarily, can already fit, as we shall see later, state economic policy with long-lasting effects into the framework of their system. Friedman is right in saying that under the circumstances of inflation it is difficult to distinguish between the change in the price level and the change in relative prices, that it is not easy to assess the change in real wages. However, he is not right in maintaining that it is only for this reason that economic policy can be effective.

One of the pillars of the natural-rate hypothesis is the paradigm of market-clearing. The change in relative prices reflects in Friedman allocational tasks related to the real sphere, and ensures harmony between the structure of demand and output, while the movement of the price level expresses a change in the monetary sphere. Namely, when the quantity of money and through it nominal aggregate demand fall, the decrease in the price level maintains the real demand which is needed to keep employment at its equilibrium level. As already pointed out above, changes in the price level do not only reflect inflationary or deflationary movements in the monetary sphere, but also changes in allocation, in the reproduction process as well as in the relation between the production of capital and consumer goods. Therefore, the even rate of money issue, hence a measure taken exclusively in the monetary sphere, cannot ensure the undisturbed development of the capitalist economy, cannot ensure that the agents of the market be able to make a distinction between changes in the price level and those in relative prices. It cannot eliminate those shocks of the capitalist economy which stem from the real sphere. Criticizing Friedman, Modigliani refers to facts, namely, "... our most unstable periods have coincided with periods of relative monetary stability."[73]

Unemployment growing since the 1970s together with increasing inflation in the developed capitalist countries means a severe blow to Friedman's natural-rate hypothesis. In his lecture held on the occasion of winning the Nobel Prize, he was compelled to admit that "the natural-rate hypothesis in its present form has not proved rich enough to explain a more recent development..."[74] However, he continues to believe in the efficiency of the capitalist real economy, and sees the source of the recent serious problems of the capitalist economies in state intervention. In order to realize full employment, or in the interest of its welfare policy, the government increases its spendings which are financed by issuing money, and thereby it causes inflation. On the other hand, under the pressure of its constituents, it pursues an anti-inflationary policy and strives to keep inflation down. This fluctuation of government policy makes both the actual and the expected rate of inflation very unstable. In addition, the government seeks to regulate price formation and diverts thereby the prices from their relative levels established by

---

[73] F. Modigliani: *op. cit.*, p. 12.
[74] M. Friedman: Nobel Lecture..., *op. cit.*, p. 470.

the market forces. All this gives rise to disturbances in all markets, as a result of which the efficiency of the economic system diminishes and unemployment grows.

In Friedman's view the recent severe diseases of the developed capitalist economies could be cured by ensuring that the market forces might play a greater role. For this purpose, and in the interest of decreasing inflation, he finds it desirable to keep down state expenditures. In reality, at the present stage of development of the capitalist economy, even if we disregard armament expenditures as Friedman did, the government is compelled to undertake a number of tasks which the private sector is reluctant or unable to perform exactly in the interest and the defence of development. And in several important branches of the economy, it was exactly development that ruled out the classical form of competition and substituted for it the "cut-throat" competition of the oligopolists, which, according to the representatives of the theory of market forms, has to be controlled by the state.

Chapter 3

THE NEW MICRO-ECONOMICS

THE SEARCH MODEL

The new micro-economics is a specific branch of monetarism. Its emergence is part of that trend unfolding since the 1960s which, ignoring the person of the Walrasian auctioneer, wishes to explain inflation and unemployment on the basis of the imperfect information of the market agents. The approach of its representatives—Phelps, Mortensen, Holt and others—is micro-economic, as is also indicated by the name of the school. All of them rely significantly on Stigler's so-called search model. Hence, before discussing their views, it is necessary to get acquainted with Stigler's model.

In Stigler's decentralized markets having no auctioneer, owing to the costliness of gathering information, it is impossible for any buyer to know all the prices at which the sellers offer their products for sale at a given point of time, nor can the sellers know the prices of all their competitors. If the buyer wants to buy at the most favourable price, he must first search for it. But the seller must also be informed about the prices of the other sellers before he sets the price of his own products. This process of gathering information is the so-called search activity. Its costliness, however, restricts the buyer in finding the seller who offers his products at the lowest possible price, but it also restricts the seller in finding out the prices of all his competitors. It is exactly owing to the imperfect information of the market agents that a product may have different prices at a given point of time. And the higher the cost the market agents are willing to spend on this search, that is, the more informed they are, the less will be the dispersion of prices.

However, despite the searching activity, the divergence of prices will persist, because the information collected becomes obsolete as a result of the changes in the demand and supply relations.

Would it not be possible to inform the buyers about the price changes, about the new prices by way of advertising?—asks Stigler. The answer is that it would not, because a typical household is likely to buy several hundred different items in a month, and even if their prices change on average only each month, the number of advertisements that a housewife ought to read would be formidable. "The seller's problem is even greater: he may sell two thousand items ... and to advertise each on the occasion of a price change ... would be impossibly expensive."[75]

Stigler maintains that, as regards information, the situation in the labour market

[75] G.J. Stigler: The Economics of Information, *The Journal of Political Economy*, June 1961, p. 223.

is similar to that in the commodity markets.[76] No worker has all the information on the wage rates and the labour conditions that he can expect to find with each potential employer. It is therefore worthwhile for him to spend his time gathering information so that he may find the wage rate and working conditions which are the most favourable for him. But the acquisition of information is only successful if the worker devotes his whole day to it and specializes in searching for new job opportunities. Therefore, he quits his earlier job and spends his time getting acquainted with job availabilities. In agreement with Stigler, Mortensen considers it worthwhile for a worker to continue his search as long as he finds a wage rate "which equates at the margin the value of time spent searching to the present value of the future benefits attributable to search"[77]. This kind of unemployment, the so-called search unemployment, plays an important role in a significant part of the neo-classical models of the 1970s. It stems not from the insufficiency of demand, but from the workers' incomplete information, and is of a voluntary character. And the case of "unemployment at full employment", namely when the number of labour searchers and the number of new job opportunities coincide, finds a novel explanation in the new micro-economics. This type of unemployment stems not only from structural discrepancy, but also from deficient information. That is, the unemployed are not informed about many of the job vacancies.

Let us characterize the search model on the basis of features shared by the representatives of the new micro-economics.

Let us set out from the market situation presented as typical in the new microeconomic model. In the various labour markets of an economy, money wage rates are widely dispersed in space and a part of the workers spend their time gathering information, that is, they—as unemployed—are searching for new job opportunities. Let us suppose that the quantity of money and with it nominal aggregate demand rises unexpectedly. The price level will rise and so will the money wage rates. But since there is no auctioneer to inform the workers free of charge about the general trend of the rise in money wage rates, "such unexpected rises induce some of the search unemployed to stop search earlier, to accept employment at the sampled wage rates..."[78], as they think they would find lower money wages elsewhere. Experiencing the growth of their money wage rates, the workers already employed will not begin to search for new jobs. However, slowly they will find out that money wages have also increased in other jobs, that a general inflationary process has unfolded and thus the originally existing differences among wage rates have not disappeared. Some of them will start to search for new jobs and unemployment will rise to its original level. That is, unemployment was decreased only temporarily by an unexpected inflationary process. And if the government wishes to maintain unemployment at a level lower than the original one, it has to increase the rate of inflation and thereby make the workers have the

[76] G.J. Stigler: Information in the Labor Market, *Journal of Political Economy*, October 1962, Part II, pp. 94–105.

[77] D.T. Mortensen: Job Search, the Duration of Unemployment and the Phillips Curve, *The American Economic Review*, December 1970, p. 849.

[78] E.S. Phelps: The New Microeconomics in Inflation and Employment Theory, *The American Economic Review*, May 1969, p. 152.

illusion that the money wage rate offered to them is higher than what they can get elsewhere.

A process in the opposite direction takes place when the government cuts the quantity of money and with it nominal aggregate demand. The price level and money wage rates will decline. And since the workers are not informed about the general fall in money wages, "some workers will refuse employment at the now (lower) market-clearing money wage rates, preferring to spend the time searching for a better relative money wage elsewhere."[79] However, the workers' expectations are adjusted also in deflation. Sooner or later they will recognize that the fall in money wage rates is general, part of them will take up work, and unemployment will fall to the level that prevailed when the original difference between money wage rates still existed. And if the government wished to maintain the increased volume of unemployment, it ought to raise the rate of deflation so that it might systematically mislead the workers.

This model is similar to that of Friedman. Also in the new micro-economics unemployment has a constant rate which, independently of the rate of inflation, persists even after the workers' expectations have been adjusted. Phelps speaks of the equilibrium rate of unemployment, which is a concept similar to the natural rate of unemployment in Friedman's model. In both models, the government can only act upon the rate of unemployment if it transitorily misleads the workers by changing the rate of inflation or deflation. Therefore, the trade-off expressed by the Phillips curve, that is, the impact of the growth of the quantity of money on real processes, exists also in the search model in the short run. "The model... provides an inverse relation between the rate of change in money wages and the employment ratio."[80] Or, as Lucas remarks, Phelps received the Phillips curve in a theoretical framework "which is neoclassical except for the removal of the postulate that all transactions are made under complete information."[81] As a result of the effect of the rise in the rate of inflation, unemployment will decrease, whereas it will increase with a rise in the rate of deflation. As soon as the rate of inflation or that of deflation becomes anticipated, the Phillips curve changes into a vertical straight line, and then the level of unemployment does not depend on the rate of inflation or deflation. "An important result is that the equilibrium unemployment ratio is found to be independent of the inflation ratio."[82] And since both the natural rate of unemployment and the equilibrium rate of unemployment depend on the magnitude of the unemployment benefit, it logically follows from both models that this rate could be diminished by decreasing the unemployment benefit.

However, the two models also differ from each other; namely, while in Friedman's model the worker, owing to his incomplete information, does not perceive the relation between his money wage and the price level, in the search model it is the relation between his money wage and the money wage expected to receive elsewhere, about which he is not informed. If the money wage changes, then in Friedman's view the worker will change the length of his leisure, whereas accord-

[79] E.S. Phelps: *op. cit.*, p. 150.
[80] D.T. Mortensen: *op. cit.*, p. 847.
[81] R.E. Lucas: Expectations and the Neutrality of Money, *Journal of Economic Theory*, April 1972, p. 104.
[82] D.T. Mortensen: *Ibid.*

ing to the search model he either starts or stops his job search. In both models, the Phillips curve is a short-term supply function of labour. In Friedman, the supply of labour is a function of the expected real wage rate, whereas in the search model it is a function of the relation between actual money wage rate and money wage rate expected elsewhere. In Friedman's model, the supply curve of labour may also shift at a given real wage rate if the worker believes that his money wage has changed in relation to the price level and thereby his real wage has also changed. In the search model, the supply curve of labour will shift at a given real wage rate if the workers think that their money wage has changed relative to the wage rate paid elsewhere. In other words, in the case of mistaken expectations, the workers in both models strive to form such a supply of labour which optimizes their position, in one on the basis of an erroneously estimated price level whereas in the other on that of the erroneously expected wage rates to be found elsewhere. Consequently, not even flexible money wage rates can clear the labour market in the short run in either model.

CRITICAL COMMENTS

The representatives of the search model claim to provide a general explanation of unemployment micro-economically, i.e. on the basis of the rational decisions of workers who have incomplete information about an imperfect market. This explanation rapidly gained ground in non-Marxian economics, in the 1970s, although it was repeatedly criticized from that side, too.

The search model, like Friedman's natural-rate hypothesis, makes unemployment appear as voluntary. Feldstein[83] points out that becoming unemployed through voluntary quits is not a general phenomenon in the capitalist economy. According to his estimates, only 15 per cent of the unemployed became jobless through voluntarily quitting their jobs in the USA in 1974. And a significant part of them did not leave their place of employment because they wanted to find a better job.

It is a fact that most workers changing their firms were not unemployed even temporarily, i.e. they went directly over to another firm and received higher wages than the job searchers. Thus the assumption that searching for jobs while being unemployed is more effective than in the case of uninterrupted employment, is not justified by experience.[84]

And with the present, developed system of communication, the worker need not first become unemployed in order to search for a new job. In Gordon's view,[85] white-collar workers can search for an alternative job on the telephone during their working hours, whereas blue-collar workers can get the necessary information, among others, in the pub after work.

The model assumes that a worker who quits his job believes that somewhere

[83] M. S. Feldstein: The Importance of Temporary Layoffs: An Empirical Analysis, *Brookings Papers on Economic Activity*, 1975/3, p. 731.

[84] See H. Gerfin: Neue Entwicklungen und Perspektiven der Arbeitsmarkttheorie, *Zeitschrift für die gesamte Staatswissenschaft*, September 1978, p. 431.

[85] R.J. Gordon: Recent Developments in the Theory of Inflation and Unemployment, *Journal of Monetary Economics*, 1976/1, p. 206.

there exists a place of employment which offers him a higher money wage rate. But giving notice to quit depends not only on the expected wage differences, but also on the likelihood—in the worker's estimate—of a vacancy for him. And as this likelihood is very little in a slump, the decision to quit will clearly depend primarily on this circumstance and not on the imagined wage differences. But in the model, the frequency of workers' quitting their jobs is taken to be anti-cyclical: the number of workers quitting their jobs increases in a downswing when money wages fall, and decreases in an upswing when money wages rise. The actual process, however, is just the opposite. This theory reflects reality only in so far as unemployment really increases during a recession. According to this theory, it takes place because the wage claims of workers, i.e. the magnitude of money wages expected elsewhere, have not been adjusted to the money wages that have fallen as a result of the downswing. But this is only a theoretical assumption which cannot be justified by practice. The adequacy of this assumption is refuted by the fact that the number of workers giving notice falls to a minimum during a recession.

The search model cannot explain why unemployment is so high in certain groups of the labour force (young people, women, coloured people) that it exceeds the average several times.[86]

If unemployment were connected only with the search for better places of employment, it would not be possible to explain, says Solow[87], why such a great number of workers queue up at the gates of factories when they are offering job opportunities in the course of a recession.

With unemployment taken to be voluntary, there is no room in the search model for the general phenomenon that it is the employer who gives notice to the worker and that it depends on the employer whether he employs the worker or not. In practice, the firms do not stimulate their abundant workers to leave by lowering their wage rate (by the way, money wages are generally not flexible downwards), instead, the employers dismiss part of their workers at unchanged wage rates. Alchian's argument[88] that the two ways of diminishing the size of the labour force have the same effect does not hold. In his view, the firm knows that if it diminishes the money wage, the worker will quit his job, and therefore it finds it easier to dismiss him without applying the market mechanism. This argument contradicts the logic of the neo-classical theory. Namely, if an enterprise does not decrease the money wage, but dismisses part of the workers and pays, along a positively upward sloping supply curve, more to the remaining workers than what is needed to keep them, it will not optimize its position.[89] Furthermore, if it dismisses a worker who would have remained at the existing wage rate, then the worker will have to switch over from an optimal supply function of his labour which is restricted only by prices and money wages, to a supply function which also implies

[86] H. Gerfin: *op. cit.*, pp. 428–430.

[87] R. Solow: On Theories of Unemployment, *The American Economic Review*, March 1980, p. 7.

[88] See A. Alchian: Information Costs, Pricing and Resource Unemployment. In: E.S. Phelps (ed.): *Microeconomic Foundations of Employment and Inflation Theory*, New York, 1969, pp. 22–52.

[89] See M. Sentomero and J.J. Seater: The Inflation-Unemployment Trade-off: A Critique of the Literature, *Journal of Economic Literature*, June 1978, pp. 522–523.

a quantity constraint (which, as we shall see later, expresses that in offering his labour, the worker also takes into account the demand for the good he produces). Thus we have entered a non-Walrasian world, and this situation cannot be analysed in the equilibrium model of the search theory.[90] And, finally, also non-Marxian criticism points out[91] that if the enterprise wishes to get rid of its redundant workers by diminishing the wage rates, the efficiency of this policy will be uncertain. Assuming non-homogenous workers, it may occur that a more qualified and more efficient worker whom the enterprise would like to retain will quit.

The search model, says Dean,[92] conceals structural unemployment which, owing to the rapid changes in technology and tastes, is significant. The structurally unemployed who search for new jobs but find no appropriate place of employment appear in this model as unemployed searching for a new job, in the same way as the workers who have become unemployed for lack of demand, with the only difference that in these cases the search will last longer.

The theory completely fails to answer the question of what endogenous factors call forth the cyclical changes in aggregate demand, which, through the movement of money wages, give rise to the fluctuations in search unemployment.

The segmented or dual labour-market theory presents a picture of the labour market which is completely opposed to the one drawn by the search model,[93] thus it also provides a criticism of the search model. According to the model of the dual labour-market theory, a primary and a secondary sector can be distinguished in the labour market. In the primary sector the places of employment are good, the earning possibilities are favourable, employment is relatively stable, as enterprises have invested "human capital" in the training of their work force, or the workers have acquired their high skills simply in the learning-by-doing process. The firms will try to keep these workers even in an unfavourable business cycle. The labour force belonging to the primary sector enjoys various advantages and has prospects for promotion in the firm. To supply appropriate labour for the more important jobs, the firms do not recruit their work force from outside. Workers rise along the stages of an internal hierarchy, whereas to outsiders it is only the lower stages that are open, and even those not to anyone. The firms apply discrimination against certain groups of the labour force.

If, during a recession, a firm is compelled to dismiss part of its workers belonging to the primary sector, then, according to Feldstein's temporary lay-off theory already discussed, a significant proportion of these workers will not try to find employment elsewhere, and will not therefore engage in a search activity either, but expect to be recalled. "The conventional model of search unemployment is inappropriate for those on temporary layoffs."[94]

[90] *Ibid.*

[91] F. Modigliani: The Monetarist Controversy or Should We Forsake Stabilization Policies? *The American Economic Review*, March 1977, p. 7.

[92] See J.W. Dean: The Dissolution of the Keynesian Consensus. In: *The Crisis of Economic Theory*, New York, 1981.

[93] See G.G. Cain: The Challenge of Segmented Labor Market Theories to Orthodox Theory: A Survey, *Journal of Economic Literature*, December 1976, pp. 1215–1257.

[94] M. Feldstein: The Effect of Unemployment Insurance on Temporary Layoff Unemployment, *The American Economic Review*, December 1978, p. 834.

The wide fluctuation of the labour force, to which the proponents of the search model refer, is typical of the secondary sector. Here the productivity of labour and the wages are low, there is hardly any promotion possibility, the firms do not make any effort to keep the labour force, as workers belonging to the secondary sector are easy to substitute. The firms have not invested "human capital" in the workers, and thus their skills are not firm-specific. Lay-offs initiated by the firm are frequent, for which insignificant changes in market relations or matters of little consequence in the worker's behaviour are sufficient. But quits are also frequently initiated by the workers. And since the alternative jobs open to the worker are not better either, this sector is characterized by a high labour turnover. However, as has been shown above, this happens for the most part for reasons different from those to which the representatives of the search model refer.

Chapter 4

THE NEW CLASSICAL MACRO-ECONOMICS

THE MAJOR CHARACTERISTICS OF THE THEORY. THE HYPOTHESIS OF RATIONAL EXPECTATIONS

The new classical macro-economics is the second wave of monetarist counter-revolution, a radical variant of monetarism. Its major representatives, Lucas, Sargent, Wallace and Barro, attack active state economic policy and through it Keynesian macro-economics, and devote in their models less space for state economic intervention than even Friedman in whose model it is possible for systematic economic policy aimed at misleading the agents of the market to be successful at least temporarily. Through the innovations carried out in the tools of analysis and in the econometric models, the new school, writes Tobin,[95] attracts the youth in the same way as Keynes did in his time.

The representatives of the new classical macro-economics borrow much from Friedman, the initiator of monetarist counter-revolution. Such is, among others, the market-clearing paradigm, the idea that at flexible prices private capitalist economy stabilizes itself. In their models, the economic agents try to make optimal use of their means and resources. In their decisions on this use they adjust only to relative prices and shift the market by their behaviour towards an equilibrium position. Given relative equilibrium prices, all agents of the market make a maximum use of the mutual advantages offered by the market. In their decisions, the price level has no role to play. The representatives of the new classical macro-economics also borrow from Friedman, among others, the natural-rate hypothesis, and the distinction between anticipated and unanticipated inflation.

On the other hand, they criticize Friedman for relying on the hypothesis of adaptive expectations. According to this hypothesis, the agents of economic life, when estimating the expected price level, project the past movement of prices into the future. They always take notice of the actual changes of the price level only with a lag. This is why the government can temporarily mislead them with its economic policy measures through which it establishes a price level that is unexpected by them.

The representatives of the new classical macro-economics substitute Muth's hypothesis of *rational expectations* for the hypothesis of adaptive expectations. Along with the market-clearing paradigm, this hypothesis is another pillar of their theoretical system.

According to the hypothesis of rational expectations, the economic agents make optimal use of all information available to them when forming their expectations. This range of information extends not only to past and current prices as is the case

---

[95] J. Tobin: *Assets Accumulation and Economic Activity*, Chicago Press, 1980, p. 22.

in the hypothesis of adaptive expectations, but is much wider, covering, among other things, knowledge of the structure of the economy and information on the reaction of the government to events known to the public, such as, for example, its reaction to unemployment; that is, it also contains what is called the feedba k rule. According to the assumption of the theory, people make use of their past observation of regularities experienced in the government's behaviour—the recognition of the rules according to which the government changes the quantity of money, among them — in order to draw conclusions therefrom for the expected change in the government's economic policy. In forming their expectations, the economic agents also rely on the new results of economics: "... expectations, since they are informed predictions of future events, are essentially the same as the predictions of the relevant economic theory."[96] The expectations in this model are not phenomena to be explained psychologically, but magnitudes which mathematically depend on the given conditions. By the designation "macro-economics" the representatives of this theory want to express that the economic agents in their models also take into account the all-economic conditions of their optimal action when shaping their expectations. And by the attribute "classical", they wish to express that it is based on the neo-classical theory.

In a stochastic model, the economic agents do not possess all the information needed to make their decision, but they use the information accessible to them in an optimal way. Thus, although rational expectations cannot provide an accurate prediction of the future price level, they give at least the best possible estimation. Thereby this model shatters the assumption of the hypothesis of adaptive expectations, namely, that expectations concerning the price level are slow to adjust.

The similarity of the available items of information and their optimal use make it possible for the agents of economic life to estimate the future in a similar way.

Owing to the insufficiency of information, the expectations may be uncertain or erroneous, but, according to this theory, the economic agents do not make systematic errors and the economic policy cannot mislead them systematically as is the case with the hypothesis of adaptive expectations: "Unlike the implications of adaptive expectations, the forecast error must be nonsystematic, nonserially correlated variables".[97] If the regular reaction of the government to a given phenomenon were estimated erroneously, this would already constitute part of the available information to be used when forming the next expectation regarding the same governmental behaviour.

As a result of the behaviour of the economic units that optimize their position and rationally estimate the micro- and macro-economic conditions of their actions, the economy develops along a stable equilibrium path even without the Walrasian auctioneer. According to the representatives of the new classical macro-economics, adaptive expectations would only make sense if there existed a stable relation between the past and future values of the aggregate variables, and thus the individuals could exclusively base their expectations on past information in a rational way. But this hypothesis becomes irrational if economic policy changes in the meantime. Relying merely on past information, it is impossible to assess

[96] J.F. Muth: Rational Expectations and the Theory of Price Movements, *Econometrica*, July 1961, p. 316.

[97] J.L. Stein: Monetarist, Keynesian and New Classical Economics, *The American Economic Review*, May 1981, p. 140.

the effect of this change. According to the hypothesis of adaptive expectations, in such cases the individuals always correct their expectations and change their decision afterwards. According to the hypothesis of rational expectations, however, the individuals take into account the expected economic policy decisions and their consequences in advance. They are able in any period to assess, for example, how monetary policy influences the quantity of money as well as the corresponding changes in the price level.

Relying on the hypothesis of rational expectations, Willes[98] doubts whether the Keynesian theory has the right foundations. In the Keynesian model expectations are irrational and, in Willes's view, Keynes could only demonstrate the existence of involuntary unemployment and the insufficiency of aggregate demand and justify state economic intervention on this basis.

Tobin[99] points out that the assumption of market-clearing is a logical necessity in the model, for the agents of the market, with the necessary information in their possession, can assess the actual formation of prices in advance. If the markets were not to be cleared automatically, actual prices would not be equilibrium prices, and the economic agents estimating them and adapting to them would not place equilibrium quantities on the market. In this case, the government would be able to act on the economic processes. But the theory wishes to prove just the opposite.

What will now happen if the government interferes in the course of the economy, increases its spending financed by money issue in order to raise employment and depress unemployment below its natural rate? It follows from the premises of the theory that this intervention is doomed to failure. If the position of all economic units, among them that of the workers too, is optimal, then government economic policy can only put them in a more unfavourable position, as a result of which the optimizing agents will try to offset the impact of economic policy. Forming their expectations rationally, and also knowing the rules of economic policy, namely, what economic policy the government pursues at the existing rate of unemployment, they will not be misled by the increase in the price level due to the growth in nominal demand. The firms will recognize that not only the price of their product but the prices of all other goods have also risen, and thus it is not worthwhile to increase their output. And the workers will recognize that, together with their money wages, the price level has also increased, and, consequently, their real wage rates have not changed, so they will not increase the supply of their labour. Hence, the homogeneity postulate proves to be valid. With the quantity of money increasing, only the price level has become higher, but neither real demand nor employment have changed. Money is completely neutral with respect to the formation of real processes.

The representatives of the new classical macro-economics speak of policy ineffectiveness and, using the initial letters of Lucas, Sargent and Wallace, of the LSW theorem. This ineffectiveness is also expressed by Lucas's aggregate supply function, $Q_t - Q_n = f(P_t - E/P_t)$, where Q_t is the actual magnitude of production, Q_n the quantity of products produced at the natural rate of unemployment,

[98] M.H. Willes: Rational Expectations as a Counter-revolution. In: *Crisis in Economic Theory*, New York, 1981.

[99] See J. Tobin: *op. cit.*, pp. 45–46.

P_t the actual price level and E/P_t the price level expected by people. Hence, the government could only act upon the magnitudes of employment and of output if it could divert the actual price level from the price level expected by people. According to Friedman, the government is able to do it temporarily. For example, not perceiving for a time the increased price level, the worker reckons with the earlier price level and experiencing the growth of his money wage, he believes that his real wage has increased; as a result, he will raise his labour supply. Unemployment will fall below its natural rate, Q_t will exceed Q_n. According to the hypothesis of rational expectations, however, E/P_t coincides with P_t, hence if P_t increases, E/P_t will also incrase. Thus, with the growth in the quantity of money, Q_t will not deviate from Q_n. That is, the actual rate of output is that quantity which exists at the natural rate of unemployment. A trade-off between unemployment and inflation, as expressed by the Phillips curve, does not exist even in the short run. The Phillips curve is a vertical straight line also in the short run. "The hypothesis formulated here implies," writes Sargent, "that there is no way that the government can operate so that it can expect to depress the unemployment rate below the natural rate even in the short run."[100] Thus "policymakers have no 'cruel choice' between inflation and unemployment..."[101] Thus Friedman's problem of the equation missing in the short run, i.e. the problem of how to divide the impact of nominal demand between output and the price level, does not even emerge in the new classical macro-economics.

DISPUTATION OF THE EFFICIENCY OF GOVERNMENT SPENDING IN THE 1970s

On the basis of the new classical macro-economics, Barro tries to demonstrate the ineffectiveness of state expenditures in a specific way.

According to Friedman's view discussed above, it is uncertain whether pure fiscal policy, in which government spending is financed by taxation or by issuing government bonds, increases aggregate nominal demand. The imposition of taxes and their spending by the government only redistribute the incomes among the various strata of the population. The government taking up loans withdraws from the population part of the available credits for the purposes of public expenditure.

Those believing in the effectiveness of fiscal policy refer, on the other hand, to the fact that the financing of government expenditure by issuing bonds increases the wealth of society. Since consumers accumulate wealth in order that later when their incomes owing to age, illness, retirement, unemployment, etc. decrease, they should not be compelled to diminish their consumption, they will cut back their savings and increase their current consumption if their wealth is growing. Moreover, Blinder and Solow hold the view that aggregate demand is further increased by the fact that the government pays interest on its bonds, and the interest income after the deduction of taxes is also a source of demand.[102]

[100] T. J. Sargent: A Classical Macroeconomic Model for the United States, *Journal of Political Economy*, April 1976, No. 2, pp. 213–214.

[101] T. J. Sargent: *op. cit.*, p. 214.

[102] A.I. Blinder and R.M. Solow: Does Fiscal Policy Matter? *Journal of Public Economics*, No. 4, pp. 319–337.

Thus, in the theoretical analysis of whether monetary and fiscal policy were effective, an inportant role was played by the question whether the public regarded government bonds as net wealth.

According to Barro, government bonds really increase wealth in the present, but tax liabilities will also grow with them in the future when the government has to repay its debts, with compound interests. Thus the consumer forming his expectations rationally, also takes account of his future liabilities, capitalizes their stream and recognizes that his wealth has not increased over time. Relying on a relationship found already with Ricardo, Buchanan speaks of *the Ricardian equivalence theorem:* "taxation and public debt issue exert basically equivalent effects",[103] that is, from the point of view of their effect on aggregate demand, it amounts to the same if the government finances its expenditures by taxation or by issuing bonds.

But the life of the consumer is limited, and thus his tax liabilities also extend into the life of the future generation. Hence, the consumer's wealth increases more than his tax liabilities in the remaining part of this lifetime. On the other hand, says Barro, assessing his future tax liabilities, the consumer reckons with the expected fall of not only his own but also of his successors' consumption. "... finite lives will not be relevant to the capitalization of future tax liabilities so long as current generations are connected to future generations by a chain of operative intergenerational transfers..."[104] The consumer does not want that the future income distribution relations affect his successors unfavourably and therefore he increases his current savings so that he may leave a greater bequest to them. Thus in the magnitude of government expenditures private savings will grow, and these expenditures will provide no contribution to a growth in aggregate demand. Their effect is the same as if they had been financed from taxes instead of issuing bonds. According to Barro, it is this increasing saving that ensures the market for government bonds and thus by means of government loans "...there is no change in interest rates, and no displaced private borrowers."[105] Aggregate nominal demand will remain unchanged not because of the crowding-out effect, but as a result of the voluntary growth in consumers' savings.

Barro maintains that "...social security payments are analogous to changes in government debt."[106] By them, the present older generation gains such incomes that are financed from taxes imposed on the present younger generation. In his view, the individual generations increase their savings in order to leave greater bequests to their successors, which are large enough to pay the social security taxes imposed on them. And he notes the following: "As in the case of changes in government debt... the impact of a marginal change in S [i.e. social security payments—A.M.] would be solely on the size of bequests and not at all on the pattern of consumption."[107]

[103] J.M. Buchanan: Barro on the Ricardian Equivalence Theorem, *Journal of Political Economy*, April 1976, No. 2, p. 337.

[104] R.J. Barro: Are Government Bonds Net Wealth? *Journal of Political Economy*, November/December 1974, No. 6, p. 1095.

[105] R.J. Barro: Reply to Feldstein and Buchanan, *Journal of Political Economy*, April 1976, No. 2, p. 347.

[106] R.J. Barro: Are Government Bonds Net Wealth? *op. cit.*, p. 1097.

[107] R.J. Barro: *op. cit.*, p. 1107.

It is worth noting the changes that have taken place in the interpretation of saving in the non-Marxian economic literature. As Bruce also asserts, saving is generally regarded as what is called forth by the difference between the magnitude of actual and desired wealth and not by consumer psychology.[108]

We shall evaluate Barro's view together with the new classical macro-economics.

THE EXPLANATION OF BUSINESS CYCLES IN THE NEW CLASSICAL MACRO-ECONOMICS

In the new classical macro-economics, the magnitude of output and employment is independent of the movement of the price level. But even the representatives of this theory cannot afford to ignore facts. It is a fact of experience that upswing and downswing alternate in the capitalist economy, in the course of an upswing, the price level and with it output and employment rise, whereas in a downswing the price level and with it output and employment fall. In other words, in the course of business cycles, the fluctuations of inflation, output and employment correlate positively with one another. This, however, means that an active economic policy is possible.

Lucas derives the cyclical fluctuations of the economy from incomplete information. If the economy experiences a monetary "shock", i.e. if the quantity of money grows, nominal demand and with it also the price level will increase. According to Lucas, both the entrepreneur and the worker will raise their supply of the product and of the labour power, respectively, because at the beginning they interpret the rise in the price level as a rise in relative prices. "... the positive association of price changes and output arises because suppliers misinterpret general price movements for relative price changes."[109] That is, the price level rises, and hence employment and output will also rise, which means that the trade-off also appears in the new classical macro-economics. In his 1968 article[110] Friedman writes that in the case of unexpected inflation, the worker experiences a change in his money wage, but does not reckon for a time with a change in the price level. He thinks that his real wage has risen and increases the supply of his labour. This was the idea that Lucas developed further in his theory concerning the inversion of the change in the price level and the change in relative prices. In his Nobel lecture held in 1977,[111] however, Friedman relied on Lucas's statement. Sargent and Wallace explain the mistake made by the economic agents by assuming that "... the suppliers receive information about the price of their own goods faster than receive information about the aggregate price level."[112]

According to the representatives of the new classical economics, the cycles and

[108] N. Bruce: The IS-LM Model of Macroeconomic Equilibrium and the Monetarist Controversy, *Journal of Political Economy*, October 1977, p. 1054.

[109] R.E. Lucas: Some International Evidence on Output-Inflation Tradeoffs, *The American Economic Review*, June 1973, p. 333.

[110] M. Friedman: The Role of Monetary Policy, *The American Economic Review*, March 1968, pp. 1–17.

[111] M. Friedman: Nobel Lecture: Inflation and Unemployment, *Journal of Political Economy*, June 1977, pp. 451–472.

[112] Th. J. Sargent and N. Wallace: Rational Expectations, the Optimal Monetary Instrument, and the Optimal Money Supply Rule, *Journal of Political Economy*, April 1975, p. 243.

instability were put into the model by state economic policy, and, in addition, changes in technology and tastes may cause further disturbances in capitalist reproduction. But Lucas holds the view that all this is merely a question of information. Namely, if appropriate information is gathered and it is used optimally, the cycles can be avoided. They are not organic concomitants of capitalist development. If appropriate information is given, only an unsystematic and unpredictable economic policy can act upon output and production, because it is only unpredictable economic policy that can mislead the economic agents who form their expectations rationally. The representatives of this theory maintain that in such cases a game-theory situation arises.

CRITICAL COMMENTS

In agreement with the statements made by Friedman and the representatives of the new micro-economics, the proponents of the new classical macro-economics assume that the mechanisms of the capitalist real economy are viable. In addition, however, they also suppose that in the possession of appropriate information, the market agents, who form their expectations rationally, perceive the market signals correctly, not only as a result of a learning process but also in the short run, and, by adjusting to them, they keep up the equilibrium development of the economy; however, they admit that unexpected surprises may upset this equilibrium temporarily. Then unemployment may deviate from its natural rate. But unemployment exceeding its natural rate is treated as voluntary in this model too; namely it is always the worker who leaves his job, and lay-offs also develop anti-cyclically. Prices and wage rates move symmetrically both in an upswing and in a recession.

Tobin justly notes that the view according to which the market system has sufficiently strong adaptive mechanisms to ensure stability at full employment, is not supported either by theory or by the long history of economic fluctuations under capitalism.[113]

In Marx, capitalist production relations transform the disturbances experienced in reproduction into cyclical movements and maintain these movements in the course of development. The first cyclical crisis leads to the subsequent ones in an endogenous way; and the equilibrium is realized only through its own incessant violation in the same way as the law of value also asserts its validity through its own violation. Can the change in the price level not eliminate the business cycles, i.e. the upswings and the recessions? It cannot, because the cycles in the competition model assumed by the representatives of the new classical macro-economics are called forth by the disruption of the proportion between the two departments of social production. And this cannot be eliminated by an immediate, general change in the price level. On the contrary, a change in the price level also reflects an allocational problem, viz. the formation of some disproportion between the two departments.

In a recession, the output of department I contracts compared to that of department II. Within aggregate supply, the supply of consumer goods will over-

[113] J. Tobin: *op. cit.,* p. 46.

575

weigh that of the means of production, but the demand for consumer goods will lag behind their supply. If the price level fell proportionately in both sectors, excess supply would continue to persist in the market for consumer goods. If, however, prices and wages decreased in such a way that demand would meet supply in the consumer market, entrepreneurs would suffer a loss. With the working class being the principal buyer of consumer goods, this market could only be cleared through a rise in real wages which, in turn, would entail a fall in real profit. This involves a conflict between the rise in the living standard of the masses and the profit interests of the capitalist class. If in this process the wealth effects were also taken into consideration, then in the model of a pure capitalist economy, which disregards government expenditures, only an inverse Pigou effect would prevail at most. With an increase in debt liabilities, owing to the debtors' greater propensity to consume, the fall in aggregate demand would become more pronounced and the recession would become deeper. Despite the designation of their theory, the representatives of the new classical macro-economics examine only the micro-conditions of obtaining maximum profit and are not interested in what the volume of the profit of the capitalist class depends on at a social level.

In practice, an upswing begins when the massive replacement of fixed capital, neglected during the recession period, starts off again. The output of department I will increase, and the demand of those engaged in department I for consumer goods will increase with it. And as the disproportion between the two departments grows as a result of the increased output of department I, aggregate demand for consumer goods will increasingly surpass the supply of these goods. If the price level rose proportionately in both departments, the excess demand for consumer goods would persist. If, however, instead of increasing their output, the capitalists of department II were only to raise the price level of consumer goods in order to clear the market of consumer goods, the disproportion in reproduction would increase. As a result of massive replacements, department I would increase its output, while the production of department II would stagnate. Wealth effects would further enhance the tension. With a fall in debt liabilities, the consumption of debtors would rise, the consumption of creditors would decline, and the inverse Pigou effect, owing to the debtors' greater propensity to spend, would further increase the price level with the rise in consumer demand.

The issue of the relation between aggregate demand and aggregate supply in the competition model assumed by the representatives of the new classical macro-economics could only be analysed on the basis of the relationship between the two departments of social reproduction, and it is incorrect to approach it merely from the aspect of the market and of the movement of the price level.

By the way, as also pointed out by Gordon,[114] it is impossible that in the case of a deviation of aggregate demand from aggregate supply, all prices, i.e. the prices of both inputs and outputs, would immediately change proportionately on the decentralized markets. If the individual producers were to decrease the price of their products in proportion to the fall in nominal demand, they would go bankrupt, that is, it is not the business cycle that would be eliminated since the suppliers of intermediate products would not adjust their prices simultaneously.

114 R.J. Gordon: Output Fluctuations and Gradual Price Adjustment, *Journal of Economic Literature*, June 1981, pp. 525–526.

Let us examine that basic statement of the new classical macro-economics according to which the rationally acting economic agents do not make mistakes systematically.

In a capitalist economy, upswings and downswings follow each other systematically. Capitalists should know that an upswing ends up in a downswing. Why do they nevertheless increase their investments during a period of upswing? Because competition compels them to do so, because in the hunt for profit each is concerned only with its own interest and not with the results of their efforts on a social scale. "Après moi le déluge!—is the watchword of every capitalist and of every capitalist nation",[115] says Marx when characterizing the capitalists' behaviour, who, in the course of the cyclical movement of the capitalist economy, systematically make mistakes in their decisions. They need not be misled, in addition, by unexpected economic policy measures.

Are the individual economic units capable of assessing in advance the formation of the price level? According to the representatives of the theory, there is a huge amount of information available to them in the trade press. In some countries the central banks publish the rate of money issues in advance. Economists compute the natural rate of unemployment by country. Reports on the economic situation publish the actual rate of unemployment.

However, the formation of the price level is a much too complex process to be derived accurately from the information available to the economic units. It depends on the development of production. But production develops cyclically under capitalist circumstances. The fact of business cycles is also acknowledged by the representatives of the new classical macro-economics, but they explain them by incomplete information and shocks that affect the economy unexpectedly. For the expected price level to be predicted, the formation of the business cycles ought to be known in advance. But their forecast is still unreliable.

Furthermore, the movement of the price level also depends on the economic policy of the governments. State expenditures directly increase nominal demand. But the effect of monetary policy on increasing nominal demand is uncertain. And it is uncertain in the case of both policies as to what extent the growth in nominal demand they create will elicit an increase in output and/or a rise in the price level. This depends on the structure of the economy, on the relation between the productive and the non-productive sector, and also on how the aggregate market is distributed among the markets in which the prices are flexible and those in which the prices are formed by means of the independent price policy of the agents of the market, that is, on how the so-called price-makers respond to the changes in nominal demand.

The formation of the price level also depends on the movement of the velocity of circulation and, under inflationary conditions, on inflationary expectations, too. Tobin[116] emphasizes that the expectations of other market agents are entirely unknown to the individual economic units. The information available to them is different. Their knowledge of economic theory also differs greatly. Thus it cannot be assumed that they will form their expectations concerning the movement of the price level in conformity. But thereby it will also become uncertain in the models

---

[115] K. Marx: *Capital*, Vol. 1, Moscow, 1954, p. 270.
[116] J. Tobin: *op. cit.*, p. 26.

of the new classical macro-economics "whose expectation, or what combination of diverse expectations, is represented by the single symbol of the model."[117]

The rate of the price increase is also influenced by the fact that the social classes in the struggle for their respective shares in national income also make use of inflation. However, the representatives of the new classical macro-economics do not take account of this, since they interpret inflation as a demand-pull inflation.

Reality, however, especially during the period of the oil-price rise, appeared to be in sharp contradiction with the logic of the new classical macro-economics. According to its representatives, the economic units infer from the growth rate of the quantity of money the likely increase in the price level. If the issue of money is wrongly estimated and the increase in the price level lags behind the expected level, a decline in output and unemployment will ensue. During the period of the oil-price rise, however, an inverse causal relationship became obvious. It was the quantity of money that had to adjust to the price level increased by the rising oil-prices. And if the central bank failed to carry out this adjustment, output fell, unemployment increased even if the agents of the market correctly estimated the growth rate of the quantity of money.

In view of the difficulties in predicting the formation of the price level, Meade justly notes that "I find this assumption [i.e. the hypothesis of rational expectations—A.M.] also very implausible, given the extreme complication of the real world in which we live..."[118] Referring to the many uncertainties after the post-1965 inflation, Fellner writes that "... the expected prices have become unpredictable".[119] Paradoxically, the hypothesis of rational expectations has appeared in non-Marxian economic literature exactly in a period when the uncertainty of the prospects of the capitalist economy has greatly increased.

And even if the economic agents succeeded in reliably calculating the expected price level, would they be able thereby to safeguard themselves against the deceptions of government economic policy?

As has been shown, changes in the price level express the disproportions of the structure of production in a capitalist economy left to itself. When increasing or decreasing their output, the capitalist firms adjust themselves not only to relative prices but also to the changes in the price level. Why would the government in an unstable capitalist economy mislead the economic agents? Instead, it will try to stabilize the capitalist economic processes by its economic policy. If its assessment of the troubles of the capitalist economy is wrong, then its economic policy will prove to be wrong, too. In this case, it has made a mistake. But Tobin's graph shows that, owing to the active role of the state, economic development in the United States after the Second World War was much more balanced than it had been in pre-war times.[120]

[117] *Ibid.*

[118] J.E. Meade: Comments on Laidler and Tobin, *The Economic Journal,* March 1981, p. 51.

[119] W. Fellner: Piaci reakciók az inflációs irányzatra: változások az amerikai magánháztartások vagyonának összetételében és a vállalatok mérleghelyzetében (Market reactions to the inflationary trend: changes in the structure of American private households and the in balance-sheet position of enterprises). In: Á. Schmidt and E. Kemenes (eds.): *Változások, váltások és válságok a gazdaságban* (Changes, transitions and crises in the economy). Tanulmányok Varga István emlékezetére (Studies in the memory of István Varga). Budapest. 1982. p. 86.

[120] J. Tobin: *op. cit.,* p. 47.

If we connect the change in the price level with changes in the structure of production, then the rise in the price level is elicited in the model of classical cycles, as we have seen, by the faster development of the output of department I compared to the output of department II. Then, in the process of general price rise, real profit does not remain unchanged either even if, despite the price rise, the costs increase. Real profit will grow, because the sum of the real consumption and the real investment of the capitalist class will grow, too. Why should in this case the capitalist class withhold its production even if it were able to foresee the movement of the price level? On the other hand, in a crisis, investment activity will fall. The level of real profit will not remain unchanged despite the fact that costs will fall together with the product prices. Real profit will decrease in reality even if the capitalist class maintains its consumption at the earlier level, simply because its investment activity has declined. In this case, the capitalist class will decrease its production even if it accurately anticipated the fall in the price level. Not only changes in relative prices, but also those in the price level exert an influence on economic decisions.

The assumption of the new classical macro-economics about flexible, market-clearing prices does not present a true picture either of the present-day capitalist markets. A great part of these markets is characterized both by an oligopolistic price formation, with a rigid profit margin added to the average cost, which the oligopolists try to keep up even in an unfavourable business cycle, and by a money wage rate which is set in a bargaining process between the trade unions and the oligopolistic capitalist organizations. As soon as non-Marxian economics renounces the market-clearing paradigm, it can fit involuntary unemployment into the theoretical model of capitalist economy, and it will turn out that in the case of involuntary unemployment, economic policy may be successful even if the economic agents can take account of its effect in advance.

Approaching the Ricardian equivalence theorem from this aspect, we come to a conclusion which differs from that of Barro. If the public—even if it entirely discounts its expected future debt liabilities in order to repay the bonds designed to cover government expenditures—can hope that its real incomes will increase as a result of a higher rate of employment and thus the repayment of government debts will be ensured, it will not cut down its consumption spendings, will not increase its savings and, as a result of government expenditures, aggregate demand will increase.[121]

121 J. Tobin: *op. cit.*, p. 61.

37*

579

Chapter 5

COST-PUSH INFLATION

The inflation theories discussed above approach the problem of inflation from the demand side: aggregate demand increases, the price level rises and, parallel with it, unemployment decreases even if, according to the neo-classical view, temporarily. Until the end of the 1960s, inflation and unemployment moved really in an opposite direction. Then, at the end of the 1960s and in the 1970s, the picture changed: the rate of inflation increased even though the growth rate of aggregate demand did not rise, and unemployment grew. This, the so-called stagflation, cannot be expressed by a negative-sloping Phillips curve; the relationship between the percentage change in unemployment and the rate of inflation is shown by a positive-sloping curve, and the loop is clockwise. This fact induced several economists to approach the problem of inflation from another side, i.e. from the side of costs.

Earlier, the theory of cost-push inflation was neglected because it was held to be unable to explain a continuing growth of the price level; it could only give explanation for a once-and-for-all increase of the price level. However, this theory experienced a revival when the process of stagflation had unfolded.

Cost-push inflation can be produced by the exogenous increase of costs when, for example, the import prices of intermediate products rise. Wages are regulated in a significant part of the labour markets not by the market mechanisms but by the bargaining processes between trade unions and capitalist monopoly organizations. The higher wages thus gained may also be a source of exogenous cost-push inflation. Under oligopolistic conditions, prices are determined not by the spontaneous working of market mechanisms, but by the individual oligopolists in such a way that they add a certain mark-up to the costs of production. Exogenous cost-push inflation may be brought about when individual oligopolists raise the mark-up, and also when the government raises indirect taxes.

Gylfason and Lindbeck point out[122] that the exogenous increase of costs can only produce continuing inflation in certain cases. However, as a result of the struggle which the organized groups that represent a market power fight for their share in the national income, both exogenous cost-push inflation as well as demand-pull inflation may change into a continuous, endogenous cost-push inflationary process.[123] R.J. Gordon also refers to the endogenous process when

[122] T. Gylfason and A. Lindbeck: The Political Economy of Cost Inflation, *Kyklos,* 1982, Vol. 35, Fasc. 3, pp. 436–437.
[123] T. Gylfason and A. Lindbeck: *op. cit.,* p. 438.

he writes that "cost-push inflation was generated ... by a struggle for income shares among any set of subgroups in society."[124] Today, inflation has become a significant instrument of rivalry for the distribution of national income in the struggle between the capitalist and the working classes on the one hand, and also in the struggle among the various capitalist groups and among the individual workers' groups on the other.

In Scitovsky's example, the oil-price rise, being an exogenous factor calling forth cost-push inflation, increases the living costs of all income groups. In the case of the producers, however, the costs of production also increase. Adding an appropriate mark-up to them, the producers charge the consumers with these costs by increasing the price of their products, "leaving wage-earners as the main victims of the rise in oil prices."[125] Workers wanting to be compensated for the higher prices of consumer goods demand higher money wages. Higher money wages further increase the costs of production, and the producers, adding an appropriate mark-up to them, further increase prices. The exogenous rise in costs started off the price–wage spiral and so it gave rise to the process of endogenous cost-push inflation.

It was, among others, Duesenberry[126] who pointed out that the wage contracts concluded in the individual industries had an effect on the wage contracts in other industries. Political pressure in certain trade unions induces the leadership to keep pace with the results attained by other trade unions even if the objective circumstances are different. That is, a competition among the different groups of workers develops. And since in a dynamic economy, wage rises always occur somewhere, other trade unions will also demand and reach wage increases. And if individual industries adjust their wage policies to an industry in which the productivity of labour increased more than in their own, their prices will be inflated. In this case, the exogenous wage rise attained by individual groups of workers will become the source of a continuing cost-push inflation. In their so-called "key-industry" hypothesis, Eatwell, Llewellyn and Tarling point out that "the overall rate of increase of money wages is linked to the rate of increase of productivity in those sectors with fastest productivity growth."[127]

The firms compete with one another through prices in order "to maintain or increase their relative prices or relative rates of return (as compared with other firms)."[128]

An economy, says Scitovsky, in which wages are set in the course of a bargaining process between the trade unions and the management while prices are determined in the product market by the price-makers, "always responds to them [i.e. changes in costs, whether they rise or decline—A.M.] with an inflationary upward drift of the price level, owing to the conflict in power relations in different markets."[129]

[124] R.J. Gordon: Recent Developments in the Theory of Inflation and Unemployment, *Journal of Monetary Economics*, 1972/2, p. 188.

[125] T. Scitovsky: Market Power and Inflation, *Economica*, August 1978, p. 225.

[126] See J. Duesenberry: *Inflation and Income Distribution*, I.E.A. Conference on "Inflation Theory and Anti-Inflation Policy", Saltsjöbaden, Sweden, August 1975.

[127] J. Eatwell, J. Llewellyn and R. Tarling: Money Wage Inflation in Industrial Countries, *The Review of Economic Studies*, October 1974, p. 516.

[128] T. Gylfason and A. Lindbeck: *op. cit.*, p. 440.

[129] T. Scitovsky: *op. cit.*, p. 227.

He assumes that a firm innovates in the hope of higher profit. As a result, productivity rises and costs fall in that firm. But its exceptional profit is only temporary, because the activity of its competitors or its workers will sooner or later reduce it to the normal level. The effect of innovations on the economy is different, depending on whether it is the firm's competitors or its workers who first perceive and respond to them. If, taking over an innovation, it is the competitors who first respond, they will increase their output and the price will fall. However, it is more typical that an innovation is first perceived by the workers of the innovating firm, who are implementing it, and the competitors perceive it only with a delay. These workers will demand higher wages for themselves. The wage rise will slowly extend over the given branch and later also over the other branches of industry. The costs, rising as a result of higher wages, will also compel the other firms to innovate, so as to regain their profits. If they do not succeed in doing so, they will raise their prices and will cause inflation thereby.

Duesenberry emphasizes that, given the presence of organized groups with a market power, the working of the law of value, optimal allocation, will materialize only through inflation. If, for example, the structure of demand changes and thus the demand for certain goods rises and for others falls, the price of the former will increase while of the latter will not decrease. As a consequence, the price level will rise. The labour force will be allocated among the various fields of use by the changes in relative wages. Money wages have to grow in industries with a shortage of labour and have to fall in others where there is unemployment. But since workers resist a fall in their wages, in the productive branches with unemployment a certain rate of inflation is needed to bring about the wage proportions required by these changes.

There are authors who point out that the downward rigidity of the price level, typical of oligopolistic markets, will also cause inflation when the overall growth rate of money wages coincides with the average growth rate of productivity. In such cases, the price rise caused by an increase in wages in industries with productivity rising at a lower than average rate cannot be offset by a price fall in industries with a growth rate of productivity above the average rate.

Gylfason and Lindbeck also treat as cost inflation that inflationary process which only ensues because the economic agents, under the conditions of inflation caused either by an exogenous increase in costs or by a growth in demand, want to maintain their respective shares. Therefore they adjust the prices and wages to the overall rate of inflation. In discussing demand-pull inflation, we have already come across this process. Demand-pull inflation induces an endogenous cost-push inflation. (And a higher nominal income is the source of a higher nominal demand.) Many authors emphasize the role that inflationary expectations play in influencing relative shares, or in the endeavours to preserve the existing real position, as soon as they have been built into the processes of price and wage setting. The rate of inflation will rise if the opposed parties, expecting higher rates of price and wage increases, increase the current rates of prices and wages; "... prices rise in part, because people expect them to rise..."[130]

In the case of a pure cost-generated inflation, there is no trade-off between inflation and unemployment: the Phillips curve is a horizontal line.

[130] J.A. Carlson and M. Parkin: Inflation Expectations, *Economica*, May 1975, p. 123.

According to Lerner,[131] the endeavour of social groups to influence their respective positions, or merely to maintain their real positions by means of inflation, may be a source of stagflation. If, for example, the government wants to curb inflation but erroneously interprets cost-push inflation as demand-pull inflation and pursues therefore a restrictive economic policy, then it will diminish the growth rate of aggregate demand. Entrepreneurs, in order to prevent the fall of their profit share in national income, will keep up the growth rate of their prices. The trade unions, however, will insist on the earlier growth rate of money wages to prevent a fall in the share of the working class. And, as a result of the restrictive economic policy, aggregate demand will prove to be insufficient to realize the price sum of the commodities produced. Entrepreneurs will diminish output, and unemployment will grow. The economy will come into the state of stagflation.

In the theory of cost-push inflation, unlike in the monetary approach, it is not the price sum of goods that adjusts to the quantity of money in circulation, but the quantity of money has to adjust to the price sum of goods. And the price level does not even decrease as a result of the fall in nominal demand; thus an appropriate magnitude of real demand cannot develop.

In their study on cost-push inflation, Gylfason and Lindbeck attack the narrow monetary approach which takes inflation to be a basically monetary phenomenon and regards its control by the quantity of money as a sufficient means of regulation. In their view, the monetary argument that cost-push inflation cannot persist in the long run without a growth in nominal demand and in the quantity of money, is not a sufficient evidence for the demand-pull character of inflation and against the concept of cost-push inflation. The main point is that in certain cases the increase of costs gives rise to inflation which is then maintained by the struggle for changing the relative shares or for keeping up the existing real position. They hold the view that it is impossible to cope with the problem of inflation if attention is paid only to its demand or monetary aspects, while the forces that drive both inflation and money creation remain ignored.

The structural changes, the increased weight of non-productive expenditure, after the Second World War elicited a demand-pull inflation. In the course of an unfolding inflationary process, the individual social groups began to use inflation as an instrument in the struggle for their shares in national income. The inflationary process, as a result of the intertwining of demand-pull and cost-push inflation, increasingly got out of the control of government authority.

How do economists wish to cure cost-induced inflation? According to the representatives of the theory of cost-push inflation, the government has to conduct such an income policy which is able to limit the struggle for the shares in national income. Incomes policy is designed to ensure a harmony among the growth of wages, of prices and of productivity.

But the trade unions have no trust in incomes policy. They see in it an attempt to force down wages.

Neither do the entrepreneurs have trust in incomes policy. They see in it state control over prices, aiming to curb their profits. The theoretical economist, on

131 See A.P. Lerner: Employment Theory and Employment Policy, *The American Economic Review*, May 1967, p. 8.

the other hand, attacks income policy on the grounds that both price and wage regulations counteract the requirement of optimal allocation.

According to experience, incomes policy has not succeeded in significantly slowing down inflation either in the United States or in the United Kingdom.

The simultaneous achievement of a high level of employment and price stability is a problem that non-Marxian economists have been unable to solve as yet. It is in this sense that Samuelson writes on this question: "Experts do not yet know how to agree on an income policy that permits us to have simultaneously the full employment and the price stability that our monetary and fiscal policies are able to create the purchasing power for."[132] The perplexity and scepticism that can be experienced today among non-Marxian economists appear to be very similar to those that prevailed in the period of the Great Depression before Keynes entered the scene with his *General Theory*. Now a new Keynes is expected to come who would unravel the unsolved problems of today's capitalist economy. But, for the time being, there is no indication of a new Keynes being in the offing. All that appears to be "new" is nothing but a revival of the old quantity theory of money under the name of monetary counter-revolution.

[132] P.A. Samuelson: *Economics*. New York–Toronto–London, 1973, p. 823.

Chapter 6

THE NEW MACRO-ECONOMICS

THE SO-CALLED NON-WALRASIAN MODEL.
THE NON-MARKET-CLEARING PARADIGM

Inflation and unemployment gave rise, as has been shown, to a reform of price theory. Friedman and the representatives of the new micro-economics, by assuming flexible prices which clear all markets, as well as those of the new classical macro-economics thought that they were able to present a true picture of the reality of capitalist economy, of the effect that government economic policy exerts on the nominal and real processes of the economy. However, when presenting the functioning of the price mechanism, they already took account of the process of inflation, of the incomplete information of the agents of the market who first interpret changes in the price level as a change in relative prices, and so they increase or decrease their output and increase or cut back the supply of labour. As a result, they realized that the free play of prices could not eliminate the fluctuations of output and employment. The basic statements of these theories, however, came, as we have seen, into conflict with the reality of capitalist economy, with the fact that there does exist involuntary unemployment, that in today's capitalist economy most prices are rigid downwards and even those moving upwards do not change continuously, only temporarily, and that government economic policy was able to influence output and the magnitude of employment successfully after the Second World War.

During the 1970s, such theories also evolved which, though standing on the basis of price theory and using the instruments of general equilibrium theory, strove to approach the reality of capitalist economy in a different way. Their representatives thought that they would draw a more accurate picture of today's capitalist economy if they rejected the assumption of flexible prices, the paradigm of market-clearing, and chose instead the non-market-clearing type of approach as their working hypothesis. Non-Marxian economics often discusses these approaches under the heading of "new macro-economics". Its proponents hold the view that prices in most markets are "sticky", "sluggish". They respond to changes in demand and supply slowly and do not clear the markets. In this case, given a divergence between demand and supply, it is not the prices but the quantities that react faster. Economists belonging to the school of new macro-economics suppose that by this approach they will be able to deduce within the framework of price theory even the relationships revealed by Keynes, with certain assumptions concerning the magnitudes of the price level and of money wages.

As commonly known, Keynes explained the existence of involuntary unemployment macro-economically, by means of aggregate concepts. He did not find it necessary to found the results of this exploration in terms of price theory, that is, to reduce them to the decisions of the economic agents wishing to optimize their positions. He presumed that the relationships explored by him would not be influenced by assuming either flexible or rigid prices and money wages.

The Keynesian statement that in the market of commodities aggregate demand and aggregate supply can be in equilibrium even at involuntary unemployment, contradicts the relationships presented in the Walrasian model. Therefore, some representatives of the new macro-economics held the view that the existence of involuntary unemployment could only be presented in a general disequilibrium model, and they also tried to reconstruct Keynes's macro-economics in the framework of this model.

The way towards this attempt had already long been prepared. In Chapter XIII of his work published in 1956, Don Patinkin[133] assumes that there is an excess supply in the commodity market, that at the prevailing prices the entrepreneurs are unable to sell that volume of commodities at which they can maximize their profits. That is, the existing prices do not clear the market. The insufficiency of demand induces entrepreneurs to diminish their output and through it employment: "... the initial decrease in commodity demand causes a corresponding decrease in the input of labour."[134] Entrepreneurs "not being able to sell all they want ... cannot employ all [i.e. workers—A.M.] they want".[135] It is not the price level, not money wages, but quantities, the volume of output and employment, that first react to the divergence between aggregate demand and aggregate supply. That is, to every real-wage level, a smaller demand for labour is attached. Thus the demand for labour in Patinkin is a function not only of real wages but also of the demand for products, of the volume of output. That is, the function of the demand for labour includes, besides real wages as an independent variable, also a new constraint, namely, a constraint which is not of a price but of a quantity character, i.e. the magnitude of the demand for and the output of commodities. Depending on the magnitude of the aggregate demand for and output of commodities, a differing magnitude of labour demand is attached to every real-wage level. And in case aggregate demand for commodities is insufficient, employment can only be increased by increasing the aggregate demand for commodities.

Patinkin seems to approach Keynes's views from the aspect of price theory.

The effect that Clower's study,[136] published in 1966, exerted on the representatives of the new macro-economics of the 1970s was much greater than the effect of Patinkin's explorations. The Walrasian-type supply function related to products presupposes that entrepreneurs can sell, at the existing prices, that quantity of output which enables them to maximize their profit; and they seek the services of the factors of production on this basis. The Walrasian-type demand function related to products presupposes, on the other hand, that the suppliers of productive services (let us restrict them, for the sake of simplicity, to workers as the suppliers of labour) are able to sell at the existing wage rate that quantity of labour at which they can optimize their position as consumers and it is the mag-

133 D. Patinkin: *Money, Interest and Prices*, Harpers International Edition, New York, 1956.
134 D. Patinkin: *op. cit.*, p. 217.
135 D. Patinkin: *op. cit.*, p. 213.
136 R. Clower: The Keynesian Counterrevolution: A Theoretical Appraisal. In: F.H. Hahn and F.P.R. Brechling (eds.): *The Theory of Interest Rates*, MacMillan, 1966.

nitude of wages obtained as the product of this quantity of labour and of the existing wage rate that is included in the demand function related to consumer goods. Clower calls the supply, demand and income determined by this assumption *notional* supply, demand and income. In the worker's notional demand function related to commodities, the magnitude of wages is the result of the worker's decision. He has decided on the quantity of labour he is willing to do at the prevailing wage rate.

According to Clower, if we give up equilibrium and focus our attention on sales and purchases at non-equilibrium prices, we shall obtain a model similar to the Keynesian one. He assumes that at the existing wage rate, supply in the labour market exceeds demand. The workers cannot sell the quantity of labour they would like to in order to optimize their position as consumers. However, then their income is no longer the result of their own decision, but that of the actual quantity of labour they can sell at the existing wage rate. This, in turn, depends on the extent to which entrepreneurs are willing to employ them at the existing demand for their products. Then the function of the workers' demand for commodities will include their actual income. This *effective demand* differs from the notional one as it also includes, besides the prices of consumer goods and the worker's wage rate, a *quantity constraint,* viz. the magnitude of employment, which is independent of the worker: "... current income flows may impose an independent restriction on effective demand, separate from those already imposed by prevailing market prices..."[137] If effective demand deviates from the notional one, through the quantity constraint Clower speaks of a *constrained* demand function. He arrived at such a demand function related to workers which is similar to Keynes's consumption function. Hence, the consumption demand of workers depends on the magnitude of their employment, on the given magnitude of their income. And insufficient demand in the labour market also acts upon the commodity market. The demand for commodities will be smaller than the notional demand, i.e. than what workers would have demanded at their notional incomes. Thus, in Clower, effective demand or supply in a given market always depends on what happens in other markets.

Making a distinction between the notional and the effective or constrained demand (or supply) functions, Clower speaks of the *dual decision* of the market agents. In the commodity market, for example, the worker decides what and how much to buy, on the basis of his notional income and the price constraints. If, however, there is excess supply in the labour market, and thus the worker cannot sell at the prevailing wage rate the quantity of labour desired, he will shift from the notional demand function to the effective demand function which already contains a quantity constraint, namely, the actual labour quantity that can be sold. This shift between functions is the gist of the dual decision.

According to Clower, Walras's law is only valid if selling and buying take place in all markets on the basis of the notional demand–supply function. It cannot be applied if supply or demand are quantitatively constrained in a market. According to Walras's law, the excess supply of individual goods, i.e., the insufficient demand for them, means an excess demand for other goods. Hence, the sum of excess demands always equals zero. If we assume, following Clower, two markets in the

137 R. Clower: *op. cit.,* p. 120.

economy, the labour and the product markets, then, according to Walras's law the "... excess supply of factors necessarily implies the simultaneous existence of excess demand for goods."[138] Interpreting Clower's statements, Leijonhufvud says that the worker supplies his labour because he wishes to buy goods for the wages he receives for it and, in this sense excess supply of labour would mean, according to Walras's law, an excess demand for goods. In the Walrasian auction market entrepreneurs would be induced by the excess demand for goods to expend output and employment. Only real wages should change until they bring in equilibrium the demand for and the supply of labour. Looking for a job, however, the worker asks for money and not for commodities, and thus the producer cannot be informed about his notional demand for goods: "...not being able to perceive this potential demand for their products, producers will not be willing to absorb the excess supply of labor at a wage corresponding to the real wage that would 'solve' the Walrasian problem above."[139]

THE DISEQUILIBRIUM MODEL OR THE EQUILIBRIUM MODEL WITH RATIONING

By using the elements discussed above, Barro and Grossman were the first to construct a general disequilibrium model[140] in 1971. In 1975, Benassy published his model of a similar character under the designation of neo-Keynesian disequilibrium theory.[141]

The most detailed elaboration of the models of this type can be found in Malinvaud's work.[142] "This model is very similar in spirit to the one introduced by R.J. Barro and H.L. Grossman."[143]

Let us select the most important relationships from his model.

He holds the view that the higher the level at which a society is organized, the less it applies that prices respond to changes in demand and supply faster than quantities. Thus, "...short-term quantitive adjustments are much more apparent and influenced than short-term price adjustments."[144] Therefore, Malinvaud assumes that prices and wage rates are exogenous, i.e., their changes are autonomous, as the development of demand and supply cannot influence them substantially.

Hicks was among the first ones to make a distinction between the so-called flex and fix price systems.[145] He maintains that a stock of goods suitable to be stored could be formed to keep prices unchanged. If demand exceds output, entrepreneurs can cut back on their stocks and prices need not rise. If, however, demand lags

[138] R. Clower: *op. cit.*, p. 121.
[139] A. Leijonhufvud: *On Keynesian Economics and the Economics of Keynes*, Oxford University Press, 1968, p. 90.
[140] R.J. Barro and H.J. Grossman: A General Disequilibrium Model of Income and Employment, *The American Economic Review*, March 1971, pp. 82–93.
[141] J.P. Benassy: Neo-Keynesian Disequilibrium Theory in a Monetary Economy, *The Review of Economic Studies*, October 1975, pp. 503–523.
[142] E. Malinvaud: *The Theory of Unemployment Reconsidered*, Oxford, 1970.
[143] E. Malinvaud: *op. cit.*, p. 37.
[144] E. Malinvaud: *op. cit.*, p. 10.
[145] J.R. Hicks: *Capital and Growth*, Oxford, 1965.

behind output, they can build up their stocks and prices need not fall: "...stock changes substitute for price changes."[146]

Relying on Hicks, Malinvaud writes that the direct effect of changes in the relationship between demand and supply may appear in order books, in waiting lists, in stocks, in delivery times, in changes in output, labour time and employment. "Such quantitative adjustments are the first signals of changes in the demand–supply relationship."[147]

In his model, the existing prices are not equilibrium prices, thus excess demand or excess supply may prevail in the individual markets, and so buyers and sellers are restricted in their transactions. At the existing prices, they cannot buy or sell as much as they would like to in order to optimize their positions. In the market, there develop a *short* and a *long* side. On the short side are those who are able to carry out their transactions at the prevailing prices, while those on the long side are restricted, *rationed,* in their demand or supply. And it is the short side that decides what quantity of business can be transacted. If buyers are on the short side and sellers are rationed in their supply, the market is a *buyers' market,* whereas in the case of a *sellers' market,* sellers are on the short side and it is the demand of the buyers that is rationed.

The fact that some agents are on the long side in one market imposes a quantity constraint upon their demand and supply in other markets. Assuming two markets, a product and a labour market, Malinvaud's model presents the following possibilities:

1. The supply of the worker is rationed in the labour market, and, given the existing prices and wages, he cannot sell the desired quantity of labour, or, to use Clower's expression, he cannot move along his notional supply function, that is, the function of his demand for goods will include a quantity constraint, namely the sold quantity of labour. And if we change the quantity of labour sold, we shall obtain the function of the demand for commodities restricted by the sold quantity of labour.

2. If the worker is rationed in his demand in the product market, he cannot buy, given the existing prices and wages, the desired quantity of goods, i.e. he cannot move along this notional demand function, and a lesser quantity of labour will be supplied in the labour market. The supply function of this labour will include the quantity of consumer goods offered for sale as a quantity constraint. If we change the quantity of consumer goods offered for sale, we shall obtain the supply function of labour constrained by the available consumer goods.

3. If the firm, given the prevailing prices and wages, cannot sell the quantity of product that would be needed to maximize its profit, i.e., if the actual supply of its product does not proceed along its notional supply function, it will diminish its demand for labour. The function of the demand for labour will include the quantity of saleable goods as a quantity constraint. And if we begin to change the quantity of saleable goods, we obtain the function of the demand for labour constrained by the quantity of saleable goods.

4. If the firm, at the given prices and wages, cannot buy as much labour as would be needed for its profit to be maximum, i.e., if it cannot move along its

146 J.R. Hicks: *op. cit.,* p. 79.
147 E. Malinvaud: *op. cit.,* p. 9.

notional demand function in the labour market, it will not be able to produce the quantity of goods that would optimize its position. The supply function of its product will include the quantity of the available labour as a quantity constraint. And if we start changing the quantity of available labour, we shall obtain the supply function of its product constrained by the quantity of labour.

Malinvaud does not regard his model as a disequilibrium model. He maintains that the Walrasian equilibrium encompasses a long period, because in the long run prices are flexible and fulfil their traditional function.[148] In his view, however, equilibrium can also be established in the short run at non-equilibrium prices and wages if the sellers and buyers correctly estimating the quantity constraints take account of them when forming their demands. This equilibrium as a short-run consistency between individual actions, "materializes by the adjustment of the exchanged quantities and not of prices."[149] In an equilibrium situation, sellers supply only as much as is the restricted demand of buyers, and buyers demand as much as is the restricted supply of sellers. In other words, firms supply as much quantity of consumer goods as workers as consumers demand at the insufficient demand for their labour, while workers as the sellers of their commodity supply as much labour as entrepreneurs demand at the insufficient demand for their product. Entrepreneurs demand as much labour as workers are willing to supply at the insufficient supply of consumer goods, while workers demand as much quantity of consumer goods as entrepreneurs are able to supply at the insufficient supply of labour.

Depending on whether the sellers' or the buyers' side is quantitatively rationed in the product and the labour markets included in the model, Malinvaud distinguishes different types of short-term, non-Walrasian equilibrium positions:

1. If the firm as buyer is rationed in the labour market and the worker as buyer is rationed in the product market, there exist excess demand and inflationary pressure in both markets, but the short-term rigidity of prices represses inflation. This is the case of *repressed inflation*. The buyer, since he cannot spend his income, carries out *forced saving*.

2. If there appears an excess supply in both markets, i.e., if the firm is rationed in the product market and the worker is rationed in the labour market, then we have to do with the case of the *Keynesian unemployment*.

3. If the worker is rationed in the labour market, and the consumer is rationed in the product market, then it is the case of *classical unemployment*.

Applying this approach, Malinvaud says "that in essence the 'Keynesian revolution' was a shift of emphasis from one type of short-run equilibrium to another type as providing the appropriate theory for actual unemployment situations."[150]

The rationing of demand or supply in one market gives rise, according to Malinvaud, to a multiplier effect. In the case of the Keynesian equilibrium, when the workers, at the existing wage rates, cannot sell the quantity of labour they would like to, they diminish the demand for consumer goods. Entrepreneurs then cut down the output of consumer goods, demand less labour, unemployment grows and the demand for consumer goods further decreases.

[148] E. Malinvaud: *op. cit.*, p. 14.
[149] E. Malinvaud: *op. cit.*, p. 12.
[150] E. Malinvaud: *op. cit.*, pp. 29–30.

The multiplier effect in the case of suppressed inflation was examined by Barro and Grossman in their study published in 1974.[151] This multiplier, unlike the Keynesian one, is a *supply* multiplier. The worker is rationed in the product market, and at the prevailing prices he is unable to have access to the consumer goods he desires to buy with his income. "He will typically respond by both increasing his effective savings and decreasing his effective labour supply accordingly... Hence, to the extent that households reduce their effective labour supply, employment and output must also decline."[152]

In the models of the new macro-economics, the market will not be cleared at sticky prices and wages, and thus Walras's law does not come into effect. Excess supply or excess demand may occur in all markets simultaneously. In this case, the sum of excess demands cannot be zero. When demonstrating the invalidity of Walras's law in the case of Keynes, Clower refers to the dual decision: if the worker cannot realize his notional supply, he will shift from the notional demand function to the function of the effective, constrained demand for goods. That is, he does not raise his demand according to the magnitude of his notional supply, and thus aggregate demand and aggregate supply cannot be equal. Hence, Walras's law loses its validity in the case of unemployment.[153]

In the models discussed above there is already room for economic policy. The government need not mislead the market agents in order to be able to pursue a successful economic policy. If it increases nominal aggregate demand, then real aggregate demand, owing to the slow adjustment of prices, will also grow. In the case of unemployment, entrepreneurs will increase their output. As a result of the sluggishness of prices, the change in the quantity of money will stop to be neutral with respect to the formation of real processes.

In contrast to the Walrasian-type models based on the relative scarcity of the factors of production, in which only certain factors can temporarily be available in excess quantity and the movement of factor prices also clears the market of the factors concerned, but all factors cannot exist in abundance simultaneously, in the new micro-models all factors can be available in excess quantity at the same time.

It was Arrow who pointed out that the reformers of neo-classical price theory, by assuming that under disequilibrium sellers cannot get rid of the desired quantity of their commodities at the prevailing market prices, shook the criterion of perfect competition which maintains that individual sellers are always able to sell at the prevailing prices any quantity of their products or productive services. Therefore, under disequilibrium, every seller is temporarily faced with a negatively sloped demand curve for his product, and thus his position is temporarily monopolistic in a non-Marxian sense, for if one seller decreases the price of his product it takes time before the other sellers are informed about it and react to the price reduction by reducing their own prices. During this period, demand for the product of the price-reducing seller will gradually increase until the information about the new price is spread among the buyers.[154]

[151] R.J. Barro and H.J. Grossman: Suppressed Inflation and the Supply Multiplier, *The Review of Economic Studies*, January 1974, pp. 87–104.

[152] R.J. Barro and H.J. Grossman: *op. cit.*, p. 88.

[153] R. Clower: *op. cit.*, p. 122.

[154] See K.J. Arrow: Towards a Theory of Price Adjustment. In: M. Abramowitz et al.: *The Allocation of Economic Resources*, Stanford, 1959.

CRITICAL COMMENTS

New macro-economics depicts a more realistic picture of the present-day functioning of the price mechanism than those economists do who have chosen the market-clearing paradigm as their working hypothesis. Today, the prices and money wages are no longer flexible in most markets. The proponents of this theory can present, by the slow adjustment of prices, such real market relationships as were impossible to be shown in the market-clearing models which assumed flexible prices.

But do they help us to better understand the nature and the causes of the serious troubles of today's capitalist economy?

What we can learn from them amounts merely to the fact that if prices and wages are sticky, they cannot balance the changes in aggregate nominal demand, and what will result is involuntary unemployment or repressed inflation.

But why does aggregate nominal demand change?

The formation of aggregate nominal demand, the explanation of which Keynes regarded as his main task, is treated in the model as an exogenous datum. Some of its representatives make aggregate nominal demand dependent on changes in the quantity of money, others on governmental expenditures, again others refer at most to the "Keynesian cross", i.e. to Keynes's definition of aggregate demand,[155] without fitting it organically into their models. Barro's statement on the contracting model of the market also applies to new macro-economics: "...the contracting model... does not explain the key features of Keynesian analysis with regard to the determination of employment and ouput."[156]

However, as has been shown, since the appearance of the *General Theory,* substantial changes have taken place in the capitalist economy. As a result, the structure of aggregate demand as well as the sphere and weight of the profit components have changed. Without an analysis of these important transformations, the major peculiarities of today's capitalist economy cannot be revealed, nor can the changes be shown that have ensued in the self-movement of the capitalist economy, a knowledge of which, however, is indispensable, since the spontaneous development of capitalist economic processes still play a significant role in today's cyclical changes. What can these models reveal from the typical features of present-day capitalist economy, from the changed character of the cycles if they lack even that depth of analysis of aggregate demand which was already achieved by Keynes? Here we cannot find even such answers to involuntary unemployment and to the insufficiency of aggregate demand as was given by Keynes in his *General Theory* published in 1936.

And why are prices and money wages sticky?

The transformation that occurred in the capitalist economy explain the changes in the functioning of the price mechanism, too. It is not the spontaneous play of the market forces that imposes the prices on the market agents, but the oligopolists who set them. And competition is waged today not in terms of prices, but rather in terms of quantities. The situation is similar with regard to money wages. They are established not as a result of spontaneous market mechanisms, but in

[155] R.J. Barro and S. Fischer: Recent Developments in Monetary Theory, *Journal of Monetary Economics,* No. 2, 1976, p. 148.

[156] R.J. Barro: Second Thoughts on Keynesian Economics, *The American Economic Review,* May 1979, p. 54.

bargaining processes between trade unions and the capitalist oligopolistic organizations, largely on the basis of the power relations of the two parties. The consequences of the stickiness of prices and wages can only be analysed in conjunction with the effect of the economic changes that have brought about this stickiness. Given sticky prices and wages, it is uncertain to what extent restrictive fiscal and monetary policy can curb inflation. But they are sure to press down output and employment. And with all its sluggishness, oligopolistic price formation is not so sticky upwards that it would not be able to absorb a large part of the nominal demand increased by governmental economic policy. In this case, the effect of economic policy on output and employment is insignificant. With sticky prices, the magnitude of unrealized commodity stocks is greater in a slump period. This circumstance deepens the crisis and makes it difficult to find a way out of it. But the crisis is not caused by the stickiness of prices and wages. A crisis of general overproduction just as involuntary unemployment also arises at flexible prices and wages.

According to Marx, if the free play of prices, owing to the disproportions evolved in production, can clear the markets only through losses, then the imbalance developed in them will spill over also to the other markets even at flexible prices. Marx describes how in a glutted cotton goods market, the stagnation in the production of cotton goods spills over to the markets of yarn, cotton, spindles, looms, iron and coal, and how it disturbs their reproduction, because the reproduction of cotton goods is a precondition of the reproduction of all these goods.[157]

New macro-economics, however, can demonstrate the lack of general demand and involuntary unemployment only at sluggish prices and wages. Thus, the source of the troubles of the capitalist economy revealed by the model is merely the dissatisfactory operation of the market mechanisms. The representatives of this theory hold the view that if prices and wages were flexible, they could counterbalance the fluctuations of aggregate nominal demand. That is, aggregate demand would never be insufficient or too abundant, and no involuntary unemployment would exist. The various neo-classical theories today, trying to prove the viability of the capitalist economy, also assert the same. Thus, there is no *substantial* difference between the views held by the representatives of the new neo-classical and those of the new macro-economic theories. Prices and wages are flexible in the long run also in the view of the proponents of new macro-economics, and thus the economic problems presented by them exist only in the short run. Involuntary unemployment and idle capacities are not possible in the long run. Krelle expresses his doubt about it by asking "whether this theory may be applied to the type of unemployment which we are confronted with now. We have unemployment for several years."[158]

The representatives of new macro-economics, although they make every effort to render even Keynes's statements on the basis of price theory, are very far from Keynes. Though in most places of the *General Theory* Keynes assumed rigid prices and wages, he attested that his statements were also valid at flexible prices and wages.

New macro-economics too, assumes that economic agents are keen on optimizing their position, else it would not be able to present economic action as a determined one in the price model. The difference relative to the Walrasian-type

[157] Marx, K.: *Theories of Surplus Value*, Part II. Moscow, 1976, pp. 522–523.
[158] W. Krelle: The Way out of Unemployment, *Kyklos,* Vol. 32, 1979, Fasc, 1/2, p. 117.

models appears only in the fact that it includes in the conditions of action not only the price but also the quantity constraints. Thus, despite its designation, it is from a micro-economic aspect that it approaches the macro-economic problems. Such an approach precludes the possibility of getting at least as far as the Keynesian theory of aggregate demand did, and therefore its proponents are compelled to take aggregate demand to be an exogenous datum. Furthermore, besides the micro-economic point of departure, the profit problem also appears at the micro-level only. In so far as entrepreneurs are on the long side, they are unable to sell that quantity of their products and to buy that amount of labour which they would need for maximizing their profit.

Several representatives of the new macro-economics generally presuppose the stickiness of prices and money wages without striving to explore its cause.

Those who do wish to reveal it refer, partly, to the oligopolistic character of the markets. They explain the downward rigidity of oligopolistic prices by saying that no oligopolist dares to diminish the price of his product for fear that the others will follow suit, and an oligopolistic price competition, a so-called "cut-throat" competition, will ensue. The downward rigidity of oligopolistic prices is also due to the fact that with a fall in output, unit costs will not diminish. On the contrary, they will probably rise, because owing to a declining capacity utilization, fixed costs per product unit will increase. Oligopolistic price formation takes place in the presentation of today's non-Marxian economic literature on the basis of the so-called "mark-up pricing" principle. Namely, the oligopolist sets the price of his product by adding a certain percentage to the unit costs, as a traditional mark-up which changes only slowly over time.

According to another explanation, prices may also be rigid downwards owing to imperfect information. Since the agents of the market cannot find out whether a fall in aggregate demand is long-lasting or only temporary, they first regard it as temporary and do not diminish the price of their product. Leijonhufvud was one of the first to profess this view.[159]

To those who insisted on the assumption of the optimizing behaviour of the economic units, the explanation of sticky prices based on oligopolistic price formation was not acceptable. The "mark-up pricing principle", with a mark-up changing only slowly over time, does not express an optimizing behaviour, at least not in the short run. Nor does the setting of wages by bargaining express it.

Those, on the other hand, who represented the principle that economic units formed their expectations rationally, found the explanation of price rigidity unacceptable because it was irreconcilable with their presupposition of rationality that economic units were unable to perceive whether aggregate demand was long-lasting or just temporary.

Others again, who in explaining the stickiness of prices and wages wanted to go beyond the sphere of the market and to penetrate into the depth of things, tried to find the right explanation of sluggish prices and wages by tracing them back to the decisions of the economic units which try to optimize their positions.

This attempt found its reflection in the *contract* theory of the market. In recent non-Marxian economic literature, the theories related to this idea are summarized under the heading of "new-new micro-economics".

[159] A. Leijonhufvud: *op. cit.*, pp. 77–78.

594

Chapter 7

THE NEW-NEW MICRO-ECONOMICS.
THE CONTRACT THEORY OF THE MARKET

The so-called new-new micro-economics claims to provide such a micro-economic explanation of a fact of experience contradicting the competition model which is in harmony with the price theory; namely, this fact is that prices and wages do not clear the market, that in a slump period entrepreneurs do not induce their workers to quit their jobs voluntarily by decreasing their money wages, but lay part of them off at unchanged money wage rates. According to a widespread view in non-Marxian economic literature, this is the only choice-theoretically founded explanation of the rigidity of prices and wages.

The theory in question has two varieties. The elaboration of the first is attached to Azariadis,[160] Baily[161] and D.F. Gordon.[162] Therefore, it is usually referred to briefly as the A-B-G- paradigm. The other variety was worked out by Okun.[163]

THE A-B-G MODEL

According to the A-B-G variety, the worker is more averse to risks than those who hold their wealth in real and financial assets. He cannot invest his labour power, his "human capital", in different forms, while the capital market makes it possible for the capitalist to hold his wealth in various assets and to decrease thereby the risk inherent in wealth holding. If, according to the cyclical fluctuations, the worker wanted to change his job, the involved geographical and professional mobility would entail extremely high costs.

The employer is willing to bear part of the worker's risk and concludes a contract with him. According to the proponents of the theory, this contract is implicit, it is not put down in writing. It contains the terms of employment declared and undertaken by the firm. The safeguard for observing the terms of the contract is the reputation of the firm. The labour contract may be a fixed-income contract, when the firm offers the workers a definite wage rate, stable employment and

---

160 C. Azariadis: Implicit Contracts and Underemployment, *Journal of Political Economy*, December 1975, pp. 1183–1202.

161 M.N. Baily: Wages and Unemployment under Uncertain Demand, *Review of Economic Studies*, January 1974, pp. 37–50.

162 D.F. Gordon: Neo-Classical Theory of Keynesian Unemployment, *Economic Inquiry*, December 1974, pp. 431–459.

163 A.M. Okun: Inflation: Its Mechanics and Welfare Cost, *Brookings Papers on Economic Activity*, 1975, II, pp. 351–390.

the commitment not to lay them off even in a recession. However, there may be contracts in which fixed wage rates are combined with varying employment (reduced man-hours, overtime, lay-offs). Baily supposes that there are two strategies open to the worker: fixed wage rates at varying employment in the contract market and uncertain wage rates and employment in the competitive market. The uncertainty of employment is, in his view, the same in both strategies: the worker's income at a fixed wage rate is more stable and thus the contract market is more favourable for him even if the expected wage rate in the competitive market is greater to a certain extent. "The more risk averse the workers, the greater is the return from the non-stochastic wage."[164] Fixed wage rates are more favourable for the firm too: it gains higher profit at lower costs. Furthermore, it is advantageous for the firm also because during the contractual period the worker renounced to make full use of his marginal product in the course of the fluctuation of demand.

However, if the expected value of the stochastic wage rate significantly exceeds the wage rate of the contract market, or when it shows even a rising trend, the worker will prefer the competitive market, provided the costs of mobility are not too high.

Thus, the inclusion of the contract in the model of the labour market serves the aim to explain at least the downward rigidity of wages on the one hand and the lay-offs on the other. In the case of a decreasing aggregate demand, the firm will not decrease the wage rate to induce thereby the workers to quit, but will rather choose to lay off part of them at unchanged wage rates, "... because of rigid wages ... reductions in employment appear as layoffs."[165]

OKUN'S MODEL

Okun wishes to explain price and wage contracts from another aspect; he refers, primarily, to the costliness of information: "... the costs of information lead to implicitly contractual long-term relationships between employees and employers and between customers and suppliers."[166] His examination covers both the product and the labour markets. He wishes to explain thereby the stickiness of not only wages but of prices, too. Prices and wages are also in his model sluggish owing to the common interest of sellers and buyers. His theory is the other variety of new-new micro-economics.

As to the product market, Okun makes a distinction between the competitive market, the so-called auction market, and the "customer" market which has its clientele. In the latter market, a lasting relationship develops between buyers and sellers as if an implicit contract existed between them. Okun explains the existence of the "customer" market, on the one hand, by the imperfect information of the buyers. Products differ both in their quality and in their prices from seller to seller. Before making their purchases, the buyers are compelled to collect information about the price and quality differences. But gathering information is

---

[164] M.N. Baily: *op. cit.*, p. 45.
[165] C. Azariadis: *op. cit.*, p. 1201.
[166] A.M. Okun: *op. cit.*, p 358.

costly. To avoid it, if the customer finds a seller whose products and prices are suitable for him, he will return to this seller in his future purchases, provided he can be confident of finding the same favourable conditions.

On the other hand, the seller is also interested in a "customer" market. It is desirable for him to keep his customers because, with an established clientele, he can use his equipment more evenly, he need not costly transform part of it to adjust it to the production of other goods and need not spend significant sums on advertisements to recruit new buyers.

The seller assumes that "if today's offer is maintained, most of today's customers will return."[167] In other words, "...yesterday's offer influences today's demand..."[168] Therefore, he thinks that if he raises the prices of his products, part of his customers will leave him and will try to collect information on the offers of other firms. Therefore, he restrains the cyclical fluctuation of this prices and responds to changes in demand with changes in his inventory, in delivery times and in production. He will only raise the price of his product if its costs of production have increased. Okun thinks that customers are also willing to accept such price increases as fair.

A contact similar to the lasting relationship between the firm and customers in the product market is established, according to Okun, between the employer and the employee in the labour market. He also distinguishes two types of the labour market: along with the competitive market, i.e. the auction market, there is the so-called "career" market which is analogous, in many respects, with the "customer" market. While in the A-B-G model differences among workers did not play any significant role, the significance of this circumstance has increased in the "career" market. In this market, it is a rational interest of the firm to establish a long-run relation with a certain group of workers.

Part of the work at a firm is firm-specific. This firm-specific skill is either acquired by the worker himself in the so-called learning-by-doing process, or the firm allocates a certain amount for the training of its workers, which then they further develop in the course of work. The firm tries to keep those workers who have proved efficient in the work assigned to them. Employers are generally interested in keeping their experienced workers, because the value they produce exceeds the value which the less experienced ones produce more than the wage difference between the two groups of workers is. Employers are uncertain about the capabilities of outside potential employees. They do know, however, who are the best, the more experienced workers among those already working at their firm. They wish to keep the wages of these workers above the nearest most advantageous possibilities offered in the labour market in order to reduce the number of their quitting. Therefore, they do not reduce the wages even under unfavourable demand conditions, because if they did so, they might lose those workers on whose employment they insist the most; instead, while keeping the wage level unchanged, they dismiss those whose work is less profitable. They will retain the most efficient and most clever workers even if their labour is momentarily not needed, because they assume that sooner or later the business cycle will turn more favourable. And when demand for the firm's products increases and it wishes to

---

[167] A.M. Okun: *op. cit.*, p. 361.
[168] *Ibid.*

employ more workers, it need not increase the wage rate to recruit the necessary labour force, because, as a result of the higher wages paid in the "career" market, workers seeking jobs will queue up at the firm's gate even at the earlier wage rates, and thus it has an ample source of labour to draw from. The experienced workers will not quit even if their wages do not rise in the upsurge, because their skills are firm-specific, which they would hardly be able to utilize in another job and thus their wages would be lower elsewhere. But there are also a number of other advantages that tie them to the firm, such as the benefits of the seniority system, bonuses, old-age pension programmes, etc. Thus, in this labour market, wage rates are relatively insensitive to the general pressure of the labour market. It is to these workers that Feldstein's already mentioned theory on temporary lay-offs applies. Feldstein has pointed out in several studies that it has generally been experienced in the industry of the United States that firms re-hire a large proportion of the same workers belonging to the "career" market as it laid off during a recession. These workers would be able to find employment at lower money wage rates or in less qualified jobs in the competitive market, but they would rather not, because they got higher wages in their earlier jobs where the work they did matched their qualification. They prefer to wait.

SOME SPECIFIC STATEMENTS OF NEW-NEW MICRO-ECONOMICS

In the contract theory of the market, if aggregate demand and the price level fall, firms do not reduce money wages, instead, they decrease their output and dismiss part of the workers even if they correctly anticipated the decline in the price level. Since the existence of the contract makes short-term adjustment difficult, in order to understand today's processes, it is necessary to project the past, which, in turn, gives the hypothesis of adaptive expectations a greater role to play. Involuntary unemployment, moreover, its various magnitudes depending on the fall in aggregate demand, could not exist in the various neo-classical models discussed so far. And if aggregate demand increases, in the contract theories of the market both output and employment will grow under the conditions of involuntary unemployment even if both employers and employees are able to predict the rise in the price level accurately. The trade-off between unemployment and inflation exists in these models even in the case of anticipated inflation. Hence, the involuntarily unemployed worker need not be misled by inflation to become willing to take up employment.

As the possibility of involuntary unemployment is assumed in the contract theories of the market, successful economic policy is also possible in the case of rational expectations. If the quantity of money changes within the contract time, the money wage, unless the contract is indexed, cannot adjust itself to the increase in the price level even if the workers anticipated it. Real wages will fall, and entrepreneurs will increase employment. And the workers of the "career" market will not reduce the supply of their labour, will not quit their jobs even if the price level is growing at unchanged money wages.

CRITICAL COMMENTS

New macro-economics wished to explain the serious troubles of the capitalist economy, even those which Keynes wanted to approach by mere macro-economic categories without relying on price theory, by way of a novel presentation of the functioning of the price mechanism. The non-Walrasian model set up by the proponents of the new macro-economic theory appeared, with its assumption of sticky prices and wages, as a negation of the Walrasian model.

Those economists who tried to explain sticky prices and wages by the existence of the oligopolies and the trade unions, referred to the typical products of today's capitalist economy. In so far, their position reflects reality. But we cannot agree with their view that involuntary unemployment, the insufficiency of aggregate demand were caused merely by the stickiness of prices and wages. These phenomena were already concomitants of free-trade capitalism.

New-new micro-economics lies on the same foundations as new micro-economics, and new classical macro-economics. It differs from them only in its conclusions. Setting out from the Walrasian model, it tries to draw non-Walrasian conclusions from it. In new classical macro-economics, expectations may be erroneous, uncertain. Economy may be affected by unexpected "shocks", by changes in technology, tastes, unexpected actions of economic policy. The economic units acting rationally soon adjust themselves to these changes. In new-new micro-economics, however, they insure themselves against the uncertainty of their expectations by contracts.

It was the basic assumption of new micro-economics that goods, labour force, work place, prices and wages were different, and thus it was worthwhile for the rational agent of the market to gather information about the opportunities before concluding any transaction. In new-new micro-economics, however, the economic units have already found each other, the firm the worker, the worker the firm, the buyer the seller, and therefore it is worthwhile for them to enter into a long-term contractual relationship in order to avoid the costs of collecting information.

In both models of new-new micro-economics it is the common interest of the market agents to give up flexible prices and wages and to replace them by sticky ones.

Risk aversion, the endeavour of the buyer to return to his reliable firm, the striving of the firm to retain its customers and its efficient skilled workers, respectively, can be found in both free-trade and monopoly capitalism. Thus, the stickiness of prices and wages in the models of new-new micro-economics is not restricted to a specific stage of capitalist development. This way of presentation contradicts historical development. The real social background, however, becomes apparent also in Okun's model, in which the firm, unless its costs have risen, takes care not to raise its prices when demand changes, because stable prices inform its buyers and keep them back from searching. Of free-trade capitalism, however, it is not the endeavour to preserve prices, but price competition that is typical. In its course, the firm can keep its customers and its position in the competitive struggle if it decreases the prices of its products. It is a typical feature of today's capitalism only that price competition has become pushed into the background.

Since the rigidity of prices and wages is derived from the rational interests of the market agents, and since the insufficiency of aggregate demand and involuntary unemployment are explained by the rigidity of prices and wages, eventually insufficient aggregate demand and rigid prices and wages can be traced back to the rational considerations of the economic units in new-new micro-economics. In this way, starting from the Walrasian model we can arrive at new-new micro-economics, that is, there is no unbridgeable gap between them. The proponents of new-new micro-economics do emphasize that the lay-offs resulting from the stickiness of wages does not deteriorate the position of the worker relative to the auction market. Furthermore, the magnitude of employment in this model does not significantly deviate either from the level of employment which is realized at flexible wages, since in concluding the contract, the parties concerned take optimal allocations into account. "Productive efficiency conditions ... are a consequence of a competition in the markets for labor contracts."[169] "The contracting approach ... does not imply that levels of employment would differ significantly from the (efficient) values that would have been obtained under flexible prices."[170]

If, however, a bridge can be built between the models based on the stickiness of prices and wages and the Walrasian model, this bridge also exists between new macro-economics and the Walrasian model. A good illustration of this statement is provided by the scientific activity of Barro who is one of the elaborators of the disequilibrium model based on the assumption of sticky prices and wages as well as a proponent of the new classical macro-economics, i.e. of the hypothesis of rational expectations. Barro's schizophrenia mentioned by Gordon[171]—namely, Gordon states that there is a contradiction between the disequilibrium model jointly elaborated by Barro and Grossman and Barro's later model[172] which is based on the hypothesis of rational expectations—may be resolved by the relationship between the two models.

It is incorrect on the part of today's non-Marxian economic literature to interpret new macro-economics as the continuation of the Keynesian theory. Although within the framework of new macro-economics and new-new micro-economics it has become possible to provide a presentation of the lasting effects of government intervention, which can also be found in Keynes, Barro asserts that these models do not prove at all the superiority of the government over private capitalist economy. "The underlying problem must reflect some deeper economic elements, such as imperfect information about the present or future, factor mobility costs or some types of significant transaction costs. ...uncertainty and mobility costs seem to imply that the allocation of resources is a difficult problem—not that the government can assist in allocation through active use of its macro-policy instruments."[173]

The explanation of involuntary unemployment within the framework of the neo-classical price model makes this deduction questionable. This has also been

[169] H.I. Grossman: Why Does Aggregate Employment Fluctuate? *The American Economic Review*, May 1979, p. 67.

[170] R.I. Barro: Second Thoughts on Keynesian Economics, *The American Economic Review*, May 1979, p. 54.

[171] R.J. Gordon: *Recent Developments in the Theory of Inflation and Unemployment*, The International Conference on "Inflation Theory and Anti-Inflation Policy", Saltsjöbaden, Sweden, August 28, 1975.

[172] R.I. Barro: *Rational Expectations and the Role of Monetary Policy*, University of Chicago, May 1975.

[173] R.I. Barro: Second Thoughts ..., *op. cit.*, p. 55.

pointed out by non-Marxian authors. Criticizing the A-B-G- model, Solow[174] and Gerfin[175] have raised the question why the risk-averse worker endeavours to stabilize only the money wage rate, and why he does not want to stabilize employment, too. In that case, his money income would also be stable. In their opinion the contract may stipulate also such a low wage rate at which the firm should pay only such a wage bill, at which it would be able to keep the redundant workers even during a recession and would not be compelled to dismiss them. Thus the rigidity of wages alone does not explain unemployment, and the conclusion that can be drawn from the model under discussion is that "unemployment cannot occur at all."[176]

New-new micro-economics finds the way out of this difficulty by assuming that the worker also has incomes other than what he receives from his employer, for instance, unemployment benefit. Hence, the wage rate cannot be fixed at such a low level that the money income paid to the worker would be less than the unemployment benefit. On the contrary, it must be higher than the unemployment benefit. In this case, however, the wage rate is higher than necessary for full employment, and thus part of the workers are involuntarily unemployed. However, actually the situation is just the reverse. It is the unemployment benefit that is computed according to the wage paid out earlier to the new unemployed worker.

Criticizing the A-B-G model, R. Gordon has also come to the conclusion that the theory can only explain involuntary unemployment if it assumes the existence of unemployment benefit. He raises the following question: if the mean of the worker's total money income paid out by the firm and the variance are equal in both markets, why is it in his interest to sell his labour in the contract market at fixed wage rates and variable working hours rather than in the competitive market where he moves along his notional supply function and where, with a fall in money wages, he can himself decrease the supply of his labour. Gordon is also of the opinion that the contract market is only superior to the competitive market if the worker has some income other than what he gets from the firm. Such is, for example, the unemployment benefit which he receives on his lay-off. And with respect to the A-B-G model he makes the critical remark that "one can question its applicability to the period before the introduction of unemployment benefits in the late 1930s."[177]

The contract theory generally gets into conflict with its own theoretical foundations when it assumes the lay-off of redundant workers at unchanged money wages. Namely, as has already been pointed out, with a positively sloping supply curve of labour, the firm pays out to the remaining workers more than it would be necessary to keep them. And this contradicts the optimizing endeavour—another evidence that despite its reform, price theory based on neo-classical foundations is not a suitable framework for the explanation of involuntary unemployment, and that it is impossible to draw non-Walrasian conclusions from it without contradictions.

[174] R. Solow: Alternative Approaches of Macroeconomic Theory: A Partial View, *Canadian Journal of Economics*, Vol. 12, 1979, pp. 339–354.
[175] H. Gerfin: Informationsproblem des Arbeitsmarktes, *Kyklos*, 1982, Vol. 82, Fasc. 3, pp. 398–429.
[176] H. Gerfin: *op. cit.*, p. 407.
[177] R. Gordon: *Recent developments ...*, op. cit., p. 207.

CONCLUSION

Having surveyed the economic theories that have evolved on the basis of the new crisis situation of the capitalist economy, we may arrive at the following conclusions:

The capability of functioning of the capitalist economy has again become a key issue in the relevant disputes. Already in 1936 Keynes regarded capitalist real economy as unstable which is unable to maintain a high level of aggregate demand and employment without the active economic policy of the state.

Indeed, the efficiency of capitalism left to itself had already been heavily shaken by the 1930s. Under the circumstances of monopoly capitalism, it was far from having the same viability and flexibility as it had had in its free-trade stage. It was this fact, and not an erroneous economic policy, that was responsible for the seriousness of the Great Depression in 1929–1933.

Price competition is no longer characteristic of the oligopolies. Non-Marxian theory gives a correct description of the price-forming practice of the oligopolists, the so-called "mark-up pricing". They add a traditional mark-up to the costs of production and they try to maintain it even in the times of recessions. On the other hand, the strengthening of the trade unions makes money wages sticky—at least in a downward direction. The stickiness of prices and wages is due to modern capitalist development and not to some rational interest of the market agents, which is independent of this development.

The maturing of productive investments increases productive capacity in the production of consumer goods. In the case of its full utilization, the supply of consumer goods considerably increases. Under modern capitalist circumstances, it is the wage- and salary earners that represent a decisive part of the purchasing power in the market of consumer goods, while the consumer demand of the capitalist class constitutes a mere fraction of the total consumer demand and, moreover, is rather inelastic—at least in the short run. The increased supply of consumer goods could only be realized in a model of pure capitalist economy, in which the economic role of the state, the weight of non-productive expenditures is insignificant, if real wages increased. But this would decrease real profit and the oligopolistic mark-up.[178] In order to maintain this mark-up, production capacities are not fully utilized, which in turn affects employment unfavourably. Furthermore, excess capacity does not stimulate investments either. Under the conditions of monopoly capitalism, the compulsion to accumulate—a typical trait of free-trade capitalism—decreases and the rate of accumulation slows down. This is the real essence of the Keynesian theoretical system and it also constitutes the basis of the stagnation theories following Keynes.

The danger of lasting stagnation, which had been threatening capitalist economies was averted after the Second World War by the strengthening of state monopoly capitalism, by increasing non-productive expenditures.

Has the efficiency of capitalist economy decreased with the greater role of the state? This is the most debated issue in today's non-Marxian economic literature.

No doubt, the growth in the weight of the state sector is accompanied by a

---

[178] P. Erdős: *Wages, Profit, Taxation. Studies on Controversial Issues of the Political Economy of Capitalism*, Akadémiai Kiadó, Budapest, 1982. pp. 261–262.

number of serious problems which had never been experienced before and have not been resolved yet. Budgetary expenditures, even if they are financed from taxes, generally have a price-increasing effect. And departure from the gold standard has made a steady rise in the price level possible. In addition, erroneous economic policies have often caused recessions and they have also played a role in the emergence of stagflation.

At the same time, capitalist economies cannot dispense with the economic activity of the state. Only the government is able and willing to cope with a significant part of the problems raised by development. The relatively higher level of aggregate demand and aggregate employment, the relatively lower amplitude of fluctuation in the reproduction cycles in post-World War II capitalist development, were to a significant extent the consequence of the greatly increased government spendings. Behind the revival of the trust in the viability of capitalist automatisms, in the various neo-classical models there figures as a realistic background the increasingly even development of economic growth which is also promoted by budgetary expenditures. In the writings of the proponents of an active governmental economic policy one can often come across the requirement that on evaluating the efficiency of governmental economic policy not only the disadvantages but also the advantages should be taken into consideration.

How is the efficiency of today's capitalist economy reflected in the writings of the representatives of the two opposed trends of economic theory discussed in this part?

Those theories which accept the market-clearing paradigm and intend to prove the inefficient or even harmful impact of government expenditures, idealize the mechanisms of the capitalist economy of a bygone period—mechanisms which were unable even in their own times to eliminate general overproduction crises and involuntary unemployment. They exaggerate the significance of those partial phenomena of the market and inflation which they have revealed. They represent a conservative ideology, they would heavily curtail or invalidate those achievements that the working masses fought out for themselves under state monopoly capitalism. In their view, the government can act upon the real economy only because the market information is imperfect and only through the unpredictability of its measures. The assumptions of their models preclude the real presentation of the serious problems of today's capitalist economies.

On the other hand, a more realistic picture of the capitalist economy, of the efficiency of governmental economic policy, is drawn by those theories which have chosen the non-market-clearing paradigm as their working hypothesis. They admit the insufficiency of aggregate demand, the existence of involuntary unemployment as well as the possibility of excess demand in all markets, including the insufficiency of labour supply, too. Hence, there exists the possibility of a successful intervention by the government. However, they can only demonstrate all this within the framework of a neo-classical price model, by assuming sticky prices and wages. They do state that at flexible prices and wages the above-mentioned troubles cannot arise. At this point, they actually share the view of those economists who idealize the automatisms of today's capitalist economy.

But what is the source of the stickiness of prices and wages in the models based on the non-market-clearing paradigm? Some of the proponents of these models simply presuppose this characteristic of prices and wages without examining it.

Others refer to the existence of the oligopolies, but the historical evolvement of the oligopolies is missing from their models and they simply take these products of the market as given. Again others try to trace the stickiness of prices and wages back to the rational decisions of the economic agents, that is, to decisions that may also have taken place in the earlier periods of capitalist development.

In this presentation, the economic activity of the state lacks any historical elements. Also missing is from these models the demonstration that state monopoly capitalism is a definite stage of capitalist development from which, like from monopoly capitalism, there is no way back to free-trade capitalism. That is why the proponents of these models cannot bring up convincing arguments against the view of those economists who idealize the freedom of competition and deny the active economic role of the state.

And the stickiness of prices and wages alone does not provide an answer to the basic question of what forces move the economic processes and cause, at sticky prices and wages, once the insufficiency of aggregate demand and involuntary unemployment whereas, at another time, too great aggregate demand and labour shortage. On referring to these phenomena, the representatives of the theory present them as exogenous factors. For example, they say that the money stock has changed as a result of monetary policy, state spending has changed owing to fiscal policy, and these changes have then caused the fall or the increase in aggregate demand.

True, the historical approach was not a strong side of Keynes, either. And he also treated some of the factors responsible for the fluctuation of economic processes as exogenous data. But these factors also stemmed from the capitalist economy and changed together with the changes in the economic situation: for example, the profit expectations of entrepreneurs, the liquidity preferences of wealth-holders. They were exogenous inasmuch as Keynes could not relate them with certain economic variables in exact functions, as he considered them to be influenced not only by economic but also by other, for example, by psychological effects.

The basic deficiency of the models in question is that they have got stuck in the framework of a reformed neo-classical price theory, and they cannot offer an alternative theoretical concept to the market-clearing paradigm—a concept which would reflect today's capitalist development at least as much as Keynes's theory did by providing an adequate picture of the capitalist economy of his age.

The crisis of preasent-day capitalist economy has not yet produced a new "Keynesian" system. And actually this is the crisis of today's non-Marxian economics.

AUTHOR INDEX

Kornai, J. 293
Krelle, W. 492, 505, 513, 517
Kuznets, S.S. 353

Lange, O. 57, 71, 179, 282
Lehmann, G. 249
Leijonhufvud, A. 196, 360, 387–388, 401, 558, 594
Lenin, V.I. 18, 248, 250, 272, 282
Leontief, W. 161, 163–164, 281–283, 298
Lerner, A.R. 78, 96, 157, 583
Lexis, W. 33
Lindahl, E. 273–274, 278, 328, 331, 333, 335–336, 338, 365
Lindbeck, A. 580, 581
Lipsey, R.G. 538
Little, I.M.D. 142, 145, 208, 210–211
Llewellyn, J. 581
Lucas, R.E. 551, 564, 569, 571, 574, 575
Lundberg, E. 493

Machlup, F. 83, 195, 245, 249, 251
Malinvaud, E. 588–590
Malthus, R. 114
Marchal, J. 121, 193
Marshall, A. 21, 26–41, 36, 38–41, 43, 52, 57, 65, 78, 83, 87–88, 90–92, 94–95, 134, 166, 184–185, 196, 200–201, 213–215, 222–233, 255, 284, 320–322, 326
Marx, K. 17–19, 43–44, 51, 56, 59, 94–95, 101, 122, 186, 190, 192, 198, 202, 212, 249, 267, 272, 278, 309–310, 317, 326, 337, 371–372, 376–377, 379, 382, 384, 393–397, 401, 414, 424, 428, 433, 439, 443–445, 453, 461, 469, 502, 529, 575, 577
Mason, E.S. 171
Matthews, R.C.O. 69, 471, 504
Mayer, H. 140
McFarland, D. 251, 254–255
Meade, J.E. 182, 206, 244, 449, 471, 474, 475, 479, 482, 489
Meltzer, A.H. 343, 533
Mendershausen, H. 293, 477
Menger, C. 15–19, 21–23, 65
Mill, J.S. 17
Minhas, D.S. 294–297
Mirrlees, J.A. 523
Mises, L. 120–121, 336
Modigliani, F. 355, 356–357, 425–426, 428, 558–560
Möller, H. 324
Moore, H.L. 282
Morgenstern, O. 46–48, 57, 138, 241–242

Mortensen, D.T. 562–564
Muth, J.F. 570
Myrdal, G. 273–274, 315, 328, 335–336

Neisser, H. 61, 101
Neumann, J. 241–242, 484
Nordhaus, W.D. 506

Ohlin, B. 273–275, 364
Okun, A.M. 595, 596–597
Olson, M. 251, 254–255
Oppenländer, K. 357, 515
Ott, A. 447, 513

Pantaleoni, M. 120
Pareto, V. 65, 123, 125–128, 130, 141, 241
Parkin, J.M. 582
Pasinetti, L. 68, 420, 430–433
Patinkin, D. 196, 315, 321–322, 324, 326, 411, 586
Paulsen, A. 278
Phelps, E.S. 69, 484–488, 490–492, 506, 519, 562–564
Phillips, A.W. 533–536, 539–540, 552
Pigou, A.C. 49, 91–92, 213, 320–322, 324, 326, 410–411, 546
Preiser, E. 73

Ramsey, F.B. 484
Reder, M.V. 245
Ricardo, D. 15–18, 45, 51, 114, 202, 211, 424, 573
Ricci, U. 267
Riese, H. 156
Ritter, L.S. 325
Robbins, L. 120, 345
Robertson, D.H. 321–322, 324, 326
Robinson, E.A.G. 79
Robinson, J. 68, 78, 88, 94, 96, 99, 145, 157, 188–191, 197–199, 219, 221, 223–224, 226–229, 252, 341, 362, 384, 418, 420, 427, 478, 483–484, 512, 527
Rogin, L. 184
Röpke, W. 249
Rosenstein-Rodan, P. 260
Runge, H. 87, 90–91

Samuelson, P.A. 59, 61, 63, 72, 83–85, 97–99, 108–115, 141–142, 180–183, 209, 261, 264, 271, 276, 343, 353, 395–396, 400, 425–426, 428, 434, 467, 484, 494, 497, 499–501, 557, 584
Santomero, A.M. 566

608

SUBJECT INDEX

609

Rate of interest, role of ~ in
    regulating the form of holding wealth
    387–390
Rational choice, logic of 119–122
Reaction curve in Cournot's duopoly 237
Real-balance effect, *see* Pigou effect
Real-cost theory 38–40, 91, 180–181, 413
Real financial effect 411
Relative income hypothesis, *see* Consumption function
Rent theory
    consumers' ~ 29, 215
    producers' ~ 188
    rent of factors 188–190
    rent of factors with alternative uses
    190–191
Representative firm 200–201
Reswitching of techniques 113–115,
    155–156, 161, 164, 338, 420, 517–518
Return, laws of
    return to proportions (principle of
    variable proportions) 70–77, 81–83, 167
    return to outlay 80
    return to scale 78–80, 172
Revealed preference 141–145
Revenue function under monopoly
    marginal ~ 222–224
    total ~ 222–224
Ricardian equivalance theorem 572–574,
    579
Risk, interpretation by Knight 98
Robinson–Amoroso proposition 224
Roundabout production 103–108

Sargant effect 39
Saving(s)
    ex-ante ~ 364–365
    ex-post ~ 364–365, 458–459
    forced ~ 334, 590
    relationship between ~ and investment in
        Keynes's theory 362–366
    neo-classical theory 39, 91–95, 329, 350
Savings function
    ~ based on the life-cycle hypothesis
    356–357
    ~ in Hicks's theory 458
    ~ in Keynes's theory 350–353
    ~ in permanent-income hypothesis
    355–356

Savings function
    ~ in neo-classical theory, 39, 91–95,
    329–331, 350
    ~ in relative-income hypothesis 354
Say's dogma 328, 347, 349, 386
Scale elasticity 79
Scitovsky paradox 209
Search model 562–565
Slutsky effect 33, 134–135
Socio-legal school, *see* Economic schools
Social marginal cost, *see* Cost
Social marginal productivity, *see* Marginal
    productivity
Space principle 79
Stagflation 540, 560, 580, 583
Statics, interpretation of ~ by
    Frisch 261
    Harrod 260
Stochastic macro-equilibrium 537
Strategic games, theory of
    maxi-min game 243
    mini-max game 242
Substitution
    elasticity of ~ 102, 157–161, 290,
    294–297, 478, 480, 484, 486, 500–504
    ex-ante ~ 69
    ex-post ~ 69
    margins of ~ in the system of isoquants
    149
Substitution effect
    equilibrium of ~ and technical effect on
    the golden-age path 481
    ~ of factor-price changes 183
    ~ of product-price changes 33, 134–136
    separation of ~ from the effect of
    technical progress in Solow's theory
    475–476
    separation of ~ from the income effect of
    price changes in Hicks's theory 134–137
Substitution parameter in the CES function
    296
Superior goods 132
Super-multiplier, *see* Multiplier
Supply
    elasticity of ~ 262, 271
    independence ~ in duopoly 238
    notional ~ 587, 589
Supply function
    aggregate ~ 346–347

Supply function
  constrained ∼ 589–590
  dynamic ∼ 262
  ∼ in the capital market 39, 59, 61, 91–95
  ∼ in the labour market 38, 59, 61, 90, 413
  long term ∼ 187
  Lucas's short run aggregate ∼ 571–572
  short-term ∼ as marginal cost function 182–183
Surrogate capital, *see* Capital
Switch points 114–115, 161, 518
Symmetry assumption 185, 229

Technical dynamism 522, 528
Technical maximum in changing factor proportions 75–76, 80
Technical optimization in the system of isoquants 154–155
Technical optimum in changing factor proportions 75–76, 80
Technical progress
  autonomous ∼ 493
  capital-augmenting ∼ 491
  classification of ∼ by
    Harrod 449
    Hicks 472–474
    Kaldor 521–522
  embodied ∼ 69, 489
  factor-augmenting ∼ 496
  induced ∼ 493–494
  innovation-possibility frontier 496
  interpretation of neutral ∼ by
    Harrod 449
    Hicks 472–473
    Kennedy 494
    Solow 491
  labour-augmenting ∼ 451, 479
  non-embodied ∼ 489
  separation of the effect of ∼ from the substitution effect in Solow's theory 475–476
  treatment of the effect of ∼
    as an endogenous factor 504–511
    as an exogenous factor 493, 504

Technologically non-effective production methods 163
Time factors in economic analysis
  delayed adjustment 266–272
  distinction between short- and long-term periods 39, 166, 172, 266, 316–317, 329, 552–554, 564
  lead 437
  period analysis in the Stockholm School 273–278
  period and rate analysis in Samuelson 263–264
  process analysis 262
  time path 262
Time preference 91–94
Trade-cycle theory
  Harrod's growth model as ∼ 453–457
  Hicks's ∼ 461–469
  Wicksell's ∼ 331–338
Transformation, marginal rate of 178
Transitivity in consumers' choice 141
Turnpike theory 484

Uncertainty, Knight's interpretation of 99
Unemployment
  explanation of ∼ by Keynes 342, 359–360
  ∼ in earlier neo-classical theory 85
  ∼ in present-day neo-classical theory 545, 552, 563–565
  involuntary ∼ 342, 359–366, 583, 586–588, 590, 596, 597
  natural rate of ∼ 545, 564
  search ∼ 563–565
  temporary lay-off 539, 567, 598
Utility
  cardinal interpretation of ∼ 33, 123, 127, 139
  ordinal interpretation of ∼ 127, 139
  revealed preference 141–145
Utility functions
  additive ∼ 48
  generalized ∼ 123, 125
  index function 127
  marginal ∼ 21–22, 23–28, 44–46, 48–49, 57, 60, 94, 124, 129, 284–286, 321
Utility-possibility curve 209–211